Prisons, Punishment, and the Family

Towards a New Sociology of Punishment?

Edited by
RACHEL CONDRY
PETER SCHARFF SMITH

OXFORD
UNIVERSITY PRESS

OXFORD
UNIVERSITY PRESS

Great Clarendon Street, Oxford, OX2 6DP,
United Kingdom

Oxford University Press is a department of the University of Oxford.
It furthers the University's objective of excellence in research, scholarship,
and education by publishing worldwide. Oxford is a registered trade mark of
Oxford University Press in the UK and in certain other countries

© The several contributors 2018

The moral rights of the authors have been asserted

First Edition published in 2018

Impression: 3

All rights reserved. No part of this publication may be reproduced, stored in
a retrieval system, or transmitted, in any form or by any means, without the
prior permission in writing of Oxford University Press, or as expressly permitted
by law, by licence, or under terms agreed with the appropriate reprographics
rights organization. Enquiries concerning reproduction outside the scope of the
above should be sent to the Rights Department, Oxford University Press, at the
address above

You must not circulate this work in any other form
and you must impose this same condition on any acquirer

Crown copyright material is reproduced under Class Licence
Number C01P0000148 with the permission of OPSI
and the Queen's Printer for Scotland

Published in the United States of America by Oxford University Press
198 Madison Avenue, New York, NY 10016, United States of America

British Library Cataloguing in Publication Data

Data available

Library of Congress Control Number: 2018942721

ISBN 978–0–19–881008–7

Printed and bound by
TJ International Ltd, Padstow, Cornwall

Links to third-party websites are provided by Oxford in good faith and
for information only. Oxford disclaims any responsibility for the materials
contained in any third-party website referenced in this work.

Acknowledgements

Our thanks first and foremost go to the many thousands of prisoners' families as well as the prisoners and prison staff across the world who have given their time and shared their experiences for the purposes of the research that informs the different chapters in this book. Without the help of all these people and their willingness to reveal and describe personal and emotional events this book would not have been possible. We hope that this collective volume does justice to their experience, and contributes to the growing recognition that prisoners' families often experience social injustice and social exclusion, and that this should be of concern to everyone in a democratic society.

We would like to thank all our contributors, who have been a pleasure to work with—we're delighted to have you all on board and look forward to future collaborations. The idea for this book grew over a number of years as a group of us began to come together at various conferences and share our work. Panels and roundtables were organized over the past four years at a number of conferences, including the British Society of Criminology conferences in 2014 and 2015 and the American Society of Criminology Annual Meetings every year since 2014. In 2015, we held a two-day international symposium on 'Prisoners' Families, Punishment, and Social Inequality' at St Hilda's College in Oxford, where the idea for this volume was developed. That event was funded by the John Fell Oxford University Press (OUP) Research Fund and we extend our thanks for that support. We held a second workshop for contributors in May 2017 at St Hilda's College where draft chapters for the book were discussed. We would like to thank St Hilda's College and the Faculty of Law at the University of Oxford for their support of these events.

Rachel would like to thank her colleagues in the Centre for Criminology at the University of Oxford for an inspiring and supportive working environment. Peter would similarly like to thank all his excellent colleagues at the Department of Criminology and Sociology of Law at Oslo University. A special thanks goes to Annica Allvin for helping with editing chapters. We are grateful to the team at Oxford University Press, the editors, the reviewers, and the production team for thorough and professional guidance and help throughout the process. Many thanks also to photographer Fredrik Clement for providing us with a fantastic cover photo.

Finally, it is of course important with a book about the ties between family members to extend our very warm thanks and appreciation to our own families and to our friends that have supported our work across the years. In a way, none of this would make much sense without you.

Contents

List of Contributors   ix

1. The Sociology of Punishment and the Effects of Imprisonment on Families   1
   Rachel Condry and Peter Scharff Smith

I. PRISONERS' FAMILIES AND SOCIAL INEQUALITY

2. Prisoners' Families and the Problem of Social Justice   27
   Rachel Condry

3. Parental Incarceration and Family Inequality in the United States   41
   Joyce A. Arditti

4. How Much Might Mass Imprisonment Affect Childhood Inequality?   58
   Sara Wakefield and Christopher Wildeman

5. 'I'm the man and he's the woman!': Gender Dynamics among Couples During and After Prison   73
   Megan Comfort

6. Missing and Missing Out: Social Exclusion in Children with an Incarcerated Parent   87
   Susan M. Dennison and Kirsten L. Besemer

7. Are the Children of Prisoners Socially Excluded? A Child-Centred Perspective   102
   Helene Oldrup and Signe Frederiksen

II. PENAL POWER AND HUMAN RIGHTS

8. Prisoners' Families, Public Opinion, and the State: Punishment and Society from a Family and Human Rights Perspective   121
   Peter Scharff Smith

9. 'The sins and traumas of fathers and mothers should not be visited on their children': The Rights of Children When a Primary Carer is Sentenced to Imprisonment in the Criminal Courts   136
   Shona Minson

10. 'Someone should have just asked me what was wrong': Balancing Justice, Rights, and the Impact of Imprisonment on Children and Families in Scotland   151
    Nancy Loucks and Tânia Loureiro

11. Eroding Legitimacy? The Impact of Imprisonment on the Relationships between Families, Communities, and the Criminal Justice System 167
Cara Jardine

12. Prisoners' Families, Penal Power, and the Referred Pains of Imprisonment 181
Caroline Lanskey, Friedrich Lösel, Lucy Markson, and Karen Souza

13. Rights and Security in the Shadow of the Irish Prison: Developing a Children's Rights Approach to Prison Visits in Ireland 196
Fiona Donson and Aisling Parkes

III. THE LIVED EXPERIENCES OF PRISONERS' FAMILIES IN EUROPE, NORTH AMERICA, AND AUSTRALIA

14. 'Everyone is in damage control': The Meanings and Performance of Family for Second and Third Generation Prisoners 213
Mark Halsey

15. The Legally Sanctioned Stigmatization of Prisoners Families 230
Marie Hutton

16. Time, the Pains of Imprisonment, and 'Coping': The Perspectives of Prisoners' Partners 244
Anna Kotova

17. Sharing Imprisonment: Experiences of Prisoners and Family Members in Portugal 258
Rafaela Granja

18. Betwixt and Between: Incarcerated Men, Familial Ties, and Social Visibility 273
Shenique S. Thomas and Johnna Christian

19. The Systemic Invisibility of Children of Prisoners 288
Else Marie Knudsen

Index 305

List of Contributors

Joyce A. Arditti is Professor of Human Development and Family Science at Virginia Tech. Her research interests include family disruption, parent–child relationships in vulnerable families, and public policy. She has published numerous empirical and review articles in therapy, human services, family studies, and criminal justice journals. Joyce recently served as the editor-in-chief of *Family Relations: The Interdisciplinary Journal of Applied Family Studies*. Her 2012 book *Parental Incarceration and the Family* was awarded the 2014 Outstanding Book Award by the Academy of Criminal Justice Sciences.

Kirsten L. Besemer holds a PhD in development studies. She has worked on a variety of research projects relating to poverty and social exclusion in Vietnam, the United Kingdom, and Australia. She is a Lecturer at Griffith University and former postdoctoral research fellow on the Vulnerable Families Project studying the effect of parental incarceration on children's developmental outcomes.

Johnna Christian is an associate professor at the School of Criminal Justice, Rutgers University-Newark. She has conducted research into incarcerated individual's familial ties, prison visitation, and prisoner re-entry. She is currently studying the role of informal social support systems, such as family- and faith-based communities, in the re-entry process.

Megan Comfort is a senior research sociologist in the Youth, Crime Prevention, and Community Justice Program in RTI International's Applied Justice Research Division. Among her research interests and areas of expertise are families and incarceration, HIV risk and prevention, and how health disparities relate to wealth distribution in urban populations. She is the author of *Doing Time Together: Love and Family in the Shadow of the Prison* (University of Chicago Press, 2008), an ethnographic study of the 'secondary prisonization' of women in relationships with incarcerated men. Her articles have appeared in *Criminal Justice and Behavior*, *Ethnography*, the *Journal of Sex Research*, *Annual Review of Law & Social Science*, *Actes de la recherche en sciences sociales*, *PLoS ONE*, and *AIDS & Behavior*, among others, and have been translated into three languages.

Rachel Condry is Associate Professor of Criminology at the University of Oxford and a Fellow of St Hilda's College. She has previously been a lecturer and British Academy Postdoctoral Fellow at the London School of Economics and a lecturer in criminology at the University of Surrey. Her work focuses broadly on the intersections between crime and the family, which has included research projects on the families of serious offenders, prisoners' families, parenting expertise in youth justice, and adolescent to parent violence. She is the author of *Families Shamed: The Consequences of Crime for Relatives of Serious Offenders* (Willan, 2007), shortlisted for the BSA Philip Abrams Memorial Prize. Rachel is a co-editor of the *Howard Journal of Crime and Justice*, a trustee of the Howard League for Penal Reform, and a member of the editorial board of the *British Journal of Criminology* and the International Advisory Board of the *Australian and New Zealand Journal of Criminology*.

Susan M. Dennison is a former ARC Future Fellow and a Professor in the School of Criminology and Criminal Justice and the Griffith Criminology Institute, Griffith University. Her research is positioned within a criminology and human development framework and focuses on the contexts affecting children's developmental systems and life outcomes, and the importance of using evidence-based research to inform policy change, prevent crime, and improve outcomes for at-risk children. Her Future Fellowship focused on the impact of parental incarceration on the family system and the mechanisms that mediate developmental outcomes for incarcerated parents, their children, and caregivers.

List of Contributors

Fiona Donson is a lecturer in the Faculty of Law, University College Cork. Her publications include *Legal Intimidation: A SLAPP in the Face of Democracy* (Free Association Books, 2000) and articles on protest, human rights, administrative justice, policing, and prisons. She has collaborated on projects funded by the British government, the Economic and Social Research Council (UK), and the Commission for the Support of Victims of Crime. Before joining UCC at the end of 2007 she worked as a child rights advocate in Cambodia for a number of years, developing child rights training for lawyers with UNICEF and running a major child rights project funded by the European Commission. She has taught at a number of law schools in the United Kingdom including Leicester and Cardiff. Her current research includes the rights of children of incarcerated parents, the legal right for citizens to participate in democratic processes, and administrative justice.

Signe Frederiksen is a researcher in the department for children and family research at VIVE—The Danish Centre for Social Science Research. She has been involved in register- and survey-based studies on wellbeing among children and youths in out-of-home care as well as studies of the long-term outcomes for these children such as educational attainment, labour market attachment, and crime. Currently she is involved in a research project on wellbeing among children with an incarcerated parent, focusing on everyday life.

Rafaela Granja is a postdoctoral research fellow at the Communication and Society Research Centre (CECS), University of Minho. Her main areas of research are governability of criminality, prison studies, and family relationships. More recently she has focused on the sociological effects of science and technology, in particular on the controversies around the intersections of family, genetics, and crime in different disciplines.

Mark Halsey is a professor of criminology at Flinders University and co-chief editor of the *Australian and New Zealand Journal of Criminology*. His key areas of interest include youth offending, repeat incarceration, gun violence, Aboriginal imprisonment, and desistance from crime. He has received, solely or jointly, five Australian Research Council grants to study these and related issues. Mark has undertaken consultancies for state and local government in areas ranging across restorative and therapeutic justice, mentoring, serious repeat youth offending, prisoner reintegration, correctional corruption, and optimizing the positive effects of prison officer work. In 2012, he was awarded a four-year Australian Research Council Future Fellowship for the project 'Generations through Prison: A Critical Exploration of the Causes, Experiences and Consequences of Intergenerational Incarceration'. His current research explores the social, economic, and cultural dimensions of Aboriginal (over)imprisonment and the process of offender reintegration in metropolitan, rural, and remote areas of Australia.

Marie Hutton is a Lecturer in Criminology at the University of Sussex. Her cross-disciplinary research explores the empirical realities of human rights legislation in the prison environment from a socio-legal perspective. She has a longstanding interest in the topic and has conducted extensive research with prisoners and their families in prisons across England, Wales and Northern Ireland. Her current research interests include family contact and human rights during imprisonment and the role of communication in the prison environment.

Cara Jardine completed her PhD at the University of Edinburgh. Her research explored which relationships are affected when a person is sentenced to a period of imprisonment in Scotland, and the impact of this particular form of punishment on relationships, families, and their perceptions of the criminal justice system. Her research interests include punishment, gender, reflexivity, and innovative research methods. Cara has recently been awarded a Leverhulme Early Career fellowship to continue her research with the University of Strathclyde.

Else Marie Knudsen is an Assistant Professor of Social Work at Trent University in Canada. Her main research interests are the criminal justice system and the sociology of punishment, with a particular focus on the experiences, impacts and policy context of parental incarceration. She holds a PhD from the London School of Economics (2017), an MSc in Social Policy (2006) and an MSW (2002). She worked as a social worker in Toronto for several years, first as a child protection investigator, and later engaged in policy and advocacy work with a criminal justice policy organization.

Anna Kotova is a Lecturer in Criminology in the Department of Social Policy, Sociology, and Criminology at the University of Birmingham. She was previously a doctoral student in the Centre for Criminology at the University of Oxford. Her teaching and research interests are in prison sociology and the collateral impact of imprisonment on families of prisoners. She has researched the impact of long sentences on partners of prisoners in the United Kingdom, and her next project is on prisoners serving sentences for sex offences in a therapeutic community.

Caroline Lanskey is a lecturer in Applied Criminology at the Institute of Criminology, University of Cambridge. Building on an earlier ESRC postdoctoral research fellowship, her work addresses the criminal justice experiences of young people and families with a particular focus on imprisonment, education, citizenship, and wellbeing. She is currently Principal Investigator of the Families and Imprisonment Research (FAIR) study, a prospective longitudinal study of resilience following parental incarceration.

Friedrich Lösel is emeritus professor and past director at the Institute of Criminology, Cambridge University (UK), and at the Institute of Psychology, University of Erlangen-Nuremberg (Germany). At both places, and at the Berlin Psychological University, he has honorary functions. He has carried out research into juvenile delinquency, violence, developmental prevention, offender treatment, prison staff, prisoners and their families, football hooliganism, school bullying, psychopathy, resilience, close relationships, family education, child abuse, extremism, and prisoners and their families. On these and other topics he has published more than 400 articles in journals and books and 38 monographs, edited volumes, and special journal issues. In recognition of his work he received the Sellin-Glueck Award of the American Society of Criminology (ASC), the Lifetime-achievement Award of the European Association of Psychology and Law, the Jerry Lee Award of the ASC Division of Experimental Criminology, the Lifetime-achievement Award of the ASC Division of Developmental & Life-Course Criminology (DLC), the Joan McCord Award of the Academy of Experimental Criminology, the German Psychology Prize, and the Stockholm Prize in Criminology. Currently he is president of the Academy of Experimental Criminology and chairman of the DLC Division of ASC.

Nancy Loucks is the Chief Executive of Families Outside, a Scottish voluntary organization that works on behalf of families affected by imprisonment. Prior to this she worked as an independent criminologist, specializing in prison policy and comparative criminology. She received her MPhil and PhD from the Institute of Criminology at the University of Cambridge and in 2012 was appointed as visiting professor at the University of Strathclyde's Centre for Law, Crime, and Justice. Nancy has conducted extensive research into human rights issues in prison, female and young offenders, prison violence and protests, addiction, suicides and self-harm, violence-risk-assessment and management, the experience of offenders with learning difficulties and learning disabilities, homelessness amongst ex-prisoners, and the maintenance of prisoners' family ties. She has researched family issues and family participation in prisoner resettlement and studied the role of prison visitors' centres, the work of family contact officers, and the experience of young parents in prison. She has conducted consultations with prisoners' families and written reviews of the literature on the needs of prisoners' families and the services they require for international journals. Nancy was awarded an OBE in the 2016 New Year's Honours list for services to education and human rights.

Tânia Loureiro was awarded and Elphinstone scholarship to conduct her PhD at the University of Aberdeen in the School of Law. Her current research focuses on the impact on families of offenders who have received an imposition of a community sentence as an alternative to imprisonment. Previously, Tânia worked as a Research Associate for the Parenting and Family Support Research Programme in the Department of Psychology at Glasgow Caledonian University, where she was a project coordinator of a randomized controlled trial. Prior to that, she worked with Families Outside conducting research into the use of child and family impact assessments in court. Building on this research, Tânia continued her work with Families Outside and, in collaboration with the Scottish Commissioner for Children and Young People, she conducted research into the experiences of children and young people who have had a family member sent to prison. With Families Outside and Barnardo's Scotland, Tânia also completed research on the support available for families of people who have committed a sexual offence in Scotland. Her research interests focus on imprisonment, alternatives to custody, and the impact of sentencing options on families and children.

Lucy Markson is a forensic psychologist for Her Majesty's Prison and Probation Service (HMPPS) and a research associate on the Families and Imprisonment Research (FAIR) study at the Institute of Criminology, University of Cambridge. Prior to this she received her PhD in developmental psychology from the University of Cambridge. Lucy's recent research focuses on the impact of paternal imprisonment on families. She is also interested in the role of psychology in prisons.

Shona Minson is a research associate in the Centre for Criminology, University of Oxford. After graduating from St.Anne's College, Oxford in Jurisprudence Shona was called to the Bar of England and Wales and practised criminal and family law from 1 King's Bench Walk, London. Her professional experience led to her research interest in the points of intersection between family and criminal law. She completed her DPhil in 2017 on the place of children in maternal sentencing decisions in England and Wales. She then worked on an ESRC Impact Acceleration Project to deliver training films to criminal justice professionals on the sentencing of mothers/primary carers, which developed from the findings of her doctoral work.

Helene Oldrup is a senior researcher at Lev Uden Vold, an organization working with preventing domestic violence. Formerly she was a researcher at VIVE—The Danish Centre for Social Science Research. Her research explores the themes of family practices, relations, and care and processes of social exclusion, focusing on vulnerable families and children. She was project leader for the research project 'Everyday life and wellbeing amongst children of prisoners'.

Aisling Parkes is a lecturer in the School of Law, University College Cork. Aisling's research interests lie in the areas of children's rights and family law as well as disability and the law. Her publications include articles on international children's rights including the rights of children with disabilities in journals such as the *Child and Family Law Quarterly, International Journal of Law Policy and the Family*, and *International Family Law*, as well as the contribution of a chapter to a book entitled *Child Protection and Welfare Social Work: Contemporary Themes and Practice Perspectives*. Her book, *Children and International Human Rights Law: The Right of the Child to be Heard*, was published by Routledge-Cavendish in 2011. Her current research includes work on the rights of children of incarcerated parents.

Peter Scharff Smith is Professor in the Sociology of Law at The Department of Criminology and Sociology of Law, Oslo University. He has previously done research at the Danish Institute for Human Rights, the University of Copenhagen, Cambridge University, and The Royal Danish Defense College. He has published books and articles in Danish, English, and German on prisons, punishment, and human rights, including works on prison history, prisoner's children, and the use and effects of solitary confinement in prisons. He has also written books and articles on the Waffen-SS and the Nazi war of extermination at the Eastern front. His publications include more than ten research monographs and edited collections and more than 70 articles and book chapters. Peter's latest book is *Scandinavian Penal History, Culture* *and Prison Practice. Embraced By the Welfare State?* (co-edited with Thomas Ugelvik), Palgrave Macmillan, 2017.

Karen Souza holds a PhD in psychology from City, University of London. Her dissertation research focused on resilience in relation to youth bystander reporting of peer violence. Karen was employed at the Institute of Criminology, University of Cambridge from 2006 to 2012. She is currently an affiliated researcher on the Families and Imprisonment Research (FAIR) study at Cambridge. She has previously published on the topics of sentencing, families and imprisonment, evidence-based practice in corrections, and restorative justice. Karen's current research interests lie in youth violence and victimization, offender risk assessment, and the effects of imprisonment on families.

Shenique S. Thomas is an Assistant Professor at the City University of New York (CUNY), Borough of Manhattan Community College. Her research sits within a criminology and human development framework and includes the social consequences of mass incarceration, race and ethnicity, and restorative justice. She has conducted research about the social implications of mass imprisonment and the utility of criminogenic risk assessments for specific offender groups.

Sara Wakefield is an Associate Professor in the School of Criminal Justice at Rutgers University. Her research interests focus on the consequences of mass imprisonment for the family, with an emphasis on childhood wellbeing and racial inequality, and she is co-author of *Children of the Prison Boom: Mass Incarceration and the Future of American Inequality* (with Christopher Wildeman). Related work examines the social networks and conditions of confinement of inmates and social/family ties during re-entry.

Christopher Wildeman is a Professor of Policy Analysis and Management at Cornell University and a Senior Researcher at the Rockwool Foundation Research Unit. His work considers the prevalence, causes, and consequences of contact with the criminal justice system and the child welfare system for families. His first book, *Children of the Prison Boom: Mass Incarceration and the Future of American Inequality* (with Sara Wakefield) was published by Oxford University Press in 2013.

1
The Sociology of Punishment and the Effects of Imprisonment on Families

Rachel Condry and Peter Scharff Smith

Introduction

The purpose of this book is to draw together some excellent scholarly work that has emerged in recent years and has begun to address the impact of criminal justice and particularly prison upon the families of offenders and the ways in which they are drawn into the realm of punishment. This research has appeared in a number of different countries and explores how imprisonment creates, reproduces, and reinforces patterns of social inequality. Much earlier work on prisoners' families was concerned with identifying the difficulties they faced and how this might be addressed through policy measures. In more recent years, studies have begun to explore deeper theoretical, legal, and sociological questions which have important implications for criminology and criminal justice, the sociology of punishment, human rights, and the broader study of social justice. This volume assembles examples of recent and ongoing research on prisoners' families and draws upon these studies not only to learn about the secondary effects and 'collateral consequences' of imprisonment but also to disentangle what the experiences and realities of prisoners' families mean for the sociology of punishment and our broader understanding of criminal justice systems. The sociology of punishment has gained very significant ground since the 1970s and we are today able to analyse and to some extent explain complicated phenomena such as penal populism, mass imprisonment, rehabilitative strategies towards offenders, and neo-liberal risk management—but this literature has often remained silent on the ways in which the families of prisoners are affected by our practices of punishment.

As the saying goes, sometimes you can't see the wood for the trees. The inability to understand a situation clearly because you are too involved in the details and lack overview is arguably more of a frequent occurrence when we deal with areas of life heavily shaped by history and tradition. The use of prisons and punishment seems to be such an area where many answers are often taken for granted, old practices are left unquestioned, and novel reform often seems difficult. Nevertheless, it is still a bewildering fact that while we have had prisons for centuries, and while the deprivation of liberty has been a central pillar in the Western mode of punishment since the early nineteenth century, we have only quite recently embarked upon serious discussion of the way imprisonment affects the families and relatives of offenders. Prisoners' families have only really begun to receive attention from researchers in the past couple of decades although millions of family members are affected yearly in the United States alone and hundreds of thousands in the United Kingdom, for example.

During the last 200 years, the effects of imprisonment on the individual prisoner (individual deterrence and rehabilitation) and the possible preventive effect on society at large (general deterrence) have been discussed intensively (Garland and Sparks,

2000, 8). In contrast the question of prisoners' relatives and children did not surface proper until late in the twentieth century and as recently as 2005 criminologists agreed that this was still a neglected area of research in great need of attention (Liebling and Maruna, 2005, 16). Since then a remarkable and quickly expanding wave of new research has produced numerous studies—qualitative as well as quantitative—which have appeared especially in Europe, Australia, and North-America. This research poses numerous fundamental questions to the sociology of punishment and the way punishment is practised and conceptualized in the Western world.

Punishment and society from the perspective of prisoners' families

With this book we take a step back to consider how punishment has come to be shaped in the way it has and how the many millions of people across the world who have the status of 'prisoners' family member' have remained relatively invisible in policy and politics, despite the recent growth in academic research. By doing so we consider the ways in which the state's power to punish is wielded disproportionality against those who are already likely to be experiencing a range of social disadvantages in their lives, providing us with a space to think about the meaning of 'justice' within criminal justice. Through the lens of prisoners' families, the various authors in this volume will discuss issues such as legitimacy, human rights, and social exclusion, and attempt a theoretical analysis of the broader relationship between prisons, punishment, family, and society. This analysis also speaks to philosophical debates about the meaning of— and justifications for—punishment in democratic societies. To understand the role of punishment in society we must attend not just to its formal content, but also to its further 'collateral' effects. These can include restrictions upon voting and full civic participation, restricted access to employment, housing, welfare benefits, healthcare, and general life-chances. These impact directly upon the primary subject of punishment, the offender, but also extend to his or her family network. In this way, collateral effects stretch both across time and through kin ties. It is important to explore whether these are incidental or deliberate consequences of punishment and whether these additional burdens can be justified.

This book has grown somewhat organically, essentially borne out of discussions which have developed over the past four years through panels organized by the editors at various conferences, including the British Society of Criminology conferences and the American Society of Criminology Annual Meetings in 2014 and 2015. These issues were explored in more depth during a two-day international symposium on 'Prisoners' Families, Punishment, and Social Inequality' organized by the editors at the University of Oxford in June 2015 and a workshop in Oxford in May 2017 where draft chapters for this book were discussed. In our view, the chapters that have emerged have benefited enormously from an ongoing dialogue over a number of years between members of a developing network of international researchers across eight countries. The resulting final chapters cover much ground but four sets of questions remain central throughout this book:

(1) In what ways does the experience of punishment extend beyond the prisoner to the family member? How might this best be understood and can it be justified? Why has this discussion been poorly reflected in the sociology of punishment?

(2) What types of inequalities and exclusions do prisoners' families experience? What theoretical tools should we employ to make sense of this? Are concepts such as social justice, social marginalization, and social exclusion useful?

(3) What does justice look like from the perspective of prisoners' families? How do they see the criminal justice system? To what degree are they treated with respect by the authorities and when and how do issues of legitimacy, trust, and fairness arise?

(4) How should we interpret the concepts of citizenship and human rights from the point of view of prisoners' families? The field of prisons and human rights is not only about prisoner rights but also involves relatives as rights holders living outside of prisons.

Towards a new sociology of punishment?

As the title of our book indicates, we hope our endeavours here will contribute to the development of a sociology of punishment that takes families seriously. Our intention is not to locate this volume in any one discipline—in fact, quite the contrary, it draws on and contributes to debates in a range of fields including criminology, sociology of law, social policy, philosophy of punishment, family studies, and so on—but rather to advocate an inclusive sociological approach to the effects of punishment. It is about the intersection of punishment with one of the most important organizing institutions in society, the family. When approached in this way it seems surprising that the *sociology* of punishment or punishment and *society* scholarship has not seen this intersection as central.

So what do we mean by a sociological approach or perspective? As David Garland reminded us over a quarter of a century ago, 'sociological perspectives view punishment as a complex social institution, shaped by an ensemble of social and historical forces and having a range of effects that reach well beyond the population of offenders' (Garland, 1991, 115). This wide reach is our concern. Calvin Morrill has described a sociological approach as comprising a number of elements: a relational approach, focusing on dynamic relationships between objects of study; attention to context, situating phenomenon in their social, cultural, and political environs; a concern with social hierarchies of all kinds, including power, domination, coercion, and inequality; and power as substantiated in racial, ethnic, gender, social class, or organizational forms (Morrill, in Harcourt et al., 2005). Our focus, then, is on these sociological elements within the intersection of the complex social institutions of punishment and the family, the effects that reach far beyond offenders to their kin, and with developing a sociological perspective that explores social, cultural, and political themes, relationships, hierarchies, and power.

Discovering the societal consequences of our penal practices

Historians normally agree that prisons have existed since the sixteenth century as institutions specifically established to incarcerate a significant number of people for prolonged periods of time (Morris and Rothman, 1998). For much of this time and especially in the last 200 years, the effects of imprisonment on prisoners have been discussed intensively. From the late nineteenth century and up until the 1960s, modern criminology saw 'the maladjusted delinquent' as 'the problem and correctional treatment was the solution' (Garland and Sparks, 2000, 8). The scope and focus of research have since broadened considerably but remarkably research on how the use of prisons affects the relatives and children of those imprisoned remained sparse up until recent decades. Given that the prison as an institution of punishment stretches more than 400 years back in time and that imprisonment has been a key sanction in Western penal practice in the last two centuries, this fact becomes even more astounding. Following Thomas Mathiesen's basic sociology of law distinction between how the law and its institutions can influence and shape society on the one hand, and is itself influenced and shaped by society on the other hand, we can certainly say that while the plight and fate of prisoners families has been heavily influenced by the legal and penal system for the last two centuries, their experience of being caught up in the turmoil of these institutions has until recently had minimal influence the other way around (Mathiesen, 2011).

Historically, the shift in the Western practice of punishment, which took place from the late seventeenth century until the early nineteenth century, gradually left a religiously defined system of public shaming and corporal punishment behind and produced a system of extreme isolation which—unlike the preceding system—had a unique ability to affect and sometimes even destroy family life. It is quite striking, to say the least, how effectively the modern system of imprisonment tends to sever the prisoner's important social relations without regard to those being cut off on the outside. In contrast, the pre-modern Western and Christian religious system of punishment—although psychically brutal and barbaric—often refrained from separating family members much longer than it took to corporally punish and publicly shame the offending part. True, the early prisons saw the light of day during the heyday of this religious system of punishment and especially the Dutch 'tuchthuis' model which spread across Europe during the seventeenth and eighteenth centuries. However, these pre-modern prisons never isolated their prisoners from the surrounding world, nor from their fellow prisoners as the nineteenth-century modern penitentiaries did, and their conditions and regimes, although dirty and unhealthy, were in many ways much more liberal and less regulated (Smith, 2014, 21 f.).

The modern penitentiary of the nineteenth century left the Western world with a system and a legacy of extreme isolation where the most basic form of interaction between prisoners and families—the prison visit—was a seldom and brief occurrence. In Denmark, for example, each prisoner was in 1919 allowed a 15-minute visit every third month (Smith, 2014, 25). The question of how to use prison visits as a way of maintaining and perhaps even developing family relationships is a much more recent phenomenon (as expressed for example in the European Prison Rules, rule 24.4) and even today some jurisdictions continue to make physical prison visits harder rather than easier through strict regimes and sometimes simply by locating prisons far away from cities and without any kind of public transportation (Reiter, 2016, 28). Indeed, recent developments suggest that some jurisdictions have considered partly replacing physical visits with Skype and video conferencing and in that sense the introduction of Information and Communications Technologies (ICTs) can be a double-edged sword. Even in countries typically associated with relatively liberal visiting policies, prisoners are sometimes placed very far from families without reasonable possibilities for regular physical visits as the Norwegian case of renting prison space in the Netherlands shows (FFP, 2015).

But why would one want to construct and continue to uphold a mode of punishment that has the capacity to ruin families, which are otherwise considered one of the most important pillars of society? Often, there is no shortage of political support for 'the family' as an institution which is generally considered to produce societal cohesion and solidarity. Indeed, 'the family has often been regarded as the cornerstone of society. In pre-modern and modern societies alike it has been seen as the most basic unit of social organization' (Haralambos and Holborn, 2004, 464). As expressed in the 1948 Universal Declaration of Human Rights, 'the family is the natural and fundamental group unit of society and is entitled to protection by society and the State' (Article 16.3). Considering this almost universal reliance on the family, it is certainly remarkable that our modern societies have chosen a method of punishing criminals that disrupts the basic life and functionality of many of the families that become swept up in the system of punishment.

Trends in research

From the 1960s to the 1990s, a limited number of studies appeared which focused upon prisoners' families and children. The most comprehensive of these early studies is Pauline Morris' pioneering 'Prisoners and their families' from 1965, which was based on, among other things, an impressive 588 interviews with wives of a wide range of prisoners from England and Wales who all had at least three months remaining of their sentence (Morris, 1965, 28 and 36). At that time the author was only able to identify one previous study which dealt with the effects of imprisonment on families (an unpublished PhD thesis) and concluded that while there had previously been 'a great deal of attention [...] on the delinquent inside an institution' their family members had been ignored (Morris, 1965, 17). Morris' study revealed several issues which we can recognize in contemporary research including, for example, the way that prisoners' partners often complained about financial problems (41 per cent regarded this as a 'major problem') and also reported 'disturbed behavior among children' as a significant challenge (Morris, 1965, 292). Indeed, the researchers regarded the latter issue as 'one of the most striking findings of the research and one meriting further systematic investigation' (Morris, 1965, 292).

During the 1970s and 1980s a few studies looked particularly at male prisoners and their families and all 'provided evidence of the benefits for parents and children of continuing contact during the prison sentence' (Boswell and Wedge, 2002, 21). Further, during the 1980s and 1990s a number of mainly qualitative studies appeared and described the situation of prisoners' children in various ways. This research was clearly important but the empirical data was typically quite limited in scope. An empirically significant study was conducted by Roger Shaw who through interviews and questionnaires sampled 415 imprisoned fathers who reported having more than 588 children (including stepchildren) (Shaw, 1987, 8 ff.). Shaw's research was carried out in a Midlands prison in England in the middle of the 1980s and showed how children of imprisoned fathers were a socially and economically very vulnerable group and how their problems were often exacerbated by the incarceration. As Shaw drily noted the 'whole basis of justice and punishment collapses when one repeatedly identifies children of prisoners who suffer more as a result of their father's sentence than did the original victim of the offence' (Shaw, 1987, 71). However, Shaw also found that the imprisonment was beneficial for some families and children (Shaw, 1987, 34 ff.)—an issue that we will return to. One of the key discussions in much of the (relatively sparse) research in this area from the later decades of the twentieth century was the extent to which parent–child ties were broken by imprisonment and the extent to which this separation was damaging, particularly for the children (Boswell and Wedge, 2002, 22 ff.; Catan, 1992; Christensen, 1999; Richards, 1992).

During the last decade and especially the last five years or so there has been a remarkable surge in literature about prisoners' families and particularly their children, and new research projects continue to emerge in different parts of the world. The at first gradual and then sudden massive increase in the volume of research in this area can be illustrated by a few numbers. A review which focused on the effects of parental incarceration on children counted 187 articles published between 1987 and 2011, three of which appeared in the 1980s, forty during the 1990s, and 144 during the 2000s (Johnson and Easterling, 2012, 344). Our own more recent search for literature has revealed that more than 260 new publications on prisoners' families, including parental incarceration and children of imprisoned parents, appeared between 2012 and September 2016, and many more have since followed. In other words, the rise of research in this area does not resemble a steady and slowly climbing curve but rather a sudden and extraordinary burst of writing after many years of minimal activity.

One can argue that much of the recent work on prisoners' children and families is part of a growing trend in research looking at the wider societal effects and inequalities associated with the use of imprisonment (Western, 2006; Western and Wildeman, 2009; Alexander, 2012; Tranæs and Geerdsen, 2008). In the United States this development has been a natural product of the phenomenon of mass imprisonment—that is, the use of incarceration on a scale hitherto unseen in the history of democratic societies. This 'prison boom' has made it apparent to even the most casual observer how imprisonment can and will affect society in many different and sometimes subtle ways—although many of these effects are likely to be found with varying intensity in most jurisdictions. As pointed out by Hagan and Dinovitzer, in 1999, at that time 'little attention' had been paid to the 'collateral effects' of the increased use of imprisonment (Hagan and Dinovitzer, 1999, 121), something which the authors themselves set out to change and in that process identified 'the impact of the imprisonment of parents on children' as the probably 'least understood and most consequential implication of the high reliance on incarceration in America' (Hagan and Dinovitzer, 1999, 122). Liebling and Maruna took a similar position six years later in a discussion of the effects of imprisonment in general when they concluded that 'there is little research emphasis on the effects of imprisonment on prisoner's families' (Liebling and Maruna, 2005, 16).

Numerous studies on the societal impact of imprisonment and mass incarceration has since followed and shown us, among other things, how prisons and jails in the United States have 'come to form part of a novel system of social inequality' (Western, 2006, xi). Recently, an overview of the consequences of mass imprisonment described how these encompass a wide range of themes including 'economic attainments, homelessness, mental health, social disability, subjective status, physical health, and political involvement' (Foster and Hagan, 2015a, 696). Nevertheless, among all these problems the question of how 'parental incarceration influences [...] children' was once again singled out as constituting a 'critical area of further research' (Foster and Hagan, 2015a, 696).

Regardless, there is no doubt that children of imprisoned parents have become the object of extensive research during the last decade or so. When viewing the recent quickly expanding literature on how the use of imprisonment affects families and children a number of topical themes stand out: the health effects of imprisonment in the family (see, e.g. Murray et al., 2009; Wakefield and Wildeman, 2014; Jones and Wainaina-Woźna, 2013); social exclusion of prisoners' families (including intergenerational and racial disadvantages (see, e.g. Foster and Hagan, 2015b; Halsey, 2017; Western and Wildeman, 2009; Wakefield and Wildeman, 2014; Siennick et al., 2014, 391; Condry et al., 2016); the (human) rights of family and children (see, e.g. Lagoutte, 2016; Lee et al., 2014; Smith, 2014; Donson and Parkes, this volume); as well as more practice and reform oriented work (see, e.g. Knudsen, 2016; Minson et al., 2015; Rossitera et al., 2015; Smith and Gampell, 2011).

This new wave of research on prisoners' families and children obviously has great relevance for criminology, the sociology of law, and the sociology of punishment in general—fields of study which have traditionally not been especially interested in prisoners' families. Even the sociology of imprisonment literature has traditionally focused more narrowly on the offender and the prison experience itself and developed influential theories about prisonization; the pains of imprisonment; the 'weight, depth and tightness' experienced by prisoners; and so forth (Clemmer, 1958 [1940]; Crewe, 2011; Sykes, 1958). As documented in this book, these theories can also be effectively applied to prisoners' families (Comfort, 2008; Aiello and McCorkel, 2017; Kotova, this volume; Lanskey et al., this volume).

There are other signs that the theme of prisoners' families might be entering into the more general literature on prisons and punishment (see Smith, this volume). But if we look at some of the standard mainstream criminological literature there appears to be little evidence that the question of prisons and families is being foregrounded, although the effects of imprisonment are of course discussed (see, e.g.: *The Oxford Handbook of Criminology*, 5th edition, 2012 and the recent 6th edition, 2017). When it comes to the sociology of law or philosophy of punishment one will have even less luck in finding relevant material in the literature (see Smith, this volume).

The literature on the effects on family and children

The existing literature has dealt with a long list of possible ways that imprisonment can influence family life and has discussed numerous concrete effects which these families and their members—partners, children, etc.—might experience. Here we will attempt to provide a brief overview of some of the central themes in the literature and how these have been categorized. Some keywords are: economic strain, stigma, shame, health, behaviour, family relations (especially parent–child), and social exclusion. The literature has treated these, and many other issues in great detail, which has included discussions about such diverse questions as infant mortality (Wakefield and Wildeman, 2014, 97 ff.), the importance of prison conditions (Smith, 2014), caregiver resilience (Arditti, 2012, 132 ff.), foster care placement (Andersen and Wildeman, 2014), parental incarceration as a risk factor for obesity among women (Roettger and Boardman, 2012), and the impact on civic participation (Lee et al., 2014), just to give a few examples.

Different authors have tried to group the various themes mentioned above (and many others) in different ways to get a sense of the general and overall effects imprisonment can have on families. For example, Braman operated with two basic categories in an essay on families and incarceration, namely (a) 'the costs of incarceration' (i.e. loss of income, loss of childcare assistance, added expenses, added stress, etc.); and (b) the changes in 'family organization' (i.e. strain on relationships, changes in gender norms, behaviour, etc.) (Braman, 2002, 118 ff.). In his later book *Doing Time on the Outside* he used three categories: (a) the effects of incarceration on family structure and relationships; (b) the material effects on social life; and (c) stigma (Braman, 2004, 10 f.). Condry et al. (2016), drawing on the work of Arditti (2012), have grouped these effects according to four categories: demographic characteristics and patterns of pre-existing disadvantage; cumulative disadvantage; institutional practices; and socio-political effects that include stigma and disenfranchisement. Arditti has also organized her discussion of the effects of incarceration on families along four further themes: (a) what she calls 'primary and secondary effects'; (b) 'traumatic separation and ambiguous loss'; (c) family contact and communications processes; and, finally, (d) family strength and resilience (Arditti, 2012, 97).

A British study identified a number of problems often experienced by prisoners' families, which could essentially be grouped into four main areas: (a) family relationships; (b) financial hardship; (c) stigmatization; and (d) the impact on children (Codd, 2008, 47 ff.). As already mentioned the classical sociology of imprisonment literature has also been used as a tool to understand and categorize the way imprisonment affects not only the prisoner but also the family (Comfort, 2008; Kotova, this volume; Lanskey et al., this volume). This, for example, includes the use of Gresham Sykes' theory on the 'pains of imprisonment' according to which deprivations of liberty, goods and services, sexual relationships, autonomy, and security are experienced by prisoners—and as originally argued by Comfort also in particular ways by their families (Comfort, 2008, 29). In her study on families of serious offenders Condry furthermore found that kin relationship, offence type, and the gender of the offender were some of the primary mediators of the effects experienced (Condry, 2007, 181).

The majority of work in this area has been focused particularly on prisoners' children and several of these studies have also attempted to categorize the effects produced by parental imprisonment. Hagan and Dinovitzer for example operated with three categories in their path-breaking review from 1999, namely: 'strains of economic deprivation, the loss of parental socialization through role modeling, support, and supervision, and the stigma and shame of social labeling' (Hagan and Dinovitzer, 1999, 123). Kruttschnitt has categorized research on the effects of parental imprisonment slightly differently within four areas: (a) insecure attachment; (b) economic strain; (c) stigma; and (d) social learning (Kruttschnitt, 2011, 831). In their 2008 review on 'The Effects of Parental Imprisonment on Children' Murray and Farrington structured their discussion about the possible associations between parental imprisonment and negative outcomes for the children along three categories: 'child antisocial behavior', 'mental health problems', and 'other adverse outcomes', where the latter included quite different things such as 'effects on child drinking, drugs, education, and employment' (Murray and Farrington, 2008). Other reviews and overviews of the possible effects have included, in addition to the already mentioned categories, themes such as, for example, the effects of imprisonment on the parent (does a prisoner become a worse parent?); the importance of prison regimes (including possibilities for contact); and the experience of social and administrative exclusion (Smith, 2014, 49 ff.).

Categorizing the effects of imprisonment on families

As we can see, there have been many attempts towards organizing an analysis of how imprisonment can impact upon families and they vary quite a bit. Some authors also differentiate between 'effects' and 'mediators' and 'moderators' of these effects—like prison conditions and national welfare policies—but the line between these categories can be blurred and of course depends on how one defines 'causes' and 'effects' and what exactly they relate to (for an explanation of moderators and mediators, see Murray et al., 2014, chapter 3). Is the act of imprisonment of a family member the sole *cause* and should everything else be termed *mediators* or *moderators*? As explained by Foster and Hagan—with regard to research on the effects of parental incarceration—most of the literature has viewed, for example, behavioural problems and low educational attainment as effects but one can 'also see these outcomes as potential mediating mechanisms [. . .] through which indirect effects are further transmitted' (Foster and Hagan, 2015b, 144). In other words, prison conditions, for example, can be very important for families and are likely to be able to produce (or mediate) effects in themselves. There is clearly a vast difference between having a family member locked up in solitary confinement hundreds or even thousands of miles away compared to having a family member in an open prison nearby, for example. Other factors that might be important include the police arrest procedures leading up the initial deprivation of liberty pre-trial and the duration of imprisonment.

Regardless, many themes recur in the different categorizations outlined above and the literature shows clear similarities in this regard. Below is an attempt to synthesize the available research and thereby suggest a way to categorize the effects and changes which have been discussed. We have used the differentiation between *effects*, *mediators*, and *moderators* in order to create a more workable and useful model even though, as noted above, it is not always clear where to draw the line between these categories.[1] Our list is not intended to be exhaustive but captures the essential issues treated in the currently available research.

Effects of imprisonment on the family—key issues:

1) Economic/material effects (financial hardship, employment, homelessness, etc.)
2) Changes in family relationships and quality (changes in family structure, lack of contact, the effects on parenting, etc.)
3) Health problems (mental health, physical health, infant mortality, etc.)
4) Behavioral changes among the children (antisocial and risk/criminal behavior, etc.)
5) Effects in relation to schooling and education (prisoners' children)
6) Social exclusion, inequality and citizenship (broader social effects and questions of democracy, rights and legitimacy)

One could say that an attempt to collapse all these effects into one category has been made with regard to prisoners' children and the use of the term 'wellbeing'—partly inspired by a human rights approach. However, indicators measuring such 'wellbeing' are typically informed by several of the issues already mentioned such as material welfare, family, and social relations (Oldrup and Frederiksen, this volume).

As already discussed, many issues can exacerbate or alleviate the above effects (moderators)—and are sometimes in themselves very important co-producers of these effects (mediators). The following two lists highlight some of the important factors in that regard. Moderators are factors that 'may indicate resilience or vulnerability to risk' and which 'precede the risk factor' (Murray et al., 2014, 39). Mediators on the other hand are 'mechanisms by which risk factor effects are produced' and they always 'occur after the risk factor and might be caused by the risk factor' (Murray et al., 2014, 34 and 39).

[1] For a slightly different way of grouping some of the below issues, see Foster and Hagan (2015b, 137 and 144 ff.). Foster and Hagan 'urge future research to attend to indirect as well as direct effects of parental imprisonment' (144) and in that spirit mention some of the below listed 'effects' as mediators (e.g. education, behavioural problems, and family resources/processes, 137).

Possible mediators—some key issues:

(1) Stigma, guilt, and shame (including secrecy, lies, and ambivalent emotions)
(2) Type of offence (the reason for the incarceration)[2]
(3) Police practices (during arrests and pre-trial detention)
(4) Prison regimes, programmes, and prison culture/conditions (including travel distances)
(5) The duration of imprisonment

Possible moderators—some key issues:

(1) Family and individual resilience (family situation, economic/social status, networks/support)
(2) Gender, ethnicity, and age
(3) Welfare policies and social services
(4) The work of non-governmental organizations (NGOs) (support from civil society)

In real life and in empirical research it can obviously be difficult to distinguish between all these categories and many of them are interwoven and closely interrelated. Furthermore, the weight with which these problems and experiences affect families will of course vary greatly, but that they can do so intensively and extensively is clear. In her study on 'fugitive life in an American city' Alice Goffman describes the fluid and often extreme reality of family life in the shadow of mass imprisonment in Black neighbourhoods and points to the creation of a culture of distrust and suspicion, which is a product of several of the above mentioned factors. According to Goffman, a 'new social fabric is emerging under the threat of confinement: one woven in suspicion, distrust, and the paranoiac practices of secrecy, evasion and unpredictability' (Goffman, 2014, 8)—a culture or 'fabric' which will often destroy 'familial and romantic relationships that are often quite fragile to begin with' (Goffman, 2014, 90).

Positive effects

Importantly, some authors also make the point that for some families' incarceration of a family member can have a positive impact—although sometimes alongside other negative impacts. This can, for example, be the case in situations where a parent has abused family members and/or is heavily drug dependent (Smith, 2014, 187 ff.; Wakefield and Wildeman, 2014, 152 f.; Wakefield and Powell, 2016). Wakefield and Wildeman, for example, found that domestic violence moderated the effects of paternal imprisonment significantly and concluded that 'the consequences of paternal incarceration in the presence of abuse are more complex than they are in its absence' (Wakefield and Wildeman, 2014, 155). A qualitative study from Portugal based on interviews showed how imprisonment can sometimes 'interrupt destructive cycles of abuse and violence and, up to a certain point and with the necessary resources, be seen by family members as an opportunity to change trajectories and to foster the reconstruction of

---

[2] This of course depends on what takes place before the arrest and incarceration (and is not a mediator in that sense). But technically the type of offence is not established until the arrested person has been before a judge where, initially, a reason for the pre-trial detention is decided, and later, when sentenced, a reason for the imprisonment of a convicted prisoner is officially established.

relationships' (Granja, 2016, 286). This is hardly surprising but nevertheless an important reminder that while the effects of incarceration on families are often negative and sometimes decidedly disruptive, this is clearly not always the case. An American study on 'relationship quality during and after incarceration' also gave somewhat mixed results and while 'paternal incarceration in the past 2 years was, by and large, associated with lower mother-reported (but not father-reported) relationship quality […] across some outcome variables, current paternal incarceration was positively associated with relationship quality' (Turney, 2015, 480). The study concluded that 'current and recent incarceration have countervailing consequences for relationship quality and, more generally, that the penal system exerts a powerful influence even among couples who maintain relationships' (Turney, 2015, 480). There is also evidence that, while visiting imprisoned parents is often extremely important for children, it can also be a very stressful experience and in some cases prove more problematic than positive for the children. In some cases, unstable imprisoned parents might even forget or ignore their children as soon as they are released (Smith, 2014, 191).

Theoretical explanations

It is beyond the scope of this introduction to look thoroughly at all the attempts to create theoretical models for analysing and explaining the way imprisonment affects family members—but authors have focused on a range of different issues such as, for example, stigma, exclusion, attachment theory, and prison conditions—a mixture of effects and moderators in other words. We find one of the most influential contributions to the understanding of how the use of imprisonment can impact family life in Megan Comfort's theory of 'secondary prisonization' (Comfort, 2008). Here Comfort draws on the classical sociology of imprisonment and expands Clemmer's theory on prisonization from 1940 to include spouses and partners by analysing 'how women with incarcerated partners undergo *secondary prisonization*, a less absolute but still powerful form of Clemmer's construct, derivate of and dependent on the primary prisonization of their partners' (Comfort, 2008, 15). In her study of relatives of serious offenders Condry drew on Goffman's notion of stigma and described how these relatives experienced a form of 'secondary stigma' and were 'deemed responsible' for both the actions of their relative and for their continued support for the offender (Condry, 2007, 62). The families and relatives studied by Condry and Comfort were clearly affected deeply, in many detrimental ways and over very long periods of time, by the imprisonment of a relative (Condry, 2007; Comfort, 2008) and later qualitative research has supported these findings (see, e.g. Aiello and McCorkel, 2017; Granja, 2016; Jardine, 2015; Kotova, this volume).

Much of the research on prisoners' children has also discussed, among other things, the stigma of being associated with an imprisoned parent (Bernstein, 2005, 193; Manby et al., 2015; Minson, 2016; Murray et al., 2014; Smith, 2014). Several studies have drawn on John Bowlby's well-known 'attachment theory', according to which separation from parents is generally detrimental to children (Murray and Farrington, 2008, 724 f.; Bjercke, 1994, 18). Murray and Farrington (2008) provide an overview of some of the theories applied to explain how children are affected by parental imprisonment and include in their discussion: trauma theories; modelling and social learning theories; strain theories; stigma and labelling theories; as well as what they call 'other mediating factors', which include perceptions of punishment, inadequate explanations, and prison visits (Murray and Farrington, 2008, 171 ff.).

Several authors are interested in the way prisoners' families and children can experience both social and administrative exclusion (Murray, 2006, 208; Smith, 2014, 79 ff.). In this spirit, Hagan and Foster adopt what they call a 'systematic social exclusion perspective' which 'recognizes and emphasizes the multiple deliberately chosen and overlapping institutional policy domains by and from which the children of incarcerated parents are excluded' (Hagan and Foster, 2015, 82; Foster and Hagan, 2015b; see also Dennison and Besemer, this volume).

Other approaches seek to theorize how the effects on families can best be understood in relation to punishment. Some have critiqued the common use of the term 'collateral' to characterize these effects (Kirk and Wakefield, 2017). Condry and Minson argue that the term 'symbiotic harms' better captures the effects on families. They suggest that these harms have five vital characteristics that are not captured by the notion of 'collateral': they are *relational*; they are characterized by *mutuality*; they are *non-linear*; families experiencing them have *agency* and are not simply passive recipients of these effects; and they are *heterogeneous* in experience and impact. Symbiotic harms follow from punishment, but are not part of punishment itself. Yet, Condry and Minson argue, they should still be given full consideration within punishment theory, first because they are significant and serious effects that are due to punishment, and second because they breach the rights of citizens who are innocent of wrong-doing (see also Condry; Minson; Smith; Donson and Parkes, this volume).

Taken together, the practice of imprisonment has during recent decades been studied extensively as a powerful force which relates to and affects society in many significant and often detrimental ways. This is certainly true with regard to how imprisonment affects families. Research tells us that these effects are significant across jurisdictions, and involve issues from economy and education to mental and physical health.

Families and prison: a definition

If we want to consider how the use of prisons and imprisonment affects families, it is as well to be clear about what 'prison' is and how we define a 'family'. Prison is often defined as a place—typically a building—where a group of inmates are placed as punishment for having committed one or more criminal acts. Furthermore, the purpose of this institution, as defined and discussed within law, criminology, and sociology, has traditionally been to rehabilitate, incapacitate, and/or deter offenders (and the public) from committing crime or, according to some, simply to deliver society's just retribution. However, prison systems normally also include various forms of pre-trial detention (jails, remand prisons, etc.) which are not always distinguished in the literature, though the effects of these institutions are certainly also relevant to the present context. For the purpose of this book 'prison', 'imprisonment', and 'incarceration' are therefore defined broadly to include not only imprisonment of sentenced prisoners but also pre-trial detention (remand imprisonment) and in principle all forms of the deprivation of liberty traditionally used within prison systems.

The question of how we define 'family' is a somewhat more contested space than the question of what constitutes imprisonment. Indeed, while part of the problems studied in this book have to do with the relative lack of reform, change, and development within the area of prisons and punishment, there is little doubt that the concept of the 'family' and the question of what this is has changed significantly during recent years, although the scale of these changes is of course culturally dependent. As pointed out by Erera, the family is not simply a social institution, but 'an ideological construct laden with symbolism and with a history and politics of its own' (Erera, 2002, 2).

In many places the family has clearly moved 'toward greater diversity in both its form and function' (Chriss, 2015, 59) and in some parts of the world a conservative and narrow definition of families has had to make way for a much more liberal understanding of this particular concept. Consequently, a variety of new and diverse forms of families have emerged including not only the 'traditional heterosexual nuclear family' but also 'single-headed households', 'blended families (including stepfamilies or multiple generations of kin living in the same household', and 'same-sex marital or domestic partners' (Chriss, 2015, 59).

There are undoubtedly many who disagree with such an expanding and liberal definition of the family and at the other end of the scale we have cultures which prefer arranged marriages and allow little or no creativity in redefining the family as an institution. In most liberal democracies it is still fair to say that 'at least at some level, biological and marital ties remain intrinsic to our cultural understandings of the family' (Holtzmann, 2008, 170). Nevertheless, we have to conclude that families, their roles, forms, and functions have developed significantly in the Western world during the last 50 years or so. According to Holtzmann 'cultural understandings of what it means to be a family have broadened considerably in recent years' and she points to a number of social changes which have caused this (Holtzmann, 2008, 168). This includes 'rising rates of divorce and remarriage', 'cohabitation', as well as 'gay and lesbian marriage and parenting'. These changes have 'helped to promote more expansive definitions of the family' and consequently, the 'family has come to reflect more than two married parents and their biological children—for many, it also includes stepfamilies, cohabiting couples, and gay and lesbian couples with or without children' (Holtzmann, 2008, 168). According to some sociologists this changing nature of the family is not always reflected in policies, and nor in research: 'Much of the sociological study of the family still views the two-adult, heterosexual, married couple, residing together with their biologically related offspring, as constituting "the family"' (Farrell et al., 2012, 296 f.). This is also the case with some of the literature on prisoners' families.

Another important change with regard to families which has importance also for those related to prisoners is the significant change in parenting cultures which has taken place during recent decades. For example, some authors talk about the development of what has been termed 'intensive parenting' (Hays, 1996; Granja et al., 2014)—that is, a parenting culture, or ideology, which 'places strenuous expectations' on parents while ignoring the implications of, for example, economic status, education, age, and ethnicity (Granja et al., 2014, 1213 f.). Needless to say, such a culture can leave imprisoned mothers and fathers increasingly incapacitated and even further removed from the ideal of a responsible and loving parent.

For the purpose of this book it will clearly not be relevant to adopt a narrow definition of the family—a strictly legal or biological definition of family is unlikely to capture the diversity of prisoners' families and will instead function as yet another exclusionary mechanism. As explained by Jardine, 'we must guard against privileging family displays that fit most comfortably within a white, middle-class framework, and ensure that the voices of all families affected by imprisonment are heard in the growing conversations about their needs' (Jardine, 2017, 1). It therefore makes sense to follow Schwartz and Scott who 'define family as any relatively stable group of people bound by ties of blood, marriage, adoption; or by any sexually expressive relationship; or who simply live together, and who are committed to and provide each other with economic and emotional support' (Schwartz and Scott, 2007, 3). This definition does not lie too far from the one offered in the *Oxford Dictionary of Sociology*: 'The family is an intimate domestic group made up of people related to one another by bonds of blood, sexual mating, or legal ties' (Scott and Marshall, 2009).

Some themes emerging in this book

As we have described, the overarching frame of this book is the intersection of the complex social institutions of punishment and the family, the effects of punishment that reach far beyond offenders to their kin, and a broadly sociological perspective that explores social, cultural, and political themes, and relationships, hierarchies, and power to understand the social harms of punishment. Within this broad focus, there are a number of emerging themes in the chapters that follow.

1. Multidisciplinary lenses and analytical frameworks

To some extent, this is the very premise of this book which is founded upon an interdisciplinary approach to making sense of the experience of prisoners' families. The authors represent different disciplines, including law, psychology, criminology, and the sociology of law; and though many of the contributors are criminologists, criminology itself brings to bear a range of disciplines to the study of crime and punishment. Here we find a variety of analytical frameworks drawn from the field of law and human rights, sociology and social policy, family studies and trauma, political and punishment philosophy, and historical analysis. Similarly, many of the contributors share a methodological approach that prioritizes direct engagement with the families themselves, for example through in-depth interviews and observation, while others use administrative or survey data, or analyse policy and legal developments or sentencing transcripts. Our approach is by definition international—contributions are from eight countries—but this is dominated, beyond Europe at least, by English-speaking countries where most work on prisoners' families is currently produced. A challenge for the future will be to expand our knowledge of the wider impact of punishment on the family beyond these countries, and particularly throughout the Global South.

2. The family and its members as the starting point

Whatever analytical frameworks are used, the research included in this book begins with the prisoners' family members as the primary focus, in contrast to studies that include families as a side-issue, and give prominence to the prisoner and the prison. It has often been the case that family members only become visible through the prisoner and the prison—when they enter the prison as visitors, for example, or for the positive contribution they bring to resettlement when the prisoner is released. Here, the family and its members are the starting point for our analyses—the individual family member's lived experience is worthy of study in its own right, and not a 'collateral' or 'secondary' issue. This follows a tradition of prisoners' families research that has strengthened considerably in recent years, as outlined earlier in this chapter. So, for example, Thomas and Christian explore how prisoners and their family members navigate complexities of a prison sentence across time, what they do with the circumstances they are placed in, and how visitation is crucial to this process. Several authors explore the creative negotiation of family involvement and how relationships are sustained across a prison sentence (Granja, this volume; Comfort, 2002, 2008; Jardine, 2017). Arditti's starting point is what she describes as a 'family perspective', with the family itself—children and their caregivers—as the unit of analysis, facilitating her account of inequality at the level of the family. Knudsen interviews children and prioritizes their own telling of their experiences, while Kotova draws upon interviews with the female partners of long-term prisoners to illuminate the particular difficulties they experience. Jardine writes about the importance of giving families who are already marginalized a voice and listening to their perspectives and views. Similarly, Dennison and Besemer emphasize the importance of studying how children of prisoners themselves experience social exclusion—the perspectives of children are often missing in the literature on social exclusion (see also Oldrup and Frederiksen, this volume). As Dennison and Besemer show, children's experiences may be quite distinct from others in the family, and those in their study prioritized such things as missing their imprisoned father, play, the activities they did together, and acutely feeling his absence at significant events. They described feeling isolated and different from their peers, and this 'missing out' took a significant emotional toll.

3. Intersectional inequality and multiple disadvantage

Part I of this book focuses specifically upon the complexities of social inequality and multiple disadvantage, and this remains a key theme throughout. It has long been recognized that the families of prisoners experience multidimensional and intersectional forms of inequality (Western and Pettit, 2010) and chapters in this volume seek to explain the processes to which they are subject and to delve into exactly what those dimensions comprise, and how they are experienced and lived. There are different ways of conceptualizing this disadvantage and authors do so using concepts such as social exclusion (Dennison and Besemer; Oldrup and Frederiksen), social and administrative exclusion (Smith), the entrenching of social inequalities and marginalization (Arditti; Jardine; Thomas and Christian), family inequality (Arditti), and threats to social justice (Condry; Lanskey et al.).

As Wakefield and Wildeman argue, the racialized nature of imprisonment in the United States (and elsewhere) and the importance of the criminal justice system for understanding the American stratification system have long been recognized. They review findings of their previous work which showed how parental incarceration translates into very large childhood inequalities that represent a potentially massive shift in the life chances of those children. Their work has shown this in relation to childhood behavioural problems (Wakefield and Wildeman 2011), homelessness (Wildeman, 2014), and infant mortality (Wildeman, 2012). In their chapter in this volume, Wakefield and Wildeman advocate the need for a more nuanced approach to race, moving beyond Black–White comparisons and thinking through how inequality may manifest in other racial/ethnic groups, including Hispanics and Native Americans. They argue that we need to study inequality within countries but also between countries, for example they note that the American–Denmark disparity in parental incarceration rivals the Black–White disparities in the United States. Wakefield and Wildeman emphasize the need to 'think about inequality in a broader sense including both other racial/ethnic groups and other nations while also interrogating variation in the incarceration experience—rather than just more outcomes'. In his chapter Halsey shows how intergenerational incarceration weaves its way through families in very different ways with devastating impact, and that this is strikingly disproportionate in indigenous communities in Australia.

Dimensions of inequality and disadvantage intersect in the lives of families of prisoners and are further worsened by their experiences of the justice system. Thomas and Christian, for example, conducted primary research on prison visiting and interviewed incarcerated men, exploring how those men and their family members navigate positions of marginality, social exclusion, and invisibility in wider society and within the prison itself. The family members who are central to enhancing the visibility and legitimacy of these men in prison are primarily women from economically disadvantaged racial and ethnic minority groups, and Thomas and Christian argue that their own marginalization is compounded through their experience of prison visiting.

Comfort turns her focus to the problem of gender and how couples navigate gender roles and expectations throughout a prison sentence and then again on release, something which is often the source of tension and struggle. Comfort explores exactly how female non-incarcerated partners of prisoners and male prisoners enact particular forms of femininity and masculinity through the prison sentence and how performing acceptable constructions of gender changes through the cycle of imprisonment and release. Within many of the chapters in this volume the visible family members—and those doing the primary supporting of prisoners—are women, and the labour involved in supporting a prisoner compounds the other care work that dominates their lives (Condry, 2007; Jardine, 2015, and this volume).

Some authors make the point that marginalization needs to be understood in terms of blocked opportunities to a meaningful quality of life. Dennison and Besemer define the socially excluded as those who 'lack access to the activities and living conditions, or participation in key activities that are customary in the society in which they live'. The Australian children of prisoners they studied experienced barriers to participation in activities resulting from the financial impacts of imprisonment, parental absence, and related practical consequences. Oldrup and Frederiksen also understand social exclusion as a complex and multidimensional process and argue for a child-oriented perspective. They use administrative data to explore the experience of social exclusion in a representative sample of children of Danish prisoners, with a focus on the importance of social relations and networks, comparing them with a sample of children from the general population in Denmark. They find that vulnerability is higher in prisoners' children across the domains of material welfare, family, school, and leisure activities.

Condry draws on the capabilities approach to show how families of prisoners are deprived of a wide range of opportunities, including for play and the enjoyment of recreational activities. Halsey argues that prisoners should be provided with consistent and structured involvement in non-trivial activities such as challenging educational courses, cutting-edge industry/training options, vibrant and sophisticated arts based workshops, and competitive sports, in order to substantively reduce the risk of prisoner discontentment and/or outright frustration and aggression. He argues that it is through such activities that prisoners might concretely demonstrate to family that there are 'real' things to discuss and that personal growth is possible even behind bars. Poverty and economic marginalization are clearly crucially important to both prisoners and their families, but quality of life is about more than addressing basic needs. Finally, our analysis of inequality and intersecting disadvantage highlights some of the gaps in our knowledge about prisoners' families. For example, most research on the partners of prisoners examines heterosexual relationships—we know very little about the relationships of those with other sexual orientations or identities. Similarly, we know little about how disability intersects with other forms of marginalization for prisoners' families.

4. Prisoners' families, the state and society

More than fifty years ago C. Wright Mills exhorted us to exercise sociological imagination in recognizing what might initially look like private troubles as public issues:

> An issue is a public matter […] It is the very nature of an issue, unlike even widespread trouble, that it cannot very well be defined in terms of the everyday environments of ordinary men. An issue, in fact, often involves a crisis in institutional arrangements […] and we may not hope to find its solution within the range of opportunities open to any one individual. (Mills, 1959, 9)

The expansion of imprisonment and the compounding disadvantage experienced by millions of family members worldwide can certainly be understood as a crisis in institutional arrangements whose solution is not to be found at the individual level—what might initially appear to be private family suffering, and an individual family paying the consequences for an offence committed by one of their own, can be seen instead as part of a crisis at the level of society. A society has an ethical and moral duty to protect innocent citizens when they are affected by the actions of others or by particular consequences that flow from the state action of punishment. Condry explores this point in her analysis of the impact of the social injustices experienced by prisoners' families for society. Individual prisoners' family members suffer harm as a consequence of their relative's imprisonment, have individual rights that are breached, and experience broader patterns of marginalization and discrimination that compound and connect to pre-existing forms. As Condry argues, their status as citizens and their ability to fully participate as political actors is impaired, yet they themselves have not committed a crime or breached any aspect of the social contract.

Part II of this volume sets out the ways in which the reach of penal power negates the fundamental human rights of families of prisoners. Smith shows how a family and human rights lens from the perspective of families and children of prisoners enables us to consider their rights to privacy and a family life, the individual rights of children to be heard, to be treated in their best interests, and not to be discriminated against. As Smith shows, very often these rights are not protected in practice, and to uphold these rights for children would have wide ranging implications for policy, practice, and legal standards when their parents are arrested, when they are sentenced, and throughout imprisonment. Smith employs the sociology of punishment and literature on public sentiments on justice to demonstrate the major problems of legitimacy created when the family perspective is neglected by the state. Smith argues that:

> [H]uman rights carry a potential strength in terms of increasing the moral credibility of criminal justice systems by making them more respectful of vulnerable groups. The central purpose of human rights is after all to protect people against abuse from the state and studies on the informed public sense of justice arguably show us that people generally respect and want to help marginalized and disadvantaged groups. Furthermore, strengthening the rights and protection of prisoners' families' vis-à-vis the criminal justice system will in turn help shape society's view and understanding of this group of people and in doing so potentially increase social cohesion.

Such an approach has been adopted in Norway, for example, where prison law has recognized the rights of prisoners' children by legally establishing children's rights to contact with their parents as a general principle and requiring that children 'shall receive special attention' during their parents' imprisonment (Smith, 2014, 233).

In their chapter, Loucks and Loureiro show that although Scotland has not incorporated the United Nations Convention on the Rights of the Child into domestic law, it is making greater progress than other parts of the United Kingdom in seeking to address those rights, though there is still some way to go. In contrast, Donson and Parkes argue that little attention has been paid by the state in Ireland to the rights of children who have a parent in prison. This is despite a general advancement in children's rights in Ireland from both a policy and law reform perspective. Children of prisoners are not identified in education or child protection policy, nor in wider criminal justice and court practice. Both Donson and Parkes and Minson in this volume show that children due to be separated from a parent by imprisonment do not have their rights considered in the same way as children separated by other measures. As Minson argues, children in society are one of the least powerful and most vulnerable groups, unable to fight for their rights to be respected—it is vital to highlight the rights of children whose parents are sentenced, and the breach of duty of care the state has towards those children.

Lanskey et al. analyse the experiences of prisoners' families through a sociological framework that focuses upon the reach of penal power into the lives of families. They draw upon concepts from prison sociology and primary research in England to show how the depth, weight, breadth, and tightness of penal power are experienced in very particular ways by family members. Lanskey et al. argue that these pains are both acute (such as shock and other intense emotions at arrest and sentencing) and chronic (longer-term hardships and concerns). Both Smith and Jardine explore one concerning effect on families of prisoners that follows repeated negative interactions with prison staff: damage to those families' sense of the legitimacy of state institutions. Smith describes a kind of 'upside-down world' for families in which society's official representatives become enemies instead of sources of support. Jardine found in her research on prisoners' families in Scotland that negative interactions between families and the prison lead to antagonistic 'us and them' relationships which were damaging to both legitimacy and citizenship. As Jardine shows, adversarial interactions can be cumulative and may also stem from other interactions with state agencies such as benefits agencies or social workers, ultimately resulting in already socially marginalized people becoming even more so. As Smith argues, antipathy towards society and agencies of the state can lead to both social and administrative exclusion for families.

Several authors in this book argue that the state has obligations to children and families of prisoners as a result of the negative consequences that follow from the punishment of the prisoner. Drawing upon Bulow (2014), Minson (2017) has argued that consideration must be given to the question of whether residual obligations arise from the breach of the rights of citizens who are harmed by imprisonment. These obligations might include financial help, housing assistance, and better visits provision. In reality, most countries fall short on these measures, and in the United Kingdom almost all direct support for prisoners' families is provided through the voluntary sector.

One time at which the state might take their obligations to children into consideration is at the point of sentencing. In her chapter, Minson shows that both case law and sentencing guidelines in England and Wales say that judges ought to consider the welfare of child dependents in adult sentencing cases, but her research suggests that this does not always happen and that Crown Court judiciary have a limited understanding of the consequences that flow to children of imprisoned mothers. Evidence from other countries shows that this can be done successfully with unique punishments for parents who are primary carers. Minson argues for a communitarian conception of justice, following Nicola Lacey (2003), which takes account of the wide-reaching implications of punishment and the suffering of those who are involved with prisoners.

Knudsen describes the 'systemic invisibility' of children of prisoners in Canada, which she traces through the children's own families, their communities, in the prison system, and in the wider society. She uses Purdie-Vaughns and Eibach's (2008) concept of 'intersectional invisibility' to explain how members of marginalized groups can become acutely socially invisible through processes of stigmatization and interrelated exclusion. The interests of children of prisoners are subordinated and this invisibility has utility for the justice system as it need not recognize any responsibilities it might have to families.

5. Heterogeneity and complexity of prisoners' families

Prisoners' families are not a homogenous group and vary in numerous ways—socio-economically, in terms of age, gender, ethnicity, sexuality, and so on. They are not all affected in the same way by the experience of a relative's imprisonment. Some family members might also be offenders themselves, and others completely law abiding. Their lived experiences might also vary by the type(s) of offences committed, criminal histories, sentence length, prison type, gender, and kin relationship, to name but a few important characteristics. We might say that there are differences between families, within families, and within individuals at different times. As Lanskey et al. argue, we need to know more about how the experiences of families of prisoners vary across time and not just view this as a static condition. Families are affected across the criminal justice process, from the point of arrest through court and trial processes, to sentencing, imprisonment, community punishments, and on release. Their experiences through these various processes are unlikely to remain constant. For example, Comfort highlights the challenges, frustration, and disappointment that can accompany men's return from prison to their families—'the post-release period is rife with complex emotions, interpersonal conflict, and a pervasive feeling of being let down—by oneself, one's partner, and society at large.'

Minson draws our attention to this heterogeneity in the experience of the children of prisoners, some of whom might experience few or even positive effects from the imprisonment of a parent while for many others the negative impact is intensified. Some children may have protective factors such as secure attachments and stable caregiving arrangements, and others may be more resilient, all of which can change across time producing further variability. Yet as Minson outlines, despite this variation, most studies find a wide variety of negative consequences for children of prisoners. When it is their mother that is imprisoned every aspect of their life is affected—they experience the loss of their primary carer, their home, and experience various forms of social marginalization and threats to identity which Minson characterizes as 'confounding grief' (Minson, 2017). The same variation in response can be found in families generally—people respond differently to the circumstances they find themselves in, and may be more resilient or protected by factors such as economic security or class advantage and social capital.

Part III of this book draws together a series of first-hand studies of the families of prisoners that show the need for careful empirical work to explore the lived experiences of prisoners' families and understand their complexities. For example, Hutton draws a contrast between her personal experience visiting a family member in prison and the way she was treated as an 'official' visitor, entering the prison as a researcher. Hutton argues that the stigmatization of prisoners' families is institutionalized in prisons and that 'courtesy stigma' (Goffman, 1963) is embodied in the national rules and local procedures of prisons and their visiting practices. She shows how prisoners' families experience less favourable and discriminatory practices compared to official prison visitors, despite the fact both groups enter the prison as outsiders. Hutton argues that 'this is reinforced by the troubling way that all of these discriminatory measures operate corporally; they mandate a more intimate engagement with the bodies of those who are more intimately connected to prisoners compared to those who are not. The rules allow social visitors' bodies to be searched more rigorously and be subjected to greater scrutiny on prison grounds.'

We need more nuanced data and research to allow us to explore these complexities and variation. Wakefield and Wildeman sum this up in their chapter: 'many of the studies in this volume demonstrate the significant heterogeneity of experiences that are typically hidden in quantitative work. The confinement experience, for example, varies tremendously across type of facility, jurisdiction, and even prisoners within the same unit may have very different incarceration experiences (Crewe, 2009; Kotova, this volume; Schaefer et al., 2017) as well as orient towards maintaining family contact quite differently (Granja, this volume). Current work does little to distinguish between jail and prison incarceration (but see Apel, 2016;) or incarceration from other forms of criminal justice contact such as arrest or conviction (but see Sugie and Turney, 2017). The creative application of new methods and original data collection have moved the field forward but there are still many questions that cannot be answered with the data infrastructure in the United States.'

At the moment, prisoners' families occupy an odd position of an increasing visibility in the academic realm (as described in this chapter), alongside an ongoing invisibility as far as many governments worldwide are concerned (though there are variations in the degree to which this is so). As Smith says in his chapter, we can no longer describe these families as 'forgotten' by the research community when we see the growth in academic literature, yet they are very often forgotten and excluded by society's official institutions. Prisoners' families do not often garner public support (though prisoners' children are sometimes given more sympathy)—relatives of prisoners rarely campaign or present a public face—and are likely left to manage their situation alone, or only receive help through specialist NGOs. The stigma and marginalization plotted by authors in this volume to some degree silences the families of prisoners, and facilitates a casual neglect on the part of the state. Yet the profound disadvantage wrought by imprisonment and the devastating consequences of punishment for innocent citizens should be of concern to all in society. Our aim in this volume is to contribute to ongoing sociological analysis of why this matters and to advocate for an inclusive sociology of punishment which sees the family (one of the most important institutions in society) as central to this endeavour.

References

Aiello, B. and McCorkel, J. 2017. 'It Will Crush You Like a Bug': Maternal Incarceration, Secondary Prisonization, and Children's Visitation'. *Punishment & Society*. Available at: https://doi.org/10.1177/1462474517697295.

Alexander, M. 2012. *The New Jim Crow: Mass Incarceration in the Age of Colorblindness*. New York: The New Press.

Andersen, S. H. and Wildeman, C. 2014. 'The Effect of Paternal Incarceration on Children's Risk of Foster Care Placement', *Social Forces*, 93(1), 269–98.

Apel, R. 2016. 'The Effects of Jail and Prison Confinement on Cohabitation and Marriage', *Annals of the American Academy of Political and Social Science*, 665(1), 103–26.

Arditti, J. A. 2012. *Parental Incarceration and the Family*. New York: New York University Press.

Bernstein, N. 2005. *All Alone in the World. Children of the Incarcerated*. New York: The New Press.

Bjercke, E. C. 1994. *Arbeidsgruppen som skal utrede forholdene for barn med foreldre i fengsel*. Oslo: Ministry of Justice.

Boswell, G. and Wedge, P. 2002. *Imprisoned Fathers and their Children*. London: Jessica Kingsley Publishers.

Braman, D. 2002. 'Families and incarceration', in Mauer, M. and Chesney-Lind, M. (eds.) *Invisible Punishment: The Collateral Consequences of Mass Imprisonment*. 117–36. New York: The New Press.

Braman, D. 2004. *Doing Time on the Outside*. Ann Arbor, MI: The University of Michigan Press.

Bulow, W. 2014. 'The Harms beyond Imprisonment: Do We Have Special Moral Obligations Towards the Families and Children of Prisoners?', *Ethical Theory and Moral Practice*, 17(4), 775–89.

Catan, L. 1992. 'Infants with Mothers in Prison' in Shaw, R. (ed.) *Prisoners' Children. What Are the Issues?* 13–28. New York: Routledge.

Chriss, J. J. 2015. *Social Control: An Introduction*. Cambridge: Polity Press.

Christensen, E. 1999. *Forældre i fængsel*. Copenhagen: SFI.

Clemmer, D. 1958. [1940]. *The Prison Community*. New York: Holt, Rinehart and Winston.

Codd, H. 2008. *In the Shadow of Prison. Families, Imprisonment and Criminal Justice*. Cullompton: Willan Publishing.

Comfort, M. 2002. '"Papa's House": The Prison as Domestic and Social Satellite'. *Ethnography*, 3(4), 467–99.

Comfort, M. 2008. *Doing Time Together. Love and Family in the Shadow of the Prison*. Chicago: University of Chicago Press.

Condry, R. 2007. *Families Shamed. The Consequences of Crimes for Relatives of Serious Offenders*. Cullompton: Willan Publishing.

Condry, R., Kotova, K., and Minson, S. 2016. 'Collateral damage: The families and children of prisoners', in Jewkes, Y. et al. (eds.) *Handbook on Prisons* (2nd ed.). 662–41. Abingdon: Routledge.

Crewe, B. 2009. *The Prisoner Society: Power, Adaptation and Social Life in an English Prison*. Oxford: Oxford University Press.

Crewe, B. 2011. 'Depth, Weight, Tightness: Revisiting the Pains of Imprisonment'. *Punishment & Society*, 13(5), 509–29.

Erera, P. I. 2002. *Family Diversity. Continuity and Change in the Contemporary Family*. Sage: Thousand Oaks.

Farrell, B., Vandevusse, A., and Ocobock, A. 2012. 'Family Change and the State of Family Sociology'. *Current Sociology*, 60(3), 283–301.

FFP. 2015. Høringsuttalelse fra For Fangers Pårørende. 9 October. Available at: https://www.regjeringen.no/contentassets/00b320df63a7415db766858d843b78bc/for_fangers_paaroerende.pdf.

Foster, H. and Hagan, J. 2015a. 'Mass Imprisonment and its Consequences', in Wright, J. D. (ed.) *International Encyclopedia of the Social & Behavioral Sciences* (2nd ed.). vol. 14, 696–701. Oxford: Elsevier.

Foster, H. and Hagan, J. 2015b. 'Punishment Regimes and the Multilevel Effects of Parental Incarceration: Intergenerational, Intersectional, and Interinstitutional Models of Social Inequality and Systemic Exclusion'. *Annual Review of Sociology*, 41, 135–58.

Garland, D. 1991 'Sociological Perspectives on Punishment'. *Crime and Justice*, 14, 115–65.

Garland, D. and Sparks, R. 2000. 'Criminology, social theory and the challenge of our times', in Garland, D. and Sparks, R. (eds.) *Criminology and Social Theory*. 189–204. Oxford: Oxford University Press.

Goffman, A. 2014. *On the Run. Fugitive Life in an American City*. New York: Picador.

Goffman, E. 1963. *Stigma: Notes on the Management of Spoiled Identity*. New York: Simon and Schuster.

Granja, R. 2016. 'Beyond Prison Walls: The Experiences of Prisoners' Relatives and Meanings Associated with Imprisonment'. *Probation Journal*, 63(3), 273–92.

Granja, R., da Cunha, M. I. P., and Machado, H. 2014. 'Mothering from Prison and Ideologies of Intensive Parenting: Enacting Vulnerable Resistance'. *Journal of Family Issues*, 36(9), 1212–32.

Hagan, J. and Dinovitzer, R. 1999. 'Collateral Consequences of Imprisonment for Children, communities, and prisoners', in Tonry, M. H. and Petersilia, J. (eds.) Prisons. Crime and Justice: A Review of Research. vol. 26, 121–62. Chicago: University of Chicago Press.

Hagan, J. and Foster, J. 2015. 'Mass Incarceration, Parental Imprisonment, and the Great Recession: Intergenerational Sources of Severe Deprivation in America'. *Russell Sage Foundation Journal of the Social Sciences*, 1(2), 80–107.

Halsey, M. 2017. 'Child Victims as Adult Offenders: Foregrounding the Criminogenic Effects of (Unresolved) Trauma and Loss'. *The British Journal of Criminology*, 58(1), 17–36.

Haralambos, M. and Holborn, M. 2004. *Sociology: Themes and Perspectives*. London: Collins.

Harcourt, B., Meares, T. L., Hagan, J., and Morrill, C. 2005. 'Seeing Crime and Punishment through a Sociological Lens: Contributions, Practices, and the Future'. *University of Chicago Legal Forum*, 289–324.

Hays, S. 1996. *The Cultural Contradictions of Motherhood*. New Haven, CT: Yale University Press.

Holtzman, M. 2008. 'Defining Family: Young Adults' Perceptions of the Parent-Child Bond'. *Journal of Family Communication*, 8(3), 167–85.

Jardine, C. 2015. *Constructing Family in the Context of Imprisonment: A Study of Prisoners and their Families in Scotland*. PhD thesis, University of Edinburgh.

Jardine, C. 2017. 'Constructing and Maintaining Family in The Context of Imprisonment'. *The British Journal of Criminology*, 58(1), 114–31.

Johnson I. E. and Easterling, B. 2012. 'Understanding Unique Effects of Parental Incarceration on Children: Challenges, Progress, and Recommendations'. *Journal of Marriage and Family*, 74(2), 342–56.

Jones, A. and Wainaina-Woźna, A. (eds.) 2013. *Children of Prisoners: Interventions and Mitigations to Strengthen Mental Health*. COPING Project, University of Huddersfield. Available at: http://childrenofprisoners.eu/wp-content/uploads/2013/12/COPINGFinal.pdf.

Kirk, D. S. and Wakefield, S. 2017. 'Collateral Consequences of Punishment: A Critical Review and Path Forward'. *Annual Review of Criminology*, 1, 171–94.

Knudsen, E. M. 2016. 'Avoiding the Pathologizing of Children of Prisoners'. *Probation Journal*, 63(3), 362–70.

Kruttschnitt, C. 2011. 'Is the Devil in the Details? Crafting Policy to Mitigate the Collateral Consequences of Parental Incarceration'. *Criminology & Public Policy*, 10(3), 829–37.

Lacey, N. 2003. 'Penal Theory and Penal Practice: A Communitarian Approach', in McConville, S. (ed.) *The Use of Punishment*. 175–98. Cullompton: Willan Publishing.

Lagoutte, S. 2016. 'The Right to Respect for Family Life of Children of Imprisoned Parents'. *International Journal of Children's Rights*, 24(1), 204–30.

Lee, H., Porter, L., and Comfort, M. 2014. 'The Collateral Consequences of Family Member Incarceration: Impacts on Civic Participation and Perceptions of Legitimacy and Fairness'. *Annals of the American Academy of Political and Social Science*, 651(1), 44–73.

Liebling, A. and Maruna, S. 2005. *The Effects of Imprisonment*. Cullompton: Willan Publishing.

Manby, M., Jones, A., Foca, L. Bieganski, J., and Starke, S. 2015. 'Children of Prisoners: Exploring the Impact of Families' Reappraisal of the Role and Status of the Imprisoned Parent on Children's Coping Strategies'. *European Journal of Social Work*, 18(2), 228–45.

Mathiesen, T. 2011. *Retten i samfunnet—en innføring i rettssosiologi*. Oslo: Pax.
Mills, C. W. 1959. *The Sociological Imagination*. New York: Oxford University Press.
Minson, S. 2017. *Who Cares: Analysing the Place of Children in Maternal Sentencing Decisions in England and Wales*. DPhil thesis, University of Oxford.
Minson, S. Nadin, R. and Earle, J. 2015. *Sentencing of Mothers: Improving the Sentencing Process and Outcomes for Women with Dependent Children*. London: Prison Reform Trust.
Morris, N. and Rothman, D. 1998. *The Oxford History of the Prison*. Oxford: Oxford University Press.
Morris, P. 1965. *Prisoners and Their Families*. New York: Hart Publishing Company.
Murray, J. 2006. *Parental Imprisonment: Effects on Children's Antisocial Behaviour and Mental Health through the Life-course*. PhD dissertation, Institute of Criminology, University of Cambridge.
Murray J. and Farrington, D. P. 2008. 'The Effects of Parental Imprisonment on Children'. *Crime and Justice*, 37(1), 133–206.
Murray, J., Bijleveld, C. C. J. H., Farrington, D. P., and Loeber, R. 2014. *Effects of Parental Incarceration on Children: Cross-National Comparative Studies*. Washington, DC: American Psychological Association.
Murray, J., Farrington, D. P., Sekol, I., and Olsen, R. F. 2009. *Effects of Parental Imprisonment on Child Antisocial Behaviour and Mental Health: A Systematic Review*. Campbell Systematic Reviews 4. Cambridge: The Campbell Collaboration. Available at: http://www.campbellcollaboration.org/media/k2/attachments/Murray_Parental_Imprisonment_Review.pdf.
Oldrup, H., Frederiksen, S., Henze-Pedersen, S., and Olsen, R. F. 2016. *Indsat far udsat barn? Hverdagsliv og trivsel blant børn af fængslede*. Copenhagen: SFI.
Purdie-Vaughns, V. and Eibach, R. P. 2008. 'Intersectional Invisibility: The Distinctive Advantages and Disadvantages of Multiple Subordinate-Group Identities'. *Sex Roles*, 59(5–6), 377–91.
Reiter, K. 2016. *Pelican Bay Prison and the Rise of Long-Term Solitary Confinement*. New Haven, CT: Yale University Press.
Richards, M. 1992. 'The Separation of Children and Parents: Some Issues and Problems', in R. Shaw (ed.) *Prisoners' Children. What are the Issues?* 3–13. New York: Routledge.
Roettger, M. and Boardman, J. D. 2012. 'Parental Incarceration and Gender-based Risks for Increased Body Mass Index: Evidence From the National Longitudinal Study of Adolescent Health in the United States'. *American Journal of Epidemiology*, 175(7), 636–44.
Rossitera, C., Powera, T., Fowlerab, C., Jackson, D., Hyslope, D., and Dawson, A. 2015. 'Mothering at a Distance: What Incarcerated Mothers Value about a Parenting Programme'. *Contemporary Nurse*, 50(2–3), 238–55.
Schaefer, D. R., Martin B., Young J. T. N., and Kreager D. A. 2017. 'Friends in Locked Places: An Investigation of Prison Inmate Network Structure.' *Social Networks*, 51, 88–103.
Schwartz, M. A., and Scott, B. M. 2007. *Marriages and Families: Diversity and Change* (5th ed.). Upper Saddle River, NJ: Pearson Prentice Hall.
Scott, J. and Marshall, G. 2009. *Oxford Dictionary of Sociology* (4th ed.). Oxford: Oxford University Press.
Shaw, R. 1987. *Children of Imprisoned Fathers*. London: Hodder and Stoughton.
Siennick, S., Stewart, E., and Staff, J. 2014. 'Explaining the Association between Incarceration and Divorce'. *Criminology*, 52(3), 371–98.
Smith, P. S. 2014. *When the Innocent are Punished: The Children of Imprisoned Parents*. Basingstoke: Palgrave.
Smith, P. S. and Gampell, L. (eds.) 2011. *The Children of Imprisoned Parents*. Copenhagen: The Danish Institute for Human Rights.
Sugie, N. and Turney, K. 2017. 'Beyond Incarceration: Criminal Justice Contact and Mental Health'. *American Sociological Review*, 82(4), 719–43.

Sykes, G. 1958. *The Society of Captives: A Study of a Maximum-Security Prison*. Princeton, NJ: Princeton University Press.

Tranæs, T. and Geerdsen, L. P. (with others) 2008. *Forbryderen og Samfundet: Livsvilkår og Uformel Straf*. Copenhagen: Gyldendal.

Turney, K. 2015. 'Hopelessly Devoted? Relationship Quality During and After Incarceration'. *Journal of Marriage and Family*, 77(2), 480–95.

Wakefield, S. and Powell, K. 2016. 'Distinguishing Petty Offenders from Serious Criminals in the Estimation of Family Life Effects'. *Annals of the American Academy of Political and Social Science*, 665, 195–212.

Wakefield, S. and Wildeman, C. 2011. 'Mass Imprisonment and Racial Disparities in Childhood Behavioral Problems'. *Criminology & Public Policy*, 10(3), 791–817.

Wakefield, S. and Wildeman, C. 2014. *Children of the Prison Boom: Mass Incarceration and the Future of American Inequality*. New York: Oxford University Press.

Western, B. 2006. *Punishment and Inequality in America*. New York: Russell Sage Foundation.

Western, B. and Pettit, B. 2010. 'Incarceration & Social Inequality'. *Daedalus*, 139(3), 8–19.

Western, B. and Wildeman, C. 2009. 'The Black Family and Mass Incarceration'. *Annals of the American Academy of Political and Social Science*, 621(1), 221–42.

Wildeman, C. 2012. 'Imprisonment and Infant Mortality'. *Social Problems*, 59(2), 228–57.

Wildeman, C. 2014. 'Parental Incarceration, Child Homelessness, and the Invisible Consequences of Mass Imprisonment'. *Annals of the American Academy of Political and Social Science*, 651(1), 74–96.

PART I

PRISONERS' FAMILIES AND SOCIAL INEQUALITY

2
Prisoners' Families and the Problem of Social Justice

Rachel Condry

Introduction

This chapter aims to explore the wide-ranging impact of imprisonment upon the lives of the families of prisoners and the entrenched social inequalities that this both generates and reinforces. The chapter considers the concept of social justice and whether it is useful to this enterprise. In this volume we will read about a catalogue of difficulties that are faced by the families of prisoners and a wide range of social harms. In this chapter I ask the question: Why does this matter? I attempt to answer this question by applying theories of social justice to the consequences experienced by families of prisoners and asking whether or not those consequences are consistent with the principles of these theories. In a democratic society that claims to be organized around principles of equal citizenship there is a need to fully consider how and why families of prisoners (as innocent citizens) are affected by punishment inflicted by the state.

I will draw upon a range of theories of social justice. Although moral and political philosophers have historically propounded individual, general theories of social justice, others have advocated hybrid theories or drawn useful lessons from a number of conceptions of the meaning of social justice. My intention is to draw upon some key principles of social justice to show that the experiences of families of prisoners should matter to anyone concerned with the fair and just organization and operation of society. I do not intend to trawl through the characteristics of each individual theory or to catalogue their continuities or points of disagreement in detail, but rather to consider how the principles identified by some of these moral and political philosophers might further enhance and develop our understanding of the impact of punishment of the families of prisoners, and why it is important.

Many of my arguments are writ large in the context of the size and scale of mass incarceration in the United States, but have salience in all countries that use prison as a primary form of punishment. I will draw upon examples of prisoners' families from a number of different jurisdictions. This is not to suggest that experience in these locations is the same, nor that some form of simplistic policy transfer is taking place between jurisdictions (Jones and Newburn, 2007) but rather that there are sufficient commonalities in the experiences of families of prisoners and the wider impact of punishment to make such an analysis valid. This has been demonstrated in a range of research studies (see Condry and Smith, this volume) and can be seen in case studies in this volume from different continents of the world. I will also refer to the broad category of 'prisoners' families' encompassing a wide range of kin relationships, although most research in this field has been focused on female heterosexual partners and children of prisoners. Clearly experiences will differ and using this broad category is not intended to suggest that the impact is the same for all family members.

Many theories of social justice focus particularly on the equitable distribution of resources as the most important way it can be achieved. While the distribution of resources is important, I am going to draw mainly upon theories which have moved beyond a sole focus on this to include other forms of inequity in their analysis. John Rawls identified the importance of fair and equal distribution of liberty, opportunity, and 'the social bases of self-respect', in addition to income and wealth (1971, 303). David Miller argues for three main principles that social justice requires: need (to not lack basic necessities), desert (appropriate reward for one's performance), and equality (society should treat its citizens as equals entitled to rights). Which of these takes precedence depends upon 'modes of relationships', the different relationships people have with each other—such as in the family, the workplace, and so on (Miller, 1999). Iris Marion Young identifies the institutional context that produces and reproduces disadvantage as the barrier to social justice, defining it as 'the elimination of institutional domination and oppression' (1990, 15). Evolving from the work of Amartya Sen (1992; 1999), Martha Nussbaum (2000; 2003; 2011) develops the Capabilities Approach asking two questions: what is each person actually able to do and to be? And what real opportunities are available to them? This moves beyond a purely resource-focused approach to argue for the importance of the basic human needs of dignity and respect. Those denied capabilities and substantive freedoms are denied human dignity and justice. Yet other authors have focused on the importance of full citizenship and civil liberties (Marshall, 1965; Margalit, 1996), and these are considered in the context of prisoners and their families. Each of these theories has important implications for understanding the harm experienced by prisoners' families, but first we can turn to consider the nature of that harm.

The harm experienced by prisoners' families

As has long been documented, and explored in detail in the previous chapter, prisoners' families are exposed to a range of harms that affect several important arenas of life. Condry et al. (2016) have drawn upon Arditti's (2012) analysis of four key characteristics of parental incarceration and applied it in the context of the general category of prisoners' families. This classification of the harm experienced by prisoners' families is useful in allowing a consideration of the circumstances of families before, during, and after imprisonment, and to delve into exactly what it is that prison *does* to the family (Condry et al., 2016). We can use this analysis to usefully summarize some of the harms that threaten social justice before moving on to examine philosophical explanations.

First, prisoners' families are more likely to share certain *demographic characteristics and patterns of pre-existing disadvantage*. Data on who the families of prisoners are is not routinely collected in the United Kingdom and in most other countries, so some of what we know in these countries has to be inferred from prisoners. There are exceptions to this: Denmark collects detailed register data on families of prisoners (see Oldrup and Frederiksen, this volume). Patterns of state punishment and imprisonment intersect strongly with race, as is well documented in the United States with mass incarceration drastically impacting upon the African-American population. Though the scale is lower, in the United Kingdom black and minority ethnic (BME) groups are also significantly over-represented in the criminal justice system and disproportionately in the prison population—about a quarter of all prisoners (Berman and Dar, 2013), much more than the proportion of the general population—1 in 11 in 2009

(Prison Reform Trust, 2014). We can therefore infer that the families of prisoners will be disproportionately from BME groups and experience marginalization and discrimination intersecting with race. Race therefore has an impact on the likelihood of being drawn into the criminal justice system, but also on treatment within it (see, e.g. Cheliotis and Liebling, 2006; Bowling and Phillips, 2007) and will therefore exacerbate the consequences of imprisonment for families in important ways.

Prisoners are much more likely to come from backgrounds of poverty, interrupted education, and other problems (Social Exclusion Unit, 2002; see also Dennison and Besemer, this volume; Oldrup and Frederiksen, this volume). Studies from both the United States and the United Kingdom suggest that prisoners' families are more likely to come from backgrounds of lower socio-economic status and be contending with a range of associated problems (see Condry, 2007; Comfort, 2008; Wakefield and Wildeman, 2014). Gender is also important to understanding patterns of pre-existing disadvantage that intersect with families' experiences. Relatives that support prisoners are often female—wives, mothers, sisters (Condry, 2007; see also Christian, 2005 and Comfort, 2008 for the US context)—and they will already be experiencing gender oppression. Women are more likely to experience poverty and be deprived of capabilities and substantive freedoms (Nussbaum, 2011). Women are subject to a prevailing conception of natural caregiving and responsibility for other families (see Condry, 2007). Caring for a person in prison requires considerable personal resources and time and this care work—like other care work—is often undervalued. Women can also be made accountable in particular ways for their relative's offending, for example as mothers or wives (Condry, 2007). Patterns of pre-existing disadvantage are therefore complex and multi-layered and will intersect in particular ways for individual prisoners' families. While prison may compound gender oppression, it may also offer some form of relief as some women benefit from the imprisonment of a partner, for example in the case of domestic violence (Condry and Smith, this volume; Smith, this volume). We should also note that this quick sketch of intersecting oppression is not exhaustive—other patterns of oppression might be important, such as discrimination based upon sexuality or disability.

The second category is that of *cumulative disadvantage*, when imprisonment itself compounds and magnifies patterns of economic, social, educational, health, and mental health disadvantage to create new problems for families. Supporting a prisoner can be very demanding in terms of time and energy and draw upon the reserves of a family member's social and personal resources. Visiting and supporting a prisoner can be expensive and compound economic disadvantage. Worries about the prisoner and his or her welfare and feelings of loss can further compound pre-existing mental health problems and create new anxieties for the family (Condry, 2007).

Institutional practices cause further harm. A body of research on prisoners' families has shown how the consequences of the punishment inflicted upon the prison reach beyond the prison walls into the lives of families. Comfort has described this as 'punishment beyond the legal offender' (Comfort, 2007), extending to prisoners' families who 'experience restricted rights, diminished resources, social marginalisation, and other consequences of penal confinement' (Comfort 2007, 7). Through her research in the United States, Comfort found that prison visitors would have to adjust their choice of clothing according to somewhat arbitrary prison regulations, and that the time devoted to visiting would consume women's lives. She describes the women in her study as fundamentally changed by their interaction with the prison, assuming the status of 'quasi-inmates' as they came under its rules and discipline, and as the boundary between home and prison became blurred. In the UK context, some prisoners' partners arrange their daily lives around supporting their imprisoned loved one, which includes waiting for phone-calls, going on visits, and writing frequent letters (Condry, 2007). Comfort (2007; 2008) has described this as 'secondary prisonization': 'a weakened but still compelling version of the elaborate regulations, concentrated surveillance, and corporeal confinement governing the lives of ensnared felons' (Comfort, 2009, 2). The organization of prisons and the ways in which relatives interact with the prison intersect to produce an institutional burden for families (see chapters in Part II and Part III of this volume).

The final category of harm is *socio-political, encompassing stigma and disenfranchisement*. This refers to the exclusionary and stigmatizing practices and 'othering' of prisoners' families and the denigration of their status as citizens. To take one example, relatives of serious offenders experience stigma and shame for a number of reasons. They are perceived to be the same as the offender because of their close association—'tarred with the same brush'—or because of a genetic connection that can provoke very primitive ideas of bad blood (Condry, 2007). Mothers of serious offenders, for example, speak of their horror that someone born of their body has committed a heinous offence, and sons worry whether they might inherit some of their offending father's traits. Family members feel they are blamed directly for their action (or inaction) (Condry, 2007). Explanations which locate the source of deviant behaviour within the family have a long history and are woven through political, media, and lay discourse, and expert and therapeutic analyses (Condry, 2007). I will return below to the detrimental effects on the political liberties and citizenship of families of prisoners.

Understanding the harm to prisoners' families through a social justice lens

The relationship between punishment (including imprisonment) and social justice is complex, not least because punishment has an important role in *upholding* social justice, by enforcing the law when offences are committed; criminal justice helps bring about social justice but also interferes with its realization (Robinson, 2010, 78). Enforcing the rule of law is necessary to achieve social justice, yet the way in which it is enforced and the extended consequences that reach beyond the offender mean that this is far from straightforward. Punishment administered to those who break the law is the ultimate exercise of state authority and needs justification in its own right—yet our concern here is not with theories of punishment, but rather with theories of the organization of society and the duties that citizens have to each other. Drawing from the literature on social justice, I here consider four dimensions in relation to the impact upon prisoners' families: equality and desert; the elimination of institutional oppression and domination; capabilities and substantive freedoms; and civil liberties and citizenship.

1. Equality and desert

Most authors define social justice as to do with equality in some sense, but the question is: equality of what? As we have seen, different positions are taken on whether resources should be distributed equally; whether this is done on the basis of skill and effort; whether equality is marred instead by oppression and marginalization; or whether equality can only be achieved through access to capabilities and freedoms. Equality can therefore be conceived of in a range of different ways. The theories of John Rawls (1971; 2003) and David Miller (1999) are instructive in this respect. Robinson (2010) examines the main theories of social justice posited by Rawls and Miller and uses them to interrogate American criminal justice, concluding that its ideals are consistent with social justice, but many actual practices make it impossible to achieve (2010, 94–5). Here we can focus particularly on practices of punishment—and more specifically, the use of imprisonment as a primary method of administering criminal justice and its consequent harms for families—and ask whether it is consistent or not in practice with principles of social justice.

For Rawls, those principles centre on the importance of equal access to basic liberties, rights, and opportunities. His theory of 'justice as fairness' comprises three main principles: that of equal basic liberties; that if inequalities exist, they must do so under conditions of equality of opportunity; and that they must also serve the interests of the most disadvantaged members of society (Rawls, 2003). Those most disadvantaged in his theory might be so because they lack 'primary goods', which might include particular rights, liberties, freedoms, power, position of authority, and the social bases of self-respect, as well as income and wealth. David Miller argues for three main principles that social justice requires: need (to not lack basic necessities), desert (appropriate reward for one's performance), and equality (society should treat its citizens as equals entitled to rights). Which of these takes precedence depends upon 'modes of relationships', the different relationships people have with each other—such as in the family, the workplace, and so on (Miller, 1999). Miller acknowledges that a theory of justice requires 'an account of the basic rights of citizens, which will include rights to various concrete liberties, such as freedom of movement and freedom of speech' (2003, 13).

In summary, for consistency with the principles of social justice expanded by Rawls and Miller, '... the practices of criminal justice institutions should respect the civil liberties of all citizens, should be applied in an equal fashion, should be based on desert, and should be arranged to the benefits of the least advantaged' (Robinson 2010, 94).

We will return later in this chapter to the question of *respecting the civil liberties of all citizens*, but at this stage can note significant harmful effects on the families of prisoners in this regard (Lee et al., 2014). I now examine the other principles in turn.

i. Should be applied in an equal fashion

A lack of equality before the law and the unequal application of sanctions to particular groups clearly contravenes social justice. This is reflected in the hugely disproportionate representation of poor and minority populations in the prison population. Crimes of the poor and minority ethnic groups are much more likely to be criminalized and vulnerable populations are not protected:

In a nutshell, to the degree that the criminal law is aimed at the crimes committed disproportionately by the poor and people of color while it simultaneously ignores the harmful and culpable acts of the powerful (e.g., wealthy whites), it is unequal, undeserved, not focused on helping people achieve their basic needs, and clearly not aimed at providing the greatest advantage to the least advantaged. Thus, it violates Rawls' and Miller's conceptions of 'need,' 'equality,' 'desert,' and the 'difference principle.' (Robinson 2010, 91)

Furthermore, differential access to social and financial capital can mean that individual defendants and their families are denied access to fair and equitable justice.

ii. Should be based on desert

The principle of desert can be questioned for the primary subjects of punishment when the criminal law is targeted unequally at poor and minority populations. However, its ongoing harmful consequences for innocent family members who are not guilty of any offence certainly violates this principle. As we have seen, prisoners and their families are already subject to a wide range of pre-existing and intersecting forms of marginalization and exclusion which could be further argued to contravene the principle of desert.

iii. Should be arranged to the benefits of the least advantaged

Prisoners' families are more likely to come from already marginalized populations of low socio-economic level and black and minority ethnic populations. There is therefore a pre-existing fundamental inequality in society that intersects with patterns of imprisonment (Western, 2007). In some cases crimes are actually driven by poverty and deprivation and inequality may therefore be a precursor to offending. Furthermore, the application of criminal justice and punishment (in the form of imprisonment, fines, probation and parole restrictions, and the collateral consequences that follow) creates further inequality, marginalization, and compounding disadvantage.

We might therefore conclude that the harm experienced by the families of prisoners (and outlined in more detail earlier in this chapter) contravenes a conception of social justice that focuses on equality and desert.

2. Elimination of institutional oppression and domination

A second conception of social justice focuses on institutional context. Iris Marion Young argues that the scope of justice is wider than the equitable distribution of resources in society. She emphasizes the importance of the institutional context that produces and reproduces disadvantage. Young defines social justice as 'the elimination of institutional domination and oppression' (1990, 15). She proposes what she describes as:

> An enabling conception of justice. Justice should refer not only to distribution, but also to the institutional conditions necessary for the development and exercise of individual capacities and collective communication and cooperation. Under this conception of justice, injustice refers primarily to two forms of disabling constraints, oppression and domination. While these constraints include distributive patterns, they also involve matters which cannot easily be assimilated to the logic of distribution: decision-making procedures, division of labor, and culture. (1990, 39)

Young further defines oppression as consisting 'in systematic institutional processes which prevent some people from learning and using satisfying and expansive skills in socially recognized settings, or institutionalized social processes which inhibit people's ability to play and communicate with others or to express their feelings and perspective on social life in contexts where others can listen' (1990, 38). Domination, in Young's analysis, 'consists in institutional conditions which inhibit or prevent people from participating in determining their actions or the conditions of their actions. Persons live within structures of domination if other persons or groups can determine without reciprocation the conditions of their actions. Thorough social and political democracy is the opposite of domination' (1990, 38).

Prison is an institutional structure of oppression and domination. By definition, prisons restrict the liberty of those imprisoned, and their freedom of expression, access to resources, self-determination, and democratic participation. How this is experienced by prisoners is beyond the focus of this chapter, but imprisonment as an institution also imposes oppression and domination upon the families of those who are imprisoned. There are myriad ways that imprisonment as an institution imposes oppression and domination upon families and some of these are explored in detail in the chapters in this volume (see also Condry and Smith, this volume).

Prisoners' families are a structural group, defined by their relationship to the prison, and experience marginalization and oppression as a result. This intersects with other forms of structural oppression and domination. As we have seen above, this is rooted in pre-existing disadvantage, cumulative disadvantage, stigma, and disenfranchisement (Arditti, 2012; Condry et al., 2016). Here Young's concept of structural injustice is important—many of the harms experienced by prisoners' families stem from state punishment. The organization of the criminal justice system, sentencing, and the predominance of prison as a form of punishment all contribute to the institutional context of harm.

3. Capabilities and substantive freedoms

Another way of understanding the social injustice faced by prisoners' families is through the Capabilities Approach, identifying how their status and treatment lead to a wide range of capability failures and denials of substantive freedoms. Nussbaum (2011, 18) describes the Capabilities Approach as an approach to a comparative quality of life assessment to theorize about basic social justice. Analysis in this approach starts with the individual—each person is seen as an end with individual choices and freedoms—the focus is on the opportunities available to each person rather than an assessment of average wellbeing. This is a helpful reminder of the heterogeneity of prisoners' families—people won't all be affected all in the same way by their experiences.

This approach is particularly concerned with entrenched social injustice and failures in capability that result from discrimination or marginalization, which has direct relevance to the experience of prisoners' families. As we have seen above, many of these families are already contending with intersecting forms of discrimination and marginalization; this is compounded by imprisonment; and impacts directly upon their capabilities and freedoms. Capabilities are often interrelated and can affect each other in positive or negative ways—Wolff and de-Shalit (2007) capture this nicely with the concepts of 'fertile functioning' and 'corrosive disadvantage'. The latter is of particular relevance to the families of prisoners and refers to types of capability failure that lead to failure in other areas, and racial discrimination and stigma are sources of such corrosive disadvantage (Nussbaum, 2011, 99). This is about how disadvantages cluster and how one can lead to another.

Nussbaum identifies a list of ten Central Capabilities that must be secured for social justice to prevail. It is worth considering these in full:

1. *Life.* Being able to live to the end of a human life of normal length; not dying prematurely, or before one's life is so reduced as to be not worth living.
2. *Bodily health.* Being able to have good health, including reproductive health; to be adequately nourished; to have adequate shelter.

3. *Bodily integrity.* Being able to move freely from place to place; to be secure against violent assault, including sexual assault and domestic violence; having opportunities for sexual satisfaction and for choices in matters of reproduction.
4. *Senses, imagination, and thought.* Being able to use the senses, to imagine, think, and reason—and to do these things in a 'truly human' way ... Being able to have pleasurable experiences and to avoid non-beneficial pain.
5. *Emotions.* Being able to have attachments to things and people outside ourselves; to love those who love and care for us, to grieve at their absence; in general, to love, to grieve, to experience longing, gratitude, and justified anger. Not having one's emotional development blighted by fear and anxiety.
6. *Practical reason.* Being able to form a conception of the good and to engage in critical reflection about the planning of one's life.
7. *Affiliation.* (A) Being able to live with and toward others, to recognize and show concern for other human beings, to engage in various forms of social interaction; to be able to imagine the situation of another. (B) Having the social bases of self-respect and non-humiliation; being able to be treated as a dignified being whose worth is equal to that of others. This entails provisions of non-discrimination on the basis of race, sex, sexual orientation, ethnicity, caste, religion, national origin.
8. *Other species.* Being able to live with concern for and in relation to animals, plants, and the world of nature.
9. *Play.* Being able to laugh, to play, to enjoy recreational activities.
10. *Control over one's environment. (A) Political.* Being able to participate effectively in political choices that govern one's life; having the right of political participation, protections of free speech and association. *(B) Material.* Being able to hold property (both land and movable goods), and having property rights on an equal basis with others; having the right to seek employment on an equal basis with others; having the freedom from unwarranted search and seizure. (Nussbaum, 2011)

By definition, the capabilities and freedoms of prisoners themselves are curtailed in many pervasive and embedded ways—though this is of course by no means inalienable. Though many of their freedoms have been removed, prison regimes can still be constructed in ways that protect some capabilities—for example, providing good healthcare and nourishing food, protecting bodily integrity by reducing opportunity for physical and sexual assault, providing meaningful work, and so on. Human rights and the principle of normalization can facilitate the organization of prison regimes with respect for prisoner rights, capabilities, and freedoms (see Smith, this volume). However, freedom and control over one's life plans and environment, affiliation, liberty, property, civic rights, and so on are clearly severely restricted through the sentence of imprisonment. Debates about the design of imprisonment and the important issue of the lack of social justice experienced by prisoners will be bracketed here and we will restrict our focus to their families.

Prisoners' family members are legally innocent. They are not the intended targets of state punishment, though they do suffer a range of secondary consequences. Looking through the list of ten capabilities, there are many that are significantly restricted for the families of prisoners. Taking the more specific example of children, concrete evidence from rigorous empirical analysis of survey data and qualitative interviews can be found in Wakefield and Wildeman's 2014 book *Children of the Prison Boom*. In the book they map the devastating impact of mass incarceration for generations of children in the United States and provide striking evidence of the impact this has on inequality in American society. Many of the examples of this impact relate directly to the Central Capabilities, for example *Life* (children of incarcerated parents have a greater chance of infant mortality before the age of one—an increase of 75 per cent compared to children without incarcerated parents, Wakefield and Wildeman, 2014, 105); *Bodily health* (they are more likely to experience mental health problems in life) and *Control over one's environment (B) Material* (they are more likely to be homeless and suffer severe material disadvantage). Overall, a basic lack of education and socio-economic detriment restricts and curtails their life chances and their access to so many of the freedoms in this list. Race is particularly important to this picture—African Americans born around 1990 had a one in four risk of parental imprisonment by their fourteenth birthday, compared with a risk of one in thirty for white children. For those African-American children whose fathers dropped out of high school there was a better than even chance of having a father imprisoned at 50.5 per cent; to put this in further context, black children are more likely to have a parent imprisoned by their first birthday than white children are before their fourteenth birthday. These children will be contending with intersecting race discrimination and marginalization of various forms. As Piachaud (2008) has highlighted, children pose very particular issues for social justice yet are often not considered in the social justice literature.

There are also significant capability failures for adult relatives of prisoners who report problems with health; a range of emotions including grief and loss, stigma and shame; restrictions on their time and control over their own lives; material loss; and loss of civic freedoms (see Condry and Smith, this volume). The burden of supporting a prisoner impedes access to many capabilities. The Capabilities Approach is a call to action for governments to ensure that citizens can access the ten capabilities—where these are curtailed, or absent, this should be of immediate concern to politicians and policy makers.

4. Civil liberties and citizenship

Our final conception of social justice centres on civil and political liberties. Citizens in a democratic society have certain rights and responsibilities, many of which are removed or curtailed when a citizen is sentenced to prison. In the United Kingdom, prisoners are disenfranchised for the entirety of their sentence, while in some states in the United States it continues for life. In the United States, 5.85 million Americans are forbidden to vote because of 'felon disenfranchisement', or laws that restrict voting rights for those convicted of felony level crimes (Uggen et al., 2012). The perception of a prison sentence constituting a civil death has its roots in the idea of the prisoner having broken the social contract and expressive punishment.

T. H. Marshall (1965) argued that citizenship had three elements: legal, political, and social. *Legal citizenship* involves citizens' rights in law; *political citizenship* is their right to vote, stand for office, and so on; and *social citizenship* includes their rights to benefits, health services, education, and so on. To this, Margalit adds a fourth dimension, *symbolic citizenship*—the sharing of society's symbolic wealth. This includes deeper questions of citizens' identification with what the state stands for, and their sense of loyalty, sharpened by powerful symbols which unite people together. However, within this dimension minority groups might be excluded—Margalit gives the example of a minority language not being recognized—and become 'second-class citizens on the symbolic level' (Margalit, 1996, 158).

Here I will argue that it is not just prisoners that experience weakened or diminished citizenship; prisoners' families too experience serious threats to a number of citizen dimensions and in very real ways become 'second-class citizens on the symbolic level'.

Patterns of marginalization and exclusion from civic life can be understood as a recasting of the relationship between the carceral state and what Lerman and Weaver (2014) describe as 'custodial citizens', a sizeable and growing group of individuals whose contact with the state is primarily through the institutions of criminal justice rather than democratic processes. They distinguish this group from the 'criminal class' as it is much larger and comprises all those who experience contact with the criminal justice system, from police surveillance and searches, to the raiding of apartment blocks, to various forms of punishment including incarceration. Many of these custodial citizens will be innocent, or responsible only for low level misdemeanors (indeed, Lerman and Weaver say in some locales the majority will be innocent of any crime in a court of law)—yet their entire sense of government and their place within it is mediated through the carceral state. Lerman and Weaver argue that custodial citizens experience a 'state-within-a-state' (2014, 8) as they are systematically denied the basic rights of full and equal American citizenship, which has devastating consequences for political inequality.

The status of 'custodial citizen' has great value in trying to make sense of the dominance of the carceral state and the processes by which an entire group—racially and socio-economically defined—is excluded from democratic citizenship. However, families of prisoners do not become custodial citizens (following Lerman and Weaver's definition) solely through their kin relationship to an offender: '… the custodial citizen is defined by his or her relationship to the state, predicated on individual behaviour (both legal and illegal), but also on the government's activities related to crime control' (2014, 32). Lerman and Weaver '… thus conceptualize the custodial citizenry as comprised of three distinct and non-mutually exclusive categories: the criminal suspect, the arrestee/misdemeanant, and the incarcerated offender' (2014, 35). The category of criminal suspect includes those not guilty of any crime, but subject to interventions from criminal justice agencies.

Family members may be part of socio-economic or racially defined communities that are subject to suspicion, and may (as we have seen) experience many of the consequences of custodial citizenship through their kin relationships to a custodial citizen (which could be defined as custodial citizenship by proxy). Lerman and Weaver acknowledge that political learning through criminal justice contact can also be secondary, as custodial citizens tend to be embedded in communities and groups that experience routine contact—but this is in addition to their own status as custodial citizens, rather than the sole cause.

To illustrate, an elderly mother of a prisoner who has never been convicted of any crime herself and does not feel under direct suspicion will likely still vicariously experience the surveillance of her kin. She might even experience stigma and disdain when prison visiting, or negative interactions with police officers when her son is arrested, but the effects extending to her are a direct consequence of the punishment imposed upon her prisoner son and flow through her relationship with him. In some communities contact with criminal justice agents may be so routine and entrenched that families too become custodial citizens (see, e.g. Goffman's 2014 account of this). It is also important to note that family members may also be offenders or suspects themselves, which would constitute the primary status of custodial citizen.

The citizenship of families of prisoners is affected in profound ways. Drawing on a range of empirical evidence from ethnographic and statistical analyses, Lee, Porter, and Comfort argue that 'having a family member incarcerated can have enduring repercussions for sociopolitical attitudes, behaviors, and perceptions' (2014, 45). Full citizenship requires both political participation and a perception that the state is legitimate and fair, both of which are transformed by the experience of having a family member imprisoned:

> Similar to the role of schools (Justice and Meares, 2014) and the military (Sapiro, 2004), the correctional system becomes a primary mode of political socialization for families of the incarcerated, particularly as they adjust to penal facilities in ways that alienate them from other socializing institutions. (Lee et al., 2014, 45)

They propose two mechanisms by which this occurs: first indirectly via the *transmission* of behaviours and attitudes from the incarcerated loved one to other family members and second, directly through a partner's or child's own experiences with the correctional system and *secondary prisonization*. Given the extent of felon disenfranchisement and the disproportionate impact on particular communities (one in four black men are disenfranchised in some states, Manza and Uggen, 2006) transmission can be an important factor—Lee et al. (2014) cite a small but growing number of studies which suggest that felon disenfranchisement laws impact the political participation of non-felons, leading to reduced voting participation for entire communities (Bowers and Preuhs, 2009; Burch, 2014; and Uggen and Manza, 2002). To this we might add a lack of political participation in the public sphere, and unwillingness or inability to stand for election or represent local communities or community groups at any level.

Lee et al. (2014) argue that family members contending with the difficulties of supporting someone in prison—which can include huge investments of time and personal resources, complex and invasive visiting procedures, and so on (Christian, 2005; Comfort et al., 2005; Condry, 2007; and Fishman, 1990)—are often treated in a disparaging manner by correctional authorities which erodes their belief in the fairness of the wider system of government and leads to a perception that all state entities are adversarial and unconcerned with the wellbeing of poor and ethnic minority populations. Furthermore, the time and energy this absorbs curtails the engagement of families with other social institutions such as houses of worship, adult education courses, or political organizations. As they argue: 'the power of other institutions—such as schools, churches, and the government—as socializing forces becomes blunted for these families through their absorption into the correctional system' (Lee et al., 2014, 50).

Other studies have pointed to the damage to legitimacy and perceptions of state authority that can occur for families of prisoners (Jardine, 2015, 2017, and this volume; Minson, 2017; Smith, 2014 and this volume). This can be particularly powerful for a child whose sense of legitimacy might be damaged by interactions with police arresting a parent or searching a property or with prison guards when visiting. For both adult and child relatives of prisoners this can lead to fatalistic attitudes and the feeling of a loss of control over one's pathway in life, which draws us back to some of the Central Capabilities above (and in particular bodily integrity; practical reason; affiliation; and control over one's environment) which are failing for these families.

In conclusion, the harms that imprisonment generates suggest it should only be used as a punishment of last resort—where it is necessary, the state might be seen to have 'residual obligations' (Bulow, 2014) to the families and children of prisoners. Many of the secondary consequences of imprisonment for families could potentially be foreseen and measures taken to attempt to compensate or ameliorate to some degree. As we have seen, prisoners' family members suffer harm as a consequences of their relative's imprisonment; they have individual rights that are breached; and that they experience broader patterns of marginalization and discrimination that compound and connect to pre-existing forms. Their status as citizens and their ability to fully participate as political actors is impaired, yet they have not committed a crime or breached any aspect of the social contract. The consequences are therefore broader than the harm experienced by individual families and are very real for the way in which we perceive the operation of democratic society. As Margalit argues, a society can be judged on how it treats its members: 'One very important question for determining if the society is a decent one is the question of whether it rejects the membership of those who are supposed to belong to it' (1996, 151). When held up against a range of theories of social justice, the unacknowledged harms experienced by the families of prisoners are inconsistent with the principles of a just democratic society.

References

Arditti, J. 2012. *Parental Incarceration and the Family: Psychological and Social Effects of Imprisonment on Children, Parents, and Caregivers*. New York: NYU Press.

Berman, G. and Dar, A. 2013. 'Prison Population Statistics', Commons Library Standard Note. Available at: http://www.parliament.uk/briefing-papers/sn04334.

Bowers, M. and Preuhs, R. R. 2009. 'Collateral Consequences of a Collateral Penalty: The Negative Effect of Felon Disenfranchisement Laws on the Political Participation of Nonfelons'. *Social Science Quarterly*, 90(3), 722–43.

Bowling, B. and Philips, C. 2007. 'Racism, Ethnicity, Crime and Criminal Justice', in Maguire, M., Morgan, R., and Reiner, R. (eds). *The Oxford Handbook of Criminology* (4th ed.). 421–61. Oxford: Oxford University Press.

Bulow, W. 2014. 'The Harms Beyond Imprisonment: Do We Have Special Moral Obligations Towards the Families and Children of Prisoners?'. *Ethical Theory and Moral Practice*, 17(4), 775–89.

Burch, T. 2014. 'Effects of Imprisonment and Community Supervision on Neighborhood Political Participation in North Carolina'. *The Annals of the American Academy of Political and Social Science*, 651(1), 184–201.

Cheliotis, L. K. and Liebling, A. 2006. 'Race Matters in British Prisons: Towards a Research Agenda'. *British Journal of Criminology*, 46(2), 286–317.

Christian, J. 2005. 'Riding the Bus: Barriers to Prison Visitation and Family Management Strategies'. *Journal of Contemporary Criminal Justice*, 21(1), 31–48.

Comfort, M. 2007. 'Punishment Beyond the Legal Offender'. *Annual Review of Law and Social Science*, 3, 271–296.

Comfort, M. 2008. *Doing Time Together: Love and Family in the Shadow of the Prison*. Chicago: University of Chicago Press.

Comfort, M. 2009. '"We Share Everything We Can the Best Way We Can". Sustaining Romance across Prison Walls'. *Transatlantica*, 1. Available at: https://journals.openedition.org/transatlantica/4281.

Comfort, M., Grinstead, O., McCartney, K., Bourgois, P., and Knight, K. 2005. '"You Can't Do Nothing in This Damn Place": Sex and Intimacy Among Couples with an Incarcerated Male Partner'. *Journal of Sex Research*, 42(1), 3–12.

Condry, R. 2007. *Families Shamed: The Consequences of Crime for Relatives of Serious Offenders*. Cullompton: Willan.

Condry, R., Kotova, A., and Minson, S. 2016. 'Social Injustice and Collateral Damage: The Families and Children of Prisoners', in Jewkes, Y., Bennett, J., and Crewe, B. (eds.) *The Handbook on Prisons* (2nd ed.). 622–41. Abingdon: Routledge.

Fishman, L. T. 1990. *Women at the Wall: A Study of Prisoners' Wives Doing Time on the Outside*. New York: State University of New York Press.

Goffman, A. 2014. *On the Run: Fugitive Life in an American City*. Chicago: University of Chicago Press.
Jardine, C. 2015. *Constructing Family in the Context of Imprisonment: A study of Prisoners and their Families in Scotland*. PhD thesis, University of Edinburgh.
Jardine, C. 2017. 'Constructing and Maintaining Family in The Context of Imprisonment'. *British Journal of Criminology*, 58(1), 114–31.
Jones, T. and Newburn, T. 2007. *Policy Transfer and Criminal Justice: Exploring US Influence over British Crime Control Policy*. Maidenhead: Open University Press.
Justice, B. and Meares, T. L. 2014. 'How the Criminal Justice System Educates Citizens'. *The Annals of the American Academy of Political and Social Science*, 651(1), 159–77.
Lee, H., Porter, L. C., and Comfort, M. 2014. 'Consequences of Family Member Incarceration: Impacts on Civic Participation and Perceptions of the Legitimacy and Fairness of Government'. *Annals of the American Academy of Political and Social Science*, 651(1), 44–73.
Lerman, A. E. and Weaver, V. M. 2014. *Arresting Citizenship: The Democratic Consequences of American Crime Control*. Chicago: University of Chicago Press.
Manza, J. and Uggen, C. 2006. *Locked Out: Felon Disenfranchisement and American Democracy*. New York: Oxford University Press.
Margalit, A. 1996. *The Decent Society*. Cambridge, MA: Harvard University Press.
Marshall, T. H. 1965. *Class, Citizenship and Social Development*. New York: Anchor.
Miller, D. 1999. *Principles of Social Justice*. Cambridge, MA: Harvard University Press
Miller, D. 2003. *Principles of social justice*. Boston, MA: Harvard University Press
Minson, S. 2017. *Who Cares? Analysing the Place of Children in Maternal Sentencing Decisions in England and Wales*. DPhil thesis, University of Oxford.
Nussbaum, M. 2000. *Women and Human Development: The Capabilities Approach*. Cambridge New York: Cambridge University Press.
Nussbaum, M. 2003. 'Capabilities as Fundamental Entitlements: Sen and Social Justice'. *Feminist Economics*, 9(2–3), 33–59.
Nussbaum, M. 2011. *Creating Capabilities: The Human Development Approach*. Cambridge, MA: Harvard University Press.
Piachaud, D. 2008. 'Social justice and public policy: a social policy perspective', in Craig, G., Burchardt, T., and Gordon, D. (eds.) *Social Justice and Public Policy: Seeking Fairness in Diverse Societies*. 33–51. Bristol: Policy Press.
Prison Reform Trust. 2014. 'Projects and Research: Race', Prison Reform Trust. Available at: http://www.prisonreformtrust.org.uk/ProjectsResearch/Race accessed November 2017.
Rawls, J. 1971. *A Theory of Justice*. Cambridge, MA: Harvard University Press.
Rawls, J. 2003. *Justice as Fairness: A Restatement* (2nd ed.). Boston, MA: Belknap Press.
Robinson, M. 2010. 'Assessing Criminal Justice Practice Using Social Justice Theory'. *Social Justice Research*, 23(1), 77–97.
Sapiro, V. 2004. 'Not Your Parents' Political Socialization: Introduction for a New Generation'. *Annual Review of Political Science*, 7(1), 1–23.
Sen, A. 1992. *Inequality Re-examined*. Oxford: Clarendon Press.
Sen, A. 1999. *Development as Freedom*. Oxford: Oxford University Press.
Smith, P. S. 2014. *When the Innocent are Punished*. Basingstoke: Palgrave MacMillan.
Social Exclusion Unit. 2002. *Reducing Reoffending by Ex-Prisoners*. London: Social Exclusion Unit.
Uggen, C. and Manza, J. 2002. 'Democratic Contraction? Political Consequences of Felon Disenfranchisement in the United States'. *American Sociological Review*, 67(6), 777–803.
Uggen, C., Shannon, S., and Manza, J. 2012. *State-Level Estimates of Felon Disenfranchisement in the United States, 2010*. The Sentencing Project. Available at: http://www.sentencingproject.org/wp-content/uploads/2016/01/State-Level-Estimates-of-Felon-Disenfranchisement-in-the-United-States-2010.pdf.

Wakefield, S. and Wildeman, C. 2014. *Children of the Prison Boom: Mass Incarceration and the Future of American Inequality*. New York: Oxford University Press.
Western, B. 2007. *Punishment and Inequality in America*. New York: Russell Sage Foundation.
Wolff, J. and de-Shalit, A. 2007. *Disadvantage*. Oxford: Oxford University Press.
Young, I. M. 1990. With new forward by Allen, D. 2011. *Justice and the Politics of Difference*. Princeton: Princeton University Press.

3

Parental Incarceration and Family Inequality in the United States

Joyce A. Arditti

Background and significance

The United States locks up more people, per capita, than any other nation, with upwards of 2.3 million people confined in state and federal prisons, local jails, and other forms of detention (e.g. youth and immigrant detainees, territorial prisons, Civil Commitments, Wagner and Rabuy, 2017). A substantial number of the incarcerated are parents to several million children. Approximately 3.6 per cent of all children under 18, or 2.7 million children, have a parent in state or federal prison, or who is jailed (Western and Pettit, 2010a). Another 840,000 people are on parole (conditional release) and 3.7 million are on probation (i.e. typically an alternative sentence, Wagner and Rabuy, 2017). Incarceration is widespread in the United States, and despite recent declines in prison population at the state level, the reach of incarceration into the lives of ordinary Americans is profound.

The costs of parental incarceration are multifaceted and rooted deeply in social inequality given well documented racial and ethnic disparities in prison and jails, and by extension, high levels of correctional control in the most disadvantaged communities (Wagner and Rabuy, 2017; Western and Pettit, 2010b). As noted criminologist Todd Clear (2008, 100) once said: 'Incarceration is not equal-opportunity'. A family perspective (Arditti, 2012b) draws attention to the implications of carceral confinement as a manifestation of social inequality as well as how widespread incarceration excludes broad segments of society from family life and how this exclusion extends to non-incarcerated family members and children. Institutional racism, colourism, and intersections between crime, race, gender, age, poverty, and health, all coalesce in hidden and complicated ways that constrain or exclude parents from family life and potentially undermine child development (Poehlmann-Tynan and Arditti, 2017). A central thesis underlying this chapter is that mass incarceration and its consequences can be thought of as a lever to perpetuate not only social inequality, but also *family inequality* when one considers children and their caregivers as the unit of analysis.

A family inequality framework acknowledges not only that 'incarceration is not equal opportunity' but articulates inequalities with regard to the opportunity for healthy and fulfilling family lives for those held in our nation's prisons and jails, those who re-enter society, and non-incarcerated family members connected to the justice-involved individual. Incarcerated parents are most obviously excluded from fully enacting parental roles due to their confinement, which is often far from family members and children (Arditti and Kennington, 2017). Exclusion that may serve to undermine efficacious parenting is also evident with regard to re-entrant parents, who are subject to 'invisible punishments'. Invisible punishments are policies and practices that exclude ex-offenders from employment, civic participation, and important benefits and resources after they serve their time (Travis, 2005). Foster and Hagan (2015) delineate these invisible punishments as 'exclusionary regimes' that serve to disenfranchise and punish those in the criminal justice system as well as those associated with incarcerated persons. Exclusionary regimes are particularly harmful to African American and poor families given their disproportionate incarceration in the United States (Mauer and Chesney-Lind, 2002). From a family lens, it is worth noting that such regimes extend beyond the incarcerated parent to his or her family, and are characterized by a process that systematically denies the disadvantaged access to capital building experiences (such as education), ineligibility for (as in certain federally funded health and welfare benefits) or temporal delays in receiving assistance, and social isolation and rejection. (Burton and Welsh, 2015). Therefore, exclusionary processes are not only a means to perpetuate and intensify social inequality for incarcerated parents and re-entrants, but extend beyond the justice-involved individual to his or her family (Condry, this volume). If the goal of social justice is full and equal participation of all groups in society whereby resources are equitable and members are 'physically and psychologically safe and secure' (Bell, 2010, 21), then clearly familial and in particular parental incarceration, translates into unequal family opportunities and childhood outcomes for the families (hereafter referred to as 'justice-involved') of incarcerated parents.

Here I argue that mass incarceration is an insidious mechanism to limit equal opportunity to freely and optimally 'do family'. Indeed, research documents a host of negative family outcomes associated with parental incarceration and children seem to be particularly vulnerable. A burgeoning literature examining child effects of parental incarceration suggests that even after controlling for other risk markers such as parental substance abuse, parental mental health, compromised parenting, and poverty, parental incarceration continues to predict externalizing (Johnson, 2009; Wildeman, 2010), internalizing problems such as depression (Dallaire et al., 2015; Murray and Farrington, 2008), child trauma symptomology (Arditti and Savla, 2013), antisocial behaviour (Will et al., 2014), and overall poor health (Lee et al., 2013). A 'Family Inequality Framework' (FIF) builds on research and theory that conceptualizes parental incarceration as an ongoing family stressor that influences critical parenting processes and indices of family functioning (Arditti, 2016). Based on family stress theory (Conger et al., 2000; Patterson, 2002) and ecological frameworks (Bronfenbrenner, 1979), the FIF points to material hardship as the main conduit through which parental (and in particular paternal) incarceration contributes to and reproduces family inequality. Similar to Wakefield and Wildeman's (2014) recent work, a FIF represents a shift in emphasis from how mass imprisonment contributes to inequality among incarcerated adults, to how parental incarceration contributes to inequality among children.

A Family Inequality Framework (FIF)

Typical definitions of family or child inequality are largely focused on (a) population dynamics specifying racial and ethnic disparities in marriage rates and (b) income dynamics and the implications of wealth inequality and income reduction (Lundberg et al., 2016). Disparities in marriage and income are seen as contributing to and maintaining children's disadvantaged social locations (Conger et al., 2000). These disadvantaged social locations are correlated with a host of adverse social, health, and intergenerational outcomes for families in general and children specifically, with intergenerational repercussions. For example, Wakefield and Wildeman (2014) documented the implications of the tremendous growth of paternal imprisonment for black children and concluded that it exacerbated racial inequalities with respect to children's wellbeing and development. Paternal incarceration was associated with increased infant mortality, homelessness, and an array of child mental health and behavioural problems.

Traditional notions of child inequality that highlight disparities in material resources and physical and mental health are expanded in an FIF to more fully encompass critical family processes that are altered or undermined as a function of parental incarceration. My hope in advancing the FIF is to more clearly articulate how parental incarceration is more than just a form of 'social exclusion' (e.g. Foster and Hagan 2015) but a mechanism of *family exclusion* that drives and perpetuates inequality with regard to relational processes and by extension, developmental trajectories of offspring. Components of the FIF framework are summarized in Figure 1.

Sources of family inequality

For the purpose of this chapter, 'family' is defined as children, their incarcerated parent, and their non-incarcerated parent(s) or caregiver(s). In identifying key sources of family inequality, I consider the ways in which incarceration, and by extension carceral policy in the United States, contributes to disparities in children's health and wellbeing by virtue of its impact on affected households. Based on existing research and theory, these effects largely flow through (a) material hardship; (b) family instability; and (c) parenting quality. The Family Stress Proximal Process Model (FSPPM, see Arditti, 2016) helps delineate these effects because it is relational and focuses on how dynamic person–environment interactions drive family adjustment and children's developmental trajectories. The FSPPM conceptualizes parental incarceration as an ongoing stressor, and is informed by family stress theory which postulates not only the implications of economic hardship for children's development, but specifies key intervening processes that serve as mechanisms of these effects (e.g. Conger et al., 2000, 2010; Neppl et al., 2016). A family inequality framework extends these ideas by more specifically focusing on how parental incarceration impacts family functions, roles, and investments in children in ways that contribute to or intensify inequality in family life.

Material hardship

Research has documented multiple ways in which parental incarceration connects with material hardship for justice-involved families. First, most prisoners already come from intense histories of disadvantage characterized by multiple risks including low education, neighborhood disadvantage, and material hardship (Arditti, 2012b; Phillips et al., 2006). Sociologists have long discussed how penal involvement 'crystallizes' social and economic inequality in that prisoners represent the least advantaged of society's members (Western and Pettit, 2010b). Beyond the fact that imprisonment itself reproduces macro level inequality, it drives everyday inequalities for families and children associated with the prisoner. The existing literature indicates that the economic situation of children prior to a parent's incarceration is already characterized by economic difficulties (Murphey and Cooper, 2015; Phillips et al., 2006; Wakefield and Wildeman, 2014). Parental incarceration seems to intensify the precarious economic situations of affected families primarily through the removal of men from their respective households.

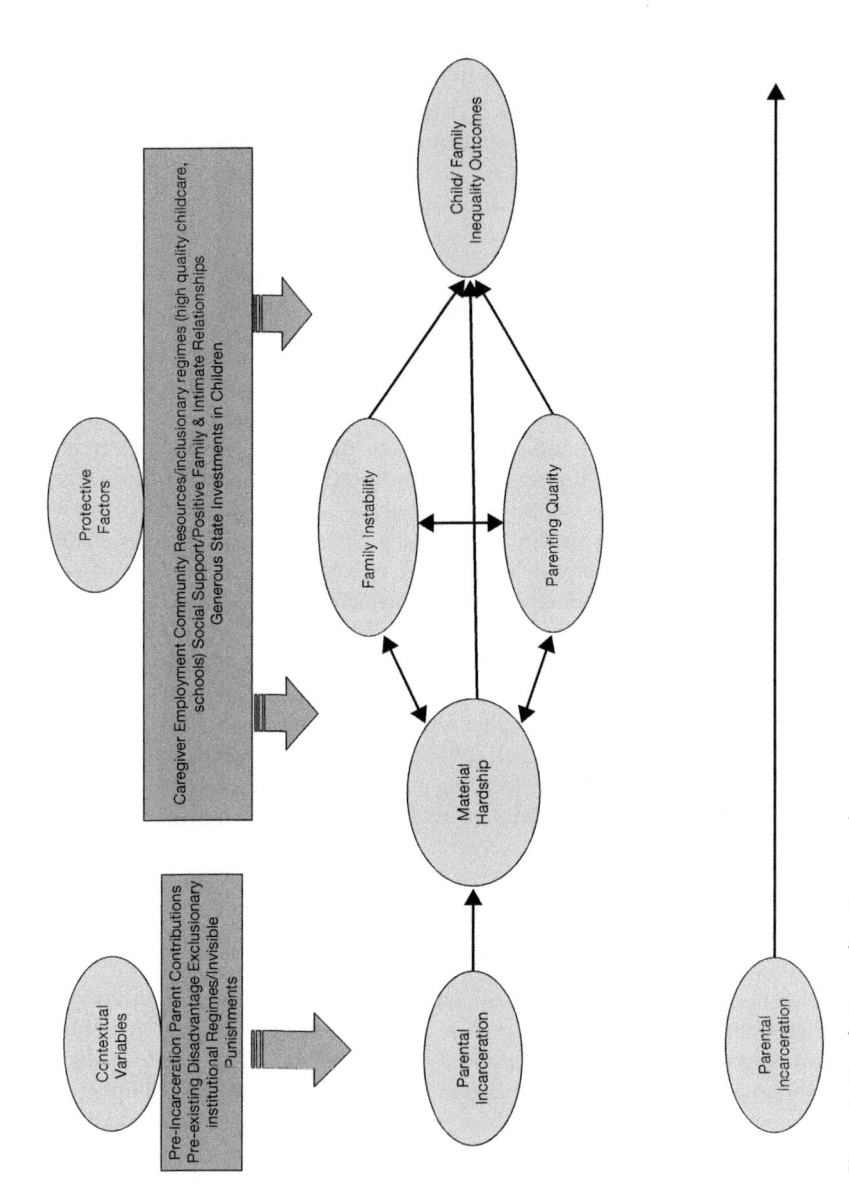

Figure 1 Family Inequality Framework.
Source: Adapted from Arditti, 2016.

The growth of the male penal population in recent decades is seen as a driving force in the formation of poor single-mother headed households (Western et al., 2004) as well as a means to compound any pre-existing material disadvantage that exists in these families. How is economic disadvantage compounded by parental and in particular paternal incarceration? Research suggests three important and direct ways this occurs. First, although most incarcerated fathers in the United States report incomes below the poverty line (Mumola, 2000), more than half of fathers in prison report that they were the primary source of financial support for their children (Glaze and Marushchak, 2008). Therefore, children stand to lose direct financial investments from parents that were contributors prior to incarceration. Second, children may lose child support as a result of parents' (most likely fathers') jail or prison time (Arditti et al., 2003; Geller et al., 2011). A lack of child support assurance for children impacted by parental incarceration further aggravates this situation as lost child-support funds are not necessarily recovered even if parents go into arrears during confinement (Brito, 2012). Finally, incarceration of a family member not only reduces resources, but is associated with financial costs in terms of maintaining contact with the incarcerated and providing them with financial support during their confinement. Family members may take responsibility for legal fees, fines, and other legal debts associated with involvement in the criminal justice system. These debts are substantial and serve to reproduce inequality among the most disadvantaged families (deVuono-powell et al., 2015; Harris et al., 2010). Additionally, families bear responsibility for expenses associated with prison visits, phone calls, and commissary—and it is women in families who are primarily responsible for these costs (Arditti et al., 2003; Comfort, 2008; deVuono-powell et al., 2015).

In addition to the direct and visible ways parental incarceration prohibits economic transfers from the incarcerated parent to the family and corresponds and necessitates financial support from families to the incarcerated, confinement contributes to the family's material hardship indirectly through its effects on caregivers. Financial strain, mental and physical health decline, and under-employment or unemployment on the part of non-incarcerated caregivers (usually mothers in the context of paternal incarceration) all stand to intensify material hardship among justice-involved families (Arditti et al., 2003; deVuono-powell et al., 2015). Research has yet to uncover the complex ways that the incarceration of a parent may impact caregivers' employment. One descriptive study examining caregivers and their children visiting a jailed parent suggested the possibility that incarceration might serve to 'trigger' caregivers' departure from paid labour (Arditti et al., 2003). Yet a larger study utilizing the Fragile Families and Child Well-Being (FFCWB) dataset found parental incarceration was associated with increased hours in paid employment for caregivers, particularly those who were married and white (Bruns, 2017). The effects are likely to be varied based on how disruptive a parent's incarceration was to family members. Bruns (2016) suspects that incarceration's impact with respect to women's employment may link to relationship dissolution or labour-market stratification.

Non-incarcerated mothers' resource management and good mental health may help buffer against financial inadequacies connected to paternal incarceration, yet these hardships seem to persist over time and the link appears to be causal (Schwartz-Soicher et al., 2011; Wakefield and Wildeman, 2014). In sum, material hardship drives child inequality primarily by stopping and prohibiting contributions from the incarcerated parent, and indirectly by straining under-resourced single parent families. Moreover, there may be additional co-occurring family conditions (such as larger family size for families impacted by incarceration; see, e.g. Acs and Gallagher, 2000; Arditti and

Savla, 2015) as well as macro policies (e.g. inadequate state safety-net expenditures) that further exacerbate economic strain among families who experience parental incarceration. To the extent that parental incarceration prohibits economic transfers from the incarcerated parent to the family, and overburdens already vulnerable caregivers or inhibits their own employment, we can see how it drives material hardship. Such hardship is a manifestation and contributor of family inequality in the day-to-day lives of parents and children experiencing parental incarceration.

Family instability

Parental incarceration can be seen as an increasingly visible form of family instability, 'distinct from other demographic trends in family life' (Turney and Wildeman, 2014, 950). Family stress theory helps situate how family instability can put children at greater risk for negative outcomes. Family instability is typically defined as repeated changes in a child's family structure, and characterized by frequent 'entrances and exits by a biological parent's romantic partners or spouses into or out of a child's household' (Fomby and Osborne, 2017, 75). In addition to parents' union formations and dissolutions, family instability also encompasses multipartner fertility (MPF)—that is, a 'parent's experience of having biological children with more than one partner during his or her lifetime' (Fomby and Osborne, 2017, 75). Parental incarceration can be both a marker and contributor of family instability through co-occurring processes associated with partner transitions and relationship dissolution, as well as multipartner fertility (Turney and Wildeman, 2014). A FIF framework, as informed by family stress theory (e.g. Fomby and Osborne, 2017), predicts that family instability in the form of a parent's union transitions and multipartner fertility, can potentially compromise child wellbeing by challenging children to adapt in the face of unpredictable and chronic changes that upset family equilibrium. In thinking about how parental incarceration contributes to unequal chances for children, the challenges posed by family instability must be considered in the context of material hardship to fully understand their implications for parenting (Gershoff et al., 2007).

Decades of literature point to the importance of stable relationships in supporting positive developmental trajectories for children (see Fomby and Osborne, 2017 for a review, but also: Bronte-Tinkew et al., 2009; Carlson and Furstenberg, 2006; Cooper et al., 2011; Osborne and McLanahan, 2007). The Urban Institute's recent report on key findings related to the importance of stable environments and relationships in promoting children's healthy development highlights how instability limits upward mobility in families and undercuts children's potential (Adams et al., 2016). In this manner instability can be viewed as a pathway for family inequality. Parental incarceration is identified as a 'trigger' for instability, which in turn can lead to damaging scenarios for children, particularly in the absence of protective socio-emotional or financial resources (Adams et al., 2016).

This triggering effect is particularly salient for families impacted by paternal incarceration in that men's confinement is often associated with frequent changes in mothers' romantic relationships (Edin et al., 2001). These frequent changes are associated with maternal distress and less optimal parenting practices such as harsh discipline and withdrawal (Arditti et al., 2010; Beck et al., 2009; Braman, 2004; Fomby and Osborne, 2017; Neppl et al., 2016). Moreover, incarceration is typically associated with relationship dissolution among incarcerated fathers (Lopoo and Western, 2005) and has spillover effects for mothers that undermine parenting (Turney and

Wildeman, 2014). None of this is optimal for children's development, particularly if it involves residential instability and material hardship (Fomby and Osborne, 2017).

Carlson and Furstenberg (2006) discussed how children 'stand to lose' parental resources in households characterized by MPF. Their multivariate analysis of the FFCWB dataset revealed several antecedents of MPF that bear on family wellbeing. MPF households, which were disproportionately African-American, were characterized by early maternal childbearing, which in turn connected with larger 'sib sized' families. Also of note was the fact that fathers' incarceration was strongly related to MPF even after controlling for a host of other known correlates. The authors discuss how these factors (larger sib size, paternal incarceration) deterred union formation and strained time and money resources across households of low-income parents diminishing the overall parental investment in children. Guzzo (2014) extended their analysis and confirmed similar findings: compared with peers that have two or more children with the same partner, men and women with MPF start childbearing earlier, have more children, are more likely to have unintended births, and are far less likely to have had their first birth in a co-residential union. These findings revealed clear differences in parental wellbeing based on MPF, ranging from higher indices for maternal depression for mothers, to less satisfied and efficacious MPF fathers.

All too often family instability seems to correspond with justice involvement of one or both parents, serves as an invisible deterrent to stable union formation (or stable single parent households), underlies structural and processual aspects of family life that can potentially undermine parenting (e.g. residential instability, see also Turney and Wildeman, 2014), and characterizes households that may already face other forms of discrimination and hardship. However, the issue of family instability is clearly one that requires an intersectional lens to help tease out underlying structural conditions (such as racism and sexism) that may underpin negative child outcomes associated with family instability. Intersectionality calls attention to how the various institutions with which minority families, and Black women in particular, must interact reinforce day-to-day social inequalities (Few, 2007). For example, research has failed to consider under what circumstances MPF and its effects may connect with family resilience and positive relational outcomes, or at the very least, not factor into family difficulties and poor child outcomes. Repartnering (particularly in conjunction with paternal incarceration) could give rise to positive parenting scenarios, stabilize the family, and even curb abuse for some women (Comfort, 2008; Sano, 2005; Turney and Wildeman, 2014).

Therefore, to the extent that relationship transitions and multipartner fertility disrupt family life and parenting in particular, or remove parents that were otherwise positive contributors to children's lives, we can broadly view instability as a mechanism through which parental incarceration contributes to family inequality. It is not my intent to pathologize families of the incarcerated here, and I want to be clear and point out that 'instability' in and of itself may not necessarily be the cause of negative conditions at play in justice-involved families. For example, one could imagine different and more positive scenarios for families with dynamic romantic union and childbearing profiles—there is always the possibility that complex families, such as those with a parent in prison, *can* thrive given sufficient resources, supports, parental competence, and positive continuity in family relationships (Adams et al., 2016; Fomby and Osborne, 2017). However, given how family instability is more often intertwined with disadvantaged social locations, it seems to be both a manifestation and contributor to family inequality among children experiencing parental incarceration.

Parenting quality

While little doubt remains regarding the importance of material adequacy and stable relationships for supporting family wellbeing and positive child development in all families, for children impacted by incarceration, the importance of non-incarcerated caregivers' parenting 'cannot be overstated' (Poehlmann-Tynan et al., 2015, 54). Parenting is implicated in virtually all studies examining childhood resilience and is also malleable to interventions predicting better family outcomes (Masten, 2014). Positive relationships between children and their primary caregivers can mediate the degree to which youth are affected by trauma experiences and promote family resilience (Federal Interagency Working Group, 2013). Parenting quality has been conceptualized as a protective and mediating process in theorizing by social scientists examining the issue of parental incarceration (Arditti, 2012a, 2012b, 2016; Parke and Clarke-Stewart, 2003; Turney and Wildeman, 2014), and therefore can be seen as a pathway for levelling the playing field with regard to promoting positive parent and child outcomes. Unfortunately, children with a parent in prison are more likely to experience caregiver risks and parenting deficiencies. Caregiver risks include mental health problems, high stress levels, and histories of victimization and substance abuse (Aaron and Dallaire, 2010; Mackintosh et al., 2006; Phillips et al., 2004; Phillips et al., 2006). Given racial disparities in the demographics of the penal population (i.e. younger African-American men) the resultant parenting impact on under-resourced Black women warrants particular attention (Christian and Thomas, 2009; Comfort, 2008; Hanlon et al., 2007) although it is important to consider caregiver 'deficiencies' in context. Western culture may judge parents within an ideological framework of intensive mothering that holds women to 'strenuous expectations' of economic and affectional support of children (Granja et al., 2014, 1214). Intensive mothering standards, which idealize women's self-sacrifice and child-centred provision, generate additional pressure for under-resourced and criminalized mothers (Granja et al., 2014). Consequences to justice-involved families can include stigmatization and role strain due to caring for any shared children (Arditti et al., 2003; Braman, 2004).

In the face of material hardship and family instability that may be triggered or intensified by a parent's incarceration, parenting quality becomes increasingly relevant in terms of explaining variation and resilience in family life. It is surprising then how little we know with regard to the nature of parenting on the part of non-incarcerated caregivers in justice-involved families given its theoretical significance. Quantitative studies suggest children with a history of parental incarceration may experience harsh punitive discipline and less parental supervision (Phillips et al., 2006). And while empirical reviews cite disproportionate numbers of children experiencing parental incarceration as being involved in the child welfare system (Berger et al., 2016; Hines et al., 2004; Phillips et al., 2004), the causal mechanisms driving the association is unclear. For example, Phillips and colleagues (2004) reported that one in eight children who were subjects of a maltreatment report had a parent who was recently arrested. A recent analysis of Milwaukee children revealed similar findings: substantial numbers (about one in three) of Child protective services-involved children had incarcerated parents in prison or jail (Berger et al., 2016). Additionally, children involved with CPS were much more likely to have an incarcerated father than mother, suggesting the reports concerned the non-incarcerated caregiver (usually mothers). Once again, social location seems relevant with the majority of maltreatment and foster-care cases involving poor minority children, reflecting disparities in the incarcerated population of parents as well as race and class disparities in CPS reporting and foster-care involvement (Berger et al., 2016; Hines et al., 2004). Indeed, macro factors such as income inequality and state expenditures on children (Isaacs and Edelstein, 2017) influences unequal distribution of maltreatment rates. Nationally, higher county level rates of child maltreatment are found in counties with the highest levels of income inequality (Eckenrode et al., 2014), suggesting pre-existing disadvantage, and material hardship contribute to poor parenting scenarios (as well as CPS involvement connected to these scenarios). Maltreatment, then, may have more to do with the secondary repercussions that surround a parent's criminal justice involvement such as high levels of maternal distress and economic hardship (Arditti, 2012b).

Compelling evidence for the meditational role of parenting processes comes from parallel literatures applying family stress sensibilities to the study of children and parents in low-income families. For example, Gershoff and colleagues (2007) utilized a national sample (N = 21,255) of children to examine the implications of income loss and material hardship on developmental outcomes. Mediational models testing the associations of material hardship on child outcomes yielded robust and negative effect on children that were almost entirely mediated by parental stress and parenting behaviour. That is, when material hardship was lessened, parental stress was reduced and parenting behaviour was characterized by more warmth, parental investment, and positive parenting behaviour (Gershoff et al., 2007). These parenting processes in turn predicted cognitive and socio-emotional competence in 6-year-old children (Gershoff et al., 2007). Similarly, Neppl et al. (2016) tested a longitudinal model that situated parental emotional distress and parenting practices as mediators of economic hardship and child externalizing behaviour (aged 6–10). Findings yielded parent distress and parenting variables as fully mediating the effects of economic pressure on child outcomes. Although these studies did not examine the issue of paternal incarceration, we can extrapolate from their findings, along with similar research that utilizes a family stress approach. Parenting *matters*, and to the extent that parental incarceration contributes to material hardship, and I would add, caregivers' emotional distress, we can expect parenting behaviours to be an important pathway of influence for children with a parent in prison or jail.

Although some evidence points to the importance of parenting for shaping child outcomes as it pertains to parental incarceration, a recent study by Turney and Wildeman (2014) examined the implications of paternal incarceration for both fathers' and mothers' parenting and found only weak average effects between fathers' incarceration and mothers' parenting. Analyses revealed increased parenting stress for mothers (similar to other mothers attached to non-resident fathers)—particularly for those mothers who resided with fathers prior to men's incarceration. Study findings also revealed that paternal incarceration was unexpectedly associated with positive parenting changes in the form of increased engagement in mothers' parenting, suggesting that mothers (who previously resided with fathers prior to men's incarceration) spent more time involved in child-centred activities after fathers' incarceration.

Nuances and variation in children's caregiving experiences also seem to be the theme with regard to the implications of maternal incarceration for children (Turney and Wildeman, 2015). Heterogeneity in these effects suggests contexts when maternal incarceration might improve children's caregiving scenarios (by removing a troubled parent from the home) or fail to disrupt parenting because children are already in positive non-parental care arrangements. For example, smaller-scale empirical studies suggest instances of maternal incarceration whereby caregivers of imprisoned women's children express positive or no change associated with mothers' incarceration (Turanovic et al., 2012) possibly due to the fact that children were already in non-parental care prior to mothers' confinement (Hanlon et al., 2005b). Hanlon's research on children with incarcerated 'drug addicted' mothers found evidence that children were doing well—living in 'peaceful and caring home' atmospheres with surrogate caregivers with whom they felt satisfied (Hanlon et al., 2005a, 83). On the other hand, grandmothers are heavily relied upon to care for children affected by maternal incarceration, which can be problematic to the extent that grandmothers are poor and infirm (Hanlon et al., 2007). Evidence suggests that grandmothers caring for children as a result of a parent's incarceration identify an array of problems among offspring under their care including health and learning difficulties and behavioural problems (Bloom and Steinhart, 1993; Harm and Thompson, 1995).

In sum, we can draw several conclusions from the research on parental incarceration as well as from findings in parallel literatures in terms of the meditational role of parenting/caregiving quality with respect to family and child inequality. First, it seems that parental incarceration, particularly fathers' incarceration, can potentially strain caregivers and contribute to parenting stress. Second, there appears to be heterogeneity with regard to how children are affected by parental incarceration, and much of this is likely to be due to nuances in parenting quality. Not all caregiving scenarios are undermined by parental incarceration—with fewer negative impacts likely in cases whereby the incarcerated parent was non-resident. The literature on maternal incarceration helps unpack this variation in that children may already be in quality care arrangements prior to mothers' incarceration. The literature on paternal incarceration suggests non-resident fathers' incarceration may not significantly impact non-incarcerated mothers' parenting and could yield positive opportunities for repartnering and mothers' engagement with children. Yet given the fact that substantial numbers of parents reside with their children prior to their incarceration (64 per cent of mothers and 44 per cent of fathers, Mumola, 2000), we can presume that the incarceration of a parent will not be so benign or insignificant when it comes to the parenting quality of the non-incarcerated caregiver.

Conclusions and recommendation to promote family equality

The inequality created by incarceration has been characterized as invisible, cumulative, and intergenerational (Western and Pettit, 2010b). In this chapter, *familial* sources of inequality are identified that contribute to an 'unequal playing field' for children and families experiencing parental incarceration in terms of their chances for optimal parenting scenarios and child outcomes. As informed by Family Stress Proximal Process theoretical concepts (Arditti, 2016), a FIF articulates more precisely that family and child difficulties are often a function of material hardships that predate and are intensified by criminal justice involvement, and that these hardships drive relationship instability and parenting problems that increase the odds for child psychopathology and less positive family relationships. Children in some families experiencing parental incarceration do better than others, likely due to variation in how well their caregivers navigate the experience and the extent to which any relational transitions bring additional resources and stability or result in added strain and 'thin out' parental investments. An 'unequal playing field' in terms family and child wellbeing is also a result of macro forces such as state spending on resources and services that support children's healthy development (Isaacs and Edelstein, 2017). Unfortunately, the upsizing of the government's carceral role has been proportionate to the downsizing of its social welfare and educational role (NAACP, 2011; Wacquant, 2010). For example, many low spending states (< $7000 a year investment per child) are also those that are more likely to have the highest population of racial and ethnic minority children *and* the highest incarceration rates, further perpetuating inequality for justice-involved families and their children (Isaacs and Edelstein, 2017; The Sentencing Project, 2014). Given these realities, policy and intervention must be multipronged and attend to disparities in state spending on children and families, as well as disparities in family life as it pertains to parental incarceration.

While critics of mass incarceration policy had reason to hope due to signs that state prison populations were declining (Glaze and Herberman, 2013) along with criminal justice reforms enacted by the Obama administration (see, e.g. Obama, 2017), optimism has been tempered by the failure of a comprehensive package of bipartisan reforms to pass the US Senate and the hardline stance of the incoming Trump administration with regard to crime and punishment. Recent reform reflected fair sentencing practices, including a series of Supreme Court decisions that made it easier for judges to depart from mandatory sentences for drug-related offences, as well as non-traditional justice approaches. Non-traditional justice approaches tend to be non-adversarial and collaborative and aimed at strengthening relational informal social controls needed to create safe and liveable communities (Gilbert, 2014). Strategies include neighbourhood-based partnerships to prevent crime and ensure public safety, victim-centred restorative justice and the reparation of harms, diversion programmes such as drug courts community-based treatment, and supportive housing programmes for female offenders and their children (see, e.g. Warren, 2008). These kinds of strategies align well with principles of developmental science that are strength based and cognizant of family processes and needs.

Broad mechanisms for promoting social justice aimed at reducing family inequality involve decreasing prison populations, enfranchisement of offenders, and support for their families. Expansion of social justice in these areas will not only help restrict inequality in the criminal justice system but also the need for penal solutions for social problems such as poverty and unemployment (Wacquant, 2010). However, promotion of child development and family wellbeing need not wait until social justice is achieved (Arditti, 2012b). Support for parents and primary caregivers, as well as upholding those ecological domains which directly affect family stability and parenting, is critically important. Kin and social networks can serve to buffer financial and emotional challenges such as the hardships experienced by justice-involved families outlined in this chapter. For example, in some circumstances, extended kin can offer families financial aid and care to offset short-term crises (Adams et al., 2016). Similarly, childcare institutions and schools that function well can go a long way to ensure families have access to needed support as well as parental respite. In addition to directly supporting parents and children, efforts to combat material hardship involve strengthening employment (particularly for non-incarcerated caregivers of children), reducing income volatility, and renewed public and political vigour to strengthen safety-net programmes in order to ensure families impacted by incarceration thrive. Stable levels of income paired with safety-net assets and benefits are essential for buffering income shocks and family instability (Adams et al., 2016). Yet concern that safety-net programmes are not functioning as well as they could, and proposed cuts or restrictions to fundamental programmes such as Medicaid, unemployment insurance, and so on, could serve to further compromise justice-involved families.

Family-centred approaches that focus on building family strengths hold particular promise with regard to supporting quality parenting and life affirming relationships. Family strengths can be defined as relationship qualities that contribute to the health and wellbeing of the family (Walsh, 2006). Strengths-based approaches maximize opportunities and family choices, are collaborative by involving parents in goal setting and treatment, and are effective in leveraging change in families with multiple problems (Olson et al., 2010; Ryan et al., 2015). Typically, strengths-based interventions, such as multi-systemic interventions and parenting programmes, look for positive features of child, parent, family, neighbourhood, and community systems and provide support in various domains over time to lead families in the direction of positive change (Eddy and Poehlmann-Tynan, 2010; Ryan et al., 2015).

In sum, while much as been written about policy and practices aimed at helping the families of incarcerated parents, budget shortfalls, social stigma, political biases, and the very real challenges faced by justice-involved families all hinder progress and perpetuate unequal chances for caregivers and their children. Parental incarceration intensifies family inequality in terms of fostering economic adequacy and family instability, and uncertain and variable parenting quality. Therefore, targeted, non-stigmatizing support that recognizes the intersections of material hardship and parental functioning, and cushions difficulties that stem from a parent's criminal justice involvement are critical for ensuring successful and promotive human development. Just as economic and parenting domains are implicated in the difficulties families impacted by incarceration have, these areas of concern can be part of the solution (Adams et al., 2016). The FIF identifies family inequality as depending largely on the economic circumstances and parenting capabilities within families and identifies key points for intervention in order to ensure positive outcomes for children and caregivers experiencing parental incarceration.

References

Aaron, L. and Dallaire, D. 2010. 'Parental Incarceration and Multiple Risk Experiences: Effects on Family Processes and Children's Delinquency'. *Journal of Youth and Adolescence*, 39(12), 1471–84. doi: 10.1007/s10964-009-9458.

Acs, G. and Gallagher, M. 2000. *Income Inequality among America's Children*. Washington, DC: Urban Institute.

Adams, G., Bogle, M., Isaacs, J., Sandstrom, H., Dubay, L., Gelatt, J., and Katz, M. 2016. *Stabilizing Children's Lives: Insights for Research and Action*. Washington, DC: Urban Institute.

Arditti, J. 2012a. 'Child Trauma within the Context of Parental Incarceration: A Family Process Perspective'. *Journal of Family Theory & Review*, 4(3), 181–219. doi: 10.1111/j.1756-2589.2012.00128.x.

Arditti, J. 2012b. *Parental Incarceration and the Family: Psychological and Social Effects of Imprisonment on Children, Parents, and Care-givers*. New York, NY: NYU Press.

Arditti, J. 2016. 'A Family Stress-Proximal Process Model for Understanding the Effects of Parental Incarceration on Children and their Families'. *Couple and Family Psychology: Research & Practice*, 5(2), 65–88. doi: 10.1037/cfp0000058.

Arditti, J. and Kennington, M. 2017. 'Families of Incarceration and Reentry' in Browning, S. and van Eeden-Moorefield, B. (eds.) *Contemporary Families at the Vexus of Research and Practice*. 201–20. New York, NY: Routledge.

Arditti, J. and Savla, J. 2013. 'Parental Incarceration and Child Trauma Symptoms in Single Care-giver Homes'. *Journal of Child and Family Studies*, 24(3), 551–61. doi: 10.1007/s10826-013-9867-2.

Arditti, J. and Savla, J. 2015. 'Parental Incarceration and Child Trauma Symptoms in Single Care Giver Homes'. *Journal of Child and Family Studies*, 24(3), 551–61. doi: 10.1007/s108.

Arditti, J., Burton, L., and Neeves-Botelho, S. 2010. 'Maternal Distress and Parenting in the Context of Cumulative Disadvantage'. *Family Process*, 49(2), 142–64. doi: 10.1111/j.1545-5300.2010.01315.x.

Arditti, J., Lambert-Shute, J., and Joest, K. 2003. 'Saturday Morning at the Jail: Implications of Incarceration for Families and Children'. *Family Relations*, 52(3), 195–204. doi: 10.1111/j.1741-3729.2003.00195.

Beck, A., Cooper, C., McLanahan, S., and Brooks-Gunn, J. 2009. 'Relationship Transitions and Maternal Parenting'. Working Paper No. 2008–12-FF. Princeton University: Center for Research on Child Wellbeing.

Bell, L. 2010. 'Theoretical Foundations', Adams, M., Blumenfeld, W., Castaneda, C., Hackman, H., Peters, M., and Zuniga, X. (eds.) *Readings for Diversity and Social Justice*. (2nd ed.). 21. New York, NY: Routledge.

Berger, L., Cancian, M., Cuesta, L., and Noyes, J. 2016. 'Families at the Intersection of the Criminal Justice and Child Protective Services System'. *The Annals of the American Academy of Political and Social Science*, 665(1), 171–94. doi: 10.1177/0002716216633058.

Bloom, B. and Steinhart, D. 1993. *Why Punish the Children: A Reappraisal of the Children of Incarcerated Mothers in America*. Atlanta, GA: Carter Center.

Braman, D. 2004. *Doing Time on the Outside: Incarceration and Family Life in Urban America*. Ann Arbor, MI: University of Michigan Press.

Brito, T. 2012. 'Fathers Behind Bars: Rethinking Child Support Policy Toward Low-income Noncustodial Fathers and their Families'. *Journal of Gender, Race and Justice*, 15(3), 617–19.

Bronfenbrenner, U. 1979. *The Ecology of Human Development*. Cambridge, MA: Harvard University Press.

Bronte-Tinkew, J., Horowitz, A., and Scott, M. 2009. 'Fathering with Multiple Partners: Links to Children's Well-being in Early Childhood'. *Journal of Marriage and Family*, 71(3), 608–31. doi: 10.1111/j.1741-3737.2009.00622.x.

Bruns, A. 2017. 'Consequences of Partner Incarceration for Women's Employment'. *Journal of Marriage and Family*, 79(5), 1331–53.

Burton, L. and Welsh, W. 2015. 'Inequality and Opportunity: The Role of Exclusion, Social Capital, and Generic Social Processes in Upward Mobility'. William T. Grant Foundation Inequality Paper. Available at: http://wtgrantfoundation.org/library/uploads/2016/01/Inequality-and-Opportunity-Burton-and-Welsh-William-T.-Grant-Foundation.pdf.

Carlson, M. and Furstenberg, F. 2006. 'The Prevalence and Correlates of Multipartnered Fertility among Urban U.S. Parents'. *Journal of Marriage and the Family*, 68(3), 718–32. doi: 10.1111/j.1741-3737.2006.00285.

Christian, J. and Thomas, S. 2009. 'Examining the Intersections of Race, Gender, and Mass Imprisonment'. *Journal of Ethnicity in Criminal Justice*, 7(1), 69–84. doi: 10.1080/15377930802711797.

Clear, T. 2008. 'The Effects of High Imprisonment Rates on Communities'. *Crime and Justice*, 37(1), 97–132. doi: 10.1086/522360.

Comfort, M. 2008. *Doing Time Together: Love and Family in the Shadow of Prison*. Chicago: University of Chicago Press.

Conger, R., Cui, M., Bryant, C., and Elder, G. Jr. 2000. 'Competence in Early Adult Romantic Relationships: A Developmental Perspective on Family Influences'. *Journal of Personality and Social Psychology*, 79(2), 224–37. doi: 10.1037/0022-3514.79.2.224.

Conger, R.D., Conger, K.J. and Martin, M.J. 2010. 'Socioeconomic Status, Family Processes, and Individual Development', *Journal of Marriage and the Family*, 72(3): 685–704.

Cooper, C., Osborne, C., Beck, A., and McLanahan, S. 2011. 'Partnership Instability, School Readiness, and Gender Disparities'. *Sociology of Education*, 84(3), 246–59. doi: 10.1177/0038040711402361.

Dallaire, D., Zeman, J., and Thrash, T. 2015. 'Children's Experiences of Maternal Incarceration Specific Risks: Predictions to Psychological Maladaptation'. *Journal of Clinical Child and Adolescent Psychology*, 44(1), 109–22. doi: 10.1080/15374416.2014.913248.

deVuono-powell, S., Schweidler, C., Walters, A., and Zohrabi, A. 2015. *Who Pays? The True Cost of Incarceration on Families*. Oakland, CA: Ella Baker Center, Forward Together, Research Action Design.

Eckenrode, J., Smith, E., McCarthy, M., and Dineen, M. 2014. 'Income Inequality and Child Maltreatment in the United States'. *Pediatrics*, 133(3), 454–61. doi:10.1542/peds.20131707.

Eddy, J. and Poehlmann, J. 2010. 'Multidisciplinary Perspectives on Research and Intervention with Children of Incarcerated Parents', in Eddy, J. and Poehlmann, J. (eds.) *Children of Incarcerated Parents: A Handbook for Researchers and Practitioners*. 1–12. Washington, DC: Urban Institute.

Edin, K., Nelson, T., and Paranal, R. 2001. *Fatherhood and Incarceration as Potential Turning Points in the Criminal Careers of Unskilled Men*. Evanston, IL: Northwestern University Institute for Policy Research. 1–33. Available at: http://www.northwestern.edu/ipr/publications/papers/2001/fatherhood.pdf.

Federal Interagency Working Group for Children of Incarcerated Parents. 2013. *Promoting Social and Emotional Well-being for Children of Incarcerated Parents*. Washington, DC: US Department of Justice. Available at: https://csgjusticecenter.org/wp-content/uploads/2013/06/Promoting-Social-and-Emotional-Well-Being-for-Children-of-Incarcerated-Parents.pdf.

Few, A. L. 2007. 'Integrating Black Consciousness and Critical Race Feminism into Family Studies Research'. *Journal of Family Issues*, 28(4), 452–73. doi: 10.1177/0192513X06297330.

Fomby, P. and Osborne, C. 2017. 'Family Instability, Multipartner Fertility, and Behavior in Middle Childhood'. *Journal of Marriage and Family*, 79(1), 75–93. doi: 10.1111/jomf.12349.

Foster, H. and Hagan, J. 2015. 'Punishment Regimes and the Multilevel Effects of Parental Incarceration: Intergenerational, Intersectional, and Interinstitutional Models of Social Inequality and Systemic Exclusion'. *Annual Review of Sociology*, 41, 135–58. doi: 10.1146/annurev-soc-073014-112437.

Geller, A., Garfinkel, I., and Western, B. 2011. 'Paternal Incarceration and Support for Children in Fragile Families'. *Demography*, 48(1), 25–47. doi: 10.1007/213524-010-0009-9.

Gershoff, E., Aber, J., Raver, C., and Lennon, M. 2007. 'Income Is Not Enough: Incorporating Material Hardship into Models of Income Associations with Parenting and Child Development'. *Child Development*, 78(1), 70–95. doi: 10.1111/j.14678624.2007.00986.

Gilbert, M. 2014. 'Restorative justice' in Mitchell Miller, J. (ed.) *The Encyclopedia of Theoretical Criminology*. 724–30. Malden, MA: Wiley & Sons.

Glaze, L. and Herberman, E. 2013. *Correctional Populations in the United States, 2012*. Washington, DC: Bureau of Justice Statistics.

Glaze, L. and Maruschak, L. 2008. *Parents in Prison and their Minor Children*. Bureau of Justice Statistics Special Report (NCJ 222984). Washington, DC: US Department of Justice, Office of Justice Programs.

Granja, R., da Cunha, M., and Machado, H. 2014. 'Mothering from Prison and Ideologies of Intensive Parenting: Enacting Vulnerable Resistance'. *Journal of Family Issues*, 36(9), 1212–32. doi: 10.1177/0192513X14533541.

Guzzo, K. 2014. 'New Partners, More Kids: Multiple-partner Fertility in the United States'. *The Annals of the American Academy of Political and Social Science*, 654(1), 66–86. doi: 10.1177/0002716214525571.

Hanlon, T., Blatchley, R., Bennett-Sears, T., O'Grady, K., Rose, M., and Callaman, J. 2005a. 'Vulnerability of Children of Incarcerated Addict Mothers: Implications for Preventive Intervention'. *Children and Youth Services Review*, 27(1), 67–84. doi: 10.1016/j.childyouth.2004.07.004.

Hanlon, T., Carswell, S., and Rose, M. 2007. 'Research on Caretaking of Children of Incarcerated Parents: Findings and their Service Delivery Implications'. *Children and Youth Services Review*, 29(3), 348–62. doi: 10.1016/j.childyouth.2006.09.001.

Hanlon, T., O'Grady, K., Bennett-Sears, T., and Callaman, J. 2005b. 'Incarcerated Drug-abusing Mothers: Their Characteristics and Vulnerability'. *American Journal of Drug and Alcohol Abuse*, 31(1), 59–77. doi: 10.1081/ADA-200037564.

Harm, N. and Thompson, P. 1995. *Children of Incarcerated Mothers and their Caregivers: A Needs Assessment*. Little Rock, AR: Centers for Youth and Families.

Harris, A., Evans, H., and Beckett, K. 2010. 'Drawing blood from stones: Legal debt and social inequality in the contemporary United States'. *American Journal of Sociology*, 115(6), 1753–99.

Hines, A., Lemon, K., Wyatt, P., and Merdinger, J. 2004. 'Factors Related to the Disproportionate Involvement of Children of Color in the Child Welfare System: A Review and Emerging Themes'. *Children and Youth Services Review*, 26(6), 507–27.

Isaacs, J. and Edelstein, S. 2017. *Unequal Playing Field? State Differences in Spending on Children in 2013*. Washington, DC: Urban Institute.

Johnson, R. C. 2009. 'Ever-increasing Levels of Parental Incarceration and the Consequences for Children', in Raphael, S. and Stoll, M. (eds.) *Do Prisons Make us Safer? The Benefits and Costs of the Prison Boom*. 177–206. New York, NY: Russell Sage Foundation.

Lee, R., Fang, X., and Luo, L. 2013. 'The Impact of Parental Incarceration on the Physical and Mental Health of Young Adults'. *Pediatrics*, 131(4), 118–1195. doi: 10.1542/peds.2012-0627.

Lopoo, L. and Western, B. 2005. 'Incarceration and the Formation and Stability of Marital Unions'. *Journal of Marriage and the Family*, 67(3), 721–34. doi: 10.1111/j.1741-3737.2005.00165.

Lundberg, S., Pollak, R., and Stearns, J. 2016. 'Family Inequality: Diverging Patterns in Marriage, Cohabitation, and Childbearing'. *Journal of Economic Perspectives*, 30(2), 79–102. doi: 10.1257/jep.30.2.79.

Mackintosh, V., Myers, B., and Kennon, S. 2006. 'Children of Incarcerated Mothers and their Caregivers: Factors Affecting the Quality of their Relationship'. *Journal of Child and Family Studies*, 15(5), 581–96. doi:10.1007/s10826-006-9030-4.

Masten, A. S. 2014. *Ordinary Magic: Resilience in Development*. New York, NY: Guilford Press.

Mauer, M. and Chesney-Lind, M. 2002. 'Introduction', in Mauer, M. and Chesney-Lind, M. (eds.) In *Invisible Punishment: The Collateral Consequences of Mass Imprisonment*. 1–12. New York, NY: The New Press.

Mumola, C. 2000. *Incarcerated Parents and their Children*. Bureau of Justice Statistics Special Report (NCJ 182335). Washington, DC: US Department of Justice, Office of Justice Programs.

Murphey, D. and Cooper, P. 2015. *Parents Behind Bars: What Happens to their Children?* Bethesda, MD: Child Trends, Inc.

Murray, J. and Farrington, D. P. 2008. 'Parental Imprisonment: Long-lasting Effects on Boys' Internalizing Problems through the Life Course'. *Development and Psychopathology*, 20(1), 273–90. doi: 10.1017/S0954579408000138.

National Association for the Advancement of Colored People (NAACP). 2011. *Misplaced Priorities: Over Incarcerate, Under Educate*. Baltimore, MD: Author. Available at: http://naacp.3cdn.net/ecea56adeef3d84a28_azsm639wz.pdf.

Neppl, T., Senia, J., and Donnellan, M. 2016. 'Effects of Economic Hardship: Testing the Family Stress Model Over Time'. *Journal of Family Psychology*, 30(1), 12–21. doi: 10.1037/fam0000168.

Obama, B. 2017. 'The President's Role in Advancing Criminal Justice Reform'. *Harvard Law Review*, 130(3), 811–66.

Olson, D., DeFrain, J., and Skogrand, L. 2010. *Marriages and Families: Intimacy, Diversity, and Strengths*. New York, NY: McGraw Hill.

Osborne, C. and McLanahan, S. 2007. 'Partnership Instability and Child Wellbeing'. *Journal of Marriage and the Family*, 69(4), 1065–83. doi:10.1111/j.1741-3737.2007.00431.

Parke, R. and Clarke-Stewart, A. 2003. 'Effects of Parental Incarceration on Children: Perspectives, Promises, and Policies', in Travis, J. and Waul, M. (eds.) *Prisoners Once Removed: The Impact of Incarceration and Reentry on Children, Families, and Communities*. 189–232. Washington, DC: Urban Institute.

Patterson, J. M. 2002. 'Integrating Family Resilience and Family Stress Theory'. *Journal of Marriage and Family*, 64(2), 349–60. doi: 10.1111/j.1741-3737.2002.00349.

Phillips, S., Burns, B., Wagner, H., and Barth, R. 2004. 'Parental Arrest and Children Involved with Child Welfare Services Agencies'. *American Journal of Orthopsychiatry*, 74(2), 174–86. doi: 10.1037/0002-9432.74.2.174.

Phillips, S., Erkanli, A., Keeler, G., Costello, J., and Angold, A. 2006. 'Disentangling the Risks: Parent Criminal Justice Involvement and Children's Exposure to Family Risks'. *Criminology and Public Policy*, 5(4), 677–702. doi: 10.1111/j.1745-9133.2006.00404.

Poehlmann-Tynan, J. and Arditti, J. A. 2017. *Developmental and Family Perspectives on Parental Incarceration*. Washington, DC: American Psychological Association.

Poehlmann-Tynan, J., Runion, H., Burnson, C., Maleck, S., Weymouth, L., Pettit, K., and Huser, M. 2015. 'Young Children's Behavioral and Emotional Reactions to Plexiglas and Video Visits with Jailed Parents', in Poehlmann-Tynan, J. (ed.) *Children's Contact with Cincarcerated Parents: Implications for Policy and Intervention*. 39–58. New York, NY: Springer.

Ryan, S., Cunningham, P., Brennan, P., and Foster, S. 2015. 'Multisystemic Therapy as a Strength Based Model for Working with Multiproblem Families', in Arditti, A. (ed.) *Family Problems: Stress, Risks, and Resilience*. 305–319. Malden, MA: Wiley-Blackwell.

Sano, Y. 2005. 'The Unanticipated Consequences of Promoting Father Involvement: A Feminist Perspective', in Bengston, V., Acock, A., Allen, K., Dilworth-Anderson, P., and Klein, D. (eds.) *Source-book of Family Theory and Research*. 355–6. Thousand Oaks, CA: Sage.

Schwartz-Soicher, O., Geller, A., and Garfinkel, I. 2011. 'The Effect of Paternal Incarceration on Material Hardship'. *Social Services Review*, 85(3), 447–73. doi: 10.1086/661925.

Sentencing Project, The. 2014. 'The Facts: State by State Data [imprisonment rate]'. Available at: http://www.sentencingproject.org/the-facts/#rankings?dataset-option=SIR.

Travis, J. 2005. *But They all Come Back: Facing the Challenges of Prisoner Reentry*. Washington, DC: Urban Institute.

Turanovic, J., Rodriguez, N., and Pratt, T. 2012. 'The Collateral Consequences of Incarceration Revisited: A Qualitative Analysis of the Effects on Caregivers of Children of Incarcerated Parents'. *Criminology*, 50(4), 913–59. doi: 10.1111/j.1745-9125.2012.00283.

Turney, K. and Wildeman. C. 2014. 'Redefining Relationships: Explaining the Countervailing Consequences of Paternal Incarceration for Parenting'. *American Sociological Review*, 78(6), 949–79. doi: 10.1177/0003122413505589.

Turney, K. and Wildeman, C. 2015. 'Detrimental for Some? Heterogeneous Effects of Maternal Incarceration on Child Wellbeing'. *Criminology & Public Policy*, 14(1), 125–56.

Wacquant, L. 2010. 'Class, Race and Hyperincarceration in Revanchist America'. *Daedalus*, 139(3), 74–90.

Wagner, P. and Rabuy, B. 2017. 'Mass Incarceration: The Whole Pie 2017'. Available at: https://www.prisonpolicy.org/reports/pie2017.html.

Wakefield, S. and Wildeman, C. 2014. *Children of the Prison Boom: Mass Incarceration and the Future of American Inequality*. New York, NY: Oxford University Press.

Walsh, F. 2006. *Strengthening Family Resilience*. (2nd ed.). New York, NY: The Guilford Press.

Warren, J. 2008. *One in 100: Behind Bars in America 2008*. Philadelphia, PA: Pew Center on States. Available at: http://www.pewtrusts.org/-/media/legacy/uploadedfiles/wwwpewtrustsorg/reports/sentencing_and_corrections/onein100pdf.pdf.

Western, B. and Pettit, B. 2010a. 'Collateral Costs: Incarceration's Effect on Economic Mobility'. The Pew Charitable Trusts. Available at: http://www.pewtrusts.org/-/media/legacy/uploadedfiles/pcs_assets/2010/collateralcosts1pdf.pdf.

Western, B. and Pettit, B. 2010b. 'Incarceration and Social Inequality'. *Daedalus*, 139(3), 8–19. doi: 10.1162/DAED_a_00019.

Western, B., Lopoo, L., and McLanahan, S. 2004. 'Incarceration and the Bond between Parents in Fragile Families', in Pattillo, M., Weiman, D., and Western, B. (eds.) *Imprisoning America: The Social Effects of Mass Incarceration*. 21–45. New York, NY: Russell Sage Foundation.

Wildeman, C. 2010. 'Paternal Incarceration and Children's Physically Aggressive Behaviors: Evidence from the Fragile Families and Child Wellbeing Study'. *Social Forces*, 89(1), 285–309. doi: 10.1353/sof.2010.0055.

Will, J., Whalen, M., and Loper, A. 2014. 'From one Generation to the Next: Childhood Experiences of Antisocial Behavior and Parental Incarceration among Adult Inmates'. *Journal of Offender Rehabilitation*, 53(3), 190–210. doi: 10.1080/10509674.2014.887606.

4

How Much Might Mass Imprisonment Affect Childhood Inequality?

Sara Wakefield and Christopher Wildeman

Introduction

In our 2013 book *Children of the Prison Boom*, we offered evidence on how mass incarceration in the United States widened existing inequalities in childhood wellbeing among Black and White children (Wakefield and Wildeman, 2013). Marshalling a variety of datasets and evidence, our work showed that mass incarceration represented a new and especially pernicious form of intergenerational inequality in the United States. While more classic works in criminology and sociology have reflected on the degree to which criminal involvement is transmitted from parent to child (Farrington, 1989; Farrington et al., 2001; Hagan and Palloni, 1990), our book emphasized how parental incarceration influences outcomes for children far beyond criminal offending or criminal justice contact. In this chapter, we first briefly remind readers of, or introduce them to, the arguments we made in our earlier work and then devote the remainder of the chapter to the potential for broadening these arguments beyond the narrow confines of the United States and the Black–White dichotomy.

Where we left off

In *Children of the Prison Boom*, we made three core arguments. First, as shown in Table 1, we demonstrated empirically that mass imprisonment had transformed the imprisonment of a father from something relatively uncommon even for the most marginalized American children to something that 25 per cent of recent birth cohorts of African-American children could expect to experience. For African-American children whose fathers did not complete high school more than 50 per cent could expect to experience paternal imprisonment. To be sure, White children also experienced increases in the risk of paternal imprisonment—from about one in fifty before the prison boom to 1 one in thirty in more recent birth cohorts—but the racial disparity in the cumulative risk of paternal imprisonment is most striking (see also Muller and Wildeman, 2016; Pettit and Western, 2004; Sykes and Pettit, 2014; Western and Wildeman, 2009; Wildeman and Wakefield, 2014).

While children also experienced greater risks of maternal incarceration, the distinctive feature of mass incarceration we noted from a demographic perspective was that paternal imprisonment (but not maternal imprisonment) had become a shockingly common experience for African-American (but not White) children in recent years.

The racialized nature of imprisonment in the United States (and elsewhere) has long been recognized, and both classic and contemporary works highlight the importance of the criminal justice system for understanding the American stratification system

Table 1 Cumulative risk of paternal incarceration by aged 14 for children born in 1978 and 1990 by child's race and parental education.

	White children		Black children	
	1978 (%)	1990 (%)	1978 (%)	1990 (%)
All non-college educated	2.9	5.6	15.6	30.2
High school dropout	4.1	7.2	22.0	50.5
High school only	2.0	4.8	10.2	20.4
Some college	1.4	1.7	7.1	13.4

Source: Wildeman 2009.

(Alexander, 2010; Muhammad, 2011; Tonry, 1995; Wacquant, 2009). A number of point-in-time comparisons show large disparities between Whites and non-Whites in the American criminal justice system but these often obscure the scope of the problem. More recent work shows how such disparities cumulate over time and include those with current criminal justice involvement as well as those with prior experience (Pettit and Western, 2004; Shannon et al., 2017). Such estimates of the cumulative risk of experiencing imprisonment (or, in our case, experiencing parental imprisonment) are staggeringly large but make it difficult to ignore the potential for long-term consequences and the implications for American inequality (Arditti, this volume; Pettit et al., 2009; Sykes and Pettit, 2014; Wildeman, 2009).

Second, having established high and unequally distributed risks of exposure, we then outlined a host of theoretical mechanisms through which paternal incarceration could affect child wellbeing. Consistent with criminological and family trauma perspectives (Arditti, 2012; Condry, 2007; Murray et al., 2012; Poehlmann, 2005; Sutherland and Cressey, 1978; Wakefield and Apel, 2017), we also highlighted some specific instances in which paternal incarceration may not harm (and may even help) children. Such instances include when a father is violent (see also Wildeman, 2010) or has significant substance abuse or mental health problems (Wakefield and Powell, 2016). Earlier interview and ethnographic work on children of incarcerated parents was immensely helpful in this regard (Braman, 2004; Christian, 2005; Comfort, 2008; Condry, 2007; Giordano, 2010; Nurse, 2002; Siegel, 2011).

Our empirical work, which considered effects on children's behavioural and mental health problems, risk of homelessness, and risk of mortality, largely bore out our predictions. We found large effects in the direction of harm of paternal incarceration for children virtually across all domains we studied and across modelling strategies. We also found that for children whose fathers had been violent toward their mothers, the effects of his incarceration on children were quite muted.

Our third core argument—and the one that we (and we think others) see as being the big move in the work—was combining these descriptive and causal estimates to generate estimates of how much mass imprisonment might have affected Black–White inequality in childhood wellbeing in the United States. The maths behind this is mundane, and so we do not dwell on that here,[1] but we believe the results shown

---

[1] Interested readers may choose to peruse the methodological appendix of our book or see Wakefield and Wildeman (2011) for more detail on how we aggregated the individual-level effects to achieve group-level inequality estimates. In essence, we used the cumulative prevalence estimates to apply individual-level estimates of harm due to incarceration to aggregate shifts in outcomes (mental health and behavioural problems, infant mortality, and homelessness). In so doing, we assess how

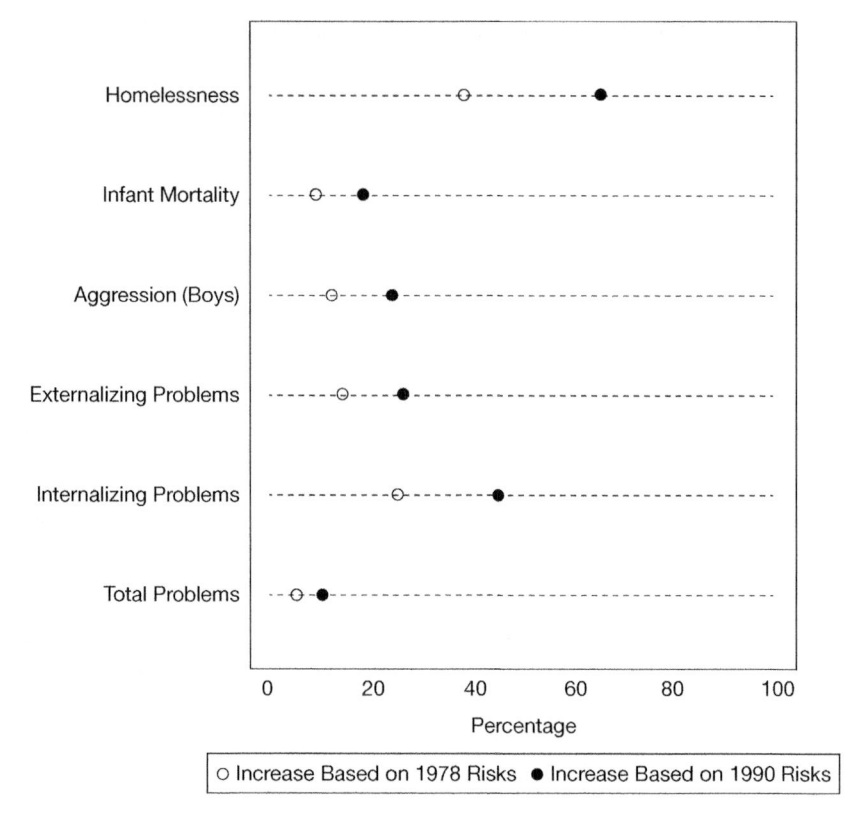

Figure 1 Estimate of increase of Black–White inequalities in child wellbeing due to paternal incarceration.
Source: Author's calculations, Wakefield and Wildeman, 2013, 146.

in Figure 1 are not. Across all of the domains we considered, we found that mass imprisonment significantly exacerbated childhood inequality, with the estimates ranging from 5 to 10 per cent for children's total behavioural problems to 30 to 65 per cent for children's risk of being homeless around the time they started school. Importantly, with the exception of homelessness (see Wildeman, 2014 for more information), we find little evidence that Black and White children respond in fundamentally different ways to paternal incarceration. That is, paternal incarceration is equally harmful for Black and White children and the inequalities that result are largely driven by differential exposure to paternal incarceration, not racial differences in responses to the experience.

Now 5 to 10 per cent might not sound like much, and so we want to very briefly go back to the past to talk about just how substantial those effects are. Evidence regarding the consequences of mass imprisonment Black–White disparities in men's earnings (Western, 2006), union formation and dissolution (Lopoo and Western,

much wellbeing gaps changed as the incarceration rate increased. Such estimates are necessarily imprecise and rely on average effects but offer a baseline for thinking through how inequalities in wellbeing grew for cohorts who came of age during the prison boom.

2005; Western, 2002, 2006), and health (Massoglia, 2008; Schnittker and John, 2007) shows large individual-level effects and striking racial disparities in the likelihood of incarceration among adult men (Pettit and Western, 2004). Yet the influence of mass incarceration in the United States on *inequality* in earnings, marriage, or health are often quite small, ranging from virtually no change to a 3 to 4 per cent shift (Wakefield and Wildeman, 2013).

Why might this be? We suggest that incarceration and inequality effects are substantially constrained by the starting distributions of adult men prior to incarceration. Put simply, even in the absence of incarceration, men at high risk for incarceration tend to earn very little, are less likely to form stable unions, and face a host of health problems. This reflects *existing* inequalities. This is not to argue that the incarceration of adult men (or women for that matter) has nothing to do with inequality. Rather, incarceration among adults represents a consequence of existing inequalities and is thus reasonably viewed as one step (and a late one at that) along a much longer path of disadvantage and marginalization.

This point is worth making twice as the mass incarceration literature is often overly mired in a narrow focus on the causal effects of incarceration—yet for scholars of inequality, it is the case that the criminal justice system reflects both existing inequalities and has the potential to create new ones. The latter appears to be the case for some, but not all, outcomes. As a result, to show that a particular group is not harmed (more) by the addition of an incarceration experience is not the same thing are arguing that incarceration (or disparities in it) is irrelevant to understanding inequality. Incarceration is a reflection of a complex set of forces—marginalization, structural racism, entrenched poverty, exposure to surveillance, bad luck, and individual failing—but among adults, it often has much smaller effects on creating *new* inequalities than one might expect.

For children, however, incarceration is very much implicated in the creation of new inequalities. In our work, we suggested that experiencing parental incarceration in childhood or adolescence creates new and substantial inequalities that represent a potentially massive shift in the life chances of youth who have yet to settle on a life path. Our own work focused on childhood behavioural problems (Wakefield and Wildeman, 2011), homelessness (Wildeman, 2014), and infant mortality (Wildeman, 2012) but other scholars have added to these outcomes, detailing a broad range of harms associated with parental incarceration in early life that should be added to the inequality ledger (Andersen and Wildeman, 2014; Foster and Hagan, 2007; Geller et al., 2012; Hagan and Foster, 2012; Haskins, 2014; Haskins and Jacobsen, 2016; Roettger and Boardman, 2012; Roettger and Swisher, 2011; Schwartz-Soicher et al., 2011; Sugie, 2012; Turney and Haskins, 2014). As a result, whereas incarceration effects among adult men may not translate into new inequalities, parental incarceration translates into very large *childhood* inequalities. Moreover, these effects may represent a lower bound of harm because small (and large) disadvantages in childhood tend to cumulate over time.

Our estimates of how much paternal incarceration has increased childhood inequalities are reproduced in Figure 1. The figure provides upper and lower bound estimates based on the risk of experiencing parental incarceration by aged 14 among cohorts of Black and White children born in 1978 and 1990. Most notably, the latter cohort entered childhood and adolescence during the peak of the prison boom in the United States. We caution that our focus was less to specify an exact point estimate for inequality effects (though in all models, we aimed for the most conservative estimate possible) but rather to show that virtually all of our estimates were in the direction of widening inequality, often by large margins. Experiencing the incarceration of a father appears to confer harms across virtually every domain we studied (as well as in domains studied by other researchers) and played a large role in widening inequalities in childhood wellbeing between Black and White children during the prison boom.

Children of the prison boom revisited

As we think back on that work nearly five years after sending the final version to the publisher, it is hard not to feel a pang of regret or two over missed opportunities (and horror at the couple typos we have found that we missed). We might have done better with some of the policy suggestions, for instance, being less naïve about how difficult letting non-violent drug offenders out of prison with no discernible supports in place might have been. We might also have spoken more about the conditions of confinement (a focus of much of our current research, collectively and individually) or tackled violence head on (Wakefield et al., 2016). We also might have specified the occasional model differently; although no one has yet contacted us to indicate that we did something wrong (or, more specifically, that we did something horrifically wrong), always a fear for first-time authors. Like other social scientists, we did not anticipate the political shift that has taken place in the United States (and Europe) and we remain uncertain as to how this will change the optimistic view for criminal justice reform we felt just a few short years ago.

More broadly, increased incarceration in the United States had countervailing effects that may be important for childhood wellbeing and we were not able to account for these in our analysis. Chief among these are findings that increases in incarceration led to non-trivial reductions in the violent crime rate (Johnson and Raphael, 2012; Levitt, 1996; Liedka et al., 2006; Western, 2006). Any intervention that makes societies less violent and more stable should have consequential effects on childhood wellbeing. The size of such an effect is an open question, however. We would point to the weight of evidence showing that reductions in the crime rate owing to increased incarceration levelled off in the 1990s, such that further increases conferred more harm without clear added benefits (Johnson and Raphael, 2012; Liedka et al., 2006). It is also the case that the children most likely to experience paternal incarceration tend to witness a shocking level of violence during early life, however low (or high) the crime rate may be at the city, state, or nation level, and such exposures are clearly harmful (see, e.g. Sharkey, 2010). In the end, it is difficult to quantify these countervailing forces but the only study that we are aware of that attempts to do so in rigorous fashion finds that the gains of the prison boom in terms of reduced homicide were counterbalanced by increases in infant mortality (Light and Marshall, 2018). We nevertheless encourage efforts to interrogate the incarceration ledger (Sampson, 2011) to assess the benefits of incarceration for crime weighed against alternative strategies (e.g. Durlauf and Nagin, 2011) and the harms imposed on those connected to inmates (Wakefield and Wildeman, 2013).

Putting aside these broader questions, we believe there are three omissions that merit significant discussion and present challenges for the field moving forward. First, we hope to join other scholars by moving beyond Black–White comparisons and thinking through how inequality may manifest in other racial/ethnic groups. As we show below, such efforts are hampered by severe data limitations and we see little sign that data infrastructure within the United States will be significantly improved (at least at the federal level) any time soon, despite a number of promising ideas for how to do so (National Academy of Sciences, 2017).

Second, recent research suggests that the effects we show in our work may be driven by children whose parents were least likely to end up in prison (Turney, 2017), suggesting that merely reducing the incarceration rate for those who would not have been incarcerated in earlier eras might yield substantial benefits. This work, along with others, also suggests that finding the right sets of levers to pull may be dependent on having much more information about the conditions of confinement, experiences prior to imprisonment, and heterogeneity in a host of other characteristics. While the goal in our original work was to provide baseline estimates for later work to complicate, we acknowledge five years on that exploration of treatment effect heterogeneity (and heterogeneity of treatments) has largely not happened (but see Andersen, 2016; Foster and Hagan, 2015; Smith, 2014; Sugie and Turney, 2017).

Third, mass incarceration in the United States is also likely to be consequential for understanding within—and across—country variation in inequality. The United States stands far behind its peers on a number of metrics, most notably in health and wellness (Wildeman and Wang, 2017). While predicting how state and federal governments choose to allocate resources is complicated, it is abundantly clear that spending on criminal justice in the United States increasingly crowds out other initiatives (Kearney et al., 2014; Western and Pettit, 2010).

1. Moving beyond Black–White comparisons

The first thing we hope to address, even if we cannot fully do so empirically, is that we should have moved beyond Black and White in our discussion of the consequences of mass imprisonment for inequality. In the book, the rare occasion on which we mention a racial/ethnic group other than Whites or Blacks, it is in passing to mention how shifts in the coding of Hispanics in federal statistics made it difficult to generate stable estimates of their risks of parental imprisonment. This unfortunately remains true but represents a substantial missed opportunity for our understanding of the links between mass incarceration and inequality in the United States.

It is virtually impossible to do the kind of analysis we presented in *Children of the Prison Boom* with other racial or ethnic groups in the United States. Hispanics are inconsistently measured during the mass incarceration era and even the most rigorous estimates would be highly unstable and error-prone. Other racial and ethnic groups were not a focus of our work because their numbers were not large enough to be able to create plausible estimates in any of the datasets we have available to us.

That said, Whites and Blacks do not represent the bounds of inequality in incarceration in the United States, Asians and Blacks do. And as the data we demonstrate bring to the fore, a greater emphasis especially on Native Americans is something sorely lacking and desperately needed in this area of research. To ignore these bounds as well as the rather large complications imposed by how Hispanic/Latino and Native populations in the United States are counted (or not) is to obscure the full picture of how the prison has emerged as a critical stratifying institution in the United States.

To provide an example of populations that remain unexamined, the population in local jails in 2000 and 2010 by race and converted to rates is displayed in Figure 2. Figure 3 provides incarceration rates by race and ethnicity in State and Federal prisons in 2015. In order to provide context, we should note that jail populations represent one of the most invisible incarcerated populations within the United States. Jails hold many people for very short periods of time so direct comparisons to State and Federal

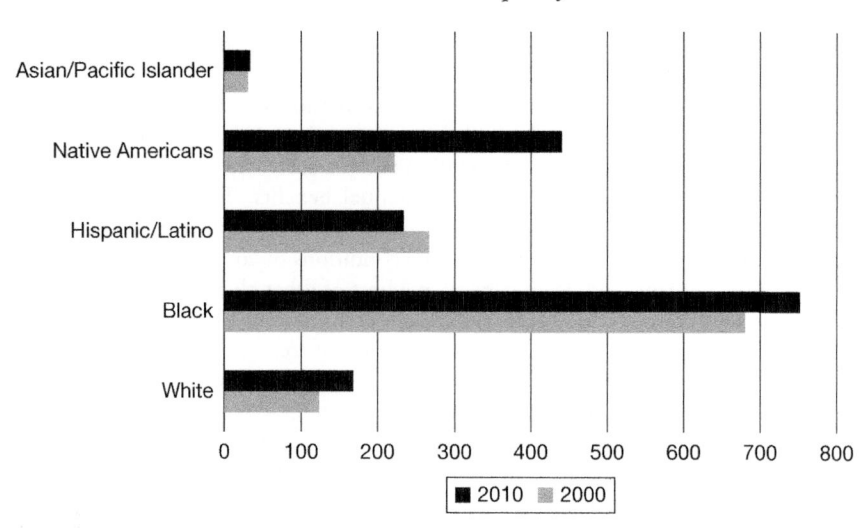

Figure 2 Jail incarceration rate per 100,000 by race and ethnicity, 2000 and 2010.
Source: Infoplease, 2017; Minton and Zeng, 2016.

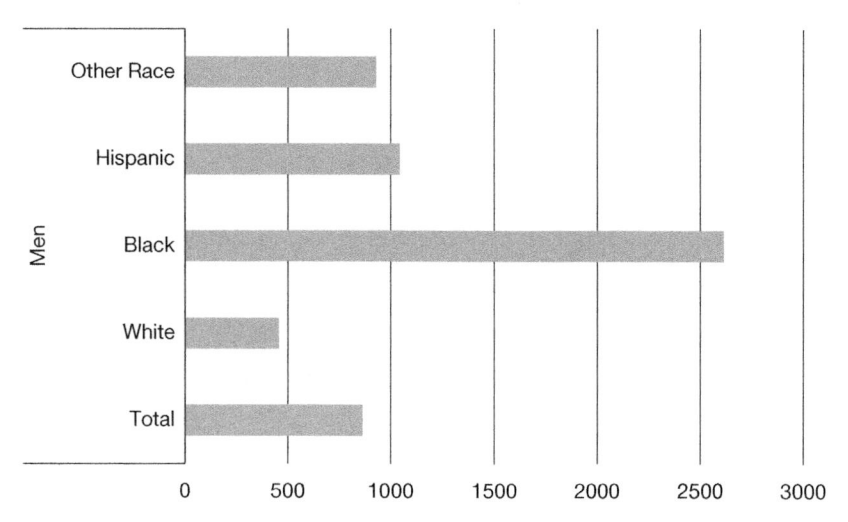

Figure 3 Imprisonment rate of sentenced state and federal male prisoners per 100,000 by race and ethnicity, 2015.
Source: Infoplease, 2017; Minton and Zeng, 2016.

prisons systems are complicated. Importantly, however, while the average daily population held in US jails is about one-half the size of the population held in State and Federal prisons, almost eleven million Americans passed through local jails in 2015 alone (Minton and Zeng, 2016). Moreover, the majority of jail inmates (~63 per cent) have not been convicted of any crime and instead are being held while awaiting case disposition (Minton and Zeng, 2016).

Several features of the figures are notable. First, we note that the rates of both Hispanics and Native Americans represent fruitful sites of future investigation for inequality scholars. With respect to the Hispanic population, the relatively high rates of jail and prison incarceration in this group falls at the midway point between the Black and White rates. These rates also exclude the very large number of Hispanic immigrants and undocumented persons that are detained in Federal facilities. At its peak in 2012, for example, the United States detained almost 480,000 unauthorized immigrants for criminal and non-criminal reasons (US Department of Homeland Security, 2016). It is not hard to imagine that such a large population bound up in the criminal justice and homeland security systems should have implications for childhood wellbeing and inequality yet the data to make such connections explicit simply do not exist (but see Patler and Branic, 2017). This represents an important hidden population standing in the way of a full accounting of the relationship between incarceration and inequality. More research on what Lansky and colleagues (this volume) call 'punishment creep' is critically needed. As one example, in light of the political shifts that have occurred in the United States, work interrogating the overlap between the carceral, immigration, and child welfare systems would move the field forward considerably (Edwards, 2016; Kirk and Wakefield, 2018; Ousey and Kubrin, 2018).

Second, turning now to the Native American population, we suggest here that Natives represent another hidden population worthy of investigation. In making this argument, we focus both on the data we have on incarceration and insights from other relevant fields. In the study of child welfare, for instance, there is a heavy, heavy emphasis on Native Americans, which is fitting since their rates of involvement in the foster-care system surpass, sometimes by up to 50 per cent, the foster-care placement rates of African-American children (Wildeman and Emanuel, 2014). Yet criminological research on this vulnerable subpopulation is nearly completely missing. The problem also appears to be worsening. In Figure 2, for example, note that the rate of jail incarceration among Native Americans grew substantially between 2000 and 2010.

Such patterns are not lost on the Bureau of Justice Statistics. Since 1998, the agency has published reports on confinement in facilities operated by the Bureau of Indian Affairs (see, e.g. Minton, 2016). Yet beyond these reports, it is difficult to get a full sense of how these high rates of detention in jails influence other outcomes. One possible way to address this core limitation, which the Bureau of Justice Statistics uses for other important subgroups that are a relatively small share of the penal population (like women and sex offenders, to name two groups) is to oversample them in order to gain stable estimates for those groups. Such a strategy—especially in combination with one that sought to publish all counts above ten for population data for the racial/ethnic groups lumped into the 'Other' category—could be cost-effective and dramatically increase our understanding of the prevalence of imprisonment among Asians and Native Americans in the United States.

2. Exploring heterogeneity

The second issue we raise concerns variation in both the treatment and outcomes. Our goal in *Children of the Prison Boom* was to provide a series of baseline estimates that future work would complicate or revise. This was perhaps overly ambitious. There were a number of outcomes that we did not choose to focus on because we made a determination that available data did not support a rigorous analysis of them. More broadly, however, many investigations of variation in treatment or outcomes are limited by the data available to researchers in the United States (Kirk and Wakefield, 2018; Wakefield et al., 2016). Beyond the challenges this presents for scholarly work, it also makes it less developed contexts masks relationships of great interest. Our search for prevalence estimates in other locales yielded few sources that could be used to do the kind of analysis that we completed in *Children of the Prison Boom* but a number of point estimates suggested their potential importance. To take one example, a report summarizing prison statistics in the United Kingdom estimated that about 200,000 children had a parent in prison in 2009 and over half of current prisoners in the country have minor children (Prison Reform Trust, 2016). Given estimates like this and coupling them with individual-level studies showing harm (Murray et al., 2014), effects like those we found in the United States are potentially relevant for other contexts.

The other contributions in this volume offer a number of avenues for further exploration along these lines. We are especially intrigued by movements to include the rights of prisoners' families alongside those of prisoners along the lines of those described by Shona Minson and Peter Scharff Smith in this volume. In the context we are most familiar with, the United States, rights related to imprisonment are enumerated in principle but rarely does this translate to clear practices or protections (and certainly these are routinely violated). More promising would be to compare how caregiving obligations are accounted for (or not) across contexts and how this translates to differences in child wellbeing outcomes (e.g. Loucks and Loureiro, this volume). Many of the other contributions in this volume detail halting (albeit inadequate) accounting for families in sentencing decisions and such reforms in the United States represent an opportunity for researchers. Beyond the large disparities in the prevalence of parental incarceration between the United States and other countries, and the obvious implications that may have for inequality, there may also be differences in the effects of parental incarceration across countries, though these may be more pronounced at the aggregate level than the individual level (Wildeman, 2016; Wildeman and Wang, 2017).

Conclusion

In our earlier work, we thought about inequality only within the US context and only in Black and White. Much, although certainly not all, of the more recent research has followed very much in the same vein, enhancing the perspective by testing for effects on an ever-growing number of outcomes. Some of these moves make good sense. Objectively measured medical conditions remain understudied, for instance, so adding those to the list seems strategically important for drawing in additional scholars from other fields. But others seem little more than an exercise in cataloguing all the harms mass imprisonment has caused. In this chapter, we hope to argue for a different move—a move toward thinking about inequality in a broader sense including both other racial/ethnic groups and other nations while also interrogating variation in the incarceration experience—rather than just more outcomes. We encourage researchers to broaden their gaze as we broaden our own.

References

Alexander, M. 2010. *The New Jim Crow: Mass Incarceration in the Age of Color Blindness*, New York: The New Press.

Andersen, L. H. 2016. 'How Children's Educational Outcomes and Criminality Vary by Duration and Frequency of Paternal Incarceration'. *The Annals of the American Academy of Political and Social Science*, 665(1), 149–70.

Andersen, S. H. and Wildeman, C. 2014. 'The Effect of Paternal Incarceration on Children's Risk of Foster Care Placement'. *Social Forces*, 93(1), 269–98.

Apel, R. 'The Effects of Jail and Prison Confinement on Cohabitation and Marriage'. *The ANNALS of the American Academy of Political and Social Science*, 665.

Arditti, J. 2012. 'Child Trauma Within the Context of Parental Incarceration: A Family Process Perspective'. *Journal of Family Theory and Review*, 4(3), 181–219.

Braman, D. 2004. *Doing Time on the Outside: Incarceration and Family Life in Urban America*, Ann Arbor: University of Michigan Press.

Christian, J. 2005. 'Riding the Bus: Barriers to Prison Visitation and Family Management Strategies', *Journal of Criminal Justice*, 21(1), 31–48.

Comfort, M. 2008. *Doing Time Together: Love and Family in the Shadow of the Prison*, Chicago: University of Chicago Press.

Condry, R. 2007. *Families Shamed: The Consequences of Crime for Relatives of Serious Offenders*. Cullompton: Willan.

Crewe, B. 2009. *The Prisoner Society: Power, Adaptation and Social Life in an English Prison*. Oxford: Oxford University Press.

Durlauf, S. N. and Nagin, D. S. 2011. 'Imprisonment and Crime: Can Both Be Reduced?' *Criminology and Public Policy*, 10(1), 13–54.

Edwards, F. 2016. 'Saving Children, Controlling Families: Punishment, Redistribution, and Child Protection'. *American Sociological Review*, 81(3), 575–95.

Farrington, D. P. 1989. 'Early Predictors of Adolescent Aggression and Adult Violence'. *Violence and Victims*, 4(2), 79–100.

Farrington, D. P., Jolliffe, D., Loeber, R., Stouthamer-Loeber, M., and Kalb, L. M. 2001. 'The Concentration of Offenders in Families, and Family Criminality in the Prediction of Boys' Delinquency'. *Journal of Adolescence*, 24(5), 579–96.

Foster, H. and Hagan, J. 2007. 'Incarceration and Intergenerational Social Exclusion'. *Social Problems*, 54(4), 399–433.

Foster, H. and Hagan, J. 2015. 'Punishment Regimes and the Multilevel Effects of Punishment: Intergenerational, Intersectional, and Interinstitutional Models of Social Inequality and Systemic Exclusion'. *Annual Review of Sociology*, 41, 135–58.

Geller, A., Cooper, C. E., Garfinkel, I., Schwartz-Soicher, O., and Mincy, R. 2012. 'Beyond Absenteeism: Father Incarceration and Child Development'. *Demography*, 49(1), 49–76.

Giordano, P. C. 2010. *Legacies of Crime: A Follow-Up of Children of Highly Delinquent Girls and Boys*. New York: Cambridge University Press.

Hagan, J. and Foster, H. 2012. 'Intergenerational Educational Effects of Mass Imprisonment'. *Sociology of Education*, 83(3), 259–86.

Hagan, J. and Palloni, A. 1990. 'The Social Reproduction of a Criminal Class in Working Class London, Circa 1950–1980'. *American Journal of Sociology*, 96(2), 265–99.

Haskins, A. R. 2014. 'Unintended Consequences: Effects of Paternal Incarceration on School Readiness and Later Special Education Placement'. *Sociological Science*, 1, 141–58.

Haskins, A. R. and Jacobsen, W. C. 2016. 'Schools as Surveilling Institutions? Paternal Incarceration, System Avoidance, and Parental Involvement in School'. *American Sociological Review*, 82(4), 657–84.

Infoplease. 2017. 'Population of the United States by Race and Hispanic/Latino Origin, Census 2000 and 2010'. Available at: https://www.infoplease.com/us/race-population/population-united-states-race-and-hispaniclatino-origin-census-2000-and-2010/.

Johnson, R. and Raphael, S. 2012. 'How Much Crime Reduction Does the Marginal Prisoner Buy?'. *Journal of Law and Economics*, 55(2), 275–310.

Kearney, M. S. et al. 2014. 'Ten Economic Facts about Crime and Incarceration in the United States'. Policy Memo. May. The Hamilton Project. Available at: http://www.hamiltonproject.org/assets/legacy/files/downloads_and_links/v8_THP_10CrimeFacts.pdf.

Kirk, D. S. and Wakefield, S. 2018. 'Collateral Consequences of Punishment: A Critical Review and Path Forward'. *Annual Review of Criminology*, 1, 171–94.

Levitt, S. 1996. 'The Effect of Prison Population Size on Crime: Evidence from Prison Overcrowding and Litigation'. *Quarterly Journal of Economics*, 111(2), 319–51.

Liedka, R. V., Piehl, A. M., and Useem, B. 2006. 'The Crime-Control Effect of Incarceration: Does Scale Matter?'. *Criminology and Public Policy*, 5, 245–76.

Light, M. T. and Marshall, J. 2018. 'On the Weak Mortality Returns to the Prison Boom: Comparing Infant Mortality and Homicide in the Incarceration Ledger'. *Journal of Health and Social Behavior*, 59(1), 3–19.

Lopoo, L. M. and Western, B. 2005. 'Incarceration and the Formation and Stability of Marital Unions'. *Journal of Marriage and the Family*, 67(3), 721–34.

Massoglia, M. 2008. 'Incarceration as Exposure: The Prison, Infectious Disease, and Other Stress-Related Illnesses'. *Journal of Health and Social Behavior*, 49(1), 56–71.

Minton, T. D. 2016. *Jails in Indian Country, 2015*. in Bureau of Justice Statistics (ed.), Washington, DC: US Government Printing Office, Bureau of Justice Statistics.

Minton, T. D. and Zeng, Z. 2016. *Jail Inmates in 2015*. in Bureau of Justice Statistics. (ed.), Washington DC: US Government Printing Office, Bureau of Justice Statistics.

Muller, C. and Wildeman, C. 2016. 'Geographic Variation in the Cumulative Risk of Imprisonment and Parental Incarceration in the United States'. *Demography*, 53(5), 1499–509.

Muhammad, K. G. 2011. *The Condemnation of Blackness: Race, Crime, and the Making of Modern Urban America*. Cambridge, MA: Harvard University Press.

Murray, J., Bijleveld, C. C. J. H., Farrington, D. P., and Loeber, R. 2014. *Effects of Parental Incarceration on Children: Cross-National Comparative Studies*. Washington, DC: American Psychological Association.

Murray, J., Farrington, D. P., and Sekol, I. 2012. 'Children's Anti-Social Behavior, Mental Health, Drug Use, and Educational Performance After Parental Incarceration: A Systematic Review and Meta-Analysis'. *Psychological Bulletin*, 138(2), 175–210.

National Academy of Sciences. 2017. *Innovations in Federal Statistics: Combining Data Sources While Protecting Privacy*. Washington, DC: The National Academies Press.

Nellis, A. 2016. *The Color of Justice: Racial and Ethnic Disparity in State Prisons*. Washington, DC: The Sentencing Project.

Nurse, A. 2002, *Fatherhood Arrested: Parenting from Within the Juvenile Justice System*. Nashville, TN: Vanderbilt University Press.

Ousey, G. C. and Kubrin, C. E. 2018. 'Immigration and Crime: Assessing a Contentious Issue'. *Annual Review of Criminology*, 1, 63–84.

Patler, C. and Branic, N. 2017. 'Patterns of Family Visitation During Immigration Detention'. *RSF: The Russell Sage Foundation Journal of the Social Sciences*, 3(4), 18–36.

Pettit, B. and Western, B. 2004. 'Mass Imprisonment and the Life Course: Race and Class Inequality in U.S. Incarceration'. *American Sociological Review*, 69, 151–69.

Pettit, B., Sykes, B., and Western, B. 2009. *Technical Report on Revised Population Estimates and NLSY-79 Analysis Tables for the Pew Public Safety and Mobility Project*. Cambridge, MA: Harvard University Press.

Phelps, M. S. 2017. 'Mass Probation: Toward a More Robust Theory of State Variation in Punishment'. *Punishment and Society*, 19(1), 53–73.

Poehlmann, J. 2005. 'Children's Family Environments and Intellectual Outcomes During Maternal Incarceration'. *Journal of Marriage and the Family*, 67(5), 1275–85.

Prison Reform Trust. 2016. 'Prison: The Facts. Bromley Briefings Summer 2016'. Prison Reform Trust.

Roettger, M. E. and Boardman, J. D. 2012. 'Parental Incarceration and Gender-Based Risks for Increased BMI: Evidence from a Longitudinal Study of Adolescents and Young Adults in the United States'. *Journal of Epidemiology*, 175(7), 636–44.

Roettger, M. E. and Swisher, R. R. 2011. 'Associations of Father's History of Incarceration with Delinquency and Arrest among Black, White, and Hispanic Males in the U.S.'. *Criminology*, 49(4), 1109–47.

Sampson, R. J. 2011. 'The Incarceration Ledger: Toward a New Era in Assessing Societal Consequences'. *Criminology & Public Policy*, 10(3), 819–28.

Schaefer, D. R., Martin, B., Young J. T. N., and Kreager D. A. 2017. 'Friends in Locked Places: An Investigation of Prison Inmate Network Structure.' *Social Networks*, 51, 88–103.

Schnittker, J. and John, A. 2007. 'Enduring Stigma: The Long-term Effects of Incarceration on Health'. *Journal of Health and Social Behavior*, 48(2), 115–30.

Schwartz-Soicher, O., Geller, A., and Garfinkel, I. 2011. 'The Effect of Paternal Incarceration on Material Hardship'. *Social Service Review*, 85(3), 447–73.

Shannon, S. K. S. et al. 2017. 'The Growth, Scope, and Spatial Distribution of People with Felony Records, 1948–2010'. *Demography*, 54(5), 1795–818.

Sharkey, P. 2010. 'The Acute Effect of Local Homicides on Children's Cognitive Performance'. *Proceedings of the National Academy of Sciences*, 107(26), 11733–8.

Siegel, J. 2011. *Disrupted Childhoods: Children of Women in Prison*. New Brunswick: Rutgers University Press.

Smith, P. S. 2014. *When the Innocent are Punished: The Children of Imprisoned Parents*. London, UK: Palgrave Macmillan.

Smith, P. S. and Ugelvik, T. 2017. *Scandinavian Penal History, Culture, and Prison Practice*. Palgrave Studies in Prisons and Penology. London: Palgrave Macmillan.

Sugie, N. 2012. 'Punishment and Welfare: Paternal Incarceration and Families' Receipt of Public Assistance'. *Social Forces*, 90(4), 1403–27.

Sugie, N. and Turney, K. 2017. 'Beyond Incarceration: Criminal Justice Contact and Mental Health'. *American Sociological Review*, 82(4), 719–43.

Sutherland, E. H. and Cressey, D. R. 1978. *Criminology*. (9th ed.). New York: J.B. Lippincott Company.

Sykes, B. L. and Pettit, B. 2014. 'Mass Incarceration, Family Complexity, and the Reproduction of Childhood Disadvantage'. *The Annals of the American Academy of Political and Social Science*, 654(1), 127–49.

Tonry, M. 1995. *Malign Neglect: Race, Crime, and Punishment in America*. New York: Oxford University Press.

Turney, K. 2017. 'The Unequal Consequences of Mass Incarceration for Children'. *Demography*, 54(1), 361–89.

Turney, K. and Haskins, A. R. 2014. 'Falling Behind? Children's Early Grade Retention After Paternal Incarceration'. *Sociology of Education*, 87(4), 241–58.

US Department of Homeland Security. 2016. *Immigration Enforcement Actions: 2014*.

Wacquant, L. 2009. *Punishing the Poor: The Neoliberal Government of Social Insecurity*. Durham, NC: Duke University Press.

Wakefield, S. and Apel, R. 2017. 'Criminological Perspectives on Parental Incarceration', in Wildeman, C., Haskins, A. R., and Tynan-Poehlmann, J. (eds.) *When Parents Are Incarcerated: Interdisciplinary Research and Interventions to Support Children*. Washington, DC: American Psychological Association.

Wakefield, S. and Powell, K. 2016. 'Distinguishing "Petty Offenders" From "Serious Criminals" in the Estimation of Family Life Effects'. *The Annals of the American Academy of Political and Social Science*, 665(1), 195–212.

Wakefield, S. and Wildeman, C. 2011. 'Mass Imprisonment and Racial Disparities in Childhood Behavioral Problems'. *Criminology & Public Policy*, 10(3), 793–817.

Wakefield, S. and Wildeman, C. 2013. *Children of the Prison Boom: Mass Incarceration and the Future of American Inequality*. Crime and Public Policy Series. New York: Oxford University Press.

Wakefield, S., Lee, H., and Wildeman, C. 2016. 'Tough on Crime, Tough on Families? Criminal Justice and Family Life in America'. *The Annals of the American Academy of Political and Social Science*, 665(1), 8–21.

Walmsley, R. 2016. 'World Prison Population List'. (11th ed.). London: International Centre for Prison Studies.

Western, B. 2002. 'The Impact of Incarceration on Wage Mobility and Inequality'. *American Sociological Review*, 67(4), 477–98.

Western, B. 2006. *Punishment and Inequality in America*. New York: Russell Sage Foundation.

Western, B. and Pettit, B. 2010. 'Collateral Costs: Incarceration's Effect on Economic Mobility'. Washington, DC: The Pew Charitable Trusts.

Western, B. and Wildeman, C. 2009. 'The Black Family and Mass Incarceration'. *The Annals of the American Academy of Political and Social Science*, 621(1), 221–42.

Wildeman, C. 2009. 'Parental Imprisonment, the Prison Boom, and the Concentration of Childhood Advantage', *Demography*, 46(2), 265–80.

Wildeman, C. 2010. 'Parental Incarceration and Children's Physically Aggressive Behaviors: Evidence from the Fragile Families and Child Wellbeing Study'. *Social Forces*, 89(1), 285–310.

Wildeman, C. 2012. 'Imprisonment and Infant Mortality'. *Social Problems*, 59(2), 228–59.

Wildeman, C. 2014. 'Parental Incarceration, Child Homelessness, and the Invisible Consequences of Mass Imprisonment'. *The Annals of the American Academy of Political and Social Science*, 651(1), 74–96.

Wildeman, C. 2016. 'Incarceration and Population Health in Wealthy Democracies'. *Criminology*, 54(2), 360–82.

Wildeman, C. and Andersen, L. H. 2015. 'Cumulative Risks of Paternal and Maternal Incarceration in Denmark and the United States'. *Demographic Research*, 32, 1567–80.

Wildeman, C. and Emanuel, N. 2014. 'Cumulative Risks of Foster Care Placement of U.S. Children, 2000–2011'. *PLoS ONE*, 9(3), e92785.

Wildeman, C. and Wakefield, S. 2014. 'The Long Arm of the Law: The Concentration of Incarceration in Families in the Era of Mass Incarceration'. *Journal of Gender, Race, and Justice*, 17, 367–89.

Wildeman, C. and Wang, E. A. 2017. 'Mass Incarceration, Public Health, and Widening Inequality in the USA'. *The Lancet*, 389(10077), 1464–74.

Wildeman, C., Turney, K., and Yi, Y. 2016. 'Paternal Incarceration and Family Functioning: Variation Across Federal, State, and Local Facilities'. *The Annals of the American Academy of Political and Social Science*, 665(1): 80–97.

5

'I'm the man and he's the woman!'
Gender Dynamics among Couples During and After Prison

Megan Comfort*

Introduction

The spectacular rise of the number of people confined in jails and prisons in the United States has become a cornerstone of contemporary penal scholarship. After hovering around 150 inmates per 100,000 residents for half a century, the national incarceration rate began inflating in 1973 and by 2015 had skyrocketed to 870 inmates per 100,000 residents aged 18 or over (Bureau of Justice Statistics, 2017), establishing the United States as one of the leaders in world incarceration (Institute for Criminal Policy Research, 2017). Yet the nation's daily count of 2.1 million bodies behind bars is not a static population: each year millions of people leave correctional facilities to return to their home neighbourhoods (Carson and Anderson, 2016; Kaeble and Glaze, 2016; Minton and Zeng, 2016). These sizeable numbers of people trying to (re)integrate into society have spurred research on their efforts to find work and shelter, grapple with addiction and access health care, and meet the conditions of parole and probation (Pager, 2007; Binswanger et al., 2011; Miller, 2014).

Through such research on the socioeconomic context of released inmates' lives, their kinship and social networks have come into sharper focus. Long stereotyped as loners, the millions of former jail detainees and prisoners returning home have brought attention to the parents, spouses, siblings, children, and other intimates who are affected by the incarceration of a loved one (Condry, 2007; Wakefield and Wildeman, 2013; Smith, 2014; Arditti, 2012; Christian and Kennedy, 2011; Codd, 2008). Furthermore, research on the family and social ties of those confined within and released from correctional facilities has transformed our understanding of incarceration as a phenomenon that predominantly affects males: although the vast majority of people in jail and prison are male, millions of females are profoundly involved with the criminal justice system through its grip on their sons, fathers, partners, brothers, and other relatives and loved ones (Halsey and Deegan, 2015; Comfort, 2008; Condry, 2007).

As scholars elucidate the scope of the 'repercussive effects' of incarceration (Comfort, 2007) with more clarity and complexity, a fertile area for exploration is

---

* I am very grateful to the people who participated in this study and shared their experiences with us. My thanks as well to Sébastien Chauvin, Jessica Fields, Ken Kolb, Reuben Miller, and Loïc Wacquant for their helpful comments on this manuscript, and to Olga Reznick, Diane Binson, Nicolas Alvarado, and John Weeks for their assistance with carrying out the study. This research was funded by grants P30 MH62246 and R01MH078743 from the National Institutes of Health. All procedures were approved by the University of California San Francisco Committee on Human Subjects Research and the RTI International Institutional Review Board.

Prisons, Punishment, and the Family: Towards a New Sociology of Punishment? First Edition. Rachel Condry and Peter Scharff Smith. © The several contributors 2018. Published 2018 by Oxford University Press.

gender and intimate relationships. Prior research has focused mainly on the construction of gender inside of correctional settings, with men's jail and prison environments being characterized as valourizing a specific set of 'manhood acts' (Schwalbe, 2005) and requiring aggression, violence, and emotional withdrawal as safety strategies (Evans and Wallace, 2008). Yet relatively little is known about how experiences behind bars shape gender dynamics in relationships between incarcerated people and their non-incarcerated partners during the custodial sentence, and likewise there is much to be learned about whether and how shifts in gender roles and relations that may occur between intimate partners while one person is confined play out in relationships post-release.

Since 1995, I have been involved in a series of studies focusing on non-incarcerated women's romantic relationships with imprisoned men and couples' relationships after men's release from prison (Comfort, 2008; Comfort et al., 2000; Comfort et al., 2005; Grinstead et al., 2008; Comfort et al., 2018; Wildeman et al., 2013). Fieldwork for these studies employed a variety of methodological approaches, including ethnography, in-depth interviewing, and longitudinal survey research. One prominent theme that emerged consistently across studies over the years is the challenge, frustration, and disappointment that accompany men's return from the penitentiary. In contrast to both personal and societal expectations for joyful reunions, relief that the custodial sentence is over, and energetic efforts at domestic and civic 're-entry,' data indicate that the post-release period is rife with complex emotions, interpersonal conflict, and a pervasive feeling of being let down—by oneself, one's partner, and society at large.

Analysis reveals that gender roles and expectations more often than not lie at the heart of couples' struggles, closely linked to matters of employment, responsibility for domestic work, and questions over household control and management. In some ways, one could assert that male former prisoners and their female partners contend with similar issues as other couples who renegotiate a division of labour within the family unit when job-seeking and home-making patterns change (Bianchi and Milkie, 2010). However, as I discuss in this chapter, people's accounts of the challenges they face when men return to the home from prison highlight particular tensions related to shifting from a masculinity constructed in accordance with the punitive constraints and dictates of the penitentiary to one that must operate within the harsh social conditions of life for impoverished people in the 'outside' world. Paradoxically, although riddled with emotional distress and responding to a brutalizing environment, the masculinity enacted during the incarceration period brings elements of fulfillment to men as well as their partners, who themselves enact an incarceration-specific femininity. By contrast, once men are home, men's and women's understandings of what it means to 'be a man' shift to encompass behaviours and achievements that are difficult for men with conviction histories to attain, and the profound dissatisfaction both parties feel about the failure to enact this manhood translates into conflict in the relationship. It therefore becomes clear that couples are navigating two contexts in which the same male bodies attempt to undertake different sets of 'manhood acts', one of which is 'strategically adapted to the realities of resource availability, individual skill, local culture, and audience expectations' (Schrock and Schwalbe, 2009) and the other of which is woefully out of synch. This analysis of gender dynamics during and after imprisonment provides a lens for deepening our understanding of how the rising use of confinement may contribute to strife within the family, and thus how the state's power to punish reverberates daily in the social roles and interactions of some of society's most vulnerable members.

Methods

Although my analysis is informed by over two decades of research with male prisoners and their female partners, I concentrate in this chapter on in-depth interviews and observations with sub-samples of participants in two studies. The first was a four-year HIV-prevention education intervention based at the visiting centre at a northern California state prison, one component of which involved conducting longitudinal in-depth interviews with women visiting incarcerated partners whom our project team had trained to be peer health educators (Grinstead et al., 2008). Either a colleague or I conducted two qualitative interviews over six months with each woman, which permitted us to obtain information from her at various points during the incarceration of the man she was visiting. Of the eight interviewees, three women had a partner in prison at the time of the first interview who was released by the time of the second; two women experienced the release of the man before the first interview but he had been reincarcerated at the time of second; two women's partners were released at the time of both interviews; and one woman's partner was released at the time of her only interview.

The second study involved a cross-sectional survey conducted with 172 male-female couples in which the male partner had been released from state prison within the previous twelve months (Comfort et al., 2014).[1] Participants were recruited from multiple sites in Oakland and San Francisco, California, including post-release information meetings and support groups, street outreach, and referrals from social service agencies. Twenty-three couples from the study were invited to participate in an in-depth interview; participating couples came to a scheduled appointment together and were interviewed separately and simultaneously by myself and a male colleague, with the exception of one woman who came alone because her partner had been reincarcerated and one man who had broken up with his partner and she had left the country (total N = 44 participants). Recruitment criteria specified that couples had been romantically involved during and after the man's most recent incarceration, and the majority had been in a relationship prior to his arrest as well.

'He probably felt a little emasculated': Constructions of masculinity behind and beyond bars

Men's prisons are notoriously hyper-macho, misogynistic environments (SpearIt, 2011). Not surprisingly, violence in prison is highly gendered (Kupers, 2010). Men who are the victims of sexual violence and men who form consensual relationships with a powerful partner who can protect them from other prisoners are called 'women', 'wives', and a host of slurs used in outside society to refer to women (Rideau and Wikberg, 1992). Struggles for power among prisoners are also frequently portrayed in gendered terms, with those who are in control being the 'men' and those who are forfeiting their food, handing over their commissary items, or even just keeping a clear

---

[1] I refer to participants as 'male–female couples' because recruitment criteria for this study did not require partners to be married, monogamous or to identify as heterosexual, but did require that one partner self-identify as female and one partner self-identify as male and neither partner self-identify as transgender.

distance on the yard being deemed 'women' who are weak, submissive, and dominated (Trammell, 2011).

Women enter this charged space via letters, phone calls, care packages, and visits. In California, each of these forms of interaction is considered a privilege by the penitentiary, and as correctional budgets have become tighter and other privileges have been stripped away, communicating with and receiving goods from outsiders have increasingly become the sole source of 'rewards' offered to prisoners (for a similar dynamic in the Portuguese context, see Granja, this volume). Such an arrangement adds to the gendered nature of how women's roles are structured by the correctional institution: they are assigned to be caretakers, providing nourishment and succour through emotional connection, provision of food and supplies, and the maintenance of family and relationship ties (see Condry, 2007 for a discussion of how such care-taking varies according to the gender of the prisoner). Being separated from their loved ones and having limited opportunities to interact with them often encourages women to rise to the occasion with attentiveness, generosity, and ingenuity as they care for incarcerated men, reinforcing the feminization of the emotional and physical nurturance received by male prisoners and promoting the image of a 'good woman' who 'stands by her man' (Mcdermott and King, 1992; Comfort, 2008; Christian et al., 2006; Jardine, 2015; Condry, 2007). Women who do not fulfill this role or attempt to subvert it are expelled, whether by a partner who seeks another relationship with someone who will tend to his needs, or by the prison authorities who bar women considered to be disruptive, unruly, or 'inappropriate' from having contact with prisoners (Comfort et al., 2005; Bandele, 1999).

Maintaining contact with a prisoner is labour-intensive and costly (deVuono-powell et al., 2015; Kotova, this volume; Granja, this volume; Jardine, this volume), and women need motivation to participate in these activities. Women often make active decisions about their level of engagement with their partner and articulate a strong sense of control in their partnerships, speaking directly about rewarding men with treats and frequent visiting to enforce certain behaviours and withholding affection, financial support, or information as leverage to produce change in others, effectively using incarcerated men's dependence on them as a means of redefining the relationships along their own terms (Comfort, 2008; Granja, 2016). Having a strong connection to people on the outside can be pivotal for surviving incarceration: communication can provide the hope and emotional support needed to preserve mental health, visits and phone calls are highlights in the monotonous routine of prison life, and receiving money and goods can not only make life more comfortable but can also keep prisoners from falling victim to exploitation by other inmates.

Hence the desire to maintain contact with partners on the outside is extremely strong. However, in their quest to retain their partners' interest, incarcerated men are obstructed from enacting stereotypical manliness for their partners: they cannot be economic providers, exhibit sexual prowess, protect women from danger, or be 'the man of the house'. Meanwhile, their partners have access to other men who may be able to assume these roles. This is one of the most salient conundrums of prison life: the carceral milieu at once glorifies and cultivates the performance of intensely macho manhood acts, while also profoundly emasculating its denizens.

In response to this dilemma, incarcerated men reach out to their partners through stereotypically *feminized* forms of communication: they write impassioned letters in which they reveal their inner feelings; they craft cards for every birthday and holiday; they sit with their partners for hours in visiting rooms and talk, asking questions, sharing memories, and maybe even shedding tears (Christian and Thomas, this volume). For couples who are able to have overnight visits,[2] three days and two nights in the simulated domestic environment of a prison trailer provide men with the opportunity to model an idealized husband role, engaging in long conversations, listening attentively with no distractions, and taking on the tasks of cooking and cleaning (Comfort, 2002). One woman summed this up, lauding her partner: '*He is a male me*! He is a male, he is sensitive, loving, *he's all of that*!' (Comfort, 2008). Indeed, women express awareness of the idea of a dualized gender identity for incarcerated men: in one realm, men are expected to be and often need to be hard-bodied, violent, and menacing, but in their interactions with their partners they express a masculinity that embraces sensitivity, emotion, and gentleness. As the incarceration goes on, the carceral environment intensifies the former, and the continued importance of retaining women's emotional and financial investment in the relationship strengthens the latter. These mounting pressures and divergent trajectories position the post-release period as a time of clash and discord, with men leaving an environment that promotes engaging in a masculine project that prizes and prioritizes qualities that are not only in opposition to each other but also differ significantly from those they and their partners expect them to exhibit once back home.

Yet men who return to their families and attempt to enact masculinity by immediately assuming the role of 'head of the household' face resentment from the wives and girlfriends who took on new financial independence, control of domestic decisions, and management of daily affairs while their partners were behind bars (Kotova, this volume). In addition, they often find themselves discredited and encounter opposition from women who are unwilling to follow their partners on a path that has proven to lead only to hardship and the penitentiary. Alfonso,[3] a man in his early thirties who had great difficulty recalling how many times he had been incarcerated in his lifetime, neatly summed up this scenario:

> I pretty much always try to be, how would you say it? [with a twang, almost as if mocking himself] 'Head honcho,' you know. 'Shot caller,' whatever. *I* tell [my wife] what to do.... But there's times where she will be like, 'Fuck that! I'm running shit around here. Because if you run shit it's going to be all fucked up and you're just going to go back to jail.'

Men who survived imprisonment by assuming a more submissive role within the carceral milieu also face challenges when reuniting with partners after release. Michael, a man in his late forties, explains that he was referred to a psychiatrist for 'severe mental depression' stemming from the trauma he experienced during his most recent incarceration when he was housed with high-level offenders despite his own low-security status. Although he claims that he did not suffer physical violence, Michael feared for his life as a series of cellmates threatened him, a situation to which he refers repeatedly and with pronounced anxiety during his interview. When not behind bars, Michael grapples with alcoholism and finding employment, the lack of which creates an uneasy imbalance in his relationship with his common-law wife, Diana, since they are unequal providers for their 10-year-old son. His portrayal of their communication since his most recent release suggests that the passive coping skills he developed while in prison continue to operate in his domestic life: 'She's kind of more forceful [than me] though. We go at it sometimes. She's kind of controlling. But I've learned how to just deal with it. Mostly I let her just think she's in total control.' For her part, Diana plays into these dynamics despite her

---

[2] Heterosexual couples who are legally married are eligible for overnight visits in California prisons if the prisoner meets multiple security requirements.

[3] All names are pseudonyms.

awareness of her husband's experiences behind bars, and in fact her view of his time inside prompts her to compensate for his perceived weakness: 'No one wants someone to have control over them like that. When you're incarcerated you don't have any words to say, you don't have anything to say.... So he probably felt a little emasculated from being in that situation as well and ... I felt like in this relationship, someone has to be strong.'

'I had to play mommy and all of that': women as a locus of discipline and surveillance

While incarcerated, men are only able to share a small portion of their lives with their partners, and the calm, controlled appearance they present during visits and phone calls may conceal a pervasive vulnerability instilled by living under the direct rule of powerful authorities, whether correctional officers or other prisoners or both (Hutton, 2016). Yet once couples transition from having highly limited, intensely supervised, and often romanticized time together during prison visits to sharing abundant and aimless 'down time' in the newly communal domestic sphere, these vulnerabilities can emerge—and are often met with impatience by women who desire competent and action-oriented partners. Rhonda, whose husband spent two years in prison, exuded confidence and good humour when she came to the visiting center to participate in our health programme. Yet when she returned after her husband's release to complete her interview, she appeared weary and irritable, in contrast to the high energy and laughter to which we were accustomed. She had brought her husband with her this time, apparently against his will but she was adamant that he get a better sense of what her life had been like while he was inside. Sending him off to 'be useful' and help other staff members while she was interviewed, she explained that she was accustomed to being on her own and was finding it hard to share her apartment with him, feeling that he had lost not only practical but also symbolic ownership of their joint household: 'Two years with my own space and I'm saying, "You're in my space now."' She then described a typical argument over her husband's inability to organize his belongings:

> [I tell him] 'Man, why don't you put those papers in there?' instead of every day, [him asking] 'What did I do with this paper? What did I do with that?'... It drives me crazy. It drives me crazy. I'm like, 'There's a drawer right there. I put all of your papers in there.' The next day he'll have them in the living room and then he'll go back. And then he asks me every day, 'Where is this paper and where is that' ... I'll go in the kitchen and start cooking and rappin' pots and he'll be in there, 'Can you come here?' I act like I don't hear him. Tune him out. Because sometimes it's too much. And I'm like, "No I'm not looking for anything today. Nope. Look yourself." [chuckles] He throws me off ... I can't take it. I'm going to blow it.

Although Rhonda's frustration is evident and understandable, one can imagine how a man who has been sharing a six-foot by eight-foot cell with another adult for an extended period of time and whose possessions were highly restricted during his incarceration would have difficulty managing his more plentiful belongings in a space with multiple rooms. Yet to explain this to his wife re-opens memories of the period of his imprisonment and focuses both of them on the humiliating experience of being stripped of possessions and privacy (Goffman, 1961), as well as on his current state of disorientation and loss of control.

In the struggle for power after prison, many women assume responsibility for their partner's behaviour and take on roles involving discipline, surveillance, and heavy-handed direction. Stephanie, a mother of three and an Oakland resident, came to visit her partner at least weekly during his time in prison, carrying their infant son on the bus as she made her way to and from the prison. After months of visiting, Stephanie told us that she had received word that her application for Section 8 housing[4] had finally come through, but rather than receiving a placement in Oakland, she would need to move to a city over a hundred miles away where she knew no one. Following much deliberation, Stephanie decided that this represented an opportunity to improve her and her children's lives, especially in light of a smattering of physical altercations with neighbours in which she and her pre-teen daughter had recently been involved. Shortly before her partner's release, Stephanie packed up her household and moved. When her partner left prison he was paroled to Oakland, but Stephanie made an effort to reconnect with him and raised the possibility of him trying to finish his parole early so that he could come join her and the children. In her efforts to help him do so, she faced resistance not only from her partner but also from his friends, who explicitly linked her actions to the correctional environment:

> *Stephanie*: I was trying my best to keep him *out* of trouble but his friends be like, 'Dang! You act like you in prison still!' and all this other stuff. So he felt probably like I was keeping him in the house or—
>
> *MC*: So his friends were saying it was like *you* had him in prison?
>
> *Stephanie*: Yeah. Like, 'Why you ain't outside with us?' See that's his whole problem. When we first got together his friends was telling him, 'Why you with her? Why you gotta go in the house by 9 or 10? Why you just can't come out here and stay with us? We need you out here. F—her.' That's basically what they said. So I guess that's what he choose now is his friends.

For all men's resentfulness of their partners' surveillance, women frequently express exasperation and dissatisfaction at being placed in this role. Pamela felt unnerved by having to watch over her partner: 'I'm seein' what I seen before he went to jail. And I'm not feelin' it.' Likewise, Rhonda described joking with the correctional officers when she visited her husband: 'The guards, they just crack up, they just love me, they do! When I go up to see my husband I said, "You know what? I'm going to kick his ass right now." So when I come in another Friday they'll say, "Is he being good?"' Once the couple was reunited, Rhonda expressed displeasure—apparently shared by her husband—with the continuation of this dynamic: 'I had to play mommy and all of that. I don't like that ... He said "You act like I'm a little kid or something." But he acts like it ... Sometimes I want to just walk out there and just go, go.' Alfonso describes a similar scenario with his wife, candidly admitting the lure of the streets and his rebellion against a life characterized by the absence of anything beyond work and family:

> [My wife] basically wants me to be a 'goody boy'. A 'A' student. Not doing nothing, not getting into no trouble. Going to work, come home and be a dad. ... We have problems. Because maybe some days I want to go out. She tells me, 'You ain't going to no clubs no more.' Or 'You're not going to this party no more because I know what's going to happen. You're going to call me from the city jail. You're going to come up with some excuse that this happened and you're in jail for six months again. It's not going to happen.' So like there be times where I get up and I take a shower and she's like, 'Where you going?' I'll be like, 'Nowhere.' So I try to sneak out the back door and she tells my

---

[4] Section 8 is a common name for a programme by the US Department of Housing and Urban Development that assists low-income people in obtaining housing. People who qualify for Section 8 pay a portion of their income toward rent, and the programme subsidizes the balance.

son, 'Go follow your daddy.' She said, 'You want to go anywhere you're taking the kids with you.' So she know my kids are gonna keep me out of trouble.

The perceived infantalization of formerly incarcerated men expressed both by the men themselves and their partners adds a new dimension to significant life events, such as childbearing, typically viewed as catalyzing a reevaluation and negotiation of gender roles within a relationship (see Sanchez and Thompson, 1997). The diminished confidence in men's abilities to be responsible for their comportment and women's sense of obligation to keep them in line undermines men's abilities to establish equity in their relationships, instead setting up dynamics of watchguard and watched. Barriers to labour-market participation further aggravate these stressors, sowing seeds of dissention around issues of economic providership and household work.

'A man's supposed to have his own': Lack of work and financial pressures

Men often speak of their time behind bars as an opportunity to reflect on their lives and to identify a new course for the future. Calvin, a 23 year old who had recently finished a two-and-a-half-year sentence, gives an account of his confinement as a time of personal transformation. Responding to a question about the impact of his most recent imprisonment on his general outlook, he asserts:

> *Calvin*: I think it was a positive experience all the way around ... Because I don't think I'd be the person I am right now if it wasn't for that. One, because it gave me time to focus ... I was thinking about how could I be a better person.... I really never had an idea of what a man was ... So I just went back, all the way just like re-evaluating myself, like, 'Man! What type of man is that? What's the definition of a man?' ...
>
> *Interviewer*: So tell me what a man is to you?
>
> *Calvin*: To me a man is honest, hardworking, a role model. I think a man is accountable, to hold himself accountable for his actions. Like I don't know, a good role model. That's what a man is to me.... Someone with integrity.

Calvin's conceptualization of what it means to 'be a man' is similar to that described by Robert, a 53 year old who completed seven years behind bars prior to his interview, in which he talked about the letters he wrote from the penitentiary to his wife:

> I wrote a lot of powerful, things that I thought were powerful, in telling her, 'I'm a changed person.... Because today I'm the man that I felt I shoulda been a long time ago in your life. Somebody who wants to take care of you and do the things that man does. I understand what a man is today.' So I would write things like that to her in the letter and she would tell me her expectations of a man. And that was right up my alley you know. Because that's what she was saying, that's how I seen me.... You're under somebody else's rule when you're in prison. You gotta do this and do this the way they want you. Get your own place! *A man's* supposed to have his own. So I told myself, 'I have to find a job. I have to do something.'

These desires to 'be a man' formulated in the peculiar environment of the penitentiary frequently pose problems when former prisoners attempt to operationalize them in the outside world. One hears in Calvin's and Robert's descriptions of manhood distinct pressures to be gainfully employed, provide for themselves and their families, and command respect from those around them. Their expectations of themselves echo the familiar American tropes of individualism and self-advancement: men stand on their own two feet, they rely on no one (Lipset, 1996). All of this can seem possible while men are still inside of the prison, especially as correctional officers and instructors in rehabilitative programming typically reinforce these messages. Yet people with criminal records face considerable difficulty legally obtaining housing and employment (Rubinstein and Mukamal, 2002; Pager, 2003) and those with health, mental-health, or substance-use treatment needs often face challenges accessing services (Richie et al., 2001; Freudenberg et al., 2006). Not surprisingly, men express high levels of stress and frustration around obtaining employment once they leave the prison, hampered by a crushing economy, the disappearance of stable blue-collar jobs, and a conviction history which effectively blocks them from being offered the scarce positions that are available. Indeed, men are often ill-prepared not only for obtaining jobs, but for the psychological pressures of chronic unemployment. Alfonso experienced a shock when he left the penitentiary and looked for work; he eventually found a position, but now lives in fear of losing it should his employer investigate his background:

> But when I came out [of prison] I see that damn, things are fucking hard! ... I already had a resume. I fixed my resume. They've got job fairs going on up there. I got back into wearing suits and ties and stuff like that. ... So I ended up getting a job at the Grocery Outlet and everything's been going cool there.... The only thing that messes me up—and [my wife] looked at this too—is my damn resume. Because I got so many years and the gaps in the dates [when I was incarcerated] and stuff they want to know what's going on. This woman where I'm working at now she was like, she kinda fished something was up but she kinda let it slide. She sees now I'm a good worker and she just don't want to let me go you know. But I know once a supervisor or some job comes up she's going to have to do a background check and that's when I have to go.

Rasheed, a 31 year old who spent his six-year sentence intensively trying to move beyond his troubled childhood and early successes selling drugs, spoke with pride of his ability to find a job within days of his release:

> [My wife] was so happy to actually have me home. She waited so long, she did everything by herself. I mean bills and everything. And I think that's what she respected about me. I came home, I got my driver's license in four days from coming home, and I was working the *next day*, no, *two days* later I was working. I came home Saturday, I was working Monday.

However, since his conviction history kept him from securing steady employment, this work consisted of informal manual labour jobs that Rasheed obtained through friends and connections he had made in prison. His desire to remain a free man restricted his work options to those in the legal economy entailing degrading work conditions and a paltry paycheck (Purser, 2006), which required a significant adjustment on his part. As he explained:

> I guess you could say from me being in the life, in the street life, selling drugs and whatnot back in the days it was like I spoiled myself. From having so much money come my way at a young age I was able to have whatever I wanted young. So by the time I let that lifestyle go and started working and trying to get it honestly it was like *man*! It was a *real* challenge. I wasn't used to managing short money.

Family members who try to help former prisoners may have trouble understanding the lingering impact of incarceration on their loved one (Haney, 2003) or the constraints placed upon them by the conditions of their parole, leaving them feeling overwhelmed, resentful, and confused (Shapiro and Schwartz, 2001; Hagan and Coleman, 2001; Halsey and Deegan, 2015). When Cornelia's husband returned to the household, she was holding down two jobs and attending night school, which left her little patience for her husband's inability to find work. Frustrated and financially strapped, she was only partially willing to attribute this to his felony record:

> It's hard for him to find a job because he has a [criminal] background. But he's letting the background be the reason, because I know there's other people who are on parole who *have* found jobs. It's just that he's not patient enough to do the footwork *to* find a job. He gets too impatient and he give up, and that's the main problem that we really have. Because I'm constantly telling him that 'It gets better as long as you do what you have to do' but it seems like that's not getting through his thick skull.

The centrality of the importance of work in her conception of manhood comes through clearly when Cornelia describes her inability to ask her family for financial help:

> Don't let me call my family. 'I thought you had a man! Why you asking me for money? You have a *man*. So you're messing with a sorry man who don't have no job? You wasn't raised like this!' That's the stuff I hear so I try not to ask them. Even though I know they would help me I know they would help me if they know that I'm doing good for myself, but if they know that I'm taking care of a man I'm not gonna get that help.

Pamela echoes Cornelia's desire to have a partner who is 'a man' in the sense of being an economic breadwinner. When talking of an ultimatum Pamela issued regarding throwing her partner out of the house if he did not secure employment within one month of his exit from prison, she emphasized: 'I need a man. I'm a single mother. I need a *man*! ... I need you to *show* me! And that's why in thirty days his ass is out! Cause you ain't showin' me nothin'!' Both Cornelia and Pamela make clear a sentiment repeated by numerous other women: the unreciprocated care-taking women shoulder during the incarceration period is due to the prison-related barriers to men financially contributing to the household, which temporarily absolved them of this duty. But as soon as men leave the correctional environment, women expect them to assume the 'manly' role of economic provider irrespective of the structural impediments to gainful employment.

Ironically, the pressure to assert one's manhood and provide for one's family can steer men back into illegal activities (in contrast to the conception of adulthood as desistence from crime, see Massoglia and Uggen, 2010). In fact, Cornelia voiced her suspicion that this had been her husband's motivation for returning to lawbreaking after a previous sentence, condemning this as a 'wrong' choice while also denigrating his current law-abiding contributions to their domestic unit:

> I don't know if he have a problem with a woman that gets more money than him, or a woman making money when he's not making money. I think he has that problem. I'm not going to say he do, but, some men really fear that, a woman making more money than them or a woman making money and they're not making enough. So I think he was trying to compete, but he went the wrong route, he went the wrong way of doing it.... [Now] he takes care of the house as far as the cooking and the cleaning, the washing. However, you know how the man brings home the bread and butter and the woman takes care of the household? *I'm* the man and *he's* the woman!

The tensions among women who want their partners to 'be men' through acts of legal economic provision, men's desires to recapture a manhood that previously was validated primarily through easy money and participation in 'the life,' the economic and legal forces that deny parolees jobs, and deep-set gender beliefs that belittle men's contributions to housework and childcare combine to tangle couples in new configurations of what Hartmann (1981) identifies as production and redistribution issues in locus of struggle that is the modern family. Faced with insurmountable odds, women yearn for the 'men' that their partners desperately want to be, and the lack of legal avenues for carrying out such acts of manhood leave both parties disillusioned, frustrated, and unhappy with each other.

Conclusion

Following couples through the cycle of imprisonment and release, and particularly observing the escalation of tensions, conflict, and hardship that arise once men leave the bounds of the penitentiary and are reunited with women who have been surviving without them, one notes the counterintuitive ways in which incarceration shifts and shapes gender roles, and thereby has a profound impact on the joint construction of masculinity undertaken within 'prisonized' relationships (Clemmer, 1958 [1940]; Comfort, 2008). For men who are denied legal means by which to perform their coveted form of manhood and then feel criticized by their partners for this failing or emasculated by women's efforts to steer them to the straight-and-narrow, the pull of 'the streets' is powerful and magnetic, even as the penitentiary looms before them. From the women's perspectives, the disappointment and unfairness of holding down the household, providing for their own and their children's needs, and supporting men through imprisonment only to find themselves still 'being the man' once their partner returns home—only now with an extra mouth to feed—often proves a bitter pill to swallow.

Through this analysis, we can see how, in a classic example of 'structural violence' (Farmer, 2003), the criminal justice system erects barriers and thwarts life chances not just for the men it confines but also for the women trying to build partnerships with them, amplifying the reach of its corrosive impact as it seeps into the fibre of their sense of self, intimate relationships, and family. Broadening our understanding of these profound transformations has implications for the sociology of punishment and related questions of social justice and social inequality. First, recognizing that incarceration alters core aspects of intimate relationships in a deep and enduring way emphasizes the importance of positioning correctional facilities as *social* institutions rather than mere sites of retribution or rehabilitation. Second, that these social institutions exert influence at the nexus of family, employment, housing, and citizenship highlights their *political* dimension beyond the determination of punishment for a specific act, but rather in the broad brush strokes of greater social and economic disadvantage for large swathes of households in areas already suffering from inequity. To reside in these areas, then, or to belong to these households, increases the likelihood that a state-funded sociopolitical institution will destabilize one's relationships, generate or exacerbate strife and conflict in one's family, and mire one in roles and interactions that feel unfulfilling and demoralizing. If the project of social justice can be conceived of as ensuring access by everyone to 'equal economic, political, and social rights and opportunities' (Van Soest, 1995), then addressing and mitigating the disruption of family life for prisoners, formerly incarcerated people, and their loved ones is integral to its advancement.

References

Arditti, J. A. (ed.) 2012. *Parental Incarceration and the Family: Psychological and Social Effects of Imprisonment on Children, Parents, and Caregivers*. New York, NYU Press.
Bandele, A. (ed.) 1999. *The Prisoner's Wife: A Memoir*. New York, Scribner.

Bianchi, S. M. and Milkie, M. A. 2010. 'Work and Family Research in the First Decade of the 21st Century'. *Journal of Marriage and Family*, 72(3), 705–25.

Binswanger, I., Nowels, C., Corsi, K., Long, J., Booth, R., Kutner, J., and Steiner, J. 2011. '"From the Prison Door Right to the Sidewalk, Everything Went Downhill": A Qualitative Study of the Health Experiences of Recently Released Inmates'. *International Journal of Law and Psychiatry*, 34(4), 249–55.

Bureau of Justice Statistics. 2017. *Key Statistics: Incarceration Rate 1980–2015*. Available at: https://www.bjs.gov/index.cfm?ty=kfdetail&iid=493.

Carson, E. A. and Anderson, E. (eds.) 2016. 'Prisoners in 2015'. US Department of Justice, Office of Justice Programs, Bureau of Justice Statistics. Available at: https://www.bjs.gov/content/pub/pdf/p15.pdf.

Christian, J. and Kennedy, L. W. 2011. 'Secondary Narratives in the Aftermath of Crime: Defining Family Members' Relationships with Prisoners'. *Punishment & Society*, 13(4), 379–402.

Christian, J., Mellow, J., and Thomas, S. 2006. 'Social and Economic Implications of Family Connections to Prisoners'. *Journal of Criminal Justice*, 34(4), 443–52.

Clemmer, D. 1958 [1940]. *The Prison Community*. (2nd ed.). New York: Holt, Rinehart, and Winston.

Codd, H. (ed.) 2008. *In the Shadow of Prison: Families, Imprisonment, and Criminal Justice*. Cullompton: Willan Publishing.

Comfort, M. 2002. '"Papa's House": The Prison as Domestic and Social Satellite'. *Ethnography*, 3(4), 467–99.

Comfort, M. 2007. 'Punishment Beyond the Legal Offender'. *Annual Review of Law and Social Science*, 3, 271–96.

Comfort, M. (ed.) 2008. *Doing Time Together: Love and Family in the Shadow of the Prison*. Chicago, IL: University of Chicago Press.

Comfort, M., Grinstead, O., Faigeles, B., and Zack, B. 2000. 'Reducing HIV Risk among Women Visiting Their Incarcerated Male Partners'. *Criminal Justice and Behavior*, 27(1), 57–71.

Comfort, M., Grinstead, O., Mccartney, K., Bourgois, P., and Knight, K. 2005. '"You Can't Do Nothing in this Damn Place!": Sex and Intimacy among Couples with an Incarcerated Male Partner'. *Journal of Sex Research*, 42(1), 3–12.

Comfort, M., Krieger, K. E., Landwehr, J., Mckay, T., Lindquist, C. H., Feinberg, R., Kennedy, E. K., and Bir, A. 2018. 'Partnerships after Prison: Couple Relationships During Reentry'. *Journal of Offender Rehabilitation*, 57(1), 188–205.

Comfort, M., Reznick, O., Dilworth, S. E., Binson, D., Darbes, L. A., and Neilands, T. B. 2014. 'Sexual HIV Risk among Male Parolees and their Female Partners: The Relate Project'. *Journal of Health Disparities Research and Practice*, 7(special issue 6), 42–69.

Condry, R. (ed.) 2007. *Families Shamed: The Consequences of Crime for Relatives of Serious Offenders*. Cullompton: Willan.

deVuono-powell, S., Schweidler, C., Walters, A., and Zohrabi, A. (eds.) 2015. 'Who Pays? The True Cost of Incarceration on Families'. Ella Baker Center, Forward Together, Research Action Design. Oakland, CA. Available at: http://ellabakercenter.org/who-pays-the-true-cost-of-incarceration-on-families accessed 20 June 2017.

Evans, T. and Wallace, P. 2008. 'A Prison within a Prison? The Masculinity Narratives of Male Prisoners'. *Men and Masculinities*, 10(4), 484–507.

Farmer, P. 2003. 'On Suffering and Structural Violence: A View from Below', in Scheper-Hughes, N. and Bourgois, P. (eds.) *Violence in War and Peace: An Anthology*. 281–9. Malden, MA: Blackwell Publishing.

Freudenberg, N., Daniels, J., Crum, M., Perkins, T., and Richie, B. E. 2006. 'Coming Home from Jail: The Social and Health Consequences of Community Reentry for Women, Male

Adolescents, and Their Families and Communities'. *American Journal of Public Health*, 95(10), 1725–36.

Goffman, E. (ed.) 1961. *Asylums: Essays on the Social Situation of Mental Patients and Other Inmates*. Harmondsworth, Penguin Books.

Granja, R. 2016. 'Beyond Prison Walls: The Experiences of Prisoners' Relatives and Meanings Associated with Imprisonment'. *Probation Journal*, 63(3), 273–92.

Grinstead, O., Comfort, M., McCartney, K., Koester, K., and Neilands, T. 2008. 'Bringing it Home: Design and Implementation of an HIV/STD Intervention for Women Visiting Incarcerated Men'. *AIDS Education and Prevention*, 20(4), 285–300.

Hagan, J. and Coleman, J. P. 2001. 'Returning Captives of the American War on Drugs: Issues of Community and Family Reentry'. *Crime & Delinquency*, 47(3), 352–67.

Halsey, M. and Deegan, S. 2015. '"Picking up the pieces": Female significant others in the lives of young (ex) incarcerated males'. *Criminology & Criminal Justice*, 15(2), 131–51.

Haney, C. 2003. 'The Psychological Impact of Incarceration: Implications for Postprison Adjustment', in Travis, J. and Waul, M. (eds.) *Prisoners Once Removed: The Impact of Incarceration and Reentry on Children, Families, and Communities*. 33–66. Washington, DC: Urban Institute.

Hartmann, H. I. 1981. 'The Family as the Locus of Gender, Class, and Political Struggle: The Example of Housework'. *Signs*, 6(3), 366–94.

Hutton, M. 2016. 'Visiting Time: A Tale of Two Prisons'. *Probation Journal*, 63(3), 347–61.

Institute for Criminal Policy Research 2017. *World Prison Brief*. Available at: http://www.prisonstudies.org/info/worldbrief/.

Jardine, C. 2015. *Constructing Family in the Context of Imprisonment: A Study of Prisoners and their Families in Scotland*. PhD thesis, University of Edinburgh.

Kaeble, D. and Glaze, L. E. (eds.) 2016. 'Correctional Populations in the United States, 2015'. US Department of Justice, Office of Justice Programs, Bureau of Justice Statistics. Available at: https://www.bjs.gov/content/pub/pdf.

Kupers, T. A. 2010. 'Role of Misogyny and Homophobia in Prison Sexual Abuse'. *UCLA Women's Law Journal*, 18(1), 107–30.

Lipset, S. M. (ed.) 1996. *American Exceptionalism: A Double-Edged Sword*. New York: W.W. Norton.

Massoglia, M. and Uggen, C. 2010. 'Settling Down and Aging Out: Toward an Interactionist Theory of Desistance and the Transition to Adulthood'. *American Journal of Sociology*, 116(2), 543–82.

Mcdermott, K. and King, R. D. 1992. 'Prison Rule 102 "Stand by Your Man": The Impact of Penal Policy on the Families of Prisoners', in Shaw, R. (ed.) *Prisoners' Children: What Are the Issues?* 50–73. London: Routledge.

Miller, R. J. 2014. 'Devolving the Carceral State: Race, Prisoner Reentry, and the Micro-politics of Urban Poverty Management'. *Punishment & Society*, 16(3), 305–35.

Minton, T. D. and Zeng, Z. (eds.) 2016. 'Jail Inmates in 2015'. US Department of Justice, Office of Justice Programs, Bureau of Justice Statistics. Available at: https://www.bjs.gov/content/pub/pdf.

Pager, D. 2003. 'The Mark of a Criminal Record'. *American Journal of Sociology*, 108(5), 937–75.

Pager, D. (ed.) 2007. *Marked: Race, Crime, and Finding Work in an Era of Mass Incarceration*. Chicago: University of Chicago Press.

Purser, G. 2006. '"Nothing but Hard-Ass Labor!": Risk and Injury among Day Laborers in the U.S.'. *Actes de la recherche en sciences sociales*, 165, 52–70.

Richie, B. E., Freudenberg, N., and Page, J. 2001. 'Reintegrating Women Leaving Jail Into Urban Communities: A Description of a Model Program'. *Journal of Urban Health*, 78(2), 290–303.

Rideau, W. and Wikberg, R. (eds.) 1992. *Life Sentences: Rage and Survival behind Bars*. New York: Times Books.

Rubinstein, G. and Mukamal, D. 2002. 'Welfare and Housing: Denial of Benefits to Drug Offenders', in Mauer, M. and Chesney-Lind, M. (eds.) *Invisible Punishment: The Collateral Consequences of Mass Imprisonment*. 37–49. New York: The New Press.

Sanchez, L. and Thompson, E. 1997. 'Becoming Mothers and Fathers: Parenthood, Gender, and the Division of Labor'. *Gender & Society*, 11(6), 747–72.

Schrock, D. and Schwalbe, M. 2009. 'Men, Masculinity, and Manhood Acts'. *Annual Review of Sociology*, 35, 277–95.

Schwalbe, M. 2005. 'Identity Stakes, Manhood Acts, and the Dynamics of Accountability', in Denzin, N. (ed.) *Studies in Symbolic Interaction*. 65–81. New York: Elsevier.

Shapiro, C. and Schwartz, M. 2001. 'Coming Home: Building on Family Connections'. *Corrections Management Quarterly*, 5(3), 52–61.

Smith, P. S. (ed.) 2014. *When the Innocent are Punished: The Children of Imprisoned Parents*. Basingstoke: Palgrave Macmillan.

SpearIt 2011. 'Gender Violence in Prison & Hyper-Masculinities in the Hood: Cycles of Destructive Masculinity'. *Washington University Journal of Law & Policy*, 37, 89.

Trammell, R. 2011. 'Symbolic Violence and Prison Wives: Gender Roles and Protective Pairing in Men's Prisons'. *The Prison Journal*, 91(3), 305–24.

Van Soest, D. 1995. 'Peace and Social Justice', in Edwards, R. L. (ed.) *Encyclopedia of Social Work*. 95–100. Washington, DC: NASW Press.

Wakefield, S. and Wildeman, C. 2013. *Children of the Prison Boom: Mass Incarceration and the Future of American Inequality*. New York: Oxford University Press.

Wildeman, C., Lee, H., and Comfort, M. 2013. 'A New Vulnerable Population? The Health of the Female Romantic Partners of Recently Released Male Prisoners'. *Women's Health Issues*, 26(3), 335–40.

6

Missing and Missing Out

Social Exclusion in Children with an Incarcerated Parent

Susan M. Dennison and Kirsten L. Besemer[*]

Introduction

Prisoners' children are often described as socially excluded, not only at the time of the imprisonment, but also many years later (Foster and Hagan, 2015a; Besemer and Dennison, forthcoming; Besemer and Dennison, 2017). However, characterizations of social exclusion vary across studies. Broadly speaking, social exclusion is a lack of engagement in the activities and living standards that are customary in conventional society (e.g. Pantazis et al., 2006; Saunders et al., 2008; Scutella et al., 2009). Some authors have operationalized this through proxy measures of social exclusion, reflecting the underlying societal processes thought to result in people's disengagement or alienation from society (e.g. Micklewright, 2002; Scutella et al., 2009; Levitas et al., 2010; Besemer and Dennison, forthcoming). Other authors have used severe forms of societal disengagement (such as homelessness and lack of healthcare coverage in Foster and Hagan, 2015a). More direct definitions of social exclusion consider children and adults' non-participation in the types of ordinary living patterns and activities that are social requirements in their national context and time (e.g. Mack and Lansley, 1985; Saunders et al., 2008; Saunders and Naidoo, 2009; Saunders, 2011; Besemer and Dennison, forthcoming). For Australian children, there is wide societal agreement that such ordinary living patterns should include, for example, children's participation in leisure activities, regular dental checks, up-to-date school books, and school clothing (Saunders, 2011).

In this chapter, we explore the concept of social exclusion and the ways that it can be used to frame discussions about the consequences of parental imprisonment for children. We review emerging findings that show that parental imprisonment may have fundamental impacts on intergenerational social exclusion. Next, we draw on narratives of children with imprisoned fathers and their caregivers to illustrate how paternal imprisonment interrupts customary practices, living patterns, and roles that a father might be expected to fulfil in contemporary family life. We thus extend the discussion beyond the typical focus on economic and health indicators of social exclusion to consider children's exclusion from daily social activities, proposing that these are essential for children's identity formation and sense of inclusion and belonging.

---

[*] This research was supported by an Australian Research Council Linkage grant (LP0776296; S. Dennison), an Australian Research Council Future Fellowship (FT0991557) for S. Dennison, as well as our partnership organizations, Queensland Corrective Services, Department of Communities, Child Safety and Disability Services, and Catholic Prison Ministry. Views expressed in this paper are those of the authors and do not necessarily represent those of the Australian Research Council or partner organizations. Where quoted or used, they should be clearly attributed to the authors.

Prisons, Punishment, and the Family: Towards a New Sociology of Punishment? First Edition. Rachel Condry and Peter Scharff Smith. © The several contributors 2018. Published 2018 by Oxford University Press.

We argue that such direct experiences of social exclusion are fundamentally harmful to children's long-term wellbeing and may mediate the lifelong disadvantage known to affect prisoners' children.

The nature of children's social exclusion

Although the term *social exclusion* itself is recent, ideas underpinning it have a much longer history. Concepts such as a 'decent life' and 'valued activities' trace back as far as Aristotle (Sen, 2000). In the eighteenth century, Adam Smith recognized that every society has items that are 'indecent for creditable people, even of the lowest order, to be without' (Smith, 1999 [1776]). In one of his examples, Smith observes that in some (but not all) cultural contexts, leather shoes are not important merely for physical comfort, but because such shoes are required to appear in public without shame. In the twentieth century, Townsend's seminal definition of poverty described poor people as unable to participate in living conditions and activities that are 'widely encouraged and approved', resulting in their exclusion from 'ordinary living patterns, customs and activities' (Townsend, 1979). This disengagement from key aspects of what is, at a particular time and place, understood as 'ordinary living' still forms the basis of most current concepts of social exclusion (Besemer and Dennison, 2017).

Despite a long tradition of time and place-specific understandings of what is now termed social exclusion, these concepts have only recently been applied to children. Traditionally, children's living standards have primarily been understood as a reflection of their families' material resources. Children's exclusion has thus often been hidden within descriptions of their overall household characteristics, typically only incorporating adults' understandings about the extent to which children's physical and social requirements are met (Main and Besemer, 2014). Given that resources are not distributed equally within families (Bennett, 2013; Main and Bradshaw, 2015), and because increasing numbers of children routinely move between households (Kelly and Emery, 2003), such understandings of social exclusion are inadequate. Parents may have a very incomplete understanding of the different activities and resources children have access to across their different household settings (Main and Besemer, 2014). In addition, children and young people are known to shield their parents from the full extent of their social exclusion by hiding their needs or by diminishing the importance of activities or possessions they are excluded from (Ridge, 2002). Most importantly, purely adult-based understandings of child poverty and social exclusion are increasingly superseded by an acknowledgement that children are not only capable of accurately describing their own living circumstances, but also whether their circumstances meet the social requirements of their own time period and context (Ben-Arieh, 2005). There has been a call for research that draws on information from both adults and children, to achieve more inclusive understandings of the living circumstances that constitute a customary contemporary childhood in different locations (Christensen and Prout, 2002; Ridge, 2002, 2006, 2011; Ben-Arieh, 2008).

Until now, purely child-derived concepts and understandings of children's social exclusion have been rare. Limited research suggests that like adults, children feel socially excluded when they are unable to participate in decisions that affect them; or when material deprivations such as shoes and clothing preclude them from taking part in social activities or cause them to stand out in social settings (Morrow, 2001; Ridge, 2011). A survey that sampled 300 children aged 8 to 15 across England identified items they thought necessary for a 'normal kind of life'. The authors found that children's 'necessary' items substantially overlapped with items adults identified as 'necessities for children' in a separate national survey (Main and Bradshaw, 2012, 2014, 2015). Overall, these findings suggest that while their practical needs may be different, children and adults' concepts of social exclusion are broadly similar, and relate to similar perceived social requirements to take part in social activities and to fit in with peers.

For the purposes of this chapter, our definition of social exclusion includes both adults and children who *lack access to the activities and living conditions, or participation in key activities that are customary in the society in which they live.* In order to identify the ways in which prisoners' children may be excluded from these customary activities and living conditions it is first necessary to consider what is regarded as customary in contemporary family life. The next section covers this literature.

Customary living conditions and activities in contemporary family life

The first study to quantitatively define what most adults regarded as minimum living standards surveyed a random sample of British adults, and asked which of a wide range of possessions and activities they felt no one should have to do without (Mack and Lansley, 1985). Similar surveys have since been carried out in a variety of countries (Halleröd, 1996; Saunders, 2003; Ahmed and Uddin, 2007; Saunders et al., 2008; Saunders, 2011; Barnes and Wright, 2012). As predicted in Smith (1999 [1776]), understandings of what constituted customary living conditions were found to be culturally and historically determined (Saunders, 2003; Gordon, 2006; Saunders and Wong, 2014). Despite these cross-national and cross-temporal differences, many commonly agreed necessities reflect similar values. For instance, the most recent Poverty and Exclusion in Modern Australia (PEMA) survey found that the vast majority of adults agreed that it was essential for children to have separate beds, to get presents from family and friends once a year, as well to have access to a local park or play area. For adults, essential items included material possessions such as furniture, but also more abstract items such as regular social contact with others (Saunders, 2011). These living patterns are likely to be customary across many contemporary developed countries.

As in the original British survey (Mack and Lansley, 1985), the majority of these societally agreed necessities are not 'essential' because their deprivation directly threatens subsistence, but because they are, at that time and place, widely considered to be necessary to feel socially included. International research has confirmed that deprivations of such ordinary living conditions are associated with detrimental psychological impacts in both adults (Payne, 2006) and children (Main, 2014). These findings are corroborated by qualitative research that shows that for children, being unable to 'fit in' and 'join in' with peers for financial reasons can be a cause of shame and sadness, and may cause children to feel deep fears of social marginalization (Ridge, 2006, 2011).

Social exclusion in prisoners' children: current research

Although in the international literature social exclusion has primarily been discussed as a manifestation or consequence of poverty, disengagement from ordinary living patterns can result from a variety of causes (Levitas, 2006). For example, incarceration excludes segments of society from family life. By separating family members from one another, imprisonment precludes not only the incarcerated, but also non-incarcerated family members, from living together as a family (Arditti, 2012). Even in situations where children were already living separately from the incarcerated parent, the incarceration may nevertheless disrupt the time and activities that children would usually enjoy with their parent, or may reduce their access to financial resources. In this section we examine and discuss research on the social exclusion of prisoners' children. Findings reveal that financial impacts of imprisonment, parental absence, as well as related practical consequences may all cause barriers to children's participation in social activities, resulting in different forms of social exclusion in their childhood as well as in their adult lives.

Although there is now a growing body of quantitative work on the social exclusion of prisoners' children, definitions of social exclusion have varied widely within this literature. For example, in relation to social exclusion in prisoners' children, Murray (2007) proposes a variety of constructs and indicators of social exclusion including: non-participation in key activities, loss of economic resources, administrative exclusion, lack of accessible information, stigma, lack of political engagement, and pre-existing disadvantage. Foster and Hagan (2007) measured prisoners' children's social exclusion during young people's transition to adulthood, by looking at homelessness, lack of healthcare coverage, and an absence of political participation. Paternal imprisonment was directly associated with all three of these negative outcomes.

In their recent study of parental imprisonment and the social exclusion of offspring, Foster and Hagan (2015a) assessed social exclusion through indicators of socio-economic inequality (i.e. personal and household income, perceived socio-economic status, and feelings of powerlessness). Having previously had a mother or father incarcerated during childhood significantly contributed to a young person's social exclusion in early adulthood (i.e. late twenties and early thirties). Besemer and Dennison (forthcoming) measured social exclusion as a combination of household-level risks, including adults' mental health, education, and financial hardship, finding that families affected by parental imprisonment were far more socially excluded across these indicators than households in the general population. Moreover, they found that most households with children that experienced family imprisonment were still socially excluded five years later (Besemer and Dennison, forthcoming). These findings demonstrate that, like Foster and Hagan (2015a) found, childhood experiences of social exclusion can become entrenched, leading to long-term social disadvantage.

Even where authors have been able to investigate the specific deprivations that cause social exclusion in prisoners' families, measurement indicators usually focus on the social exclusion of the caregiver as a proxy measure of children's own experiences. For example, Besemer and Dennison (2017) compared the social exclusion of caregivers of children affected by paternal incarceration with a nationally representative Australian sample and a matched sub-sample. They found that caregivers of prisoners' children were much more socially excluded than adults in the general population on most indicators. Caregivers of children affected by paternal imprisonment were far more likely to say they did not have family holidays, an experience considered essential for adults and children by over half of the Australian population (Saunders, 2011). Caregivers were also more likely than adults in the general population to live without a telephone or a car (Besemer and Dennison, 2017).

Although few qualitative studies have used the concept of social exclusion to understand the experiences of prisoners' children, a number of qualitative studies have identified behaviours and effects of imprisonment that are suggestive of social exclusion. For instance, Bocknek et al. (2009) described children with imprisoned relatives as 'feeling isolated and different from those around them', lacking in social support and having problematic relationships with peers. Other qualitative studies of prisoners' children describe abuse from other children as well as bullying and social rejection (Beck and Jones, 2008; Nesmith and Ruhland, 2008; Shlafer and Poehlmann, 2010; Dawson et al., 2012). By enforcing the sense that children are not conforming to normal living patterns, and by invoking feelings of shame and social rejection, such experiences are severe forms of social exclusion in and of themselves. Moreover, both the fear and the experience of social rejection have been shown to result in children's and adults' disengagement from social activities (Braman, 2004; Condry, 2007; Nesmith and Ruhland, 2008).

Until now, few studies of social exclusion in prisoners' children have focused on the broader ways that children may be unable to participate in their social worlds. While existing work is important in emphasizing the contexts of inequality and disadvantage that result in a highly unequal distribution of imprisonment across society (see also Arditti, this volume), some of these concepts of social exclusion may be far removed from the way children themselves experience it. Although children's social exclusion is undeniably interwoven with that of their household, in that many of children's needs are provided by adults, children's own experiences may nevertheless be quite distinct. While children have many similar priorities as adults, they may still have different understandings about the extent to which their specific needs are met, or about what those needs are (Main and Bradshaw, 2012). Internationally, few studies have directly interviewed children about their own experiences of imprisonment, and used children's own words to describe the meaning of such experiences to their lives (see Knudsen, in this book).

Social exclusion in prisoners' children: extracts from *The Vulnerable Families Project*

In this section, we focus on some of the specific deprivations prisoners' children may experience by drawing from quotes obtained during interviews for the *Vulnerable Families Project*—a mixed-methods study of forty-three caregivers of ninety-four children with an imprisoned father in Queensland, Australia.[1] Semi-structured interviews were conducted with all caregivers and twelve children. Together, children's and caregivers' descriptions of the ways that they are 'missing out' on a variety of customary living conditions and activities paint a fuller picture of social exclusion. Names have been changed and identifying information omitted.

In the *Vulnerable Families Project* both adults and children provided accounts of the daily experience of paternal imprisonment and the effect that the father's removal had on children's ability to engage in leisure activities and unstructured play. Nine-year-old Evie described how she missed seeing her father every day: 'Because he would always play with us and we'd have something to do ... We would always play outside and he would play soccer with us and he would run around.' Ryan, also 9, said that the hardest thing about missing his father was that he missed out on the things they usually did together: 'Um, well not getting to like kick the footy with him and play active things and ride motorbikes and do stuff with him.' Emma, aged 11, said 'just miss with my sports like soccer and kick the ball around with him ...'

---

[1] Details of this study can be found in Besemer and Dennison (2017).

Children's regular playful contact with their parents is a widely held societal expectation. It is also important for healthy child development—physically, socially, emotionally, and cognitively (Ginsburg, 2007). Deprivation of these normal practices of family life can have severe emotional consequences for children and interrupt the development of enduring parent–child relationships (Bronfenbrenner and Evans, 2000; Ginsburg, 2007). In addition, the time that parents spend playing with their children provides opportunities for parents to learn about their child's world (Ginsburg, 2007). High levels of paternal involvement through shared interactions, their presence and availability for their child, as well as more task-oriented activities are beneficial for children's cognitive and socio-emotional development (Cabrera et al., 2007). Furthermore, the physical and at times unpredictable nature of play that is more often present in the way fathers interact with their children is developmentally beneficial, contributing to secure parent–child attachment, emotional regulation and coping resources, skilfulness in social interactions, and reduced aggressive behaviour (Parke, 2002; Wilson and Prior, 2011).

In a study of sixty-four imprisoned fathers in Queensland, Australia (Dennison and Smallbone 2015), 76 per cent of fathers reported that they used to be involved in the day-to-day care of at least one of their children, and 55 per cent of fathers reported that they used to regularly play with at least one of their children. However, paternal incarceration severely compromises opportunities for fathers to interact with their children in meaningful and developmentally promotive ways due to distance, financial costs, prison regulations, the unsatisfactory nature of most prison visits (Arditti et al., 2003; Comfort, 2003; Arditti et al., 2005), and the removal of the parent from the child's environment. Children therefore have few opportunities to interact with their fathers in fun, play-based ways. Evie didn't always want to visit her father because of the long drive, the many security procedures, and because the visiting room was 'dirty and yuck'.

> I like seeing my dad but I don't like the place where we have to go. […] We have to go in and sign in and then we have to go to another room and then another one and then another one to get into—to see him. […] Sometimes I don't go every week […] I don't like being there and it's ages to drive and sometimes I'm really tired.

Aside from missing out on normal contact, for some children their father's absence meant they missed out on outings and leisure opportunities more generally. In some cases, this was because of a lack of financial resources, or because their mother was unable to take children to their usual social activities. Daniel, aged 16, was worried he would no longer be able to play soccer after his stepfather's imprisonment.

> I don't know if I can play soccer this year now because she [Mum] can't—I won't have transport to my games and training and stuff like that. So that's pretty disappointing. Just all stuff like that. But if I don't play soccer then, oh well.

Comments such as Daniel's are important, because more than 90 per cent of Australians think it is essential for all children to have access to a hobby or leisure activity (Saunders, 2011). However, prisoners' families often face financial stress. Such hardship may be caused by a loss of the parent's legal and illegal income in combination with high levels of expenses related to prison contact, commissary accounts, and visitation (Hagan and Dinovitzer, 1999; Murray and Farrington, 2008; Schwartz-Soicher et al., 2011; Lee et al., 2014). The causal effect of material hardship on social exclusion is intuitive and well established. Many social activities have costs directly associated with them, such as transport costs, money for food and drinks, or costs of entrance. Consequently, major reductions in families' residual income curtail adults' and children's opportunities for social engagement (Besemer and Dennison, 2017).

By being deprived of a regular sports activity, children like Daniel may also miss out on important peer interactions and opportunities to build positive identities. Participating in conventional activities may help keep young people connected to prosocial individuals, protect them from delinquent peer influences, and may reduce their opportunities to engage in risky or delinquent behaviour (Hartmann and Depro, 2006; Nesmith and Ruhland, 2008; Luther, 2015). Deprivations from social activities may also cause conflicts between children in the family. Jodie describes the tension between her older son Jordan and his 16-year-old brother Dylan, who feels he can't enjoy the same things his brother used to do.

> I've got to keep saying 'No, I can't afford it'... and where Dylan's feeling 'Well Jordan was allowed when he was this age, where I don't get it.' And I'm thinking, 'We had two incomes, it's only me now.' I've got to keep saying 'No, no, you'll see what's at the end of my pay'. So it is that way, it's depressing and it's affecting him as well.

For some children, while they could still participate in the same types of activities as they did before their father's imprisonment, the father's absence nonetheless caused them to feel differently within those contexts. In many social situations, such as at sporting events but also at family celebrations, having parents present is a widely held social expectation. For many children, parental imprisonment implies the loss of a parent who may have been significantly involved in their lives, and who may have lived with them. The sudden and often traumatic removal of a parent from a child's life can be highly distressing, as may their ongoing absence (Saunders, 2017). Eleven-year-old Madison describes how she feels about the absence of her father at important events in her childhood.

> I don't know, it's just different without having a dad because most of it—like when I go to sporting events—when I go to sporting events I don't have a dad around to be there. He's missed all my birthdays, all Christmases, never actually seen me grow up properly. Like, he's seen me grow up but not really.

Erin found that her 7-year-old son struggled heavily with the absence of his father, especially at his rugby games. She felt that his distress was affecting his school performance, where he was struggling academically, showing disruptive behaviour, and had problems with other children.

> So I think he was having trouble with kids at school being mean to him but I think deep down it all stems from his dad being gone. We had a big chat and he ended up having a big breakdown and cry, and said that he just is upset because he doesn't have his dad here. [...] He doesn't have his dad to take him on his bike or do boys stuff with him [...] Yeah and he'd just had his first year of rugby, which dad wasn't here for the whole thing, which I think was very hard for him. [...] To go—yeah, to go to a sport where your dad usually takes you and everyone else has their dads there but he didn't.

Chelsea, a mother of four children, decided to postpone many of the Christmas celebrations until after their father returned, so that they could have their real family Christmas together.

> Because he missed out on Christmas as well so we've got still half of the Christmas presents sitting in the cupboard because we said that we'd do Christmas when he got out.

Across narratives, there is clear evidence of the emotional impact of having Christmases, birthdays, and other key family events without the father. Such absences are likely to be felt just as significantly, if not more so in some instances, during maternal incarceration, due to mothers more often being the primary caregiver prior to incarceration (Maruschak et al., 2010). In their study of social exclusion, Lee et al. (2016) found that children who reported that a parent had been incarcerated were more likely to experience material exclusion, incarceration, and multiple forms of exclusion. They also found that the effects were greater for maternal incarceration rather than paternal incarceration (Lee et al., 2016). The authors suggest that disruption to the socialization role that is usually provided more actively by mothers may explain children's higher risks for the more severe forms of social exclusion that were found in the research (Lee et al., 2016). For children, parental absence may cause them to be unable to participate in extracurricular activities, or to feel different from other children at public events where parents are often present. These accounts speak to the many ways that children may 'miss out' on developmentally important social experiences and interactions. For prisoners' children these experiences may be particularly acute and relate not only to the absence of social interactions but also to the inability to make memories with an incarcerated parent. Erin describes her frustration with not being able to take a family picture on her daughter's birthday, which is not possible at his prison.

> It was Evie's birthday the other day, and she said 'I'd love to be able to just get a photo with my dad for my birthday.' You'd think in this day and age—to how the visits are to ten years ago when—it's still the same.

Through the father's absence in family photographs and in their family memories, children miss out on common, everyday practices of family life. For example, Jodie described how, due to the restricted nature of the visits with her incarcerated husband, who has been convicted of a sexual offence, her younger son feels excluded from the family. Although his adult brother is allowed to visit, she has not been able to get permission for her underage son. As a consequence, he has not seen his father for over two years.

> I think he feels like, how can you say it, rejected, like, pushed aside. That he's got no say in the family, he's not a part of the family. Because when they have a family day like in the prison, well, he's still not allowed to go. He's got to stay home and we're up there. And all he gets is a photo of the three of us.

Notwithstanding special visiting restrictions associated with sexual offences, the general restrictions in parent–child contact imposed by parental imprisonment far exceed those that might affect children who are separated from their parents for other reasons, such as divorce. Though children with divorced parents may spend less time with a parent than if they were living together daily, the nature of their interactions when together is, usually, unrestricted. Ironically, for children of prisoners, the absence of children's fathers may be most poignant at visits. Here children are unable to engage in normal playful contact with their parent because of the restrictions imposed by the surroundings, and because of the limited duration of their contact (e.g. Dennison et al., 2017; see also Hutton, this volume, and Halsey, this volume, for a comprehensive discussion of prison visitation restrictions and their effects on family life). Luke, aged 12, found prison visits very stressful and struggled to deal with his father's absence.

> [I'm] worried before I see him. […] How he's going to look and how he's changed. […] How tall he's gotten …if he's gotten skinnier. […] Then when I leave it just all breaks down and makes me feel upset. […] Because he's not allowed to come back with us. We have to leave him there.

Luke's distress about having to leave his father in prison illustrates the uniquely upsetting circumstances surrounding parental imprisonment. Parental imprisonment is also likely to be distinct from other forms of parental absence, such as divorce, parental death, or military services, because of the shame and stigma that is often attached to it (Lowenstein, 1986; Arditti et al., 2003). For some children, this meant that they didn't talk about their father to friends or adults outside the family.

Emma had only told her best friend that her father was in prison, but felt afraid that other children might find out. This made her anxious about any conversation with other children in which she might have to talk about him. 'Oh like when kids at school they talk about their father and then they say 'what about your dad?' and I just go like ... "err"' Daniel lied to his friends or teachers about his father's imprisonment. '[I tell them] that he's away working. Because it makes me angry that he knows—that he's been letting us down. [...] I just make it out that he's doing—he's succeeding in life. But he's actually not.' Other research has found that shame and stigma attached to imprisonment can severely impact social interactions, and may even result in social isolation (May, 2000; Condry, 2007; Beck and Jones, 2008).

Consequences of social exclusion and 'missing out' for prisoners' children

Overall, the above statements taken directly from children affected by imprisonment, as well as the statements from their caregivers, show that paternal imprisonment may heavily disrupt children's ability to engage in normal living patterns and activities, causing them to feel socially excluded. Such social exclusion, most notably through the denial of access to resources provided by shared interactions with a parent, reduces the acquisition of capabilities necessary for healthy physical, socio-emotional and cognitive development (see, e.g. Bynner, 2001; Bynner and Parsons, 2002). From the current literature on paternal imprisonment as well as from the wider social exclusion literature, it is difficult to gauge the long-term significance of these exclusions from normal childhood experiences. Although there is a growing literature on the long-term consequence of multiple disadvantage and associated psychological stress in the lives of children growing up in poverty (e.g. Evans and Kim, 2013), social exclusion from causes other than poverty has not been well researched. Within the child poverty literature, however, the profound importance of children's ability to engage in normal, everyday childhood experiences and interactions is well-established, and is thought to have severe, long-term effects on children's wellbeing (Morrow, 2001; Ridge, 2002, 2006, 2011).

Further evidence of the potential for long-term risk to prisoners' children is the continuity that occurs in social exclusion (e.g. Besemer and Dennison, forthcoming), with early exclusion leading to subsequent exclusion through mutually reinforcing processes and the accumulation of risk (Bynner, 2001). Foster and Hagan (2015b) proposed that social exclusion can come from, and be reinforced through, the multiple domains of children's lives. They built on existing research on the effects of parental imprisonment on children and drew on ecological and life course perspectives to develop a comprehensive framework to examine system effects on child inequality and social exclusion. The authors proposed that state and cross-national regimes are either exclusionary (e.g. state termination of parental rights) or inclusionary (e.g. state welfare supports) in their functions and exacerbate or reduce the social exclusion of children.

School regimes, including school policies and delinquency levels, are impacted by macro-level factors and policies that then have direct effects on family and child social exclusion but also on proposed mediating influences. These mediating factors include education, emotional and behavioural problems, family resources and processes, and social psychological factors.

Contemporaneous risk factors associated with paternal imprisonment likely interact with pre-existing risk factors for social exclusion such as a prisoners' history of unemployment, lack of basic skills, mental health problems, substance abuse, marital problems, childhood experiences of abuse and neglect, and a household history of severe material hardship (Social Exclusion Unit, 2002; Murray and Farrington, 2008; Geller et al., 2009; Schwartz-Soicher et al., 2011). In Australia, children are more likely to have experienced insecure housing situations prior to paternal imprisonment, and are much more likely to be Indigenous, both of which are statistically associated with a higher risk of poor developmental outcomes, independent of incarceration (Dennison et al., 2013). A number of authors have suggested that by disproportionally impacting on the lives of adults and children who are already disadvantaged across multiple domains, incarceration may severely exacerbate existing social problems and widen social inequalities (Clear, 2007; Wakefield and Wildeman, 2013). Moreover, it has been argued that these harms to prisoners' relatives represent a breach of their basic rights as members of their own society (Condry, this volume).

There is a large body of literature that demonstrates that exposure to childhood adversity is not deterministic of poor developmental outcomes (Bynner, 2001; Schweinhart et al., 2005; Farrington et al., 2016). Childhood risks can be countered by protective factors that reduce children's vulnerability to adversity, such as strong parental attachments (Fergusson and Horwood, 2003). While families can be sources of risk, they can also provide a critical role in providing protection and engaging in positive shared interactions to promote healthy development (Bynner, 2001). However, families' ability to create the conditions necessary for positive development and social inclusion are influenced by external circumstances (e.g. macro-level policies, institutional policies) as well as individual and family characteristics.

Benson and colleagues (2006) argue that to facilitate positive youth development, the developmental attentiveness of contexts needs to be increased (see also France et al., 2010). Following the incarceration of a parent, prisons become a context that will shape children's development. In the current chapter and in previous research, we see that prison typically undermines the kind of family interactions and social supports that children need. As most prisons are not developmentally attentive environments, there are clear opportunities to address polices that unnecessarily inhibit the way children experience prison visits and other forms of contact with their imprisoned parent. The narratives of caregivers and children from the *Vulnerable Families Project* also demonstrated that at a broader level, prison destabilizes the concept of family. Both children and parents were left out of family interactions; their absence in family photos both symbolic and tangible evidence of missed opportunities for shared, developmental interactions. We know that positive, dynamic, and sustained interactions between parents and their children are essential for forming strong parent–child bonds and the long-term wellbeing of children. Failure to develop policies and practices that facilitate positive shared interactions and allow for parent–child bonds to be maintained, and even strengthened, risks increasing children's experience of social exclusion and an accumulation of childhood adversity.

Conclusion

Social exclusion of families of prisoners is frequently described as an outcome of parental incarceration with consequences for long-term disadvantage and inequality. In this chapter we moved beyond the typical focus on economic and service use indicators of social exclusion by thinking more broadly about how prisoners' children might *lack access to the activities and living conditions, or participation in key activities that are customary in the society in which they live*. That is, we considered how the incarceration of a parent might lead to children's exclusion from more nuanced social and interpersonal activities that are nevertheless important for positive youth development. Drawing on narratives of caregivers and children from the *Vulnerable Families Project*, we found that there are very social ways that children with imprisoned parents may miss out on the living conditions that are customary in the society in which they live. Missing out on play-based activities with fathers, feeling isolated and different from peers due to the absence of the incarcerated parent from sporting and social activities, and being unable to share customary traditions like birthdays and Christmas were examples of how young people experienced social exclusion. These experiences of 'missing out' took a significant emotional toll on children. Arguably, an inability to have shared positive interactions and the almost inevitable deterioration in parent–child bonds during the imprisonment period leave children more vulnerable to the effects of other adversities that are often present in their lives. By conceptualizing social exclusion of families of prisoners as, at least in part, a consequence of punishment regimes that deliberately isolate incarcerated parents from family life, we highlight the need to reconsider current prison policies with a view to becoming 'developmentally attentive' institutions.

References

Ahmed, A. and Uddin, M. 2007. 'Consensual Poverty in Britain, Sweden and Bangladesh: A Comparative Study'. *Bangladesh e-Journal of Sociology*, 4(2), 56–77.

Arditti, J. A. 2012. *Parental Incarceration and the Family: Psychological and Social Effects of Imprisonment on Children, Parents, and Caregivers*, New York, NY: New York University Press.

Arditti, J. A., Lambert-Shute, J., and Joest, K. 2003. 'Saturday Morning at the Jail: Implications of Incarceration for Families and Children'. *Family Relations*, 52(3), 195–204.

Arditti, J. A., Smock, S. A., and Parkman, T. S. 2005. ' "It's Been Hard to Be a Father": A Qualitative Exploration of Incarcerated Fatherhood'. *Fathering: A Journal of Theory, Research, and Practice about Men as Fathers*, 3(3), 267–87.

Barnes, H. and Wright, G. 2012. 'Defining Child Poverty in South Africa Using the Socially Perceived Necessities Approach', in Minujin, A. and Nandy, S. (eds.) *Global Child Poverty and Well-Being: Measurement, Concepts, Policy and Action*. 135–54. Bristol: The Policy Press.

Beck, E. and Jones, S. J. 2008. 'Children of the Condemned: Grieving the Loss of a Father to Death Row'. *OMEGA—Journal of Death and Dying*, 56(2), 191–215.

Ben-Arieh, A. 2005. 'Where Are the Children? Children's Role in Measuring and Monitoring Their Well-Being'. *Social Indicators Research*, 74(3), 573–96.

Ben-Arieh, A. 2008. 'The Child Indicators Movement: Past, Present, and Future'. *Child Indicators Research*, 1(1), 3–16.

Bennett, F. 2013. 'Researching within-Household Distribution: Overview, Developments, Debates, and Methodological Challenges'. *Journal of Marriage and Family*, 75(3), 582–97.

Benson, P. L., Scales, P. C., Hamilton, S. F., and Sesma, A. 2006. 'Positive Youth Development: Theory, Research, and Applications', in Lerner, R. M. (ed.) *Handbook of Child Psychology*. 894–41. Australia: John Wiley & Sons, Inc.

Besemer, K. L. and Dennison, S. M. forthcoming. 'Intergenerational Social Exclusion in Prisoners' Families', in Hutton, M. and Moran, D. (eds.) *Handbook on Prison and the Family*. Basingstoke: Palgrave.

Besemer, K. L. and Dennison, S. M. 2017. 'Social Exclusion in Families Affected by Paternal Imprisonment'. *Australian and New Zealand Journal of Criminology*.

Bocknek, E. L., Sanderson, J., and Britner, P. A. 2009. 'Ambiguous Loss and Posttraumatic Stress in School-Age Children of Prisoners'. *Journal of Child and Family Studies*, 18(3), 323–33.

Braman, D. 2004. *Doing Time on the Outside: Incarceration and Family Life in Urban America*. Ann Arbor, MI: University of Michigan Press.

Bronfenbrenner, U. and Evans, G. W. 2000. 'Developmental Science in the 21st Century: Emerging Questions, Theoretical Models, Research Designs and Empirical Findings'. *Social Development*, 9(1), 115–25.

Bynner, J. 2001. 'Childhood Risks and Protective Factors in Social Exclusion'. *Children and Society*, 15(5), 285–301.

Bynner, J. and Parsons, S. 2002. 'Social Exclusion and the Transition from School to Work: The Case of Young People Not in Education, Employment, or Training (Neet)'. *Journal of Vocational Behavior*, 60(2), 289–309.

Cabrera, N. J., Shannon, J. D., and Tamis-Lemonda, C. 2007. 'Fathers' Influence on Their Children's Cognitive and Emotional Development: From Toddlers to Pre-K'. *Applied Development Science*, 11(4), 208–13.

Christensen, P. and Prout, A. 2002. 'Working with Ethical Symmetry in Social Research with Children'. *Childhood*, 9(4), 477–97.

Clear, T. R. 2007. *Imprisoning Communities: How Mass Incarceration Makes Disadvantaged Neighborhoods Worse*. New York: Oxford University Press.

Comfort, M. L. 2003. 'In the Tube at San Quentin: The "Secondary Prisonization" of Women Visiting Inmates'. *Journal of Contemporary Ethnography*, 32 (1), 77–107.

Condry, R. 2007. *Families Shamed: The Consequences of Crime for Relatives of Serious Offenders*. Cullompton: Willan Publishing.

Dawson, A. Jackson, D., and Nyamathi, A. 2012. 'Children of Incarcerated Parents: Insights to Addressing a Growing Public Health Concern in Australia'. *Children and Youth Services Review*, 34(12), 2433–41.

Dennison, S. and Smallbone, H. 2015. '"You can't be much of anything from inside": The implications of imprisoned fathers' parental involvement and generative opportunities for children's wellbeing'. *Law in Context*, 32, 61–85.

Dennison, S., Smallbone, H., and Occhipinti, S. 2017. 'Understanding How Incarceration Challenges Father-Child Relationships Using a Bioecological Paradigm: Perspectives of Imprisoned Fathers'. *Journal of Developmental and Life-Course Criminology*, 3(1), 15–38.

Dennison, S., Stewart, A., and Freiberg, K. 2013. 'A Prevalence Study of Children with Imprisoned Fathers: Annual and Lifetime Estimates'. *Australian Journal of Social Issues*, 48(3), 339–62.

Evans, G. W. and Kim, P. 2013. 'Childhood Poverty, Chronic Stress, Self-Regulation, and Coping'. *Child Development Perspectives*, 7(1), 43–8.

Farrington, D. P., Ttofi, M. M., and Lösel, F. A. 2016. 'Developmental and Social Prevention'. *What Works in Crime Prevention and Rehabilitation, Criminology & Public Policy*, 16: 415–49. doi: 10.1111/1745-9133.12298.

Fergusson, D. M. and Horwood, L. J. 2003. 'Resilience to Childhood Adversity: Results of a 21-Year Study', in Luthar, S. (ed.) *Resilience and Vulnerability: Adaptation in the Context of Childhood Adversities*. 130–55. Cambridge: Cambridge University Press.

Foster, H. and Hagan, J. 2007. 'Incarceration and Intergenerational Social Exclusion'. *Social Problems*, 54(4), 399–433.

Foster, H. and Hagan, J. 2015a. 'Maternal and Paternal Imprisonment and Children's Social Exclusion in Young Adulthood'. *Journal of Criminal Law and Criminology*, 105(2), 387–430.

Foster, H. and Hagan, J. 2015b. 'Punishment Regimes and the Multilevel Effects of Parental Incarceration: Intergenerational, Intersectional, and Interinstitutional Models of Social Inequality and Systemic Exclusion'. *Annual Review of Sociology*, 41, 135–58.

France, A., Freiberg, K., and Homel, R. 2010. 'Beyond Risk Factors: Towards a Holistic Prevention Paradigm for Children and Young People'. *British Journal of Social Work*, 40(4) 1192–210.

Geller, A., Garfinkel, I., Cooper, C. E., and Mincy, R. B. 2009. 'Parental Incarceration and Child Well-Being: Implications for Urban Families'. *Social Science Quarterly*, 90(5) 1186–202.

Ginsburg, K. R. 2007. 'The Importance of Play in Promoting Healthy Child Development and Maintaining Strong Parent-Child Bonds'. *Pediatrics*, 119(1), 182–91.

Gordon, D. 2006. 'The Concept and Measurement of Poverty', in Pantazis, C., Gordon, D., and Levitas, R. (eds.) *Poverty and Social Exclusion in Britain*. 29–70. Bristol: University of Bristol.

Hagan, J. and Dinovitzer, R. 1999. 'Collateral Consequences of Imprisonment for Children, Communities, and Prisoners'. *Crime and Justice*, 26, 121–62.

Halleröd, B. 1996. 'Deprivation and Poverty: A Comparative Analysis of Sweden and Great Britain'. *Acta Sociologica*, 39(2), 141–68.

Hartmann, D. and Depro, B. 2006. 'Rethinking Sports-Based Community Crime Prevention'. *Journal of Sport and Social Issues*, 30(2), 180–96.

Kelly, J. B. and Emery, R. E. 2003. 'Children's Adjustment Following Divorce: Risk and Resilience Perspectives'. *Family Relations*, 52(4), 352–62.

Lee, H. P., Lauren C., and Comfort, M. 2014. 'Consequences of Family Member Incarceration: Impacts on Civic Participation and Perceptions of the Legitimacy and Fairness of Government'. *The Annals of the American Academy of Political and Social Science*, 651(1), 44–73.

Lee, R. D., Fang, X., and Luo, F. 2016. 'Parental Incarceration and Social Exclusion: Long-Term Implications for the Health and Well-Being of Vulnerable Children in the United States', in *Inequality after the 20th Century: Papers from the Sixth Ecineq Meeting*. 215–34. Bingley, United Kingdom: Emerald.

Levitas, R., Pantazis, C. E., Fahmy, Gordon, D., Lloyd, E., and Patsios, D., 2010. *The Multi-Dimensional Analysis of Social Exclusion*. Department of Sociology and School for Social Policy, Townsend Centre for the International Study of Poverty and Bristol Institute for Public Affairs, University of Bristol.

Levitas, R. 2006. 'The Concept and Measurement of Social Exclusion', in Pantazis, C., Gordon, D., and Levitas, R. (eds.) *Poverty and Social Exclusion in Britain*. 123–60. Bristol: Policy Press.

Lowenstein, A. 1986. 'Temporary Single Parenthood: The Case of Prisoners' Families'. *Family Relations*, 35(1), 79–85.

Luther, K. 2015. 'Examining Social Support among Adult Children of Incarcerated Parents'. *Family Relations*, 64(4), 505–18.

Mack, J. and Lansley, S. 1985. *Poor Britain*, London: George Allen and Unwin.

Main, G. 2014. 'Child Poverty and Children's Subjective Well-Being'. *Child Indicators Research*, 7(3), 451–72.

Main, G. and Besemer, K. 2014. 'Children's Material Living Standards in Rich Countries', in Ben-Arieh, A., Casas, F., Frønes, I., and Korbin, J. E. (eds.) *Handbook of Child Well-being: Theories, Methods and Policies in Global Perspective*. 1445–81. Heidelberg: Springer.

Main, G. and Bradshaw, J. 2012. 'A Child Material Deprivation Index'. *Child Indicators Research*, 5(3), 503–21.

Main, G. and Bradshaw, J. 2014. 'Child Poverty and Social Exclusion: Final Report of 2012 Pse Study'. *PSE Report*. Available at: http://www. poverty. ac. uk/pse-research/pse-uk-reports.

Main, G. and Bradshaw, J. 2015. 'Child Poverty in the UK: Measures, Prevalence and Intra-Household Sharing'. *Critical Social Policy*, 36(1), 38–61.

Maruschak, L. M., Glaze, L. E., and Mumola, C. J. 2010. 'Incarcerated Parents and Their Children: Findings from the Bureau of Justice Statistics', in Eddy, J. M. and Poehlmann, J. (eds.) *Children of Incarcerated Parents: A Handbook for Researchers and Practitioners*. 33–54. Washington: The Urban Institute Press.

May, H. 2000. '"Murderers' Relatives"—Managing Stigma, Negotiating Identity'. *Journal of Contemporary Ethnography*, 29(2), 198–221.

Micklewright, J. 2002. Social Exclusion and Children: A European View for a US Debate'. Innocenti Working Paper No. 90. UNICEF Innocenti Research Centre: Florence.

Morrow, V. 2001. 'Young People's Explanations and Experiences of Social Exclusion: Retrieving Bourdieu's Concept of Social Capital'. *International Journal of Sociology and Social Policy*, 21(4–6), 37–63.

Murray, J. 2007. 'The Cycle of Punishment: Social Exclusion of Prisoners and Their Children'. *Criminology and Criminal Justice*, 7(1), 55–81.

Murray, J. and Farrington, D. P. 2008. 'Parental Imprisonment: Long-Lasting Effects on Boys' Internalizing Problems through the Life Course'. *Development and Psychopathology*, 20(1), 273–90.

Nesmith, A. and Ruhland, E. 2008. 'Children of Incarcerated Parents: Challenges and Resiliency, in Their Own Words'. *Children and Youth Services Review*, 30(10), 1119–30.

Pantazis, C., Gordon, D., and Levitas, R. 2006. 'Introduction', in Pantazis, C., Gordon, D. and Levitas, R. (eds.) *Poverty and Social Exclusion in Britain*. 1–25. Bristol: University of Bristol.

Parke, R. D. 2002. 'Fathers and Families', in Bornstein, M. H. (ed.) *Handbook of Parenting: Being and Becoming a Parent*. 27–74. London: Lawrence Erlbaum Associates, Publishers.

Payne, S. 2006. 'Mental Health, Poverty and Social Exclusion', in Pantazis, C., Gordon, D., and Levitas, R. (eds.) *Poverty and Social Exclusion in Britain*. 285–311. Bristol: University of Bristol.

Ridge, T. 2002. *Childhood Poverty and Social Exclusion: From a Child's Perspective*. Bristol: Policy Press.

Ridge, T. 2006. 'Childhood Poverty: A Barrier to Social Participation and Inclusion', in Tisdall, E. K. M., Davis, J. M., Hill, M., and Prout, A. (eds.) *Children, Young People and Social Inclusion: Participation for What*. 23–38. Bristol: The Policy Press.

Ridge, T. 2011. 'The Everyday Costs of Poverty in Childhood: A Review of Qualitative Research Exploring the Lives and Experiences of Low-Income Children in the UK'. *Children and Society*, 25(1), 73–84.

Saunders, P. 2003. 'Stability and Change in Community Perceptions of Poverty: Evidence from Australia'. *Journal of Poverty*, 7(4), 1–20.

Saunders, P. 2011. *Down and Out: Poverty and Exclusion in Australia*. Bristol: Policy Press.

Saunders, P. and Naidoo, Y. 2009. 'Poverty, Deprivation and Consistent Poverty'. *Economic Record*, 85(271), 417–32.

Saunders, P. and Wong, M. 2014. 'Locational Differences in Material Deprivation and Social Exclusion in Australia'. *Australasian Journal of Regional Studies*, 20(1), 131–58.

Saunders, P., Naidoo, Y., and Griffiths, M. 2008. 'Towards New Indicators of Disadvantage: Deprivation and Social Exclusion in Australia'. *Australian Journal of Social Issues*, 43(2), 175–94.

Saunders, V. 2017. 'Children of Prisoners—Children's Decision Making About Contact'. *Child and Family Social Work*, 22. (S2), 63–72.

Schwartz-Soicher, O., Geller, A., and Garfinkel, I. 2011. 'The Effect of Paternal Incarceration on Material Hardship'. *Social Service Review*, 85(3), 447–73.

Schweinhart, L. J., Montie, J. Xiang, Z. Barnett, W. S., Belfield, C. R., and Nores, M. 2005. *Lifetime Effects: The High/Scope Perry Preschool Study through Age 40*. Monographs of the High/Scope Educational Research Foundation, 14. Ypsilanti, MI: High Scope Press.

Scutella, R., Wilkins, R., and Horn, M. 2009. 'Measuring Poverty and Social Exclusion in Australia: A Proposed Multidimensional Framework for Identifying Socio-Economic Disadvantage'. Paper provided by Melbourne Institute of Applied Economic and Social Research, The University of Melbourne, Melbourne Institute Working Paper Series.

Sen, A. 2000. 'Social Exclusion: Concept, Application and Scrutiny'. *Office of Environment and Social Development, Asian Development Bank, Social Development Papers*, 1(6), 1–48.

Shlafer, R. J. and Poehlmann, J. 2010. 'Attachment and Caregiving Relationships in Families Affected by Parental Incarceration'. *Attachment & Human Development*, 12(4), 395–415.

Smith, A. 1999 [1776]. *The Wealth of Nations Books IV–V*. London: Penguin Books.

Social Exclusion Unit. 2002. *Reducing Re-Offending by Ex-Prisoners*. London: Office of the Deputy Prime Minister.

Townsend, P. 1979. *Poverty in the United Kingdom: A Survey of Household Resources and Standards of Living*. Berkeley and Los Angeles: University of California Press.

Wakefield, S. and Wildeman, C. 2013. *Children of the Prison Boom: Mass Incarceration and the Future of American Inequality*. Oxford: Oxford University Press.

Wilson, K. R. and Prior, M. R. 2011. 'Father Involvement and Child Well-Being'. *Journal of Paediatrics and Child Health*, 47(7), 405–7.

7

Are the Children of Prisoners Socially Excluded?

A Child-Centred Perspective

Helene Oldrup and Signe Frederiksen

Introduction

Until recently, no specific provisions have been made to care for the children of prisoners, as the state has regarded them as the responsibility of the family, either under the care of other family members or joining their incarcerated parent in prison. This has meant that children's needs and interests were hidden in the private sphere of the family and rendered invisible in the policy process. However, during the last fifteen years these children have begun to be identified as needing child protection, particularly by NGOs, local and regional organizations, and sometimes also by the penal authorities, for instance, in Denmark and Finland (Enroos, 2015; Smith, 2014). Provisions and policies have, not surprisingly, focused on supporting prisoners in their role as parents and in improving visiting facilities and opportunities (Shlafer et al., 2015). However, a children's rights perspective is increasingly being applied to this group of children, with provision and support directly responding to children's needs (e.g. Loucks and Loureiro, this volume; Minson, this volume; Smith and Gampell, 2011).

This chapter seeks to build on and extend this child-oriented perspective by focusing on the social exclusion experienced by this particular group of children, as social relationships are crucial to child wellbeing. Thus, the chapter examines whether the child is socially excluded from important relationships in children's lives, such as in school, with friends, and in leisure-time activities, and less on the child's encounter with the criminal justice system. This is done not only by adopting a child-centred perspective, as just noted, but also by using children as informants in a survey from a representative sample of Danish children of prisoners.

Turning to studies of the children of prisoners, a considerable body of research exploring what parental imprisonment means for children now exists, as Smith (this volume) points out. Different themes and approaches are adopted in this multidisciplinary body of research. One strand of research has focused on the consequences of parental imprisonment for children by looking at the emotional, behavioural, and cognitive development of children caught up in these circumstances and demonstrating the emotional problems they may have, such as depression and anxiety, behavioural problems, and their own criminal justice convictions, and poorer educational outcomes (Murray et al., 2007; Murray et al., 2012). This mapping of negative outcomes has made the psychological and emotional violence of these children visible by drawing attention to their special needs.

A second strand of this research focuses on these children's encounters with the criminal justice system whenever a parent is imprisoned, from the parent's arrest to his or her sentencing and imprisonment (Smith, 2014). For instance, research within this strand has explored how children experience parental imprisonment (Lanskey et al., 2016; Nesmith and Ruhland, 2008) and examined how different types of visiting affect children (Poehlmann-Tynan, 2015). Also, a children's rights approach has been developed for how to incorporate children's perspectives into the criminal justice system itself in order to take account of their needs and interests when a parent enters the system. A third strand of research examines the family as an important social context for these children, focusing on how imprisonment influences child–parent relationships in respect of, for instance, family stability and the quality of parenting (Arditti, 2012; Arditti, this volume; Codd, 2008; Geller, 2013), which in turn influences child wellbeing. A fourth strand of research examines children's experiences of stigma among their peers (Boswell, 2002) and the secrecy surrounding parental imprisonment (Knudsen, this volume).

Thus, research on children tends to focus more on the consequences of parental imprisonment in the separate social contexts of their everyday lives than on the combination of social relationships across the various contexts of those lives. However, extensive research shows that social relations and networks in the form of personal, familial, and community-level relationships are crucially important to children as they grow up (Belle and Benenson, 2014). For instance, social research on children demonstrates the importance of including children's worlds outside the family as central (Ridge, 2003). Thus, the aim of this chapter is to examine the social inclusion and exclusion of these children across the domains of their everyday lives and to compare them in these respects with children from the general population, thus making the patterns of relations visible. Furthermore, as the family is shown to be a critically important context for the children of prisoners, we also compare their social exclusion according to the type of family they live in and look for differences within this group of children. Our focus is on the children of imprisoned fathers, because fathers constitute by far the largest proportion of imprisoned parents, in Denmark reaching a figure of 95 per cent of imprisoned parents (Olsen and Frederiksen, 2015).

Studies giving voice to children's experiences of their parents' imprisonment are often conducted using qualitative methods, while much of the solid evidence on children has been uncovered by retrieving information from adults (i.e. parents, caseworkers), not from the children themselves. However, in quantitative child-centred research as well, the children's own perspective should be in focus. We therefore proceed by drawing on a survey based on a representative sample of children whose fathers were in prison in the preceding year, and who may or may not have been released at the time of the survey (Oldrup et al., 2016). This allows us to retrieve the children's own perspectives on their situations.

The study is set in Denmark, where it is estimated that 5–6 per cent of every birth cohort experiences parental imprisonment during childhood (ages 0–17) and that the share of children facing this strain is similar to that of children taken into care or living in poverty (Olsen, 2013). Experiencing parental imprisonment may, whether alone or taken together with other factors, contribute to the child's social exclusion. Children experiencing paternal incarceration are not only challenged by that very fact, but also have fewer socio-economic resources than children from among the general population do (Johnson and Easterling, 2012; Nesmith and Ruhland, 2008). A Danish study confirms this finding. It also shows that incarcerated fathers are poorer, have a weaker labour market position, and are more likely to have been diagnosed with mental health problems. Similarly, the children's mothers (the remaining parent) are more likely to be lone mothers, as 61 per cent of these mothers are single (compared to 18 per cent of mothers in the general population) (Oldrup et al., 2016).

National context matters for the children of prisoners, as the child's development can be enhanced by the adoption of public policies and practices that create additional settings and social roles conducive to family life (Bronfenbrenner, 1979). For the children of prisoners, the welfare context and the penal context are both important. This study is set in Denmark, a social-democratic welfare state with an extensive welfare system, one with a large degree of redistribution and with government-sponsored programmes and interventions that are accessible to all, regardless of economic means, thus possibly compensating for the influence of parental imprisonment. For instance, pre-school childcare is almost universally adopted.

As for its penal system, Denmark has been located within what has been called 'Nordic exceptionalism' (Pratt, 2007), that is, has lower rates of imprisonment and a more humane prison service, including better visiting facilities and opportunities, than those in English-speaking countries. Indeed, during the last decade, the Danish prison and probation services have launched various initiatives to support prisoners in their role as parents and to improve visiting facilities. However, critics argue that the idea of Nordic exceptionalism is subject to qualification, as a third of all prisoners in Denmark are on remand and thus have less contact with the outside world (including typically having supervised visits and no use of phones) and a high incidence of short sentences, as more than half of new sentences are of less than four months duration compared to Anglo-Saxon systems (Kriminalforsorgen, 2015; Smith and Jakobsen, 2017). In addition, the children of prisoners in Denmark are faced with the same challenges as children in other countries, as they continue to be unable to visit their incarcerated fathers unless accompanied by an adult, and they often have great distances to travel. Nevertheless, being a social-democratic welfare state at the forefront of a more family-friendly prison regime makes Denmark an excellent case for exploring the wellbeing of this particular group of children.

A child-centred research approach to children's social exclusion

The concept of social exclusion was developed in the 1990s to capture the complexity and character of social problems in society, which were not adequately captured by traditional measurements focusing on material poverty (Redmond, 2014). A more comprehensive understanding was proposed, where social exclusion was understood as a complex and multidimensional process. While poverty is understood as a lack of or low access to material resources, social exclusion concerns non-participation in a much broader sense, including being unable to participate in relationships and social activities, whether in economic, social, cultural, or political arenas (Levitas, in Ridge, 2003). Social exclusion is therefore about non-participation more broadly and being in or out of various social domains or arenas, for example, the family or the labour market. Thus, we find the concept useful, as it draws attention to the complex and multidimensional nature of exclusion.

However, the tradition of social exclusion grew out of policy discussions at EU level about marginalized adults, and does not specifically address the lives of children. Instead, it focuses on adult experiences and where children appear in this policy agenda, it is as adults-to-be (Ridge, 2003). However, children experience social exclusion within the immediacy of childhood among their peers as well. Thus social exclusion is also exclusion from what matters for children, from the perspective of their daily lives and from the norms and customs of children's society (Ridge, 2003).

A child-centred approach to children's social exclusion has been developed in the international field of child indicator research, which measures the 'state of the child' (Ben-Arieh, 2010). Child indicator research builds on the UN Convention on the Rights of the Child (UN, 1989), where the focus is not only on the basic needs of children such as food and housing, but also on children's lives, which are seen in a rights perspective, with the right to be included in society and to be heard. In this approach, the term 'wellbeing' has been proposed: 'Children are human beings with rights and entitlements, including the right to wellbeing. Child wellbeing encompasses quality of life in a broad sense. It refers to a child's economic conditions, peer relations, political rights and opportunities for development' (Ben-Arieh, 2010).

This approach also builds on ecological theories of child development, which argue that children's development and wellbeing must be seen from a multidimensional perspective, stressing the family's role for children's lives, but also relationships in other domains and other systemic levels, such as the nursery, school, local community, and peer groups (Bronfenbrenner, 1979). Finally, it draws on the 'new sociology of childhood', which stresses that considerations of children's wellbeing should concentrate on their current life situations, and not only on their future development, thus representing a shift from becoming to being.

These underpinnings in child indicator research have had methodological implications for practical research. Thus, in child indicator research there is a focus on including indicators that measure not only future life chances, but also the current conditions that the child is experiencing. There is also a focus on both negative and positive factors and behaviours, and on achieving a balance between stressors and resources. Finally, as this perspective stresses the need for children to be heard, research should use children rather than parents or other adults as the primary source of information. Indeed, many studies in child indicator studies has children as main respondents rather than adults.

To examine the social exclusion of prisoners' children, we build on the child-centred approach developed in child indicator research. In this chapter, we have chosen to include relationships in these key domains in the child's life:

(1) Material welfare
(2) Family and social relations
(3) School
(4) Leisure and risk behaviour

In the following, we present each of these domains as they relate to the lives of children in general and the children of prisoners in particular.

Material welfare

A vast literature on material welfare and child wellbeing has documented the fact that material deprivation may have negative outcomes for children, including poorer health, lower educational attainment, and fewer employment chances as adult (Bradshaw, 2016). Likewise, such deprivation influences children's abilities to take part in social activities at the same level as their peers. There is general agreement in Denmark that absolute poverty (referring to the deprivation of basic needs such as food and poor housing conditions) no longer exists (Bak and Larsen, 2015), but that relative poverty does. Relative poverty refers to a lack of resources with which to participate in activities and obtain recognized standards of living, and second, having resources so far below the average of what an ordinary family has that one is excluded from typical life patterns, actions and activities (Bradshaw, 2016).

Studies show that lower levels of material welfare and poverty are a common childhood condition for the children of prisoners, both before, during, and after parental incarceration (Arditti, this volume; Johnson and Easterling, 2012; Oldrup et al., 2016). Research also suggests that the economic situation of families may be destabilized by parental imprisonment, as the family loses an income and has increased expenses such as transport costs when visiting (Smith, 2014).

Family

Numerous studies have shown that the quality of family relationships is consistently related to child wellbeing and outcomes (Thompson, 2014). Parents provide children with resources such as material assistance, affection, physical comforting, listening, guiding, advice, and reassurances of their worth (Belle and Benenson, 2014). The quality of such relations not only provide children with essential resources, it may help prevent demoralization in times of stress and increase children's options when confronting change and loss. Parental roles change in line with the child's age and development, but adolescent children continue to need parents' attention in respect of, for instance, advice, guidance, and intimacy. Outside the close family, potential networks such as other family members, child-carers, educators, friends, and others may provide additional support or compensate when parents are not able to care.

The children of prisoners will often experience challenging family relations. Parental incarceration may influence family life, as well as the child, during imprisonment, as the non-incarcerated parent becomes a sole carer, both practically and emotionally (Arditti, 2012 and this volume). The quality of care in the family may change as the remaining parent becomes more isolated and emotionally influenced by imprisonment. Overall, imprisonment also increases the risk of divorce (Apel, 2016). However, the family may also be influenced before imprisonment by the fathers' crime and court case, as well as afterwards, when the father is being reintegrated either into family life or into having regular contact with the child again (Lanskey et al., 2014). Research on the children of prisoners has examined aspects of relations between the children and their incarcerated parent, but more rarely relations with the non-incarcerated parent. This research show that the bonds of attachment are weakened between the incarcerated parent and the child (Poehlmann, 2005b; Poehlmann, 2005a), and increased family conflicts may arise after a parent's release from prison (Aaron and Dallaire, 2010).

School

School plays an important role in children's wellbeing for both their life chances and social mobility in the long term, but also for their wellbeing and social participation during childhood (Bacete et al., 2014).

Research on the children of prisoners shows that they are at greater risk of not doing well at school in acquiring academic skills and knowledge as measured by school marks. Studies also show that these children are often more difficult to teach, because they find it difficult to concentrate, are aggressive, or absent themselves from school (Murray et al., 2012; Jones and Wainaina-Woźna, 2013). Other research suggests that some children experience more bullying by peers (Boswell, 2002; Murray and Farrington, 2006).

Leisure and risk behaviour

Leisure time is time not spend with the family or at school and can be positive, such as spending time in organized activities, for example, sports, music, or drama, or may be negative, such as spending time in risky activities, for example, smoking, drinking, stealing, or violence. Research shows on the one hand how organized leisure activities are associated with enhanced wellbeing, as participation in such activities may improve children's physical and psycho-social wellbeing, academic performance, and social connectedness (Ommundsen et al., 2014; Blank, 2014). In addition, it may prevent anti-social behaviour and secure well-functioning integration. On the other hand, research has also documented that risk-oriented behaviour may have negative long-term outcomes for children and young people, including criminality, lower school attainment, and problems finding or keeping employment (Gruber, 2001).

Research on the children of prisoners has focused in particular on the risk of their carrying out criminal behaviour or becoming criminals themselves It has been shown that the children of prisoners do in fact have a higher risk of committing youth crime or becoming criminals in adulthood (Murray, 2005; Murray et al., 2007; Rakt et al., 2012; Murray et al., 2012). Other studies have looked at their susceptibility to alcohol or drug abuse, but they do not show any systematic connection between parental incarceration and the risk of such abuse (Murray et al., 2012). The role of organized leisure activities for the children of prisoners has not been examined systematically, but qualitative studies suggest that such activities may provide an escape from a difficult home situation for the children (Dawson et al., 2012; Nesmith and Ruhland, 2008).

Having outlined these four domains, we now turn to present our study and analysis, starting with a consideration of methods.

Methods

One challenge in carrying out child-centred research on this group of children is gaining access to them—that is, both identifying and subsequently recruiting them. In this chapter we exploit administrative data, which provide a unique opportunity to identify a representative sample of prisoners' children.

All children aged 11, 13, 15, and 17 years who for some or all of 2013 had an imprisoned father were invited to fill out a questionnaire in spring 2015. The children were identified through Statistics Denmark, which collects administrative information on the whole population. Combining incarceration data with data on families, 3,744 children were identified and invited to participate in the study. For comparison we use survey data on children from the general population (i.e. with no incarcerated father) at the ages of 11, 13, 15, and 17. The questionnaire was carefully constructed to consist of general questions on the children's lives, such as family structure, family life, friends, school, mental wellbeing, leisure time, and risk behaviour. A filter question was included directing only those children who had confirmed that their fathers had been absent due to incarceration to questions concerning paternal incarceration. This was to ensure that if any of the children were unaware of their father's imprisonment, this was not revealed to them.

Of the invited children, 43 per cent answered the questionnaire. The non-respondent analysis reveals that those prisoners' children who did not answer the questionnaire were older and more disadvantaged regarding their own characteristics (registered in psychiatry, placed in out-of-home care, receiving preventive measures) and parents' characteristics (mother's and father's ethnic origin, none or only basic education, father with multiple periods of imprisonment, or a mother with mental health problems). Even though the questionnaire was sent to a representative sample of the children of incarcerated fathers, the non-respondent analysis shows that the data provide information primarily about the most advantaged children of prisoners.

The great advantage of identifying prisoners' children through register data is that the sample is representative of such children. However, as with all empirical data, this collection strategy has its drawbacks. Importantly, when we draw a sample from administrative data, we do not know in advance which children have contact with their fathers. Of those children who answered the survey, 79 per cent did not live with their fathers, though 40 per cent of those had contact with him. This leaves a relatively large number of children with seemingly no contact with the imprisoned father (as discussed in e.g. Smith, 2014). It is important to bear this in mind, but it does not pose a problem for this analysis. The focus in this chapter is on the social relationships of the children of prisoners in general, and not only a selected group with a specific type of contact with an imprisoned father. Thus, we assume that all prisoners' children are necessarily more exposed than children in general.

In this chapter, we include four domains and nineteen indicators. In the material welfare domain the children were asked only one question on the role of resources for peer activities. The family and social relations domain concentrated on family structure, the nature of family relations, and practices, and the frequency of contact with grandparents and friends. When reporting answers in this domain, we treat a frequency of 'at least once a month' as very low. As we assume that higher frequencies of interaction matter in the creation and maintenance of social relations, unusually low frequencies make maintaining social relationships and ties challenging.

As school takes up a large amount of time in a child's life, functioning well at school is important for both performance and social relationships. The school domain measured the child's own perception of his or her performance. Questions as to how children view school and their own academic performance there inform us about their opportunities for learning and wellbeing, as do questions of whether a child skips school or feels bullied while there.

The leisure time and risk behaviour domain consists of both stressors and measures of resources. Participating in activities outside family and school helps children form new relations with peers or strengthen existing ones. As with the domains of family and social relations, the frequency threshold of activities used is 'at least once a month'. This is a high threshold indicating whether children are at risk of social exclusion. At the same time, hours not spent in school or with the family are potentially also hours where crime or risk-taking behaviour can occur. We asked the children whether they had been the victims of theft, threats, or beatings, as well as the perpetrator of any of them, or both.

Results

The first part of the analysis compares prisoners' children with children within the general population to examine whether children with an incarcerated father have weaker social relationships than do other children. The second part of the analysis examines social relationships of prisoners' children according to the type of family they live in. Research has well established that care is given differently in different family types: nuclear family, stepfamily, or single-parent. By using this lens, we are able to investigate whether type of family matters for the social relationships that the children have in- and outside the family.

The social exclusion of the children of prisoners compared to children in general

Table 1 shows the answers given by both the children of prisoners and the comparison group of children in general.

1. Material welfare

Table 1 show that 8 per cent of 17-year-old children of prisoners refrained from going out with friends due to money trouble, compared with 1 per cent of children in general. Indeed, using an objective measure shows that children of prisoners in Denmark live in families with few material resources as children of prisoners are three times more likely to live in poor families than children in general; 22 per cent receive under 50 per cent of the median income (compared to 7 per cent of mothers in the general population) (Oldrup et al., 2016). Mothers of children of male prisoners in Denmark are also more likely to consider their economic situation to be bad than mothers of children in general. They more often refrain from buying clothes, shoes, going on holiday, or going to the dentist or hairdresser, and also tend to have more difficulties paying rent and bills on time. Thus, from both an objective point and a maternal perspective, children of prisoners grow up in families with fewer resources than children in general. From the children's own perspective they tend to participate less in social activities due to financial restrictions.

2. Family and social relations

Table 1 shows that the children of prisoners report that their mothers are very important to them (77 per cent) and that they always feel loved by their mothers (91 per cent) to a greater degree than children in general (71 per cent and 88 per cent respectively). Conversely, children in general more often report feeling loved by their fathers (85 per cent) than the children of prisoners (81 per cent). These high percentages show that both the children of prisoners and children in general mostly feel close to their parents. However, the findings indicate that the children of prisoners are closer to their mothers than children are in general. One explanation for this may be that their father's absence has strengthened their bond with their mother. For relationships beyond the family, Table 1 shows that the children of prisoner appear to have fewer relationships, reporting that they see their grandparents less (63 per cent) compared to children in general (75 per cent). In addition, the children of prisoners do not

Table 1 Comparison between children of prisoners and children in general (per cent).

Domains and questions	Children of prisoners	Children in general	t-test[1]
Material welfare			
Refrain from being with friends due to money trouble[2]	8	1	***
Family and social relations			
Mother is *very* important	77	71	***
Always feeling loved by mother	91	88	***
Always feeling loved by father	81	84	**
Sees grandparents at least once a month	63	75	***
Chats with friends at least once a month	88	88	
Having friends at home at least once a month	80	90	***
Feeling lonely (often/very often)	10	5	***
School			
Likes school very much for the time being	90	95	***
Doing really well in school	19	27	***
Has skipped school within the last year	35	19	***
Has been bullied within the last six months	17	9	***
Leisure and risk behaviour			
Attends sport activities at least once a month	64	76	***
Attends other leisure at least once a month	15	23	***
Has things taken from him/her (clothes, cell phone, iPod, etc.)	52	38	***
Has been beaten or threatened by someone he/she doesn't know	21	9	***
Has taken things from others	12	7	***
Has beaten or threatened others	16	6	***
Number of observations	1133	3524	

[1] * p < 0.05, ** p < 0.01, *** p < 0.001.
[2] Question directed at 17 year olds only. Percentage is based on 143 children of prisoners and 211 children in general.

have friends at home as frequently (80 per cent) as children in general (90 per cent). Once again, the levels at which both the children of prisoners and children in general see friends and grandparents are relatively high, but the children of prisoners still see friends and grandparents to a significantly lesser degree.

3. School

Although most children value their school positively, we do find differences between the children of prisoners and children in general. Table 1 shows that 95 per cent of children in general report that they like their school very much, as do 90 per cent of the children of prisoners. Yet when asked how well they think they do in school, a higher proportion of children in general think that they are doing really well (27 per cent) than the children of prisoners do (19 per cent). As for skipping school (from a few times to all the time), 35 per cent of the children of prisoners report skipping school as opposed to 19 per cent of children in general. Finally, when asked if they had been bullied, more children of prisoners had experienced bullying (17 per cent) compared with children in general (9 per cent). Thus, despite the fact that most children of prisoners like school, they experience more academic challenges, more frequently skip school, and are more often subject to bullying.

4. Leisure and risk behaviour

An important factor in children's lives and in forming social relationships is leisure activities. Table 1 show that fewer children of prisoners engage in either sport or other activities than children in general. Hence, 76 per cent of children in general engage in sports at least once a month, and 23 per cent attend other leisure activities such as drama or music, while 64 per cent of the children of prisoners engaged in sport and 15 per cent engage in other leisure activities at least once a month. Further, the children of prisoners have a more risk-oriented behaviour. On the one hand, they are more often offenders, with 12 per cent having taken things not belonging to them compared to 7 per cent of children in general. Sixteen per cent of prisoners' children have beaten or threatened others compared to 6 per cent of children in general. On the other hand, they are more frequently victims, as 52 per cent of them have had things stolen from them (e.g. clothes from the locker room, cell phones, iPods). In comparison, 38 per cent of children in general have had things stolen from them. Prisoners' children have also been threatened or beaten more often by someone they do not know (21 per cent), compared to only 9 per cent of children in general. Thus, the children of prisoners engage in leisure activities less frequently than children in general and are more often both victims and offenders.

In sum, Table 1 shows that both the children of prisoners and children in general have high levels of close relations with parents, grandparents, and friends, and high levels of satisfaction with school. However, the level for the children of prisoners is significantly lower than for children in general across relationships in all four domains, thereby confirming earlier research and showing that prisoners' children are vulnerable across all the domains of their everyday lives. Importantly, it also shows that children are vulnerable outside the family, in children's domains, whether at school, at leisure, or in respect of peer relations.

Differences between the children of prisoners according to family type

The children of prisoners do not form a homogenous group. Conditions other than the incarceration of their fathers influence the wellbeing of these children. In line with ecological theory, the closest relationship influencing these children is that with the family, most likely the non-incarcerated parent or caregiver. One way to zoom in on the differences among prisoners' children is therefore to focus on their different family situations. In general, nuclear families appear to offer the best environment for upbringing. Research has shown that children brought up in single-parent families or step-families experience more disadvantages in terms of psychological functioning, behavioural problems, education, and health (Kamerman et al., 2003).

Indeed, the type of family the children of prisoners live in differs markedly from the families of children in general. Table 2 shows that 18 per cent of the children of prisoners live in nuclear families, 22 per cent in step-families, and 47 per cent in single-parent families, with 14 per cent living alone or with grandparents, relatives, foster parents, in institutions, or with friends. Yet for children in general, this distribution is

Table 2 Family structures of children of prisoners and children in general (per cent).

Family type	Children of prisoners	Children in general
Nuclear family	18	64
Stepfamily	22	8
Single parent	47	14
Others or alone	14	15
Number of observations	1137	3544

different, as 64 per cent of them live in nuclear families, 8 per cent in step-families, 14 per cent in single-parent families, and 15 per cent with others or alone.

This finding suggests not only that prisoners' children live in much more complex families than other children do, but also, given that so many live with a single parent, that they have weaker family relations than other children. This likelihood helps explain why the mother is more important for these children: she is their main carer. Thus, family type is an important structural difference between the children of prisoners and other children. We next examine what characterizes the social exclusion or wellbeing of prisoners' children when they are categorized according to family type.

Table 3 shows the difference between different groups of prisoners' children, according to family type. At first glance, we see that the differences between family types are not large. This may have to do with the fact that the children of prisoners are already a selected group, making the three comparison groups initially more alike, than when comparing the children of prisoners with children in general. However, some differences across family types can be detected. The group of children living in nuclear families stands out regarding school, leisure, and risk behaviour. They tend to like school more and skip school less than children in step-families or single-parent families. They are also bullied less often than children in step-families. They engage in sports activities more often, are not victims of theft, beatings, or threats as frequently, and do not have things stolen as often as children in step-families and single-parent families. Therefore, children living in nuclear families also have more positive social relationships and activities outside the family, at school, and during leisure time: they are less excluded than other children of prisoners across the different domains in their lives.

However, when examining the character of family and social relationships across family types, children in step-families stand out. Fewer children in step-families report that their mother is very important to them, and fewer still report that they always feel loved by their father than children in nuclear families or in single-parent families, indicating that the complexity inherent in step-families makes relationships less intense. Children in single-parent families report seeing less of their grandparents than children in either nuclear families or step-families, which is in line with other findings showing that children in divorced families suffer from a loss of kin in the non-custodial parent's family (van Eeden-Moorefield and Pasley, 2013), suggesting that they have fewer social ties.

When children in general are examined by family type (table not shown), we see a similar pattern, meaning that children in general living in nuclear families have more social relationships, are more satisfied with school, engage in leisure activities more frequently, and show less risky behaviour than their peers in both step-families and single-parent families. However, wellbeing among children in general across the different family types is higher than that of the children of prisoners.

Table 3 Comparison between by family types among children of prisoners (per cent).

Domains and questions	Nuclear Family	Step family	t-test[1]	Nuclear family	Single parent	t-test[1]	Step family	Single parent	t-test[1]
Family and social relationships									
Mother is *very* important	84	73	***	84	80		73	80	**
Always feeling loved by mother	94	90		94	91		90	91	
Always feeling loved by father	88	75	***	88	83		75	83	**
Sees grandparents at least once a month	69	71		69	62	*	71	62	**
Chats with friends at least once a month	87	90		87	89		90	89	
Having friends at home at least once a month	82	79		82	83		79	83	
Feeling lonely (often/very often)	7	8		7	10		8	10	
School									
Likes school very much for the time being	96	89	***	96	88	***	89	88	
Doing really well in school	19	21		19	19		21	19	e
Have not skipped school within the last year	27	36	*	27	38	***	36	38	
Have been bullied within the last six month	13	20	*	13	17		20	17	
Leisure and risk behaviour									
Has things taken from him/her (clothes, cell phone, iPod. etc.)	45	54	**	45	55	**	54	55	
Has been beaten or threatened by someone he/she doesn't know	13	22	**	13	22	**	22	22	
Has taken things from others	5	14	**	5	11	*	14	11	
Has beaten or threatened others	13	17		13	14		17	14	
Attends sport activities at least once a month	71	62	**	71	63	**	62	63	
Attends other leisure at least once a month	14	12		14	17		12	17	**
Number of observations	201	247		201	530		247	530	

[1] * p < 0.05, ** p < 0.01, *** p < 0.001.

Importantly, Table 3 shows that, despite there being little difference in the character of family relationships across family types, differences appear to matter in domains outside the family, namely relationships, school, and leisure activities. This means that children in the more vulnerable family types, single-parent and step-families, are also more vulnerable in the domains outside the family. In addition, more children of prisoners are likely to live in these family types.

Discussion

This chapter has presented a child-oriented perspective for analysing children's social relationships and the social exclusion of prisoners' children by drawing on the approach developed in child-indicator research. Using this perspective, we have investigated children from a representative sample of the children of male prisoners in Denmark using a survey comparing them with children in the general population.

The analysis shows that a higher proportion of prisoners' children are more vulnerable than children in general across all four domains. This finding is not surprising, as it confirms previous studies that document the different ways in which the children of prisoners are vulnerable. However, our study reveals that significantly more children of prisoners are more vulnerable across the domains of material welfare, family, school, and leisure activities. Although the study includes children whose fathers have a broad range of sentences (short and long), it clearly shows that a larger group of these children are vulnerable. While being vulnerable in one or two domains might not amount to actual exclusion, vulnerability in three or more domains must be regarded as showing that a greater proportion of the children of prisoners are indeed socially excluded (Redmond, 2014). Thus, while this survey cannot confirm the nature of the link between parental imprisonment and children's wellbeing, it does confirm that this is a vulnerable group.

Studying family type, we are able to paint a more complex picture of the social exclusion of children of prisoners. Indeed, children from nuclear families appear less vulnerable than those from step- or single-parent families. This is a pattern also seen amongst children in general. However, children in general thrive at a significantly higher level than children of prisoners.

While there are significant differences between the children of prisoners and children in general, it could be argued that these are relatively slight. However, it should be noted that there is a degree of selection in respect of which children participated in the survey. The non-respondents have fewer socio-economic resources, which presumably increases the real differences between the two groups of children. In addition, the moderate difference between the two groups could also be explained by the particular national context, as Denmark represents a national context characterized by a social welfare state with a great deal of family support which is likely to mediate some of the consequences of paternal imprisonment for children.

The child-centred research perspective on the children of prisoners confirms the significance of including indicators relevant to children's everyday lives and of asking questions of the children themselves. As qualitative research suggests (Lanskey et al., 2014) that prisoners' children might not want to be defined in terms of their fathers' imprisonment, future research needs to find ways of conducting such research with these children without defining them in terms of their fathers' imprisonment.

In our introduction, we argued that a child-focused policy needs child-oriented research. As research repeatedly shows, the children of prisoners are vulnerable to the effects of penal policies, and not only family and social security policies. To develop a child-centred policy response, the relevant authorities must understand and acknowledge the issues concerning the children of prisoners. Without an informed awareness of the pressures that prisoners' children experience in their everyday lives, policies directed at these children run the risk of failing to respond adequately to their needs (Ridge, 2003).

Indeed, the analysis has policy implications. Continued focus on fathers' parental skills and improving visiting facilities is important, but looking beyond the prison into children's daily lives outside the family are also critical. While finding that the children of prisoners tend to value their mothers more than other children is positive, it also suggests that these children are more isolated outside the family and that supporting children in their daily lives at home, at school, and in respect of their relations with their peers is valuable. Doing this will require cross-sectoral co-operation between the prison service, the school authorities, and the social welfare authorities.

References

Aaron, L. and Dallaire, D. H. 2010. 'Parental Incarceration and Multiple Risk Experiences: Effects on Family Dynamics and Children's Delinquency'. *Journal of Youth and Adolescence*, 39(12), 1471–84.

Apel, R. 2016. 'The Effects of Jail and Prison Confinement on Cohabitation and Marriage'. *Annals of the American Academy of Political and Social Sciences*, 665, 103–26.

Arditti, J. A., 2012. *Parental Incarceration and the Family: Psychological and Social Effects of Imprisonment on Children, Parents and Caregivers*. New York: New York University Press.

Bacete, F. J. G. et al. 2014. 'Effects of School on the Wellbeing of Children', in Ben-Arieh, A. et al. (eds.) *Handbook of Child Well-being*. 251–1306. Dordrecht: Springer Netherlands.

Bak, C. K. and Larsen, J. E. 2015. 'Social Exclusion or Poverty Individualisation? An Empirical Test of Two Recent and Competing Poverty Theories'. *European Journal of Social Work*, 18(1), 17–35.

Belle, D. and Benenson, J. 2014. 'Children's Social Networks and Children's Well-Being', in Ben-Arieh, A. et al. (eds.) *Handbook of Child Well-being*. 1335–64. Dordrecht: Springer Netherlands.

Ben-Arieh, A. 2010. 'From Child Welfare to Child Well-Being: The Child Indicators Perspective', in Kamerman, S. B., Phipps, S., and Ben-Arieh, A. (eds.) *From Child Welfare to Child Well-Being: An International Perspective on Knowledge in the Service of Policy Making*. 9–25. Dordrecht: Springer Netherlands.

Blank, J. 2014. 'Artistic Activity and Child Wellbeing in Early Schooling', in Ben-Arieh, A. (ed.) *Handbook of Child Well-being*. 941–56. Dordrecht: Springer Netherlands.

Boswell, G. 2002. 'Imprisoned Fathers: The Children's View'. *The Howard Journal of Criminal Justice*, 41(1), 14–26.

Bradshaw, J. 2016. *The Wellbeing of Children in the UK*. Bristol: Policy Press.

Bronfenbrenner, U. 1979. 'Contexts of Child Rearing: Problems and Prospects'. *American Psychologist*, 34(10), 844–50.

Codd, H. 2008. *In the Shadow of the Prison: Families, Imprisonment and Criminal Justice*. Cullomptom: Willan Publishing.

Dawson, A., Jackson, D., and Nyamathi, A. 2012. 'Children of incarcerated parents: Insights to addressing a growing public health concern in Australia'. *Children & Youth Services Review*, 34(12), 2433–41.

van Eeden-Moorefield, B. and Pasley, B. K. 2013. 'Remarriage and Stepfamily Life', in Peterson, G. W. and Bush, K. R. (eds.) *Handbook of Marriage and the Family*. 517–46. New York: Springer.

Enroos, R. 2015. 'From Invisibility to Protection: Children in Prison with their Parent in Finland'. *Children and Society*, 29(5), 399–409.

Geller, A. 2013. 'Paternal Incarceration and Father-Child Contact in Fragile Families'. *Journal of Marriage & Family*, 75(5), 1288–303.

Gruber, J. E. 2001. *Risky Behavior Among Youths: An Economic Analysis*. Chicago: University of Chicago Press.

Johnson, E. I. and Easterling, B. 2012. 'Understanding Unique Effects of Parental Incarceration on Children: Challenges, Progress, and Recommendations'. *Journal of Marriage & Family*, 74(2), 342–56.

Jones, A. D. and Wainaina-Woźna, A. E. 2013. *Children of Prisoners: Interventions and Mitigations to Strengthen Mental Health*. Huddersfield: University of Huddersfield.

Kamerman, S. B., Phipps, S., and Ben-Arieh, A. 2003. *From Child Welfare to Child Well-Being: An International Perspective on Knowledge in the Service of Policy Making*. Dordrecht: Springer Netherlands.

Kriminalforsorgen. 2015. *Kriminalforsorgen—Statistik 2014*. Copenhagen: Justitsministeriet & Direktoratet for Kriminalforsorgen.

Lanskey, C. et al. 2014. 'Re-framing the Analysis: A 3-dimensional Perspective of Prisoners' Children's Well-being'. *Children and Society*, 29(5), 484–94.

Lanskey, C. et al. 2016. 'Children's Contact with their Imprisoned Fathers and the Father–Child Relationship Following Release'. *Families, Relationships and Societies*, 5(1), 43–58.

Levitas, R. 1998. *The Inclusive Society: Social Exclusion and New Labour*. Basingstoke: Macmillan

Murray, J. 2005. 'Effects of Imprisonment on Families and Children of Prisoners', in Liebling, A. and Maruna, S. (eds.) *The Effects of Imprisonment*. Cullompton: Willan Publishing.

Murray, J. and Farrington, D. P. 2006. 'Evidence-Based Programmes for Children of Prisoners'. *Criminology & Public Policy*, 5(4), 721–35.

Murray, J., Farrington, D. P., and Sekol, I. 2012. 'Children's Antisocial Behavior, Mental Health, Drug Use, and Educational Performance After Parental Incarceration: A Systematic Review and Meta-Analysis'. *Psychological Bulletin*, 138(2), 175–210.

Murray, J., Janson, C.-G., and Farrington, D. P. 2007. 'Crime in Adult Offspring of Prisoners: A Cross-National Comparison of Two Longitudinal Samples'. *Criminal Justice and Behavior*, 34(1), 133–49.

Nesmith, A. and Ruhland, E. 2008. 'Children of Incarcerated Parents: Challenges and Resiliency, In Their Own Words'. *Children & Youth Services Review*, 30(10), 1119–30.

Oldrup, H. et al. 2016. *Indsat far—udsat barn: hverdagsliv og trivsel blandt børn af fængslede [Incarcerated Father—Vulnerable Child. Everyday Life and Wellbeing Amongst Children of Prisoners]*. Copenhagen: SFI—Det Nationale Forskningscenter for Velfærd.

Olsen, R. F. 2013. *Invisible Consequences of Punishment: Parental Imprisonment and Child Outcomes. Politicas ph.d.-serie*. Aarhus: Aarhus University Press.

Olsen, R. F. and Frederiksen, S. 2015. 'Growing Up With an Incarcerated Mother: Life Course Trajectories of Children of Incarcerated Mothers in Denmark', in Bijleveld, C. and Kruttschnitt, C. (eds.) *Lives of Incarcerated Women: An International Perspective*. 73–88. London: Routledge.

Ommundsen, Y., Løndal, K., and Loland, S. 2014. 'Sport, Children and Wellbeing', in Ben-Arieh, A. et al. (eds.) *Handbook of Child Well-being*. 911–40. Dordrecht: Springer Netherlands.

Poehlmann-Tynan, J. (ed.) 2015. *Children's Contact with Incarcerated Parents: Implications for Policy and Intervention*. Cham: Springer International Publishing.

Poehlmann, J. 2005a. 'Incarcerated Mothers' Contact With Children, Perceived Family Relationships, and Depressive Symptoms'. *Journal of Family Psychology*, 19(3), 350–7.

Poehlmann, J. 2005b. 'Representations of Attachment Relationships in Children of Incarcerated Mothers'. *Child Development*, 76(3), 679–96.

Pratt, J. 2007. 'Scandinavian Exceptionalism in an Era of Penal Excess: Part I: The Nature and Roots of Scandinavian Exceptionalism'. *British Journal of Criminology*, 48(2), 119–37.

Rakt, M. v. d., Murray, J., and Nieuwbeerta, P. 2012. 'The Long-Term Effects of Paternal Imprisonment on Criminal Trajectories of Children'. *Journal of Research in Crime and Delinquency*, 49(1), 81–108.

Redmond, G. 2014. 'Poverty and Social Exclusion', in Ben-Arieh, A. et al. (eds.) *Handbook of Child Well-being*. 1387–426. Dordrecht: Springer Netherlands.

Ridge, T. 2003. *Childhood, Poverty and Social Exclusion*. Bristol: Policy Press.

Shlafer, R. J., Loper, A. B., and Schillmoeller, L. 2015. 'Introduction and Literature Review: Is Parent–Child Contact During Parental Incarceration Beneficial?', in Poehlmann, J. (ed.) *Children's Contact with Incarcerated Parents*. 1–21. Madison: Springer International Publishing.

Smith, P. S. 2014. *When the Innocent are Punished: The Children of Imprisoned Parents*. London: Palgrave Macmillan.

Smith, P. S. and Gampell, L. 2011. *Children of Imprisoned Parents*. Skive: The Danish Institute for Human Rights.

Smith, P. S. and Jakobsen, J. 2017. *Varetægtsfængsling: Danmarks hårdeste straf?* [*Remand Imprisonment: The Hardest Punishment in Denmark?*] Copenhagen: DJØF.

Thompson, R.A. 2014. 'Why are Relationships Important to Children's Wellbeing?', in Ben-Arieh, A. et al. (eds.) *Handbook of Child Well-being*. 1917–54. Dordrecht: Springer Netherlands.

LEGISLATION

UN, 1989. *Convention on the Rights of the Child*.

PART II

PENAL POWER AND HUMAN RIGHTS

8

Prisoners' Families, Public Opinion, and the State

Punishment and Society from a Family and Human Rights Perspective

Peter Scharff Smith

Introduction

The historical roots of our current prison systems explain the way partners and children are typically isolated from their imprisoned family members. It has, since the nineteenth century, been a general trait of the Western and increasingly global practice of imprisonment to de facto punish relatives of offenders by harming many of their families in very significant ways. In reality, prisoners' families not only risk suffering numerous secondary effects of imprisonment—they also often encounter a system where their concepts of justice and legitimacy do not make sense and have never even been considered. For some partners and children the imprisonment of a relative can be beneficial but research demonstrates that the negative effects are more common and often severe. These families risk experiencing the criminal justice system not only from beneath—as the weaker part—but also as a kind of upside-down world in which society's official representatives become enemies instead of sources of support. An illustration of this is the way that the laws and rules regulating the penal system typically only attempt to balance the use of state power against the rights of prisoners but seldom take the rights of their families into account. But can we construct legitimate criminal justice systems in such a manner and do these practices actually reflect the public sense of justice? By using a partly Durkheimian approach this chapter will attempt to move focus from the offender-state binary to a broader discussion about the relationship between penal policies, prisons, and society. Finally, it will be suggested that interpreting and implementing the rights of prisoners' children and families provides a perspective on criminal justice systems, which can potentially change the current state–offender dynamic.

When the state becomes the enemy

Growing up most of us learn that if a person does something very bad the police will come, apprehend the responsible party, and send him or her to prison. When we are old enough we understand that a judge is responsible for interpreting the law and in doing so has to decide if and how to punish. At some point we will probably also realize that prison officers work in prisons to keep prisoners from escaping and ideally to rehabilitate them. Most likely we will get the impression that all this is essentially done

Prisons, Punishment, and the Family: Towards a New Sociology of Punishment? First Edition. Rachel Condry and Peter Scharff Smith. © The several contributors 2018. Published 2018 by Oxford University Press.

to keep us safe. The trust in criminal justice systems varies quite considerably from one country to another (ESS, 2011; Justitsministeriets Forskningskontor, 2016) but generally in democracies most people will adopt the understanding that the police, judges, courts, and prison staff are here to protect society. Such an understanding is arguably very important, if not essential, for creating cohesion in our societies. As others have argued, 'consent is constitutive of legitimate authority' (Bottoms and Tankebe, 2012, 134) and such consent requires a certain amount of trust in the authorities in question and arguably also a certain amount of shared values (an issue which I will return to later when discussing Durkheim).

But not everyone will feel that they are part of society and some people are even likely to view representatives of the criminal justice system as opponents. This may be the case if you have knowingly decided on pursuing a criminal career but there can be other reasons involving groups of people who have not themselves chosen marginalization or exclusion. 'I remember clearly when the officer said: "Visiting time is over." I regarded him as a stupid pig who just enjoyed bothering us', tells a son who recollects visiting his father in a Danish prison (Grøftehauge, 2004, 86). Here the prison officer, whose official and legal function is to help protect society, becomes 'a stupid pig' and the enemy of an innocent boy who has committed no crimes. Similarly a 10-year-old girl's traumatic recollection of her father's arrest meant that afterwards she 'was scared for a long time' every time she saw a police car (Christensen, 1999, 38). Hence the police, a primary societal source of protection and safety, instead become a dangerous opponent threatening the family and the most intimate private life of a child. As I will return to below, not all families of offenders will experience the criminal justice system this way and several factors, including the nature of the family relationships in question and the crime committed, can be important in that regard. But qualitative research clearly demonstrates that prisoners' families and children can develop animosity towards society. As explained in another study 'deep feelings of loss and anger' on the part of prisoners' children can end up being 'directed at legal authorities' (Boswell and Wedge, 2002, 61). On a similar note, Jardine found 'adversarial interactions' between families visiting in prison and the 'criminal justice professionals' who they met and she argues that this 'can create, or reinforce, a view that the prison system is operating without sufficient regard to what might be seen as fair or just from the perspective of families, and therefore risk undermining the legitimacy of the system as a whole' (Jardine, 2015, 233; see also Halsey, this volume; Jardine, this volume).

Few have tried to study how this can be experienced by these 'legal authorities' and 'criminal justice professionals' themselves but there are examples which clearly illustrate the above and also indicate that this mechanism of alienation can sometimes be problematic for these authorities as well. For example, a Danish police officer remembers an experience which still haunted him almost thirty years later:

Once, many years ago, I had to carry out an arrest of a female drunk-driver together with another officer. Unfortunately, she managed to get into her apartment before we could get hold of her. When we rang the doorbell, she opened the door and was clearly very intoxicated. Her husband, who didn't appear to be under the influence, stood behind her with their almost five-year old son. We asked the husband to go into another room with the child and explained: 'We just need to chat with your wife and take her down to the station for a blood test. It won't take that long'. But he refused and remained standing where he was. The woman did certainly not want to go to the station and began kicking and hitting. She was a very heavy-built and strong lady and very infuriated, so we couldn't get her to come with us just like that. We continued to urge the husband to leave with the child, but he refused. The situation with the woman developed and it all ended very unfortunately by having to get her to lie down and almost having two officers sitting on top of her out in the stairwell. And if that wasn't enough, the husband wouldn't go away with the boy; he didn't even have a proper hold on him. Suddenly, the boy attacked me and beat furiously on my back while shouting, 'Get away from my mother! Get away from my mother!' I will never forget the boy's eyes and I often wonder where he is today, how it has affected him and what he thinks about the police and about the episode. It's almost twenty-eight years ago, so he is an adult man now. (Smith, 2014, 4)

In other words, family members of prisoners risk experiencing a sort of upside-down world where allegiance and support can be very difficult to locate within the system of official authorities.

The 'upside-down' world of prisoners' families

Traditionally discussions, research, court judgments, etc. within the field of prisons and human rights, have almost exclusively been a matter of balancing the state's legitimate use of power and security concerns against the individual prisoners' rights. The question of whether, how, and to what degree the use of imprisonment has also affected the rights of persons outside of prison has for many years been left out of consideration. This has up until recently certainly been the case with prisoners' children—a group of people whose rights are clearly affected by the use of imprisonment (Condry et al., 2016; Lagoutte, 2016; Smith, 2014). A prisoner's right to a family life, and deriving from that especially the right to receive visits from family members, is well established within human rights law and within many national jurisdictions—but this right has traditionally been viewed and interpreted from the prisoner's perspective and less so from that of the families and relatives (Lagoutte, 2016, 206; Smith, 2014, 84 and 103 f.). The perspective of these families and children has generally been left out of consideration, which includes *their* rights to, for example, privacy and a family life, and in case of the children all their individual rights to be heard, to be treated in their best interest, not to be discriminated, etc. Hence, a prisoner has the right to receive visits whereas a child's or a family member's right to visit is seldom mentioned in penal law or elsewhere. As I will return to below this almost complete lack of attention within the legal system and its institutions (the police, prisons, etc.) is very likely a major reason that this group of people have experienced severe forms of exclusion and serious hardship throughout the history of the prison (Smith, 2014).

Today, we know a lot about prisoners' families and children and based on the extensive research which has surfaced especially in recent years we can conclude that prisoners' families constitute a very vulnerable group and risk experiencing both social and administrative exclusion (Comfort, 2008; Condry et al., 2016; Hagan and Foster, 2015; Murray, 2006; Oldrup and Frederiksen, this volume). Prisoners' families, and especially the involved children, have often been described as a 'forgotten' or 'invisible' group of people who have fallen victims to the way our criminal justice system works and become collateral damage along the way as partners, fathers, and mothers have been arrested, sentenced, and imprisoned (Hagan and Dinovitzer, 1999; Murray and Farrington, 2008, 133). Especially the last decade has witnessed a massive and international surge in research within this area which has documented very convincingly how these families are affected in extensive and often very detrimental ways. This has especially been shown with regard to the children of imprisoned parents (Miller and Barnes, 2015; Murray and Farrington, 2008; Smith, 2014; Wakefield and Wildeman, 2014) but also with regard to spouses and partners (Apel, 2016; Comfort, 2008; Condry, 2007; Jardine, this volume; Kotova, this volume). Interestingly, we in fact know much less about exactly when and under what circumstances parental/partner imprisonment will be *positive* for family members on the outside and when contact with an imprisoned parent is *not* in the child's best interest (Smith, 2014, 187 ff.; Condry and Smith, this volume).

Taken together the above means that in terms of research we can no longer call these families and their children 'forgotten'. But unfortunately they are still very often forgotten and excluded in practical terms and are typically neglected as a group by society's official institutions. One illustration of this is the lack of routinely recorded data about prisoners' families and children. In other words, although there is still much research to do in this area, the biggest and most immediate challenge now is how we change our criminal justice systems and penal practices to reflect the knowledge we have gathered about prisoners' families and the ways in which they are treated and affected when a partner/parent etc. is arrested and imprisoned.

A possible reason why prisoners' children have generally not been the object of political and legal interest can be that some of the most basic conceptions of justice and guilt, around which the penal system is built, are turned upside down when the focus turns to prisoners' families and especially their children. On the one hand it is arguably part of some of our most basic instincts and values to consider some acts criminal and to want the guilty party punished, while on the other hand the children of imprisoned parents who are often severely harmed are obviously completely innocent of any crime. At first glance this looks like a Gordian knot facing the use of imprisonment and hence the practice of punishment today (Smith, 2014, 7). As touched upon in the above we have created a system of punishment which to a significant extent will cause exclusion and alienation of numerous such family members. Arguably, this problem has only become worse in many jurisdictions in recent years as a result of the political rhetoric about longer and tougher sentences, which currently characterize the legal-policy debate in many countries (Roberts et al., 2003; Ryberg and Roberts, 2014; Frøseth et al., 2016). This 'penal populism' means that politicians often refer to public opinion and public sentiments on justice as an argument for longer sentences as well as harsher and stricter policies towards offenders. But this 'tough on crime' language can potentially lose legitimacy if the perspective of prisoners' families and children is adopted. This is one of the issues which I will return to below in an effort to align and incorporate the experience of prisoners' families with the sociology of punishment.

Prisoners' families and the sociology of law and punishment

So how do we bring the perspective, experience, and rights of prisoners' families into the machinery of our criminal justice systems? From a researcher's point of view—a researcher who is interested in ways to inform and produce penal reform—one way to approach this issue would be through the literature on the sociology of punishment. This makes sense, since the sociology of punishment evolved as a response to traditional 'penological' and 'philosophical' discussions about punishment and did so in an attempt to 'conceptualize punishment as a social institution' (Garland, 2000, 381). According to Garland such an approach should, among other things, enable us to answer questions regarding the 'unintended social effects' and 'wider social costs' of punishment (Garland, 2000, 381). In other words, the very issues in which we are interested in the present context.

But although the literature on prisoners' families has multiplied in recent years there are few signs that it has entered far into mainstream criminology and general textbooks on the sociology of law. Take, for example, *The Oxford Handbook of Criminology*, where neither the 5th edition (Maguire et al., 2012), or the recent 6th edition (Liebling et al., 2017), deals specifically with prisoners' families. In fact, when looking at the 5th edition as well as the recent 6th edition you will not even find the word 'family' in the index—not by itself nor sub-indexed under 'prison'. Based on a look at the indexed words as well as the chapter themes, it seems fair to say that the crime and the offender, including the sanctions directed towards him or her, are still the main focus (Maguire et al., 2012; Liebling et al., 2017). The perspective of prisoners' families and the way they are affected by the criminal justice system are clearly not considered a major issue although these individuals far outnumber the otherwise huge number of prisoners worldwide. Indeed, prisoners' children alone are likely to equal or outnumber the incarcerated (Smith, 2014, 43 ff.). When it comes to the sociology of law one will have even less luck in finding relevant material in the mainstream textbook literature (see, e.g. Banakar and Travers, 2013) and even in those titles which clearly acknowledge social control, crime, and punishment as being part of the sociology of law (see, e.g. Deflem, 2010). As far as the more specialized literature on prisons goes the result appear somewhat different. Indeed, the most recent edition of the Palgrave Handbook on prisons (Jewkes et al., 2016) includes a chapter on 'Collateral damage: The families and children of prisoners' (Condry et al., 2016), and the previous edition had a chapter on 'Prisoners' families' (Jewkes, 2007).

If we look at the more specialized literature on the sociology of punishment we will find, that although it is extremely sophisticated and has taught us a great deal about punishment and society, the issue of prisoners' families and children has typically been overlooked. In other words, while 'concepts from the wider literature on the sociology of the prison […] can fruitfully be applied to the experiences of families affected by imprisonment' at the same time 'greater attention should be paid to the experiences of families by those researching other aspects of the criminal justice system' (Jardine 2015, 234). Again, there are signs that things might be changing (Muller and Wildeman, 2013). On a general note, one could say that a critical sociological literature on prisons and their relation to society appeared during the 1970s in which prisons have been studied as a reflection of society and modernity. This more or less 'Foucauldian' discourse and other critical interpretations have generally produced a very interesting theoretical literature on power technologies, 'governmentality', etc.— and theories of punishment in general—but have certainly not lead to any focus on prisoners' relatives and children (Smith, 2014, 9). So how do we achieve this? How do we infuse the sociology of punishment with the experiences of prisoners' families? And how do we go from there to policy and practice in order to ensure that our criminal justice systems will include—and not exclude—the plight of prisoners' families?

When looking broadly at the sociology of punishment and the sociology of law there are of course countless possible sources and stepping stones for an analysis of contemporary practices. In his seminal work on 'Punishment and Modern Society', originally from 1990, David Garland discussed the work of Durkheim, Weber, and Foucault, as well as that of Rusche and Kirchheimer (Garland, 1991). While these great thinkers can be very inspirational in different ways one, in my opinion, seems to be of more immediate relevance when trying to take into account the experiences of a large group in society in risk of exclusion. Focus on processes of rationalization (Weber), the system of production (Rusche and Kirchheimer) or technologies of power (Foucault) have arguably informed the sociology of punishment to a large degree throughout half a century or more, while the Durkhemian perspective on solidarity and social cohesion has featured far less prominently. The latter should however be of great interest to anyone interested in taking into account feelings of alienation and injustice produced by punishment since Durkheim studied punishment as a 'moral phenomenon' and as the 'embodiment of society's moral order' (Garland, 1991, 24 and 25).

In fact, the relative lack of interest in the Durkhemian perspective on criminal justice and the traditional focus on the offender-state binary (and the corresponding lack of interest in prisoners' families) might be two sides of the same coin. As explained by Katja Franko, 'until recently criminological writing has primarily focused on utilitarian, reformative and crime control aspects of punishment rather than on its emotive, passionate and moralizing sides' (Franko, 2013, 81 f.). Interestingly, however, there are signs that this is now changing, and recently several authors 'have pointed out the growing importance of expressive justice and of populist sentiments in contemporary penality' (Franko, 2013, 81 f.). As I will return to below, I think that much of this recent interest has been sparked by the rising prominence of 'penal populism' and emotional criminal justice policies and while this research is extremely interesting—such as studies of the public sense of justice (Balvig, 2006; Ryberg and Roberts, 2014; Frøseth et al., 2016)—it has not yet been discussed in relation to prisoners' families. In the following I will try to do just that—that is, attempt to view the experiences of prisoners' families through a semi-Durkhemian lens and include *their* situation and sense of justice in a discussion of the public sense of justice. Following that, I will argue that a human rights based analysis provides a possible answer on how to operationalize such a family-oriented perspective on criminal justice.

A normative turn? From utilitarianism to legitimacy and the public sense of justice

'In the past 20 years, criminologists have become more interested in normative compliance with the law, and especially the concept of legitimacy: that is to say, citizens' recognition of the rightness of the authority of criminal justice officials, and the consequences of this recognition for behaviour' (Tankebe and Liebling, 2013, 1). One example is found within literature on prison conditions and prison regimes and how these are experienced by prisoners (Sparks et al., 1996). Indeed, some of this literature (Liebling and Arnold, 2004) demonstrates 'that legitimacy can also generate prisoner well-being through a staff commitment to justice' (Tankebe and Liebling, 2013, 1). We are in other words moving towards increasing academic acceptance of the importance of some of the more normative elements of law and criminal justice and 'especially in relation to policing and prisons' (Bottoms and Tankebe, 2012, 119). This is a very interesting development, but once again it has so far taken place without significant interest in the role of prisoners' relatives and families—indeed, one can argue that this literature in a way replicates the state-offender binary by arguing that 'prisoners' and 'the general public' are two distinct groups that have significantly different priorities with regard to legitimacy and justice (Bottoms and Tankebe, 2012, 123). In any case, when it comes to prisons research, the focus has primarily been on legitimacy within the prison walls and between staff and prisoners (Sparks et al., 1996; Liebling and Arnold, 2004). Nevertheless, this current criminological interest in legitimacy is clearly interesting in the present context (see also Jardine, this volume).

Of course, as always one is tempted to say, the recent interest in legitimacy and punishment is not completely new. For example, when Thomas Mathiesen put 'Prison on trial', originally in 1972, he also discussed whether or not prisons produced 'justice' although he did that without discussing prisoners' families and the broader collateral consequences of imprisonment (Mathiesen, 2006). Since then a sophisticated literature on principled sentencing has also evolved which clearly accepts a normative approach to questions of punishment (see, e.g. Hirsch and Ashworth, 2000). The literature on restorative justice could be another interesting example of a field which has paid attention to questions of justice as well as the more emotional and normative side of punishment. Authors concerned with procedural justice have also looked into questions of legitimacy (Bottoms and Tankebe, 2012). Again, however, this literature has not been especially interested in aligning the level of punishment with the way it affects prisoners' relatives.

In fact, for inspiration it makes sense to go even further back in history to the late nineteenth-century work of Durkheim. As explained by Garland, Durkheim saw the function of the 'institutions of penality […] less as a form of instrumental rationality and more as a kind of routinized expression of emotion, like the rituals and ceremonies of a religious faith' (Garland, 1991, 32). According to such an approach, thinking of punishment 'as a calculated instrument for the rational control of conduct' would be 'to miss its essential character, to mistake superficial form for true content' since the 'essence of punishment is irrational, unthinking emotion fixed by a sense of the sacred and its violation' (Garland, 1991, 32). As explained by Durkheim himself, in his work on 'The division of labour', the 'real function' of punishment 'is to maintain inviolate the cohesion of society by sustaining the common consciousness in all its vigour' (Durkheim, 1984, 63). For Durkheim this understanding entailed that if the system and level of punishment comes out of touch with the dominating values in society—the collective consciousness—a problem will arise which can potentially create an 'anomic' situation (Durkheim, 1984). Here it is important to bear in mind that prisoner's families are not an obscure minority but a significant group in society which far outnumber those incarcerated. In other words, how well does the legal system represent the common consciousness if one in four black children born in the United States in 1990 risk paternal imprisonment by aged 14 (Wakefield and Wildeman, 2014, 33) and 5–6 per cent of all children born in Denmark experience parental imprisonment at some point during their lives (Oldrup et al., 2017, 5)—and the sentiments of these children and their families are not properly reflected in the criminal justice system?

Bearing the present issue in mind, one way to approach such a problem would be to examine public sentiments on justice while making sure that the experience and sentiments of prisoners' families are fed into such a study. Although we have a significant literature on public sentiments on justice this has to my knowledge not been attempted yet.

Prisoners' families and the public sense of justice

There is little agreement among scholars exactly as to how—or indeed whether or not—public sentiments on justice are relevant and should feed into actual policies on, and practices of, punishment. Ryberg and Roberts distinguish between three different models in that regard: (a) a 'direct importation model', according to which 'community values should be directly imported into sentencing practice'; (b) an 'exclusionary model', according to which 'community values are explicitly excluded from the evolution of any penal policies'; and (c) a 'qualified public input' model which represents 'an intermediate position' between the other two (Ryberg and Roberts, 2014, 5). Several authors follow the latter model (Ryberg, 2014) and that is also a starting point for the following discussion. In my opinion, that would also be the natural position for anyone inspired by Durkheim's approach as previously outlined.

I think it would be fair to say that from the classic discussions of 'moral panics' (Cohen, 1972) to more topical debates over 'penal populism' (Pratt, 2007) the most prominent criminological perspective on the relation between criminal policy and the public sense of justice has been rather sceptical leaning towards the 'exclusionary model' just described (with writings on principled sentencing as the probably most obvious exception). A now well-developed literature on penal populism and late modern cultures of control has certainly underlined the way that the publics (alleged) moral values and sense of justice is often used to justify harsher sentencing and tough on crime policies. Indeed, despite insufficient or opposing documentation, it is often taken for granted that the public wants more revenge and not more lenient sentences and prison practices (Ryberg, 2006; Balvig, 2006; Olaussen, 2014). This is also the case if we look at, for example, Danish prison law—that is, the Danish Sentence Enforcement Act—where consideration of public sentiments on justice figures only as purely punitive considerations. In other words, when the law requires that public sentiments on justice are taken into account—for example when the prison service has to approve or reject a release on parole—referring to public sentiments will always weigh against the prisoner and fulfil the role as society's revenge (Engbo, 2006, 58). Strictly speaking, this is absurd since one could in many cases just as well refer to the public sense of justice as an argument for more lenient sentencing and sentence enforcement (Balvig, 2006). But such thoughts have apparently not been on the minds of the legislators. This is just one concrete way of illustrating that a reference to the public sense of justice is often—both politically and legally—the same as arguing for more or tougher punishment. Again, this is a perfect example of how the legal and penal system can facilitate social and administrative exclusion of prisoners' families. Another way of phrasing this problem would be to say that the sense of justice of many families of prisoners is neglected completely while the public sense of justice is assumed to be purely punitive. For example, when the then Danish Minister of Justice, Lene Espersen, published a bill in 2005, which, based on the Danes' alleged public sense of justice, ordered three months' home leave suspension for prisoners who appeared late for their commitment to prison, she stated: 'I think it has a pedagogical effect if you cannot visit your family for three months or participate in your child's birthday' (Smith, 2014, 222). The Minister of Justice in other words focused exclusively on the prisoner and completely failed to even consider how the children would feel about such legislation. Breaking the contact between children and parents was on the contrary—in this particular context—framed as something, which was positive for the state and allegedly reflected the public sense of justice. On the same occasion, another political party profiled itself by proposing that prisoners who appeared too late for their prison sentence should have a total prohibition on home leave for the duration of the entire sentence (Smith, 2014, 222). Such political initiatives are striking illustrations of how families affected by imprisonment are excluded from the collective consciousness further reinforcing an antagonistic relationship between the state (which in that type of statement is assumed to equate to the public) and prisoners' families.

In terms of the public sense of justice the problem we are dealing with here seems to be that the politicians are feeding on what has been termed the *uninformed* public sense of justice instead of the *informed* sense of justice (Balvig, 2006; Balvig et al., 2015). The former is what you pick up on in, for example, telephone surveys, with questions like 'Do you think the level of punishment is too low?', 'Do you think that prisoners have too many benefits?' etc. It is a sort of bottomless punitive pit in the sense that across jurisdictions people will almost always want *more* and not *less* punishment when asked in that fashion (Balvig, 2006). Remembering Durkheim and the moral nature of punishment, a positive way to interpret this mechanism might be to say that people value justice and want to see it 'done'. Indeed, we do know from research that there are 'widely shared intuitions about the relative blameworthiness of different cases, at least with regard to a "core" of wrongdoing, involving, for example, physical aggression and theft' (Robinson, 2014, 62). But of course, justice is a complicated thing, and if researchers study the *informed* sense of justice they tend to find that people will punish much less. That is, when they know the circumstances of a given case they will often see matters from the offenders perspective as well and wish to punish much less. A recent study of the *uninformed* and the *informed* sense of justice in the Nordic countries clearly demonstrated the substantial difference in the two categories and the results they bring to the table in terms of crime, justice, and punishment (Balvig et al., 2015). For example, these Nordic studies uniformly showed how in six different cases of criminal behaviour people in fact tended to punish milder than the courts would when they knew the facts and circumstances surrounding the case—that is, when their informed sense of justice was probed (Balvig et al., 2015). The problem is that these informed attitudes are generally not uncovered or included in the daily media/political debate on crime and punishment. On the contrary, the politicians are speaking directly to the uninformed sense of justice when they campaign for more and tougher punishment.

Such problems have arguably worsened in many jurisdictions in recent years due to the rise of penal populism. But if mum or dad ends up in prison then popular political catch phrases such as 'zero tolerance' and 'tough on crime' will often make poor sense for the children and families concerned. From this perspective public and political debate on crime can therefore appear decidedly hostile. This clearly produces a risk of reinforcing the 'them' and 'us' tendency, which already at the outset can thrive in a situation of imprisonment in the family. As already described this can have very concrete results in terms of how prisoners' children view society and society's representatives. The French psychologist, Alain Bouregba, argue that a child's sense of community can be destroyed when a parent is imprisoned and the loss replaced by withdrawal, narcissistic tendencies, and isolation, which can again result in antipathy towards society (Smith, 2014, 81). If this is the case, it must certainly be very important that representatives of state and society step into the arena on the children's side as well. Otherwise, prisoners' children are likely to develop animosity and lack of loyalty towards society. Of course, not all prisoners' children risk being caught up in these mechanics. Some of these children have minimal contact or no relation at all to the imprisoned parent and for some families the imprisonment and lack of contact is beneficial (Smith, 2014, 187 ff.; Condry and Smith, this volume). Furthermore, many families and even children might find the imprisonment fair given the acts committed. But the point here is that the way the punishment—in this case the imprisonment—is carried out matters and the important question is whether the needs of the families are neglected or not, not whether or not it is fair to meet out some kind of punishment. As explained by a former spokesperson for the prisoners in Jyderup State Prison—an open Danish prison: 'It is, in my opinion, in society's short-term and long-term interest to [...] ensure that children of prisoners do not become defiant towards society, which can be the result when children experience that contact to their parents is hindered and that the contact which does take place, occurs under conditions that do not promote a positive dialogue between child and parent' (Smith, 2014, 81). What we are dealing with here is, in other words, a possible process towards social and administrative exclusion.

From the 'uninformed' to the 'informed' sense of justice

So if we want to acknowledge and incorporate the emotions and experiences of prisoners' families in a model of 'qualified input' of public sentiments on justice we should, in other words, disregard the *uninformed* and turn to the *informed* public sentiments on justice. Here we can certainly locate a milder and more balanced view on punishment. This is all very well, but so far nobody has shown interest in actually informing the *informed* sense of justice with the sentiments of prisoners' families. Once again, the focus of studies on the *informed* sense of justice has been on the offender, not his or her relatives. Similarly, the academic interest in principled sentencing, and those who have tried to measure the harshness of sentencing with a view to the public sense of justice, seems to have focused almost exclusively on the effects of punishment (including imprisonment) on the offender while leaving out the broader effects on the community (perhaps apart from looking at how prisonization can disrupt rehabilitation of offenders; Bagaric, 2014, 95). In that sense, the problem of the state-offender binary mentioned above seems to have been repeated.

But this need not be the case of course. If we accept the 'qualified public input' model outlined earlier, and then proceed using the *informed* sense of justice, while at the same time informing this with perspective of prisoners' families, then this arguably makes for a very sensible way of imbedding the sentiments of prisoners' families in our criminal justice systems and practices. In order to do that systematically we would of course have to study their views on justice and punishment empirically. It is beyond the scope of this chapter to do this thoroughly, and for now we will therefore have to rely on the studies quoted and referenced above, which (a) document the social exclusion experienced by prisoners' families; and (b) illustrate how they risk experiencing the criminal justice system as an upside-down world, where the state and its officials becomes the enemy. As already described this body of evidence clearly illustrates that we need to reform our penal policies and practices. In the following I will argue that a human rights approach is a possible way of doing that.

A human rights approach

Criminologists have been relatively slow to acknowledge and show interest in the field of human rights (Weber et al., 2014). Ironically the same has up until quite recently been true for scholars dealing with the sociology of law (Madsen and Verschraegen, 2013). Similarly van Zyl Smit argues that 'in research on legitimacy and criminal justice relatively little attention has been paid to the international [human rights] standards that seek to shape the implementation of punishment in national jurisdictions' (van Zyl Smit, 2013, 267). However, looking at the field of prisons and human rights from a perspective of rights holders outside of prison is not common (for an exception, see Engbo and Smith, 2012). Court judgments as well as research reports and monographs on prisons and human rights reflect this. The latter tend to deal systematically with prisoners' rights in most areas of prison life, but the question of the rights of others outside of prison seldom arises (Smith, 2014, 86 f.).

Nevertheless, human rights conventions and soft law clearly express the rights to private life, family life, and children's rights. All three areas can be of crucial importance to prisoners' families and children. The original Universal Declaration of Human Rights from 1948, which paved the way for the later legally binding UN Covenants, contained an article for the protection of family and private life: 'No one shall be subjected to arbitrary interference with his privacy, family, home or correspondence, nor to attacks upon his honour and reputation. Everyone has the right to the protection of the law against such interference or attacks' (Article 12). The International Convention on Civil and Political Rights (ICCPR) elaborated on these principles and established that the 'family is the natural and fundamental group unit of society and is entitled to protection by society and the State' (Article 23.1). In the same covenant, it is furthermore made clear that children have their own independent rights: 'Every child shall have […] the right to such measures of protection as are required by his status as a minor, on the part of his family, society and the State' (Article 24.1). The child's rights have since been furthered primarily in the Convention on the Rights of the Child (CRC), which went into effect in 1990. It states that participant states 'shall take all appropriate measures to ensure that the child is protected against all forms of discrimination or punishment on the basis of the status, activities, expressed opinions, or beliefs of the child's parents, legal guardians, or family members' (Article 2.2). The requirement in Article 3 is equally fundamental: 'In all actions concerning children, whether undertaken by public or private social welfare institutions, courts of law, administrative authorities or legislative bodies, the best interests of the child shall be a primary consideration' (Article 3.1). Family rights expert Stephanie Lagoutte concludes that three principles in the CRC are central for children of imprisoned parents: (1) the protection of the best interest of the child; (2) the right of the child to express his or her view and to be heard in matters affecting the child; and (3) the principle of non-discrimination (Lagoutte, 2016).

It is beyond the scope of this chapter to enter into a detailed discussion of to what degree these rights are upheld when it comes to prisoners' families (for such a discussion with regard to children of imprisoned parents, see Smith, 2014 and Lagoutte, 2016). For now it is sufficient to state what has already been alluded to earlier, that very often these rights are *not* protected in practice when it comes to prisoners' families. Regardless, they provide a systematic and analytical starting point in the present case: a method and a concrete approach which can be directed at all levels of the criminal justice system and used to analyse—legally, sociologically, and criminologically—how the police, courts, prisons, etc. relate to prisoners' relatives and what outcomes this produce. For example, an analysis of the rights of prisoners' children (Smith, 2014) reveals that upholding these rights will have implications for policy, practice, and legal standards within the following areas:

(1) The arrest of parents:
    (a) How are the children treated and how do they experience the arrest situation?
    (b) Are the children informed about the arrest and the possible separation that subsequent imprisonment will entail?
    (c) Are the social authorities notified with a view to assessing the children's situation?
(2) Sentencing a parent:
    (a) Length of prison term/regime/choosing alternatives to imprisonment etc.
(3) During imprisonment:
    (a) How are the remaining family members and children assured in a financial respect?

(b) How is direct and regular contact maintained between the imprisoned parent and his or her child/children? (questions concerning prison regimes, visiting policy/practice, use of telephone, other forms of contact, etc.)
(c) Choice of prison and the question of stationing (where is the parent placed)
(d) Living with mum (or dad) in prison—what is in the best interest of the child?

Importantly, the above is not only a list of legally relevant issues, it is also a draft model for incorporating the perspective of prisoners' families into the criminal justice system in general. A human rights approach (in this case more specifically that of family rights and children's rights) can be used in that way to map all areas of interest and relevance from a child and family perspective. Indeed, within all the above areas not only legal standards but also policy and, most importantly, practice should be reformed to take the perspective of prisoners' families and children into account. In that sense, a rights based approach is a potential analytical tool for locating weak spots in the system—where prisoners' families are forgotten, neglected, marginalized, etc.—and through that process working to achieve a morally just equilibrium which will avoid creating alienation and social as well as administrative exclusion. Needless to say, this is a normative approach but we embarked on that road when accepting the policy relevance of the *informed* public sense of justice and the importance of the experience of exclusion on the part of prisoners' families.

From rights and research to practice

We need to remind ourselves, of course, that human rights do not solve anything by themselves. They are merely a mechanism, a perspective, and a possible vehicle for reform, among many others (Smith, 2015). The most obvious way of recognizing the rights of prisoners' families and children would be to change our punishment practices fundamentally and start reducing prison populations significantly across jurisdictions. Regardless of whether or not this is achieved there are countless other practices and legal standards that need to be reformed. This includes, for example, implementing police protocols for carrying out arrests of parents, promoting alternatives to imprisonment, improving visiting policies and conditions in prisons, enhancing possibilities for communication, etc. (see also Donson and Parkes, this volume). Examples of such initiatives do exist in different jurisdictions—sometimes as national policies although more often as local initiatives in specific regions, prisons, districts, etc. Some of these practices have been developed based on a human rights perspective—often that of children's rights. This is, for example, the case with children's officers in Scandinavian prisons (Smith, 2014) and this is also the reason that Norwegian prison law now recognizes the rights of prisoners' children by legally establishing children's right to contact with their parents as a general principle and requiring that children 'shall receive special attention' during their parents' imprisonment (Smith, 2014, 233).

In terms of creating legitimacy, one of the strengths of human rights standards is that they are international and gradually developed in a process between states and with ongoing input from practitioners and experts. In that sense, human rights standards tap into global expertise and practice as well as global public sentiments on justice. In addition the legitimacy of these standards is constantly tested in national, regional, and international courts, as well as in media and in the political arena. The normative aspects of these questions have previously caused scepticism among scholars—for example within the sociology of law (Madsen and Verschraegen,

2013)—but if accepted as relevant, human rights carry a potential strength in terms of increasing the moral credibility of criminal justice systems by making them more respectful of vulnerable groups. The central purpose of human rights is after all to protect people against abuse from the state and studies on the *informed* public sense of justice arguably show us that people generally respect and want to help marginalized and disadvantaged groups. Furthermore, strengthening the rights and protection of prisoners' families' vis-à-vis the criminal justice system will in turn help shape society's view and understanding of this group of people and in doing so potentially increase social cohesion. After all, as Robinson reminds us, 'the most powerful force that comes from a criminal justice system with moral credibility is its power to shape societal norms and to cause people to internalize those norms' (Robinson, 2014, 57). In other words, by recognizing and implementing family rights and children's rights in our criminal justice systems these will arguably become more just, reduce their capacity to marginalize and exclude people, and increasingly help create cohesion in our societies.

References

Apel, R. 2016. 'The Effects of Jail and Prison Confinement on Cohabitation and Marriage'. *Annals of the American Academy of Political and Social Science*, 665(1), 103–26.
Bagaric, M. 2014. 'Proportionality in Sentencing: The Need to Factor in Community Experience, Not Public Opinion', in Ryberg, J. and Roberts, J. (eds.) *Popular Punishment: On the Normatice Significance of Public Opinion*. New York: Oxford University Press.
Balvig, F. 2006. *Danskernes syn på straf*. Copenhagen: Advokatrådet.
Balvig, F., Gunnlaugsson, H., Jerre, K., Tham, H., and Kinnunen, A. 2015. 'The Public Sense of Justice in Scandinavia: A study of Attitudes Towards Punishments'. *European Journal of Criminology*, 12(3), 342–61.
Banakar, R. and Travers, M. (eds.) 2013. *Law and Social Theory*. Oxford: Hart Publishing.
Boswell, G. and Wedge, P. 2002. *Imprisoned Fathers and their Children*. London: Jessica Kingsley Publishers.
Bottoms, A. and Tankebe, J. 2012. 'Beyond Procedural Justice: A Dialogic Approach to Legitimacy in Criminal Justice'. *Journal of Criminal Law and Criminology*, 102(1), 119–70.
Christensen, E. 1999. *Foroeldre i fængsel—en undersøgelse af børns og forældres erfaringer*. Report no. 99/5. Copenhagen: Socialforskningsinstituttet.
Cohen, S. 1972. *Folk Devils and Moral Panics: The Creation of the Mods and Rockers*. London: MacGibbon and Kee Ltd.
Comfort, M. 2008. *Doing Time Together: Love and Family in the Shadow of the Prison*. Chicago: University of Chicago Press.
Condry, R. 2007. *Families Shamed: The Consequences of Crime for Relatives of Serious Offenders*. Cullompton: Willan Publishing.
Condry, R., Kotova, A., and Minson, S. 2016. 'Social Injustice and Collateral Damage: The Families and Children of Prisoners', in Jewkes, Y., Bennett, J., and Crewe, B. (eds.) *The Handbook on Prisons*. (2nd ed.). London: Routledge.
Deflem, M. 2010. *Sociology of Law. Visions of a Scholarly Tradition*. Cambridge: Cambridge University Press.
Durkheim, E. 1984. *The Division of Labour in Society*. Basingstoke: Macmillan.
Engbo, H. J. 2006. 'Ret og etik i straffuldbyrdelsen', in Kühle, L. and Lomholt, C. (eds.) *Straffens menneskelige ansigt?* Copenhagen: ANIS.
Engbo, H. J. and Smith, P. S. 2012. *Fængsler og menneskerettigheder*. Copenhagen: Jurist- og Økonomforbundets Forlag.

ESS (European Social Survey). 2011. *Trust in Justice: Topline Results from Round 5 of the European Social Survey*. Available at: https://www.europeansocialsurvey.org/docs/findings/ESS5_toplines_issue_1_trust_in_justice.pdf.

Franko, K. 2013. *Globalization and Crime*. London: Sage.

Frøseth, A. M., Gröning, L., and Wandall, R. H. (eds.). 2016. *Rettsfølelsen i strafferettssystemet*. Oslo: Gyldendal.

Garland, D. 1991. *Punishment and Modern Society: A Study in Social Theory*. Oxford: Oxford University Press.

Garland, D. 2000. 'Sociological Perspectives on Punishment', in Hirsch, A. von and Ashworth, A. (eds.) *Principled Sentencing. Readings on Theory and Policy*. Oxford: Hart Publishing.

Grøftehauge, M. 2004. *Fangebørn*. Århus: CDR-Forlag.

Hagan, J. and Dinovitzer, R. 1999. 'Collateral Consequences of Imprisonment for Children, Communities, and Prisoners', in Tonry, M. and Petersilia, J. (eds.) *Prisons. Crime and Justice: A Review of Research* vol. 126, 121–62. Chicago: University of Chicago Press.

Hagan, J. and Foster, H. 2015. 'Mass Imprisonment and Its Consequences', in Wright, J. D. (ed.) *International Encyclopedia of the Social & Behavioral Sciences*. (2nd ed.). 696–701. Amsterdam: Elsevier.

Hirsch, A. von and Ashworth, A. (eds.) 2000. *Principled Sentencing. Readings on Theory and Policy*. Oxford: Hart Publishing.

Jardine, C. 2015. *Constructing Family in the Context of Imprisonment: A study of Prisoners and their Families in Scotland*. PhD thesis, University of Edinburgh.

Jewkes, Y. (ed.) 2007. *Handbook on Prisons*. Cullompton: Willan publishing.

Jewkes, Y., Bennet, J., and Crewe, B. (eds.) 2016. *Handbook on Prisons*. Basingstoke: Palgrave.

Justitsministeriets Forskningskontor. 2016. 'Tryghed og holdning til politi og retssystem. Justitsministeriet'. Justits Ministeriet, January. Available at: http://justitsministeriet.dk/sites/default/files/media/Arbejdsomraader/Forskning/Forskningsrapporter/2016/tryghed_og_holdning_2016.pdf.

Lagoutte, S. 2016. 'The Right to Respect for Family Life of Children of Imprisoned Parents'. *International Journal of Children's Rights*, 24(1), 204–30.

Liebling, A., and Arnold, H. 2004. *Prisons and their Moral Performance: A Study of Values, Quality, and Prison Life*. Oxford: Oxford University Press.

Liebling, A., Maruna, S., and McAra, L. (eds.) 2017. *The Oxford Handbook of Criminology*. Oxford: Oxford University Press.

Madsen, M. R. and Verschraegen, G. 2013. 'Making Human Rights Intelligible: An Introduction to a Sociology of Human Rights', in Madsen, M. R. and Verschraegen, G. (eds.) *Making Human Rights Intelligible: Towards a Sociology of Human Rights*. 1–22. Oxford: Oxford University Press.

Maguire, M., Morgan, R. and Reiner, R. (eds.) 2012. *The Oxford Handbook of Criminology*. Oxford: Oxford University Press.

Mathiesen, T. 2006. *Prison on Trial*. Winchester: Waterside.

Miller, H. V. and Barnes, J. C. 2015. 'The Association Between Parental Incarceration and Health, Education, and Economic Outcomes in Young Adulthood'. *American Journal of Criminal Justice*, 40, 765–84.

Muller, C. and Wildeman, C. 2013. 'Punishment and Inequality', in Simon, J. and Sparks, R. (eds.) *The SAGE Handbook of Punishment and Society*. 169–85. London: Sage.

Murray, J. 2006. *Parental Imprisonment: Effects on Children's Antisocial Behaviour and Mental Health through the Life-course*. DPhil dissertation, Institute of Criminology, University of Cambridge.

Murray, J. and Farrington, D. P. 2008. 'The Effects of Parental Imprisonment on Children'. *Crime and Justice*, 37(1), 133–206.

Olaussen, L. P. 2014. 'Concordance between Actual Level of Punishment and Punishments Suggested by Lay People—But with Less Use of Imprisonment'. *Bergen Journal of Criminal Law and Criminal Justice*, 2(1), 69–99.

Oldrup, H., Frederiksen, S., Henze-Pedersen, S., and Olsen, R. 2017. *Indsat Far. Udsat Barn? Hverdagsliv og Trivsel Blandt Børn af Fængslede*. Copenhagen: SFI.

Pratt, J. 2007. *Penal Populism*. Abingdon: Routledge.

Roberts, J., Stalans, L., Indermaur, D., and Hough, M. 2003. *Penal Populism and Public Opinion*. Oxford: Oxford University Press.

Robinson, P. H. 2014. 'The Proper Role of Community in Determining Criminal Liability and Punishment', in Ryberg, J. and Roberts, J. (eds.) *Popular Punishment. On the Normatice Significance of Public Opinion*. New York: Oxford University Press.

Ryberg, J. 2006. *Retsfølelsen. En bog om straf og etik*. København: Roskilde.

Ryberg, J. and Roberts, J. (eds.) 2014. *Popular Punishment. On the Normatice Significance of Public Opinion*. New York: Oxford University Press.

Smith, P. S. 2014. *When the Innocent are Punished: The Children of Imprisoned Parents*. New York: Palgrave Macmillan.

Smith, P. S. 2015. 'Reform and Research—Re-connecting Prison and Society in the 21st Century'. *International Journal for Crime, Justice and Social Democracy*, 4(1), 33–49.

Sparks, R., Bottoms, A., and Hay, W. 1996. *Prisons and the Problem of Order*. London: Clarendon Press.

Tankebe, J. and Liebling, A. (eds.) 2013. *Legitimacy and Criminal Justice. An International Exploration*. Oxford: Oxford University Press.

van Zyl Smit, D. 2013. 'Legitimacy and the Development of International Standards for Punishment', in Tankebe, J. and Liebling, A. (eds.) *Legitimacy and Criminal Justice. An International Exploration*. 267–92. Oxford: Oxford University Press.

Wakefield, S. and Wildeman, C. 2014. *Children of the Prison Boom: Mass Incarceration and the Future of American Inequality*. Oxford: Oxford University Press

Weber, L., Fishwick, E., and Marmo, M. 2014. *Crime, Justice and Human Rights*. Abingdon: Routledge.

9

'The sins and traumas of fathers and mothers should not be visited on their children'

The Rights of Children When a Primary Carer is Sentenced to Imprisonment in the Criminal Courts

Shona Minson

Introduction

This chapter focuses on the rights of dependent children when their parents are sentenced for criminal offences. The chapter begins with an introduction to the harms which children suffer as a consequence of the imprisonment of their parents and in particular their mothers or primary carers. The chapter considers whether sentencers, when sentencing primary carers of dependent children in England and Wales, take into account the impacts of a custodial sentence on those children. It examines the application of the United Nations Convention on the Rights of the Child 1989 to children whose parents are facing imprisonment due to criminal convictions. The way in which the rights of a child to non-discrimination (Article 2), primary consideration (Article 3), participation (Article 12), and special assistance when separated from a parent (Article 20) are given consideration in adult sentencing proceedings is examined and this is contrasted with the treatment of children separated from their parents by the state in proceedings under section 31 of the Children Act 1989. The approach of the South African Constitutional Court in the case of *M v The State* [2007] illustrates the way in which children's rights can be upheld within the adult sentencing process. The chapter concludes with a discussion of the implications of disregarding the rights of children rather than adopting an approach which upholds their rights.

The impacts of parental imprisonment on dependent children

Since the 1980s concern has been expressed that the children of prisoners are adversely affected by their parents' imprisonment. Their fast track to crime and delinquency has been alleged and children of imprisoned parents are said to be as much as six times more likely than other similarly situated children to enter the criminal justice system (Barnhill and Dressel, 1991 in Sandifer and Kurth, 2000). Shaw referred to the pain inflicted on children by the sentencer of their father as 'institutionalised child abuse' (Shaw, 1987, 64). There is consensus that parental imprisonment is linked to harms or disadvantages to children although 'a thorough understanding of the causal nature of this does not currently exist' (Flynn, 2013, 216; Travis and Waul, 2004, 17). It is of course important to note that there are children whose lives are improved by the imprisonment of their parent, but for many more children the loss of a parent is experienced negatively, as no matter the strength or quality of the relationship the parent and child bond is usually one of a child's primary attachments (Wakefield and Wildeman, 2014). In this chapter I will not rehearse the extensive evidence of the harms caused to children by parental imprisonment, as the introduction to the volume provides an overview and there is discussion of the harms throughout this volume (see Arditti, this volume; Lanskey et al., this volume; Loucks and Loureiro, this volume; Knudsen, this volume; Donson and Parkes, this volume). Instead, I will examine the situation of children whose mother is imprisoned in England and Wales, before considering the court's understanding of the implications of sentencing a child's primary carer to imprisonment, and the way in which this intersects with children's rights.

The reason for focusing on maternal imprisonment is that mothers are more likely to be the primary carers of children. When a mother goes to prison in England and Wales very few children remain in the family home (Caddle and Crisp, 1997), whilst only 9 per cent are cared for by their fathers (Corston, 2007, 20), in contrast with the situation of children of imprisoned fathers who generally remain with their mothers in the family home (Boswell and Wedge, 2002). A child with an imprisoned mother is likely to suffer more negative effects of parental imprisonment than a child with an imprisoned father (Dallaire, 2007b; Murray and Farrington, 2008; Murray, 2010; Gilham, 2012), and there is evidence to suggest that although fewer mothers are imprisoned, the threshold at which their absence has an impact upon their children is lower than that of fathers (Kruttschnitt, 2010). The negative effects of maternal imprisonment may also be increased for children due to the social constructions of motherhood and the perceptions of mothers who are involved in criminal activity, resulting in both harsher punishments of women and greater stigmatization of their children (Hagan and Foster, 2012). As with children of imprisoned fathers, children of imprisoned mothers are not a homogeneous group and although some general patterns have emerged, there can be variations in research findings. For example, a recent study in the United States found that for children most likely to experience maternal incarceration it had a null or even positive effect (Wildeman et al., 2016), perhaps because those children have the protective factors of pre-existing secure attachments, social support, and hopefulness (Dallaire, 2007a), or in those families the family caregiving processes are of higher quality or are less likely to be disrupted by maternal incarceration, or the most disadvantaged children are the most resilient, although this should 'never be an excuse to "do nothing"' (Arditti, 2015, 9). Some children have pre-existing promoting factors which intensify the negative impacts of maternal imprisonment (Dallaire, 2007b), and the complex 'interacting trajectories followed by parents, alternative caregivers, and children across time' (Parke and Clarke-Steward, 2001) inevitably produce variability. The literature from the United States and Europe does however link maternal imprisonment to a wide variety of negative consequences for children, diminished future outcomes due to disrupted primary attachments in childhood (Dallaire, 2007b), disrupted education (Dallaire and Wilson, 2010; Cho, 2011; Hagan and Foster, 2012), difficulty in following a 'pro-social' pathway (Hirschi, 1969; Fox and Benson, 2000; Green and Scholes, 2004), a very high aggregate, in number and range, of worrisome adversities and risk factors (Cunningham and Baker, 2003; Dallaire, 2007b; Miller, 2014), a greater risk of future criminality or antisocial behaviour when a mother rather than a father is imprisoned (Murray and Farrington, 2008), and care arrangements which may not be in the child's best interests (Caddle and Crisp, 1997; Poehlmann, 2005).

The first major research study on the children of imprisoned mothers in England and Wales (Caddle and Crisp, 1997) found that for 85 per cent of the children it was the first time they had been separated from their mother. During the imprisonment, 44 per cent of the children had behavioural problems, 30 per cent became withdrawn, 27 per cent had problems sleeping, 26 per cent developed health problems, 22 per cent had problems with eating, 18 per cent began to experience nighttime enuresis, and 17 per cent had problems with their friendships. The problems increased when children were separated from their siblings, and became more serious, or more apparent, the older the child. When children experienced a change of home due to maternal imprisonment, 33 per cent had a problem with the new home and 20 per cent a problem with the new area. With children over 10 years of age, 17 per cent responded to their mother's imprisonment by 'mixing with the wrong crowd', with 4 per cent drinking alcohol and 3 per cent taking drugs. Thirty-one per cent had to change school and for a third of the children that was problematic both for schoolwork and attendance. Twenty-nine of the mothers had children who were living by themselves as a consequence of the mother's imprisonment, with 10 per cent of those children caring for younger siblings. Most children lost their principal carer and one-third, their only carer (Caddle and Crisp, 1997).

The most recent study on children of imprisoned mothers in England and Wales (Minson, 2017) found that children continue to experience the same physical, relational, and social difficulties when their mother is imprisoned. A child experiences physical changes in carer, home, and education as they lose their mother's physical presence and in parallel with her change of physical location, they too undergo a change of residence. The mother and child relationship becomes constrained by the regulations of the prison and their other relationships are altered both inside and outside the family, and third, the children are socially marginalized because of the negative attributes, which attach to the label 'children of imprisoned parents'. This has consequences for their mental health and social identity (Link and Phelan, 2001, 287–94) and contributes to the secrecy which they build around themselves (Knudsen, this volume), and the 'confounding grief' which they experience (Minson, 2017). Every aspect of a child's life is affected by the imprisonment of their primary career, and the next section of the chapter examines the consideration of these impacts within maternal sentencing decisions in England and Wales.

Consideration of dependent children in the sentencing process in England and Wales

Sentencers in England and Wales have two main sources of authority when they make sentencing decisions, sentencing guidelines, and sentencing authorities (case law). In 2004 the 'Overarching Principles, Seriousness' guideline was issued by the Sentencing Guidelines Council, and it referenced section 166(1) of the Criminal Justice Act 2003 which makes provision for a sentencer to take account of any matters that 'in the opinion of the court, are relevant in mitigation of sentence', thus giving permission for dependents to be considered if a judge believes it to be relevant, and for the sentence to be reduced accordingly. In 2011, the 'Assault Definitive Guideline' was the first sentencing guideline to include 'Sole or primary carer for dependent relatives' in the list of 'Factors reducing seriousness or reflecting personal mitigation' (Sentencing Council, 2011). This factor has been included in every subsequent guideline and can be taken into account as a mitigating factor when prescribing sentence. In 2017, the 'Imposition of Community and Custodial Sentences: Definitive Guideline 2017' stated that:

For offenders on the cusp of custody, imprisonment should not be imposed where there would be an impact on dependants which would make a custodial sentence disproportionate to achieving the aims of sentencing.

Additionally included in the list of factors which may make it appropriate for a sentence to suspend a custodial sentence is that: 'Immediate custody will result in significant harmful impact upon others.'

Turning to case law, a defendant's primary care responsibilities, and the duties of the court to consider them, have been specifically addressed in a series of Court of Appeal decisions. There are four principles to follow, first, the sentencing of a parent for a criminal offence engages the Article 8 right to family life of both the parent and the child, as the right is not lost automatically by reason of criminal conviction (*R (on the application of P and Q) v Secretary of State for the Home Department* [2001] paragraph 78). Second, any interference by the state with a person's right to family life must be in response to a pressing social need, and proportionate to the legitimate aim pursued (*R v Secretary of State* [2001], paragraph 87). Third, the more serious the interference the more compelling the justification must be, and it cannot be much more serious than the act of separating a mother from a very young child (*R v Secretary of State* [2001], paragraph 78 (iv); *R (on the application of Amanda Aldous) v Dartford Magistrates Court* [2011]; *R v Petherick* [2012]). Fourth, non-custodial sentences are preferable for women with dependent children, with custodial sentences to be considered when the offence is serious or violent or the woman represents a continuing danger. Even when that is the case, a custodial sentence should only be given after considering the best interests of the child or children, whilst ensuring that appropriate provision has been made for their care (United Nations 'Bangkok Rules', 2010; UNCRC, 1989, Article 3). Subsequent decisions have provided clear guidance on the application of the above principles. The sentencing court must obtain sufficient information to allow it to balance the punishment of the offender against the impact of the offender's punishment on the child, and it is the court's responsibility to seek further information if necessary to allow the sentencer to make a properly informed judgment (*R v Bishop* [2011]). The case of *R v Petherick* [2012] set out the process the court should follow in such cases. Where the right to family life applies, the court should ask first, is there an interference with family life? Second, is the interference in accordance with law and in pursuit of a legitimate aim, and third, is the interference proportionate given the balance between various factors (*R v Petherick* [2012], paragraph 18)? In a case which is on the threshold between a custodial and non-custodial or suspended sentence, the impact on a dependent child can tip the scales, and a proportionate sentence can become disproportionate (*R v Petherick* [2012], paragraph 22). Finally, the welfare of the child must be a primary consideration of the court *(ZH (Tanzania) (FC) Appellant v Secretary of State for the Home Department* [2011], paragraphs 25–6; see also Minson et al., 2015).

It is clear from a preliminary investigation of case law and sentencing guidelines that judges ought to consider the welfare of child dependents in adult sentencing cases, but on a review of a sentencing appeals on which data was available, heard in the Court of Appeal between 2003 and 2011 by mothers who had been sentenced to imprisonment, in twenty-one of the twenty-seven cases in which sentence was reduced, the mitigation of sentence due to dependent children was a specified factor leading to that reduction. This indicated that the lower courts were not conducting the correct balancing exercise and were passing sentences of imprisonment on mothers which were disproportionate when the harm the children would suffer due to maternal imprisonment was considered alongside the appropriate punishment for the crime (Minson and Condry, 2015). Epstein (2012) found, in a similar review of sentencing decisions, that sentencers were not conducting the Article 8 balancing exercise as required by the case law.

In recent research it was found that members of the Crown Court judiciary had a very limited understanding of the consequences which flow to children from the imprisonment of their mothers (Minson, 2017). The majority of those interviewed thought that other than separation from their parent and perhaps their siblings, children did not suffer harm unless they were taken into local authority care, were very young, or had a 'good' mother. They made no reference to issues of education, behavioural problems, attachment issues, overcrowded housing, unsuitable carers, anxiety, stigma, or stress (Minson, 2017).

The next section of the chapter focuses on the universally held rights of children that have particular application for those whose parents are sentenced in the criminal courts. The United Nations Convention on the Rights of the Child (UNCRC 1989) has been ratified by the United Kingdom, and its Articles form the main body of rights to be considered. In addition, Article 8 of the European Convention on Human Rights has been incorporated into the Human Rights Act 1998 and provides a right to family life for all citizens. It is important to note however that England 'experiences an ambivalent cultural relationship to fundamental rights' (Lazarus, 2004), which extends to the bodies which enforce those rights, most notably the European Court of Human Rights with which the United Kingdom has had an uncomfortable relationship since its inception (Madsen, 2016). The UNCRC has been ratified by the United Kingdom, but the seriousness with which it is regarded differs even between countries within the United Kingdom. Although international conventions are regarded as 'hard law' in most countries, in England the view seems to be taken that they are persuasive rather than binding, and they are attributed the same status as general comments which are non-binding 'soft law' (Fottrell, 2015). For example, the Scottish Government is working towards full incorporation and implementation of the UNCRC 1989 whilst the English Government has failed to implement the recommendations of the Universal Periodic Review of Human Rights (Loucks and Loureiro, this volume), and seems to act under a belief that the Children Act 1989 provides all the protection needed by children, despite the fact that it only applies to proceedings taking place in the family courts (Hansard, 2010; Minson, 2017). After a number of bruising confrontations it appears that the European Court of Human Rights is giving England and Wales more discretion in the application of domestic law, but this has had the consequence that the decisions of the court are disregarded (Madsen, 2016). Despite this context of ambivalence the UNCRC 1989 should have application in England and Wales, as the 'minimum standards for the treatment of children' (Donson and Parkes, this volume), and the next section of the chapter examines the Articles of the Convention which directly relate to the treatment of children whose parents are sentenced in the criminal courts.

The rights of children whose primary carers are sentenced in the criminal courts

Article 8 of the Human Rights Act 1998 states that everyone has the right to respect for his private and family life, and this right can only be interfered with under certain conditions which include 'the prevention of disorder or crime, for the protection of health or morals, or for the protection of the rights and freedoms of others'. There has been very little mention of the rights of children of prisoners in the academic and practitioner literature since the ratification of the UNCRC 1989. It has been suggested that legislative bodies should consider the rights of these children, but these suggestions have not been given further consideration or implementation (Child Right's Development Unit, 1994; Carlen and Worrall, 2004; Silvestri, 2006; Lagoutte, 2016; Smith, 2016). Within the UNCRC 1989, Article 9 states that children have a right to live with their parents but that right can be overridden if separation is in the child's best interests as determined by competent authorities 'in accordance with applicable laws and procedures', but in UK-focused discussions about the legislative implications of Article 9 children of prisoners are not included in the lists of children to whom this article applies (Department for Children, Schools and Families, 2007). When children of prisoners are referred to it is usually with respect to maintaining relationship with a parent in prison, and not with reference to their rights under the UNCRC 1989 to non-discrimination (Article 2), primary consideration (Article 3), participation (Article 12), and special assistance when separated from a parent (Article 20) (Van Bueren, 1995; Freeman, 1996; Fottrell, 2000; Franklin, 2001; LeBlanc, 2005; Fortin, 2009; Choudry and Herring, 2010; MacDonald, 2011).

The judges in the case of *R v Petherick* [2012] did not make a determination regarding the relevance of Article 3 to adult sentencing decisions but did refer to the case of *ZH v Secretary of State for the Home Department* [2011], the judgment of which states that Article 3 of the UNCRC applies to *any* court in England and Wales whose actions will have the consequence of separating a child from their parent (paragraph 26), and therefore this ought to mean that in the criminal courts when a parent is sentenced, the welfare of any children that she has should be a 'primary consideration' of the court. There is, in existence already, a mechanism by which a judge can gain information about the child's needs and welfare: a Pre-Sentence Report can be requested from the probation service, such a report potentially providing to the court information about the defendant's background, family circumstances, and family responsibilities. However, research has found that judges are unaware of their Article 3 obligations, and do not consistently request Pre-Sentence Reports (Epstein, 2012; Minson, 2013, 2017). Therefore a child may be separated from her primary or sole carer by a judge in the criminal courts who, in some instances, may not even be aware of the existence of the dependent child, and in other instances, although aware, regards it to be of such limited significance that no mention is made of the child in the sentencing remarks and the child is not considered at all in the sentencing decision (Minson and Condry, 2015). The right of a child to have their welfare treated as a primary consideration in all actions concerning them does not seem to be upheld within the adult criminal sentencing process.

Article 12 of the CRC 1989 requires a child's views to be heard in any judicial proceedings 'affecting' them, with due weight then accorded to those views. The issue of whether adult criminal sentencing is a proceeding 'affecting' a child is discussed in the *Implementation Handbook of the Convention on the Rights of the Child*:

'Any judicial proceedings affecting the child' covers a very wide range of court hearings, including all civil proceedings such as divorce, custody, care and adoption proceedings, name changing, judicial applications relating to place of residence, religion, education, disposal of money and so forth, judicial decision making on nationality, immigration and refugee status and criminal proceedings, it also covers States' involvement in international courts. Arguably, it covers criminal prosecutions of parents, the outcome of which can affect children dramatically. (Hodgkin and Newell, 2002)

It would seem that it is intended that criminal sentencing of dependent parents is a proceeding 'affecting' a child to which Article 12 applies, but it is not the practice of the probation officers who author Pre-Sentence Reports to speak directly with children of a defendant in order to ascertain their views. There is no legislative requirement within national laws for the court to give consideration to the child's views, and therefore in many cases children are separated from their parent without the court giving regard to the child's wishes, feelings, and needs, or the effect on the child of any possible change in circumstances which might result from their decision.

Despite the requirement of Article 20 that any child who is without their family is 'entitled to special protection and assistance provided by the State', and the obligation on the state to provide such children with alternative care, and the availability of a mechanism by which the state could meet that duty (Children Act 1989, section 17; Children Act 2004), children of imprisoned parents are not given special protection or assistance by the state during the period in which they are separated from their primary carer. When a custodial sentence is given it is common for no preparation to have been made for the separation between parent and child. Men and women are not systematically asked if they have dependent children and it is often the case that the state only becomes aware of the existence of these children when the families who take on their care contact the local authority to ask for help. The Corston Report, a review of women with particular vulnerabilities in the criminal justice system, found that in a group of 1,400 women serving a first sentence in Holloway Prison, forty-two women did not know who was looking after their children (Corston, 2007). This is in clear breach of Article 20 of the CRC 1989.

It is apparent that both in the literature and in practice children are barely visible when parental separation takes place due to criminal sentencing, and their status as rights holders is entirely overlooked. Thus children who may lose their primary or sole carer (in one third of cases when a mother is imprisoned she is the sole carer for children (Social Exclusion Unit, 2002)) are deprived of the rights to have their welfare considered, to be heard, and to receive special care and protection from the state. Even if it is argued that the CRC 1989 is persuasive rather than binding, the cases on the separation of children from their parents, when held alongside the state duty of care towards children which has existed for centuries in England and Wales (Minson, 2017) and the section 17 provisions of the Children Act 1989 which obligate local authorities to care for 'children in the need', demonstrate that the state does have a duty of care towards children of imprisoned mothers, arising from both statute and rights. This duty requires the state to consider the welfare of children of defendant parents within sentencing decisions and following their separation from their primary carer if she is sent to prison. Such disregard for the rights of children whose parents face imprisonment within the sentencing process has the appearance of discriminatory behaviour by the state, in breach of its obligations under Article 2 of the CRC (1989):

2(1). States Parties shall respect and ensure the rights set forth in the present Convention to each child within their jurisdiction without discrimination of any kind, irrespective of the child's or his or her parent's or legal guardian's race, colour, sex, language, religion, political or other opinion, national, ethnic or social origin, property, disability, birth or other status.

2(2). States Parties shall take all appropriate measures to ensure that the child is protected against all forms of discrimination or punishment on the basis of the status, activities, expressed opinions, or beliefs of the child's parents, legal guardians, or family members.

The Article 2 right to protection from discrimination is referred to directly in conjunction with children whose parents are accused of criminal behaviour in *The Implementation Handbook for the Convention on the Rights of the Child*:

> In its examination of reports, the Committee has noted a variety of examples of the child suffering discrimination ... Implementation requires States to ensure that any existing Constitution, relevant legislation, court decisions and administrative policy and practice comply with this principle. For example, are 'all appropriate measures' taken to protect children from discrimination or punishment when their parents are subject to action on the ground of criminal behaviour? (Hodgkin and Newell, 2002)

It is my contention that the state in England and Wales is in breach of Article 2 both procedurally and in practice as there is differentiated treatment between children separated from their parents by the state in proceedings under section 31 of the Children Act 1989 in the family courts and children separated from their parents by the state in criminal sentencing proceedings. In proceedings under section 31 of the Children Act 1989 children are represented by lawyers and a guardian ad litem, their best interests are the 'paramount consideration' of the court under section 1 of the Children Act 1989, and they have the legislative protection of that act. This contrasts with children whose existence may not even have been acknowledged by the court sentencing their parent for criminal acts:

> There is a lack of consciousness on the part of both the judiciary and policy makers about this issue and consequently the state is discriminating against a group of children by its failure to recognise their existence and their rights in court proceedings and by its failure to offer them protection and special assistance when they are separated from their mother. (Minson, 2017, 175)

Consideration of dependent children in the sentencing process in other jurisdictions

In a number of countries, unique punishments are available for parents who are primary carers of dependent children. In Germany, mothers can have any sentence less than two years suspended, and probation can last for between two and five years. In Italy mothers with children up to the age of 10 are permitted in some circumstances to serve their sentence at home in order to look after their child. The country which has most notably altered its sentencing practices to give regard to the children of adult defendants is South Africa, which changed its treatment of children whose primary carer was before the court as a defendant following the landmark case of *M v the State* [2007], heard in the Constitutional Court of South Africa. Justice Albie Sachs gave the leading judgment on an appeal to determine whether the sentencing courts had paid appropriate attention to the constitutional provision that in all matters concerning children, the children's interests should be paramount. The defendant was a 35-year-old single mother of three boys aged 16, 12, and 8, who was convicted of a large number of fraud offences and sentenced to imprisonment. She appealed the decision on the basis that section 28 of the Constitution required sentencing courts 'to give specific and independent consideration to the impact that a custodial sentence in respect of a primary caregiver would have on minor children' (*M v State* [2007], 4). The National Director of Public Prosecution refuted this claim, replying that the current procedures in the courts already took account of the interests of children (*M v State* [2007]). The section 28 requirement of the Constitution stemmed from the CRC 1989 and the African Charter on the Rights and Welfare of the Child 1990. It required all courts to consider children's rights and embedded the paramountcy principle in law. It was not unlike the obligations that currently exist in England and Wales under the CRC 1989 and the Children Act 1989. Sachs J acknowledged the broad-reaching nature of the provision and stated in paragraph 15 of his judgment that 'statutes must be interpreted and the common law developed in a manner which favours protecting and advancing the interests of children', and that courts must function 'in a manner which at all times follows due respect for children's rights'. In his judgment he emphasized the citizenship of children:

If a child is to be constitutionally imagined as an individual with a distinctive personality, and not merely as a miniature adult waiting to reach full size, he or she cannot be treated as a mere extension of his or her parents, umbilically destined to sink or swim with them. The unusually comprehensive and emancipatory character of section 28 presupposes that in our new dispensation the sins and traumas of fathers and mothers should not be visited on their children. (*M v State* [2007], paragraph 18)

He referred to the state's duty to minimize the harms which children suffer when their parents are unable to care for them properly:

It follows that section 28 requires the law to make best efforts to avoid, where possible, any breakdown of family life or parental care that may threaten to put children at increased risk. Similarly, in situations where rupture of the family becomes inevitable, the State is obliged to minimise the consequent negative effect on children as far as it can. (*M v State* [2007], 20)

The counsel for the state argued, as it would be argued in the courts of England and Wales, that the impact of children was already taken account of by looking at the crime, the criminal, and the community:

She contended that sentencing courts as a matter of routine consider the personal circumstances of the criminal, including their parental obligations, and weigh them against the gravity of the crime and its impact on the community. Hence, it was said, no change in present sentencing practice is called for. (*M v State* [2007], 29)

The 'amicus' acting on behalf of the children responded to that statement:

A child of a primary caregiver is not a 'circumstance', but an individual whose interests needed to be considered independently. The weight to be given to those interests and the manner in which they were to be protected would depend on the particular circumstances. But ... these interests were not to be swallowed up by and subsumed into the consideration of the culpability and circumstances of the primary caregiver. (*M v State* [2007], 30)

Sachs J. addressed the question of whether such consideration of children gave an unfair advantage of leniency to parents. He made it quite clear that this was not the case. It was not the punishment of the parent for wrongdoing which violated the rights of the child, rather it was the form which that punishment took which could violate the child's rights:

The purpose of emphasising the duty of the sentencing court to acknowledge the interests of the children, then, is not to permit errant parents unreasonably to avoid appropriate punishment. Rather, it is to protect the innocent children as much as is reasonably possible in the circumstances from avoidable harm. (*M v State* [2007], 35)

Ultimately the court decided that insufficient attention had been paid to the children's interests in the lower courts, the appeal was allowed, and the case set an important precedent. It has been followed in other South African cases including the case of a father who pleaded guilty to the culpable homicide of his wife and was sentenced to 'periodic imprisonment of 2000 hours', meaning that he was imprisoned every weekend between 6pm Friday and 2pm Sunday, so that he could look after his children and continue to work and provide income for his family (*S v Ntikedzeni* [2011]). The South African case law very clearly addresses the concerns which have been raised in the jurisdiction of England and Wales about the adoption of a more intentional focus on the best interests of the child. I interviewed Sachs J in December 2014 and discussed with him the concerns of judiciary that such a change would make them a 'welfare court' rather than a criminal court. He articulated the burden which falls upon the sentencing court in relation to dependents:

> In some cases, in rare cases it [consideration of the child's interests] can actually make a difference whether to go to jail. It can be a tipping point which encourages a non-custodial sentence ... I think it happens and it should be acknowledged and I think it should become part and parcel of the jurisprudence. In other cases if you know that the children exist, they've been very dependent, it's going to be a shock, then it's not for the judge to make arrangements but just to ensure that the relevant authorities are informed ... and you can't say I wash my hands of it. State action is producing that result. A necessary result but the state action must also encompass the ripple effect in as much as it relates to children ... the prosecution have a duty too. It's a serious part of their function, to ensure that the children who are going to lose their primary carer as a result of state action initiated by the prosecution are not left high and dry... I explain to the judges they are not being called on themselves to provide protection to the children. They are called upon to ensure that the impact on the children will be dealt with ...They are all officers of the court and the courts are the upper guardians of children. (Sachs, 2014)

The way forward, extending punishment or extending justice?

The justice system in England and Wales is based on liberal rather than communitarian values, and 'the institutional framework of modern penology tends to narrow our perceptions of the phenomenon and obscure the social ramifications of punishment' (Garland, 1990, 1). Liberal theories of justice and punishment focus on the individual, and are evident in the binary nature of sentencing processes in England and Wales which regard the assessment of guilt and the punishment of the offender as a matter between the state and the offender. It is only relatively recently that victims were given regard within the process. For other affected third parties to be taken into consideration within the justice system liberal thinking will have to give way to a communitarian understanding of justice and punishment which acknowledges that punishment has wider societal implications. A communitarian conception 'recognises human identity as a fundamentally social construction' (Lacey, 2003, 186), and a communitarian approach to punishment would:

> give real consideration to the inevitable suffering of those who are materially and emotionally involved with prisoners, people whose position is generally ignored in both theoretical and policy debates. In abandoning a totally individualistic perspective, we become aware of the nature of imprisonment as a penal measure that inevitably leads to punishment of innocent parties. (Lacey, 2003, 192)

The imprisonment of a particular population, primary carers of dependent children, has wide-reaching implications which will ultimately reduce social cohesion. These issues are currently unaddressed within a punishment framework focusing on the individual, but they are disregarded at a cost to communities:

> If the proper social functions of punishment have to do with the maintenance of and respect for fundamental community values, then any inhumanity in a prison system must be seen as directly, both symbolically and instrumentally, counterproductive. (Lacey, 2003, 190)

Children whose mothers are in prison speak about their loss of trust in the criminal justice system, including the police, and it is apparent that many children lose their faith in civic society, and no longer feel part of the community (Minson, 2017; Jardine, this volume). Secondary stigmatization causes them to isolate themselves from others, as they feel they can no longer trust other people. This lack of trust is problematic at a societal level. Barker describes trust as 'a basic building block of society' which is:

> intimately tied to norms of reciprocity, the practice of mutual exchange between interdependent parties. It holds societies together by making cooperation possible. By having confidence in others, believing that others will not take advantage of one's vulnerability (Misztal, 2011), and engaging in reciprocity, trust eases our more mundane daily exchanges and enables more complex forms of collaboration across all areas of social, economic, political and private life. (Barker, 2016, 82)

I would suggest that children of imprisoned mothers lose their confidence in others, and are taken advantage of because of their vulnerability (Misztal, 2011). Children are one of the least powerful and most vulnerable groups in our society, and therefore when their needs are not met, or their rights are overridden, they do not have the standing to address that. Consequently, they no longer trust that if they do no wrong they will be protected. In addition, the suffering of unfair and unjustified hardship may impact upon a child in ways which will influence their future responses to the state and their community, and it is arguable that their loss of trust and enhanced vulnerability may be contributing factors to their longer-term outcomes. The dangers of allowing children to experience punishing circumstances as a consequence of their mother's imprisonment are partially known. The likelihood of future criminogenic behaviour is increased (Murray and Farrington, 2008), as is the likelihood of experiencing addiction and mental health problems (Tasca et al., 2014). If punishment is intended to promote social good then consequential effects which detract from that reduce the value of punishment.

A child who suffers the loss of their mother due to her imprisonment is unlikely to take from that experience positive understandings of the need for wrongdoing to be punished. Instead, their suffering will obfuscate all else:

> Harsh punishment of a child frequently produces strong emotional reactions in that child even while the undesired behaviour is being suppressed. Hostility, fear, screaming and crying are not unusual responses to harsh punishments. One problem is that these emotional reactions may interfere with the learning of competing behaviours and the extinction of the undesirable behavior.... we can expect the hostility and fear that one experiences while being punished to become classically conditioned responses to all sorts of characteristics associated with the punishment,—the person, the setting, the institution. This may make future positive reinforcements very difficult to deliver. (Huesmann and Podolski, 2003)

As more children experience the imprisonment of their parents, it might be wise to heed the warnings coming from the United States about the societal impacts of mass imprisonment of adults (Wakefield and Wildeman, 2014) alongside the insights from psychology. Reflecting on these should cause us to question the value of imprisoning primary carers. Not only is there a risk that the children develop 'hostility and fear ... to all sorts of characteristics associated with the punishment—the person, the setting, the institution' (Huesmann and Podolski, 2003), but the imprisoned parents, who feel the pain of their children's suffering, also develop hostility towards the criminal justice system. By ignoring these costs it is likely that our society will gain an ever-increasing number of disenfranchized citizens (Lacey and Pickard, 2015), which in turn will weaken our communities. In addition, we must not forget that our state is actively discriminating against a group of children whom it has a specific duty to protect (CRC 1989, Article 2).

It is time for change. The state in England and Wales needs to recognize that it is currently in breach of its duty of care towards a population of its most vulnerable citizens through its denial of Article 2, 3, 12, and 20 rights to children of primary carers who are before the courts for sentencing. Punishment is not an act which applies only to an individual, and in order to prevent longer-term individual and societal harm, the rights of children whose parents are sentenced must no longer be ignored.

References

Arditti, J. 2015. 'Family Process Perspective on the Heterogeneous Effects of Maternal Incarceration on Child Wellbeing'. *Criminology and Public Policy*, 14(1), 1–14.
Barker, V. 2016. 'Civic Repair and Penal Reform, The Role of the State in Rebuilding Trust', in Farrall, S., Goldson, B., Loader, I., and Dockley, A. (eds.) *Justice and Penal Reform: Re-shaping the Penal Landscape*. 81–98. Abingdon: Routledge.
Barnhill, S. and Dressel, P. 1991. 'Three Generations at Economic Risk When Daughters go to Prison'. Conference Paper at the Association of Black Sociologists, August, Cincinnati, OH.
Boswell, G. and Wedge, P. 2002. *Imprisoned Fathers and Their Children*. London: Jessica Kingsley.
Caddle, D. and Crisp, D. 1997. *Imprisoned Women and Mothers*. Home Office Research Study 162. London: Home Office.
Carlen, P. and Worrall, A. 2004. 'Analysing Women's Imprisonment', in *UK Agenda for Children, a Systematic Analysis of the Extent to Which Law, Policy and Practice in the UK Complies with the Principles and Standards Contained in the UN Convention on the Rights of the Child*. Cullompton: Willan.
Child Right's Development Unit. 1994. *Child Right's Development Unit*. London.
Cho, R. M. 2011. 'Understanding the Mechanism Behind Maternal Imprisonment and Adolescent School Dropout'. *Family Relations*, 60(3), 272–89.
Choudry, S. and Herring, J. 2010. *European Human Rights and Family Law*. Oxford: Hart.
Corston, J. 2007. *The Corston Report, A Review of Women with Particular Vulnerabilities in the Criminal Justice System*. London: Home Office.
Cunningham, A. and Baker, L. 2003. *Waiting for Mommy, Giving a Voice to the Hidden Victims of Imprisonment*. Ottawa: National Crime Prevention Centre.
Dallaire, D. 2007a. 'Children with Incarcerated Mothers: Developmental Outcomes, Special Challenges and Recommendations'. *Journal of Applied Developmental Psychology*, 28(1), 15–24.
Dallaire, D. 2007b. 'Incarcerated Mothers and Fathers: A Comparison of Risks for Children and Families'. *Family Relations*, 56(5), 440–53.
Dallaire, D. and Wilson, L. 2010. 'The Relation of Exposure to Parental Criminal Activity, Arrest, and Sentencing to Children's Maladjustment'. *Journal of Child and Family Studies*, 19(4), 404–18.
Department for Children, Schools and Families and Ministry of Justice. 2007. *Children of Offenders Review*. London: DCSF/MOJ.
Epstein, R. 2012. 'Mothers in Prison: The Sentencing of Mothers and the Rights of their Child'. *Coventry Law Journal Special Issue Research Report*. Coventry, Coventry Law School.
Flynn, C. 2013. 'Understanding the Risk of Offending for the Children of Imprisoned Parents: A Review of the Evidence'. *Children and Youth Services Review*, 35(2), 213–17.
Fortin, J. 2009. *Children's Rights and the Developing Law*. Cambridge: Cambridge University Press.

Fottrell, D. 2000. *Revisiting Children's Rights*. The Hague: Kluwer Law International.
Fottrell, D. 2015. 'The UNCRC in the Supreme Court—The impact of SG v Secretary of State for Work and Pensions'. Family Law Week. Available at: http://www.familylawweek.co.uk/site.aspx?i=ed144937.
Fox, G. L. and Benson, M. L. 2000. *Families, Crime and Criminal Justice*. Amsterdam: Oxford, JAI.
Franklin, B. 2001. *The New Handbook of Children's Rights*. London: Routledge.
Freeman, M. 1996. *Children's Rights: A Comparative Perspective*. Aldershot: Dartmouth.
Garland, D. 1990. *Punishment and Modern Society: A Study in Social Theory*. Oxford: Clarendon Press.
Gilham, J. J. M. 2012. 'A Qualitative Study of Incarcerated Mothers' Perceptions of the Impact of Separation on their Children'. *Social Work in Public Health*, 27(1–2), 89–103.
Green, M. and Scholes, M. 2004. 'Education for What? Attachment, Culture and Society', in Green, M. and Scholes, M. (eds.) *Attachment and Human Survival*. 37–51, London: Karnac.
Hagan, J. and Foster, H. 2012. 'Children of the American Prison Generation, Student and School Spillover Effects of Incarcerating Mothers'. *Law & Society Review*, 46(1), 37–69.
Hansard, 2010. Written Ministerial Statement, Education, Children's Commissioner Review. Available at: https://www.theyworkforyou.com/wms/?id=2010-12-06a.5WS.1.
Hirschi, T. 1969. *Causes of Delinquency*. London: Transaction.
Hodgkin, R. and Newell, P. 2002. *Implementation Handbook for the Convention on the Rights of the Child*. New York: UNICEF.
Huesmann, L. R. and Podolski, C. L. 2003. 'A Psychological Perspective', S. McConville (ed.) *The Use of Punishment*. 55–88. Cullompton: Willan.
Kruttschnitt, C. 2010. 'The Paradox of Women's Imprisonment'. *Daedalus*, 139(3), 32–42.
Lacey, N. 2003. 'Penal Theory and Penal Practice: A Communitarian Approach', in McConville, S. (ed.) *The Use of Punishment*. 175–98. Cullompton: Willan.
Lacey, N. and Pickard, H. 2015. 'To Blame or to Forgive? Reconciling Punishment and Forgiveness in Criminal Justice'. *Oxford Journal of Legal Studies*, 35(4), 665–96.
Lagoutte, S. 2016. 'The Right to Respect for Family Life of Children of Imprisoned Parents'. *International Journal of Children's Rights*, 24, 204–330.
Lazarus, L. 2004. *Contrasting Prisoners' Rights: A Comparative Examination of England and Germany*. Oxford: Oxford University Press.
LeBlanc, L. J. 2005. *The Convention on the Rights of the Child*. Lincoln, NE: University of Nebraska Press.
Link, B. G. and Phelan, J. C. 2001. 'Conceptualising Stigma'. *Annual Review of Sociology*, 27, 363–85
MacDonald, A. Q. C. 2011. *The Rights of the Child*. Bristol: Family Law.
Madsen, M. R. 2016. 'The Challenging Authority of the European Court of Human Rights: From Cold War Legal Diplomacy to the Brighton Declaration and Backlash'. *Law and Contemporary Problems*, 79(1), 141–78.
Miller, K. M. 2014. 'Maternal Criminal Justice Involvement and Co-occurring Mental Health and Substance Abuse Problems: Examining Moderation of Sex and Race on Children's Mental Health'. *Children and Youth Services Review*, 37, 71–80.
Minson, S. 2013. *Mitigating Motherhood: A Study of the Sentencing of Mothers in England and Wales*. London: Howard League for Penal Reform.
Minson, S. 2017. *Who Cares? Analysing the Place of Children in Maternal Sentencing Decisions in England and Wales*. DPhil thesis, Oxford: University of Oxford.
Minson, S. and Condry, R. 2015. 'The Visibility of Children Whose Mothers are Being Sentenced for Criminal Offences in the Courts of England and Wales'. *Law in Context*, 32, 28–45.
Minson, S., Nadin, R., and Earle, J. 2015. *Sentencing of Mothers: Improving the Sentencing Process and Outcomes for Women with Dependent Children*. London: Prison Reform Trust.

Misztal, B. 2011. 'Trust, Acceptance of, Precaution Against and Causes of Vulnerability'. *Comparative Sociology*, 10(3), 358–79.

Murray, J. 2010. 'Longitudinal Research on the Effects of Parental Incarceration on Children', in Eddy, J. M. and Poehlmann, J. (eds.) *Children of Incarcerated Parents: A Handbook for Researchers and Practitioners*. 55–73. Washington, DC: Urban Institute.

Murray, J. and Farrington, D. 2008. 'Effects of Parental Imprisonment on Children', in Tonry, M. (ed.) *Crime and Justice, A Review of Research* (37). 133–206. Chicago, IL: University of Chicago Press.

Parke, R. D. and Clarke-Steward, K. A. 2001. *Effects of Parental Incarceration on Young Children*. Conference Paper at the 'From Prison to Home, the effect of incarceration and re-entry on children, families and communities' Conference. US Department of Health and Human Services.

Poehlmann, J. 2005. 'Children's Family Environments and Intellectual Outcomes during Maternal Incarceration'. *Journal of Marriage and Family*, 67(5), 1275–85.

Sachs, A. 2014. Interviewed by Minson, S. at University College Cork, December.

Sandifer, J. and Kurth, S. 2000. 'The Invisible Children of Incarcerated Mothers', in Fox, G. L. and Benson, M. L. (eds.) *Families, Crime and Criminal Justice: Charting the Linkages*. Contemporary Perspectives in Family Research, vol. 2. 361–80. New York: Emerald Press.

Sentencing Council. 2011. *Assault Guidelines*. London: Sentencing Council.

Sentencing Council. 2017. *Imposition of Custodial and Community Sentences Definitive Guideline*. London: Sentencing Council.

Shaw, R. 1987. *Children of Imprisoned Fathers*. London: Hodder and Stoughton.

Silvestri, M. 2006. 'Gender and Crime: A Human Rights Perspective', in Heidensohn, F. (ed.) *Gender and Justice*. 222–42. Cullompton: Willan.

Smith, P. S. 2016. 'Prisons and Human Rights: Past, Present and Future Challenges', in Weber, L., Fishwick, E., and Marmo, M. (eds.) *The Routledge International Handbook of Criminology and Human Rights*. 525–35. London: Routledge.

Social Exclusion Unit. 2002. *Reducing Re-offending by Ex-prisoners*. London: Social Exclusion Unit.

Tasca, M., Turanovic, J. J., White, C., and Rodriguez, N. 2014. 'Prisoners' Assessments of Mental Health Problems Among Their Children'. *International Journal of Offender Therapy and Comparative Criminology*, 58(2), 154–73

Travis, J. and Waul, M. 2004. *Prisoners Once Removed, The Impact of Incarceration and Re-entry on Children, Families, and Communities*. Chicago: Urban Institute Press.

Van Bueren, G. 1995. *The International Law on the Rights of the Child*. Dordrecht: Springer.

Wakefield, S. and Wildeman, C. 2014. *Children of the Prison Boom: Mass Incarceration and the Future of American Inequality*. Oxford: Oxford University Press.

Wildeman, C., Turney, K., and Youngman, Y. 2016. 'Paternal Incarceration and Family Functioning, Variation across Federal, State and Local Facilities'. *Annals of the American Academy of Political and Social Science*, 665, 80–97.

CASES

HH v Deputy Prosecutor of the Italian Republic, Genoa [2012] UKSC 25.

J v C [1970] HL, [1970] AC 668, [1969] UKHL 4, [1969] 3 WLR 8.

R (on the application of Amanda Aldous) v Dartford Magistrates' Court [2011] EWHC 1919 (Admin).

R (on the application of P and Q) v Secretary of State for the Home Department [2001] EWCA Civ 1151.

R v Bishop [2011] WL 84407.

R v Mills [2002] All ER (D) 24 (Jan).

R v Petherick [2012] EWCA Crim 22.
Re J (a child) [2013] EWHC 2694 (28) (Fam).
ZH (Tanzania) (FC) Appellant v Secretary of State for the Home Department [2011] UKSC 4.

SOUTH AFRICA

M v The State [2007] CCT 53/06 ZACC 18.
S v Ntikedzeni [2011] CC26\2010 ZALMPHC 2.

STATUTES

Children Act 1989.
Children Act 2004.
Criminal Justice Act 2003.

CHARTERS AND CONVENTIONS

United Nations Convention on the Rights of the Child 1989.
United Nations Rules for the Treatment of Women Prisoners and Non-custodial Measures for Women Offenders ('the Bangkok Rules') 2010.

10
'Someone should have just asked me what was wrong'
Balancing Justice, Rights, and the Impact of Imprisonment on Children and Families in Scotland

Nancy Loucks and Tânia Loureiro

Introduction

The impact of imprisonment is not a single process but a continuing one that can be very disruptive and has an impact on families in terms of finances, housing, social stigma, and family dynamics (Armstrong and Weaver, 2013; Christian and Kennedy, 2011; Dickie, 2013; Light and Campbell, 2007; Loucks, 2004; Murray and Farrington, 2008). In Scotland, about half of prisoners have dependent children, in which two in five have one child and a third have two children (Carnie and Broderick, 2015). When looking specifically at women in Scottish prisons, two-thirds reported having children (Gavin et al., 2016).

In 2012, Scottish Justice Government Analytics estimated that around 27,000 children in Scotland each year experienced a parent's imprisonment (Holligan, 2012). This means that, in Scotland, more children experience a parent's imprisonment each year than parental divorce (Families Outside, 2009). We must therefore think about the long-term consequences that this impact could bring on the child's life.

Following the landmark case in the South African Constitutional Court of *S v M* (2007), which required the judiciary to take into account the impact of a prison sentence on a parent's children, children's rights organizations and other interest groups in Scotland have been questioning how the impact of custody on the remaining family can be assessed and taken into account. This includes identifying these families early, getting a clear picture of how decisions in the criminal justice process are likely to impact upon them, and consequently ensuring that appropriate support and information are available to them. While not controversial in principle, the questions of who would conduct such assessments and to what purpose have been challenged continuously, with opponents arguing that perceived interference with the independence of the judiciary, the risk that children will become a 'get out of jail free card' (Justice Committee, Scottish Parliament, 2010), and the potential cost negates the benefits of such assessments. Other jurisdictions have taken the opposite approach, with probation services in the United States deliberately including impact assessments as part of their court reports to inform sentencing decisions (Cramer et al., 2015), and caring responsibilities cited as a mitigating factor in the Sentencing Guidelines in England and Wales. The UN Committee on the Rights of the Child, meanwhile, has recommended the use of impact assessments for both custodial and non-custodial sentences (Robertson, 2012).

Scotland has no sentencing guidelines at present, with the courts relying on legal precedent to inform its judgments. However, the first ever Scottish Sentencing Council was launched in 2015 and is working to establish clear principles of sentencing. An early discussion of the Sentencing Council focused on the sentencing of parents, with the discussion reflecting not *whether* children should be taken into account in adult criminal courts—something the Council appeared to accept—but rather *how* and *to what purpose* they should be taken into account (Scottish Sentencing Council, 2017). The Criminal Justice (Scotland) Act 2016 (described below) also took tentative steps towards highlighting and addressing the needs of children when a parent goes to prison. Like the rest of the United Kingdom, Scotland has fallen short of incorporation of the United Nations Convention on the Rights of the Child (UNCRC) into domestic law, However, the Children and Young People (Scotland) Act 2014 places a duty on the public sector to report what they are doing to realize the rights set out in the UNCRC, and discussion of full incorporation remains live (arguably more so than in other parts of the United Kingdom). Scotland seems to be teetering on the edge of significant positive change regarding support for children with imprisoned parents.

This chapter explores the current debate in Scotland into the attempt to introduce Child and Family Impact Assessments (C&FIA) at key stages in the criminal justice process. It compares this to current international practice in taking the impact of a parent's imprisonment on children into account, then questions what further improvements could be made.

What do we know about children affected by imprisonment?

The need to assess and address the impact of imprisonment on the children and families left behind is clear from the existing research on its effects. Most families experience having a family member in prison as traumatic, and when families have the opportunity to talk about their experience, they often describe feeling blamed, as if they have also committed a crime (Comfort, 2003).

Research conducted specifically on the impact of parental imprisonment shows that the imprisonment of a parent can leave a tremendous mark on a child's life, and with no appropriate levels of support, children may not recover from those consequences (Robertson, 2007). In fact, the impact of parental imprisonment and consequent separation from a parent have been considered as an experience with deep, long-lasting negative effects (Hagan and Dinovitzer, 1999), and imprisonment of a household member is included as one of the ten Adverse Childhood Experiences critical to health outcomes in later life (originally Felitti et al., 1998). Minson's chapter in this volume mentions in more detail some of the harms children face as a consequence of the imprisonment of their parent.

Evidence about the long-term effects on families, particularly on children affected by imprisonment, remains limited overall (Loucks, 2004; Seymour and Hairston, 1998) but has been growing in the last decade (McGillivray, 2016). What the research has shown throughout, however, is that this impact is multifaceted and diverse. Some of the outcomes for children highlighted on research include the stigma and negative social labelling (Boswell and Wedge, 2002),[1] fear of

---

[1] For an overview on stigma and families of prisoners, see Hutton's chapter in this volume.

discovery[2] (Martynowicz, 2011), anxiety and depression associated with parental separation (Murray and Murray, 2010), breakdown of family relationships, and adjustments to care arrangements (Smith et al., 2007; Murray, 2007). The imprisonment of a parent may also mean losing financial contributions from that person (Lee et al., 2014), which may lead to socio-economic disadvantage (Arditti et al., 2003). Financial concerns are usually associated with accommodation, expenses related to the justice process, and travel costs in order to maintain contact with the parent in custody (Dickie 2013; Hairston 2002; Smith et al., 2007).

These effects on children are dynamic, and the consequences also depend on which parent was arrested, whether the child was living with the parent before the arrest (Murray and Farrington, 2008; Parke and Clarke-Stewart, 2002), and whether the child was present at the time of the arrest (Kampfner, 1995). In addition, parental incarceration can produce several negative consequences in children such as unhappiness, anxiety, loss (Robertson, 2007), relationship problems between the mother and child (Thompson and Harm, 2000), antisocial behaviours, difficulties at school, and mental health problems (Murray and Farrington, 2008). The impact is not limited to older children but can have negative consequences for toddlers, babies, and even antenatally (Galloway et al., 2014).

Child and Family Impact Assessments in Scotland

Various organizations have been looking at how the impact of imprisonment on families can be evaluated and taken into account at various stages of sentencing process. In Scotland, some initiatives in research have focused on children of imprisoned parents and more specifically on the promotion and safeguarding of the children's rights.

The United Nations Convention on the Rights of the Child (UNCRC)[3] speaks very clearly of the need to take the best interest of the child into account for any decision that affects them (Article 3.1). This includes prisons, yet we tend to overlook children when we think about prisons. Similarly, Article 12 states that:

1. States Parties shall assure to the child who is capable of forming his or her own views the right to express those views freely in all matters affecting the child, the views of the child being given due weight in accordance with the age and maturity of the child.
2. For this purpose, the child shall in particular be provided the opportunity to be heard in any judicial and administrative proceedings affecting the child, either directly, or through a representative or an appropriate body, in a manner consistent with the procedural rules of national law.

This includes administrative decisions, yet these take place in (and out of) prisons on a regular basis with no involvement of the family, let alone specific consideration of children.

The first work looking at how Scotland was putting into practice these children's rights and interests as stated by the UNCRC (Article 3.1) was by Kathleen Marshall, then Scotland's Commissioner for Children and Young People (SCCYP) (Marshall, 2008). Her report, *Not Seen, Not Heard, Not Guilty*, recommended the use of Child and Family Impact Assessments (C&FIAs) to inform sentencing. In this report she

---

[2] See also Knudsen and her chapter in this volume on the secrecy and invisibility of children of prisoners.
[3] All UN member states other than the United States have signed and ratified the UNCRC.

argued that, under the Scottish Law, children have the same rights as adults to protection and recommended that, in keeping with Article 3.1 of the UNCRC, all people and organizations concerned with children of incarcerated parents should take into account a child's interests as a primary consideration in any decision that affects them (Marshall, 2008).

This pioneer work led to other projects focusing on the impact of parental imprisonment and C&FIAs. In 2009, Loureiro conducted research focusing on the use of C&FIAs in court. The purpose of this research was to learn how sentencers might get to know more about the impact their decisions are likely to have on the remaining family, again in keeping with Article 3.1 of the UNCRC. Fifteen interviews were undertaken with several stakeholders (e.g. Criminal Justice and Children and Family Social Workers, a lawyer, a Sheriff, as well with other professionals from different organizations such as the Scottish Prison Service, national Scottish charity Families Outside, the Salvation Army, South West Scotland Community Justice Authority, and SCCYP) (Loureiro, 2009). Some of the key questions of this research included who might have responsibility for conducting a C&FIA; whether sentencers were likely to use the information provided; what the focus of these assessments should be; and in what circumstances such assessments should be used.

All interviewees agreed that, despite the lack of straightforward answers to these questions, the impact of parental imprisonment is an important issue that needs to be resolved and something that sentencers should take into account when considering their decisions. This impact should be considered on a case-by-case basis, always bearing in mind the consequences to the children and in accordance with UNCRC, Article 3.1. Interviewees also agreed that it is not easy for sentencers to make a decision when they have to balance the offence committed, the appropriate punishment, public safety, and the impact on family. Therefore, it is important to standardize how a C&FIA should be taken into consideration (Loureiro, 2009).

With regard to who should be responsible to conduct the C&FIA and in what cases they should be used, interviewees had different opinions. They agreed, however, that children's needs should be highlighted in the assessments and that existing reports provided to the court are not enough to recognize and assess the impact of the imprisonment of a parent on children (Loureiro, 2009).

In 2010, Loureiro conducted further research specifically looking into the impact of having a family member sent to prison from children's and young people's perspectives. She conducted twenty qualitative semi-structured interviews with children, young people, and some of their carers in order to learn more about the impact the imprisonment of a parent had on their lives and how their views might be taken into account. Most of the participants involved in this research showed that the imprisonment of a parent leaves a tremendous mark on a child's life. The children and young people exhibited concerns regarding their imprisoned parent and revealed how important it was for them for sentencers to listen their opinions. Moreover, '... when listening to the children, it was clearly evident that many clung to the hope that their feelings would make a difference to the sentence given by the judge' (Loureiro, 2010, 41). When asked about the best way to share their views with sentencers, opinions varied from talking to the judges themselves, having someone speak for them, or writing a letter (Loureiro, 2010). The research concluded that, although courts do not regularly request information regarding children's views, these should be considered (as stated under the UNCRC, Article 12), and that children's interests must therefore be a primary consideration in any decision that affects them (as stated under the UNCRC, Article 3.1) (Loureiro, 2010).

Child and Family Impact Assessment tools

After conducting research on the views of key stakeholders regarding the use of C&FIAs in court and the perspectives of children and young people regarding the impact of parental imprisonment, two social work students from the Netherlands developed an assessment tool on behalf of Families Outside (van Haaften and Sijtsma, 2011). The purpose of their research was to develop a tool for social workers and other professionals to identify needs of children of prisoners in Scotland. To achieve that, interviews were conducted with social workers and other professionals in two areas (Edinburgh and North Ayrshire). The tool van Haaften and Sijtsma then developed aimed to help Criminal Justice Social Workers (CJSW) gather information to identify children and their families' needs, as well as to assess the potential impact on children before a parent being sent to prison. It was intended to inform sentencers about the impact the imprisonment may have on the family; it would then be up to each judge's discretion whether they used the information.

From this research, three tools were developed: two Court Assessments (for children with a parent at risk of prison custody) and one Care Assessment (for children with a parent already in custody). The Court Assessments were divided into a short version—to be used by CJSWs in Court when they have limited time to speak with the family—and a fuller version, categorized into SHANARRI wellbeing indicators (Safe, Healthy, Achieving, Nurtured, Active, Respected, Responsible and Included), in accordance with *Getting It Right For Every Child* (GIRFEC) (Scottish Government, 2015b) and now encompassed in the Children and Young People (Scotland) Act 2014.[4] Meanwhile, the Care Assessment is an even more comprehensive tool that can be used by other professionals when a parent is already in custody (van Haaften and Sijtsma, 2011).

This C&FIA tool has not been tested in practice on more than an ad hoc basis. Only with a more comprehensive trial of this tool will we know whether the courts will take this additional information into account and, indeed, whether the child's interests are paramount for any decision that affects them. This lack of evidence on the utility of such impact assessments is commonplace: the Urban Institute in the United States notes that:

> Although family impact statements appear to hold promise for mitigating some of the trauma children face when their parents are involved in the justice system, no empirical studies on the topic have been done. Data also are lacking about how many children are affected by pre-sentence investigations, so it is impossible to determine the full scope of the problem. (Cramer et al., 2015, 11)

In the United States, and with an opposite approach to developments in Scotland (see below), C&FIAs are starting to be introduced by probation services to inform the sentencing process.

Despite the Children's Commissioner's recommendation for the use of Child and Family Impact Assessments, in 2010 the Justice Committee of the Scottish Parliament rejected their introduction. Scotland's Commissioner for Children and Young People reiterated its recommendation for C&FIAs in 2011, but again to no avail. Equally, in 2012 the Angiolini Commission on Women Offenders (Scottish Government, 2012b)

---

[4] The SHANARRI framework, now embedded in *The Children & Young People (Scotland) Act 2014*, is used by social workers and other professionals in Scotland to obtain a good overview of children's needs.

did not include C&FIAs as a recommendation, this time in the belief that court reports fulfilled this role.[5]

However, the courts began to reflect decisions that took the impact on children into account. For example, the Court of Appeal in *R v Rosie Lee Petherick* (2012)[6] gave guidance based on Article 8 of the European Convention on Human Rights (the right to family life) to balance the effects of sentencing on the remaining children and family.[7] The case of *Slovakia v Denise Srponova* (January 2013, unpublished) successfully argued that the deportation to Slovakia and imprisonment of a single mother who had breached a probation order, and consequent placement of her 18-month-old child in an orphanage, would have a disproportionate impact on her child's right to family life under Article 8 of the Human Rights Act. The case of *Stuart Gorrie v PF Haddington* (2014) went to appeal partly on the basis that the court reports had not taken adequate consideration of the impact of a single father's imprisonment on his teenage son, with the appeal successfully overturning the prison sentence and replacing it with a community-based penalty. Other cases occasionally come to light in which judges take the needs of children into account, such as allowing carers to make arrangements for their children prior to entering prison (Currie, 2011), as per the terms of the UN Rules for the Treatment of Women Prisoners (the Bangkok Rules 2010). However, no standard means of taking these circumstances into account are in place, and such cases remain exceptional.

Various attempts to introduce Child and Family Impact Assessments in Scotland

Following recommendations to use C&FIAs in court from SCCYP's report (Marshall, 2008) and the UN Committee's concluding observations (Committee on the Rights of the Child, 2008), Scotland has made some progress in terms of its policy and practice. A report entitled *Do the Right Thing* from the Scottish Government (2009) started to be published annually,[8] outlining priorities and the developments towards the implementation of the UNCRC in Scotland. The Scottish Government also started to support Together Scotland[9] in publishing reports regarding the UK's progress on implementation of the UNCRC. One of Together Scotland's reports recommended that Scotland:

… address inconsistencies in the implementation of the UNCRC across local authorities and professions. It should ensure the principles of the UNCRC are at the heart of policy and practice in work with all children. (Together, 2011, 2)

To this recommendation, Aileen Campbell, then the Minister for Children and Young People in Scotland, stated the commitment 'to ensuring that children's rights feature

---

[5] Personal correspondence with the Commission on Women Offenders.
[6] This was a Court of Appeal case in England, though courts in Scotland can take such cases into account.
[7] For more information on human rights and family, see Scharff Smith's chapter in this volume.
[8] Despite the commitment for annual publication, only two reports were produced (the report in 2009 and an additional one in 2012—setting out the progress made in the priorities identified in 2009.
[9] Together Scotland (Scottish Alliance for Children's Rights) is an organization of children's charities in Scotland that work together in order to improve consciousness, understanding and application of the UNCRC.

in the planning, development and review of policies and services across Scotland' (Scottish Government, 2012c, 7).

The Scottish Government's consultation on the Children and Young People Bill (Scottish Government, 2012a)—now the Children and Young People (Scotland) Act 2014—was announced in 2012. In this Bill, the Government showed its intention to develop legislation regarding a child rights impact assessment process. The Government, in conjunction with Together Scotland and SCCYP, also established a group to develop implementation and progress of the UNCRC called the Scottish Children's Rights Implementation Monitoring Group (SCRIMG).

Focusing on children of imprisoned parents, the UN Committee on the Rights of the Child held a Day of General Discussion in 2011. From this discussion the Committee recommended the use of child impact assessments in both custodial and non-custodial sentences:

Child impact assessments should be available whenever considering placing or releasing parents from custody ... Non-custodial sentences should also be assessed for their impact on children ... When a sentence causes parents to be separated from children for whom they are caring, they should be given sufficient time to make arrangements for those children. (Robertson, 2012, 16 and 17)

In 2012, Together Scotland, SCCYP, and Families Outside gathered support from other member states and together submitted a paper to the United Nations Universal Periodic Review of Human Rights (UPR)[10] highlighting the issues faced by children of prisoners. The briefing was supported by thirty-four children's groups, thirteen MSPs,[11] and twenty other interested professionals. The UPR process requires other governments to ask specific questions to the United Kingdom. The briefing suggested recommendations that the United Kingdom could make to improve support for children of prisoners. Following contact with embassies to highlight the briefing, interest in the issues raised was shown by Slovenia, Germany, and Uruguay. Slovenia submitted a question on children of prisoners in advance of the UPR, which was supported by Germany and Uruguay. Interestingly Slovakia then made the suggested recommendation to the UK Government (Families Outside, 2012).

By accepting the recommendations made from other countries, the United Kingdom is obliged to review its policies regarding children of prisoners, and in this case improve the support to children with a parent in prison. A recommendation from the UPR made a stronger case for children's organizations to push UK and Scottish governments into action (Families Outside, 2012). Following this recommendation, the UPR mentioned that the UK Government needs to 'take all measures necessary to fully implement the CRC' and therefore must ... 'establish Child Rights Impact Assessments, promoting a systematic approach to considering the UNCRC throughout Government, in all legislation and decision-making' (Together, 2013, 2). The UPR also recommended that '... the best interests of the child are taken into account when arresting, detaining, sentencing, or considering early release for a sole or primary carer of the child' (Together, 2013, 3). In addition, it stated that the UK Government should use Child and Family Impact Assessments for all type of sentences (custodial and non-custodial), starting at the moment of the arrest through to the prisoner's release (Together, 2013).

---

[10] The UPR is used by the Human Rights Council to examine the human rights situation in all Member States of the United Nations.
[11] Members of Scottish Parliament.

Although the UK Government stated its agreement with these recommendations, they have not yet been implemented. This may be based on the assumption that the United Kingdom is already considering the impact on children through court reports, as the members of the Angiolini Commission believed, though cases such as *Stuart Gorrie v PF Haddington* (2014) demonstrate that this is not the case.

In 2014, and through the Children and Young People (Scotland) Act, the Scottish Parliament extended the Commissioner for Children and Young People in Scotland's role, allowing the Commissioner to undertake investigations on behalf of individual children and young people.[12] The Commissioner's new powers took effect from April 2016, allowing children and young people to go directly to the Commission's office to make individual complaints of alleged violations of their rights (Children and Young People's Commissioner Scotland, 2015). Although the Scottish Parliament has passed the Children and Young People (Scotland) Act 2014, in which Scottish Ministers now have the obligation to take children's views into account as well as to promote public awareness and understanding of children's rights, the need for a specific legal measure for children in Scotland whose UNCRC rights are violated remains. Still missing is full incorporation of the UNCRC into Scots law[13] (Together, 2016). While the 2014 Act is considered a welcome step, it does not 'ensure that the principles and provisions of the Convention are directly applicable and justiciable' (Convention on the Rights of the Child 2016, paragraph 7a), leaving this to Ministers' discretion. To this matter, Scotland's First Minister stated that she is open to 'exploring implementing and incorporating into Scots law some of the key international human rights treaties' (Sturgeon, 2015), including the UNCRC.

In addition to these measures, from June 2015 the Scottish Government started to use Child Rights and Wellbeing Impact Assessments (CRWIA) to assess how the impact on children and young people have been met by Scottish Government policies. The CRWIA is to be used to assist Ministers in achieving their responsibilities under the Children and Young People (Scotland) Act 2014 and the articles stated under the UNCRC (Scottish Government, 2015a).

All of these steps are positive moves forward but do not yet address the impact on children and families when someone goes to prison. The principle of proportionality remains unaddressed, failing to recognize that the imprisonment of a parent is likely to have much more damaging and longer-term consequences on innocent parties than the imprisonment of people without children or other dependents. Impact assessments can also address proportionality when prison is inevitable due to the seriousness of the offence: such an assessment can identify the likely impact, allowing measures for support to be put in place at the earliest possible stage. Scotland still falls behind much of the practice internationally, increasing the importance of seeking examples of good practice from elsewhere.

Good practice internationally

Although Scotland does not yet have a requirement in place to apply impact assessments to children of imprisoned parents, some good practice examples are worth mentioning.

---

[12] Scotland's Commissioner for Children and Young People (SCCYP) changed its name to the Children and Young People's Commissioner Scotland in 2014 and the latter will be used from now on to reflect that change.

[13] Similar issues are raised in Donson and Parkes' chapter in this volume on children of prisoners and their rights in all stages of the criminal justice process in Ireland.

One example of good practice comes from a Scottish charity called Circle.[14] This organization has been delivering information to sentencers regarding the potential impact to children in case their parents are sent to prison, with the charity stating that this information has been well received by judges. The fact that a Sheriff allowed a mother to return home in order to make child arrangements before serving her sentence in a Scottish prison (Currie, 2011) is also an example of good practice in Scotland—again, something agreed to under the Bangkok Rules 2010 (United Nations, 2010), but not yet widely used in practice in the United Kingdom.

Other countries tend to take a more general approach to reducing the impact of a parent's imprisonment on children. For example, countries such as Germany, Italy, and Argentina place mothers of very young children under house arrest rather than sending them to prison. Slovenia allows parents to alternate serving their sentences if both are sentenced, to provide care for their children. Serbia allows caring responsibilities as a mitigating factor in sentencing, as is the case in England and Wales.

A particularly well-developed approach, promoted by Children of Prisoners Europe, is the Italian Memorandum of Understanding (MoU) between the Ministry of Justice, the National Ombudsman for Childhood and Adolescence, and the NGO Bambinisenzasbarre. The MoU was originally agreed in 2014 but has since been renewed. The agreement requires judges to take into account the rights and requirements of underage children when making a decision about detaining someone with parental responsibility, using non-custodial measures where possible (Article 1). It also requires systematic collection of data about the number and age of children whose parents are detained, 'along with any other relevant information', and that aggregate statistics on the number and ages of children must be made available to the public (Article 6). Argentina, Croatia, Portugal, and The Netherlands are considering a similar model, with research in The Netherlands specifically calling for the use of impact assessments (Reef et al., 2015). The MoU does not promote a specific method of assessment such as a Child and Family Impact Assessment tool but, in requiring questions to be asked, should in theory achieve the same outcome.

The most developed standard on this issue (Brett, 2017) is the African Charter on the Rights and Welfare of the Child. Article 30 of the Charter makes specific provision for expectant mothers and mothers of young children, but interprets this to apply to all sole or primary caregivers, including other family members such as grandparents or foster parents. The Charter states that the best interest of the child must be *the* primary consideration (rather than *a* primary consideration as per Article 3.1 of the UNCRC) in relation to 'all actions that may affect children whose parents are in conflict with the law', and that this applies to all stages of the criminal justice process. The wording of this is important: the Article 3.1 of the UNCRC refers to actions *concerning* children rather than *affecting* children—a difference that has not yet been tested in court but which may be enough to exempt consideration of children in an adult criminal justice court, if a judge interprets 'concerning' as being *about* a child rather than *affecting* a child.

Following the landmark case of *S v M* in 2007, international courts are also making strides towards greater recognition of the impact of imprisonment on the children and families left behind. In 2011, for example, the High Court of Gujarat ordered State support for a prisoner's family because the imprisonment had caused them 'untold misery and deprivation without any fault on their part' (*The Times of India*, 2011). In

---

[14] Circle is a Scottish charity organization that works with children and families in deprived communities across central Scotland.

Ioan Pop and others v Romania (2016), the European Court of Human Rights ruled that a 12-year-old child being left unattended overnight after witnessing the arrest of his parents qualified as degrading treatment under Article 3 of the European Convention. Most recently, the *Case of Polyakova and others v Russia* (2017) in the European Court ruled that housing prisoners so far from their family home that it prevented them from receiving visits breached their right to family life under Article 8.[15]

While courts are beginning to ask questions in individual cases, Children of Prisoners Europe (COPE) highlights the importance of systematic data collection (2016), promoting the requirement for this in the Italian Memorandum of Understanding (above) and noting its inclusion in the 2009 Council of Europe Parliamentary Resolution on Women in Prison. COPE notes that:

> Good data collection allows us to get a better picture of the number of children affected and allows us to point to a real, identifiable population that need our help … Most importantly, however, good data on children of prisoners allows governments, charities and NGOs to target their efforts and resources where they are needed most. It also permits the long-term evaluation of support initiatives for children of prisoners … (Council of Europe, 2009, 1)

Aggregate data collection such as this is highly beneficial—yet this is not the same as an assessment that reflects the impact on an individual, taking into account and supporting the personal strengths and needs a child may have when someone goes to prison.

Importantly the UN Standard Minimum Rules for the Treatment of Prisoners (the Nelson Mandela Rules 2015) recognize the importance of data collection regarding the children and families of prisoners. Rule 7(f) requires that '… The names of his or her family members, including, where applicable, his or her children, the children's ages, location and custody or guardianship status … shall be entered in the prisoner file management system upon admission of every prisoner.' This does not go as far as a requirement to assess impact, nor does the Rule state how the information should be used, but it requires a systematic collection of information about children and families not currently conducted in most jurisdictions.

Potential pitfalls

As noted earlier, the Sentencing Guidelines in England and Wales recently added caring responsibilities as a mitigating factor in sentencing (Minson, 2015). This specifically applies to the 'sole primary carer for dependent relatives'—but again, as a guideline, such consideration is not mandatory. More information on consideration of dependent children in the sentencing process in England and Wales can be found in Minson's chapter in this volume.

Brett (2017) emphasizes the need for mandatory, systematic collection of information, as guidelines are not always followed. Donson (2015) and Geiran (2015) noted this problem in the Irish criminal justice system (CJS), in which child impact statements are possible but remain discretionary. Sweden faces a similar difficulty in that consideration of the child in sentencing is not universal and is only required when the child is the victim (Schiratzki and Sköndal, 2015). A case in Switzerland highlighted problems with the lack of systematic data collection to tragic effect when a mother went to prison, leaving her 2-year-old daughter alone in the house and, in an effort to

---

[15] For a discussion of more relevant case law, see Lagoutte, 2016 and Smith, 2014.

prevent the involvement of social services, did not say anything and instead left a coded message for a friend. The friend did not understand the message, and the child died of dehydration (Schekter, 2014).

Fear of involvement with officials is a real concern for families who may not have had the most positive contact with state authorities (see Jardine's chapter in this volume on the impact of imprisonment on the relationships between families and CJS). Philbrick notes that:

For information to be freely given, the prospective prisoner needs to trust the person they are giving information about their children to, and be confident that this information will be well used. (2015, 3)

The requirement for a Child and Family Impact Assessment alone is not enough: we must also consider who will ask these questions; when will they ask; whom will they ask; what will they ask; how will they ask; and what will they do with the information. If the process itself is not sympathetic to the needs of, and pressure on, children and families, the risk is that families will suppress information, which potentially prevents them from receiving vital information and assistance (Loucks, 2017). Further, if a parent or carer has not yet spoken to a child about the potential for imprisonment at the time of assessment, who (if anyone) has the right to tell the child, especially if it risks damaging the relationship with the parent (Philbrick, 2015).

Finally, clarification of the purpose of a Child and Family Impact Assessment is critical to its use. If, as COPE argues, such data collection allows support organizations to target their efforts and resources where they are needed most, this is very different from the 'instrumentalizing' of children (Philbrick 2015, 4) as a tool in determining the outcome of their parent.

Recent developments in Scotland

Progress towards Child and Family Impact Assessments has not quite mirrored the progress elsewhere. In 2015, Mary Fee MSP (Member of the Scottish Parliament), with support from with Barnardo's Scotland, Families Outside, and the National Society for the Prevention of Cruelty to Children (NSPCC) developed a draft proposal for The Support for Children (Impact of Parental Imprisonment) (Scotland) Bill. A consultation on this Private Member's Bill received 102 responses (Fee, 2015).[16] Aiming to improve support and outcomes for children of imprisoned parents, the proposed Bill was intended for courts *after* the sentencing process to take into account the impact of a custodial measure on children and also to guarantee that children with a parent in prison received the appropriate level of support (Fee, 2015). The use of C&FIAs *after* the sentencing process was proposed due to politicians arguing that the use of C&FIAs before sentencing interfered with the independence of the judiciary. This is despite the fact that defence agents already include similar information as a case for mitigation during the course of a trial and that the Guidelines published by the Sentencing Council for England and Wales (2008) specifically identify 'caring responsibilities' as a mitigating factor. Developing practice in the United States also provides an interesting contrast to the reservations in Scotland about C&FIAs prior to sentence, as noted above.

---

[16] Responses to the consultation are available at: http://www.parliament.scot/S4_MembersBills/20150907SummaryFinal.pdf.

Unfortunately, and even though Mary Fee worked closely with Barnardo's Scotland, Families Outside, and the NSPCC to amend the Criminal Justice (Scotland) Bill to ensure C&FIAs are conducted, the Justice Committee rejected the call for child and family impact assessments in September 2015 (*The Herald Scotland*, 2015). To this rejection, Scotland's First Minister Nicola Sturgeon assured the Government's 'full consideration' to proposals for assessments to be conducted on children and young people who have a parent in prison *(The Herald Scotland,* 2015). Subsequently an amendment by Mary Fee was accepted, with section 107 of the (now) Criminal Justice (Scotland) Act 2016 requiring notification of the Named Person[17] when the parent of someone under the age of 18 goes to prison. While not meeting the full aims of an impact assessment—the parent must already be in prison before the impact on the child is considered—it created a systematic mechanism for the first time for identifying and providing support for children with a parent in prison in Scotland.

Unfortunately, legal challenges to the role of the Named Person in Scotland, and specifically to information sharing with the Named Person (*The Christian Institute and others v The Lord Advocate* (Scotland) (2016)), have resulted in delays to the implementation of this part of the Criminal Justice (Scotland) Act 2016. In response to the UK Supreme Court's request for further clarity on information sharing, the Scottish Government conceded that information sharing would not be mandatory, and further legal challenges are possible.

Conclusions

Despite the Scottish progress and achievements in terms of compliance with the UNCRC, there is still considerable work to be done to guarantee that children's rights are considered and that their voices are heard (Baillie, 2015). As one of the examples of what should be addressed immediately, Tam Baillie, the then Children and Young People's Commissioner for Scotland, mentioned the lack of guidance for Scottish Ministers to know how they should put in practice their responsibilities regarding the voice and participation of children and young people required in the Children and Young People (Scotland) Act 2014. Scotland has yet to incorporate the UN Convention on the Rights of the Child into domestic law, despite a commitment within the Children and Young People Act to raise awareness of the UNCRC. With little legislative leverage to protect the rights of children in this context, and with no one yet asking about the impact on children and families in a systematic and sensitive way when someone is at risk of imprisonment, children and families remain at risk of being the invisible victims of crime and the penal system.

References

Arditti, J. A., Lambert-Shute, J., and Joest, K. 2003. 'Saturday Morning at the Jail: Implications of Incarceration for Families and Children'. *Family Relations*, 52(3), 195–204.

Armstrong, S., and Weaver, B. 2013. 'Persistent Punishment: User Views of Short Prison Sentences'. *The Howard Journal of Criminal Justice*, 52(3), 285–305.

---

[17] The Named Person is usually the head teacher of a child's school, or the health visitor for children too young to be in school, identified in the Children & Young Person (Scotland) Act 2014 as the focal point for information that affects a child's wellbeing.

Baillie, T. 2015. *Submission to the Joint Committee on Human Rights Inquiry into the UK's compliance with the United Nations Convention on the Rights of the Child*. Edinburgh: Scotland's Commissioner for Children and Young People (SCCYP). Available at: http://dera.ioe.ac.uk/22890/1/evidence-to-JCHR-Mar15.pdf.

Boswell, G. and Wedge, P. 2002. *Imprisoned Fathers and their Children*. London: Jessica Kingsley Publishers.

Brett, R. 2017. 'Best Interests of the Child when Sentencing a Parent: Some reflections on international and regional standards and practice'. Unpublished.

Carnie, J. and Broderick, R. 2015. *Prisoner Survey 2015: 15th Series Research Strategy and Innovation*. Edinburgh: Scottish Prison Service.

Case of Polyakova and Others v Russia (2017) European Court of Human Rights Applications nos. 35090/09 and 3 others, Judgment 7 March 2017.

Children and Young People's Commissioner Scotland. 2015. *Annual Report 2014–2015*. Edinburgh: Children and Young People's Commissioner Scotland.

Children and Young People (Scotland) Act 2014.

Children of Prisoners Europe. 2016. Data Collection and Children with Imprisoned Parents. Available at: http://childrenofprisoners.eu/2016/06/27/data-collection-and-children-with-imprisoned-parents/.

Christian, J. and Kennedy, L. W. 2011. 'Secondary Narratives in the Aftermath of Crime: Defining Family Members' Relationships with Prisoners'. *Punishment & Society*, 13(4): 379–402.

Comfort, M. 2003. 'In the Tube at San Quentin: The 'Secondary Prisonization' of Women Visiting Inmates'. *Journal of Contemporary Ethnography*, 32(1), 77–107.

Committee on the Rights of the Child. 2008. *Consideration of Reports Submitted by States Parties under Article 44 of the Convention. Concluding Observations: United Kingdom of Great Britain and Northern Ireland*. Available at: http://www2.ohchr.org/english/bodies/crc/docs/AdvanceVersions/CRC.C.GBR.CO.4.pdf.

Committee on the Rights of the Child. 2016. *Concluding Observations on the Fifth Periodic Report of the United Kingdom of Great Britain and Northern Ireland*. Available at: http://tbinternet.ohchr.org/_layouts/treatybodyexternal/Download.aspx?symbolno=CRC/C/GBR/CO/5.

Convention on the Rights of the Child. 1989. Available at: http://www.ohchr.org/Documents/ProfessionalInterest/crc.pdf.

Council of Europe. 2009. *Women in Prison*. Resolution 1663 (2009). Available at: http://assembly.coe.int/nw/xml/XRef/Xref-XML2HTML-en.asp?fileid=17733&lang=en.

Cramer, L., Peterson, B., Kurs, E., and Fontaine, J. 2015. *Toolkit for Developing Family Impact Statements: Children of Incarcerated Parents Project*. Available at: http://www.urban.org/research/publication/toolkit-developing-family-impact-statements-children-incarcerated-parents-project.

Currie, G. 2011. 'Sent Home to Warn Daughter She's Off to Jail'. *The Sun*. Available at: https://www.thesun.co.uk/archives/news/407999/sent-home-to-warn-daughter-shes-off-to-jail/.

Dickie, D. 2013. *The Financial Impact of Imprisonment on Families*. Edinburgh: Families Outside.

Donson, F. 2015. 'Whose Rights? What Impact? The Potential for the Development of Child Impact Statements in the Irish Criminal Justice System'. *European Journal of Parental Imprisonment: Child Impact Assessments and Sentencing*, Winter, 10–13.

Families Outside. 2009. 'Support and Information for Children Affected by Imprisonment.' *In Brief* 4. Edinburgh: Families Outside. Available at: https://www.familiesoutside.org.uk/content/uploads/2011/02/FO-In-Brief-No4-Single-Pages.pdf.

Families Outside. 2012. *Universal Periodic Review*. Edinburgh: Families Outside.

Fee, M. 2015. *Proposed Support for Children (Impact of Parental Imprisonment) (Scotland) Bill*. Available at: http://www.parliament.scot/parliamentarybusiness/Bills/86482.aspx.

Felitti, V J., Anda, R. F., Nordenberg, D., Williamson, D. F., Spitz, A. M., Edwards, V., Koss, M. P., and Marks, J. S. 1998. 'Relationship of Childhood Abuse and Jousehold Dysfunction to Many of the Leading Causes of Death in Adults'. *American Journal of Preventive Medicine*, 14(4): 245–58.

Galloway, S., Haynes, A., and Cuthbert, C. 2014. *All Babies Count: Spotlight on the Criminal Justice System—an Unfair Sentence*. London: NSPCC.

Gavin, M., Broderick, R., and Carnie, M. J. 2016. *Women in Custody 2015. 15th Survey Bulletin Research, Strategy and Innovation*. Scottish Prison Service.

Geiran, V. 2015. 'Child Impact Statements and the Irish Probation Service'. *European Journal of Parental Imprisonment: Child Impact Assessments and Sentencing* (Winter 2015), 8–9.

Hagan, J., and Dinovitzer, R. 1999. 'Collateral Consequences of Imprisonment for Children, Communities, and Prisoners'. *Crime and Justice*, 26, 121–62.

Hairston, J. C. F. 2002. 'Prisoners and Families: Parenting Issues During Incarceration'. In *From Prison to Home Conference*. National Institutes of Health: US Department of Health and Human Services.

Holligan, C. 2012. *Freedom of Information Request*. Scottish Government Justice Analytical Services.

Ioan Pop and others v Romania (2016) European Court of Human Rights, *Affaire Ioan Pop et autres c. Roumanie*, 6 décembre 2016 (Requête no 52924/09).

Justice Committee. 2010. Scottish Parliament Justice Committee debate, Criminal Justice (Scotland) Bill 2010.

Kampfner, C. J. 1995. 'Post-Traumatic Stress Reactions in Children of Imprisoned Mothers', in Johnston, D. and Gabel, K. (eds.) *Children of Incarcerated Parents*. 89–102. New York: Lexington Books.

Lagoutte, S. 2016. 'The Right to Respect for Family Life of Children of Imprisoned Parents'. *International Journal of Children's Rights*, 24(1), 204–30.

Lee, H., Porter, L. C., and Comfort, M. 2014. 'Consequences of Family Member Incarceration: Impacts on Civic Participation and Perceptions of the Legitimacy and Fairness of Government'. *The Annals of the American Academy of Political and Social Science* 651(1), 44–73.

Light, R. and Campbell, B. 2007. 'Prisoners' Families: Still Forgotten Victims?' *Journal of Social Welfare and Family Law*, 28, 297–308.

Loucks, N. 2004. *Prison without Bars: Needs, Support and Good Practice for Work with Prisoners' Families*. Edinburgh: Tayside Criminal Justice Partnership and Families Outside.

Loucks, N. 2017. 'Data Collection and the Right to Privacy: Which Way Forward?' Workshop presentation, INCCIP Inaugural Conference, Rotorua, New Zealand, 22 March.

Loureiro, T. 2009. *Child and Family Impact Assessments in Court: Implications for Policy and Practice*. Edinburgh: Families Outside.

Loureiro, T. 2010. *Perspectives of Children and Young People with a Parent in Prison*. Edinburgh: Scottish Commissioner for Children and Young People and Families Outside.

Marshall, K. 2008. *Not Seen. Not Heard. Not Guilty. The Rights and Status of the Children of Prisoners in Scotland*. Edinburgh: Scotland's Commissioner for Children and Young People (SCCYP).

Martynowicz, A. 2011. *Children of Imprisoned Parents*. Denmark: The Danish Institute for Human Rights.

McGillivray, C. 2016. *Rendering Them Visible: A Review of Progress Towards Increasing Support of Prisoners' Families*. Edinburgh: Families Outside. Available at: http://www.familiesoutside.org.uk/content/uploads/2016/04/Rendering-Them-Visible-FINAL.pdf.

Minson, S. 2015. *Sentencing of Mothers: Improving the Sentencing Process and Outcomes for Women with Dependent Children*. London: Prison Reform Trust.

Murray, J. 2007. The Cycle of Punishment: Social Exclusion of Prisoners and their Children. *Criminology & Criminal Justice*, 7(1), 55–81.

Murray, J. and Farrington, D. P. 2008. 'The Effects of Parental Imprisonment on Children'. *Crime and Justice,* 37(1), 133–206.

Murray, J. and Murray, L. 2010. Parental Incarceration, Attachment and Child Psychopathology. *Attachment & Human Development,* 12(4), 289–309.

Parke, R. and Clarke-Stewart, K. A. 2002. 'Effects of Parental Incarceration on Young Children'. In *From Prison to Home Conference.* National Institutes of Health: US Department of Health and Human Services.

Philbrick, K. 2015. 'Assessing the Impact on a Child When Their Parent is Imprisoned: Some Ethical Questions'. *European Journal of Parental Imprisonment: Child Impact Assessments and Sentencing,* Winter, 3–4.

R v Rosie Lee Petherick (2012) EWCA Crim 2214.

Reef, J., Nieuwbeerta, P., and Dirkzwager, A. 2015. 'Children's Well-Being Prior to Paternal Incarceration'. *European Journal of Parental Imprisonment: Child Impact Assessments and Sentencing,* Winter, 25–27.

Robertson, O. 2007. *The Impact of Parental Imprisonment on Children.* Geneva: Quaker United Nations Office.

Robertson, O. 2012. *Collateral Convicts: Children of incarcerated parents. Recommendations and Good Practice from the UN Committee on the Rights of the Child Day of General Discussion 2011.* Geneva: Quaker United Nations Office.

S v M (2007) Constitutional Court of South of Africa. *S v M* (CCT 53/06) [2007] ZACC 18; 2008 (3) SA 232 (CC).

Schekter, V. 2014. Plenary Discussion, Children of Prisoners Europe Conference, Edinburgh.

Schiratzki, J. and Sköndal, E. 2015. 'Swedish Children's Rights Lacking When Sentencing Their Parents.' *European Journal of Parental Imprisonment: Child Impact Assessments and Sentencing,* Winter, 23–4.

Scotland's Commissioner for Children and Young People. 2011. *Not Seen. Not Heard. Not Guilty: Review: the Rights and Status of the Children of Prisoners in Scotland.* Edinburgh: SCCYP.

Scottish Government. 2009. *Do the Right Thing: A Report for Under 18s on Scottish Government Priorities in Response to the UK Concluding Observations 2008.* Available at: http://www.gov.scot/Publications/2009/08/27133115/3.

Scottish Government. 2012a. *A Scotland for Children: A Consultation on the Children and Young People Bill.* Available at: https://www.gov.scot/Publications/2012/07/7181.

Scottish Government. 2012b. *Commission on Women Offenders: Final Report 2012.* Available at: http://www.gov.scot/About/Review/commissiononwomenoffenders/finalreport-2012.

Scottish Government. 2012c. *Do the Right Thing—A Progress Report on the Scottish Government's Response to the 2008 Concluding Observations from the UN Committee on the Rights of the Child.* Available at: http://www.gov.scot/Publications/2012/05/3593/downloads.

Scottish Government. 2015a. *Child Rights and Wellbeing Impact Assessment (CRWIA).* Available at: http://www.gov.scot/Topics/People/Young-People/families/rights/child-rights-wellbeing-impact-assessment.

Scottish Government. 2015b. *What is GIRFEC?* Available at: http://www.gov.scot/Topics/People/Young-People/gettingitright/what-is-girfec.

Scottish Sentencing Council. 2017. Report on 'Sentencing of Parents' Event. Available at: https://www.scottishsentencingcouncil.org.uk/news-and-media/news/report-on-sentencing-of-parents-event/.

Sentencing Council for England and Wales. 2008. *Magistrates' Court Sentencing Guidelines.* Available at: http://www.sentencingcouncil.org.uk/publications/item/magistrates-court-sentencing-guidelines/.

Seymour, C. and Hairston, C. F. 1998. *Children with Parents in Prison: Child Welfare, Policy, Program and Practice Issues.* New Brunswick: Transaction Publishers.

Slovakia v Denise Srponova (January 2013, unreported). Edinburgh Sheriff Court.

Smith, P.S., 2014. *When the Innocent are Punished: The Children of Imprisoned Parents*. New York: Palgrave Macmillan
Smith, R., Grimshaw, R., Romeo, R., and Knapp, M. 2007. *Poverty and Disadvantage Among Prisoners' Families*. York: Joseph Rowntree Foundation. Available at: https://www.jrf.org.uk/report/poverty-and-disadvantage-among-prisoners-families.
Stuart Gorrie v PF Haddington (2014) HCJAC 10.
Sturgeon, N. 2015. *SNAP Human Rights Innovation Forum*. Available at: https://news.gov.scot/speeches-and-briefings/snap-human-rights-innovation-forum.
The Christian Institute and others (Appellants) v The Lord Advocate (Respondent) (Scotland) [2016] UKSC 51.
The Herald Scotland. 2015. 'Nicola Sturgeon vows to consider Labour's family impact assessment proposals'. 10 September. Available at: http://www.heraldscotland.com/news/13712312.Nicola_Sturgeon_vows_to_consider_Labour_s_family_impact_assessment_proposals/.
The Times of India. 2011. 'HC directs govt to take care of families of poor prisoners'. 31 October. Available at: http://articles.timesofindia.indiatimes.com/2011-10-31/ahmedabad/30341579_1_jail-inmates-prisoners-vadodara-central-jails.
Thompson, P. J. and Harm, N. J. 2000. 'Parenting from Prison: Helping Children and Mothers'. *Issues in Comprehensive Pediatric Nursing*, 23(2), 61–81.
Together. 2011. *State of Children's Rights in Scotland*. Available at: http://www.togetherscotland.org.uk/pdfs/Together_Report_2011_PDF.pdf.
Together. 2013. *Universal Periodic Review. Children's Rights Recommendations: Priorities for Government*. Available at: http://www.togetherscotland.org.uk/pdfs/UPR%20Scottish%20mid-term%20report%20JH.pdf.
Together. 2016. *State of Children's Rights in Scotland*. Available at: http://www.togetherscotland.org.uk/pdfs/TogetherReport2016.pdf.
United Nations. 2010. United Nations Rules for the Treatment of Women Prisoners and Non-custodial Measures for Women Offenders (the Bangkok Rules). Available at: https://www.hri.global/contents/811.
United Nations. 2015. Standard Minimum Rules for the Treatment of Prisoners (the Nelson Mandela Rules). Available at: http://www.unodc.org/documents/justice-and-prison-reform/Brochure_on_the_UN_SMRs.pdf.
van Haaften, G. and Sijtsma, C. 2011. *Child Punishment: The Other Side of the Coin of Parental Imprisonment*. Unpublished thesis. Edinburgh: Families Outside.

11

Eroding Legitimacy? The Impact of Imprisonment on the Relationships between Families, Communities, and the Criminal Justice System

Cara Jardine

Introduction

The imprisonment of a family member can affect virtually every element of family life, causing disruption to housing, finances, relationships, and caring arrangements; particularly where families choose to undertake the demanding task of supporting the person in custody (Comfort, 2016; Light and Campbell, 2006). Further, there is a now an emerging consensus that the damaging effects of imprisonment stretch far beyond individual families, also having a pronounced, negative effect at a societal level. Much of this research originates from the United States, a jurisdiction which has experimented with a large-scale and highly racialized use of imprisonment, often termed Mass Incarceration (Foster and Hagan, 2015; Christian and Thomas, 2009; Alexander, 2010). Such widespread use of imprisonment has been shown not only to have contemporaneous negative consequences for children, but to also reinforce the structural inequalities that limit future life chances, thus further entrenching racial and social inequalities (Wakefield and Wildeman, 2014).

The effects of mass incarceration are highly geographically concentrated, serving to undermine the capacities and resources of many of the poorest communities. As residents cycle in and out of the prison in large numbers, this creates increased mobility and social isolation, eroding social capital and collective efficacy (Clear, 2002). Opportunities for families affected by imprisonment to participate in their community are reduced, as the large investments of time required to support a family member in custody limit their chances to engage with other civic institutions such as schools, churches, or community life. Consequently, these families are less likely to participate politically (Sugie, 2015), creating a set of circumstances whereby the criminal justice system becomes a key agent of political socialization (Lee et al., 2014).

Importantly, the disproportionate contact between such marginalized communities and the criminal justice system also serves to undermine trust and confidence in formal agencies of social control (Clear, 2002). This distrust has been conceptualized as 'legal cynicism', or the feeling that the law lacks relevance to a person's everyday life and concerns, which is cultivated and exacerbated in communities which experience highly concentrated levels of individuals returning from custody (Kirk, 2016). Such mistrust can then become heightened still amongst families affected by imprisonment, as poor or degrading treatment by criminal justice professionals—either of the person in custody or the family themselves—fosters a view that both the criminal justice systems lack legitimacy and cannot be trusted (Lee et al., 2014).

In sum, this body of literature raises important questions about the role of criminal justice agencies within these families and communities, and how social inequalities consequently become heightened and entrenched. Yet, while mass incarceration may be unique to the United States, it cannot be assumed that analogous processes are not operating within a European or UK context. For example, Scotland's imprisonment rates are amongst the highest in Western Europe (Scottish Prisons Commission, 2008), with a pronounced over-representation of the most deprived communities amongst its prison population (Houchin, 2005). Scottish police have also been found to disproportionately warn, charge, or stop and search white working-class boys and young men *because* of their social marginality and class position, rather than the utility of these approaches in detecting or reducing offending (Lennon and Murray, 2016; McAra and McVie, 2005); and there is a large body of evidence to show that poor interactions with UK criminal justice professionals are damaging to legitimacy (Brunton-Smith and McCarthy, 2016; Jackson et al., 2012; Hough et al., 2010). Perhaps most crucially, all jurisdictions which use imprisonment as a primary form of punishment will necessarily have to confront these questions (Condry, this volume).

In this chapter, I will attempt to address these issues through the conceptual lens of legitimacy. This theoretical framework was first applied in the context of imprisonment by Sparks, Bottoms, and Hay to better understand order and compliance in prisons (Sparks et al., 1996). In their landmark study, *Prisons and the Problem of Order*, Sparks et al. argue that prison officers cannot simply impose their authority. Rather the terms of these power relations should be defined by clear rules, consented to by prisoners, and also justifiable from their perspective (Sparks and Bottoms, 1995; Beetham, 1991). These arguments are instructive here as they highlight not only the importance of justice, fairness, and respect in achieving legitimacy, but also the damaging effects when these qualities are absent from seemingly 'everyday' interactions:

Every instance of brutality in prisons, every casual racist joke and demeaning remark, every ignored petition, every unwarranted bureaucratic delay, every inedible meal, every arbitrary decision to segregate and transfer without giving clear and well-founded reasons, every petty miscarriage of justice, every futile and inactive period of time is deligitimizing. (Sparks and Bottoms, 1995, 607)

Further, recent scholarship has demonstrated that legitimacy is not a 'single transaction', rather it is ongoing, dialogical, and relational (Bottoms and Tankebe, 2012). Consequently, each time those in a position of power make a claim of authority, this must be justified to their wider audiences, who may accept or reject such a claim (Bottoms and Tankebe, 2012). When such claims to legitimacy are rejected, the audience in question are then less likely to comply with the demands of those in power. This is because legitimacy enhances the moral nature of the relationship between social actors, creating normative reasons for compliance (Beetham, 1991; Sparks and Bottoms, 1995). Thus, where prison officers are seen as unfair or unjust in their decision making, motivation to follow or accept their instructions are reduced. Low levels of legitimacy also erode trust, communication, and the quality of relationships with criminal justice institutions (Liebling, 2011).

As the imprisonment of a family member brings families into regular contact with the prison, much of which is often boring, distressing, frustrating or even overtly disrespectful (Hutton, 2016, and this volume; Flynn, 2014; Arditti, 2003) the risk that families will reject the legitimate authority of the prison is clear. While these arguments can equally be made with regard to *all* families affected by imprisonment (see Jardine, 2015), they become increasingly troubling when the experiences of already marginalized families are considered. These families are not only disproportionately likely to experience the imprisonment of a family member, but this can exacerbate the cumulative social disadvantages they experience, raising important questions about the role of criminal justice institutions in these communities, and the wider implications for justice, fairness, and legitimacy.

Background and methods

These are ambitious questions, and are not the issues which I initially sought out to address. The aims of this research were more modest; predominantly to examine who is affected when a custodial sentence is imposed, and how is this experienced in the Scottish context. In short, I intended to explore who the term 'families affected by imprisonment' might refer to by applying a more critical lens to the concept of family (see Jardine, 2017). To do so, I conducted in-depth interviews with families visiting a person in prison, and also men and women who were serving a custodial sentence.

With regard to the latter, the majority of these interviews were conducted at HMP Greenock, situated in the West of Scotland. Family members were recruited through the Visitors' Centre at HMP Edinburgh, a separate, purpose-built facility situated inside the prison grounds. Thus, almost all of the prisoners and family members were unknown to each other. Towards the end of the fieldwork a small number of additional interviews were conducted in HMP Edinburgh in an attempt to capture the views of *both* the family and the person they were visiting, however this was only achieved in one instance. In total, ten men and four women were interviewed in custody, and nineteen individuals from fourteen families were interviewed in the Visitors' Centre.[1]

As my fieldwork progressed, it quickly became clear that I needed to become a regular presence in the Visitors' Centre both to gain the trust of potential participants, and to be available to conduct interviews at a time that suited them. Thus, over the course of the project I spent upward of 350 hours 'hanging around' the Visitors' Centre conducting interviews, but also chatting to families, playing with children, tidying the Centre and making notes of my daily observations. Visitors' Centre Staff (n = 4) and prison officers (n = 8) were also interviewed.

This strategy of 'hanging around' led to the recruitment of a particular group of families who, first and foremost, had made the decision to maintain their relationships by actively visiting the prison. Not all families affected by imprisonment will choose to do so, and many relationships break down over the course of a custodial sentence (Woodall et al., 2009). Further, at the time of the research, the Visitors' Centre delivered a range of support expressly informed by the principles of community education; a pedagogical approach characterized by shared learning and working together to meet the social, political, and personal needs of the group in question (Ceesay, 2012). Perhaps because of this, many of the families who made the greatest use of the Centre, and were therefore also happy to participate in my research, were a particularly marginalized group. It is their experiences, and the implications for penal legitimacy, which this chapter will explore.

---

[1] Where permission was given, interviews were digitally recorded and transcribed in full; and where this was withheld contemporaneous notes were taken (see Jardine, 2015 for a fuller discussion). For those unfamiliar with the Scottish vernacular, a guide to common expressions can be found in the glossary at the end of this chapter.

Families, social marginality, and legitimacy

Supporting a family member in custody can be a long and arduous task, requiring a considerable investment of time, effort, and financial resource (Condry, 2007; Christian, 2005). This exposes families to the power of the prison, even when not physically visiting the establishment, as they must wait at home for telephone calls, shop for items for the person in custody, and seek to devise creative strategies to continue their family relationships (Comfort, 2008; Jardine, 2017). Importantly, these burdens weigh most heavily on the families perhaps least able to withstand them (Halsey and Deegan, 2015; Braman, 2002).

Indeed, participants placed considerable importance on providing material supports to the person in custody, even when this was to the detriment of their own wellbeing. Ensuring the supply of visits, phone cards, and contributions to the person's Prisoner Personal Cash (PPC) account (which funds purchases from the prison canteen such as tobacco or chocolate) was seen by families as an important tool for demonstrating their ongoing love and commitment. Consequently, families would dedicate a considerable proportion of their already scarce resources to this task. For example, Tracey, who was visiting her partner, told of how she had experienced considerable hardship in her own life, including recovering from heroin addiction, serving short periods in custody, and becoming homeless only a few weeks before our interview, when her partner was remanded in custody. Yet despite her own difficulties and limited resources, Tracey attended all six visiting sessions permitted to remand prisoners each week, and made financial contributions over and above the maximum limit set by the prison by also paying money into her partner's friend's account:

> *Tracey*: But now he knows I will stand by him 110% I mean I have been up here since October six days a week do you know what I mean ... ken like a day saver a day is £3.50 so my bus fares are like £17 a week and I still do it and it doesnae bother me. And on a Wednesday night I don't get in until half ten, quarter to eleven but I still do it ... And the amount of times that I have came up to visits and put money into other people's properties because he has wanted I dunno extra tobacco but he has wanted munchies so he is like 'will you put a fiver in somebodies property for me so I can get tobacco and I can buy munchies as well ...
>
> *CJ*: Why does it need to go in somebody else's?
>
> *Tracey*: Because he can only spend a certain amount—so somebody who doesn't get money, he'll get it put it in theirs and then he'll let them buy, what they'll want to buy is a half ounce of baccy so he'll let them buy a half ounce of baccy and he just fills their shop sheet out with sweeties and things like that that he wants. He doesnae do it all the time, it's like maybe once a month or something.

As Tracey explains, these financial contributions and time spent travelling to and attending visits are a means of demonstrating that she is '110%' committed to her partner, despite his imprisonment. However, the poverty experienced by these participants does not only mean that they have fewer resources available to dedicate to supporting their family member, and fewer still left for themselves. Their social marginalization also makes providing this support increasingly costly, both in terms of time and money. For example, if the person in custody does not already own clothes that meet the prison's security requirements, or as some participants noted these no longer fit as a consequence of a prison diet, new—but also affordable—clothes must be found and purchased. This may require repeated shopping trips, often undertaken with small children, and multiple journeys made on public transport to bring these items to the prison.

As the resources which might ease this process—such as childcare, stable incomes, their own transportation or shopping for convenience rather than cost (Holligan, 2016)—were not accessible to participants, it is perhaps unsurprising that tensions could arise between families and prison officers when these items of property were not accepted, payments to PPC accounts were processed incorrectly, or visits were booked but then missed due to court appearances, lateness, or a lack of acceptable identification. The frustration that can arise when such significant investments of time and money prove to be ultimately fruitless is evident in the account of Sophie, a mother of two small children and one of the most amiable but reserved young women to participate in the research. To our amusement, as the events she describes are so out of character, Sophie tells me how she had lost her temper after she and her young daughter travelled to the prison in the rain, whilst Sophie was heavily pregnant, with the sole purpose of handing in property, for this to be refused because her partner had not supplied the correct paperwork:

> *Sophie*: its such stupid rules ... you have to have proforms to hand clothes in—I came up one day, it was pissing it down with rain and I brought up clothes for him because that's what he wanted, he never told me I need a proform. And they were like 'No, he can't have them because you got no got a proform.' And I was like 'But I've come all this way with all these clothes in the pissing rain and you're saying I can't because he's not got a special form.' I went mental at them ... I was like 'That's not my fucking fault he's not got a proform.' And I was like 'I'm sorry for being so angry but I'm heavily pregnant, I've just came up in the rain and now you're telling me I can't even put in what I need to put in.' And he was like 'There's nothing we can do.'... [Laughter.]
>
> *CJ*: I can't imagine you losing your temper [laughing].
>
> *Sophie*: Because I was so angry. But obviously being heavily pregnant I was I just want to do what I need to do so I can leave—I didn't have a visit that day so

However, our amusement at this encounter belies a more serious point, which must also be recognized. For it is not only the practical and financial costs of imprisonment that can be exacerbated for family members who are already experiencing social marginalization, but also the emotional ones. It is now well established that the imprisonment of a family member can prompt a range of often difficult emotions—encompassing fear, guilt, distress, and relief (Lanskey et al., 2015; Arditti et al., 2003). Yet, for families already experiencing difficult circumstances, these additional strains can have catastrophic consequences, particularly in the absence of appropriate professional support, as both the accounts of family members and the observational data demonstrate:

I have been guided by the prison staff and the people here and they have all been fantastic. I was hearing voices about suicide all the time so without the help I am 99% sure I would have killed myself. Sometimes I want to bash my head against the wall stop the voices, but I've managed to stop myself from doing that. [Bill, visiting his step-son in prison.]

A young woman came into the office to speak to the Visitors' Centre staff—she was stressed and upset because her partner had told her on the visit that he as being moved to another prison. She was in the office for about an hour and was in tears twice. She seemed very vulnerable: her baby is in care; she takes large amounts of prescription medication daily; she is on dialysis; she had a miscarriage and feels like everything is falling apart because she doesn't know where he is going to be tomorrow and cannot settle while he is on remand. (Fieldnote, March 2014)

While these are perhaps extreme examples, similar themes flowed through the accounts of other participants: of the sixteen adults who participated in interviews, seven reported experiencing anxiety, depression, or engaging in self-harm. That quality of relationships with prison officers and Visitors' Centre staff can provide much needed information or support (as they did for Bill) or can exacerbate feelings of distress, powerlessness, or frustration (as in the latter example) is clearly of normative importance. However, in keeping with the wider literature on legitimacy, perceived unfair treatment can also cause families to question or reject the authority of prison officers, as the account of one young woman attests:

> *Brooke*: they have got the uniform on but they are no the police. They really really annoy me. Put it this way—to be fair I have no respect for them either because what respect do they show us? They dinnae show us any respect so the way I see it is I treat people the way they treat me. And I tell you if I treated them the way they treat us, they wouldnae like it, I would be barred from this place I tell you, I wouldnae get away with swearing at them and 'do this' and 'do that'.

Thus, the legitimacy of the prison is eroded when families feel they have been treated disrespectfully. As the manner in which criminal justice actors exercise their authority communicates to a citizen their value and status within society (Jackson et al., 2012), Brooke's strong reaction is perhaps unsurprising. However, this is not to suggest that officers at HMP Edinburgh deliberately sought to treat families poorly or that examples of positive interactions, such as the support provided to Bill, were not observed. Rather, these tensions are fostered by the complexity of the prison officer role, a focus on prison security, and the difficulties of embedding a families-rights perspective within prisons (Jardine, 2015; Donson and Parkes, this volume; Smith, this volume). Consequently, the prison *as an institution* can impose 'legally sanctioned stigma' upon visitors, characterized by inferior treatment, suspicion, and the stigmatization of families (Hutton, this volume).

Social marginality and prolonged criminal justice contact

As the prison population is disproportionately drawn from Scotland's poorest areas, families already experiencing social disadvantage are more likely to experience this stigma. Indeed, one member of the Visitors' Centre team rejected the assertion that imprisonment of a family member has less of an impact where the family has experienced this on multiple occasions. Rather, this participant argued that this served to create an oppositional or 'us and them' relationship between families affected by imprisonment and criminal justice agencies, which could be reinforced by the tensions and frustrations described above:

> *Jamie* (VISITORS' CENTRE): I think there is a funny sort of dynamic between prisoners and families, and prisoners and partners ... there is always a very funny emm feeling that a lot of the visitors don't think their partner should be here—most of them don't think that their partner should be here. Most of them don't think that they've not done it because most of them do know that they have done things but they will say 'this shouldn't really have happened' and 'he shouldn't be in a place like this' and it's almost as if they don't really have a sense of citizenship if you get me. Which isn't really their own fault because it is the fault of structure but there is definitely a really common hostility towards the state for having done this, which is reinforced by the relationships that they have between the prison officers and themselves.

That Jamie links this antagonistic relationship between the families and the prison to a lack a full citizenship is insightful and important, and resonates with arguments that poor interactions with the criminal justice system are damaging to both legitimacy and citizenship (Lee et al., 2014; Jardine, 2015; Condry, this volume; Smith, this volume). As Condry observes, this erosion of citizenship cannot be separated from the cumulative disadvantages experienced by many families, as the prison itself exacerbates and compounds these difficulties (Condry, this volume). It is notable, then, that almost a third of participants reported multiple instances of supporting a family member in custody, and that these women were also experiencing acute social marginalization. For instance, Tracey, who as noted above has herself struggled with homelessness, addiction, and previous incarceration, explained that she had been visiting various people in custody for over twenty years:

> *Tracey*: I have been coming up here since I was fifteen, so that is like 20 years of my life ... 20 years of my life I have been coming to this jail, do you know what I mean.
>
> *CJ*: To see lots of different people?
>
> *Tracey*: At first it was my brother, and then it was like partners do you know what I mean, and it was just friends. Most of them were just friends—one partner and then most of them were just friends except my brother and my brother-in-law and then it was my man ... I've been with him ten years, I think I was with him two years, three years and then he ended up getting his first sentence do you know what I mean. I think this is his third, this will be his fourth sentence that he is looking at now in the ten years that I have been with him and it's going to be like a flipping killer.

Each of the small interactions that occur over Tracey's twenty years of visiting will impact on her cumulative view as to whether the power exercised over her is fair, just, and transparent. Poor interactions with prison officers may be painfully felt, even if they are relatively few and far between. As one woman who seemed particularly distressed at visiting told me, while an officer had only once in the four years she had been visiting her son refused her a visit and made her cry, she had always remembered how this felt. Such enduring distress and discomfort when visiting the prison resonates with arguments that while the conduct criminal justice professionals can quickly undermine legitimacy, rebuilding this can prove more challenging (McNeill and Robinson, 2013).

Importantly, the perceived legitimacy of the prison amongst families is not only influenced by the experiences of individuals *themselves*. The intimate and connected nature of family life inevitably means that disrespectful or disinterested treatment of those closest to us can also erode the legitimate authority of the prison (Jardine, 2015). This is particularly problematic for families residing in communities characterized by disproportionate criminal justice contact, as broader and deeper connections to the prison are made through their social networks. For example, when I showed Alisha the information sheet for the project—illustrated with a jigsaw denoting the various forms family relationships might take such as cousin, aunt, friend, partner, or child—she remarked that she had visited nearly all of these relations in prison.

The detrimental effects of these multiple connections with regard to the legitimacy of the prison are further illustrated by the accounts of Brooke and Darcy. These two young women were both visiting their partners in custody, both had fathers who were also in prison and had become friends through their regular visits, and were therefore interviewed together. Given these multiple connections to the prison, over the course of a single interview Darcy spoke of officers who had insulted her father, how her partner was targeted and picked on by the police, and how her friend, Brooke, was treated unfairly when visiting the prison. Importantly, their regular visits had only served to entrench this negative view of the criminal justice system:

> *Brooke*: see without this place [the Visitors' Centre] honestly I would be barred from here I would have ended up head butting one of them I really would have. And I just walk out of there [the jail] and walk over here [the Visitors' Centre] but ken they shouldn't make me feel like that—they shouldn't manage to get me that angry that that is the way that I want to be. And they shouldn't be able to speak to us like we are shit because we are no. No offence but we could have better jobs than them, but they just look at everyone like …
>
> *Darcy*: you are visiting a jail.
>
> *Brooke*: So prison officers have got no respect whatsoever for visitors. Or children—I have seen them asking to empty bairns pockets, but only certain bairns.

Cumulatively, then, their own experiences, together with those of others in their social networks, led Brooke to conclude that she was amongst a group of families held in particular contempt by prison officers. The strength of these hostile views are notable, given the young age of Brooke and Darcy (who were in their late-teens and early-twenties) and that both had experienced parental imprisonment. Their animosity towards the prison arguably reflects the process of social and administrative exclusion detailed by Smith (2014, also this volume), whereby young people grow up feeling that state agencies do not work to protect their safety and wellbeing, but instead ignore or exacerbate their distress.

Similar themes also flowed through the ethnographic data, as the following (summarized) extract from my research diary illustrates. Each of these interactions occurred within a three-hour period when the afternoon visiting sessions are held; and while this day was not typical in the sense that *every* day I observed was like this, neither was it atypical (see also Hutton, this volume):

- The first visit has just gone over … one woman was very upset by the way that she was spoken to by the gate officers—this was her first time she and her uncle (who was elderly and disabled) had visited the prison … and she had gone up to the 'bubble' to hand in property … she came back to the Visitors' Centre in tears saying that she thought 'she wasn't going to get in' because she didn't know what to do and the officers had been 'horrible' to her. By this time she was late for her visit and needed help putting her things in the her locker.
- A woman in her thirties came back from the visit very angry saying she had been spoken to in a way that was 'rude' and 'unacceptable'. The Visitors' Centre staff tried to phone a visits manager but couldn't track one down. When they did the visits manager said the woman would have to go to the prison because he would not go to the Visitors' Centre. In the end, someone from the centre went over with her.
- This sparked off a discussion between other visitors about how the officers can be rude to them 'even though they are not guilty' and how last week one of the officers had made them wait outside because they were early and 'now they were too scared to go up'.
- A woman and a man who were on a visit came storming back into the Visitors' Centre. She was crying because she had been accused of passing drugs … they put in a formal complaint.
- Another visitor told us that an officer had told her 'you will respect the uniform'. She then said 'why should we respect them when they don't respect us?'

Crucially, this extract from my research diary illustrates how negative or adversarial interactions between families and prison staff can not only be highly distressing for families, but can also cause them to reject the authority of those officers. As the third and fifth examples demonstrate, discussion amongst visitors broadens out the impact of the initial interaction to include more people than were originally involved. That such discussions generate questions as to why families should comply with prison officers or regulations further underscores the importance of relationships between families and officers, and that these seemingly small interactions cannot be ignored when considering broader questions as to the impact of imprisonment on families and communities.

Families affected by imprisonment and the criminal justice system

Finally, in contrast to many academics who may choose to focus on one area of the criminal justice system (be it policing, sentencing, or imprisonment), by the time they come to visit somebody in custody each family will have encountered nearly every agency involved in the criminal justice process. This is significant as an individual's previous experiences with one agency—be they positive or negative—do not only seep through their current and future interactions with the agency in question, but can also impact upon their views of another (Bottoms and Tankebe, 2012; Franke et al., 2010). Consequently, many participants did not only hold negative views of the prison; they also described their distress at judges who are '*heartless*' and '*ruin lives*', police who stop their children and social workers and other criminal justice agencies who '*dinnae help you*'.

Indeed, social marginalization may increase the intensity and frequency of contact with not only the prison, but also a wide range of state agencies. While the individual histories of participants were diverse, all but one of adults visiting the prison were women, and only one of these women were in stable employment, with the remainder deriving their income from state benefit entitlement. There is a growing coalescence of criminal justice and social welfare policy in the United Kingdom as fiscal austerity has become entrenched, subjecting women in receipt of benefits to surveillance, scrutiny, and moral censure of their lives, choices, and often their parenting (Povey, 2017, 272). These families are widely denigrated by politicians, the media, and the wider public (Levitas, 2012; Skeggs and Loveday, 2012); and other families affected by imprisonment have been found to distance themselves from such recidivist or 'criminal families' as a means of claiming such moral authority (Condry, 2007).

This cumulative, stigmatizing, and often overlapping intervention of state agencies in the lives of marginalized families can have profound effects. Parents who were interviewed in custody worried deeply about how their imprisonment would influence their children's views of the criminal justice system and their own place in society. For example, one mother felt that her ex-partner's refusal to bring her daughter to visit the prison was partly motivated by a desire to punish her, but also by a fear that visiting the prison could lead her daughter to conclude that the police are '*bad people*':

I can understand from his point as well because she's old enough now—she knows what the officers look like and they are like police and she'll be asking questions about why is mummy with the police. So he [her father] doesn't want to bring the wean up for that reason; but at the same time I just think it would be nice sometimes if they had an establishment where there are family officers but just in normal plain clothes, do you know what I mean. Like so the weans are coming up and they are not having this thought in their head of they are police, why is my mummy with the police and then they think that the police are not letting their mummy come home, so then they hate the police and that's not a nice thing for a wean growing up to think that the police are bad people do you know what I mean. (Lorna, short-term sentence)

As noted previously, these concerns that repeated contact with the prison can further entrench adversarial relationships between families and criminal justice agencies also flowed through the accounts of Visitors' Centre staff. These participants explained that regularly hearing families express negative views about criminal justice professionals had lead them to develop a programme of community education projects around the theme of citizenship. One example of this was the 'Meet the Police' project. This initiative was run every few months at the Visitors' Centre to allow children and families to interact with the police in a non-threatening environment, as the Centre staff placed a considerable emphasis on fun (e.g. meeting the police dogs, dressing up, drawing and painting, seeing the police car, and bringing in balloons and food) while also trying to foster a dialogue between families and police officers.

Following the conclusion of the research, the Visitors' Centre staff sought to expand this work through the development of an information booklet for parents entitled '*My Daddy and the Police*'. This booklet was written '*by prisoners for prisoners*' by a team of fathers in custody with the support of Visitors' Centre staff, prison officers, and Police Scotland. The purpose of this booklet is to assist children in understanding various elements of the criminal justice process, for example: why their parent was arrested, why their house may have been searched, what a police station is like, why a prison sentence is given, and why a parent cannot return home until their sentence has passed. The last message from parents in custody to any child reading the booklet is as follows:

So we can't blame the police?
No, they are just doing their jobs to make sure people are not harmed or frightened, and they offer protection to everyone. Just because they are doing their jobs that doesn't make them bad people. You need to know, and should know, that if, or when, you are in danger, or need help, you can and should go to the police. You should not be frightened of them because the police help people too ... Your daddy just made some bad choices and that is why I have been put in jail. I want you to make good choices and not the mistakes I have made. (John, Gary, James, Mikey, and Robert, 2016)

That the final message these parents wished to communicate is that children should not blame the police for parental imprisonment, and that they should not be frightened of officers or scared to ask for help underscores the harms of prolonged or repeated criminal justice contact. However, the development of this booklet is also illustrative of an important means of promoting penal legitimacy. As a sense of procedural fairness and the ability to explain *why* seemingly unfavourable decisions have been taken is central to legitimacy (Bottoms and Sparks, 1997), providing families with such information in a format which is accessible, inclusive, and relevant to their concerns is key to limiting the risks to penal legitimacy outlined above. By allowing the voices of prisoners and their families to be heard in these discussions, this booklet is an important step forward to realizing a dialogical model of legitimacy in practice.

Importantly, their inclusion demonstrates to families that their voices and experiences are heard and valued, providing the moral recognition that is central to legitimacy (Liebling, 2011; Sparks et al., 1996). However, *My Daddy and the Police* goes beyond simple acknowledgement or consultation, as the co-productive approach to its development allowed families to *actively* contribute to the growing discussion surrounding families and the criminal justice system. Indeed, the pedagogical principles of community education underpinning this work not only reject unequal power relations, but also expressly seek to be both personally empowering and socially transformative (Freire, 1996). This initiative can therefore be conceptualized as recognizing and celebrating the capabilities of these families, thus supporting social justice (Condry, this volume). Finally, the very act of recognizing that prisoners and their families have a valuable contribution to make to such debates serves an important communicative function not only to the families themselves but also other audiences, challenging the stereotypical depictions of marginalized families and reinforcing their identities as valued citizens.

Conclusions

The interactions between families and criminal justice professionals described in this chapter demonstrate that the ways in which families feel they are treated by criminal justice professionals can have important implications for how fair, just, and legitimate they view the criminal justice system to be. By adopting a conceptual lens of legitimacy, we see that a perceived absence of fairness or respect can cause families to reject the legitimate authority of prison officers, therefore reducing normative motivations for compliance. While such arguments can be made with regard to any family affected by imprisonment, the risks to penal legitimacy are heightened amongst the most marginalized families, who are more likely to experience repeated contact with the prison through multiple members of their family and social networks. This creates greater opportunities for tensions between families and prison officers to occur, particularly as these families lack the social, economic, and symbolic capital that might ease such interactions. The ensuing lack of trust between families and prison officers can inform relationships with other criminal justice agencies, creating or entrenching an oppositional or antagonistic view of the criminal justice system.

The delegitimizing effects of tensions between families and prison officers must be understood and situated within the casual, routine, and everyday stigmatization of these families. Moral authority is a key component of legitimate power relations, yet this is often denied to these families as their structural and social marginalization is depicted as individual or personal failings in popular and political narratives surrounding poverty. For these families, then, the costs of imprisonment can go beyond financial loss, practical upheaval, and emotional distress that many families affected by imprisonment experience. Rather, these strains created by the imprisonment of a family member are compounded by a fundamental erosion of their feelings of safety, justice, and their own civic value. Thus, for the most marginalized families, imprisonment does not only compound their social disadvantage by draining their financial resources, it also undermines the social and political status which they perceive themselves to hold.

However, while the costs of such tensions between the families and criminal justice agencies are evident, it also clear that they are not necessarily inevitable. By allowing these most marginalized families a voice in debates of penal legitimacy, we see that these families do not want to be in conflict with the professionals with whom they interact. Parents do not want their children to be afraid of the police, and as participants such as Sophie observe, families visiting the prison '*just want to do what I need to do so I can leave*'. For many participants, the more neutral setting of the Visitors' Centre served as an important resource here, providing the information, advice, and a café to wait in that could ease their relationships with prison officers. The community education ethos of the Centre allowed families to become part of a dialogical model of penal legitimacy, as the projects described above help families to understand *why* particular decisions are taken by criminal justice professionals, and communicate to them that their concerns are seen to be valid by criminal justice authorities. Given our only partial understanding of the wider effects of imprisonment on families and communities placing the most marginalized families at the centre of such dialogues is essential. Without this space to contribute to such debates it is likely that the issues that matter most to marginalized families and communities will continue to be overlooked, yet again entrenching social disadvantage and political invisibility.

Glossary

Expression	*Meaning*
Aye	Yes
Bairns	Children, babies
Dinnae, doesnae	Do not, don't
The jail	Colloquial expression for the prison; often used in place of 'prison/custodial sentence' e.g. 'my son got the jail'.
Ken	Know, you know
Nae	No, not
Nae bother	No problem, OK
Wean	Child, baby
Willnae	Will not, won't

References

Alexander, M. 2010. *The New Jim Crow.* New York, NY: New Press.
Arditti, J. A. 2003. 'Locked Doors and Glass Walls: Family Visiting at a Local Jail'. *Journal of Loss and Trauma*, 8(2), 115–138
Arditti, J. A., Lambert-Shute, J., and Joest, K. 2003. 'Saturday Morning at the Jail: Implications of Incarceration for Families and Children'. *Family Relations*, 52(3), 195–204.
Beetham, D. 1991. *The Legitimation of Power.* London: Macmillan.
Bottoms, A. and Sparks, R. 1997. 'How is Order in Prisons Maintained?', in Liebling, A. (ed.) *Security, Justice and Order in Prison: Developing Perspectives.* 14–31. Cambridge: University of Cambridge Institute of Criminology Cropwood Conference Series.
Bottoms, A. and Tankebe, J. 2012. 'Beyond Procedural Justice: A Dialogic Approach to Legitimacy in Criminal Justice'. *Journal of Criminal Law & Criminology*, 102(1), 119–70.
Braman, D. 2002. 'Families Incarcerated', in Mauer, M. and Chesney-Lind, M. (eds.) *Invisible Punishment: The Collateral Consequences of Mass Imprisonment.* 117–35. New York: The New York Press.
Brunton-Smith, I. and McCarthy, D. 2016. 'Prison Legitimacy and Procedural Fairness: A Multilevel Examination of Prisoners in England and Wales'. *Justice Quarterly*, 33(6), 1029–54.
Ceesay, N. 2012. *Understanding the Needs of Prison Visitors: Edinburgh Prison's Visitors' Centre.* Edinburgh: The Carnegie Trust.
Christian, J. 2005. 'Riding the Bus: Barriers to Prison Visitation and Family Management Strategies'. *Journal of Contemporary Criminal Justice*, 21(1), 31–48.
Christian, J. and Thomas, S. 2009. 'Examining the Intersections of Race, Gender, and Mass Imprisonment'. *Journal of Ethnicity in Criminal Justice*, 7(1), 69–81.

Clear, T. 2002. 'The Problem with Addition by Subtraction: The Prison—Crime Relationship in Low Income Communities', in Mauer, M. and Chesney-Lind, M. (eds.) *Invisible Punishment: The Collateral Consequences of Mass Imprisonment*. New York: The New York Press.

Comfort, M. 2008. *Doing Time Together: Love and Family in the Shadow of the Prison*. Chicago; London: University of Chicago Press.

Comfort, M. 2016. '"A Twenty-Hour-A-Day Job": The Impact of Frequent Low-level Criminal Justice Involvement on Family Life'. *The Annals of the American Academy of Political and Social Science*, 665(1), 63–79.

Condry, R. 2007. *Families Shamed: The Consequences of Crime for the Relatives of Serious Offenders*. Cullompton: Willan Publishing.

Flynn, C. 2014. 'Getting There and Being There: Visits to Prisons in Victoria—The Experiences of Women Prisoners and Their Children'. *Probation Journal*, 61(2), 176–91.

Foster, H. and Hagan, J. 2015. 'Punishment Regimes and the Multilevel Effects of Parental Incarceration: Intergenerational, Intersectional, and Interinstitutional Models of Social Inequality and Systemic Exclusion'. *Annual Review of Sociology*, 41, 135–58.

Franke, D., Bierie, D., and MacKenzie, D. L. 2010. 'Legitimacy in Corrections'. *Criminology and Public Policy*, 9(1), 89–117.

Freire, P. 1996. *The Pedagogy of the Oppressed*. London: Penguin.

Halsey, M. and Deegan, S. 2015. '"Picking up the Pieces": Female Significant Others in the Lives of Young (Ex)incarcerate'. *Criminology & Criminal Justice*, 15(2), 131–51.

Holligan, C. 2016. 'An Absent Presence: Visitor Narratives of Journeys and Support for Prisoners During Imprisonment'. *The Howard Journal of Crime and Criminal Justice*, 55(1–2), 94–110.

Houchin, R. 2005. *Social Exclusion and Imprisonment in Scotland: A Report*. Glasgow: Glasgow Caledonian University.

Hough, M., Jackson. J., Bradford, B., Myhill, A., and Quinton, P. 2010. 'Procedural Justice, Trust, and Institutional Legitimacy'. *Policing*, 4(3), 203–10.

Hutton, M. 2016. 'Visiting Time: A Tale of Two Prisons'. *Probation Journal*, 63(3), 347–61.

Jackson, J., Bradford, B., Hough, M., Myhill, A., Quinton, P., and Tyler, T. R. 2012. 'Why do People Comply With the Law? Legitimacy and the Influence of Legal Institutions'. *British Journal of Criminology*, 52(6), 1051–71.

Jardine, C. 2015. *Constructing Family in the Context of Imprisonment: A Study of Prisoners and their Families in Scotland*. PhD thesis, University of Edinburgh.

Jardine, C. 2017. 'Constructing and Maintaining Family in the Context of Imprisonment', *British Journal of Criminology*, 58(1), 114–31.

John, Gary, James, Mikey, and Robert with Gunn, T. and Ceesay, N. 2016. *My Daddy and the Police*. Edinburgh: Police Scotland and the Scottish Prison Service.

Kirk, S. 2016. 'Prisoner Reentry and the Reproduction of Legal Cynicism'. *Social Problems*, 63(2), 222–43.

Lanskey C., Lösel. F., Markson, L., and Souza, K. 2015. 'Re-Framing the Analysis: A 3-Dimensional Perspective of Prisoners' Children's Well-Being'. *Children and Society*, 29(5), 484–94.

Lee, H., Porter, L., and Comfort, M. 2014. 'Consequences of Family Member Incarceration: Impacts on Civic Participation and Perceptions of the Legitimacy and Fairness of Government'. *The Annals of the American Academy of Political and Social Science*, 651(1), 44–73.

Lennon, G. and Murray, K. 2016. 'Under-Regulated and Unaccountable? Explaining Variation in Stop and Search Rates in Scotland, England and Wales'. *Policing and Society*, 28(2), 157–74. doi: 10.1080/10439463.2016.1163359.

Levitas, R. A. 2012. 'There May Be "Trouble" Ahead: What We Know About Those 120,000 "Troubled" Families'. *Poverty and Social Exclusion in the UK*. Available at: http:http://www.poverty.ac.uk/policy-response-working-papers-families-social-policy-life-chances-children-parenting-uk-government.

Liebling, A. 2011. 'Distinctions and Distinctiveness in the Work of Prison Officers: Legitimacy and Authority Revisited'. *European Journal of Criminology*, 8(6), 484–99.

Light, R. and Campbell, B. 2006. 'Prisoner's Families: Still Forgotten Victims?'. *Journal of Social Welfare & Family Law*, 28(3–4), 297–308.

McAra, L. and McVie, S. 2005. 'The Usual Suspects? Street-Life, Young People and the Police'. *Criminal Justice*, 5(1), 5–36.

McNeill, F. and Robinson, G. 2013. 'Liquid Legitimacy and Community Sanctions', in Crawford, A. and Hucklesby, A. (eds.) *Legitimacy and Compliance in Criminal Justice*. 116–37. Abingdon: Routledge.

Povey, L. 2017. 'Where Welfare and Criminal Justice Meet: Applying Wacquant to the Experiences of Marginalised Women in Austerity Britain'. *Social Policy and Society*, 16(2), 271–81.

Scottish Prisons Commission. 2008. *Scotland's Choice: Report of the Scottish Prison Commission*. Edinburgh: Scottish Prisons Commission. Available at: https://www.gov.scot/Publications/2008/06/30162955/0.

Smith, P. S. 2014. *When the Innocent are Punished: The Children of Imprisoned Parents*. Basingstoke: Palgrave Macmillan.

Skeggs, B. and Loveday, V. 2012. 'Struggles for Value: Value Practices, Injustice, Judgment, Affect and the Idea of Class'. *The British Journal of Sociology*, 63(3), 472–90.

Sparks, R. and Bottoms, A. E. 1995. 'Legitimacy and Order in Prisons'. *The British Journal of Sociology*, 46(1), 45–62.

Sparks, R., Bottoms, A., and Hay, W. 1996. *Prisons and the Problem of Order*. Oxford: Oxford University Press.

Sugie, N. 2015. 'Chilling Effects: Diminished Political Participation Among Partners of Formerly Incarcerated Men'. *Social Problems*, 62(4), 550–71.

Wakefield, S. and Wildeman, C. 2014. *Children of the Prison Boom: Mass Incarceration and the Future of American Inequality*. New York: Oxford University Press.

Woodall, J., Dixey, R., Green, J., and Newell, C. 2009. 'Healthier Prisons: The Role of a Prison Visitors' Centre'. *International Journal of Health Promotion and Education*, 47(1), 12–18.

12

Prisoners' Families, Penal Power, and the Referred Pains of Imprisonment

Caroline Lanskey, Friedrich Lösel, Lucy Markson, and Karen Souza

Introduction

Prison—it doesn't affect just one person, it affects everyone. I feel I have had a harder sentence (partner of prisoner).

The act of sending someone to prison also binds to the carceral domain the people they are close to, yet the impact on families is infrequently taken into account in sentencing decisions (Condry et al., 2016). For a long time the hardships prisoners' families faced were obscured by the traditional binary justice paradigm of 'state versus offender' but with the increasing use of imprisonment as a disposal in many countries including the United States, the United Kingdom, and Australia, its 'collateral consequences' (Hagan and Dinovitzer, 1999) became difficult to ignore. In an attempt to address the 'administrative exclusion' (Smith, 2014) by criminal justice bureaucracies and policies, research began to illustrate how the pains associated with imprisonment were not confined by institutional bars; they extended to families, children, and friends—in short, anyone who cared for those held in prison (Arditti et al., 2003; Braman, 2004; Haney, 2006).

This chapter develops the analysis of this 'punishment beyond the legal offender' (Comfort, 2007a). From the research findings we present here, we illustrate how parental imprisonment was experienced differently within and across families, and while not all experiences were negative, there were common experiences of hardship. With reference to the work of Crewe (2011), Goffman (1961), and Sykes (1958) and building on the analysis of secondary pains (Haney, 2006) and secondary prisonization (Comfort, 2007b) we call these personal and social hardships 'referred pains of imprisonment' as they stem from the 'depth', 'weight', 'breadth', and 'tightness' of penal power, institutional processes of self-mortification, and the deprivations of 'autonomy', 'safety', relationships', and 'goods and services'. Our analysis shows how these experiences were shaped by the direct contact families had with criminal justice agents, the strength of the relationship with the imprisoned parent, and the anticipated and actual response of others within the local community. It introduces a distinction between 'acute' pains that were experienced in the early stages of engagement with the criminal justice process (the arrest, trial, and removal of the father from the family) and 'chronic' pains that persisted and burdened family members over the longer term.

These referred pains can be conceptualized as 'punishment creep', for they stem from the state's administration of punishment to the offender. The concluding discussion reflects on the implications for social justice of the widespread inattention to the encroachment of punishment into family life and considers how it might be addressed. In this way the chapter aims to contribute to the growing analysis of the wider social implications of imprisonment and of the intersection between criminal and social justice.

Penal power and the pains of imprisonment

To capture the experience of imprisonment researchers have drawn on metaphors of scope, space, and sensation: 'depth' (Downes, 1993), 'weight' (King and McDermott, 1995), 'breadth' (Cohen, 1985), and 'tightness' (Crewe, 2011). These descriptors of penal power have been used to explain the dominant psychosocial burdens of imprisonment that have largely replaced physical pains of earlier eras (Sykes, 1958; Crewe, 2011).

Building on the conceptualization developed by Downes (1993), King and McDermott characterize 'depth' as the '*extent to which a prisoner is embedded into the security and control systems of imprisonment*' (1995, 89). The deepest conditions are found in maximum security prisons where prisoners may be literally housed underground (Alford, 2000) although prisoners may experience deep conditions such as segregation in more open prison environments (Crewe, 2011). The pains associated with the depth of imprisonment are linked to prisoners' physical, psychological, and social isolation from the outside world, including contact with partners and children. However, prisons 'at the shallow end' of the prison system may generate their own pains too. Open prisons, which provide prisoners with freedoms without being fully free can trigger confusion, ambiguity, and anxiety about contact with the outside world (see Shammas, 2014).

The concept of 'weight' symbolizes the burdens prisoners experience that arise from the constraints and conditions of the prison regime; '*the degree to which relationships, rights and privileges, standards and conditions serve to bear down on them*' (King and McDermott, 1995, 90). These burdens can be generated by the over or under use of power by prison officers (Crewe and Liebling, 2017) and by the mass of rules and regulations of which it is easy to fall foul. Such conditions, over which prisoners have little control, can be experienced as threatening to their personal safety and security (see Sykes, 1958).

Crewe (2011) expanded the analysis of penal power to include 'tightness' which he argued captured more accurately the character of its more recent manifestation. With resonances of Foucault's 'disciplinary gaze' (1977) this power is ever-present; it pervades the prison anonymously, 'wrapping up' prisoners in a '*web of regulation and self-government*' (Crewe, 2015, 59) and using the discourse of risk to control and manage. It creates pains of uncertainty and self-government because the criteria by which prisoners are judged are often nebulous and unpredictable, shrouded and protected by the elevated status of psychological discourse and subject to the caprice of prison staff. This form of penal power has a particular grip on the prisoner's future and hopes for release: it is never quite known how a conversation or interaction will be judged, recorded, and used in decisions about release dates and licence conditions (Crewe, 2011).

Penal power does not stop at the prison gate; its reach into the community outside the prison is denoted by the term 'breadth' (Cohen, 1985; Downes, 1993). After release, the freedom of ex-prisoners continues to be restricted by practical curbs imposed by administrative policies such as supervision requirements, licence conditions, and criminal records; by psychological and social barriers generated by self-induced or socially imposed stigma (Goffman, 1963); and by processes of institutionalization such as 'self-mortification' (Goffman, 1961) and 'prisonization' (Clemmer, 1940). Penal power beyond the prison gate is also 'tight' and opaque. It resides in the discretion given to probation staff to recall to prison all who do not continue to demonstrate self-regulation in the community, for example, by not attending probation appointments punctually.

Prisoners' families, penal power, and the pains of imprisonment

Viewing the experiences of prisoners' families through the lens of the pains of imprisonment has served to raise awareness of the wider social ramifications of mass incarceration. In his critique of penal policy in the United States, Haney (2006) refers to the unintended consequences of imprisonment for families and close relatives as *'indirect or secondary forms of prison pain'* (2006, 12). He argues that it is possible to think of penal policies as *'too painful'* if they are harmful to those who are not its legitimate targets such as *'family members of loved ones who suffer as a result of their relationship to incarcerated persons'* (2006, 11). His argument is supported by Murray et al.'s (2014) review of research on the effects of parental incarceration for children. Their cross-country comparative analysis pointed to the long-term adverse outcomes of parental imprisonment particularly in harsh penal and social contexts. They contend that although *'some "pains" of incarceration are unavoidable for those closely involved'*, reform policies should aim to reduce *'the long-lasting harms'* parental imprisonment leaves behind (2014, 160).

Comfort's (2007b) sociological analysis identifies how penal power affects the lives of adults and children connected to people in the US criminal justice system resulting from their direct contact with criminal justice agencies and from the unintended consequences of penal policy. She documents the changes they are required to make in their behaviours and expectations, the negative impact on physical and mental health, the curtailment of economic and social opportunities as well as the social support they receive from penal welfare services. In an earlier analysis (Comfort, 2003) she extends the concept of 'prisonization' developed by Clemmer (1940) to the experiences of women visiting inmates at San Quentin State Prison in California. Invoking security requirements, the prison attempted to corral these women into compliance and transform them into *'an obedient corps of unindividuated, nonthreatening entities ... organized according to the prison's rules'* (Comfort, 2003, 80). 'Secondary prisonization', defined as *'a form of socialization to carceral norms'* (Comfort, 2007, 279) is used to describe the process by which women adapted to the impositions of penal power: the rigidity and unpredictability of the prison's demands on their time, their dress, and behaviour. Drawing on Sykes' analytical framework (1958), these impositions are presented as 'pains of imprisonment' linked to deprivations of autonomy and of goods and services. In this way Comfort illustrates how the dishonouring and mortifying processes of penal power reduce the status of women who visit to that of *'quasi-inmates'*.

Comfort's work demonstrates the insights that can be generated from an analysis of penal power and how it affects the lives of people with close ties to prisoners. The following discussion develops this theorization by drawing on the broader body of literature on the pains of imprisonment described earlier and by illustrating empirically how the different dimensions of penal power, its 'depth', 'weight', 'breadth', and 'tightness' illuminate and differentiate the experiences of prisoners' relatives and friends in different contexts.

The research studies

Our analysis is based on data from two research studies from the United Kingdom. The primary research was a prospective longitudinal study investigating risk and protective factors in the resettlement of imprisoned fathers with their families. It employed a mixed method approach combining semi-structured interviews, standardized assessments, and statistical data. Separate interviews were conducted with fathers, mothers, and children, aged 4 to 18 years on two occasions, the first was within four months of the father's release from prison, the second was up to six months after the father's release. Interviews took place in family homes or in a location nearby apart from the father interviews at Time 1 which took place in prison. The sample at Time 1 in 2010 consisted of fifty-four (step)fathers, fifty-four (step)mothers and ninety children. The sample at Time 2 comprised forty fathers, forty-nine mothers and eighty children. The families were recruited when the fathers were in prisons in East Anglia or London. Details of the recruitment process and sample characteristics are described in Lösel et al. (2012). The fathers' sentences ranged from eight months to six years. They all had contact with one or more of their children, so they were a group of imprisoned fathers who had some active involvement in the lives of their partners or ex-partners and their children.

The subsidiary research study was a small-scale evaluation of a school-based support service for children with mothers or fathers in prison in 2016 to 2017 (Lanskey, 2017). The evaluation research collected and analysed data on the operation and outcomes of the service from January to December 2016. It had a mixed method design including interviews with seven children and their parents outside (including one mother who had been released from prison) and documentary analysis of fifty-one case records of children seen over the twelve-month period. The interviews all took place in the family home. The children were aged between 5 and 15 years and had all been referred for support due to the parent's imprisonment. The parents' sentences ranged between a few months to over ten years.

This discussion draws on the qualitative data from the interviews with fathers, mothers, and children (aged between 4 and 18 years) in the primary study, and from the children and parent interviews and the case records of the subsidiary study. The data from the two studies were analysed thematically (Braun and Clarke, 2006) using a framework based on the concepts of 'depth', 'weight', 'breadth', and 'tightness' identified in the research literature on penal power and the pains of imprisonment, but with flexibility to allow new ideas to emerge from the data (Layder, 2013).

Penal power in the lives of the research families

The imprisonment of a partner, father, or mother generated pains for members of the families in the two research studies in different ways. In both studies, the imprisoned parent had played an active role in family life whether or not still in a relationship with the partner, and the closeness of the relationships with individual family members varied. There were both similarities and differences in the ways penal power shaped the lives of the partners and children in comparison to the imprisoned parent. Some pains and emotions were *vicarious*, in the sense that they were derived from a concern for how penal power affected the wellbeing of the parent inside. Other pains and emotions were a consequence of *direct* experiences of penal power by the partner or the child outside. The following discussion considers these different experiences exploring how the dimensions of penal power: 'depth', 'weight', 'breadth', and 'tightness' affected the lives of the partners and children outside, and the vicarious and direct pains it generated in the short and longer term. It considers together the experiences of partners and children as many responses to the different forms of penal power were similar but highlights where experiences of adults and children varied due to their role within the family and their social status.

1. Depth, darkness, and distance

The pains and emotions families experienced varied depending to some extent on how 'deeply' the imprisoned parent was felt to be 'buried' within the prison system. 'Depth' was associated with 'darkness', the 'blackout' resulting from a lack of information about the imprisoned parent and 'distance' resulting from the coercive removal of the parent from family life.

Partners spoke about the 'secrecy' of the system and the difficulties of not having anyone to call and ask for news of how the imprisoned parent was getting on: '*[I felt] lost when he was away. [There] was no one to call and ask news.*' The anxiety generated from this lack of information was particularly acute in the early stages of the parent's involvement with the criminal justice system, when parents were 'taken away' suddenly and the partners and children outside had no one to contact: '*[It was] really hard … when he went away. [The] children [were] upset, withdrawn, didn't understand. [There was] no one to talk to. [It was] quite shocking. [I] struggled at first.*'

In contrast to King and McDermott's definition (1995) the level of contact did not always equate to the security categorization of the prison; it could also be associated with geographical distance of the prison from the family home. For example, one imprisoned mother in the second study was felt to be more deeply embedded within the system in the open prison she was in towards the end of her sentence because her family could not visit her there, in contrast to the closed prison she had first been sent to which was closer to home. The 'depth' of penal power thus also invoked pains of 'distance' and how deeply a parent was felt to be embedded within the prison system was linked to the amount of contact with the family.

The imprisoned parent's physical absence was painful for families who had close relationships. Partners spoke of the social isolation they felt: '*I'm used to talking to him every day*'. They lived with a profound feeling of loss: '*my other half is missing*'. Many children also found the physical absence difficult. Some were anxious that the parent might never be returned: '*I feel worried in case he might not come (back)*' (Callum,[1] 8 years). Their fears were linked to a lack of understanding about what had happened to the parent and to their inability to change it. The anxiety at the separation from the imprisoned parent led some to worry that they would lose the other parent at home too (see also Murray and Murray, 2010). One child had witnessed the police arresting and falsely accusing the mother following the imprisonment of his father. These children became 'clingy' to the parent at home, wanting to sleep in their bed or not go to school for fear that the other parent would not be there when they came out. For

---

[1] Pseudonyms are used to preserve anonymity.

other children the shock of the sudden distancing of the parent from their lives was responded to with anger and aggression towards others. Others were confused about their own agency in the process and felt that in some way they might be responsible: '*Sometimes I think it's my fault that dad's away*' (Lydia, 8 years).

In the absence of information about what was happening to the parent and a broader lack of knowledge about the prison system some families became anxious about the wellbeing of the parent in prison: '*(I) worry how he's coping in there*' (partner). For partners, the anxiety could be heightened by their perception of the vulnerabilities of the imprisoned parent: '*I'm worried about his health*'. For children, anxieties were made worse by their limited understanding of prison life which was often based on common myths and exaggerated representations of prison in the media (see also Boswell and Wedge, 2002).

There were moments during a prison sentence when the worlds inside and out met—in the liminal spaces (Moran, 2013) created by prison visits or home leave. There were opportunities in some of these spaces to rekindle a past normality of physical closeness: hugs, embraces, playing games together. However, some visits did not dispel children's concerns about their parent's wellbeing as one mother explained: '*It was very hard seeing their dad in prison ... It's scared the children ... they were asking if he was being fed ... they thought the cells were like dungeons.*' The temporary nature of the spaces generated its own problems too. Similar to the pains of open prison that Shammas (2014) describes, there were frustrations and confusions arising from the mirage of free interactions and the inevitable separation could be challenging and difficult to contend with: '*It felt very distressing when he went back to prison*' (partner); '*When I leave I'm a bit upset*' (Jodie, 8 years).

'Depth' was experienced differently by children within as well as across the families in the research studies. Some older brothers or sisters were allowed contact with the parent whilst the younger ones were not, which exacerbated feelings of frustration and helplessness in the younger children and could affect relationships between siblings. Some children were not allowed contact with their parent in prison for child protection reasons whether or not they wanted it. Children's experiences of the 'depth' of imprisonment were thus also affected by other forms of social control associated with the state's welfare function, their age, and status within the family.

The extent to which the 'depth' of the parent's imprisonment was experienced as painful also depended on the quality of the relationship between the incarcerated parent and individual family members. For some families, the physical and psychological separation was reassuring rather than anxiety-inducing or sorrowful. Where there had been violence or conflict in the family, between the partners or between the incarcerated parent and the child, the home was perceived to be a safer space without him or her (Lanskey et al., 2016). Thus the referred pains from the 'depth' of imprisonment could be experienced intensely but not always.

2. Weight

The families in the research studies experienced the 'weight' of penal power in two ways. The first was when families had direct contact with the prison through prison visits. This experience aligns closely with the concept of 'secondary prisonization' (Comfort, 2003). The 'weight' was generated by the complex rules and regulations surrounding the visitation process which were often difficult to negotiate and varied from prison to prison. It was not uncommon for things to go wrong and for a visit to be denied. For example, delays in getting to the prison by public transport could result in turning up too late to be admitted, or if a child's name was missing from the visitor's list, the whole family would be turned away. One parent was transferred without the family's knowledge resulting in a futile trip to the prison. The regulations and processes within the prison to which families were subject could also be stressful. This included the obligatory searches and walking through the prison: '*(It was) quite scary when ... dogs had to sniff me and a bit scary going to the library today through the prison*' (Sara, 10 years), or the requirement in ordinary visits not to move from the designated table and not to have physical contact with the imprisoned parent. On ordinary visits, in contrast to the specially organized family visits, there might be no or little food and long waits to get into the visits hall: '*I feel bored when it's a normal visit and I have to wait a long time*' (Sam, 7 years) and shorter visiting times as a result: '*[It's] meant to be 2 hour visit but by the time things get sorted, visits are only 1.5 hours*' (Jake, 15 years). Resonating with Comfort's (2003) analysis of 'secondary prisonization' the continual 'deprivations of autonomy' for children and parents and the absence of 'goods and services' (Sykes, 1958) were experienced as demeaning and a debasement of their identity: '*I hated how prison staff would treat you like you're the criminals*' (partner). So although visits could bring some temporary respite from the pains associated with the 'depth' of imprisonment, they were replaced with pains associated with its 'weight' in terms of the rules and regulations of visits, the administrative disregard of the prison to families' situations and needs, and the degradation of their social status.

The second experience of 'weight' was an inverse consequence of penal power; that is, the increased demands on the family in the imprisoned parent's absence. The 'weight of absence' affected partners' responsibilities: '*Everything now rests on me*'; '*if he was here it would halve my problem.*' Many partners were faced with the sole responsibility of running the household, looking after children, and paying bills, and additionally providing for the imprisoned parent. Some said they felt unsafe alone at night and there were additional worries about their children's wellbeing: '*It's a worse nightmare, watching what the children are going through.*'

The weight could be exacerbated by financial and material hardship: '*I had huge financial problems ... had to call Ghana to get help financially and to visit, had to leave the younger child in Ghana. I did not know how to fill in forms for money, pay bills etc.*' (partner). These constraining conditions could be experienced as a form of imprisonment on the outside with the concomitant deprivations of liberty and autonomy (Sykes, 1958): '*[There is] absolutely no freedom ... They go to prison and we get left with all the rest of it ... you have no choice but to deal with it*' (partner). For those families with little support, the additional burdens imposed by the parent's absence affected the partner's and the children's wellbeing. At a time when children might need extra support, some partners admitted they were '*sloppy with childcare*' and struggled to cope themselves: '*At first [I] couldn't sleep ... had a headache for a month and a half ... had to have tablets.*'

The majority of the families in the two studies experienced the imprisonment of a father but the additional burdens felt by the partners at home, the worries to be able to bring money in and to care for the children were similar whether the mother or father was in prison. As with other pains related to penal power, the 'weight of absence' was not felt in the same way by all. Some families had support from relatives and friends or from voluntary organizations and other partners and children found that they grew stronger with the additional responsibilities: '*I've always been able to cope on my own but [his] being away has made me stronger*' (partner). In some cases, the imprisoned parent or their offending had been felt as a greater burden so the 'weight of absence' was comparatively easy to bear: '*All the debts went with him when he went to prison—it was a relief*' (partner).

3. Tightness

Amongst the research families the sensation of 'tightness' was not confined to the imprisoned parent alone. The anxieties induced by the ubiquity and unpredictability of this form of penal power were also transmitted to and shared by the family. Partners and children could be highly sensitive to the continual monitoring and recording of contact with the parent in prison and were fearful that they could say or do something that would delay the release date: *'Calls are monitored and recorded, [we] can't speak with confidence. We're always careful what we say. We're terrified of jeopardizing my coming out … [it's] caused difficulties between me and her as [we] cannot talk properly'* (father). Once out in the community, the sense of tightness did not fully dissipate, it lingered around the ex-prisoner in the ever-present threat of recall. The uncertainty during the transitional period of licence affected all within the close family circle. One partner described the strain of the police frequently calling round unannounced to question the father about new crimes they suspected he was linked to. She said it was particularly distressing for their son who worried that he would be taken away again. The reach of penal tightness beyond the prison gate created the need for support after release too, as partners were called on to provide reassurance: *'He's paranoid. (He) thinks they're going to come back to get him. I have to tell him—it's not real, it's like he's re-living it'* (partner).

Yet although this form of penal power was deployed by agents of the criminal justice system, it was not uniquely invoked by them. It could be and was harnessed by some partners in retaliation to disputes with the other. A phone call to the police could be sufficient to return the parent to prison. One father reported being very angry about the system of recall. He said that probation believed his partner without any justification because of his past record. He said she regretted telling police he had hit her *'(cos I didn't)'*. His partner acknowledged: *'Drink is … the main source of arguments. I can be a bit of a bitch when I have a drink.'* The indiscriminating accessibility to this power by all apart from the convicted parent meant that what was experienced as 'tightness' for one could be experienced as 'liberating' or 'empowering' by another. The distinction hinged on the relationship between the parents and the extent to which they viewed themselves as a couple and 'on the same side'.

In the United States, Comfort (2007) has also highlighted how some families derived benefit from penal power, at least in the short term, by means of the social support the prison provided to the incarcerated parent: food and shelter, medical treatment, drug and alcohol rehabilitation programmes, which is not commonly available in the community. This carceral welfare enabled some parents whose existence prior to prison had been chaotic and/or violent, to stabilize their lives and renew ruptured bonds with partners and children during their sentence (see Clark, 1995; Edin et al., 2004).

4. Breadth

In addition to the family pains associated with 'tightness' described above, the 'breadth' of penal power affected family members in two ways: through the stigma associated with the parent being in prison, and in the challenges of re-establishing a life together after the parent's release. These challenges were linked both to structural and social barriers, and to the processes of institutionalization and mortification of the self that took place in prison (Goffman, 1961).

One of the most debilitating consequences of parental imprisonment was the secondary or 'courtesy' stigma that partners and children experienced. Close relatives became caught up in a 'web of shame' (Condry, 2007) created by perceived and actual social responses to the prison sentence, and the offence the parent was convicted of. Stigmatization was an isolating process and it was emotionally and physically painful.

Concerns to minimize the pain for children underpinned some parents' attempts not to tell them about the prison sentence: '*[We don't] want her stigmatised at school*' (father); '*I felt my child was too young ... and would have felt ashamed if she said it to someone*' (mother). However, the extent to which partners could protect themselves or their children from stigmatization was limited. Such news travelled fast, via reports in the media or rumours in the community which spread across and within families, and from parents to children. State welfare services actively discouraged parents' attempts at protecting their children in this way. One mother in the second study did not tell her son about her husband's sexual offence and deliberately avoided social activities for herself and her son because of the shame she felt and the fear that he would be hurt by the comments of others. Her efforts to protect herself and her child from social stigma were judged to be poor parenting by a social worker and the possibility of taking the child into foster care was mooted unless she changed her approach.

It was difficult to erase the stigmatizing mark once it was visible. Partners reported being verbally abused by others in public: '*I've had threats, people shout at me in the streets.*' Schools became risky places for some children (Lanskey et al., 2015) and for some places to avoid: '*When is a good day? ... When I'm ill and don't have to go to school*' (Alesha, 5 years). Other children in the school became the agents of social control, isolating and marginalizing the prisoner's child verbally and physically: '*Some people took the Mickey out of me as I haven't got a Dad*' (Max, 11 years); '*They said I hadn't got a proper Dad*' (Roy, 9 years); '*They call me names sometimes about my Dad being in prison ... sometimes I get into fights*' (Ellen, 8 years). When children resisted through fighting back or by self-withdrawal, the labels of 'troubled' or 'aggressive' and the resulting actions by the school authorities often served to further set them apart from others. In these ways, the forces of social control deployed through the media, community, and school talk and the welfare services worked together rendering publicly visible the mark of carceral power. The stigmatized identities attributed to the families could be seen as part of wider '*disciplinary processes*' serving to '*reproduce social order through the regulation of conduct*' (Toyoki and Brown, 2014, 718). However, not all families spoke about stigma and there were different experiences depending on personal and local community attitudes towards imprisonment. As Fishman (1990) identified in families that were in social circles where incarceration was common, stigmatization was less of a problem.

The process of readjusting to life outside prison could be painful for both the parent leaving prison and other family members. For the released parent, although the physical bars of the prison were left behind, psychological bars remained as they, too, were curbed and segregated. After having adapted to the routines and demands of living in prison, the process of adjusting to life outside could be challenging: '*When you come out of prison ... and used to being told to move, to shower, to eat, everything ... you have to get yourself self-motivated—get yourself into another routine*'; '*I was used to peace and quiet. The first few days were hard, like carnage!*'

Re-establishing relationships with the family was part of the process of undoing the mortifying effect of prison life (see also Grounds, 2004). It was easier in families where there had been contact during the prison sentence (see Lanskey et al., 2016) but the first few months could be hard for everyone: '*Sometimes he's a grumpy old man because he's tired*' (partner); '*He doesn't play with me much. He tells me off quite a lot*' (Laura, 7 years). The process of adjustment was mutual and coping with the legacy of prison had as much to do with changes that had taken place in the family over the time of the prison sentence as the 'self-mortification' (Goffman, 1961) of the incarcerated parent. While for some, the parent's return felt like the family was restored, others had grown more independent and become accustomed to a lifestyle without the parent: '*[It was] strange at first, having a man in the house, ... having to let go of my independence*' (partner).

The structural barriers left by the carceral branding of the released parent's identity could add to the pains of adjustment for the family as well as the prisoner. The convicted parent's licence restrictions after release could limit contact with the family or activities that the family could do together: '*It was a bit difficult seeing him when he had his tag*' (Julia, 18 years). The stresses that the released parent experienced at not being able to find work were shared: '*Finding a job with a criminal record is a nightmare*'; '*He's out of breath going from here to there.*' There were barriers too set in place for the partner's career: one mother was not able to be a childminder because she would not receive official accreditation from the inspection services due to the father living back in the family home. In this way, because of their associations with a former prisoner, the lifestyles and opportunities of other family members could also be restricted by the reach of carceral power into the community.

Thus the pains associated with the breadth of penal power cast a shadow over the families of prisoners and ex-prisoners (Condry, 2007; Codd, 2008). Viewed as risky subjects who posed a potential threat to the established norms and practices of child and adult society, they were isolated through social and structural processes of marginalization. Some who internalized the normalizing power of society kept themselves in the shadows. Others who employed strategies of protection or resistance were countered with stringent responses from welfare and educational authorities which served to label and often isolate further.

5. Acute and chronic pain

The seeming permanency of stigmatization highlights a temporal dimension to the pains of imprisonment for families and raises questions about the extent to which they remained constant or transformed over time. From the stories of family members it was evident that their experiences of pain changed at different stages of the parent's imprisonment and release.

The pains experienced at the early stages of the process—the arrest and sentencing in court—were often acute; shock was accompanied by intense sadness or anger. Over time, partners and children developed strategies for coping but for many the continued absence of the parent left an ongoing sadness or anger which had to be managed: '*[I] mostly keep it bottled inside; [I] don't think it helps to talk about it because it won't get him out any sooner*' (Leah, 16 years); '*[When I feel sad] I want to go out and beat people up and rob people but I don't. I talk to my girlfriend and go outside*' (Kwesi, 18 years). The stresses of enforced single parenthood and additional financial burdens were long-term hardships too that had to be endured. There were also ongoing effects of earlier insecurities resulting from the parent's incarceration: despite the return of this father, one 17-year-old said he still did not like being '*home alone*' and '*felt safer*' when '*someone stays in the house with me*' (Peter, 15 years). The collective impact of the acute and chronic pains of imprisonment experienced by families generated further pains of regret: '*I wish we could go back 2 years and change everything so my Dad didn't go away*' (Leah, 16 years). Yet despite the pains and deprivations endured, many families were forward-looking and worked steadily at rebuilding their lives together: '*He's been out about five months. It took about three months to get fully used to it. He had to build up a relationship with all of them, spending time with them individually and as a family*' (partner). There is therefore much more to understand about how the referred pains of imprisonment shift and transform over time, about the strategies families employ to address them and about their longer-term consequences for the resilience of the family.

Discussion: referred pains of imprisonment and social justice

> We speak of the individual and his environment, of the child and his family, of individual and society ... without clearly reminding ourselves that the individual forms part of his environment, his family, his society (Elias, 1978, 13).

The findings from our two research studies highlight the extent to which imprisonment is a family experience and how the wellbeing and lifestyles and opportunities of family members are affected by the vicarious and direct pains related to the incarceration of a close family member. Theoretically, they suggest the relevance of a broader analytical lens than has been used previously to understand the pains of imprisonment; bringing the family into the analytical frame reveals a more comprehensive picture of the range and extent of the hardships that imprisonment generates.

The referred pains that families experienced were related to the 'depth', 'weight', 'breadth', and 'tightness' of penal power but were individuated and varied across and within families. They changed in intensity and form over time and were shaped to a large extent by the quality of the relationship with the imprisoned partner or parent. Some were similar to those experienced by the imprisoned parent, such as anxieties generated by a lack of contact or concerns about the adverse impact of imprisonment on other family members. Others were qualitatively different, such as the 'weight' or burden generated by the absence of the imprisoned parent from family life outside. While penal power was often experienced as painful, it was not always so. The imprisonment of the parent or partner brought some families respite from conflict and the stresses of debt or drug/alcohol addictions.

The analysis of the families' experiences also identified the multiple levels at which penal power is shaped and distributed within and outside the prison: in national sentencing, penal, and social policies; in rules and regulations of employment, educational, and social institutions; and in individual interactions between family members and criminal justice agents, professionals from other services, and people in the local community. It revealed too the complex interactions of penal power with other forms of social control deployed formally by welfare and education agencies, and informally by other adults and children in the local community.

Although some families derived benefits from the parent's imprisonment, the variant forms of penal power were most frequently experienced as punitive. This 'creep' of state punishment beyond the offender created or exacerbated personal, social, and economic hardships. The findings from the studies discussed here thus support the calls of earlier writers for greater attention to be given to the social injustices prisoners' families face (e.g. Arditti, 2012; Codd, 2008; Condry et al., 2016; Kotova, 2014). This matter has acquired particular salience given the rapid increase in prison populations in many countries over the past decade (Walmsley, 2016) and the correspondingly large number of families affected.

The contribution of the referred pains of imprisonment analysis to the social justice agenda is that it establishes a conceptual link between the punishment of imprisonment administered to offenders and the experiences of their families. It reveals the unintentional consequences of penal policies and an approach to criminal justice which takes insufficient note of the social reality of human interdependence. It thus highlights the limitations of a perspective of imprisonment as punishment of an offender only (see also Kotova, this volume) and invites consideration of how the adverse effects of the 'depth', 'weight', 'breadth', and 'tightness' of penal power on prisoners' families might be addressed.

Amartya Sen's 'idea of justice' (2009) is informative to this discussion. Sen argues for a pragmatic approach to social justice that works from the actual world that emerges from institutions and rules rather than an idealized vision of what could be. This approach, which equates to the Indian concept of justice '*naya*', is not subject to overly-ambitious assumptions about how well ideals can be translated into practice (Sen, 2009). Sen's conceptualization of justice as a matter of degree and not as a dichotomous category supports our differentiated findings on family experiences. It also circumvents the challenge of disentangling the impact of penal power from other forms of social control which fall outside the official remit of the criminal justice system. Adopting this pragmatic perspective, some preliminary considerations for current criminal justice and welfare practice are outlined below.

From a sentencing perspective, awareness of the collective phenomenon of referred pains of imprisonment raises questions about whether the perceived severity of imprisonment as a form of punishment is under-estimated. This issue is considered by Hayes (2018) who proposes a proximity model of sentencing policy which would require sentencing authorities to take note of '*as wide a range of pains as possible*' in their decision-making, including what he terms '*contextual pains*' of punishment within which category the referred pains of imprisonment would arguably lie. Confronting the whole institution of punishment '*as it actually is*' and taking account of '*the subjective pains [punishment] actually engenders*' (2017, 16) could lead to a more comprehensive evaluation of the impact of imprisonment, to upward adjustments of perceptions of the severity of a custodial sentence and, arguably, to a fairer use of it as a sentencing disposal.

There is also scope to consider how each of the different referred pains might be removed or alleviated through the policies and practices of criminal justice and welfare agencies. Such a development would parallel the widening of criminal justice policy perspectives that has taken place in many countries over recent decades to include the suffering and procedural rights of victims and their relatives (Vanfraechem et al., 2014). For example, the referred pains associated with the 'depth' of imprisonment could be given greater priority in policy decisions about the placing of convicted parents within the secure estate in order to allow possibilities for face-to-face contact with partners and children. This is a particularly relevant issue for convicted mothers as recent closures of female prisons in England and Wales have increased the likelihood that women will be placed a long way from their home area (Women in Prison, 2015). At an institutional level, prisons might consider whether there are regular opportunities for quality communication with families and, taking account of the acute anxiety often experienced at the early stages of separation, ensure that there are good communication possibilities from the first hours of a person's admission. Prison family liaison officers, and professionals from welfare organizations could be given greater resources to ensure that all family members are kept well-informed, and receive support in their contacts and dealings with the prison. However, there is a deeper issue to be addressed, too; in order to mitigate the vicarious pains associated with concerns for the wellbeing of the parent in prison, it would be necessary not only to facilitate regular and quality communication but also to demonstrate that the prison was a safe and humane living environment.

With regard to pains associated with the 'weight' of imprisonment, greater recognition of the needs of prisoners' families could be given in policy-making to alleviate the burdens (financial, social, personal) directly associated with the imprisoned parent's absence. Local welfare organizations could set up networks to support partners and children and prisons might review their visiting policies and practices to ensure that families feel welcome, respected, and reassured in their interactions with prison staff.

Consideration of the adverse effects related to the 'breadth' of penal power might direct attention to removing structural barriers to re-entry such as in employment legislation. Community services and schools could increase advocacy and support for partners and children and work publicly to reduce the stigma associated with imprisonment. A more transparent approach to the decision-making processes of release and recall combined with a more stringent review process could reduce the arbitrariness in the use of penal power associated with the pain of *tightness*. Similarly ensuring that families had a clear understanding of the role and authority of professionals they come into contact with (prison and probation officers, social workers, and welfare professionals) might remove some anxieties associated with the opaqueness of state power. There is a deeper issue here too however, which relates to the actual distribution of power amongst criminal justice agents and the discretion they have to make judgements about extensions to prison sentences or recalls.

It is important therefore to acknowledge that the referred pains of imprisonment rarely result from '*intentional abuses of power or derelictions of duty, so much as side-effects of deliberate policies*' (Crewe, 2011, 524). Initiatives that operate only at the surface of criminal justice activity are unlikely to address the deeper penal and social dynamics underlying the pains that families experience. Attention therefore needs to be given to the policies and practices that *unintentionally* make their lives painful: specifically those related to sentencing, risk management, and security which dominate the landscape of criminal justice in England and Wales.

These policies do not operate in isolation but in a cultural context where people who commit crime are regularly stigmatized. Criminal justice policies alone will not therefore be able to address the deep-seated attitudes and values which result in the social stigmatization of offenders and by association their families. The findings from these research studies suggest that the interests and concerns of prisoners' families would be well placed within the decision-making framework of social as well as criminal justice policy. Such positioning might go some way to minimizing the distress, disrespect, and disruption many currently experience.

References

Alford, C. F. 2000. 'What Would It Matter If Everything Foucault Said about Prison Were Wrong? "Discipline and Punish" After Twenty Years'. *Theory and Society*, 29(1), 125–46.

Arditti, J. A. 2012. *Parental Incarceration and the Family: Psychological and Social Effects of Imprisonment on Children, Parents and Caregivers*. New York: New York University Press.

Arditti, J. A., Lambert-Shute, J., and Joest, K. 2003. 'Saturday Morning at the Jail: Implications of Incarceration for Families and Children'. *Family Relations*, 52(3), 195–204.

Boswell, G. and Wedge, P. 2002. *Imprisoned Fathers and Their Children*. London: Jessica Kingsley.

Braman, D. 2004. *Doing Time on the Outside: Incarceration and Family Life in Urban America*. Ann Arbor, MI: University of Michigan Press.

Braun, V. and Clarke, V. 2006. 'Using Thematic Analysis in Psychology'. *Qualitative Research in Psychology*, 3(2), 77–101.

Clark J. 1995. 'The Impact of the Prison Environment on Mothers'. *Prison Journal*, 75(3), 306–24.

Clemmer, D. 1940. *The Prison Community*. Boston: Christopher Publishing.

Codd, H. 2008. *In the Shadow of Prison: Families, Imprisonment and Criminal Justice*. Cullompton: Willan Publishing.

Cohen, S. 1985. *Visions of Social Control: Crime, Punishment and Classification*. Cambridge: Polity Press.

Comfort, M. 2003. 'In the Tube at San Quentin: The "Secondary Prisonization" of Women Visiting Inmates'. *Journal of Contemporary Ethnography*, 32(1), 77–107.

Comfort, M. 2007a. 'Punishment Beyond the Legal Offender'. *Annual Review of Law and Social Science*, 3(1), 271–96.

Comfort M. 2007b. *Doing Time Together: Love and Family in the Shadow of the Prison*. Chicago: University of Chicago Press.

Condry, R. 2007. *Families Shamed: The Consequences of Crime for Relatives of Serious Offenders*. Cullompton: Willan Publishing.

Condry, R., Kotova, A., and Minson, S. 2016. 'Social Justice and Collateral Damage: The Families and Children of Prisoners', in Jewkes, Y., Crewe, B., and Bennett, J. (eds.) *Handbook on prisons*. 622–40. Abingdon: Routledge.

Crewe, B. 2011. 'Depth, Weight, Tightness: Revisiting the Pains of Imprisonment'. *Punishment & Society*, 13(5), 509–29.

Crewe, B. 2015. 'Inside the Belly of the Penal Beast: Understanding the Experience of Imprisonment'. *International Journal for Crime, Justice and Social Democracy*, 4(1), 33–49.

Crewe, B. and Liebling, A. 2017. 'Reconfiguring Penal Power', in Liebling, A., Maruna, S., and McAra, L. (eds.) *Oxford Handbook of Criminology*. (6th ed.). 889–913. Oxford: Oxford University Press.

Downes, D. 1993. *Contrasts in Tolerance*. Oxford: Oxford University Press.

Edin, K., Nelson, T. J., and Paranal, R. 2004. 'Fatherhood and Incarceration as Potential Turning Points in the Criminal Careers of Unskilled Men', in Pattillo, M., Weiman, D., and Western, B. (eds.) *Imprisoning America: The Social Effects of Mass Incarceration*. 46–75. New York: Russell Sage.

Elias, N. 1978. *What is Sociology?* Transl. Mennell, S. and Morrissey, G. New York: Columbia University Press.

Fishman, L. T. 1990. *Women at the Wall: A Study of Prisoners' Wives Doing Time on the Outside*. Albany, NY: SUNY Press.

Foucault, M. 1977. *Discipline and Punish: The Birth of the Prison*. Tr. Sheridan, A. London: Penguin Books.

Goffman, E. 1961. *Asylums: Essays on the Social Situation of Mental Patients and Other Inmates*. London: Penguin Books.

Goffman, E. 1963. *Stigma: Notes on the Management of Spoiled Identity*. Englewood Cliffs, NJ: Prentice Hall.

Grounds, A. 2004. 'Psychological Consequences of Wrongful Conviction and Imprisonment'. *Canadian Journal of Criminology and Criminal Justice*, 46(2), 165–82.

Hagan, J. and Dinovitzer, R. 1999. 'Collateral Consequences of Imprisonment for Children, Communities and Prisoners', in Tonry, M., and Petersilia, J. (eds.) *Crime and Justice: An Annual Review of Research* (7). 121–62. Chicago, IL: University of Chicago Press.

Haney, C. 2006. *Reforming Punishment: Psychological Limits to the Pains of Imprisonment*. Washington, DC: American Psychological Association.

Hayes, D. 2018. 'Proximity, Pain, and State Punishment'. *Punishment & Society*, 20(2), 235–54.

King, R. D. and McDermott, K. 1995. *The State of Our Prisons*. Oxford: Clarendon Press.

Kotova, A. 2014. 'Justice and Prisoners' Families'. Howard League What is Justice? Working Papers 5/2014. Available at: https://howardleague.org/wp-content/uploads/2016/04/HLWP_5_2014_2.pdf.

Lanskey, C. 2017. *Evaluation of the Ormiston Families' 'Breaking Barriers' Service in Bedfordshire, Cambridgeshire and Essex.* Cambridge: University of Cambridge Institute of Criminology.

Lanskey C., Lösel, F., Markson, L., and Souza, K. 2015. 'Re-framing the Analysis: A 3-Dimensional Perspective of Prisoners' Children's Well-being'. *Children and Society,* 29(5), 484–94.

Lanskey, C., Lösel, F., Markson, L., and Souza, K. 2016. 'Children's Contact with Their Imprisoned Father and the Father–child Relationship after his Release'. *Families, Relationships and Societies,* 5(1), 43–58.

Layder, D. 2013. *Doing Excellent Small-scale Research.* London: Sage Publications.

Lösel, F., Pugh, G., Markson, L., Souza, K. A., and Lanskey, C. 2012. *Risk and Protective Factors in the Resettlement of Imprisoned Fathers with their Families.* Norwich: Ormiston Children and Families Trust.

Moran, D. 2013. 'Between Outside and Inside? Prison Visiting Rooms as Liminal Carceral Spaces'. *GeoJournal,* 78(2), 339–51.

Murray, J. and Murray, L. 2010. 'Parental Incarceration, Attachment and Child Psychopathology'. *Attachment & Human Development,* 12(4), 289–309.

Murray, J., Bijleveld, C. C., Farrington, D. P., and Loeber, R. 2014. *Effects of Parental Incarceration on Children: Cross-national Comparative Studies.* Washington, DC: American Psychological Association.

Sen, A. 2009. *The Idea of Justice.* London: Allen Lane.

Shammas, V. L. 2014. 'The Pains of Freedom: Assessing the Ambiguity of Scandinavian Penal Exceptionalism on Norway's Prison Island'. *Punishment & Society,* 16(1), 104–23.

Smith, P. S. 2014. *When the Innocent are Punished: The Children of Imprisoned Parents.* London: Palgrave Macmillan.

Sykes, G. 1958. *The Society of Captives: A Study of a Maximum-security Prison.* Princeton, NJ: Princeton University Press.

Toyoki, S. and Brown, A. D. 2014. 'Stigma, Identity and Power: Managing Stigmatized Identities Through Discourse'. *Human Relations,* 67(6), 715–37.

Vanfraechem, I., Pemberton, A., and Ndahinda, M. F. 2014. *Justice for Victims: Perspectives on Rights, Transition and Reconciliation.* Abingdon: Routledge.

Walmsley, R. 2016. 'World Prison Population List: 11th edition'. Institute for Criminal Policy Research, World Prison Brief. Available at: http://www.prisonstudies.org/sites/default/files/resources/downloads/world_prison_population_list_11th_edition_0.pdf.

Women in Prison. 2015. *State of the Estate: Women in Prison's Report on the Women's Custodial Estate.* (2nd ed.). London: Women in Prison. Available at: http://www.womeninprison.org.uk/research/reports.php?s=2015-11-19-state-of-the-estate.

13
Rights and Security in the Shadow of the Irish Prison
Developing a Children's Rights Approach to Prison Visits in Ireland

Fiona Donson and Aisling Parkes

Introduction

On 24 April 1916, Padraig Pearce read the Irish Proclamation of Independence outside the General Post Office (GPO) in Dublin. It stated:

The Republic guarantees religious and civil liberty, equal rights and equal opportunities to all its citizens, and declares its resolve to pursue the happiness and prosperity of the whole nation and all of its parts, *cherishing all of the children of the nation equally*, and oblivious of the differences carefully fostered by an alien government, which have divided a minority from the majority in the past.

Over 100 years on, the question remains to what extent the children of Ireland are cherished equally, in particular children with a parent in prison. While much work has been done in recent years by the Irish Government in the area of children's rights both from a policy and law reform perspective, little attention has been paid by the state to the rights of children who have a parent in prison. The protection afforded children under Article 42A of the Irish Constitution (inserted in 2015) is extremely limited and does not provide a straightforward mechanism to actively support the protection of the rights of this group beyond a general statement that:

The State recognises and affirms the natural and imprescriptible rights of all children and shall, as far as practicable, by its laws protect and vindicate those rights.

Beyond this basic commitment, the Constitution provides for some specific rights protections, however these are not directed at children with a parent in prison. In considering Ireland's need to protect the rights of children in this area we must look at obligations that recognize them as persons with rights that deserve attention and protection.

At a policy level, there has been some progress in recognizing this group of children. The Irish Government published a policy statement on children and young people living in contemporary Ireland entitled: *Better Outcomes, Brighter Futures: The National Policy Framework for Children and Young People 2014–2020* (DCYA, 2014) which includes a government commitment to '[e]nsure adequate access by children to an imprisoned parent, in a child-friendly setting'. However, this remains the only central government acknowledgement of responsibility towards children with a parent in prison. Thus, children with a parent in prison are not mentioned in the Department of Children and Youth Affairs (DCYA) Statement of Strategy 2016–2019; nor are they noted in its annual reports. This is despite the department's stated commitment to relevant factors such as 'early intervention and prevention', the need to 'listen to and involve children' and 'cross-government and interagency collaboration' (DCYA, 2017). Indeed, children with a parent in prison are, as a group, not formally identified in education policy, child protection policy, and wider criminal justice and court practice.

Unfortunately, Ireland is not alone in failing to adequately recognize the needs of this group. It has been noted that elsewhere there is a 'systemic blindness of the criminal justice system to the existence of children' of prisoners and this ultimately 'has the effect of diminishing their "dominion"' (Wallis and Dennison, 2015: 107). It is well established that '[t]he many discussions on the effects of prisons and punishment have typically focused on either the effects on the individual prisoner (individual deterrence and rehabilitation of prisoners) or the possible preventive effect on society at large (general deterrence)' (Smith, 2014). This lack of visibility for children with parents in prison in Ireland extends to all aspects of the criminal justice system from arrest through to detention and post release. Yet it is recognized that 'Children are as much the recipients, albeit indirectly, of "justice" as the adults who are incarcerated' (Flynn et al., 2015, 24). Moreover, the lack of attention to 'the rights and interests of children of prisoners robs them of their ability to be heard on matters that significantly affect them during the criminal justice system process' (Wallis and Dennison 2015, 107).

In recent times, arguments have been made in the context of research and advocacy against the use of 'too much of a quantitative, categorical approach based on generalized and simplistic assumptions about incarcerated parents and their children' (Genty, 2012, 37). Instead, an approach which is of a more individualized nature is warranted that is balanced and based on accurate information concerning the children and families of prisoners (Genty, 2012, 37). The adoption of a children's rights-based approach is ideal in achieving this aim in relation to these children given that it warrants looking at the process of imprisonment through the lens of an individual child. The purpose of this chapter, therefore, is to explore the potential for adopting a children's rights based approach when dealing with issues relating to children impacted by parental incarceration. It will be argued that the adoption of such an approach allows for the development of policies and services that are rooted in respect for justice and dignity. The extent to which children's rights are understood by staff within the Irish Prison Service (IPS) will also be explored as well as the possibility of a more instrumental approach to family visits which are seen as supporting offender rehabilitation. The chapter highlights the need for criminal justice agencies and policy makers to directly acknowledge the rights of children with a parent in prison and, in turn, for them to develop policies that uphold those fundamental rights independent of the rights and interests of their parents. In this way, it mirrors other chapters within this volume which explore the role of rights in relation to prisoners' families (Loucks and Loureiro, this volume; Minson, this volume; Smith, this volume).

Origins of state obligations towards children with a parent in prison

Under the UN Convention on the Rights of the Child 1989 (CRC), all children and young people are entitled to have their rights protected by states parties. Thus, all state institutions and agencies are duty bearers responsible for ensuring that the provisions of the CRC are adhered to in practice. This includes the prison authorities when the parent of a child is incarcerated. As the most highly ratified treaty in the world, the provisions of the CRC still represent the minimum global standards as far as the rights of children are concerned. The CRC is unique as a human rights treaty in that it encapsulates both the civil and political rights as well as the economic, social, and cultural rights of a child. Moreover, it is a holistic document which means that no one provision is stand-alone, each of the rights contained therein must be interpreted in tandem with the other CRC provisions. The CRC is unique as it clearly enshrines the importance of the relationship between parent and child and very clearly sets out states parties obligations towards children in the event that parents cannot fulfil those obligations. Moreover, where the state has made a decision that results in the parent–child relationship being interrupted, for example through parental incarceration, it has a responsibility to ensure that the rights of such children are protected throughout the process and thereafter.

The Committee on the Rights of the Child, the international body responsible for overseeing the implementation of the Convention worldwide, has set out four general principles which should guide the implementation of the Convention. These include: the principle of non-discrimination (Article 2); the best interests principle (Article 3); the right to life, survival, and development (Article 18); and the principle of respect for the views of the child (Article 12).

Article 2 requires that children with an imprisoned parent should not be discriminated against on the basis of the actions of their parents. Despite this, in the Irish context at least, these children do experience discriminatory practice. For example, the need to protect the rights of children in family law proceedings is well recognized, such as where decisions are being made which affect the child in childcare proceedings (Parkes et al., 2015). Contrast this with cases where the state has decided to incarcerate a parent for wrongdoing; a decision which directly affects the child. Currently in Ireland, there is little or no awareness of the need to protect the rights of the child in this context. Research by the authors has highlighted that current sentencing practice delivers inconsistent and discretionary outcomes in this area with the courts primarily regarding the existence of family responsibilities as a mitigation factor belonging to the offender, rather than as a matter relating to the best interests of the offenders children (Donson and Parkes, 2016). As a result, in reality, children likely to be separated from a parent because of a prison sentence appear to fall outside the rights discussion, despite the fact that a fundamental decision affecting the child's life has been made. For a detailed examination of the issues arising in this context, see the chapter by Minson in this volume.

The best interests standard set out in Article 3 has formed a fundamental feature of all decision-making systems affecting children. Requiring, as it does, that in any decision-making process which affects a child, the best interests of the child are considered as part of the process, it is critical to the effective safeguarding of children's rights. Despite lacking a clear definition, its relationship with the substantive rights of the CRC makes it a critical rights provision (Lagoutte, 2016). However, without a recognition of the fact that the rights of these children are relevant to decision making in this area, it remains highly unlikely that the best interests are even noted let alone considered as an essential component.

Of particular significance in the context of parental incarceration is the child's right to life, survival, and development recognized under Article 6 CRC. Every child has the right to develop physically and psychologically in a healthy way. The state is under an obligation to ensure that this right of the child is protected from the time they are born to the point at which they reach adulthood. Indeed, well documented psychological research points to the negative effects of parental incarceration on the development of a child resulting in serious issues in adulthood (Murray and Farrington, 2008; Lee et al., 2013).

Also fundamental to effective rights protection, Article 12 CRC provides for a child's right to have their views respected. This operates not only as a substantive right but also procedurally, providing a means by which children can access their CRC rights. Much has been written on Article 12 in recent years from a variety of different perspectives (Parkes, 2013), including the adoption of a General Comment by the UN Committee on the Rights of the Child (2009). While the UN Committee explores in detail the significance of this right for a range of children, the statement fails to outline the significance of Article 12 for children with a parent in prison in particular (Lagoutte, 2016). This is unfortunate since there is therefore no guidance for states parties seeking to implement this right in areas such as sentencing, prison visits, and child/parental access.

While each of the provisions set out above are significant in developing an overarching approach to supporting children and young people with a parent in prison, others are of particular import in this area. Article 9(3) provides that states parties should 'respect the right of the child who is separated from one or both parents to maintain personal relations and direct contact with both parents on a regular basis, except if it is contrary to the child's best interests'. Article 9(4) goes on to provide more detail as to how the right should operate:

Where such separation results from any action initiated by a State Party, such as the detention, imprisonment, exile, deportation or death ... of one or both parents or of the child, that State Party shall, upon request, provide the parents, the child or, if appropriate, another member of the family with the essential information concerning the whereabouts of the absent member(s) of the family unless the provision of the information would be detrimental to the well-being of the child.

Contact can be subject to restrictions and monitoring under national prison regulations (Lagoutte, 2016). However, best practice requires that limitations should be done in a way that still facilitates contact and should be justified (European Prison Rules, rule 24.2).

Finally, Article 18(2) sets out key elements regarding state party responsibilities for supporting parents and legal guardians 'in the performance of their child-rearing responsibilities' requiring 'the development of institutions, facilities and services for the care of children'.

It is important to acknowledge the fact that the CRC was drafted in the 1980s and practically speaking, it is an outdated document. Significantly, while the drafters were cognisant of the need to specifically recognize the rights of particular groups of children with special circumstances such as children with disabilities, they did not see fit to include a dedicated provision to recognize the rights of children with a parent in prison. This reflects the limited engagement with this group of children which has dominated law, policy, and practice until recently. Nevertheless, all the rights set out in the CRC are of course applicable to this group of children and the protections can be extrapolated and adapted to respond to their specific needs.

Of course, direct engagement with a particular group of children's needs and rights allows for a more nuanced and developed approach. This was in part rectified by the Committee on the Rights of the Child when it held a Day of General Discussion on the issue in 2011. The report and recommendations produced represent an authoritative statement on how the existing provisions of the CRC should be interpreted to protect the rights of this particular group of children. Arguably, however, they are both partial and outdated, and in reality should be seen only as a starting point for understanding children's rights in this area. Furthermore, the report does not have the same status as a General Comment which provides essential interpretative tools on specific children's rights provisions and themes. Unfortunately, the slow pace of engagement by the Committee on the Rights of the Child with this area is a common characteristic where this group of children is involved. While their vulnerability is generally recognized, rights based responses have been slow to develop, not only at national levels but also at the international level.

Critical to the debate on the Day of General Discussion was an emphasis on the 'inherent dignity of children and their best interests' in relation to situations where their needs are not met. The Committee recommends that in relation to visits, measures need to be taken by state bodies to ensure that prison visits for children are 'respectful to [their] dignity and right to privacy'. These concerns are to be balanced, as we will discuss later in the chapter, with the prison authority's obligation to ensure security within the prison context.

At a regional level, rights frameworks have also provided some protection for the rights of children with a parent in prison. The African Charter on the Rights and Welfare of the Child 1990 contains a specific provision relating to children of imprisoned mothers (ACRWC, Article 30) which was the subject of a General Comment by the African Committee of Experts on the Rights and Welfare of the Child (ACERWC, 2013). While focused on children of incarcerated mothers, the African committee acknowledged that it can be extended to apply to children affected by the incarceration of their sole or primary caregiver—this may be another family member such as a grandparent or a foster parent (ACERWC, 2013, paragraph 10). Significantly the Comment highlights the need to avoid 'formalistic determinations of children's best interests' and notes the wide variation in situations and responses needed to support children in this situation. The Comment is stronger than the Committee on the Rights of the Child report cited earlier, focusing as it does on a specific provision which sets out a number of provisions protecting children with imprisoned parents.

At the European level, the focus has been on respecting family life under Article 8 of the European Convention on Human Rights (ECHR). However, cases decided under this provision by the European Court of Human Rights primarily focus on these rights as belonging to the prisoner, or at best, the prisoners' partner/spouse. Indeed, for the most part, the court has not effectively engaged with the rights of children in this area (Smith and Gampell, 2011; Donson and Parkes, 2012; Lagoutte, 2016; Boudin, 2011). However, the Court has, in recent years, begun to identify the role of children's rights as part of the Article 8 right to family life and prison visits (*Khoroshenko v Russia*, 2015; Smith, 2014).

The above discussion indicates that there has been slow movement in developing a rights based approach to this particular group of children. However, this is not to suggest that children's rights have not had an impact in this area. Smith acknowledges the important role that children's rights have played in terms of prison reform in Sweden, Norway, and Denmark (2015). In particular, he notes the importance of institutions such as the Children's Ombudsman in Norway and Sweden as well as the Children's Council and the Danish Institute for Human Rights in Denmark, all of which have successfully pursued a children's rights agenda in the prison reform context. Norway has adopted an especially progressive approach in this regard by incorporating children's rights directly into the domestic prison laws (Smith, 2014).

In addition, UN and European prison rules, particularly those focused on women, have included provisions seeking to support child/parent contact (Bangkok Rules, 2010; Mandela Rules, 2015). The Council of Europe has also addressed this issue in its Resolution on Women in Prison which covers a number of matters including visiting conditions, search procedures and staff training (Women in Prison, 2008) while the Strategy for the Rights of the Child makes specific reference to children of imprisoned parents (COE Strategy, 2016). Most recently, the Committee of Ministers of the Council of Europe adopted Recommendation CM/Rec(2018)5, which is specifically dedicated to the rights of children with a parent in prison, marking a positive move towards formally recognizing the rights as well as needs of this group of children in various sectors of society (Council of Europe, 2018).

Children's rights within the Irish prison visiting system

At the outset of this chapter, reference was made to the latest policy document adopted in Ireland concerning children and young people in Ireland. *Better Outcomes, Brighter Futures* highlights one of the main outcomes aspired to between 2014–2020 that:

Inequalities [should be] addressed across all sectors, including health, education and justice. Children and their parents [should not] face discrimination of any kind, irrespective of membership of the Traveller Community, race, gender, sexual orientation, gender identity, civil status, disability, birth or other status. All children in need [should] have equality of access to, and participation in, a range of public services.

There is no doubt that children and young people with a parent in prison are at serious risk of unequal treatment and overall disadvantage in Ireland.

One of the few areas where this group of children in Ireland have been directly acknowledged is in relation to prison visits. As a result, the authors undertook research funded by the Irish Research Council to examine the extent to which prison visits in Ireland are being developed and operated by using the minimum children's rights standards provided for under the CRC. Interviews took place in 2015–2016 and involved a purposive sample of relevant professions as well as those directly impacted upon by the imprisonment of a family member. The study was designed to ensure that diverse perspectives on parental imprisonment were presented in a fair and balanced way. A total of thirteen participants volunteered to take part in this study, eight were employed by the IPS, three were from community stakeholders, and three were family members of imprisoned parents. Data was gathered through the use of semi-structured interviews. The research was subject to appropriate ethical approvals and confidentiality was assured to all those that participated.

The research examined aspects of the IPS's work in relation to children and families of prisoners. At management level, the organization has acknowledged the need to support families and children with family members in prison. However, a recent review of the culture and organization of the IPS highlighted the fact that there is currently 'a disconnect between the culture which exists in the headquarters of the IPS and that in the 13 prisons in Ireland' (Office of the Inspector of Prisons, 2015).

The power and remit of individual prison governors, and the inherent impact of prison cultures, is critical in terms of effective and entrenched implementation of policies, particularly in situations where those policies are in tension with the traditional prison security orientation. During interviews, one governor reflected the extent of his power to adopt a localized approach—'I do what I do ... We're independent serfdoms, call it what you like' (Governor 1, County A). The result of this can be that despite the development of policies, there is a risk of inconsistent implementation at local level. Another governor spoke of the resistance that was shown to decisions aimed at making visiting spaces more visually attractive for children and made the point that changes may only last as long as a particular person in charge is in post:

> anything that we've achieved here is because I'm here. And that shouldn't be the way. It shouldn't depend on me ... It shouldn't be about ... [Individual personalities and their own ethos] ... Because when I walk away from here, that should continue. It shouldn't roll back and say, well, look, thank god that lunatic's gone, because now we can get it back to a secure prison and put the eggshell paint back on the walls. (Governor, County C)

This individualized approach results in children and young people experiencing differential visiting conditions depending on their geographical location.

Child visits and Irish prison policy

Like most jurisdictions, Ireland has no recorded statistics on the number of children and young people with parents in prison. This is unfortunate, since knowing the number of children involved would ensure greater visibility of this group in terms of policy development, financial provision, as well as practical implementation. The effects of parental imprisonment on children are wide and varied. Indeed, a litany of research now exists exploring these and much is addressed in this volume. For example, incarceration is associated with families who face severe hardship, where the children suffer unmet material needs, residential instability, and behaviour problems (Geller et al., 2009). The fact that parental imprisonment is one of ten factors which can be indicative of childhood trauma is a significant factor in and of itself (Felitti et al., 1998).

In Ireland, 2012 marked a critical turning point in awareness, as far as prison visits and children's rights are concerned. The Irish Penal Reform Trust's report, *'Picking Up the Pieces': The Rights and Needs of Children and Families Affected by Imprisonment*, while conducted on a small scale, provided the first comprehensive consideration of the impact of imprisonment on families and children in Ireland. In response, the IPS established the Families and Imprisonment Group (FIG) to review research and practice in the area with a view to developing an applied response to be adopted by the IPS. Central to the latter task was a stated recognition that visits should be regarded as a positive intervention which can 'support prisoners and their families, aid resettlement and reduce offending ...' (FIG, 2014). It should be noted that the IPS was starting from a low base in its response to families as prior to the creation of FIG there was no prison policy on visits. Moreover, there was limited engagement with the broader responsibility of the prison service to visitors and families of offenders. That a response has been developed is therefore to be commended.

A key recommendation of FIG has been the adoption of a formal visits policy which is to have as a core aim 'the promotion of visits, and family visits in particular'. Their report notes the strong evidence that supports the view that visits, especially family visits, can play a 'critical' role in 'ameliorating the negative consequences of imprisonment both for incarcerated parents and for their children, in reducing inter-generational offending, in reducing recidivism and in aiding resettlement' (FIG, 2014, 8). The view of family ties as an important desistance factor is subject to significant critique and discussion in academic literature, and there is not the space here to discuss this in detail. However, there is a need to be cautious in this regard not least because of the burden it can place on families if they are left unsupported (Jardine, 2015). In addition, our emphasis on the need to recognize children of prisoners as independent rights holders coincides with a growing body of research, echoed through many of the chapters in this volume, that children and families of prisoners should be considered in relation to their own experiences, not merely as an extension of the prisoner (Jardine, 2015; Hutton, this volume).

The report sets out a framework by which the IPS would develop a multipronged approach focusing on visits and parenting programmes. This is a welcome development, particularly the adoption of a formal policy and an acknowledgement that family visits in particular are beneficial to all members of a family of a prisoner. However, when reviewing the work from a children's rights perspective, the change in position is constrained by the strong IPS focus on the prisoner and prison security. Despite the fact that the FIG report acknowledges the existence of the 'rights of children to have quality access to their imprisoned parents', it is immediately counterweighted by security concerns:

and, in so far as security considerations permit, they are provided with the kind of access to their imprisoned parent that allows them maintain and develop these relationships. (FIG, 2014)

Ultimately this is a narrow conception of the rights of the child which is immediately limited by the focus on security.

The lack of a children's rights focus in the prison service approach is visible in the core pillars of the FIG report. The (currently draft) policy contains five pillars upon which the new approach is to be based: communication (with visitors); facilities; staff support and training; family-related courses; and community organization partnerships. Absent from the approach is a direct reference to children, the inclusion of their voices, or a direct acknowledgment of their rights. Arguably critical to any proactive rights based approach is the reference to 'interventions' and the significance of this perspective on the implementation of the policy will be discussed below.

Standard prison visits in Ireland currently operate under the Prison Rules and formally allow sentenced prisoners to have one visit a week lasting thirty minutes (Prison Rules, 1997, rule 35). Rule 37(7)(a) provides that the default visit should take place in facilities which 'allow a prisoner and visitor to see and talk to one another but which prevent, through the use of screens or otherwise, physical contact' between them. Physical contact is allowed at the discretion of the governor under rule 37(7)(b) once s/he is satisfied that 'such contact will not facilitate the entry into the prison of controlled drugs or other prohibited articles or substances'. The default visiting arrangement allows for a minimal quality visit, with improvements being earned by the prisoner. There is no recognition within this element of the regime that children and families may be direct rights owners in relation to visits. However, visiting arrangements are often described as flexible and can be adapted both on a prison basis and to suit individual prisoner needs at the governor's discretion.

The IPS has now developed family visits, available to enhanced prisoners and operating under a more relaxed visiting arrangement. These superior visits are seen as a method of reducing reoffending and aiding resettlement. However, the adoption of family visits is also seen as a 'child centred intervention' by the IPS:

there's a big difference between a family visit, which is in a kind of a family room on couches, and there is physical contact with a kind of child-centred approach, to the actual bench, the traditional type visit. (Governor, County B)

Unfortunately, there is no clear engagement with the meaning of a 'child-centred' approach and what it would require in changing both visiting arrangements. While there is insufficient space in this chapter to explore this in detail, we would stress that it should be one which adheres to basic children's rights principles.

Access to family visits of this kind appears to be tied, at least in part, into participation in parenting courses. This is the second strand of the FIG approach—a dual family visit/parenting strategy. By tying the two components together, the right of access to family visits again appears to belong to the prisoner. There is no correlative right provided for the child or partner outside the prison. This is seen in the pilot operation of the Family Links Programme, undertaken in Limerick Prison from 2014 to 2016. The programme adopted an approach whereby poor behaviour by prisoners meant that participation in the programme was terminated—something that had a direct impact upon their families outside the prison who were co-participating in the programme. As the evaluation of the project noted:

poor prisoner behaviour resulted in partners and children not being able to participate further in the programme would appear to be directly at odds with the programme: an ethos that aims to ensure that families do not pay for the father's bad behaviour. (Bradshaw and Muldoon, 2017)

During the current study, one interviewee reflected on this approach placing responsibility for the impact of removal from the programme on the fathers, noting the need for them to 'man up' and take responsibility for the impact on their families. This approach disregards the prisons' responsibility to children and highlights the prisoner-centred focus of these initiatives. In turn, it fails to capture the potential harm that can be done to children in the name of positive interventions when the rights of those children are left unrecognized and unembedded in their design and implementation.

The role of children's rights in prison visit development

1. Prison perspectives

The analysis undertaken as part of our prison visits research sought to explore the level of engagement with, and understanding of, children's rights on the part of those working within the Irish prison system. Given that this project was focused on visiting arrangements, and was carried out against a background of change in this area by the IPS, it was expected that there would be some level of engagement by prison staff with a basic understanding of children's rights.

As part of the research, prison staff were therefore asked about their understanding of the rights of children in circumstances where a family member is in prison. While one interviewee noted a child's 'right to visit, … a right to be in a safe environment, that [visiting] … should be child friendly, that they shouldn't feel unsafe in that environment' (Governor, County C), the primary response of prison staff at all levels was to focus on child protection reflecting a traditional and limited view of children's rights. For example, interviewees highlighted concerns around the use of children to smuggle drugs into the prison. The dominance of this approach is unsurprising given the existence of child protection legislation: Children First Act 2015 and Criminal Justice (Withholding of Information on Offences against Children and Vulnerable Persons) Act 2012. Paradoxically, at the time of the research, the IPS had no formalized child protection policy in place.

For some interviewees, there was an acknowledgement that the prison service was on 'a journey' (Governor 2, County A) to including the rights of children in their polices and service provision; there was progress, but also still a long way to go. However, despite the desire to see change, there was little direct engagement with the specifics of what children's rights require of the prison authorities. One interviewee did engage with the need to broaden the IPS's understanding in this area:

> [W]e are very much focused on child protection here; it's around child protection rather than about development ... I don't think society has gone on to the whole development of a child thing yet.... We've got the child protection, which took us 100 years to get to, and now we're looking at protecting the child first and we haven't gone on to children's rights yet. And it's an awareness that some people have but I don't think we've even got there. I don't think society have got there, really. (Governor, County B)

This difficulty reflects in some way the distance between the IPS engagement with its core group—the prisoners. In not recognizing a responsibility to the children of prisoners (beyond child protection), the IPS has had difficulty in acknowledging, let alone implementing, a children's rights based approach. However, this ignores the fundamental legal requirement that state institutions are expected to comply with the rights provisions of children recognized in the CRC. Thus, while the positive steps taken by the Irish prison service in terms of moving towards recognizing their obligations towards child protection are commendable, this does not go far enough. As a state institution, the IPS is obliged to adhere to, and promote, the minimum standards set out under the CRC. Unfortunately, prison personnel acknowledged that children's rights were simply not part of the context of visits:

> We haven't stepped over into thinking about children's rights at any stage. (Governor, County B)

One officer noted that she had 'no understanding of any law relating to children' and that she had been told nothing about such rights in training (Prison Officer, County C).

This lack of engagement with children as rights holders unsurprisingly goes against the approach promoted by the Committee on the Rights of the Child in its Day of General Discussion recommendations noted earlier in this chapter. Thus, the Committee 'emphasises that children have the right to regularly visit their parent(s)' and that measures should be adopted to 'ensure that the visit context is respectful to the child's dignity and right to privacy' (UN Committee on the Rights of the Child, 2011, paragraph 28). In addition to this, there is an important body of soft law relating to prison standards (such as the UN Prison Rules) that emphasises the need for visits to be of a sufficient quality to support effective contact (Smith, 2014; Lagoutte, 2016).

2. Family visits as interventions

Significant within the changes adopted by the IPS in relation to visits is their connection with parenting courses. The creation of parenting courses can be viewed in a functional way—as an intervention that assists prisoners in their rehabilitation. A significant amount of research has been carried out in assessing the benefits of parenting courses as well as visits in supporting prisoner 're-entry' (Mitchell et al., 2016; Poehlmann et al., 2010; Mowen et al., 2016).

However, some interviewees regarded family visits as being a more fundamental and embedded component of the prison system. Recent IPS changes, including training for staff, were therefore associated with improved outcomes for all including a shift in prison staff attitudes towards prisoners

> [Y]ou need [to] train your staff to think differently ... We're not just here to incarcerate prisoners; we're here to rehabilitate and change them. And part of that is being a better parent. And understanding why the cycle isn't being broken. (Governor, County C)

So presenting a different vision of prison officers to child visitors is understood by some as being part of a positive intervention in situations where intergenerational crime is identified as a concern:

> [I]f [children] see us ... as screws, and the opposition, and the nasty man in the blue uniform or the nasty lady in the blue uniform, what are we changing? Nothing. It's vital that we start to think differently. (Governor, County C)

This view recognizes the IPS changes as being positive beyond a focus on a traditional rehabilitative function. However, they do not fully engage with the rights of this group of children. Indeed, the failure to see the children as independent parties in this situation is a key impediment to recognizing the rights of this group of children and the relative benefits they can bring. Research on parenting courses has indicated that children are rarely directly involved in either the development of such courses nor a major part of evaluations regarding their impact (Poehlmann et al., 2010). The failure to engage with the fundamental core aspects of children's rights such as the best interests principle and facilitating the voice of the child in the development of child and family initiatives reinforces their exclusion from the overall process. Prison and prisoner ownership of such initiatives as rehabilitative interventions prioritizes and justifies the security and disciplinary components noted above.

An alternative child-centred approach was rarely found in the research even among interviewees from support organizations. However, one interviewee encapsulated the way a shift in perspective to see the child as a child can have an important impact. Discussing bad visiting practice, she noted that 'labelling children as "a visitor"' was problematic; seeing them as children was the priority

> I think they have a need to be heard as well like do you know, this thing of just bringing ... I often seen them, they're lost in the process. (Child support worker, County C)

Seeing the process from the child's perspective including their needs results in a view that all children should have access to enhanced visits

> I know it's used as an incentive for prisoners to be good prisoners and I understand that there's a reasoning behind that too or else there would be all out anarchy but anyway I just think for the kids' sake, they haven't done anything wrong, screen visits and the other visits are quite hard on the children. (Child support worker, County C)

Contrast this view with that of management where a description of a child-friendly visiting regime is immediately classified as an intervention

> [The visit] would be as child friendly as possible. It would be open, it would be sort of round table type visits where parents are seen as if it's a normative environment and the visit is seen as an intervention as opposed to a visit and that there's some use going to come out of this for everybody by the way, not just the child but also the adult. (Management interviewee)

The perspective remains rooted in the prisoner—*their* responsibility for their children, *their* rehabilitation. In this context, it is unsurprising that children get 'lost in the process'; they are not recognized as rights holders requiring an institutional approach which responds to their dignity and needs.

Conclusions—tensions and opportunities

In this chapter, the lack of a children's rights approach has been noted within recent changes to the visiting regime in Ireland. It has been argued that the value of adopting such an approach would be the resultant shift in focus from a functional/instrumental position (normally adopted by prison systems to visits), to a more fundamental rights-based approach. Prison authorities see children and families through an intervention lens that supports prisoner rehabilitation and reintegration. Ireland is not unique in this way, but in developing policy that formally recognizes family within its visiting operation, it is currently missing an opportunity to adopt practice that is in line with the children's rights under the CRC, COE Guidance and more broadly in the soft law prison rules.

The current approach highlights the fact that prison service actions in this area are bounded by the system's natural risk aversion and a prisoner-security focus which results in a failure to recognize the rights of children and families. Moreover, it is clear that the extent to which 'child-friendly' approaches operate in practice tend to be reliant upon an individual governor's adoption at a local level. There is therefore no consistency across the prison estate, leading to discriminatory practice. This is reflective of approaches in other jurisdictions, where 'the focus is haphazard and relies heavily on individualized approaches and the strength of the stakeholder's professional networks' (Trotter et al., 2015, 59). These interventions do not belong to the children, they are 'owned' by the prison and 'used' by the prisoners (and partners).

The effect of this approach is ultimately that changes are potentially unsustainable in the face of security problems, resourcing, and pressures on the prison system such as overcrowding. The latter is supported by our research where senior staff see improved conditions around visits and families as being possible only because the system was not in crisis:

> It's just like people haven't really focussed on it. I suppose when you had a packed up prison system, massive overcrowding, massive slopping out, children were incidental. They weren't ... so now that our numbers have come down by almost 1,000 and we have pretty well eliminated slopping out, you know now you can start thinking about some of this quality stuff like children and like what effect has imprisonment on children and I mean it's unreasonable for a chaotic prison service to be expected to think about the wider system when actually its own system is in crisis as we have seen over the last ... the numbers in prison ... like it's just unmanageable. (Management interviewee)

So despite the recognition of children's rights in the IPS approach to families (FIG, 2014), the prioritization of parenting courses as 'interventions' with an emphasis on offender rehabilitation rather than practical commitments to upholding children's rights, ensure that there is limited engagement with children's rights. The result appears to be that there has been a lack of training in this area leaving prison staff at all levels with little or no understanding of children's rights either in principle or in practice. The result is that changes are neither informed by, nor reflective of, the responsibility of the IPS to act in accordance with children's rights. This is unsurprising given the failure to engage in a discussion around children's rights or provide training that engages with it. Additionally, there is a lack of policy development or implementation that conform with even basic children's rights requirements. A commitment to family visits without a coherent statement of what those visits demand in practice is ultimately somewhat of a hollow promise. The language of 'child-friendly' interventions masks a disconnect with the reality of implementation. Ultimately, improved visiting conditions need to engage with an understanding of the rights of children entering the state's prisons. That engagement is not a luxury but is demanded of state bodies by the CRC.

References

African Committee of Experts on the Rights and Welfare of the Child (ACERWC). 2013. General Comment No. 1 on Article 30 of the ACRWC: 'Children of Incarcerated and Imprisoned Parents and Primary Caregivers', 8 November.

Boudin, C. 2011. 'Children of Incarcerated Parents: The Child's Constitutional Right to the Family Relationship', *Journal of Criminal Law & Criminology*, 101(1), 77–118.

Bradshaw, D. and Muldoon, O. 2017. *'Family Links' Evaluation Report*. Childhood Development Initiative, Dublin.

Bunreacht na hÉireann (Constitution of Ireland, enacted in 1937), Article 42A (on the rights of children).

Children of Prisoners Europe. 2014. *Children of Imprisoned Parents: European Perspectives on Good Practice*.

Council of Europe. 2006. Committee of Ministers, Recommendation Rec(2006)2 of the Committee of Ministers to Member States on the European Prison Rules, 11 January, Rec(2006)2.

Council of Europe. 2008. Council of Europe and European Parliament Resolution of 13 March 2008 on the particular situation of women in prison and the impact of the imprisonment of parents on social and family life, 2007/2116(INI).

Council of Europe. 2016. *Strategy for the Rights of the Child (2016–2021)*. Available at: *https://rm.coe.int/168066cff8*.

Council of Europe. 2018. Council of Europe Recommendation concerning children with imprisoned parents, CM/Rec(2018)5.

Department of Children and Youth Affairs. 2014. *Better Outcomes, Brighter Futures: The National Policy Framework for Children and Young People 2014–2020*. Dublin: Government Publications Office.

Department of Children and Youth Affairs (DCYA). 2017. *Statement of Strategy 2016–2019*. Dublin: Government Publications Office.

Donson, F. and Parkes, A. 2012. 'Changing Mindsets, Changing Lives: Increasing the Visibility of Children's Rights in Cases Involving Parental Incarceration'. *International Family Law*, 4, 408–13.

Donson, F. and Parkes, A. 2016. 'Weighing in the Balance: Reflections on the Sentencing Process from a Children's Rights Perspective'. *Probation Journal*, 63(3), 331–46.

Families and Imprisonment Group (FIG). 2014. Report to Director General. Dublin: Irish Prison Service.

Felitti, V. J., Anda, R. F., Nordenberg, D., et al. 1998. 'The Relationship of Adult Health Status to Childhood Abuse and Household Dysfunction'. *American Journal of Preventive Medicine*, 14(4), 245–58.

Flynn, C. et al. 2015. 'Responding to Children When Their Parents are Incarcerated: Exploring the Responses in Victoria and New South Wales, Australia', *Law in Context*, 32, 4–27.

Geller, A. et al. 2009. 'Parental Incarceration and Child Wellbeing: Implications for Urban Families'. *Social Science Quarterly*, 90(5), 1186–202.

Genty, P. M. 2012. 'Moving Beyond Generalizations and Stereotypes to Develop Individualized Approaches for Working With Families Affected by Parental Incarceration'. *Family Court Review*, 50(1), 36.

Irish Penal Reform Trust. 2012. *'Picking Up the Pieces': The Rights and Needs of Children and Families Affected by Imprisonment*. Dublin: IPRT.

Jardine, C. 2015. *Constructing Family in the Context of Imprisonment: A study of Prisoners and their Families in Scotland*. PhD thesis, University of Edinburgh.

Lagoutte, S. 2016. 'The Right to Respect for Family Life of Children of Imprisoned Parents'. *International Journal of Children's Rights*, 24(1), 201–30.

Lee, R., Fang, X., and Luo, F. 2013. 'The Impact of Parental Incarceration on the Physical and Mental Health of Young Adults'. *Pediatrics*, 131(4), 1188–95.

Mitchell, M., Spooner, K., Jia, D., and Zhang, Y. 2016. 'The Effect of Prison Visitation on Re-entry Success: A Meta-analysis'. *Journal of Criminal Justice*, 47, 74–83.

Mowen, T. and Visher, C. 2016. 'Changing the Ties that Bind: How Incarceration Impacts Family Relationships'. *Criminology and Public Policy*, 15(2), 502–28.

Murray, J. and Farrington, D. 2008. 'The Effects of Parental Imprisonment on children', in Tonry, M. (ed.) *Crime and Justice: A Review of Research*. 133–206. Chicago: University of Chicago Press.

Office of the Inspector of Prisons. 2015. *Culture and Organisation in the Irish Prison Service: A Road Map for the Future*. Dublin: Government Publications Office.

Organization of African Unity (OAU). 1990. African Charter on the Rights and Welfare of the Child, 11 July, CAB/LEG/24.9/49.

Parkes, A. 2013. *Children and International Human Rights Law: The Right of the Child to be Heard*. Abingdon: Routledge.

Parkes, A., Caroline, C., O'Mahony, C., and Burns, K. 2015. 'The Right of The Child to be Heard? Professional Experiences of Child Care Proceedings in the Irish District Court', *Child and Family Law Quarterly*, 27(4), 423–44.

Pearse, P. 1975. *The Easter Proclamation of the Irish Republic, 1916*. Dublin: Dolmen Press.

Poehlmann, J., Dallaire, D., Booker Loper, A., and Shear, L. D. 2010. 'Children's Contact with their Incarcerated Parents: Research Findings and Recommendations'. *American Psychologist*, 65(6), 575–98.

Smith, P. S. 2014. *When the Innocent are Punished: The Children of Imprisoned Parents*. Basingstoke: Palgrave.

Smith, P. S. and Gampell, L. (eds.) 2011. *Children of Imprisoned Parents*. Denmark: Danish Institute for Human Rights.

Trotter, C., Flynn, C., Naylor, B., and Eriksson, A. 2015. *The Impact of Incarceration on Children's Care: A Strategic Framework for Good Care Planning*. Clayton, Vic.: Monash University, Criminal Justice Research Consortium.

UN Committee on the Rights of the Child. 1991. Guidelines for Submitting Initial Reports, UN Doc. CRC/C/5.

UN Committee on the Rights of the Child. 2009. General Comment No. 12: The Right of the child to be heard, CRC/G/GC/12.

UN Committee on the Rights of the Child. 2011. Report and Recommendations of the Day of General Discussion on 'Children of Incarcerated Parents', 20 September.

UN General Assembly. 1989. Convention on the Rights of the Child, 20 November. United Nations, Treaty Series, vol. 1577.

UN General Assembly. 2010. United Nations Rules for the Treatment of Women Prisoners and Non-Custodial Measures for Women Offenders (the Bangkok Rules), 6 October, A/C.3/65/L.5.

UN General Assembly. 2015. United Nations Standard Minimum Rules for the Treatment of Prisoners (the Mandela Rules), 29 September, A/C.3/70/L.3.

Wallis, R. and Dennison S. 2015. 'Out of the Shadows: Republican Criminology and the Children of Prisoners'. *Law Context*, 32, 86–107.

CASES

Khoroshenko v Russia, App. no. 41418/04 (ECtHR 30 June 2015).

PART III

THE LIVED EXPERIENCES OF PRISONERS' FAMILIES IN EUROPE, NORTH AMERICA, AND AUSTRALIA

PART III

14

'Everyone is in damage control'
The Meanings and Performance of Family for Second and Third Generation Prisoners

Mark Halsey[*]

Introduction

In this chapter I draw on data from the *Generations Through Prison* project to explore the familial impacts of incarceration from the perspectives of second and third generation prisoners. Focusing on the intimate relations lost, 'suspended', or recreated, I examine how intergenerational incarceration intensifies the pains of imprisonment (Sykes, 1958). My argument is that irrespective of the ties among those who serve time with immediate and/or extended family members, the deleterious effects of incarceration outweigh the positive dimensions. Further, for intergenerational prisoners serving time 'on their own'—that is, without the 'dividend' of extended or immediate family—the search for close ties remains key to coping with prison life. As shall be seen, most of the participants in this research had very few, if any, intimates in the community who supported them while incarcerated or who would offer support once released. This has concrete implications for how each prisoner (of second, third, or even fourth generation) transitions from a milieu built in accordance with 'argot roles' (one's position in the prison hierarchy) to those built around conventional social roles (one's status as, e.g. capable guardian, economic provider, reliable employee, and so forth).

The chapter proceeds across four sections. The first section, 'Background and relevant literature', provides background data on intergenerational incarceration and links this to the literature on prisoners' families. The second section 'Data' briefly outlines the *Generations Through Prison* project and the nature of data informing the chapter. In the third section 'Key themes', I relay the main areas emerging from interviews with second and third generation prisoners concerning the performance and meaning(s) of family within prison and beyond. Central here are the following: adjusting to prison life, the nature and impact of visitation, negotiating relationships with (ex)intimates, losing the moral high ground with regard to one's children, grappling with the ripple effect of crime on family members, and conceiving of prison as a second home. The final section, 'Implications for reintegration and familial wellbeing', examines the ramifactions of those themes for post-prison life and the likely role of family in the reintegration process.

---

[*] Centre for Crime Policy and Research, Flinders University. The *Generations Through Prison: A Critical Exploration of the Causes, Experiences and Consequences of Intergenerational Incarceration* project is funded by the Australian Research Council, Centre for Crime Policy and Research, Flinders University (FT120100284).

Prisons, Punishment, and the Family: Towards a New Sociology of Punishment? First Edition. Rachel Condry and Peter Scharff Smith. © The several contributors 2018. Published 2018 by Oxford University Press.

Background and relevant literature

Intergenerational incarceration is—or, more accurately, should be—a key correctional and social policy issue (Halsey, 2017). As far back as 1988, the US Bureau of Justice Statistics published the self-report data of 2,621 participants drawn from fifty youth custodial facilities across twenty-six US states. One quarter (24 per cent) reported their father as having been incarcerated and 9 per cent reported the incarceration of their mother (Beck et al., 1988, 3). More than two decades later, Novero et al. (2011, 767) found that nearly half (46 per cent) of 459 prisoners from ten facilities across two US states had a mother or father who had spent time in prison or jail. In the United Kingdom, the 1991 National Prison Survey in England and Wales showed 30 per cent of respondents experienced the incarceration of one or both parents (Farrington et al., 1996, 47–8). In Australia, of 1,011 prisoners randomly selected on admission to Australian prisons during 2015, 26 per cent of Indigenous and 13 per cent of non-Indigenous participants reported experiencing, in their childhood, the incarceration of any parent or primary career (Australian Institute of Health and Welfare, 2015, 32; see also Quilty, 2005).

The statistics on intergenerational incarceration connect directly to the literature on prisoners' families (see Travis and Waul, 2003; Woodward, 2003; King, 2005; Mills and Codd, 2007; Condry 2007). Attention has been paid to the *children of incarcerated parents* (Larman and Aungles, 1993; Hagan, 1996; Mumola, 2000; Boswell and Wedge, 2002; Quilty et al., 2004; Schirmer et al., 2009; Harris et al., 2010; Eddy and Poehlmann, 2010; Wildeman and Western, 2010; Comfort et al., 2011; Wakefield and Wildeman, 2014; Arditti, 2012; Smith, 2014), *problems specific to being an incarcerated father* (Arditti et al., 2005; Dyer, 2005; Maldonado, 2006; Fairchild, 2009) or *an incarcerated mother* (Brown, 1991; Greene et al., 2000; Poehlmann, 2005; Dallaire, 2007; Michalsen et al., 2010), and to problems related to *commencing or resuming the role of a parent post-release* (Nurse, 2000; Foster and Hagan, 2009). It is this literature that informs much of my thinking below. Given that around half of all prisoners in countries such as the United States, Australia, and the United Kingdom are parents of minor children (Glaze and Maruschak, 2008; Corrective Services New South Wales, 2013; Evans, 2015), it is essential that correctional and political officials reflect critically on the unintended consequences of incarceration—including the sometimes stabilizing but more often destructive effects on prisoners' children (and grandchildren).

Data

Data for this chapter stems from the *Generations Through Prison* project which sought: (a) to capture the range of circumstances surrounding incarceration episodes within particular families, and (b) to understand whether and how past incarceration episodes of previous generations impact the life-course opportunities and incarceration episodes of subsequent generations. Primary data was collected via surveys and in-depth interviews during the years 2013 to 2016 across all juvenile and adult custodial facilities in South Australia. The survey was designed to take around twenty minutes to complete and covered three broad areas: 'information about yourself', 'your knowledge of family members who have been locked-up', and 'getting in touch for a possible interview'. Basic demographic data (e.g. age, gender, educational attainment, offence history, experience of foster care, housing situation, employment history) was also requested and respondents were asked to indicate the extent of their families' carceral histories (including their own), as well as the effect of these episodes on the 'family unit' and on their own lives. Respondents nominating for interview were asked to record their prisoner number or, if release was imminent, provide contact details to enable follow-up.[1]

A total of 282 completed surveys were returned with 240 respondents reporting two or more generations of incarceration (this from a prison population of around 2,200). 10 per cent of adult respondents (mean age 35.4 years) had been incarcerated across their life-course for more than twenty years and 63 per cent had served time in juvenile facilities. Of the 214 adult prisoners who met the eligibility criteria for interview (i.e. having at least one family member from a *different* generation who was or is incarcerated and who could be contacted), 110 (51 per cent) so nominated. In selecting interviewees, respondents were ranked in order of generational depth (with third, fourth, and fifth generation prisoners given priority) as well as the quantum of family members ever incarcerated. Interviews were conducted in prison and community settings from late 2014 with data for this chapter based on completed transcripts as at mid-2015 (n = 39) (see Table 1).[2]

At interview, participants were asked to tell of the key turning points in their lives (Abbott, 1997; Laub and Sampson, 2003) and to narrate how the incarceration of other family members impacted (or not) their life-course and/or their own experience of prison and post-release life. A grounded approach to data analysis was used (Dey, 2007; Glaser and Strauss, 1976) with all interviews transcribed verbatim and read for emergent common themes as well as disparities. Coding for this chapter focused on the nature of family and social belonging in the context of intergenerational incarceration.

Key themes

Across interviews (thirty-four males, five females), several themes of direct relevance to the familial impacts of imprisonment emerged. Each of these, discussed in succession below, need to be placed in the context of intergenerational incarceration and, more specifically, the depletion of familial capital so often associated with such.

> *Can you just list for me, the people in your family that have actually done time in prison?...*
>
> My father, my mother, my mother's two brothers, one of them committed suicide in [prison], ... and the [other] ... ended up overdosing on heroin.... There's one cousin up at Port Augusta [Prison] doing ... 13 years.... There's another one at Mobilong [Prison] and another in and out all the time. And then you've got my brother.... [T]hen ... I've got [another cousin], he's in and out of gaol [and another who's] doing a stretch now. Then [there's another] first-cousin, ... [plus three others]. (A, five years)[3]

The relative number and strength (resilience) of family members left to pick up the pieces (Halsey and Deegan, 2014) following each incarceration episode proved a key

---

[1] A written agreement stipulated that surveys would not be opened by prison staff except where the security/good order of the prison was believed to be in jeopardy. To the best of my knowledge, no surveys were opened for such purposes.

[2] Ind = Indigenous; Direct = e.g. grandfather, father, son; Indirect = e.g. grandfather, uncle, son. With regard to life-time effect of incarceration: 3 = totally determined my life, 2 = major effect on my life, 1 = some effect on my life, and 0 = no effect on my life. Fam Prev = number of family members ever incarcerated.

[3] Excerpts are followed by interviewee code and length of sentence.

Table 1 Interviewees and Prevalence of Prison

Age	Gender	Ind. Status	Effect	Direct	Indirect	Fam. Prev.
33	F	NI	2	3	3	13
40	F	Ind.	2	3	3	13
30	M	Ind.	3	4	3	12
58	M	Ind.	3	3	3	11
25	M	Ind.	3	3	3	11
34	M	NI	2	5	2	11
32	M	Ind.	2	2	3	10
32	F	Ind.	3	2	3	10
34	M	Ind.	3	2	3	10
43	M	Ind.	3	2	3	9
37	M	Ind.	2	3	2	9
21	M	Ind.	2	2	3	9
45	M	NI	2	3	3	9
36	M	Ind.	1	2	3	8
26	F	Ind.	1	3	2	8
38	M	Ind.	3	2	3	7
33	M	Ind.	3	3	2	7
38	F	Ind.	2	3	2	7
27	M	Ind.	1	3	2	7
45	M	Ind.	2	2	3	6
37	M	NI	1	3	2	6
32	M	Ind.	2	2	2	6
34	M	Ind.	2	2	2	6
48	M	Ind.	1	2	3	6
24	M	Ind.	1	2	2	6
31	M	Ind.	2	3	2	6
44	M	NI	1	3	1	5
32	M	NI	2	2	2	5
31	M	NI	0	3	2	5
42	M	Ind.	2	2	2	5
24	M	NI	1	2	2	5
43	M	NI	3	2	3	4
47	M	Ind.	2	2	2	4
34	M	NI	3	2	2	4
39	M	NI	3	1	2	4
33	M	NI	2	2	2	4
25	M	Leb.	2	2	2	4
64	M	NI	2	3	1	3
39	M	NI	3	2	1	2

issue among most interviewees. Indigenous survey respondents shouldered the bulk of this burden with 50 per cent reporting from six to nine family members as ever incarcerated—five times the rate of non-Indigenous prisoners. Further, more than 80 per cent of Indigenous participants reported the *current* incarceration of a family member (an average of 3.8 family members per survey respondent), whereas just one-third of non-Indigenous participants reported other family members as being currently locked up (an average of 1.8 per respondent). Even allowing for the nature of Indigenous kinship networks and a very broad definition of 'family', these are quite remarkable statistics. Accordingly, there are complex issues surrounding how to measure and ascribe particular qualities to the familial capital both within and beyond custody for Indigenous and non-Indigenous prisoners—something well beyond the scope of this chapter but which will be dealt with in detail elsewhere (see Halsey, forthcoming). For now, it is sufficient to note the extent to which some families seem overwhelmingly if reluctantly entwined with, if not reliant upon, the prison.

1. Adjusting

Irrespective of the number of previous incarceration episodes, interviewees spoke of the reckoning process that attends any sentence (short or long). Many chose the path of active isolation as a means for steeling themselves to the routines of prison life. This meant shutting out all ideas of freedom or the world beyond prison walls for an extended period. As one participant remarked:

> Once you get sentenced you think, 'Right, I'm going to be in for a very long time. Outside does not exist, only what's behind these bars, the door [of my cell], "Yes, sir, no, sir", count, tea, and the lockup.' That's all that exists. (B, Lifer)

For others, commencing a sentence was commensurate with reflecting deeply on things lost. In that vein, one interview captured the measure of things by remarking, 'I would rather be poor, have my daughter, be a father, and be free, than have nothing' (HX, twelve years). As mentioned previously, how and to what extent prisoners tried to attenuate the pain of separation from one's family, was a defining feature of prison life. Phone calls and letter writing were possible portals for contact, but the lion's share of energy was invested in thinking through the benefits and drawbacks of prison visits.

2. Playing the visits game

Among interviewees, those who had served many sentences were well versed in the visits game—called such due to the procedures and general 'hassle' associated not only with gaining approval for one's list of potential visitors, but also actually being able to book, receive a visitor, and have it go well (see Hutton, this volume; Donson and Parkes, this volume). A smooth visit equated to the least amount of humiliating moments for the prisoner or visitor at the hands of officers (including, especially, gatehouse staff). The following illustrates the perverse nature of the system for a family whose three sons were serving life sentences.

> *Father:* On this particular visit they decided to change the rules without informing anybody [so that] on the second visit you had to show ID [to get back into the visit area].... So we produced our ID. They've turned around to us and they said, 'You're not booked in on the second visit.' ...
>
> *Mother:* I said, 'Excuse me, I've done these bookings for four years.... Do you think we're going to do a 400-kilometre trip for one 45-minute visit? Are you crazy?'
>
> *Father:* They wouldn't listen to reason. (Parents of Three Lifers)

On account of hard learned lessons, some made the decision to call quits on visits, preferring instead to leave behind the psychological baggage associated with them.

> I'd rather them [i.e., my daughters] not come. I don't want them having to see me there. I don't like it.... It hurts me more [when] I see them go. Everyone's in tears.... I just got to deal with my gaol ... and concentrate on that rather than what's going on outside. (C, eight months)

Others ensured regular visits with their children took place, and went to extraordinary efforts to disguise the real nature of the visit area.

> [A]t one stage I had [my son] convinced that when I was at [mentions prison] that I was working in a zoo.... I didn't want him to know I was in gaol. I just wanted him to think that dad's gone away for work for nine months and then come home.
>
> *So ... how would you get the idea of a zoo across [while] sitting in the visit room?*
>
> [T]here's a little window on one side of it, [and] there'd be a couple of birds [outside] ... and he'd say, 'Where are the rest of the animals?' I'd say, 'They're in their cages sleeping', and stuff like that. It worked for a while until ... the lady at his school said, 'Your dad's in gaol'. But it worked quite well. I mean, if he came here [to this particular prison], he'd know straight away that this is a gaol because of the entrance. (D, Remandee)

Some prisoners viewed visits as a vehicle for demonstrating the tolerable nature of prison life. This was done mainly for the benefit of family rather than the prisoner her/himself.

> [W]hen my mum and my aunty used to come and visit when I was first in, you lie to each other backwards and forwards: 'How are you coping in here?' 'Alright.' ... [Well] that's you telling them what they want to hear. You put their mind at ease by lying to them. You ask them how they're doing. And they lie to you by saying everything's alright, the kids are good. And it's this backwards and forwards. You're not being truthful to them because no one wants to hurt each other, nobody wants to get hurt. So everyone is in damage control.... And that's the rest of your life. (E, Lifer)

It is difficult to comprehend—let alone judge—the role of visits in situations where people are serving (or have served) sentences in excess of thirty years (as is the case immediately above). Even if something of a charade (see Knudsen, this volume) where small talk is the norm, and where no one really ever says the unsaid—that a life sentence is permanently devastating for all concerned—the ritual of contact with family members is critical to maintaining some semblance of prisoner and familial wellbeing. They are, without doubt, frequently sombre affairs where, as indicated, the pain associated with watching a loved one walk away (without the capacity to follow in their footsteps) is too much to bear. In such circumstances, prisoners fall back on their own company for the duration, or turn to other prisoners for social connection and belonging (see Glaze and Maruschak, 2008).

3. (Ex)intimates

The role of intimates—particularly partners/spouses—in supporting prisoners' families is undeniable (Halsey and Deegan, 2014, 2015). They are not infrequently the 'invisible' hand that holds things together when partners (usually men) go (back) to prison.

> My son's 12 and my daughter is five. She was eight months old when I come in, so I've lost all of that.... I've seen her in the last four and a half years maybe no more than ten times.... I've written a lot and I ring when I can. I always put money on the phone each week so I can ring my children.
>
> *Do the children know what has gone on? ...*
>
> My son knows what's going on. He knows that I'm in gaol [and] why I am in gaol. But he's got a good mum. She's preventing him from doing all of the things that I've done. She punishes him if he's bad at school—you know, consequences. I never had any of that sort of stuff. So he's growing up good. He's growing up with sports and things like that, where[as] I never had any of that. (F, ten years)

Similarly, the following excerpt speaks to the unpayable social and emotional debt owed to one's partner in the context of very lengthy sentences and confirms just how rare it is for relationships to survive such monumental upheaval.

> She's done every step of the gaol with me.... But it just tears me up.... I appreciate it and I love it that she's stuck by me because I don't know of any other long-termers, maybe one or two, that have had a missus stay [around].
> (G, ten years, previously Lifer)

Some prisoners spoke of themselves and their partners taking matters into their own hands in order to avoid being entirely at the mercy of the incarceration–release–reincarceration machine.

> When I got out that [last] time I said [to my partner], 'If I go back in, I'm doing the rest of my time. I've had enough of this being taken away from you and all that.' She's agreed with me. And so she's put it to all of the kids. I said, 'Do you want me to do a longer time in gaol so [that] I can be out permanently with you, or would you like me to get out again with the chance of being taken away again?' All of them said do the time in gaol and then get out so you can be at home for good.
>
> *It's a shame it had to be like that.... [But] it must make you feel good to know that they are on your side?*
>
> Yeah, I haven't had a family in 30 years in my eyes. (H, eight years)

The ties between prisoners and their partners were rarely this strong or this organized. In fact, most interviewees spoke of quite toxic relationships and of having to 'get past' their 'ex' in order to obtain any type of relationship with their children (see Smith, 2014, 180–6).

> *Is it important for you to stay in touch with your kids?...*
>
> I asked the mother of my son to ... send me pictures. I just wanted one little picture for in here.... And it never really happened. I've had a smattering of pictures across my 16 years. I've not had 16 years worth of pictures. Of my son, I've had one. (I, Lifer)

One of the most psychologically destructive issues faced by interviewees was the (further) demonization of their character carried out by ex-partners in the presence of their children. Reputation, as Katz (1988) reminds, is social, and on that account it is rarely if ever entirely within an individual's own capacity to manage. The prison—premised as it is on the *deprivation of the right of reply*—makes this particularly true. There are, in short, few if any immediately effective measures for restoring one's name in the prison milieu. How prisoners (re)assemble their reputation in the eyes of one's children residing many (hundreds of) miles away is a task fraught with obstacles.

> *[So what you're saying is] stories can be told that you have no right of reply to ...*
>
> Both of my kids are having stuff put in their head. And I can't sit down and explain to them what's happened.... They're only hearing things from her, whereas when I get out, if they ask me questions about stuff, I'll tell them the truth.... Simple little things, like, I can't send birthday cards or Christmas cards because she sends them back with a message on them saying, 'You're in breach of your restraining order.' ... She actually opens it up and then writes a nasty little message inside the card that I've sent to my kids.... When I was [last] out ... my oldest son was at my house on the weekend, and one of his friends turned around and said to me, 'You're not the monster that [his] mother says [you are].'... (J, eight years)

This situation drives a further wedge in the notion of family, and created psychological unrest among many prisoners. The sense of powerlessness felt by interviewees in this situation was palpable during interview. All that could be done was to wait until their release (often years away) and try to ensure their behaviour put paid to the character slurs and rumours. Restoring or maintaining a sense of dignity and respect in the eyes of their children (particularly in relation to minors) was an absolute priority for incarcerated fathers and mothers. But the tenuousness of their control over the situation was also all-too-apparent for most.

4. Loss of moral high-ground

Prisoners—perhaps especially those conscious of the history of incarceration in their family—are often concerned to stop their offspring heading down the criminal path. But a complicating factor is the extent to which imprisoned parents detect or experience a loss of the moral high-ground. Here, the dictum 'Do as I say, not as I do' is seemingly writ large in each letter, phone call, or visit with their children.

> *How do you speak to your older daughter on the phone? [Like], how do you stop the next generation from going to prison? ...*
>
> It's very hard.... Like, I've got a handful of letters [from my ex] saying, 'She's following in your footsteps, she's taking after you, she's doing this. It's all your fault'. When I got the letters I sit down and think, 'What can I do?' And in here, I've got no right to say anything.... There's a good chance that she will end up in juvey because she's running amok.... But I feel, to say anything to her, I have no right. (K, nine years)

The dilemma here is real and certainly not uncommon. And it is one that all parents face to one degree or another at various times. But the stakes are particularly high in the context of trying to intervene in lineages of intergenerational violence and crime. The following excerpt illustrates the implications of a father who exposed his son to the techniques and proceeds of crime only much later to realize the 'hypocrisy' associated with pleas for him to cease offending.

> [My son is] 15.... I showed him a lot of stupid shit, like ... I had a lot of money around me, he's seen guns and ... things that I didn't really want him to see.... I did talk to him and ... I said, "Look, don't get in trouble. I don't want you to do these things ... that I've done." At the same time, I don't want to just preach to him.... I don't want to start to preach.... I've just got to start doing the things and showing him, you know.... Because some of the [bad] things that I've shown him, I think it's going to have an effect on him and impact him for the rest of his life.... (A, five years)

A corollary of parental imprisonment is that prolonged absence—along with events witnessed or vicariously experienced—risks the *parentification* of children (Halsey and Deegan, 2015). Children who are forced into adult roles ahead of the normal course of time may well feel they have an additional right to ignore their (incarcerated) parents' newly calibrated moral compass.

> Well basically, with my kids, they were shattered. They copped the brunt of it, they copped a big sentence in the sense that they had no one. They'd been left to bring themselves up. (L, nineteen years)
>
> [My son has] seen the effects [of prison] ... because when I was in gaol his mother was really full-on into the heroin. And it's had a major effect on him.... He's had to ring the ambulance when he was six. She was overdosing and he's had to ring the ambulance and get her to hospital. (M, five years)

Exposure to violence and parental dysfunction can steel children against ever slipping into the same patterns of behaviour. And sometimes, against the odds, children manage to extricate themselves from these patterns. But many do not (Halsey, 2017; Widom, 1989, 1995). For the latter, the effects of parental imprisonment ripple ineluctably through their lives.

5. Ripple effects

Intergenerational incarceration weaves its way through families in very different ways and can impact those in succeeding or *prior* generations. Across the majority of interviewees and survey respondents, mothers emerged as those perceived as most negatively effected by their offspring's incarceration.

> Well there's a saying that gets around that … when you come to gaol your mother does the time as well.… My mum ended up quitting her job and became a recluse.… She didn't want to go anywhere or see anybody for fear of having to answer that question, 'Oh, how is your son going?'… '[Well], he's locked up for murder.' … Once she went to the local supermarket and saw the victim's family there, so after that she could never go to that supermarket again. And she'd be fearful of going to any other place in case they might be there. She'd have panic attacks. (H, Lifer)

Ironically, the closer the family, the harder it is to deal with the incarceration of a loved one. Such closeness—and the desire to see that it prevails throughout the sentence—can bring all manner of emotional duress.

> Your family suffers.… [A]t the end of the day, your family, your kids, and your wife—they all do time with you. Their time stands still too. It's not just your time that stands still, it's your family's, your kids'. They've got to be there for you, for your phone calls and visits. (N, four years)

Prison puts family members on a schedule entirely beyond their own choosing. Partners and children organize their day in order to be next to the phone at the right time to take a call. They travel long distances—often on poorly maintained and irregular public transport—to get just an hour or so with their loved one (only to find, not infrequently, that the prison is on lockdown). They try to make ends meet in the absence of the person who—even though their earnings stemmed from crime—nonetheless helped sustain the family's housing, food, and clothing needs. They try to keep track of how their incarcerated family member is doing and go to extraordinary lengths to obtain the smallest piece of information about why they weren't able to call or write, or why a parole date had been refused or delayed, or why they have been transferred to another facility, or why visits must suddenly be of the non-contact variety.

All of this is psychologically and emotionally exhausting. In the best-case scenario, it can lead to some measure of reassurance that things might, in the long run, work out for the best. But more typically, it is the feeling of powerlessness that tends to predominate among prisoners' families. This is especially so when correctional officials see fit to delay or flatly refuse the provision of information that could otherwise ease the pains of secondary imprisonment (i.e. the pain of prolonged absence and uncertainty of a loved one's wellbeing). One interviewee summarized the destructive long-term effects of imprisonment in the following way:

> You can't possibly imagine. There's a massive ripple effect.… There's no sympathy in a murderer's family doing it a bit hard.… You know, 'Tough fucking luck.' Just that act of coming to gaol, be it for however long, whether it's a lifetime [or not], it destroys people for a lifetime.… [My] three boys, … their partners, their parents.… Grandkids. Like it just keeps going. It just keeps getting bigger and bigger. (E, Lifer)

The cascading effect of this prisoner's crimes was immense. Managing the infamy of heinous events that make national headlines is not something any unsuspecting family is equipped to deal with (Condry, 2007). The brother of this prisoner commented that two sons developed various 'personality disorders' making them unfit to work and wholly reliant on government support. A third son retreated into drugs and is also on a support pension but managed to settle down after struggling for more than two decades with the implications of his father's crimes. The mother and father, though, appeared to suffer the most: '[dad] just shut down and my mum shut down for a long time'. There is even the lingering suspicion that the magnitude of the crimes caused the early death of the father.

> Yeah, ... I think that happened to my dad. And it was well on the way to happening to my mum except, at the end of nine months, everyone literally basically said, 'You are getting out of the chair. You are going back to work. You are going to start functioning,' and over a period of time she did. She didn't want to and she resisted but she did. (O, Brother of Lifer)

Critically, shame was not the decisive element that forced these parents to retreat into inactivity. Instead—and this is an under-researched issue—it was the *trauma* of realizing their child had committed the worst of crimes and that his fate was absolutely beyond their control. As the brother remarked:

> I wouldn't say—and I hope I'm not doing their memory injustice here—I wouldn't say that it was shame that did it [i.e., that caused their early demise/death] because I don't think they ever felt shame. I think they were traumatised for him because he was their little boy. He was the one that lived with them and they were just in disbelief that this would happen to him. So ... it wasn't, 'What are the neighbours going to think?' I don't think they would have cared about that. That was not important. It was more, 'What's going to happen to [our child]?'

The ripple effect of imprisonment flows deep into families—especially those that lament the civil death of their loved one. The sister of three brothers serving life sentences spoke in heart-wrenching terms about trying to find the motivation to carry on the basic rituals of family life.

> I have constant bad days.... We lost everything when my brothers went away. We didn't celebrate Christmas. We didn't celebrate Easter, Mother's Day, Father's Day, birthdays, nothing. I brought that back into our family. I started taking my parents out for their birthdays, for their anniversaries. It's hard 'cause I don't have my brothers here. I don't have them to celebrate with us. We have to send them in photos and stuff. That's hard. (Sister of Three Lifers)

There is no permanent recovery from this type of enforced separation. And even though the separation was briefly attenuated through prison visits (see above), this brought its own trauma for the family. For five years a choice had to be made ahead of each visit concerning who would sit opposite which son: '[I]f dad sat with [one of his sons], dad was only allowed to speak to [that son].... If we got up to speak to him ... we got into trouble' (Sister of Three Lifers). There is a particular cruelty—one that exceeds any claim to security—involved in such a scenario. And it was eventually shown to be nothing but a cruel ruse when a new prison manager saw the situation, questioned why it was happening, and then permitted the family to sit and converse freely with each other. Such small acts can help restore dignity and normality for families who are, in a very real sense, also 'doing time' (Comfort, 2009).

6. 'Home'

One of the paradoxes of imprisonment is that such spaces—even with their deprivations—become familiar if not preferred environments for some prisoners. Whether this is due to *prisonization* or the active 'embrace' of custodial life is an open and complex question (and one not resolvable here) (Clemmer, 1958 [1940]). Without doubt though, the things offered or supplied through incarceration are often preferable to life on the streets and living, literally, hand to mouth. Here the principle of less eligibility does a curious about-face.

> [Prison] preserves me.... This is a second home for me and it's all because out there I don't eat, and I don't sleep, and I'm aware that's no good.... I just want to go back to gaol.... I want to forget about the bullshit. (P, eleven months)
>
> It's my first home. (Q, three years)

The difficult political (and academic truth) is that prisons provide social stability for some people. This is *not* to say that prisons should be used as the answer to societal ills. Or that prisons—especially those of the supermax variety—are not harsh and psychosocially damaging environments. But it would be foolish to ascribe all prisoners who narrate the prison as a positive institution in their lives as exhibiting a false consciousness or as masking their 'true' feelings. The following exchange speaks to this:

> *What do you think about ... being in here now? ...*
>
> I don't regret nothing, it's just how it is.... I've met a lot of people in gaol.... They're good to me.... I'm happy to be here. It doesn't bother me whether I'm in gaol or out, it's just the way it is. That's how I've made my life, it's just how it is. (R, five years)

Many participants referred to their early experiences of being locked up. And what they consistently spoke of was recognizing their own story in those around them. It was this that ultimately formed the basis of belonging within and beyond custody.

> *So they put you in [a juvenile training centre], and you were required to stay there?*
>
> Yeah, ... it was like a little gaol for youths. And it didn't do nothing, it made me worse.
>
> *Tell me about that, how did it make you worse?*
>
> All the kids that was there were my cousins, so there were a lot of Aboriginals there. Also, it was all multi-cultural, and we all got on 'cause we was all young. And we all rebelled, cause what they went through I went through too.
>
> *So there was a camaraderie there?*
>
> Yeah. A few of us escaped from there too. They caught us and took us back. And it just made it worse. They didn't give us counselling, they didn't ask us what was wrong, why we was doing this. They never asked us. Maybe if they'd asked us that back then, then I wouldn't be sitting here....
>
> *So what do you think you would have said to them back then if they'd asked you 'Why are you doing this?'*
>
> Mate, I would have said because I've got no mother and father, you know, I've got no stable home. I'd go to school and be depressed and that, and I couldn't stop because I had no one.... Friends would ask me, 'Where's your mum?', and I said 'I don't know.'
>
> *Does it create a sense of loss? ...*
>
> Yeah, I think it does, especially when you're a kid. That's why I acted out. I was a good person, but I acted that way so no one could hurt me, you know, no one could touch me. It worked for so many years until I got older and started realising that it's not the right thing to do.
>
> *I guess [your time in juvenile prison] really interrupted your schooling? ...*
>
> Yeah. There was schooling in there, but it wasn't as good.... I was always thinking, 'Where's my family?' ... So I wasn't really in my right mind. I was unsettled. They'd

always tell me to sit and do something, but I couldn't because I was always worried about something else. I was always searching. (S, twelve years)

The bond between particular prisoners—particularly those who 'graduate' together from juvenile to adult facilities—is a well-documented dimension of incarceration (Irwin, 1985; Warr, 2002; Crewe, 2009). How correctional agencies might harness the peer-oriented approach to surviving imprisonment as a positive force in the reintegration process emerges as an important question. While work on *co-desistance* is in its infancy (Weaver, 2016) the concept might hold particular relevance for those in need of social buffering in the days and weeks leading up to and following release. One interviewee captured the essence of what is at stake:

> [Y]ou're dealing with people who are offending and who have a history of damage.... And when you [take] those people [and put them in] prison, all that does is damage them further. And then you are damaging the families as well—breaking ties with children and their parents, and creating a situation where you've got damaged people, damaging them more, and then kicking them out of the door and expecting something to be different next time. (H, Lifer)

On balance, imprisonment demonstrably causes more pain than it attenuates. But equally—and for so many of its occupants—the prison is one of several well-trod domains where struggles for survival and human dignity unfold. Given that the overwhelming majority of prisoners come from backgrounds defined by extreme social marginalization, the search for dignity and belonging can be equally pointed (if not brutal) beyond the prison gate (Wacquant, 2009; Contreras, 2012). It is little wonder, therefore, that the bonds formed within custody—the sense of 'brotherhood' and 'sisterhood' pertaining among groups—are so difficult to relinquish on release.

Implications for reintegration and familial wellbeing

The interview themes elaborated above need to be viewed in the context of the larger *Generations Through Prison* dataset. Of note is that the 240 survey respondents reported a total of 829 family members as ever incarcerated—563 of whom served more than one year in a single stretch. Survey respondents also reported 234 family members as currently incarcerated with cousins, uncles, brothers, nephews, and fathers featuring most prominently. Accordingly, on any day, roughly 20 per cent of prisoners in South Australia have another family member doing time. It is not unreasonable to think that similar situations apply in other jurisdictions. This situation brings a new sense to Foucault's (1980, 42, emphasis added) observation that:

> Prison professionalised people. Instead of having nomadic bands of robbers— often of great ferocity—roaming about the countryside, as in the eighteenth century, one had this *closed milieu of delinquency*, thoroughly structured by the police: an essentially urban milieu, and one whose political and economic value was far from negligible.

Consistent with this closed milieu of delinquency, one third of survey participants reported that imprisonment had been 'an ongoing issue' in their family for more than twenty years and a further 10 per cent indicated the prison had been a dominant institution in their lineage for more than forty years. One third of participants also reported that the 'effects of lock-up' had impacted their life in 'major' (negative) fashion with an additional 10 per cent indicating that the effects of incarceration had 'totally determined' their life course. While a sizeable proportion reported familial history of incarceration as either having 'some effect' (n = 38 per cent) or 'no effect' (n = 19 per cent) on their life course, the odds of all families staying in tact are slim. This is chiefly because prisons exist to *control* those within its perimeter at the expense of caring for those who might legitimately connect with them beyond the gate. Adding to the complexity of the situation is that families who evince two, three, or even four generations of imprisonment tend not only to have, at minimum, one family member locked up, but others perpetually on the cusp of being incarcerated. There is, in other words, a constant flow into and out of custody that makes any kind of stability nigh on impossible in such people's lives (Comfort, 2016).

The implications of these flows for (future) employment, housing, and education—and therefore for reintegration following release—are significant (Maruna and Immarigeon, 2004). While two thirds of project participants had ever held a full-time job, the average total time spent in full-time work was just over three years for Indigenous respondents and seven and half years for non-Indigenous respondents. With an average age of thirty-five years, this means that just 15 per cent and 37 per cent, respectively, of these respondents' 'work-age' lives, was spent in regular employment (most commonly in the labouring, hospitality, or factory sectors). This is to say nothing of those prisoners (one third of respondents) who had little or no work history to speak of. With regard to housing, just over half of all participants had been homeless at some point and of these one third had 'slept rough' (i.e. on the streets) for more than one year continuously. In descending order, escaping familial violence, lack of money, and a dearth of emergency accommodation beds were nominated as the primary reasons for homelessness. Participants who were homeless also evinced more extensive histories of familial incarceration. In relation to education, more than half (59 per cent, n = 40) of Indigenous participants did not reach year ten, compared with a third (34 per cent, n = 61) of non-Indigenous participants. Respondents' level of educational attainment also declined in accordance with the level of intergenerational incarceration. Here, third, fourth, and fifth generation respondents recorded significantly lower educational attainment with less than 60 per cent completing nine years of schooling (compared to 80 per cent of second generation prisoners). After year ten, educational attainment declined even further. Only *one* Indigenous respondent completed year eleven and only thirteen non-Indigenous respondents graduated from high school (twelve years of schooling). Collectively, these statistics lend considerable force to Jock Young's (1999, 154) contention that '[I]t is not the family which is the locus of the causes of [crime and] delinquency but the wider social forces of economic deprivation, racism and other forms of social injustice—all else is scapegoating and mis-targeting.'

The *Generations Through Prison* data shows unequivocally that family is central to the experience(s) of imprisonment. Families torn apart by violence and abuse are more likely to push children away from the home environment and into sub-optimal out-of-home care scenarios (foster homes, community residential care facilities, juvenile training facilities, and prison). The children of this 'displaced generation' are more likely themselves to head down the imprisonment path—not because their parents were overtly violent or abusive towards them (although that is certainly in the mix of things) but because the parents were absent during formative years. Intergenerational incarceration levies a heavy toll on the number and proximity of capable guardians in children's lives. Families are not always destroyed, but they are often severely and irrevocably depleted of the social and bridging capital needed to 'get on' in life. Family, in this context, is performed through the prism of prison. The following exchange with a third generation prisoner captures this dimension.

> *One thing that occurs to me is that we are sitting in [this] prison and your dad is also in prison here.... Did you ever think that would be the situation?*
>
> Well, a couple of weeks ago, I was sitting where you get strip-searched for court, for a video link-up.... I was sitting in that cell, waiting for my turn to walk up and get strip-searched, and I was ... thinking to myself, 'This was my dad sitting here. Over 20 years ago he was sitting here, walking up and down this raceway. And now it's me.' ... Yeah, [I was] thinking ... I used to visit him and now it's me and my son. (T, twenty-two years)

Prisoners in such situations need multiple and ongoing resources to keep the threads of family together. More particularly, for intergenerational prisoners—and this is borne out in the overwhelming majority of interviews—measures for addressing deep-seated trauma and loss issues have to be a key point on the path to successful reintegration and to any familial rapprochement that might then occur: 'That's why I acted out. I was a good person, but I acted that way so no one could hurt me, you know, no one could touch me' (S, twelve years) (see also Van der Kolk, 1987). Additionally, day-to-day opportunities for 'becoming-social' need careful and ongoing attention. Prison visits need to be normalized as far as practicable. Phone calls should be permitted well out of earshot of other prisoners and officers. Materials for letter writing should be plentiful and posted promptly. Photographs of family members should not be arbitrarily limited to merely one or two images.

Above all, though, connection to family needs to be buoyed by prisoners' consistent and structured involvement in *non-trivial* activities—things such as challenging (including face-to-face delivery of higher) educational courses, cutting-edge industry/training options, vibrant and sophisticated arts-based workshops, competitive sports, and the like. These—as much as, for example, completion of any cognitive behavioural module—help to substantively reduce the risk of prisoner discontentment and/or outright frustration and aggression. Above all, this is where the real work of 'turning prisoners into citizens' begins (Maruna, 2011, 4). And it is through such activities that prisoners might concretely demonstrate to family (who may be on the cusp of abandoning them) that there are 'real' things to discuss and that personal growth is possible even behind bars. Even—perhaps especially—those who have spent extended time in prison, yearn for some sense of family. As one interviewee explained:

> I've been in gaol for the last 15 years.... The thing that I have missed the most is not being able to experience a proper relationship, living a normal life, going to work, coming home at the end of the day to my partner, or having my partner go to work and having my partner come home to me.... Maybe, if the parole board decides to let me out, I can have that life I dream of—him going to work, coming home at the end of the day, I'll have meals on the table for him, me experiencing a proper relationship and having a normal life. That's what I want. (U, Lifer)

Prison administrators would do well to work with not against such desire. That way, some of the damage wrought through incarceration might be controlled if not mitigated.

References

Abbott, A. 1997. 'On the Concept of Turning Point'. *Comparative Social Research*, 16, 85–105.
Arditti, J. 2012. *Parental Incarceration and the Family*. New York: New York University Press.
Arditti, J., Smock, S., and Parkman, T. 2005. ' "It's Been Hard to Be a Father": A Qualitative Exploration of Incarcerated Fatherhood'. *Fathering*, 3, 267–88.

Australian Institute of Health and Welfare. 2015. *The Health of Australia's Prisoners 2015*. Canberra: AIHW.
Beck, A. J., Kline, S. A., and Greenfield, L. 1988. *Survey of Youth in Custody 1987*. Washington, DC: Bureau of Justice Statistics.
Boswell, G. and Wedge, P. 2002. *Imprisoned Fathers and Their Children*. London: Jessica Kingsley.
Brown, D. 1991. 'The Professional Ex-: An Alternative for Exiting the Deviant Career'. *The Sociological Quarterly*, 32, 219–30.
Clemmer, D. 1958 [1940]. *The Prison Community*. New York: Rinehart.
Comfort, M. 2009. *Doing Time Together*. Chicago: University of Chicago Press.
Comfort, M. 2016. '"A Twenty-Hour-A-Day Job": The Impact of Frequent Low-Level Criminal Justice Involvement on Family Life.' *The Annals of the American Academy of Political and Social Science*, 665, 63–79.
Comfort, M., Nurse, A., McKay, T., and Kramer, K. 2011. 'Taking Children Into Account: Addressing Intergenerational Effects of Parental Incarceration'. *Criminology and Public Policy*, 10, 839–50.
Condry, R. 2007. *Families Shamed: The Consequences of Crime for Relatives of Serious Offenders*. Cullompton: Willan.
Contreras, R. 2012. *The Stickup Kids*. Berkeley: University of California Press.
Corrective Services New South Wales. 2013. 'Statistical Profile: Characteristics of NSW Inmates'. Available at: http://www.correctiveservices.justice.nsw.gov.au/Documents/Statistical-Profile-Characteristics-of-NSW-Inmate-Receptions.pdf.
Crewe, B. 2009. *The Prisoner Society*. Oxford: Oxford University Press.
Dallaire, D. 2007. 'Children With Incarcerated Mothers: Developmental Outcomes, Special Challenges and Recommendations'. *Journal of Applied Developmental Psychology*, 28, 15–24.
Dey, I. 2007. 'Ground Theory', in Searle, C., Gobo, G., Gubrium, J., and Silverman, D. (eds.) *Qualitative Research Practice*. 80–94. London: Sage.
Dyer, J. 2005. 'Prison, Fathers, and Identity: A Theory of How Incarceration Affects Men's Paternal Identity'. *Fathering*, 3, 201–19.
Eddy, M. and Poehlmann, J. 2010. *Children of Incarcerated Parents: A Handbook for Researchers and Practitioners*. Washington, DC: Urban Institute.
Evans, J. 2015. 'Locked Out: Children's Experiences of Visiting a Parent in Prison'. Barnardo's Believe in Children, Report. Available at: https://www.barnardos.org.uk/locked-out-report.pdf.
Fairchild, S. 2009. 'Attachment Representations and Parental Memories of Incarcerated Fathers'. *Child and Adolescent Social Work Journal*, 26(4), 361–77.
Farrington, D., Barnes, G., and Lambert, S. 1996. 'The Concentration of Offending in Families'. *Legal and Criminological Psychology*, 1(1), 47–63.
Foster, H. and Hagan, J. 2009. 'The Mass Incarceration of Parents in America: Issues of Race/Ethnicity, Collateral Damage to Children, and Prisoner Re-entry'. *The Annals of the American Academy of Political and Social Science*, 623, 179–94.
Foucault, M. 1980. *Power/Knowledge: Selected Interviews and Other Writings*, ed. Gordon, C. New York: Pantheon.
Glaser, B. G. and Strauss, A. L. 1976. *The Discovery of Grounded Theory*. Chicago: Aldine.
Glaze, L. and Maruschak, L. 2008. 'Parents in Prison and Their Minor Children'. *Bureau of Justice Statistics Special Report*, Washington, DC: US Department of Justice. Available at: https://www.bjs.gov/content/pub/pdf/pptmc.pdf.
Greene, S., Haney, C., and Hurtado, A. 2000. 'Cycles of Pain: Risk Factors in the Lives of Incarcerated Mothers and Their Children'. *The Prison Journal*, 80(1), 3–23.
Hagan, J. 1996. 'The Next Generation', in *The Unintended Consequences of Incarceration*. Papers from a conference organized by the Vera Institute of Justice Arden House, Harriman, New York. Available at: https://www.vera.org/publications/the-unintended-consequences-of-incarceration-papers-from-a-conference-organized-by-vera.

Halsey, M. 2017. 'Child Victims as Adult Offenders: Foregrounding the Criminogenic Effects of (Unresolved) Trauma and Loss'. *British Journal of Criminology*, 58(1), 17–36.

Halsey, M. forthcoming. *Generations Through Prison*. London: Routledge.

Halsey, M. and Deegan, S. 2014. '"Picking Up the Pieces": Female Significant Others in the Lives of Young (Ex)Incarcerated Males'. *Criminology and Criminal Justice*, 15(2), 131–51.

Halsey, M. and Deegan, S. 2015. *Young Offenders: Crime, Prison and Struggles for Desistance*. London: Palgrave.

Harris, Y., Graham, J., and Carpenter, G. (eds.) 2010. *Children of Incarcerated Parents: Theoretical, Developmental, and Clinical Issues*. New York: Springer.

Irwin, J. 1985. *The Jail*. Berkeley: University of California Press.

Katz, J. 1988. *Seductions of Crime*. New York: Basic Books.

King, D. 2005. *National Evaluation of the Prisoners and their Families Program*. Canberra: Australian Government Attorney-General's Department.

Larman, G. and Aungles, A. 1993. 'Children of Prisoners and Their Outside Carers: The Invisible Population', in Easteal, P. and McKillop, S. (eds.) *Women and the Law*. Proceedings of a conference held 24–26 September 1991. Canberra: Australian Institute of Criminology Available at: https://aic.gov.au/publications/proceedings/16.

Laub, J. H. and Sampson, R. J. 2003. *Shared Beginnings, Divergent Lives: Delinquent Boys to Age 70*. Cambridge: Harvard University Press.

Maldonado, S. 2006. 'Recidivism and Paternal Engagement'. *Family Law Quarterly*, 40(2), 191–211.

Maruna, S. 2011. 'Reentry as a Rite of Passage'. *Punishment and Society*, 13(1), 3–28.

Maruna, S. and Immarigeon, R. (eds.) 2004. *After Crime and Punishment*. Cullompton: Willan.

Michalsen, V., Flavin, J., and Krupat, T. 2010. 'More Than Visiting Hours: Maintaining Ties Between Incarcerated Mothers and Their Children'. *Sociology Compass*, 4(8), 576–91.

Mills, A. and Codd, H. 2007. 'Prisoners' Families', in Jewkes, Y. (ed.) *Handbook on Prisons*. 672–95. Cullompton: Willan.

Mumola, C. 2000. 'Incarcerated Parents and Their Children'. Bureau of Justice Statistics Special Report. Washington, DC: US Department of Justice. Available at: https://www.bjs.gov/content/pub/pdf/iptc.pdf.

Novero, C., Loper, A., and Warren, J. 2011. 'Second-Generation Prisoners: Adjustment Patterns for Inmates With a History of Parental Incarceration'. *Criminal Justice and Behaviour*, 38(8), 761–78.

Nurse, A. 2000. 'Coming Home: The Transition From Incarcerated to Paroled Young Father', in Fox, G. and Benson, M. (eds.) *Families, Crime and Criminal Justice*. 281–308. New York: Elsevier.

Poehlmann, J. 2005. 'Incarcerated Mothers' Contact With Children, Perceived Family Relationships, and Depressive Symptoms'. *Journal of Family Psychology*, 19(3), 350–7.

Quilty, S. 2005. 'The Magnitude of Experience of Parental Incarceration in Australia'. *Psychiatry, Psychology and Law*, 12(1), 256–7.

Quilty, S., Levy, M., Howard, K., Barratt, A., and Butler, T. 2004. 'Children of Prisoners: A Growing Public Health Concern'. *Australian and New Zealand Journal of Public Health*, 28(4), 339–43.

Schirmer, S., Nellis, A., and Mauer, M. 2009. 'Incarcerated Parents and Their Children: Trends 1991–2007'. Washington, DC: The Sentencing Project. Available at: http://www.sentencingproject.org/doc/publications/publications/inc_incarceratedparents.pdf.

Smith, P. 2014. *When the Innocent Are Punished*. London: Palgrave.

Sykes, G. 1958. *The Society of Captives*. Princeton: Princeton University Press.

Travis, J. and Waul, M. (eds.) 2003. *Prisoners Once Removed: The Impact of Incarceration and Reentry on Children, Families, and Communities*. Washington, DC: Urban Institute.

Van der Kolk, B. (ed.) 1987. *Psychological Trauma*. Washington, DC: American Psychiatric Publishing.

Wacquant, L. 2009. *Punishing the Poor*. Durham: Duke University Press.
Wakefield, S. and Wildeman, C. 2014. *Children of the Prison Boom*. Oxford: Oxford University Press.
Warr, M. 2002. *Companions in Crime*. Cambridge: Cambridge University Press.
Weaver, B. 2016. *Offending and Desistance*. London: Routledge.
Widom, C. S. 1995. 'Victims of Childhood Sexual Abuse: Later Criminal Consequences'. Research in Brief. March. National Institute of Justice, US Department of Justice.
Widom, C. S. 1989. 'Child Abuse, Neglect, and Adult Behavior: Research Design and Findings on Criminality, Violence, and Child Abuse'. American Journal of Orthopsychiatry, 59(3), 355–67.
Wildeman, C. and Western, B. 2010. 'Incarceration in Fragile Families'. *The Future of Children* 20(2), 157–77.
Woodward, R. 2003. 'Families of Prisoners: Literature Review on Issues and Difficulties'. Occasional Paper No. 10. Canberra: Australian Government Department of Family and Community Services. Available at: https://www.dss.gov.au/sites/default/files/documents/05_2012/op10.pdf.
Young, J. 1999. *The Exclusive Society*. London: Sage.

15

The Legally Sanctioned Stigmatization of Prisoners Families

Marie Hutton

Introduction

For the first twenty-two years of my life I regularly visited a relative as he served several sentences in prisons across England, ranging from Categories A to C.[1] Each time, I visited I was searched, and our every interaction in the communal visits hall was overseen by security cameras, prison staff, and other prisoners and their visitors. The rationale for this was not something I questioned at the time. It was standard practice and a condition of entry to the prison and access to my relative. Ten years after my last visit, I began my foray into prisons research. In an uncanny coincidence, the first prison I entered as an official researcher was the last I had entered as a social visitor. I remembered that last social visit vividly, as in addition to searching me, the visits staff did something 'new': they swabbed our hands for drug residue. Despite remaining a picture of serenity to not arouse suspicion, internally I panicked; not because I had consumed or secreted drugs about my person, but in case I had inadvertently come into contact with any drug residue during my working life as a barmaid. Had a customer paid with a note that someone had used to snort cocaine? Would that transfer show up on the test? The odds of this were remote but rational thinking was not at play here. My panic was predicated on the consequences of a positive test in an environment where security was paramount. I would likely have been refused entry or offered a closed visit,[2] and any lack of culpability on my part would have been of little consequence. Thankfully the test was negative.

Thus, when I arrived at this same prison for my first day there as a researcher, I was ready and had steeled myself to what I assumed would be a rigorous security vetting before I was permitted entry. On that day my hands were definitely clean. But the psychological labour I had expended proved unnecessary. The officer checked that the name on my Passport matched that on the list and I was ushered through with a smile along with the rest of the team. I was not searched and neither were my bags. After years as a domestic visitor this was a revelation. But reduced, or at best perfunctory, security processing proved a regular occurrence whenever I entered a prison in an 'official' capacity. I frequently wondered why? I was still essentially the same person; the only difference was this shift in status from entering as a 'social' to an 'official' visitor. In

---

[1] For reasons of confidentiality I will name neither my relative nor the establishments he was imprisoned in.
[2] A closed visit would have meant sitting in a cubicle separated from my relative by a pane of plastic whilst spending most of the visit shouting into a microphone. A deeply unpleasant and dehumanizing experience to be avoided if possible, especially as we had travelled some sixty miles on public transport at considerable cost for the one visit a month we were entitled to.

Prisons, Punishment, and the Family: Towards a New Sociology of Punishment? First Edition. Rachel Condry and Peter Scharff Smith. © The several contributors 2018. Published 2018 by Oxford University Press.

her study of an American prison Comfort (2007) describes this as the transition from 'prisonised visitor' to 'professional outsider'. That shift transformed me from an inherently untrustworthy body that needed to be searched and constantly surveilled within the prison walls to a trustworthy one who did not.

It is this conundrum that I wish to interrogate in this chapter, drawing on my doctoral research conducted in two prisons in England and Wales. It is frequently documented that prisoners' families are subject to a 'courtesy stigma' (Goffman, 1963, 44), akin to a guilt by association for choosing to remain connected to an imprisoned loved one. Numerous studies have highlighted the stigmatization experienced by prisoners' romantic partners (Davies, 1980; Fishman, 1990; Girshick, 1996; Lanskey et al., this volume) that often manifests by way of 'disrespectful' prison visits practices (Liebling, 2004; Hutton, 2016) or as part of their 'secondary prisonization' (Comfort, 2007). For an insightful socio-legal take, see Codd (2008). Important work has also highlighted the stigmatization of families where a loved one has committed a particularly serious crime (May, 2000; Condry, 2007). Others have highlighted the stigmatization of prisoners' children (Smith, 2014; Knudsen, this volume) and how this contributes to their pathologization (Knudsen, 2016). Important insights have also been made as to the wider and longer-term consequences of this stigmatization for families (Condry, this volume; Lanskey et al., this volume). However, to date, there has been little examination in the literature of the extent to which this courtesy stigma is embodied in the national rules and local procedures of prisons in their visiting practices. This piece addresses that lacuna.

This chapter will demonstrate empirically how the five elements of stigma identified in Link and Phelan's (2001) classic schema (labelling, negative stereotyping, seperateness, status loss, and discrimination) manifested in the rules and procedures around visiting and was therefore legally sanctioned. I will begin by highlighting the ways in which prisoners' families' were labelled, misguidedly treated as a 'separate' group within society, and negatively stereotyped. Then I will describe how upon entering the prison as social visitors, families suffered a loss of status as their 'outside' identities were erased while simultaneously being subjected to a form of (associative) discrimination bought most clearly into focus when comparisons were drawn between how social and official visitors (such as legal advisors) were treated, and more importantly, trusted by the prison system. Despite both groups entering the prison as 'outsiders', there were important differences around how they were processed, the extent to which they were searched, and the location and conditions under which their visits took place. These differences were always to the detriment of prisoners' families who were ultimately treated as untrustworthy and inferior bodies in comparison to those entering for 'official' purposes. Thus this chapter concludes that prisoners' families are spuriously treated less favourably than official visitors, not because of who they are but because of who they are related to prisoners. Therefore what follows is a comprehensive, empirically driven, socio-legal analysis of the 'subtleties, complexities and contextual nature' (Macleod and Austin, 2003, 117) of how this not so courteous stigma manifests and is literally written in to the rules and procedures governing prisons.

Research context and approach

This chapter draws on my doctoral research conducted in two category B/C local prisons in England and Wales. For the purposes of this chapter I have named them HMP Anon and HMP Fermington. Over nine months, I conducted sixty-one semi-structured interviews with prisoners and a range of visitors, predominantly family members. When recruiting visitors there were no specific criteria for participation beyond a personal connection to the prisoner. Similarly, with prisoners, I recruited those who received visits and a small number who did not (although those experiences are not recounted here). Later on in the study, I employed theoretical (or purposive) sampling to capture the experiences of those who engaged in specific types of visits such as family days and closed visits. All interviews were conducted in private ensuring the confidentiality of participants whose identities have been anonymized in this study. I also conducted ad hoc, informal interviews with prison staff alongside extensive observation of each stage of the visiting process in both prisons. Interviews were recorded, transcribed, analysed, and coded thematically using NVivo.

The purpose of the study was to deepen understandings of the 'empirical reality of human rights law including its doctrinal technicalities' (Murphy and Whitty, 2013, 13), in particular how Article 8 of the European Convention on Human Rights 1950 (ECHR), the right to respect for one's private and family life, operates and is understood in the prison environment. Much of the guidance issued to prisons on how to interpret their obligations under Article 8 ECHR is contained in Prison Service Instructions, more commonly, and henceforth, referred to as PSIs. PSIs are policy documents that contain the 'rules, regulations and guidelines by which prisons are run' (MoJ, 2017). Thus, although they often contain guidance and examples of 'best' practice for prisons to aspire to beyond the scope of their legal obligations, PSIs are legal instruments and a prison's failure to adhere to a PSI can form the basis for judicial review (Von Berg, 2014). During data analysis it became clear that whilst directing prisons as to their obligations under Article 8 ECHR (see Hutton, 2017), another, previously unexplored, narrative emerged around the extent to which the PSIs embodied and facilitated the institutionalized stigmatization of prisoners' families.

Conceptualizing stigma

Goffman famously defined stigma as 'an attribute that is deeply discrediting ... a special kind of relationship between an attribute and a stereotype' that reduces those subjected to it 'from a whole and usual person to a tainted, discounted one' (Goffman, 1963, 12). Later iterations of the concept have characterized stigma as a characteristic contrary to the norm of a given social unit (Stafford and Scott, 1986); as akin to a 'mark' linking a person to undesirable characteristics (Jones et al., 1984); and an 'attribute' or 'characteristic' conveying a devalued social identity in a particular context (Crocker et al., 1998). In an excoriating critique, Manzo (2004) complained that despite years of attempts to achieve conceptual and definitional clarity, stigma remained a term that was utilised liberally but rarely satisfactorily defined. Helpfully, in a comprehensive literature review, Pescosolido and Martin synthesize these definitions and conclude:

> Stigma, proper, is the mark, the condition, or status that is subject to devaluation. Stigmatization is the social process by which the mark affects the lives of all those touched by it. (Pescosolido and Martin, 2015, 91)

Taking earlier critiques around the definitional ambiguity of stigma into account, in an influential meta-analysis, Link and Phelan (2001) identified four inter-related components which when present resulted in the stigmatization of the group in question; (i) labelling (the distinguishing and labelling of human differences); (ii) negative stereotyping (when labelled persons are linked with undesirable characteristics due to dominant cultural beliefs); (iii) separating (a degree of separation into 'us' and 'them' by the distinct characterization of the labelled); and (iv) status loss and discrimination (leading to unequal outcomes).

It is somewhat trite to state that being (or having been) a prisoner would be considered by many a devaluing mark, condition, or status; indeed, Goffman (1963) included this circumstance within the remit of stigma from the outset. But as Goffman (1963, 44) highlighted, for prisoners' families the nature of this stigma is a vicarious one; a 'courtesy stigma' whereby they are stigmatized, not because of their own actions but rather by their close association with the one whom the stigmatized attribute has been ascribed to. What follows then is a close examination of the rules and procedures that govern prison visiting applying Link and Phelan's (2001) schema to illuminate empirically examples of when prisoners' families were explicitly labelled; negatively stereotyped; treated as separate; and suffered status loss and discrimination. In short, all the ways in which prisoners' families, as social visitors, are subjected to a legally sanctioned form of courtesy stigma. Link and Phelan's (2001) study also highlighted the tendency for earlier conceptualizations of stigma to be overly focused on individuals with only a limited recognition of the structural factors that facilitated the stigmatization. Therefore there is an important shift here away from individual practices to expose the extent to which this stigmatization is embedded in the rules and procedures that govern establishments.

Labelling, negative stereotyping, and separateness

The first component of stigma Link and Phelan (2001) identify is the labelling of a group, defined as the distinguishing and labelling of human differences that have been selected for their social salience. The second of their criteria is when the group is treated as separate (defined as a degree of separation into 'us' and 'them' by the distinct characterization of the labelled). That prisoners, families are labelled as 'different' and treated as a separate group in policy terms is best exemplified by the recent PSI on corruption that states:

> There is an increased risk of corruption where relationships are formed between staff and offenders and/or with an offender's family or friends. In some instances such relationships may be inappropriate and could constitute or involve criminal conduct (such as the common law criminal offence of Misconduct in Public Office), therefore they are included in the remit of this instruction. (PSI 05-2016 on corruption)

In the corruption PSI above, prisoners' families are treated as completely separate from those who work in prisons. This 'absoluteness' is a misguided position that fails to recognize that in many cases this dichotomy is a false one. Contrary to Prison Service logic, the two states are not mutually incompatible and I encountered a number of prison officers and senior managers who had prisoners or ex-prisoners in their families. What is also unacknowledged here, as Maguire (2016) found, is that often there is a geographical congruence between prison staff and prisoners; they are frequently from the same areas, so their 'knowing' prisoners' families is inevitable. That aside, this highlights that in policy prisoners' families are labelled and treated as a distinct and separate group, and it is not uncommon to see reference to prisoners' families throughout HMPPS literature.

The third element that Link and Phelan (2001) identify is negative stereotyping (when labelled persons are linked with undesirable characteristics due to dominant cultural beliefs). A number of my participants spoke of and sensed that they were negatively stereotyped during their interactions with prison establishments:

> Trust, there is no trust is there? They think because you are coming to see a criminal, that you are kind of in those circles but I'm not. (Garth, prisoner's father, HMP Fermington)

Here, Garth encapsulates what is at the nub of the 'courtesy stigma' experienced by prisoners' families: the perception that they are equally as criminal as those they visit and consequently are inherently untrustworthy. That prisoners' families are negatively stereotyped was recently acknowledged by the Prison Reform Trust who told the All-Party Penal Affairs Parliamentary Group:

Prisoners' families come from all walks of life and it is important to avoid crude stereotyping which can be stigmatizing and harmful. (Prison Reform Trust, 2014)

But this aspect of institutionalized courtesy stigma was rarely stated explicitly by staff or in policy; instead my participants sensed it instinctively, albeit intangibly and generally by inference from the way the rules operated on families or staff behaviours towards them (e.g. by way of more onerous searching conditions, as will be discussed below).

However, that some staff held stereotyped views of prisoners' families did become clear as, similar to Maguire (2016), I witnessed occasions when prison staff utilized these crude stereotypes of prisoners' families, albeit often only when they thought I was out of earshot as the following fieldnote demonstrates:

> I'm in the visits hall, an officer is next to me but I don't think she realises I can hear her as she calls a kid who looks about seven years old 'mini me C&R kid' and tells her colleagues to keep an eye on that one. She adds 'he's delights' in a sarcastic tone. (Fieldnote at HMP Anon)

The reference to C & R is to the control and restraint procedures prisons use to physically restrain 'unruly' prisoners. Here then is an officer characterizing the behaviour of a bored child in a sparse visits hall as worthy of punitive measures; the child is the problem, not the visiting system. At this same prison I was frequently informed that prisoners' families' testimony to me about visiting conditions was not to be trusted. One officer warned me of the need to keep an open mind 'because they [prisoners' families] lie … they will have an agenda'. What was most interesting about this exchange was the underlying presumption that there was no obvious contemplation of the possibility that I could have been a member of a prisoners' family and a researcher. Thus the attitudes of some staff very clearly labelled prisoners families, treating them as separate and worthy of negative stereotyping.

In policy, the PSI on corruption above is a rare example of this negative stereotyping of prisoners' families manifesting quite so explicitly. As stated, in the PSI, the mere act of prison staff 'knowing' a prisoner's family is treated as a security risk per se. Incredibly, within the PSI there is no justification as to why the presumption is made that all prisoners' families are inherently likely to be criminal enough to warrant such an extreme precaution with respect to preventing corruption. In the absence of any validating evidence, it is hard to see this provision as anything more than a manifestation of the unjust negative stereotyping of a group of people HMPPS actually know very little about. Of the families I met, only two had criminal records or involvement in criminal activities. The vast majority were law-abiding and working professionals; from hairdressers to civil servants to small business owners. The idea that they would be involved in 'corruption' or any kind of illicit dealings within prisons was anathema to them (Hutton, 2016).

However, *explicit* examples of negative stereotyping such as in the PSI on corruption are rare. In the next section, I will demonstrate that the differences in the rules around social and official visitors are an *implicit* manifestation of this negative stereotyping to be inferred from the status loss and discrimination prisoners' families suffer in comparison to official visitors when interacting with establishments.

Status loss

Link and Phelan (2001, 371) consider that an axiomatic consequence of the separating, labelling, and negative stereotyping of a group is their downgrading in the status hierarchy as they suffer status loss. Visits from legal advisors, police officers, probation officers, authorized researchers, pastoral visits from faith leaders, immigration officials, consular officials, the Crown Prosecution Service, and Veterans organizations such as the British Legion all fall under this category of 'official visitor'.[3] As this extensive list demonstrates, the designation of official visitor extends to a wide number of professions but they are all characterized by the 'official' capacity under which they wish to enter the prison and their status as 'professionals'. Throughout their time in the prison, they remained defined by this 'outside' status and retained the trust and respect that comes by virtue of their profession.

In contradistinction, social visitors take on a transitory and anonymized identity. When prisoners' families enter the prison, who they were before the prison gate becomes irrelevant as they take on the singular identity of 'social visitor'. From that point forward they are only seen through the narrow lens of the prison and their role as the family member of the deviant contained within. Any previous 'status' is not only lost but erased.

This status loss, this erasure of who prisoners families 'are' before the prison gates, leads to the facilitation of their treatment as 'polluted and inferior' bodies (Comfort, 2007, 63) compared to the treatment of official visitors as 'superior' bodies. Thus for social visitors the area where they are processed before entering the prison becomes a 'border region':

the site of contested personhood, an intermediary zone where [social] visitors continually define and defend their social and physical integrity against the degradation of the self required by the prison as a routine condition for visiting. (Comfort, 2007, 22)

One especially troubling practice that exemplified this process of status loss was the habit of 'stamping' the hands of all social visitors at HMP Anon as they were processed into the prison. All social visitors to the prison were 'stamped' with a mark that could be seen under an ultra violet light, ostensibly as a security measure to prevent prisoners swapping places with their visitors and escaping. But it was only prisoners' families who were deemed to represent a risk in this way as, remarkably, legal visitors were not 'stamped' reinforcing their status as superior bodies. HMP Anon was an establishment that only housed adult men over the age of 21 and yet, every social visitor was 'stamped', irrespective of gender or age. Perhaps most disturbingly, HMP Anon deemed it necessary to place this mark on very small children and babies who could in no way have been capable of being utilized for an escape plan. Thus the stamping was for many a gratuitous and unnecessary act yet, reflecting the status loss endured by prisoners' families, no discretion was exercised by prison staff. All prisoners' social

---

[3] A comprehensive list is available in PSI 16-2011, 'Providing Visits and Services to Visitors'.

visitors were treated as one homogenous, collectively untrustworthy group. So while official visitors remained unsullied, the simple fact of having a more intimate connection to a prisoner necessitated the 'stamping' of social visitors invoking an unfortunate symmetry with Jones et al.'s (1984) classification of the stigma as a mark.

Discrimination

The final component of stigma described by Link and Phelan (2001) is the consequent discrimination against the group who have suffered this status loss. This discrimination can manifest in a number of ways; individual discrimination (overt interpersonal acts of discrimination), status loss as a source of discrimination (where discrimination leads to, e.g. reduced life chances) and, what will be the main focus here, structural discrimination. Structural discrimination occurs when, irrespective of whether individuals deliberately intend to discriminate, institutional practices embody and reinforce the stigmatization of groups (Link and Phelan, 2001). I am arguing that the labelling and treatment of prisoners' families as a separate group, their negative stereotyping as inherently untrustworthy (and potentially criminal) bodies, combined with their status loss, facilitates institutional practices that discriminate against them. In essence, that the rules and procedures of prisons 'act to endorse and reinforce stereotypes, and disadvantage those labelled' (Pescosolido and Martin, 2015, 92). This discrimination is bought sharply into focus when comparisons are drawn between the treatment of social visitors (prisoners' families) and official visitors, particularly when we consider differences in how both groups are processed and searched as they enter the prison and the location and condition of visits they are entitled to. As Crocker et al. (1998) noted, these structural factors are often context and spatially specific and transient in their application. Accordingly here the focus will be on illuminating important differences in treatment not only between social and official visitors but also between the two establishments.

Processing and searching

This differential treatment manifested itself in the rules around which level of search visitors could be subjected to as a condition of entry. All visitors (official and social) are generally required to undergo some kind of 'rub-down' search by a prison officer to detect attempts to convey illicit items into the prison. The rules on searching allow for two levels of search; Level A and Level B.[4] Both level A and level B searches involve officers running their hands over specified areas of a visitor's fully clothed body (similar to the body search one might experience at airport security). However the Level A search is designed to be more invasive and permits a more direct engagement with a visitors' physicality. In addition to the basic 'rub-down' officers were instructed to:

Search the [visitors] head by running your fingers through her/his head and round the back of her/his ears, or asking her/him to shake out her/his hair and run her/his fingers through it. Unpin long hair if necessary.

Look around and inside her/his ears, nose and mouth. You may ask her/him to raise her tongue so that you can look under it.

Ask her/him to remove footwear and search thoroughly. Check the soles of the feet.

---

[4] See PSI 67-2011, 'Searching of the Person'.

This more invasive Level A search is reserved for only two categories of persons in the prison as a matter of routine; prisoners and social visitors. The rules are clear that official visitors are not to be subjected to this extra layer of security, albeit with no explanation as to why. Here then at a national policy level, prisoners and their social visitors are conflated and treated as equally untrustworthy, necessitating the need for an enhanced level of search compared to official visitors. This is the embodiment of legally sanctioned stigma writ large in visiting policy.

The rules do allow for an element of discretion and prisons are able to forgo the more stringent searching conditions if it is decided at a local level that it is not necessary. Interestingly, although both my research prisons were Category B/C and local establishments, only one (HMP Anon) had chosen to exercise this discretion and not subject social visitors to the enhanced search. However, that HMP Fermington had chosen to implement the enhanced search for social visitors was noted by a number of my participants. Many of my participants experienced these additional requirements as an inconvenience that added to the labour of visiting. This was especially so for female visitors made to take down their carefully crafted hairstyles in order to prove that they were not conveying illegal items in their hair and were instead just trying to look as attractive as possible for their partners. But perhaps the most galling aspect of this additional layer of search for many was the requirement that unlike official visitors, they, as social visitors, had to remove their shoes before entering the metal detector. Their shoes had to be x-rayed, after which they had to walk barefoot across what they described as 'that filthy floor', leaving many feeling exposed and unclean.

Others noted that the requirement that social visitors remove their shoes, to which official visitors such as legal visitors were not subject, was discriminatory practice. As Calvin noted:

> For instance, my missus was out there the other week and she was walking through and there was these two men walking in and staff said 'oh, you don't have to take your shoes off'. So my missus said 'why do I have to take my shoes off?' And it was like discrimination between the solicitor and her. If you look at the wall up there you'll see a solicitor on the wall who brought cocaine in his shoes so why don't they have to take their fucking shoes off? They are more or less saying you have to take them off because you're going to bring drugs in and it does happen but .... (Calvin, prisoner, HMP Fermington)

What Calvin was alluding to here was that at the time of the fieldwork there had recently been a case where a solicitor had been sentenced to six years' imprisonment. He had been caught smuggling a cornucopia of illicit substances (including skunk cannabis, mephedrone, and electronic scales) into two different prisons (that the authorities are aware of!) (Cheston, 2012). In order to smuggle the illicit items in, he had taken advantage of the fact that official visitors were not required to remove their shoes and bought shoes that were three sizes too big to accommodate his haul. Thus Calvin and his wife's indignation was clear; despite the very obvious case of an official visitor using the rules of the prison to facilitate illegality, it was his wife, not the legal visitors who must still remove her shoes. The presumption remained that compared to official visitors, his wife (who had no criminal record nor nefarious intent) was inherently more likely to engage in illicit activity simply by dint of being related to a prisoner; him.

A further irony was that on a second occasion this misbehaving solicitor was known to have attempted to smuggle drugs into a prison, he had been on bail for his previous attempt. Thus, despite pending legal proceedings launched after he had been caught with drugs in his possession on prison grounds, the sollicitor was still able to enter another prison and minister to his clients. This highlights another important difference in standards set for the banning of visitors as a consequence of being caught attempting to smuggle illicit items into a prison. The current rules are somewhat contradictory as to the appropriate response for prisons who discover a social visitor to be smuggling drugs, mobile phones (or any other list A or B prohibited items). One the one hand, the rules state that irrespective as to whether the visitor is a family member or friend, '*a ban must be the normal response*'.[5] Therefore, it appears that social visitors will be axiomatically excluded from visiting, normally for a minimum of three months. But confusingly, the same document also states that, because any decision to impose a ban (or closed visits) engages Article 8 ECHR, the principle of proportionality should be applied and decisions should be made on an individual basis.[6] Notably the guidance on official visitors takes a more emphatic, less contradictory tone:

> There will be times when a dog indicates on an official visitor/Independent Monitoring Board (IMB) members or a member of staff/contracted staff etc. It is *vital* that prison management makes their response to the indication based on the *individual circumstances. Any decision to ban an official visitor or discipline a member of staff must be justifiable.* (PSI 67-2011, 'Searching of the Person')

In contrast to the rules for social visitors, therefore, when dealing with a possible incursion of the rules by an official visitor to prison it is 'vital' that they are given the benefit of doubt and more importantly, the very clear presumption of innocence.

What was troubling during my fieldwork was that even though the rules clearly allowed prisons to exercise discretion and apply the principle of proportionality where social visitors were caught with illicit items, in practice both prisons automatically applied a three-month ban from the establishment. One incident in particular stands out. A woman with impaired hearing had attached her mobile phone to her chest with gauze so that she could feel it vibrate when being contacted. When it was discovered during searching, she had claimed that she had left it there by accident. The visits staff not only believed in her innocence, but because they pitied her sat with her and comforted her. However, as far as the consequences of this indiscretion were concerned, the prison staff believed their hands were tied and said that they had no choice but to impose a ban from the prison for three months, most likely followed by three months on closed visits. Here, then, for a social visitor, acknowledged innocence and the lack of nefarious intent was no defence to the charge of attempting to smuggle illicit items into the prison.

The knowledge that prisons would take a strict liability approach was noted by many of my participants and they were especially troubled by the way normally innocuous items, such as money, could be transformed into illegal items just by entering a prison with them. Although cash was allowed to be taken over to the visits hall, the amount permitted was restricted. Therefore any money found over that limit left visitors open to sanction and accusations of an attempt to smuggle cash into the prison. That this was a mistake that could easily be made was something many visitors were conscious of:

> Lowe's brother, he had been on a night out and he had a five pound note all scrunched up in his back pocket and he didn't realise it was there. So the police were called for that and he got a caution and I think he was barred. Lowe's girlfriend ended up on a closed visit, and you thought, well that is bad. (Dennis, prisoner's father, HMP Fermington)

---

[5] PSI 15-2011 on management and security at visits.   [6] PSI 15–2011.

In this case the transgressor was not only banned from the prison but also received a criminal sanction; his fellow visitor (despite not carrying the money herself) was also penalized with a closed visit. However, from the prison's perspective, although five pounds is not a particularly large amount of money, the decision to take a strict liability approach was predicated on the notion that this attempt could have been a 'test run'. The concern for the prison was that this attempt was a precursor and the next time the sum involved could be higher. But it is troubling that while the rules are unambiguous as to the benefit of the doubt to be accorded official visitors in these unfortunate circumstances, the rules on social visitors are anything but. The danger here is that this ambiguity leaves prisoners' families at a disadvantage and at risk of an automatic ban, irrespective of the individual circumstances.

Location and conditions of visits

In both establishments, although domestic and official visitors were initially processed in the same space, their paths diverged as their visits took place in different areas. Social visitors would be directed to a communal visits hall and official visitors would progress to a series of cubicles. At HMP Anon, an important consequence of this bifurcation was that social visitors were subjected to an extra layer of security on the way to the communal visits hall that official visitors were not—sniffer dogs. Conversely, at HMP Fermington, when sniffer dogs were deployed it was at a point in the searching process that would enable them to detect illicit substances on *all* visitors. However, at HMP Anon dogs were, as a matter of routine, only deployed on social visitors just before they entered the communal visits hall. At HMP Anon, it was not uncommon for those negatively 'indicated' by the sniffer dogs to be asked to undergo a full body search, previously known as strip searching. A full body search of visitors exactly mirrors those carried out on prisoners. The visitor is made to remove the garments on the top half of their body in the presence of two officers of the same gender. The visitor is then scrutinized by the staff members from the waist up. The visitor is then permitted to cover their top half and remove the clothes from the bottom half of their body, again so that they can be scrutinized by prison staff. Thus, a practical consequence of official visitors not passing by the sniffer dogs was that they were significantly less likely to be singled out for full body searching. Therefore, although, prima facie, the power to conduct a full body search was applicable to all visitors, in reality, this was not the case at HMP Anon. Again, a subtle indicator of the designation of domestic visitors as inherently more untrustworthy than official visitors. To be clear, I am in no way trying to imply here that any visitor should be subjected to a full body search, indeed I have argued elsewhere the inappropriateness of such an extreme measure being available to prisons at all (Hutton, 2016; and see Codd, 2008). I am simply highlighting that the most punitive and degrading measure that could be imposed on a visitor by a prison was only likely to be imposed on social visitors.

Another important difference arose in the conditions of visits. As the PSI, 'Providing Visits and Services to Visitors' (PSI 2011-16), decrees 'social visits *must* take place within hearing range and sight of staff'.[7] Prisons are therefore mandated to ensure a lack of privacy for prisoners and their social visitors that allows for every moment of their time in the prison to be surveilled by prison staff. Accordingly, social visitors

---

[7] Emphasis added.

would be led to a 'main' or communal visits hall where their visits would be conducted in a large, very public space, where at any one time, particularly at weekends, some forty to fifty visits could be taking place at the same time. This meant that in addition to staff surveillance they could be seen and potentially overheard by other prisoners and their visitors. An additional layer of oversight was provided by security cameras that roamed overhead monitored by a team outside of the visits space. In contradistinction, where privacy is to be kept at a minimum for social visits, the standards for official visits place a premium on facilitating privacy. Prisons are tasked with ensuring:

Measures are in place to ensure that official visits—particularly those from legal advisers and consular officials—*should take place within sight but out of hearing range of staff*, other prisoners and their official visitors. (PSI 2011-16 'Providing Visits and Services to Visitors')[8]

In short, prisons were obligated to ensure official visits could be seen but not heard. Therefore, official visitors would progress to a designated space for official visits in a separate part of the prison comprised of cubicles; one per each official visit. Unlike the communal visits hall, the spaces for official visits were discreet, not communal, and the only persons present were those relevant to the discussion at hand. There were no security cameras overhead and although the cubicles had Perspex windows into which staff could see, they had to open the door to gain entry and it was only then that they would be able to overhear any discussion. Even the staff surveillance took on a different tone in this context. I conducted a number of interviews in the official visits area at both prisons I researched in. Although an officer was present at all times, for the most part they remained seated at a desk at the end of the corridor. Unlike the visits hall where they were omnipresent, in this area their presence was intermittent—an occasional walk along the corridor. They would not stare directly into the room, but instead would glance discreetly as they walked past to ensure all was well. This meant that official visitors were allowed a degree of privacy that was unimaginable and unattainable for prisoners during their social visits. One of the biggest concerns for my participants was the impact that the lack of privacy during social visits had on their relationships. Unsurprisingly, the high levels of surveillance inhibited conversation and made it difficult to engage in private and sensitive discussions. And yet here we see that while privacy is prioritized for official visitors, for family members, whose relationships with prisoners would be equally, if not more important, it is not. The incongruity of this circumstance is best demonstrated by the fact that members of veterans' organizations, as official visitors, are authorized entry under these privileged conditions to discuss resettlement issues with prisoners. However, the family members who many prisoners will be living with after release are not. Thus the rules decree that the most personal form of relationships, those between prisoners and their families, attract the least degree of privacy whereas the more anonymous relationships between prisoners and their official visitors are afforded the most.

Conclusion

In this chapter I have interrogated some of the ways in which the rules contained in nationally applicable Prison Service Instructions and local procedures of prisons in England and Wales reinforce and sanction the courtesy stigma experienced by prisoners' families. The above demonstrates that social visitors and official visitors are clearly not treated as equals despite the fact both groups enter the prison as outsiders

[8] Emphasis added.

not least because the national rules and specific procedures at both establishments categorized social visitors in need of additional scrutiny and surveillance. Thus, these additional requirements position prisoners' families as 'inferior bodies' by inference, simultaneously reinforcing negative stereotypes of prisoners' families as inherently more likely to be criminal and untrustworthy. This is reinforced by the troubling way that all of these discriminatory measures operate corporally; they mandate a more intimate engagement with the bodies of those who are more intimately connected to prisoners compared to those who are not. The rules allow social visitors' bodies to be searched more rigorously and be subjected to greater scrutiny on prison grounds. It is hard to ignore the Lombrosian undertones at play here. Undoubtedly then, all of these additional measures for social visitors discriminated against them by placing them at a comparative disadvantage to official visitors. And yet, these institutional practices of discrimination were not personal. Indeed, how could they be when prisons know so little about the characteristics of social visitors or who prisoners' families are before they enter the prison? Therefore, I argue this discrimination emanates from their homogenized collective identity as prisoners' families and the negative stereotypes attributed to that status. Just as Goffman (1963) talked of 'courtesy stigma' as stigma by association, this discrimination operates in a similar way and is analogous to 'discrimination by association' (or associative discrimination) under the Equality Act 2010. Associative discrimination occurs where someone is subjected to discrimination not on the grounds of their own protected characteristic (such as race or gender) but because they are associated with one who does (Taylor and Emir, 2015). Similarly, I argue that as social visitors are treated as inherently less trustworthy than official visitors based on little, if any, empirical evidence this discrimination stems not from who they are, but because of who they choose to remain connected to.

The next step is to think about precisely why this differential treatment between social and official visitors has been and remains the status quo. In short, is this institutional associative discrimination justified? This will inevitably be speculative as no justification is forwarded in the policy documents I have referenced above. One potential explanation could be that many of the professional visitors who enter the prison are subject to codes of conduct or ethics as part of their role. For example, solicitors are obliged to 'uphold the rule of law', 'act with integrity', and 'behave in a way that maintains ... trust' (Solicitors Regulation Authority Code of Conduct, 2011). But such a justification would be flawed on a number of counts. Although I am by no means tarring all lawyers with the same brush, we know from the incident described above that lawyers have been found to smuggle illicit items into prisons. So, an obligation to abide by a code of ethics does not automatically translate into exemplary behaviour. Similarly, this is not to deny that some prisoners' families do use visits as a means to smuggle illicit items into prisons, but this, as with official visitors, is an ill-intentioned minority. Further, not all of those within the category of official visitors are employed in professions with a code of conduct, such as the veterans' organizations who are included in this remit. Finally, any reliance on the 'professional' status of official visitors to justify this differential treatment could only be grounded in the assumption that all prisoners' families *are not* members of such professions. Therefore, such a wide-ranging justification based on 'professional' status alone would clearly be predicated on fallacious logic and unjustifiable.

Link et al. (2004) emphasize that the presence of stigma depends heavily on social, economic, and political power permitting differences to be identified. To this I would add the previously unconsidered way that the legal powers around visitation vicariously stigmatize prisoners' families. What is important here is that the stigmatizing processes described in this chapter depend not on the vagaries of the actions of individuals within prisons, they are structural and embedded into the rules that govern prison visits. It is these rules that unjustifiably label prisoners' families, treat them as a separate group, and embody negative stereotypes that translate into status loss and discrimination upon their entering the prison. As such, the rules and procedures around prison visits ultimately designate prisoners' families as inferior and untrustworthy bodies compared to official visitors constituting and facilitating a form of legally sanctioned courtesy stigmatization of prisoners' families. Accordingly, I have written this chapter in the hope that prisoners' families will eventually be afforded the same basic courtesy of trust and benefit of the doubt afforded to those who enter the prison as official visitors. This chapter is a plea to prisons and policy makers to recognize and address gratuitous stigmatizing rules and practices in visiting procedures. A plea that prisoners' families not be subjected to unjustifiable, unfair, and unwarranted discriminatory practices based not on who they are but simply because of the imprisoned loved one with whom they choose to remain connected.

References

Cheston, P. 2012. 'Lawyer Jailed for Smuggling Drugs into Prison in Big Shoes'. *Evening Standard*, 12 March. Available at: https://www.standard.co.uk/news/crime/lawyer-jailed-for-smuggling-drugs-into-prison-in-big-shoes-7562630.html.

Codd, H. 2008. *In the Shadow of Prison: Families, Imprisonment and Criminal Justice*. Cullompton: Willan.

Comfort, M. 2007. *Doing Time Together: Love and Family in the Shadow of the Prison*. Chicago, IL: University of Chicago Press.

Condry, R. 2007. *Families Shamed: The Consequences of Crime for Relatives of Serious Offenders*. Cullompton: Willan.

Crocker, J., Major, B., and Steele, C. 1998. 'Social Stigma', in Gilbert, D. T., Fiske, S. T., and Lindzey, G. (eds.) *The Handbook of Social Psychology*. 504–53. Boston, MA: McGraw-Hill.

Davies, R. 1980. 'Stigmatization of Prisoners' Families'. *Prison Service Journal*, 40, 12–14.

Fishman, L. T. 1990. *Women at the Wall. A Study of Prisoners' Wives Doing Time on the Outside*. Albany: State University of New York Press.

Girshick, L. B. 1996. *Soledad Women: Wives of Prisoners Speak Out*. Wesport, CT: Praeger.

Goffman, E. 1963. *Stigma: Notes on the Management of Spoiled Identity*. New York: Simon and Schuster.

Hutton, M. A. 2016. 'Visiting Time: A Tale of Two Prisons'. *Probation Journal*, 63(3), 347–61. doi: 10.1177/0264550516663644.

Hutton, M. A. 2017. 'Prison Visits and Desistance: A Human Rights Perspective', in Van Ginneken, E. and Hart, E. L. (eds.) *New Perspectives on Desistance*. 187–209. Basingstoke: Palgrave MacMillan.

Jones, E. E., Farina, A., Hastorf, A. H., Markus, H., Miller, D. T., and Scott, R. A. 1984. *Social Stigma*. New York: WH Freemann.

Knudsen, E. M. 2016. 'Avoiding the Pathologizing of Children of Prisoners'. *Probation Journal*, 63(3), 362–70.

Liebling, A. (assisted by Arnold, H.) (eds.) 2004. *Prisons and their Moral Performance: A Study of Values, Quality and Prison Life*. Oxford: Oxford University Press.

Link, B. G. and Phelan, J. C. 2001. 'Conceptualizing Stigma'. *Annual Review of Sociology*, 27, 363–85.

Link, B. G., Yang, L. H., Phelan, J. C., and Collins, P. Y. 2004. 'Measuring Mental Illness Stigma'. *Schizophrenia Bulletin*, 30(3), 511–41.

Macleod, J. S. and Austin, J. K. 2003. 'Stigma in the Lives of Adolescents with Epilepsy: A Review of the Literature'. *Epilepsy & Behavior*, 4(2), 112–17.

Maguire, D. 2016. *Learning to Serve Time: Troubling Spaces of Working Class Masculinities in the UK*. DPhil thesis, University of Oxford, unpublished.

Manzo, J. F. 2004. 'On the Sociology and Social Organization of Stigma: Some Ethnomethodological Insights'. *Human Studies*, 27(4), 401–16.

May, H. 2000. '"Murderers' Relatives" Managing Stigma, Negotiating Identity'. *Journal of Contemporary Ethnography*, 29(2), 198–221.

Ministry of Justice (MoJ). 2017. *Prison Service Instructions (PSIs)*. Available at: https://www.justice.gov.uk/offenders/psis accessed 19 April 2017.

Murphy, T. and Whitty, N. 2013. 'Making History Academic Criminology and Human Rights'. *British Journal of Criminology*, 3(4), 568–87.

Pescosolido, B. A. and Martin, J. K. 2015. 'The Stigma Complex'. *Annual Review of Sociology*, 41, 87–116.

Prison Reform Trust. 2014. Minutes of the All-Party Penal Affairs Parliamentary Group held on 1 April 2014, House of Commons. Available at: http://www.prisonreformtrust.org.uk/PressPolicy/Parliament/AllPartyParliamentaryPenalAffairsGroup/April2014pactPrisonersFamilies.

Smith, P. S. (ed.) 2014. *When the Innocent are Punished*. Basingstoke: Palgrave Macmillan.

Stafford, M. C. and Scott, R. R. 1986. 'Stigma, Deviance, and Social control', in Ainlay, S. C., Becker, G., and Coleman, L. M. (eds.) *The Dilemma of Difference*. 77–91. New York and London, Plenum Press.

Taylor, S. and Emir, A. 2015. *Employment Law: An Introduction*. New York: Oxford University Press.

Trust, P. R. 2014. Minutes of the All-Party Penal Affairs Parliamentary Group held on 1 April 2014 at 5.00 pm in Committee Room 5, House of Commons.

Von Berg, P. (ed.) 2014. *Criminal Judicial Review: A Practitioner's Guide to Judicial Review in the Criminal Justice System and Related Areas*. Oxford: Hart Publishing.

16

Time, the Pains of Imprisonment, and 'Coping'

The Perspectives of Prisoners' Partners

Anna Kotova*

Introduction

The numerous difficulties faced by prisoners' families have been well-documented since the 1960s, when Morris (1965) conducted a large-scale study on the experiences of wives of prisoners. As outlined in the introduction to this volume (Condry and Smith, this volume) these difficulties include financial impact such as the loss of a breadwinner's income (Smith et al., 2007; Harman et al., 2007), feelings of loss, loneliness, and grief (Fishman, 1990; Daniel and Barrett, 1981; Arditti, 2003), and the practical difficulties associated with visiting and otherwise keeping in touch (Condry, 2007; Comfort, 2008). Stigma (Condry, 2007; Codd 2000; Arditti, 2003), too, is a serious problems identified in the literature. As Hutton (this volume) identifies, families could be stigmatized not only in the community but by prison officers when visiting their relatives in prison.

Thus far, there have been very few studies on long-term prisoners' families, even though Condry (2007), in her work on serious offenders' families, has suggested that the problems faced by prisoners' families could be exacerbated by a long sentence. Merriman (1979) found that although some relatives of long-term prisoners appeared to recover from the initial trauma of imprisonment quickly, others remained in a state of chronic bereavement throughout the long sentence. Yet as her article did not provide any empirical evidence and did not describe the methodology, the bases for these conclusions are unclear. Her work raises a number of important questions. Do the pains of imprisonment (e.g. Lanskey et al., this volume) become in some way easier to bear with time? Or do they continue to be just as painful years into the sentence, and does imprisonment, therefore, create an ongoing, quasi-permanent state of continued suffering? Moreover, do long sentences create unique problems for those outside?

There is also some evidence of long sentences being transformative for families outside. Comfort (2008), in her ethnographic study of families visiting prisoners in San Quentin in the United States, discussed the processing procedures prison visitors undergo. She suggested that long-term exposure to penal power and the penal pains inherent in these processing procedures can alter visitors in deep, complex ways over time:

* This work was supported by a research grant from the Sir Halley Stewart Trust. All views expressed here are those of the author and not necessarily those of the Trust. I would like to thank Dr Rachel Condry, Professor Peter Scharff Smith, and all those contributors to this volume who attended the second symposium on prisoners' families and social justice in Oxford (May 2017), for their feedback on an earlier version of this chapter.

Prisons, Punishment, and the Family: Towards a New Sociology of Punishment? First Edition. Rachel Condry and Peter Scharff Smith. © The several contributors 2018. Published 2018 by Oxford University Press.

When the experience of being processed is particularly intense or humiliating, one can posit that recurrent exposure to this ordeal will itself become a transformative course, especially if each occurrence is followed by immersion in a distinctively abrasive and depersonalising environment constructed to modify and control behaviour. (Comfort, 2008, 28)

In order to explore how a sample of women experienced, and were transformed by, a husband's or boyfriend's long-term imprisonment, this chapter draws on theoretical tools provided by research on long-term imprisonment specifically, including emerging work on how long-term prisoners experience the pains of imprisonment over a long sentence. Lanskey et al. (this volume) suggest that some pains of imprisonment may be 'acute' for families outside—that is, these pains could persist throughout the sentence. This chapter explores *how* these acute pains are experienced over a long sentence by partners. As it has already been shown that sociological work on imprisonment provides excellent theoretical tools for examining the experiences of families (Comfort, 2008; Kotova, 2015; Lanskey et al., this volume), research on *long-term* imprisonment specifically was chosen as it, too, will help us to understand the experiences of partners outside.

1. Theoretical framework: the pains of long-term imprisonment and coping/adaptation

In their recent study on life-sentenced prisoners, Hulley et al. (2016) explored how these long-term prisoners experienced the pains of imprisonment over a long sentence. They revealed that the initial psychological adjustment to a long sentence was indeed difficult for many prisoners, with pains associated with various deprivations (of social life, sexual intimacy, etc.) being more acutely felt in the early stages of the sentence. The authors argued that over time, life-sentenced prisoners developed coping strategies and grew used to the various deprivations associated with prison life. So although prisoners reported feeling the pains of imprisonment less strongly as time went on, the authors posited that this may be because they were fundamentally transformed by these pains. They argued that 'the everyday pains of imprisonment are "felt" less sharply because, in some sense, they have been internalised into the prisoner's being' (Hulley et al., 2016, 788). This does not, however, indicate that the pains are felt to be in any objective sense less painful. Rather, they become a normal part of the prisoner's everyday existence as the conceptual divide between 'self' and 'problem' is blurred. This process of internalization—whereby one gets used to or numbed to the pains of imprisonment as they become a part of one's everyday existence—will be key to understanding the experiences of long-term prisoners' partners.

Recent work on the pains of imprisonment has also explored the increasingly 'tight' and uncertain nature of these pains (see Lanskey et al., this volume, for an overview). For the purpose of this chapter, it is important to note that modern punishment is characterized by minute, numerous rules and regulations (Crewe, 2009, 2011, 2015). Prisoners are increasingly uncertain as to when this power will be activated and have described themselves toeing an invisible line and existing within a complex and psychologically wearisome web of penal power (Crewe, 2009, 2015). This chapter reinforces Lanskey et al.'s findings, which confirm that families, too, experience this tightness of penal pains. It develops the discussions further by exploring the experiences of *long-term* exposure to these minute, complex prison rules.

Beyond simply longer-term exposure to the pains of imprisonment, long sentences may also create unique problems for prisoners and their families. For example, some long sentences in the United Kingdom are indeterminate, such as life sentences and

Imprisonment for Public Protection (IPP) sentences.[1] This gives rise to further 'pains of indeterminacy' (Crewe, 2011) in a very direct sense: the prisoners and their families do not know when the sentence will end. How do partners outside experience this indeterminacy? There is a link to be made here, also, with the concept of 'ambiguous loss' (Boss, 2004), which has been applied to the experiences of prisoners' families (Arditti, 2012). Ambiguous loss is the type of loss which is defined by lack of clarity and closure (Boss, 2004). In the prison context, the prisoner is said to be physically absent but psychologically present. He is, therefore, removed from the family, but not in any way that provides for closure. If he had died, for example, the family would be able to grieve, and the funeral would provide a degree of closure (Arditti, 2012). When a sentence is long, however, he is not simply physically absent, he is removed for an uncertain period of time. This is likely to make the family's loss doubly ambiguous. This chapter examines this long-term, double ambiguity from the perspective of prisoners' partners.

In order to explore coping and adaptation, this chapter will draw on the concept of 'institutionalization', which is when the prisoner takes on 'the folkways, mores, customs and general culture of the penitentiary' (Clemmer, 1958 [1940], 299). This process has been identified as a key coping mechanism used by prisoners in general to adapt to the pains of imprisonment (Clemmer, 1958 [1940]). Research on long-term imprisonment specifically has examined how long-term prisoners adapt to the pains of imprisonment. First, over time, they can become more introverted as a way of coping with long-term separation from their families and friends, and with the other daily pains of imprisonment (Sapsford, 1978; Heskin et al., 1973). This finding has also been reinforced by more recent qualitative studies—Crewe (2009), for instance, found that those serving the longest sentences were less likely to have friendships in prisons and generally kept themselves at a distance from other people. Liem and Kunst (2013), in a study of long-term prisoners post-release, found evidence of what they called 'post-incarceration syndrome'. This included institutionalization and difficulties with social interactions. What kinds of changes might partners outside undergo? This chapter shows that they, too, can become institutionalized, but also become, in other ways, more independent—an interesting paradox.

Hulley et al. (2016) also found evidence of introversion, adherence to institutional rules, and distancing amongst their sample of life-sentenced prisoners. Yet they developed the analysis further by showing that coping with the pains of imprisonment results in fundamental, identity-level changes in the long-term prisoner. He does not simply adapt; the coping mechanisms are transformative. Hulley and her colleagues were not concerned so much with the customs, routines, and mores that become internalized by long-term prisoners. Rather, their argument is that the process of adaptation is more than a surface-level coping strategy: the pains of imprisonment and adapting to them changes the prisoner as a person, on a fundamentally deep level. How partners may be similarly changed has not yet been explored.

Developing the themes of long-term exposure to the pains of imprisonment and transformation, this chapter also explores how the women's views of the criminal justice system were transformed following a prolonged exposure to the pains of imprisonment. Lee et al. (2014) noted that a family member's imprisonment damaged families' trust in the criminal justice and the state. Jardine (this volume) posits that *prolonged* exposure to perceived lack of fairness when it comes to interactions with prison staff could be especially damaging to families' trust towards prison officers and

---

[1] These sentences were abolished in 2012, but not retrospectively.

the criminal justice system. This chapter develops this theme further, exploring it from the perspective of long-term prisoners' partners and arguing that long sentences could be especially damaging to partners' trust in the prison system.

A further important finding from Hulley et al.'s (2016) recent study is that some adaptation techniques used by prisoners could be, in the long run, maladaptive outside of the prison setting. For example, social and emotional withdrawal inside the prison could help the prisoner survive a long sentence. Yet it could also result in difficulties in maintaining social relationships outside, especially upon release. Anecdotal evidence drawn from first-hand accounts of long-term prisoners (e.g. Warr, 2012) suggests this could indeed be the case. Again, however, whether coping mechanisms used by partners outside may be maladaptive needs to be considered.

Methods and sample

This paper draws on interviews conducted with thirty-three female partners (married and unmarried) of long-term male prisoners serving a determinate sentence of at least ten years[2] or an IPP of life sentence. The participants were recruited via charitable organizations, social media, and an advertisement placed in *Inside Time*, a national prison newspaper. There was no minimum time served stipulated as this could have made the sample too narrow, and so participants were at different stages of what one called 'the prison journey'. However, all had experienced at least one year of a partner's imprisonment, with the longest being twenty-eight years. In a small number of cases, the prisoner had been released before the interview.

All but three interviews were conducted face-to-face, with three conducted over the phone due to practical challenges of meeting in person (such as a participant's ill health). Most were audio-recorded and transcribed in full. Three of the women opted for handwritten notes instead as they did not want their voices to be recorded. The face-to-face interviews took place in neutral private locations, which included private function rooms in cafes and conference rooms in hotels. The women interviewed lived all over England and Wales, with one living in Scotland and one in Northern Ireland. They thus provided their views on different prisons in different parts of the country. Some women visited prisons regularly, some less regularly, and a very small number were unable to visit for health-related reasons, or because it was too far to travel.

It should be noted that it took twenty-four months to access the participants and conduct the interviews, which is not surprising considering that this population is hidden and often stigmatized. As such, a flexible approach to recruitment was necessary. The vast majority of the women were in ongoing relationships with the prisoners, although what this meant was not always straightforward. One participant was in a complex co-parenting relationship with the imprisoned father of her children, though she felt she was no longer in an intimate relationship with him, and another was the ex-partner of a long-term prisoner. Their stories were nonetheless valuable and were therefore included. Participants who met their partners while working in a prison were also included, but it was stipulated that they must have been in a relationship with the prisoner for at least a year. Even though these women had not experienced the arrest and sentencing of a partner, they still felt many of the pains of imprisonment, and also had to cope with a partner's long-term imprisonment. All but one of the women

---

[2] One participant's husband was serving a sentence that fell just short of the ten-year minimum. Since the shortfall was minimal, it was decided that her interview would be included.

reported having little to no prior experience of the criminal justice system, and only one had been in prison herself.

The participants were overwhelmingly White British. One was Mixed British and another Black British. Most of the women were aged 40 and above, with eight participants in their 20s and 30s. Although no claims to generalizability can be made due to the self-selective nature of the sample, the interviews do provide unique insights into the experiences of partners over a long sentence. After all, many of the pains of long-term imprisonment, such as indeterminacy, are likely to be experienced by all partners, regardless of their age, ethnicity, and socio-economic backgrounds. Where appropriate, however, this chapter refers to the specific characteristics of this sample. It will be recognized also that female partners' experiences may be in some ways different to those of other prisoners' relatives: for example, the loss of a prisoner's everyday physical presence may be more acutely felt by a partner whose household he shared than by relatives who only saw him occasionally. Gender, too, may play a role where women had enacted a traditional gender role prior to imprisonment—this too will be recognized.

'They kept on saying, numbers and numbers ...'

For the women in this sample, a partner receiving a prison sentence was in and of itself a deeply traumatic event (Lanskey et al., this volume; Condry, 2007). However, the length of the sentences exacerbated this. The length of the sentence was often overwhelming for the women, because their minds struggled to comprehend the meaning of this long period of time of separation.

> *Amanda*: It's like, when [husband] got sentenced, I don't remember ... I was just numb. I just sat there, and I couldn't even cry. Cos they kept on saying, numbers and numbers, and I was thinking, this isn't right, this ... I couldn't even sort of take it in, how many years they'd actually said, in the end. It was my niece that told me, she said—'that's 18 years!'

This was the case even for those women who met their partners during the current prison sentence, and therefore had not gone through the arrest and sentencing stages. Realizing that they were in love with someone serving a long sentence was difficult for these women, and one reason for this was precisely because they knew their new partner was serving not just a prison sentence, but a long one at that. Lisa, for example, said that realizing she was in love with a life-sentenced prisoner was 'deeply shocking' for her, partially because of the length of his sentence.

A further reason why the length of the sentence was felt to be so problematic was precisely its ambiguity. If a sentence was determinate but long—that is, if the release date was known—there was, at times, uncertainty surrounding the relationship. Some of the women could not always be sure whether they would stay in the relationship as it was difficult to plan that far ahead when they could not be sure how they and/or their partners would change over time. There is strong empirical evidence of long sentences changing prisoners, as discussed earlier in this chapter, and the women realized that the man who went in might not be the man who came out after a long sentence. Unlike biological family, the women had a degree of choice as to whether they continued to maintain the relationship or not. Unlike mothers, fathers, and other relatives, partners can elect to permanently sever their ties to the prisoner. This element of choice made the long sentence, for them, more complexly ambiguous. Mary, for example, was looking forward to her boyfriend being released. Their relationship was, at the time of the interview, positive, but she felt some uncertainty about the future. Others, such as

Elizabeth, explicitly said they could not guarantee they would sustain the relationship over the entire sentence, as it was simply too long to make those guarantees.

> *Mary*: But we talk about the future, we plan the future, so our assumption is that we're gonna be together. But like with any relationship, you never know. Because he might come out and completely have a meltdown, or, you know, not be able to handle the change and stuff after all these years.
>
> *Elizabeth*: I mean I've always, always said to him—'I cannot guarantee that I'm gonna be around. I can't.' D'you know what, nobody can guarantee. Even if you were in a married relationship where it [the relationship] was perfectly normal.

When a sentence was indeterminate, such as a life sentence or IPP sentence, the loss was doubly ambiguous. First, like all prisoners' partners, the women experienced ambiguous loss in the sense that the prisoner was physically absent but psychologically present. Martha described having a partner in prison as 'a bereavement, but without that finality of death', confirming Arditti's (2012) analysis of the ambiguity of loss arising out of imprisonment. Another participant described herself as living in a 'limbo', also highlighting the lack of resolution or finality when it comes to having a partner in prison.

Secondly, these women knew that this state of 'limbo' would continue *indefinitely* if the sentence was indeterminate. Planning for the future was thus near impossible, as the women and their partners did not know when the imprisoned partner would be released. Sarah described the uncertainty that came along with this loss when the sentence was indeterminate.

> *Sarah*: It's that uncertainty, you know? [...] As I've explained to a friend of mine, not being funny, anyone with a fixed sentence, they're in a situation where they can say to themselves—'well, my husband is gonna get out in four or five years', or whatever. [...] But for lifers and IPPs, they can't do that. Because they don't know when they're gonna get out.

'You settle into it. You adapt.'

This study confirms much of the earlier work on the pains of imprisonment as experienced by prisoners' families (see Condry et al., 2016 for an overview). In summary, the women who participated in this study discussed being 'secondarily prisonized' (Comfort, 2008), that is, being exposed to muted and temporary versions of the pains of imprisonment prisoners experience. Visiting was often practically and financially difficult, and time-consuming, even if the distances the women had to travel were shorter than those reported in the United States (Christian, 2015). Likewise, the overwhelming majority experienced a decrease in their disposable income following their partners' imprisonment. This occurred because they lost their own jobs due to stigmatization, or lost income through the loss of their partners' wages or welfare benefits. When visiting, the women were exposed to numerous prison rules and supervision, and their communication with the prisoner (phone calls and letters) was also scrutinized. The findings, therefore, reinforce the findings discussed by a number of contributors to this volume (e.g. Hutton, this volume).

Moreover, the women also described themselves becoming tangled up in the web of penal power, further reinforcing Lanskey et al.'s findings (this volume). The partners had to become used to numerous, and at times discretionarily applied, visiting rules and other prison regulations. For example, one woman said some officers would allow her to wear a belt to visit and others did not, and concluded that she felt some officers were 'playing' and 'making things a bit ridiculous'. Others said they were never sure when phone calls would be listened to by officers, and what these officers were listening out for. What kind of impact did this have over the course of a long sentence?

One of the key questions this study sought to examine was whether these pains of imprisonment became less painful over time. Certainly, it comes as no surprise that arrest and sentencing were traumatic for most partners (see Condry, 2007; Comfort, 2008; Lanskey et al., this volume). The participants also discussed visiting being stressful and upsetting in the early stages of the sentence. As most of them had never visited a prison before, they found visitation rules to be complex, some officers to be abrupt and abrasive, and the visiting environment stressful and tense due to the high levels of supervision and their lack of familiarity with the prison setting. This section is concerned with what happened when these pains were experienced for a long time.

As time went on, the women got used to visiting and got to know the numerous prison rules and regulations. When they were asked if the 'prison journey' became easier as time went on, many initially responded with an unequivocal 'yes'. Yet, this was not quite so simple. Upon a careful analysis of the interviews, it became clear that the pains of imprisonment did not become objectively less painful. Like the prisoners in Hulley et al.'s (2016) study, the women indicated that these pains became interwoven with the very fabric of their everyday lives. Although, in practical terms, things got easier as the women became well-acquainted with the prison rules, on an emotional level they still felt the 'sting' of penal power well into the sentence.

This complex nature of adjusting the pains of imprisonment over a long sentence was highlighted by the women who struggled to give a clear response to the 'does it get easier' question. Words such as 'settle into' and 'adapt' were used to describe the process of adaptation. These phrases evoke a sense of longevity, of imprisonment becoming a part of the women's lives. Yet these words do not imply that the pains are felt any less sharply; rather, they are still there, simmering in the background. Consider the following quote, which shows that getting used to something unpleasant does not make in any less painful:

> *Martha:* D'you know what, I don't think it gets easier. I think you settle into it. You adapt.

In fact, some women themselves struggled to understand whether they were still suffering or not. They got so used to a state of being inclusive of the pains of imprisonment and the associated stressors that, over time, they started to forget what their lives were like before imprisonment. As Casey described below, the pains became so normal that the women's reference points changed. Living with the pains of imprisonment became the norm for them.

> *Casey:* I don't actually know if I am still suffering as much or whether I've just got used to it [her partner's imprisonment]. It is difficult. I do know, deep down, that I am suffering. You know, I am suffering with depression, I can't sleep. I am on tablets, and the time I would be sleeping I ... I suffer with anxiety and I get spots and stress migraines and things like that. I think it's happened for so long I'm just sort of getting used to it.

Again, ambiguity may help us understand why the pains of imprisonment did not seem to become less painful over the course of a long sentence. When a sentence is long, and especially when it is long and indeterminate, there is no sense of an ending and little closure. The women were separated from their partners but still in touch with them, however infrequently. The sense of loss the women felt, for example, did not get any less painful. This was because the loss was not concrete, as with loss through a partner's death, and the period of grief became a quasi-permanent one. It is also possible that partners feel this ambiguous loss more sharply than other prisoners' relatives because the physical absence of a partner could be more acutely felt than the physical absence of another relative. Partners, after all, are more likely to spend more of their time together, especially if they share a household and if the relationship was in general stable and positive (the majority of the participants in this study described precisely such relationships). Therefore, when a partner is imprisoned, his other half may feel the loss to a greater extent than relatives who care for the prisoner just as much, but who did not share his daily life with him and for whom, therefore, his physical absence may not have been as pronounced as for partners. This was explained by Casey:

> *Casey*: I don't mean to say that a partner's pain is worse, but you have got to understand that if you're partners with someone in prison, you do share your whole life with them. It's not just … Obviously, they [other relatives] might love them a bit more because they're family, you know, but the point is, yeah, you share everything with that person. So once they go, you sort of … It's like your life's been cut right in half. It's not just something's been cut out of it, it's like everything's just gone. When they go, everything goes.

Moreover, the partners outside were exposed to the pains of imprisonment when they visited, received phone calls, and wrote letters. This state of being was to continue for years to come, and when sentences were indeterminate the women did not know when their exposure to the pains of imprisonment would end. Combined with the ambiguity of a physically absent but psychologically present partner/ex-partner, this was challenging indeed. Elly described feeling this dread of being quasi-permanently exposed to the pains of imprisonment prior to getting married to her life-sentenced husband:

> *Elly*: I think a bit of me knew [before the wedding] what was going to happen. A bit of me knew that I was actually going to become part of this prison thing. I can't express it very well, and what the consequences of that would be. And I didn't want it [the prison experience]. No normal person would want that. Being told when you can see your husband, the conditions when you can see him, where you can talk to him … Not really actually having a life with him that hasn't been observed by others …

The fact that the pains of imprisonment were tight in nature, as discussed in the previous section, also meant that the women were kept constantly 'on edge'. They had to continuously navigate complex, minute prison rules and regulations, and appeared to be unable to simply settle into their 'prison journey'. Esther, below, describes the frustrations that came along with a decade of what she felt were arbitrarily applied visiting rules. The lack of clarity surrounding the application of penal power was frustrating for her, and she saw officers as using this lack of clarity in order to play power games with prisoners and their partners.

> *Esther*: The Prison Service, to me, is the biggest, most … I dreaded, for years, I think, how am I gonna be treated this week? What sort of rubbish am I gonna have to contend with with these people? […] Every single week, I think, what type of person is gonna search me today, is it gonna be one that's gonna be polite and smile or one that's gonna say 'you can't wear your scarf this week' … I've worn a scarf last week. 'No you didn't! We don't allow scarves.' I said—'I've worn a scarf last week.' 'No, you can't, go back and put it in your locker.'[3]

At times, moreover, the pains of imprisonment struck out with renewed strength. The experience of imprisonment the women described was not simply a highly traumatic

---

[3] Quote previously published (in part) in Kotova (2015).

early stage followed by a process of adaptation. Many of the women likened their experiences to an 'emotional rollercoaster', a phrase that came up time and again. A wedding song might remind the partner outside of the fact that her partner is in prison and sharply bring out feelings of sadness and loneliness, for example:

> *Martha*: You know, anniversaries are always a bit of a rough one ... Yeah, it's just hard, you know, they're not there. They're not there to celebrate it.

In addition, prison institutions in this country do not operate on the basis of identical rules. Thus, adapting to a partner's imprisonment is not as simple as just getting used to the practicalities of staying in touch with him. If the partner is moved, the woman outside has to re-adjust to new rules, new staff, and new institutional attitudes. This could cause a renewed emotional upheaval. Lisa, for instance, said that she found it 'difficult to adjust to a different routine' every time her partner was moved to a different prison.

The rollercoaster metaphor, however, also implies the presence of emotional highs. Notably, most of the women focused on the lows—the lonely special occasions, the nights they could not sleep, and the failed appeals. It seemed that there were many more lows than highs, suggesting that, perhaps, the experience was less of a rollercoaster and more of an initial period of shock, followed by an emotional plateau with a number of troughs. There were, however, some examples of emotional highs. For instance, permission to appeal the conviction being granted, a positive visit, or the prisoner being transferred to a prison closer to where his partner lives, thereby making visitation easier for her, could all evoke feelings of joy and relief. These, however, could also transform into feelings of crushing defeat if the appeal was unsuccessful, for example.

'And you change because of it ...'

This section turns to the theme of transformation. We know that prisoners are transformed by long sentences, but are partners outsider similarly changed? The women who participated in this study did not just internalize the pains of imprisonment. This internalization resulted in them being changed. Adapting to the pains of imprisonment, thus, had a 'deep and profound impact on the person so that the process of coping leads to fundamental changes in the self' (Hulley et al., 2016, 789). Lisa confirmed this in her interview:

> *Lisa*: You do it [undertake the 'prison journey'] because you have to do it, and then you get used to it. And you change because of it, and you become someone who, that's part of your identity, the fact that you've done this, the fact that you've survived this.[4]

Yet in what ways were the women transformed? One sense in which they were changed was, quite simply, the fact of the prison becoming a normalized part of their existence. This is made clear in the quote above. Most of the women described themselves as coming from ordinary, relatively untroubled backgrounds, which made visiting prisons, adhering to prison rules and experiencing penal power as something alien and unusual. After a time, the prison wove itself into their lives and identities as the women adjusted to the pains and deprivations. Holly said, for example, that 'this'—the prison—was now her life.

Furthermore, some of the women became, to various degrees, institutionalized themselves. They, in this sense, became 'secondarily prisonized' (Comfort,

---

[4] Quote previously published in Kotova (2015).

2008) because they adopted some of the prison norms, such as prison language and prison routines. Some used terms such as 'screws' (officers), 'prop' (property), 'canteen' (prison shop), and so on. Most were extremely knowledgeable about the prison routine and described highly structured patterns of communication with their partners. Having this degree of knowledge was necessary because the women needed to know when their partners would call them. Some would structure their days, to varying degrees, around this prison routine, in order to ensure they were be available to receive a phone call. When this routine was interrupted, the partners could get anxious or distressed, which shows the extent to which they became dependant on the prison routine over time:

> Judy: You get so much into a routine of they phone on this day, they phone at that time, they write on this day. And when that doesn't happen … […] You sit and you count down, you know, what lock-up times are. So, you know … So between quarter past twelve and quarter past two I can go out 'cos he's in bang-up for lunch. And then he goes back in bang-up about five, he goes back out at quarter to six, but he's back in bang-up for night at quarter to seven … So I can do something between these hours. The prison shapes our lives as well, very much so. Because we work around their bang-up times. And you get a day when they don't fit into the routine that we're in, because we're so institutionalised by it, and it's panic. Absolute panic. Has he been moved? Is he down the block? Does he not love me anymore? Have I been dumped? The world's gonna end! [laughs]

Despite becoming to some extent institutionalized, the women who had lived with their partners prior to being imprisoned described becoming, in their daily lives, more independent. Unlike prisoners, who are deprived of their outside lives, the women had to go to work, look after children, maintain the household, and otherwise keep their lives going without the presence, support, and help of their partners (see Codd, 2000). This meant that they *had* to become more independent. After all, they could not just put their lives on hold until their partners were released—the sentences were too long for that. For the women who had, prior to imprisonment, enacted traditional gender roles, this independence was a significant change. Whereas they were used to sharing everything with their husbands or boyfriends, they now had to live independent, separate lives. Yet it would be wrong to suggest that they were simply passive subjects and that independence was forced upon them. Many realized that independence would make their 'prison journey' easier, and explicitly chose it as a coping mechanism. Anne, for example, was beginning to travel without her husband and enjoying herself without him. She discussed at length her active attempts at going out alone and enjoying the small pleasures of everyday life, such as going out for a walk alone and travelling without her husband:

> *Anne*: I need to enjoy doing that [doing things like travelling] without him. I haven't taken a holiday, now, since he went in. We would have taken a couple of holidays, like, maybe only weekend to a hotel in Ireland. And a foreign holiday or something. But now his sixteen-year-old daughter and I are going to Rome in the summer, for just a five-day thing. […] But I know that next year, why, I might go on my own! And I would enjoy it.

The above is more likely to be a stronger theme for partners than for other relatives. As discussed earlier, other relatives are less likely to have shared their daily lives with the prisoner prior to imprisonment. Partners are more likely to need to become independent as they may need to do everything they used to do with their partner, alone. Of course, this may not necessarily be the case if they had not lived with the prisoner or if the prisoner did not contribute much to the household in practical terms. However, the women who participated in this study primarily described tightly entwined, close relationships, and for them, especially those who had enacted traditional gender roles, having to become more independent was a significant form of transformation. Some described having to learn household maintenance skills, for example.

The tight nature of the pains of imprisonment also meant that the women had to become more assertive and more independent in order to navigate the prison system. Complex prison rules and lack of clarity as to when and how these rules will be applied meant that some women felt they had to learn to stand up for themselves. Esther, quoted in the previous section, said she had gotten 'braver' over the years, and described making three official complaints against officers. Paradoxically, however, this could be seen as further evidence of her becoming entangled in the prison system: she appeared to be very knowledgeable when it came to prison regulations and the complaints process. Tightness could, therefore, lead to further entanglement in the web of penal power if partners feel like they need to become further entangled in order to navigate the complexities of prison rules.

A minority of the women discussed making conscious decisions to live lives that were primarily independent of the prison system and its routines. This usually occurred well into the sentence, as the women became aware of having become entangled in the prison regime to an extent they were not happy with. Again, this shows that the women were active agents using independence to make their situations more bearable. Elly had met her husband in prison, and they had been married for more than a decade at the time of the interview. She said that she was ensuring her daily life was no longer shaped around the prison routine, partially because she was unhappy for it to be thus shaped:

> *Anna*: So your daily routine isn't really dictated by the prison routine?
>
> Elly: I think no, not anymore … I think, it's something that happened a few years ago, the wake-up call—is that the term? Where you think—what have I done? You know, what have I done? I've spent all these years and I've got nothing for it. I think that … I probably had a turn-round in my attitude then and thought—I'm not going to let what goes in prison … Well, I'm not going to let what [husband] does in prison bother me so much.

Codd (2000), in her research on older partners of prisoners, raised the question whether such independence could be short-lived and whether, upon their partners' release from prison, the women might return to traditional gender roles. The women in this sample indicated that the change was a deep-rooted one. It may be that when a sentence is long, independence as a coping mechanism is internalized to the point where it changes the women permanently. For example, Sandra's husband had been released shortly before the interview and she found that she had become so used to living alone and being independent that having him back was 'like having an alien in the house'. This echoes the theme of permanent, deep transformation that occurs over the course of a long sentence as discussed by Hulley et al. (2016) in their work on long-term prisoners.

Hulley et al. (2016) argued that some adaptation strategies could be maladaptive. There was a sense in which greater independence, specifically, could be damaging for the relationship post-release. The prisoner and his partner may struggle to adapt to living together if she has become accustomed to living her own life and making independent decisions—a concern echoed by a number of the participants, such as Martha, quoted below. This was already happening to Sandra at the time of her interview, as discussed above.

> *Martha*: I can see some barneys happening [when her partner is released]. Because I think I've become a much stronger, more independent person, as I said … So I'd hate

it to come to the stage where it's a battle of the wills, almost. [...] I think it's gonna be a lot of getting to know each other all over again.

Likewise, the fact that the women adapted to imprisonment by becoming prisonized could be seen to be maladaptive. Their lives were often negatively affected by this in the sense that their daily schedules were shaped around the prison schedule, which, as discussed earlier, resulted in distress when these routines were interrupted. The women certainly did not feel this was a positive development themselves, but were resigned to this secondary institutionalization. As one participant said, 'you have to do it [embark on the prison journey]'.

Furthermore, some became very mistrustful of the prison system and its staff, which could certainly be seen as a maladaptive coping mechanism if they, in general, saw the state and penal authority as being unworthy of their trust. Esther, quoted earlier in this chapter, certainly saw prison officers as unpleasant people who were deliberately playing power games with visitors. This quasi-permanent state of suspicion and tension could also be maladaptive if it completely transforms how the women see the criminal justice system. Certainly, some maintained that their 'prison journey' meant they would never trust the police and other criminal justice agents again. Some of this was possibly due to so many participants maintaining their partners were victims of false accusations and injustice, but *numerous, repeated* negative experiences of interactions with prison staff reinforced the view that the system on the whole was not worthy of their trust. As Lee et al. (2014) note, this loss of trust could mean families were less willing to participate in other systems of governance.

Concluding thoughts

As this chapter has shown, imprisonment can have a dramatic and often highly negative impact on the lives of prisoners' partners. This has been well documented in earlier research on this topic and in numerous chapters in this volume. To develop this literature further, this chapter considered the experiences of long-term prisoners' partners specifically, and explored the temporal aspect of the pains of imprisonment. It showed that long sentences can be transformative for partners outside. Over time, the prison weaves itself into the daily lives of the partners, changing them on an identity level. Yet as time draws on, the pains of imprisonment do not becomes less painful. Like long-term prisoners (Hulley et al., 2016), the women spoke about getting used to the pains of imprisonment—sometimes to the point where they themselves were unsure if they were suffering anymore. The pains became so normalized that they faded into the background, but still continued to be felt. Prolonged exposure to these penal pains was also, in numerous and complex ways, transformative for partners outside.

These findings show that sociology of imprisonment can benefit greatly from further understanding of the experiences of prisoners' families. Prisons are, after all, not hermetically sealed institutions. Penal power reaches into the lives of those outside, and when a sentence is long, this reach could be even more acutely felt, and for a long period of time. In order to understand the full impact of long sentences, we need to consider how everyone is affected by them, not just prisoners and prison officers. The need to explore the perspectives of prisoners' families and communities in order to gain a full understanding of imprisonment as a method of punishment has already been recognized by prison sociologists such as Ben Crewe (2009, 2015) and Alison Liebling (2004).

Finally, as the analyses in this and Lanskey et al.'s chapter (this volume) show, prison sociology provides useful theoretical tools for exploring the lives and experiences of prisoners' families. By explicitly drawing on prison sociology, the perspectives of families can be put more firmly on the agenda of prison sociology and therefore inform debates surrounding imprisonment and punishment more broadly.

References

Arditti, J. A. 2003. 'Locked Doors and Glass Walls: Family Visiting at a Local Jail'. *Journal of Loss and Trauma: International Perspectives on Stress and Coping*, 8(2), 115–38.

Arditti, J. A. 2012. *Parental Incarceration and the Family: Psychological and Social Effects of Imprisonment on Children, Parents and Caregivers*. New York: New York University Press.

Boss, P. 2004. 'Ambiguous Loss Research, Theory, and Practice: Reflections After 9/11'. *Journal of Marriage and Family*, 66(3), 551–66.

Christian, J. 2015. 'Riding the Bus. Barriers to Prison Visitation and Family Management Strategies'. *Journal of Contemporary Criminal Justice*, 21(1), 31–48.

Clemmer, D. 1958 [1940]. *The Prison Community*. New York: Holt, Rinehart and Winston.

Codd, H. 2000. 'Age, Role Changes and Gender Power in Family Relationships'. *Women and Criminal Justice*, 12(2–3), 63–93.

Comfort, M. 2008. *Doing Time Together: Love and Family in the Shadow of the Prison*. Chicago, IL: University of Chicago Press.

Condry, R. 2007. *Families Shamed: The Consequences of Crime for Relatives of Serious Offenders*. Cullompton: Willan Publishing.

Condry, R., Kotova, A., and Minson, S. 2016. 'Social Injustice and Collateral Damage: The Families and Children of Prisoners', in Jewkes, Y., Bennett, J., and Crewe, B. (eds.) *Handbook on Prisons*. 622–40. Abingdon: Routledge.

Crewe, B. 2009. *The Prisoner Society: Power, Adaptation and Social Life in an English Prison*. Oxford: Oxford University Press.

Crewe, B. 2011. 'Depth, Weight, Tightness: Revisiting the Pains of Imprisonment'. *Punishment and Society*, 13(5), 509–29.

Crewe, B. 2015. 'Inside the Belly of the Penal Beast: Understanding the Experience of Imprisonment'. *International Journal for Crime, Justice, and Social Democracy*, 4(1), 50–65.

Daniel, S. W. and Barrett, C. J. 1981. 'The Needs of Prisoners' Wives: A Challenge for the Mental Health Professions'. *Community Mental Health Journal*, 17(4), 310–22.

Fishman, L. T. 2009. *Women at the Wall: A Study of Prisoners' Wives Doing Time on the Outside*. Albany: State University of New York Press.

Harman, J. J., Smith, V. E., and Egan, L. C. 2007. 'The Impact of Incarceration on Intimate Relationships', *Justice and Behaviour*, 34(6), 794–815.

Heskin, K. J., Smith, F. V., Banister, P. A., and Bolton, N. 1973. 'Psychological Correlates of Long-term Imprisonment: Personality Traits', *British Journal of Criminology*, 13(4), 323–30.

Hulley, S., Crewe, B., and Wright, S. 2016. 'Re-examining the Problems of Long-term Imprisonment', *British Journal of Criminology*, 56(4), 769–92.

Kotova, A. 2015. '"He has a life sentence, but I have life sentence to cope with as well": The Experiences of Intimate Partners of Offenders Serving Long Sentences in the United Kingdom', in Arditti, J. A. and Le Roux, T. (eds.) *And Justice for All: Families & the Criminal Justice System*. 85–104. Ann Arbor, MI: Michigan Publishing.

Lee, H., Porter, L. C., and Comfort, M. 2014. 'Consequences of Family Member Incarceration: Impacts on Civic Participation and Perceptions of the Legitimacy and Fairness of Government'. *The Annals of the American Academy of Political and Social Science*, 651(1), 44–73.

Liebling, A. (assisted by Arnold, H.) 2004. *Prisons and Their Moral Performance*. Oxford: Clarendon Press.

Liem, M. and Kunst, M. 2013. 'Is there a Recognizable Post-Incarceration Syndrome Amongst Released "Lifers"?'. *International Journal of Law and Psychiatry*, 36(3–4), 333–7.

Merriman, P. 1979. 'The Families of Long-term Prisoners'. *Probation Journal*, 26(4), 114–20.

Morris, P. 1965. *Prisoners and Their Families*. London: Allen & Unwin.

Sapsford, R. J. 1978, 'Life Sentence Prisoners: Psychological Changes during Sentence', *British Journal of Criminology*, 18, 128–45.

Sapsford, R. J. 1983. *Life Sentence Prisoners: Reaction, Response and Change*. Milton Keynes: Open University Press.

Smith, R., Grimshaw, R., Romeo, R., and Knapp, M. 2007. *Poverty and Disadvantage Among Prisoners' Families*. Joseph Rowntree Foundation. Available at: https://www.prisonlegalnews.org/media/publications/uk%20report%20-%20poverty%20and%20problems%20re%20prisoners%20families.pdf accessed 8 April 2017.

Warr, J. 2012. Afterword, in Crewe, B. and Bennett, J. (eds.) *The Prisoner*. 142–8, London: Routledge.

17

Sharing Imprisonment

Experiences of Prisoners and Family Members in Portugal

Rafaela Granja

Introduction

In the last decade, the body of literature that focuses on the effects of imprisonment beyond prison walls has been expanding. There has been a consolidation of perspectives that challenge prisons' physical boundaries and point to a need to place correctional institutions in permanent articulation with its several implications both inside and outside walls (Combessie, 2002; Gowan, 2002; Marchetti, 2002; Comfort, 2007; Cunha, 2014). So far, most of the academic debate has focused on mapping the forms whereby prisoners' relatives negotiate relationships and experience a wide range of economic, relational, social, and material implications during imprisonment (Aungles, 1994; Girshick, 1996; Braman, 2004; Christian, 2005; Condry, 2007; Comfort, 2008; Touraut, 2012; Smith, 2014; Jardine, 2017) However, there has been little understanding of prisoners' own views regarding the challenges associated with the upholding of family ties during custodial sentences (Dixey and Woodall, 2012; Thomas and Christian, this volume).

Prisons constitute a complex and multifaceted reality. Besides being embedded in and shaped according to specific historical periods, socio-political contexts, and institutional management styles (Foucault, 1975; Barak-Glantz, 1981; Wacquant, 2000), the ways whereby correctional facilities are experienced by distinct social groups is plural. Gresham Sykes, in one of the prison studies' seminal texts, highlighted the rich multiplicity of perspectives that necessarily frames research focused on correctional environments. According to the author, the exploration of different points of view, which sometimes complement and other times contradict each other, allows to discern the most significant elements of the several dimensions of prison social life and structure.

The realities of imprisonment are […] multi-faceted; there is not a single true interpretation but many, and the meaning of any situation is always a complex of several, often conflicting viewpoints. This fact can actually be an aid to research concerning the prison rather than a hindrance, for it is the simultaneous consideration of divergent viewpoints that one begins to see the significant aspects of the prison's social structure. One learns not to look for the one true version; instead, one becomes attuned to contradiction (Sykes, 1958, 148).

The contributions of such seminal text have been widely incorporated in contemporary literature. Present-day studies take into consideration dissimilar types of involvement with the criminal justice system, such as professionally oriented (Liebling, 2000; Crawley, 2004; Bennett and Crewe, 2008), motivated by social and familial ties (Aungles, 1994; Condry, 2007; Comfort, 2008; Touraut, 2012), and imposed by conviction (Crewe, 2009; Rowe, 2011). Simultaneously, studies have also been incorporating the diverse experiences of imprisonment through the differentiated lens of gender (Carlen and Worrall, 2004; Almeda, 2005; Bandyopadhyay, 2006), age (Codd, 2000; Crawley, 2007), and race and ethnicity (Woldoff and Washington, 2008; Western and Wildeman, 2009; Haskins and Lee, 2016).

Drawing upon the importance of taking into consideration the plurality of perspectives and social positioning factors, in this chapter I shall focus on prisoners and relatives' narratives to analyse how they negotiate relationships in the shadow of prison and to explore their views on the relational, familial, social, and economic implications of imprisonment. Engaging in a constant balance between the elements that articulate the prison world and its external social perimeter enables the adaptation, diversification, and enrichment of the analytical gaze, turning it sensitive to the different gradations that permeate the socio-familial implications associated with imprisonment, both behind and beyond prison walls.

The analysis is based in the Portuguese context, a country that has been witnessing a substantial increase in the prison population and currently has a total prison population rate of 135 prisoners per 100,000 inhabitants, which, in the European scenario, positions it as a very punitive country.[1] Among the information publicly available about the socio-demographic characterization of the Portuguese prison population, there is no data on family-related dimensions, such as marital status, number of children, or composition of the household in the period prior to imprisonment. The absence of a method that collects, analyses, and disseminates information about the familial situation of prisoners is representative of the invisibility of the theme on the public debate, further reproduces its marginality in the political agenda, and poses several challenges to research (Knudsen, this volume). In addition to being invisible in the institutional domain, academic research on prisoners' families in Portugal is just taking its first steps. The existing contributions consist of the study of Manuela Ivone Cunha that analyses how familial relationships are reconfigured behind and beyond prison walls upon scenarios of concentrated incarceration in heavily penalized lower-class neighbourhoods (Cunha, 2008), and one small-scale research that has analysed the impact of imprisonment on intimate relationships from the perspective of prisoners and their wives (Carmo, 2008). Therefore, this is the first in-depth and comprehensive Portuguese research that jointly takes into consideration prisoners' and relatives' views on the social and familial implications of imprisonment.

In Portugal, the construction of the welfare state was delayed until the 70s, after the fall of the dictatorial regime (1933–74). In spite of the welfare state expansion during the last few decades, in Portugal, welfare state mechanisms are still largely underdeveloped (Alves, 2015). Taking into consideration this rudimentary state support, several scholars have been characterizing Portugal as a 'welfare society' (Santos, 1993), that is, a society that is largely characterized by the prevalence of family provision as a way of compensating for the shortcomings and inadequacies of the welfare State system (Portugal, 1999; Wall et al., 2001). The relevance of informal networks, and especially of family support, in Portugal hence makes it a very relevant case study for exploring how social support is enacted upon imprisonment (Cunha, 2008; Granja, 2016).

[1] http://www.prisonstudies.org/country/portugal.

Imprisonment and family: (in)visibilities

In recent years, there has been a growth, in scope, impact, and depth, of studies focused on prisoners' families. Contributions are increasingly anchored on different socio-geographic contexts, thus extending the analytical focus to variable legal, penal, and social settings, as this edited collection illustrates in a particularly elucidative manner. This body of literature is, therefore, increasingly aware of the specific implications of imprisonment to different social groups—such as children of prisoners (Knudsen, 2016; Smith, 2014; Wakefield and Wildeman, 2013; Minson, this volume; Oldrup and Frederiksen, this volume), prisoners' partners (Codd, 2000; Comfort, 2008; Fishman, 1990; Girshick, 1996; Kotova, this volume), prisoners' extended family (Braman, 2004; Condry, 2007; Christian and Kennedy, 2011; Touraut, 2012), and communities highly affected by imprisonment (Clear, 2007; Cunha, 2008).

In general, studies have been showing how prisoners' relatives hold in common a wide range of experiences, such as re-orienting routines and deferring future plans (Christian, 2005; Touraut, 2012), dealing with the reverberations of social stigma (Condry, 2007; Hutton, this volume), rearranging family responsibilities (Turanovic et al., 2012), actively maintaining and constructing displays of affection and commitment (Granja, 2016; Jardine, 2017), addressing issues related to prison visitation (Hutton, 2016), facing a reduction of available resources (Grinstead et al., 2001; Smith et al., 2007), experiencing the repercussions of punitive surveillance and control on their own lives (Comfort, 2008; Jardine, this volume), and managing the paradoxical (de)stabilizing effects of imprisonment (Comfort, 2008; Godoi, 2010; Sampson, 2011; Touraut, 2012; Turanovic et al., 2012; Smith, 2014, 187–93; Turney, 2015). Nevertheless, the particular constellation of difficulties and challenges that each family face upon imprisonment is dependent on several elements. That is, imprisonment constitutes a polysemous force whose social, economic, and relational implications vary according to the type of crime committed by prisoners, the kind of structural disadvantage that individuals face(d) previous and during imprisonment, and the pre-existing and current social and relational dynamics (Morris, 1965). In this regard, in the United Kingdom, drawing upon the experiences of relatives of serious offenders, Rachel Condry has shown how these individuals deal with particular issues related to social exclusion and stigma. According to the author, relatives of serious offenders suffer several experiences of stigmatization that range from personal shame towards other people' avoidance, verbal abuse, and even physical attack (Condry, 2007). However, these experiences of discrimination are not homogenous among different social contexts and distinct social groups (Hutton, this volume). Analysing the Portuguese context, Manuela Ivone Cunha has shown how in certain urban neighbours, highly segregated and levelled by poverty and social exclusion, the centralized action of law enforcement institutions—legitimized by specific criminal prosecution policies aimed at controlling retail drug trafficking—has led to the concomitant and consecutive detention of individuals from the same social networks (Cunha, 2008). In these particular social environments, the recurrent presence of imprisonment implies an additional blurring of the connotations associated with criminal and prison stigma, not because it becomes dissipated—in certain social contexts it continues to limit opportunities (Petersilia, 2001; Opsal, 2011)—but because prison becomes 'normalized' within social networks that share a disadvantaged social and economic position (Cunha, 2008). Regarding the relational impacts of imprisonment, the ethnographic research of Megan Comfort in the United States has shown how penal scrutiny and prison rules place prisoners' intimate partners in a quasi-imprisonment situation, by eroding the boundaries between home and prison and changing the forms whereby intimacy, love, and romance are experienced. Nonetheless, adopting an approach attentive to the macro-structural vulnerabilities that shape the lives of most of these women, Comfort also shows how imprisonment may sometimes represent to certain disadvantaged groups one of the ways to regain some form of control over highly disturbed relationships (Comfort, 2008).

Although this body of literature has been developing significantly in recent years, capturing and analysing how prisoners' relatives manage relationships in the shadow of imprisonment, there is an apparent scarcity of contributions that look to the same kind of negotiations inside prison walls. Sociological accounts of prison life have been developing in the last few decades (Crewe, 2009; Cunha, 2014), addressing issues such as the reproduction of social, economic, and material inequalities among prisoners (Marchetti, 2002), the dynamics of prison suicide (Liebling, 2007), the idiosyncrasies of women' imprisonment (Carlen and Worrall, 2004; Almeda, 2005; Rowe, 2011; Fili, 2013), and the social effects of concentrated incarceration of lower-class communities in prison life (Clear, 2007; Cunha, 2008). Although some of these studies directly or indirectly address issues related to the negotiation of familial relationships during imprisonment, its contributions remain widely dispersed. That is, the detailed exploration of how prisoners conceive and manage social bonds remains an under-researched aspect of prison life (see also Thomas and Christian, this volume). In general, such line of research has been narrowly focused on how imprisoned women and men deal with the experience of being separated from their children (Enos, 2001; Hairston, 2002; Nurse, 2002; Arditti et al., 2005; Celinska and Siegel, 2010; Easterling and Feldmeyer, 2017). This implies that other social significant relations to prisoners—such as ties with extended family and intimate partners—have been disregarded and enclosed in a grey box in which it is difficult to discern specificities (Leverentz, 2011).

In order to broaden the sociological approach on the social and familial impacts of imprisonment and to break with some of these limitations that have compartmentalized this body of literature, I thereby contribute, in this chapter, to an embryonic and promising field of research that sheds light on the ways whereby both prisoners and family members negotiate relationships during imprisonment (Christian and Kennedy, 2011; Dixey and Woodall, 2012; Hutton, 2016). This kind of approach allows outlining lines of continuity between two groups that experience variable degrees of correctional confinement and penal surveillance. Drawing on narratives of Portuguese prisoners and relatives, I thereby argue that these individuals share an experience of imprisonment on the basis of a mutual situation of social-economical vulnerability, a collective sense of concern and powerlessness, a joint effort to invigorate strategies that creatively recreate presence at a distance, and a common recognition of the complex effects of imprisonment.

Methodology

This chapter draws from a research study conducted in Portugal that aimed to explore the familial and social impact of imprisonment from the point of view of prisoners and their relatives. The analysis presented here uses data gathered from seventy interviews: forty were conducted with prisoners (equal numbers of men and women) and thirty with prisoners' relatives (twenty-three of them women), all of them Portuguese.

Selection and recruitment of interviewees was made in two autonomous processes. Regarding prisoners, during the fieldwork conducted in two prisons (one for the male population, and the other for imprisoned women), upon request, the prison administration provided me with a list of individuals convicted for more than six months. On the basis of this list I consulted prisoners' individual processes to select a diversified group of potential interviewees in terms of criminal records, crime leading to conviction, and familial configurations. Prisoners' relatives were recruited in the vicinity of those two Portuguese prisons during visiting periods. I selected a heterogeneous group of interviewees on the basis of sex, familial configurations, life trajectories, and previous experiences with the criminal justice system. These differentiated processes of selection and recruitment implied that interviewed prisoners and family members are not necessarily related to each other: among the thirty relatives who participated in the study only five are related to interviewed prisoners. The participants' verbal and written consent to conduct the interviews was obtained after they were informed about the study's aim and that their anonymity was guaranteed. The names used in the section that presents our analysis are fictitious, to ensure the respondents' anonymity.

Interviews with prisoners were conducted in closed and private rooms in prison facilities and interviews with prisoners' relatives took place at various locations chosen by participants, such as the waiting room for prison visits, cafes, and their homes. On average, the interviews were ninety minutes long. Wherever possible, interviews were audio recorded and the tapes were transcribed verbatim. When certain contexts prevented audio recording, I registered in writing phrases and expressions used by the participants. The interviews focused on personal trajectories and familial life before prison detention; perceptions of the relational, familial, social, and economic implications associated with imprisonment; and future prospects. For the purposes of this chapter, using a qualitative content analysis approach (Mayring, 2004), data were systematically compared, contrasted, synthesized, and coded in three main dimensions associated with the shared experience of imprisonment: (i) the economic and familial implications associated with imprisonment; (ii) the creative negotiation strategies mobilized for sustaining family involvement; and (iii) the complex effects of imprisonment.

Economic and familial implications associated with imprisonment

In the period prior to imprisonment most prisoners held active familial responsibilities in one or more domains, such as economic provision, elderly care, and childcare. Upon their imprisonment families therefore undergo a process of reallocation of responsibilities and re-organization of resources. In this regard, both prisoners and relatives' narratives outline two main implications associated with imprisonment: reduction of available resources (Smith et al., 2007) and restructuring of childcare configurations (Turanovic et al., 2012). On most occasions, the diminution of available economic resources results from the combination of two dimensions: suspension of the prisoner's income and additional expenditures emerging from the maintenance of contact with imprisoned relatives (Grinstead et al., 2001).

Regarding the interruption of prisoners' financial involvement, although not all prisoners contributed significantly to the household income, most of those that did describe how the disruption of their provider role tends to leave dependent relatives in vulnerable positions. These situations generally promote feelings of powerlessness among prisoners, exacerbated when relatives are facing challenging situations on the outside and they cannot directly assist them. Sandra, aged 25 and sentenced to seven years for theft, lived with her mother, father, and brothers prior to imprisonment and contributed significantly to the household maintenance. After being imprisoned, the loss of Sandra's income left the family, and especially her mother who is 64-years-old and retired due to disability, in poverty. This situation fostered guilt and anxiety that even led Sandra to attempt suicide in prison.

> In my head, I was responsible for my family's misfortunes. The troubles that my mother started to have after I was imprisoned, starving, not having this, not having that. I was to blame for that. That's what I thought.

Concerning the costs associated with maintenance of contact with prisoners, these are mainly related to prison visitation (Dixey and Woodall, 2012; Hutton, 2016). Going to prison generally entails a significant channelling of economic resources due to the costs associated with transportation, provision of goods (such as food, entertainment items, and toiletries) and delivery of variable amounts of money to prisoners. Family members tend to consider these kinds of provisions as a 'cushion' that might soften the harshness of prison life for their imprisoned relatives. However, visiting on weekly, biweekly, or monthly bases poses a substantial burden on scarce household budgets. In this sense, as also noticed by Johnna Christian (2005), in order to be able to sustain basic needs on the outside—such as expenses related to food, housing, health, children's education, among others—sometimes prisoners' relatives are compelled to decrease the delivery of goods or, in more extreme cases, reduce the frequency of prison visitation to protect the familial economic situation. Raúl, aged 63, whose son and daughter in law have been imprisoned for more than eight years, explains how the frequency of visits varies according to the resources available.

> [The frequency of visits] is according to the money I have [available]. For example, on the past, I went to [prison] visits every week, then things got complicated on my side and I went there every 15 days with the bag full of food. Nowadays, being alone with my grandchildren, I just go there whenever I can. I don't have a specific frequency and I don't even take a bag.

Besides posing several emotional challenges to prisoners' relatives—who feel uncomfortable for decreasing the support provided to prisoners—reducing prison visitation and/or lessening delivery of goods also tends to put prisoners in a vulnerable situation. Deprived of the resources and affective support that relatives are able to provide through frequent visits, prisoners face challenging situations, being dependent on the scarce earnings of prison work or, in cases where this is not available, of solidarity networks among other prisoners. Confronted with such situations, some prisoners prefer to conceal the problems they face within prison so as not to enhance family members' concerns about their wellbeing—a strategy also noted by Rachel Condry (2007, 60). This is the case with Rosa, aged 41, facing a prison sentence of five years in a correctional facility located more than 300km away from where her family lives. Due to the scarcity of visits from her family, she prefers to keep her problems away from them since sharing her problems with relatives would only promote feelings of impotence. According to her, this in an implicit shared strategy between her, her mother, and other members of her extended family.

> I do not tell [them] anything that happens here. Just as my mother does not tell me anything serious on the outside. [...] [She says that] if I'm in here I cannot solve things, so she won't tell me the bad things that happen on the outside. [...] I do the same [...] because they cannot solve anything and they're going to be suffering.

In addition to the socio-economic vulnerability shared by prisoners and relatives, one other dimension of the impacts associated with imprisonment concerns the reconfiguration of arrangements for the care of children (Turanovic et al., 2012). Participants' narratives consistently show that, prior to imprisonment, most women bore extensive responsibilities of childcare, being the main or sole caretakers of their children—as also showed by other studies (Enos, 2001; Celinska and Siegel, 2010). On a differentiated scenario, shaped by traditional gender norms, men generally carried out different roles, such as financial support and caregiving, and had different levels of involvement with children from different mothers (Hairston, 2002). Upon detention, in the case of women's imprisonment, children generally stay under the care of their grandmothers or other female relatives; as a result of men's confinement, mothers usually continue to provide the childcare. It is therefore clear that, regardless of the sex of the imprisoned individual, childcare tends to be provided by kinship networks and particularly by women.

Independently of the particular childcare configurations, upon imprisonment, the boundaries and contexts of parental relationships are entirely redrawn in the shadow of prison, posing challenges both to prisoners (Enos, 2001; Hairston, 2002; Nurse, 2002; Arditti et al., 2005; Celinska and Siegel, 2010; Easterling and Feldmeyer, 2017) and their caregivers (Turanovic et al., 2012). Prisoners' narratives generally highlight how the scarcity of opportunities to interact with offspring during imprisonment has the potential to detach, or further disconnect, prisoners from their children. In this regard, Jorge, aged 29, sentenced for nineteen years for aggravated robbery, describes the most emotional challenging moments he faces during his imprisonment in relation to his child.

> Sometimes I'm talking with my son on the phone, and he's calling 'father' to his grandfather and it hurts. […] But the thing that has hurt the most here in prison was when my son entered in visit walking. I didn't saw my son first steps, I didn't hear my son first word, and that's what hurts me. I lost everything.

The description of the emotional challenges associated with childcare during parental imprisonment are also vividly present in the ways in which caretakers explain routinely dealing with minor children. As well as referring to the wide variety of challenges associated with taking care of children during the imprisonment of one or both parents—such as routine modifications, difficulties posed by health conditions, and household changes (Turanovic et al., 2012)—these individuals also outline the difficulties associated with explaining imprisonment to children and managing prison visitation. In this regard, Beatriz explains the reflection she underwent before deciding if she would take her 5-year-old son to prison to visit his father, and her current daily struggle with household maintenance and prison visits financial management.

> Before I bring him here [to prison], I reflected a lot. […] I decided to bring him [here because] I didn't want my son to grow up angry without knowing his father. […] Nowadays in order to go to the [prison] visit I sometimes have to activate the credit, I know it is a stupid thing and I should not do it but otherwise I am not able to go. […] Last weekend I told my son 'This weekend we can't go see dad' […] but he started to cry and I can't [stand it].

One of the transversal elements of prisoners' and relatives' narratives is the forms whereby imprisonment has further aggravated—or, in less frequent cases, catalysed—socio-economic vulnerability (Marchetti, 2002; Smith et al., 2007). Besides posing challenges to the management of daily life, in some cases jeopardizing the response to basic needs (Christian, 2005), and to the ways that individuals cope with imprisonment, social economic situations also (in)directly influence the type and frequency of contact between prisoners and relatives. This thus implies a permanent inconstancy and changeability of family contact patterns according to resources' availability, which, as a result, poses several challenges to families' ability to remain engaged with loved ones and sustain emotional bonds.

Creative negotiation of family involvement

Enacted in a context framed by paucity of resources, institutional restraints, and scarce structural support to the maintenance of social ties, the management of relationships in prison is inscribed into a nexus of absence, powerlessness, and vulnerability. Prisoners and relatives outline how altogether these elements present challenging scenarios and variable threats to the sustaining of meaningful relationships. Nevertheless, as also explored by Cara Jardine (2017), participants in this study also describe how they are actively engaged in creatively renegotiating involvement with family during imprisonment. That is, in order to prevent the dilution of emotional bonds, prisoners and relatives seek possibilities of exercising family roles through prison walls, keeping abreast of daily dynamics and routines and reinventing ways of sharing activities through distance. These kinds of strategies help to sustain a sense of belonging, represent a source of hope and symbolize a major motivation to the future. One of the ways whereby prisoners seek to remain engaged in their families' lives during imprisonment is by providing emotional and developmental support to their relatives on the basis of exchange of letters, phone calls, and prison visitation (see also Thomas and Christian, this volume). João, aged 38, sentenced to three years and six months due to qualified theft, has a 6-year-old son. In his narrative, he explains how he is trying to actively participate in his son's development, by encouraging him educationally and building an emotional connection through small gifts and actions.

> He is learning to speak English, he knows has all the numbers in English and the whole alphabet, I train here with him. Now I began to teach him a few mathematical rules. I'm here but it's like if I was outside. [. . .] My son sends letters to me with drawings. Every week he asks daddy for a surprise, I do a drawing or I try to give him a lollypop or a Kinder egg. A simple paper airplane, a doll made of paper. He gives such a huge value to that, I feel really happy.

A similar effort of fostering connectedness and closeness is enacted by relatives on the outside. Aware of the potential of prison environment weakening prisoners' bonds to the outside, these individuals attempt to sustain bridges between the home and the prison (Comfort, 2002). Besides keeping prisoners abreast of the several dimensions of family life—such as news from close and extended family; familial routines in terms of food, hygiene, and schedules; and options and strategies taken in terms of household income—, these elements also attempt to punctuate prison life with several elements reminiscent of life beyond prison, such as photographs from home and loved ones, books, magazines, music playlists, familiar smells in freshly washed cloths, perfumes in letters, body care products, home-made food, amongst others. Overall, these elements aim to 'display' and strengthen the bonds between the prison and the home by being representative of the care, affections, desires, and commitments of family life (Jardine, 2017). However, besides being dependent on the availability of resources, the provision of these objects is also constricted by prison regulations. In Portugal, although most of these items are allowed in correctional facilities, recently there have been some changes in the regulation of prisons that pose limits on the delivery of goods. Among those changes, the one that caused most indignation to both prisoners and relatives was that of imposing new restrictions on the amount and type of food relatives were permitted to bring in for prisoners. In this regard, Tânia, aged 49, whose son is imprisoned, expresses her exasperation with the recent prison rules that prohibited the bringing-in of homemade food into prisons, especially during special occasions, such as Christmas.

> Especially at Christmas, it was ridiculous what they did because in previous years we could take food to prison. This year they only allowed deserts because they made the lunch and we had to pay to go. There was no longer that occasion for being there, being able to take him [son] a homemade meal, the food he loves. Because, in the end, we don't go to prison to eat! We seize the opportunity to take food for him!

Similar frustration about the limitations imposed on the admission of food are expressed by prisoners for whom food represents a living memory of home and a way of connecting to familial memories (Ugelvik, 2011). In order to avoid the pervasive influence of prison regulations on the possibilities of sustaining familial ties during imprisonment, some prisoners and family members thus resort to alternative strategies of recreating involvement (Comfort, 2002; Jardine, 2017). That is, instead of solely make use of forms of contact provided by prison to sustain family ties—namely, prison visits, phone calls, and letters—some participants also describe how they mobilize creative ways of blurring the boundaries between presence and absence. For prisoners, some of these strategies include, for example, the recreation of daily family-life moments in the semi-privacy of their cells. With photographs, music, smells, and other significant elements prisoners engage in personal rituals that enable them to evoke the presence of their loved ones into the solitude of their cells. In this regard, Cláudia, aged 35, serving a four year, eight months' sentence due to drug trafficking, explains how every night she recreates the presence of her daughter in her cell by playing her favourite games.

> Inside my cell, I have tazos [a children game] and everything I did in the street with my daughter I do here too. I put a picture of her on the floor ... but I'm not crazy, but I'm not crazy! With her picture on the floor I play with the marbles as I played with her, I play with tazos, and I speak as if she was there. I know she is not here but it's my thing.

Similarly, several family members also describe their strategies to symbolically maintain the presence of their imprisoned relatives into daily routines. Less constrained by prison limitations than prisoners, these individuals resort to various strategies that seek to keep vivid the past memories of a shared life (Condry, 2007; Comfort, 2008; Touraut, 2012). This may include keeping prisoners' rooms untouched, evoking prisoner's presence in daily meals by reserving a seat for them at the table, and/or carrying around, at all times, symbols that corporify prisoners' absent presence. In this regard, Cristina, aged 40, describes how she is permanently surrounded by photos of her imprisoned husband, both when she's working—in her wallet and on her mobile phone—as well as at home, especially in their room.

> In the bedroom, I have photographs of him on both sides of the bed and I also at the foot of the bed, this way I am always surrounded by him. [...] He being there [in prison] does not mean that I don't take him here: in my heart and close to me at all times.

Actively engaging in family dynamics, sharing elements that strengthen the bonds between the home and the prison, and recreating presence at a distance are some of the ways that prisoners and relatives strive to creatively negotiate a space within which familial bonds are sustained during imprisonment. Performing these kinds of acts thus, to a certain extent, makes prison walls permeable to fluxes of persons, objects, places, activities, smells, tastes, and memories that help to sustain vivid emotional bonds and symbolically subvert the physical, geographical, temporal, and communication limitations imposed by imprisonment (Comfort, 2002; Jardine, 2017).

Complex effects

Prior to imprisonment, most interviewed male and female prisoners faced a broad constellation of social problems. In some cases, these individuals were for several years victims of domestic violence and/or addicted to substances consumption (Carlen and Worrall, 2004; Edin et al., 2004). Although these issues posed several challenges and problems to family life and to other significant relationships, few men and women had resorted to social services and/or law enforcement agencies to address them. Within this framework, imprisonment emerges as the factor that compulsorily withdraws individuals from the cumulative pressures that characterized their lives, imposing a highly constrained and limited context (Christian and Kennedy, 2011). Facing such a scenario, some prisoners thus highlight how imprisonment interrupted destructive cycles of abuse and, to a certain point, is conceived as an opportunity to change previous life trajectories. For example, Joaquina, aged 37 and sentenced to 14 years for robbery, describes how she was a victim of abuse by her husband for more than ten years. Her narrative explains how, while in prison, being away from her abuser and exposed to professional counselling, Joaquina began to address violence differently. This 'violence awareness' has empowered her to deal with abuse in new ways, including the way it is perceived in retrospect and projected in the future.

> Imprisonment has opened my eyes. When I entered here it was like I was blind, he was always beating me and I didn't reacted. Now I say bad things to him too. [...] The psychologist here helps me a lot [...] For me it was better to be imprisoned. If I wasn't arrested maybe at this point I was already dead. He was sick, I swear.

Besides functioning as a peculiar site of protection for victims of domestic violence, as also noted by Abigail Rowe (2011, 579), one other dimension of the complex effects of imprisonment highlighted by prisoners is the discontinuance of drug abuse while in prison (Edin et al., 2004). Although this interruption does not necessarily result from specific resources available in prisons, some prisoners describe how, during imprisonment, they were able to temporarily control their substance abuse. As a result, in specific cases, prisoners describe how, at least in the short term, imprisonment enabled the reconstruction of previously deeply distressed family relationships (Comfort, 2008). Paulo, aged 43, sentenced to seven years for qualified fraud, stopped his problematic drug use during imprisonment. He describes how this helped him to regain the trust of his father, with whom he had not had a relationship for several years.

> Gradually I managed to conquer [my family's trust], slowly, I understand the fragilities, the suspicions, the uncertainties, small things that I can say, they stay in doubt but I clarify immediately. But I realize how 25 years' addiction will not be solved in 3 years, no way. [...] For my relationship with my father it was very important. We had not talked for two years and it was here [in prison] that I manage to get my father to talk to me again. [...] And now we are inseparable, I am his boy again.

These kinds of complex effects also have direct implications on family members' views and experiences associated with imprisonment. When their imprisoned relatives are abusive and/or addicted to substance consumption, prisoners' relatives tend to perceive and describe imprisonment as a less troubled period than the one they faced previously (Christian and Kennedy, 2011). The description of imprisonment as a stabilizing force that allows instituting control in prisoners' life trajectories and, by extension, on family life is, for example, present in the narratives of relatives who suffered domestic violence, as the case of Filipa, aged 35 whose father is imprisoned, illustrates:

> I didn't had a childhood, I had a life of terror, panic, this forced us to grow very fast! [...] We slept dressed because we already knew that in the middle of the night we were going to have to run away from my father. [...] For us it is a peace of mind that he is here imprisoned.

These kinds of narratives therefore emphasize how imprisonment may paradoxically present to several individuals, both inside and outside prison walls, a particular platform for protection and/or for addressing the complex problems they faced (Comfort, 2008; Godoi, 2010; Sampson, 2011; Touraut, 2012; Turanovic et al., 2012; Smith, 2014, 187–93; Turney, 2015). However, recognizing prisons' complex effects implies adopting an ambiguous position that is visible in participants' narratives. On the one hand, prisoners and their relatives describe the forms whereby imprisonment further exacerbates scenarios of socio-economic vulnerability and poses a wide range of challenges to the sustenance of meaningful relationships. On the other hand, some respondents also describe how, in particular cases, penal confinement might emerge as a possibility for interrupting previous dangerous cycles of abuse that posed several threats to prisoners' life and families' wellbeing. Tânia, aged 49, with an imprisoned son who had a severe drug addiction problem, illustrates the coexistence of these controversial and paradoxical implications of imprisonment. According to her, although imprisonment represents a less troubled period than the one she was facing prior to her son's imprisonment, it also involves experiencing great distress and apprehension about her son.

> [Imprisonment] was a good thing, it was. If he continued outside as he was I think my son was already dead, [imprisonment] was the form for him to leave the drugs and leave the life in which he was. [...] At this moment he feels happy. We feel very happy. Despite everything, as I say, there is something positive, in the midst of this disgrace there is a good thing and in this case, is that he left drugs. At least that.

The narratives of prisoners and relatives sharing experiences of imprisonment show how prison institutions are accumulating and overlapping a wide range of social functions that range from penal punishment to prisoners' social rehabilitation. However, taking into consideration that prisons' potential to deal with complex social problems and provide specialized therapeutic intervention is undoubtedly dominated by the punitive 'nature' that dominates the penal environment, prison institutions are enacting social roles that would probably be more adequately exercised outside its walls (Almeda, 2005; Comfort, 2008).

Conclusion

This chapter aimed to explore how prisoners and relatives experience the relational, familial, social, and economic implications associated with imprisonment and negotiate relationships in the shadow of prison. Although these groups have, traditionally, been addressed in separate frameworks due to the differentiated levels of penal involvement they are subjected to, in this chapter I aimed to outline particular realities where their views and experiences might intersect and converge. This contribution therefore pushes forward a renewed agenda within studies addressing the social implications of imprisonment, which is based on multifaceted perspectives that take into serious consideration the wide variability of family configurations (Jardine, 2017), the gendered implications of imprisonment (Aungles, 1994; Condry, 2007; Touraut, 2012), as well as the paradoxal implications of imprisonment (Comfort, 2008). I argue that such grounded perspective on the views and experiences of prisoners and family members is central when addressing this theme from a human rights' perspective (Smith, this volume) that fits with the key principles of social justice (Condry, this volume).

Based on prisoners' and family relatives' narratives, data shows that, although subjected to variable degrees of penal surveillance, both of these groups experience direct and indirect implications of the socio-economic vulnerability aggravated or catalysed by imprisonment, share feelings of powerless to assist and protect their loved ones, mobilize creative strategies to reinvent familial connectedness, and face realities that recognize the coexistence of (de)stabilizing effects of imprisonment. Such common experiences thereby collapse prison immanent physical boundaries in two main interrelated dimensions. The first regards the ways whereby the vulnerabilities faced on the outside of prison have direct implications on inside life, and vice-versa. For example, scenarios of socio-economic vulnerability might prevent relatives from maintaining frequent contact with prisoners; and, on the opposite side, prisoners cessation of substance abuse while serving prison sentences might foster more stable scenarios of family life on the outside—as also noted by Megan Comfort (2008). The second form whereby the social and familial implications associated with imprisonment collapse prison physical limits concerns the ways that prisoners and relatives' strategies for re-creating involvement are able to make prison walls permeable to the circulation of affections, objects, spaces, smells, and tastes. That is, prisoners and relatives actively negotiate imprisonment-imposed limitations in a way that constructs porous walls, able to defy, recreate, and resignify notions of presence of absence.

References

Almeda, E. 2005. 'Women's Imprisonment in Spain'. *Punishment & Society*, 7(2), 183–99.
Alves, S. 2015. 'Welfare State Changes and Outcomes—The Cases of Portugal and Denmark from a Comparative Perspective'. *Social Policy and Administration*, 49(1), 1–23.
Arditti, J. A., Smock, S. A., and Parkman, T. S. 2005. '"It's Been Hard to Be a Father": A Qualitative Exploration of Incarcerated Fatherhood'. *Fathering*, 3(3), 267–88.
Aungles, A. 1994. *The Prison and the Home: A Study of the Relationship between Domesticity and Penality*. Sydney: The Institute of Criminology Monograph Series.
Bandyopadhyay, M. 2006. 'Competing Masculinities in a Prison'. *Men and Masculinities*, 9(2), 186–203.
Barak-Glantz, I. L. 1981. 'Toward a Conceptual Schema of Prison Management Styles'. *The Prison Journal*, 61(2), 42–60.
Bennett, J. and Crewe, B. 2008. *Understanding Prison Staff*. Cullompton: Willan Publishing.
Braman, D. 2004. *Doing Time on the Outside: Incarceration and Family life in Urban America*. Ann Arbor: University of Michigan Press.
Carlen, P. and Worrall, A. 2004. *Analysing Women's Imprisonment*. Cullompton: Willan Publishing.
Carmo, I. 2008. *O Impacto da Prisão na Conjugalidade*. Master thesis. Lisbon: Instituto Universitário de Lisboa.

Celinska, K. and Siegel, J. A. 2010. 'Mothers in Trouble: Coping with Actual or Pending Separation from Children due to Incarceration'. *The Prison Journal*, 90(4), 447–74.

Christian, J. 2005. 'Riding the Bus: Barriers to Prison Visitation and Family Management Strategies'. *Journal of Contemporary Criminal Justice*, 21(1), 31–48.

Christian, J. and Kennedy, L. W. 2011. 'Secondary Narratives in the Aftermath of Crime: Defining Family Members' Relationships with Prisoners'. *Punishment & Society*, 13(4), 379–402.

Clear, T. R. 2007. *Imprisoning Communities: How Mass Incarceration Makes Disadvantaged Neighborhoods Worse*. Oxford: Oxford University Press.

Codd, H. 2000. 'Age, Role Changes and Gender Power in Family Relationships: The Experiences of Older Female Partners of Male Prisoners'. *Women & Criminal Justice*, 12(2–3), 63–93.

Combessie, P. 2002. 'Marking the Carceral Boundary: Penal Stigma in the Long Shadow of the Prison'. *Ethnography*, 3(4), 535–55.

Comfort, M. 2002. ' "Papa's House": The Prison as Domestic and Social Satellite'. *Ethnography*, 3(4), 467–499.

Comfort, M. 2007. 'Punishment Beyond the Legal Offender'. *Annual Review of Law and Social Science*, 3(1), 12.1–12.26.

Comfort, M. 2008. *Doing Time Together: Love and Family in the Shadow of the Prison*. Chicago: University of Chicago Press.

Condry, R. 2007. *Families Shamed: The Consequences of Crime for Relatives of Serious Offenders*. Cullompton: Willan Publishing.

Crawley, E. 2004. *Doing Prison Work. The Public and Private Lives of Prison Officers*. Cullompton: Willan Publishing.

Crawley, E. 2007. 'Imprisonment in Old Age', in Jewkes, Y. (ed.) *Handbook on Prisons*. 224–24. Cullompton: Willan Publishing.

Crewe, B. 2009. *The Prisoner Society: Power, Adaptation and Social Life in an English Prison*. Oxford: Oxford University Press.

Cunha, M. I. 2008. 'Closed Circuits: Kinship, Neighborhood and Incarceration in Urban Portugal'. *Ethnography*, 9(3), 325–50.

Cunha, M. I. 2014. 'The Ethnography of Prisons and Penal Confinement'. *Annual Review of Anthropology*, 43(1), 217–33.

Dixey, R. and Woodall, J. 2012. 'The Significance of "The Visit" in an English Category-B Prison: Views from Prisoners, Prisoners' Families and Prison Staff'. *Community, Work & Family*, 15(1), 29–47.

Easterling, B. A. and Feldmeyer, B. 2017. 'Race, Incarceration, and Motherhood'. *The Prison Journal*, 97(2), 143–65.

Edin, K., Nelson, T. J., and Paranal, R. 2004. 'Fatherhood and Incarceration As Potential Turning Points in the Criminal Careers of Unskilled Men', in Pattillo, M., Weiman, D., and Western, B. (eds.) *Imprisoning America: The Social Effects of Mass Incarceration*. 46–75. New York: Russell Sage Foundation.

Enos, S. 2001. *Mothering from the Inside: Parenting in a Women's Prison*. New York: State University of New York Press.

Fili, A. 2013. 'Women in Prison: Victims or Resisters? Representations of Agency in Women's Prisons in Greece'. *Signs*, 39(1), 1–26.

Fishman, L. 1990. *Women at the Wall: A Study of Prisoners' Wives Doing Time on the Outside*. Albany: State University of New York Press.

Foucault, M. 1975. *Surveiller et punir*. Paris: Gallimard.

Girshick, L. B. 1996. *Soledad Women: Wives of Prisoners Speak Out*. Wesport, CT: Praeger.

Godoi, R., 2010. 'Para uma reflexão sobre os efeitos sociais do encarceramento'. *Revista Brasileira de Segurança Pública*, 5(8), 138–55.

Gowan, T. 2002. 'The Nexus: Homelessness and Incarceration in Two American Cities'. *Ethnography*, 3(4), 500–34.

Granja, R. 2016. 'Beyond Prison Walls: The Experiences of Prisoners Relatives and Meanings Associated with Imprisonment'. *Probation Journal*, 63(3), 273–92.

Grinstead, O., Faigeles, B., Bancroft, C., and Barry, Z. 2001. 'The Financial Cost of Maintaining Relationships with Incarcerated African American Men: A Survey of Women Prison Visitors'. *Journal Of African American Men*, 6(1), 59–70.

Hairston, C. F. 2002. 'Fathers in Prison: Responsible Fatherhood and Responsible Public Policies'. *Marriage & Family Review*, 32, 111–35.

Haskins, A. R. and Lee, H. 2016. 'Reexamining Race When Studying the Consequences of Criminal Justice Contact for Families'. *The ANNALS of the American Academy of Political and Social Science*, 665(1), 224–30.

Hutton, M. 2016. 'Visiting Time: A Tale of Two Prisons'. *Probation Journal*, 63(3), 347–61.

Jardine, C. 2017. 'Constructing and Maintaining Family in The Context of Imprisonment'. *The British Journal of Criminology*, 58(1), 114–31.

Knudsen, E. M. 2016. 'Avoiding the Pathologizing of Children of Prisoners'. *Probation Journal*, 63(3), 362–70.

Leverentz, A. 2011. 'Being a Good Daughter and Sister: Families of Origin in the Reentry of African American Female Ex-Prisoners'. *Feminist Criminology*, 6(4), 239–67.

Liebling, A. 2000. 'Prison Officers, Policing and the use of Discretion'. *Theoretical Criminology*, 4(3), 333–57.

Liebling, A. 2007. 'Prison Suicide and its Prevention', in Jewkes, Y. (ed.) *Handbook on Prisons*. 423–46. Cullompton: Willan Publishing.

Marchetti, A. 2002. 'Carceral Impoverishment: Class Inequality in the French Penitentiary'. *Ethnography*, 3(4), 416–34.

Mayring, P. 2004. 'Qualitative Content Analysis', in Flick, U., von Kardoff, E., and Steinke, I. (eds.) *A Companion to Qualitative Research*. 266–9. London: Sage.

Morris, P. 1965. *Prisoners and Their Families*. London: George Allen and Unwin.

Nurse, A. M. 2002. *Fatherhood Arrested: Parenting From Within the Juvenille Justice System*. Nashville, TN: Vanderbilt University Press.

Opsal, T. D. 2011. 'Women Disrupting a Marginalized Identity: Subverting the Parolee Identity through Narrative'. *Journal of Contemporary Ethnography*, 40(2), 135–67.

Petersilia, J. 2001. 'Prisoner Reentry: Public Safety and Reintegration Challenges'. *The Prison Journal*, 81(3), 360–75.

Portugal, S. 1999. 'Family and Social Policy in Portugal'. *International Journal of Law, Policy and the Family*, 13(3), 235–246.

Rowe, A. 2011. 'Narratives of Self and Identity in Women's Prisons: Stigma and the Struggle for Self-Definition in Penal Regimes'. *Punishment & Society*, 13(5), 571–91.

Sampson, R. J. 2011. 'The Incarceration Ledger: Toward a New Era in Assessing Societal Consequences'. *Criminology & Public Policy*, 10(3), 819–28.

Santos, B. S. 1993. *O Estado, as Relações Salariais e o Bem-Estar Social na Semi-Periferia- O Caso Português*. Porto: Afrontamento.

Smith, P. S. 2014. *When the Innocent are Punished: The Children of Imprisoned Parents*. Hampshire: Palgrave Macmillan.

Smith, R., Grimshaw, R., Romeo, R., and Knapp, M. 2007. *Poverty and Disadvantage among Prisoners' Families*. London: Joseph Rowntree Foundation.

Sykes, G. M. 1958. *The Society of Captives*. New Jersey: Princeton University Press.

Touraut, C. 2012. *La famille à l'épreuve de la prison*. Paris: Presses Universitaires de France.

Turanovic, J. J., Rodriguez, N., and Pratt, T. C. 2012. 'The Collateral Consequences of Incarceration Revisited: a Qualitative Analysis of the Effects on Caregivers of Children of Incarcerated Parents'. *Criminology*, 50(4), 913–59.

Turney, K. 2015. 'Hopelessly Devoted? Relationship Quality During and After Incarceration'. *Journal of Marriage and Family*, 77(2), 480–95.

Ugelvik, T. 2011. 'The Hidden Food: Mealtime Resistance and Identity Work in a Norwegian Prison'. *Punishment & Society*, 13(1), 47–63.

Wacquant, L. 2000. *Prisons of Poverty*. Minneapolis: University of Minnesota Press.

Wakefield, S. and Wildeman, C. 2013. *Children of the Prison Boom: Mass Incarceration and the Future of American Inequality*. New York: Oxford University Press.

Wall, K., Aboim, S., Cunha, V., and Vasconcelos, P. 2001. 'Families and Informal Support Networks in Portugal: The Reproduction of Inequality'. *Journal of European Social Policy*, 11(3), 213–33.

Western, B. and Wildeman, C. 2009. 'The Black Family and Mass Incarceration'. *The ANNALS of the American Academy of Political and Social Science*, 621(1), 221–42.

Woldoff, R. and Washington, H. M. 2008. 'Arrested Contact: The Criminal Justice System, Race, and Father Engagement'. *The Prison Journal*, 88(2), 179–206.

18

Betwixt and Between

Incarcerated Men, Familial Ties, and Social Visibility

Shenique S. Thomas and Johnna Christian

Introduction

Extensive reliance on incarceration for over three decades has had significant and far-reaching impacts on American society (Clear, 2009; Travis et al., 2014). In the United States, one in every thirty-seven adults is under correctional supervision and 870 per 100,000 residents are imprisoned in State or Federal prisons or local jails (Kaeble and Glaze, 2016). Families and communities of colour are disproportionately impacted by incarceration. Sixty-eight per cent of Black men who do not complete high school are incarcerated by the age of 34 (Pettit and Western, 2004) and half of Black women have a family member who has been incarcerated (Lee et al., 2015). Growing bodies of research have identified connections between parental incarceration and adverse child outcomes (Knudsen, this volume; Wakefield and Wildeman, 2014), diminished mental health among the partners of incarcerated men (Wildeman et al., 2012), and increased levels of psychological distress for mothers of the incarcerated (Green et al., 2006). Men who have been incarcerated experience psychological disorders related to exposure to violence during incarceration (Boxer et al., 2009) and encounter myriad hardships in their reintegration to family and community after incarceration (Porter and Novisky, 2016; Western et al., 2015).

Studies of the extended consequences and aftermath of incarceration are vital, but the incarceration period itself has great import as an experience that is exceedingly harsh, degrading, and 'painful,' as the classic prison sociologist Gresham Sykes (1958) described. Sykes argued that prison inflicted not only a physical separation from society, but social isolation and rejection—powerful symbols of moral condemnation and deeply painful invisibility from the rest of society. One way to bridge this invisibility and separation for incarcerated men is visits from family members. Prison visitation is oft cited as a means of occupying prisoners' time and facilitating ties to the outside world, yet scholars still grapple with questions about the permeability between prison and the free world, and how specifically incarcerated people mitigate the isolation of the prison environment.

Extant research about visitation has focused extensively on the family members on the outside, highlighting the difficulties they encounter in the process of getting to correctional facilities and the way they are treated by authorities once inside of the prison (Arditti, 2005; Christian, 2005; Comfort, 2008; Kotova, this volume). Other studies have examined outcomes such as the relationship between visitation and in-prison infraction rates (Cochran, 2012) or recidivism upon release (Brunton-Smith and McCarthy, 2016; Cochran, 2014). Contributions anchored on the incarcerated individual's perspective are rare (see Granja, this volume; Pierce, 2015; Smith, 2014;

Prisons, Punishment, and the Family: Towards a New Sociology of Punishment? First Edition. Rachel Condry and Peter Scharff Smith. © The several contributors 2018. Published 2018 by Oxford University Press.

Thomas, 2011 for exceptions), as is work about the content, nature, and aftermath of visits (Cochran and Mears, 2013; Smith, 2014; Tasca et al., 2016).

The current research aims to advance understanding of the meaning of visitation for incarcerated men through a qualitative study of their experiences of visitation. Analysing twenty-five in-depth, semi-structured interviews with incarcerated men at various stages of their sentence, twelve hours of observations at prison visitation sessions, and a focus group conducted at a prison in the Northeastern region of the United States, we present a framework for analysing visitation as a mechanism by which incarcerated men experience belonging and visibility otherwise denied to them. Participants' accounts indicate humanistic potential of interaction with family members through visits as they make emotional connections with people who care about them, provide input to family life and decisions, and feel respected and valued. At the same time, there is a complex duality at play, as time with family is potentially transcendent, but also highlights men's and their family members' subjugation within the prison, in addition to the men's compromised roles within their families while incarcerated and invisibility in society-at-large. By theorizing about these multilayered exchanges, we aim to more squarely integrate research about visitation with critical work about social justice and family members of the incarcerated. We next situate our analysis in extant research about the prison, as well as family relationships within the context of visitation.

Literature review

1. Inmates' experiences of the prison environment

Sykes (1958) argued that incarcerated men experienced 'pains of imprisonment' such as deprivation of liberty, goods and services, autonomy, security, and heterosexual relationships. He explained that the deprivation of liberty entailed a loss of freedom, but also represented a putting away and containment by society—physical separation as well as moral judgement and condemnation. The sense of otherness, no longer belonging to family, friends, or society was particularly painful. In contrast, Irwin's (1987) importation theory held that the outside world permeated the prison environment as inmates 'imported' street identities and personas into prison. Even Irwin's importation theory, however, acknowledged that inmates' ties to the outside world became attenuated, giving greater salience to their contacts with other inmates. Such questions of separation, permeability, and invisibility are arguably even more complex in the era of mass incarceration, as inmates have cycled through correctional institutions repeatedly, and consequently more people on the outside are also connected to the carceral system (Kotova, this volume; Lee et al., 2015; Wacquant, 2001).

Building on these classic works, contemporary research about prisons has presented nuanced explanations of power dynamics (Crewe, 2011), masculine identity (Ricciardelli et al., 2015) and the social meaning of different physical spaces within the prison (Crewe et al., 2014). Crewe argued that inmates' lives are shaped by the 'depth, weight and tightness' of the prison regime, and that there is indeed a great deal of variation in inmates' experiences, particularly considering the 'emotional geography' of the prison in which specific settings elicit different personas and adaptations to the environment (Crewe et al., 2014). Crewe et al. (2014) found that men presented a softer side of themselves during visits with family members, and that other inmates respected the visit room as a 'safe space' where vulnerability and emotions could be displayed. Even after visits were over, men allowed each other opportunities to grieve the separation from family and engaged in quiet times of reflection. This was in contrast to other spaces in the prison that required traditional expressions of toughness and masculinity.

Additional research has shown how prisons might be configured to promote inmate wellbeing and satisfaction. Liebling's (2004) comprehensive study of the 'moral performance' of prisons found that inmates value 'relationship dimensions' such as respect, humanity, trust, and support, and 'regime dimensions' such as fairness, order, safety, and family contact. The relationship dimensions referred primarily to their interactions with correctional officers and other staff, and the regime dimensions to opportunities for self-improvement and comfortable overall environment. Liebling's work demonstrated the interplay of environmental aspects of the prison such as rules, regulations, and how they are communicated to inmates and enforced, and relational aspects such as how they are treated by officers and opportunities for interaction with the outside world.

Toch and Gibbs' (1992) transactional theory suggested that inmates, and in fact all people, seek congruence between their needs and environment. Inmates vary as far as which type of prison environment is most suitable for their individual needs, and the facility can accommodate the range of preferences creating a safer experience with increased levels of inmate satisfaction. Toch and Gibbs (1992, 70) suggest that for those who value emotional feedback via intimacy, 'in total institutions, the immediate environment may not only be a perceived source of emotional feedback, but also a mediator of feedback from the "outside"'. Research about humanistic corrections has indicated that inmates' experience of the prison is not immutably harsh and degrading. Notably, prison visitation is a peculiar setting within the institution in which multiple dimensions of inmates' lives converge; visitation is highly constrained by administrative rules, yet the very presence of outsiders, and particularly family members to whom inmates have emotional attachments, leads to ambiguity and possibly discomfort. Visits, and connections to the outside, thus take on a meaning and value far beyond utilitarian purposes such as decreasing infraction rates or recidivism after release.

2. Family relationships in the context of prison visitation

Research about prison visitation has described family members' experiences in the visitation process (Arditti, 2005; Christian, 2005; Comfort, 2008), as well as the impact of visitation on prisoner outcomes such as receipt of disciplinary infractions within the institution and recidivism after release (Cochran, 2012). Unfortunately, there are fundamental questions about visitation that are still unanswered, such as the average frequency of visits, relationships of visitors, and the specific nature and content of visits (Cochran and Mears, 2013; Smith, 2014). Comparative analyses are virtually non-existent, but would be informative, as there is variation in the rules for visitation between states and even within the same jurisdiction. Moreover, work from the perspective of the incarcerated individual[1] is limited, yet their voices are essential for understanding the mechanisms behind various outcomes, and for a fuller picture of inmates' experiences of the conditions of confinement.

---

[1] Historically, posing a challenge to this body of literature, US corrections agencies and authorities have limited researchers' access to this population for protection of the institution and purportedly the incarcerated.

Such invisibility is exacerbated by the difficulties family members encounter as they try to maintain connections to the incarcerated with prisons located far from the US urban cores from which prisoners hail (Eason, 2017). The sanctioned policies of the European Prison Rules, that stipulate, 'prisoners must, as far as possible, be placed in a prison close to their homes or near the place where their reintegration into society is supposed to take place' (rule 17.1) are of remarkable exception (Smith, 2014, 107). Moreover, conjugal or extended stay visits are not common practice stateside, with only four of fifty states authorized to permit conjugal visits between prisoners and their families.

In a US national survey of incarcerated parents' contact with their children, Glaze and Maruschak (2008) found that 52 per cent of State prisoners have a child under the age of 18. Of the 78.6 per cent of parents in State prison who had contact with their children, 53 per cent communicated through phone calls, 70 per cent sent and/or received letters from their children, and 42 per cent had received a visit since admission. Visits stood out as the least frequent mode of contact, likely because they required the most resources such as time, money, and emotional availability. These data referred to visits with children; it is less clear who else visited incarcerated people and with what frequency, though incarcerated women had fewer visitors than incarcerated men, and were more likely to be visited by friends and relatives than male romantic partners (Casey-Acevedo et al., 2004).

In summary, the scarcity of research focalized on the complexities and dimensions of prisoners' lived experiences and visitation has demonstrated that incarcerated men are physically and psychologically excluded from society, but still exist within it through relationships, such as those with members of their families of origin and/or formation (Comfort, 2008). Inmates move between prison and their home communities, at the same time that their family members navigate life on the outside with intervals of time in prison spaces (Comfort, 2008). Since the prison environment is vastly different from the world outside, family members experience 'secondary prisonization' within the carceral environment (Comfort, 2008), parallel to the adjustment faced by prisoners. Moreover, Crewe et al. (2014) illustrate how incarcerated individuals navigate spaces *within* the prison, and indeed visits with family take on a different 'emotional geography' from other spaces in which norms of masculinity and toughness are paramount. Yet, while scholars have investigated this process for friends and family members who transition from the outside world to the prison, less is known about how inmates contend with absolute boundaries between prison and the outside world, particularly through the context of visitation. Our research addresses this critical knowledge gap by demonstrating that while incarcerated men experience prison as degrading and harsh, visitation is an avenue, a vehicle, for connection, belonging, and visibility allowing them to transcend the everyday prison experience.

Methods

This research is based on data from twenty-five in-depth, semi-structured interviews with incarcerated men at various stages of their sentence, twelve hours of observations at prison visitation sessions, and a focus group with incarcerated men, conducted at a prison in the Northeastern region of the United States in 2006 and 2007.[2] The

---

[2] Participants were drawn from a random sample of the general population, excluding those in special units of the prison such as the gang units, administrative segregation, and the psychiatric stabilization units.

participants met with the first author of the chapter in private rooms within the prison where the study was explained and the consent process completed. Because prison officials did not permit audio recording, hand written notes were taken during the interview, and then a detailed account of each participant's responses was written immediately after the researcher left the setting. On average, the interviews were sixty minutes long. The focus group was held in a classroom without prison staff present. The researcher observed visitation sessions and wrote detailed field notes after each session.

Interview questions focused on prison experiences, life prior to incarceration, strengths and deficits in family relationships, men's concept of their roles within the family, and experiences with family contact through phone, letters, and visits. Given the focus on visitation encounters from the perspective of family members in prior research, we were interested in how men defined the process of visiting, with special attention to the positive and negative aspects of visits. This focus allowed us to delve beyond utilitarian facets of visits such as whether they decrease disciplinary infraction rates or recidivism after release, to the content and nature of visits, the emotions evoked, and men's thick descriptions of what visits meant to them. Several questions elicited responses related to men's experience of visitation such as frequency of family visits, preferences for different modes of contact such as calls, mail or visits, and aspects the men favoured most and least about visiting as a process. Coupled with this query, questions not explicitly about visitation often elicited relevant information, such as when a participant remarked on officers' interactions with prisoners in the context of visiting or when explaining the reasons for the lack of familial contact.

1. Setting

During weekend contact visiting sessions, the prison under study hosted visits for 150 incarcerated men, allowing four visitors per person,[3] space permitting.[4] Each visiting session ran approximately 1.5 hours.[5] Contrary to studied international facilities (i.e. Denmark), supervision officers were deprived the use of discretion to extend visits (Smith, 2014) however, as expected, officers could terminate visits for rule violations. The weekend contact visits were held in a large, open, multiuse shared space—the gymnasium. The visiting hall (i.e. prison gymnasium) held approximately twenty-four rows of eighteen plastic, interlocking, primary-coloured chairs. Murals covered portions of the pale blue gymnasium walls and served as backdrops for family photos. At times, facility staff would create a makeshift child-friendly area and feature a suitable film. When the weather permitted, families were able to access a small, enclosed outdoor area. This space was coveted by visitors and the incarcerated men, alike, because it offered a more intimate visit, allowing for an opportunity to smoke and sit side-by-side as opposed to the non-smoking, stale, indoor area where they were required to sit back in their chair, across from each other with hands visible to officers at all times.

---

[3] The regulations do not specify the limit on the number of children allowed to visit.

[4] According to a review of publicly available information about the Department of Corrections guidelines, the general policies pertaining to visiting have not significantly changed in the time since data were collected. The agency has made additional material available online for visitors to review prior to arrival (e.g. outlining the dress code). Additionally, the Department of Corrections provides information for those offenders with visiting restrictions (i.e. lists type of visit restraint and expiration date of restriction).

[5] Conjugal visits were not permitted at this facility. As of 2016, only four states allow extended overnight, conjugal visits.

Visitors gathered in line to register for the visiting session at least two hours prior to the start time. To account for long lines and unforeseen circumstances (e.g. denied entry due to attire), it was common practice for family members to meet in the parking lot as early as 6am for an 8.45am visit. At the beginning of each visitation period, expectant prisoners were seated together in one section until their visitor cleared security and was granted admission. With anticipation, inmates spotted and joined their visitor as s/he entered the gymnasium. Collectively, the incarcerated member and visiting party sought seating away from the waiting crowd of incarcerated men, because an increased number of inmates in one area signified heightened security. Pairs were permitted to momentarily hug and kiss their loved one at the beginning and end of the visit.

2. Participant characteristics

Demographic factors including race and ethnicity, age, time served, sentence length, length of time at the prison, prior criminal history, and visiting patterns were self-reported (see Table 1). Data pertaining to the current conviction were obtained from the Department of Corrections. Self-reported data were matched to publicly available information.[6]

Twenty-one of the participants were Black (84 per cent). The mean age of the men was 38 years old, ranging from 29 to 62 years; the average participant age at the time of the current incarceration was 27 years old. Fourteen of the interview participants were under the age of 25 at the time of their current incarceration, and four of these fourteen participants were under 18 years old at the time of incarceration. The participants had a wide range of time served, from eighteen months to twenty-seven years. On average, the men served eleven years in prison and faced sentences ranging from five years to Life. At the time of the interview, the men spent about four years at the specific correctional facility under study. More than half of the men had been previously incarcerated at least one time. The majority (88 per cent) of the men were serving a mandatory minimum sentence. According to the data provided by the Department of Corrections web resource, 56 per cent of the incarcerated men were convicted of a violent offence, 28 per cent of a drug-related crime, and 12 per cent of a property crime.

Findings

This chapter addresses critical knowledge gaps in our understanding of the meaning and value of visitation for incarcerated men by demonstrating that while they often experienced prison as a platform for degradations and harsh customs, visitation provided a reprieve from the carceral environment, and was an avenue for connectedness and belonging to their family members and society-at-large. Clearly, visitation was not a 'panacea for alleviating the pains of imprisonment' (Holligan, 2016, 94), but rather it provided at least temporary relief from these pains, with the capacity to emotionally transport men beyond the prison walls. Hence, we begin by analysing men's accounts of the visit as a reprieve from other aspects of the prison environment.

---

[6] The Department of Corrections website provides detailed inmate information. However, the indicated sentence length may not reflect the most current and/or accurate imposed sentence. Also, time served can be unclear since inmates may have concurrent sentences.

Table 1 Participant characteristics and incarceration history.

	PARTICIPANTS
	Percentage (Frequency)
Male	100.0 (25)
Race/Ethnicity	
Black, non-Hispanic	84.0 (21)
White, non-Hispanic	8.0 (2)
Hispanic	8.0 (2)
Asian	–
Criminal Justice History	
Serving a mandatory minimum	88.0 (22)
Prior incarceration	56.0 (14)
Incarcerated at other facilities	92.0 (23)
Conviction	
Violent	56.0 (14)
Drug-related	28.0 (7)
Property[1]	12.0 (3)
Sentence Lengths (years)	
5–9	24.0 (6)
10–14	12.0 (3)
15–19	20.0 (5)
20–24	20.0 (5)
25–29	–
30–39	20.0 (5)
40–49	–
50–59	–
> 60	4.0 (1)
	Mean(SD)
Age	38.1 (9.2)
Time Served (years)	11.24 (7.1)
Length of time at facility (years)	4.4 (3.1)
Times previously incarcerated	1.3 (1.8)

[1] Carjacking recorded as a property offence if not in combination with armed robbery.

1. 'A touch of freedom': visits as a reprieve

Visitation was one way that incarcerated men cultivated authentic and meaningful experiences that transcended the prison environment. They described these events as a mental escape from the institutional restrictions, power dynamics, and emotional constraints of the prison setting, fostering their interaction with the outside world, and psychologically transporting them from the prison. The men described visitation sessions as a gateway and passage to a humanizing experience. For these men, the intimate moments shared in the seemingly sterile visiting hall were enough to 'just take you away from jail, just for that moment ... you feel like you are part of the outside. That's a good feeling!' (Calvin, 42 years old, seventeen and a half years served). Undeterred by the unwelcoming visiting conditions, the performance of visiting was a commodity, a diversion and interruption to the regularly scheduled programming of the Department of Corrections and cultivated a channel for humanity to exist and persist in spite of being squeezed out in other settings of the prison. 'Visits take you out of here. If it's female company, I like to kick it, be eye-to-eye' (Barry, 35 years old, four years served). Another participant explained: 'We are all close. So, it's like we all share the visits, we are all talking, it's like we not even in there. My mother and sister are loud, so they always trying to get their point across' (Christopher, 33 years old, fifteen years served).

The visiting period was a hurried escape that momentarily melted away anxiety, trepidation, uneasiness, fear, ambivalence, and acknowledged and affirmed incarcerated men's visibility, personhood, and connectedness to non-carceral networks, and provided the ability to exercise various forms of limited control and authority within their family. As a part of this humanizing process, the men considered their eagerness, comfort, and relief to shed the emotional mask and physically aggressive persona deemed necessary for survival in the institution as powerful and liberating. Vincent, a 31 year old who was 18 years of age when sentenced to serve his first term of thirty years in prison, explained, 'I gotta go back to the unit. I don't feel any depression (during visits).' He consistently received visits from family members and friends every Saturday and Sunday.

Sixty-two-year-old Roberto, however, highlighted the dynamic nature of the 'relief' afforded by visits. He said about himself prior to incarceration, 'I wasn't too good of a husband. It wasn't a big part of my life. I was a good provider, a lousy parent, and a terrible husband. I've been married 3 times.' He described how the separation due to incarceration continued to sever his familial relationships:

> You are torn away in here. There's no social bond. So you become socially distant with your family, when you're around them you don't know what to say. It took a couple of months to feel comfortable sitting and conversing with somebody.

Still, he described visiting as having a moderating and liberating effect. Temporarily, the men were able to indulge in 'freedom', autonomy, and separation from the control of the state.

> In general, they help to keep the family unit together, to build ties, not only for the incarcerated, but a mutual give and take support system. Men in here ... the visits give a touch of freedom, like they're on the outside, they are able to communicate with children on the outside.

Though visiting sessions may have served as a reminder of unattainable freedom, they were also a cue that freedom existed. Visits reinforced the men's presence apart from the 'shadow of imprisonment' (Granja, this volume) and relevance to a meaningful network. Richard, an incarcerated grandfather who received monthly visits expressed, 'My daughter, mother, my sister, couple of grandsons, my son that's here, his mother, they all came up at one time. They surprised me, we talked about past times, up-to-date times, turned a bad situation to a right situation' (Richard, 44 years old, six years served).

Forty-two-year-old Calvin had been incarcerated for twenty-five years. During his incarceration, Calvin's two sisters, brother, and common-law wife died, and his remaining family moved to a nearby state. His father was his most frequent visitor. The visits with his father reminded him that he mattered beyond the confines of the prison. Calvin explained:

> Connection to the outside ... You get the feeling like you are still alive, it motivates you more, the feeling that someone is still there, that you got love, some guys don't get visits at all ... I look at them, I wanna help them. Outside communication shows you're loved.
>
> When we talk on a visit, I get mushy, but you wanna be loved and miss 'em so much, I get that, 'I wanna be home' feeling every time. I try not to change that too much,

cause if it changes or I do something different, they gonna wonder what's going on. A man ain't supposed to cry, that's a lie, but I cried … so many, too many times.

Being an active participant in the social process of communication and interacting with a loved one during a visit fortified these men, reinforcing their connections to others. These connections also fostered a bridge to visibility and even a sense of accountability to others. Richard further explained:

> Gives them a chance to know me, the person I become or didn't become. Time don't stop, my life keeps going, gives us time to be updated on each other. See what the plans are, what each other's goals are.

Marcus, 33 years of age, grew up visiting his older brother in prison, claiming that he 'just got caught up at an early age, 13'.

> I've visited my brother. My older brother was doing time. He's deceased now … died in motorcycle accident. I would visit the prison once every 2 months. I was about 19 years old. I would just say to myself, 'I can't see myself doing time.'

Now, finding himself incarcerated and on the receiving end of visits, Marcus created special moments with his teenage daughter and niece by shifting indoor visiting sessions to the coveted outdoor space, with fewer restrictions, allowing for increased intimacy. He made these moments constructive by talking with the girls about relationships and home life while expressing his own expectations as a father and uncle.

> I wish I was able to be there for my daughter. That's what bothers me the most, like a father is supposed to be there. I mean I do ask how she is doing, if anyone is treating her wrong, but since I've been locked up, I only see her every other weekend. See them leave and not being able to leave with them, I feel the hurt. My daughter said that she is sad … Visits play a big role, supportive. Since I've been in here, it makes the time go by smoother, they are there for you, it plays a really big part.

Lastly, visits provided a semblance to being home and living their lives as though unrestrained:

> Feel good as hell … when some of my friends come up, I like talking to them, when I see them … we were all similar in characteristics growing up, so now I like getting visits cause I could imagine how I would be if I was home. They all have jobs … I could see me outside on the streets. It makes me feel good. (Vincent, 31 years old, thirteen years served)

Vincent thus illuminated how visits connected him to his life beyond the prison.

2. Belonging and visibility

We next further expand on how visits oriented the participant's sense of belonging and visibility to his family irrespective of the mechanisms used to socially, physically, and politically isolate and exclude imprisoned people from broader society. The men yearned to belong to a unit external to the penal system; incarcerated men deprived of their 'perceptual salience' (Breyer, 2015) engaged in habits intended to resurrect their previously held identity, reaffirm their self-image, personality structure, role expectations, and familial obligations.

As previously noted of the visiting conditions, the incarcerated men and visitors were required to sit across from each other and permitted to momentarily hug and kiss at the start and close of the session. Roberto described a visiting episode:

> Sure … joy, laughter, haven't seen someone in a while, hear about who passed away, moved, weddings that you missed, the whole gamut of emotions. (Roberto, 62 years old, twenty-three years served)

Richard elaborated about the value of kinship, acknowledgment, and belonging:

> Yeah, my grandkids make cards ... family keep me in prayers, let me know what's going on with the family. Make sure the young ones know who I am. There's only so much you can do, when you in here and they out there. I'm satisfied with what I'm doing right now, 'til I get there. (Richard, 44 years old, six years served)

Along with the usual exchanges, catching up on family gossip, unions, and deaths and sharing of meals produced by the vending machines, families were also observed in spiritual practices (i.e. prayer). In most instances, a mother was praying with/for her incarcerated son. In other examples, the visible parts of his body were under scrutiny and close examination for bruises or noticeable changes in appearance, allowing family to demonstrate care and concern. Being tended to by a visitor signalled an immediate recognition of self, social and physical visibility, and inclusion into a non-penal network. The totality of their 'being' was of importance and cause for concern, protection, and nurturing.

Twenty-nine-year-old Jackson, a former college student who had 'compromised everything' by being incarcerated and claimed that he is 'the only knucklehead in the family that do dumb stuff,' entered prison for his current sentence at the age of 22. His evangelist mother and father visited monthly from a nearby state. During visiting sessions, his mother prayed and attempted to groom him. Jackson explained:

> Sometimes I get out there and pray, but it doesn't seem right and don't sit right with me. And once your family see something different about you, they may check on it. If they hear something different in your voice and they know that you were growing and progressing ... they will sense it, they will know if you're crazy.

Jackson's experience illustrated how visitation served as a mechanism of inclusion, in contrast to the constant othering and isolation of imprisonment. He was 'seen' during visits, and valued to an extent that people who cared about him would show concern if something changed.

Undeterred by their liminal status (Arditti, 2005; Comfort, 2008), visitors showed the men both explicitly and implicitly their worthiness for physical touch, dignified treatment, communication, and encouragement. As Ivan, incarcerated for eleven years noted, 'Nothing beats a hug from your family. You get that genuine feeling of love, it's not the fake stuff back in the tier' (Ivan, 45 years old, eleven years served). Shaheem attested:

> If I see my mother in the visits, I was going through something, I try to hug her, but I told her I have to hug her or kiss when I leave. I was going through something with my son, he's a diabetic ... but the best part is that you get to spend some time, physically, with people you really love and care about. (Shaheem, 31 years old, three and a half years served)

These scheduled and short interactions reduced anxiety and loneliness and introduced a window to practice empathy and understanding. Richard echoed the sentiment of others, 'Visits, you want to see how they doing, how they sound. To see and touch someone, besides prisoners or prison guards.' Even seemingly minimal periods of contact triggered feelings of validation, legitimacy, and belonging, thereby mitigating a sense of being disposable and invisible. The dignity, humanization, and respect transmitted during visits contributed to an identity beyond prisoner.

Fifty-one-year-old David was incarcerated as a juvenile and completed four jail and three prison terms. At age 13, his involvement with drugs and criminal activity damaged his relationship with his mother and siblings. His mother later died in 1982 during his incarceration and he last spoke with his father in the 'summer of '78'. He said of his life:

> I stayed with my mother 'til I was 13. I started getting incarcerated and doing bad things since I was 13. I've been in jail and prison, since I was 13. All of my adult life, I say I've been in prison. (David, 51 years old, two years served)

Because of his repeated incarcerations from a young age, David never had an opportunity to develop a sense of belonging within his family. Amid his few free years in the community prior to his current sentence, David met and proposed to his now fiancée. His extensive history of incarceration impaired previous relationships, but visits with his current fiancée helped to bridge his isolation from the outside world. He talked at length about how she continued to positively influence him:

> My life began all over again when we met… She brought a lot into my life, stability, respect, a little God in my life. She knew if I didn't change, I would be dead. What I saw in her I never saw in another woman before. We talk and talk and talk like no one else was there. I knew from that point, that she was someone I wanted to get to know … She really put a lot of stability in to place in my life.

Visits reinforced David's connectedness to his fiancée and her son, bringing his sense of belonging directly into the prison and providing both a physical and mental escape:

> Looking into her eyes, holding her, and then when after you leave, after, I wish I could walk out the visit with her. You just have to hold it in your mind in your memory. When the door close, my doors close, like to heaven, we go back to the visiting hall, but not in person.
>
> Visits, it's different cause when I am looking at her, holding her, looking into her eyes, it makes me feel real good, like a warm summer breeze.

Visits were not always welcomed because they left men vulnerable as they worked to push past emotional baggage and feelings of worry, and many encountered contradictory feelings about visits. For 31-year-old Amir, visits offered a relational opportunity that he did not initially seek at the start of his sentence.

> Jail is a microcosm, and then the streets, and everything that's with it, I couldn't do both … Me, I can do one thing and excel at it. My first bid, I couldn't do it … now that I'm 14 years in, I can do it.

Further, Ivan explained:

> I can't deal with family and what goes on in here. I am not afraid of prison, my heart, I'm not like them, in here I don't have problems, but I'm afraid of getting my heart turned black … (Ivan, 45 years old, eleven years served)

At some point in their sentence, some participants felt incapable of managing or balancing their in-prison lives with that of their familial roles and expectations (Nurse, 2002). Nurse (2002) described this process as 'hard timing', in which incarcerated men reserve and allocate physical and emotional resources exclusively to the performance of prisoner, and dissociate or terminate any conflicting relationships. In such a strategy, the men, of their own request, implored family members not to visit.

According to Amir, it was also necessary to 'cut off' contact with his family and friends to sustain his sanity. He justified his divorce and forced exclusion from the outside world:

> I had to cut off the nonsense ... when in camp[7] I will be able to deal with it. I can't live in both worlds now ... after cutting off, I haven't been in touch. The disconnect was harsh and abrupt. But, that's what I needed to do and saw as the only option at that time. When I was getting visits or talking to my boys and friends, I was a feeling like, 'Ya'll are killing me.'
>
> *Interviewer*: What was going on?
>
> My friends were having problems and were going to parties that I wanted to be at. I used to be the life of the party ... when problems would come up, I was the youngest of the clique, but I would solve the problems. But I wasn't there. I felt like my hands were tied, helpless. I never been in a situation like this before.
>
> I had a girl, but I cut that off. Now that I am about to finish, it may be different. But, immediately, I couldn't do both ... I couldn't deal with them while I was dealing with this ... one had to go, and I chose the streets.

Amir's detachment from family and friends was associated with his own frustrations at not being able to engage in or share experiences with those outside. He was an 'other' as a prisoner, living in situations unfamiliar to his family and friends. He discerned that his limited interaction with visitors affected his temperament, 'Prison reverses everything. I was social on the streets, but now, I'm anti-social in here.' With the fear of losing his mother to the terminal diagnosis of stage 4 lung cancer, the closeness and familiarity embodied in visits became particularly important to him:

> Very important. I get to smile, the face to face contact, I get to be around someone I'm familiar with. Being in here, tires you. I get tired of being around people I don't know, I want to talk with someone who can relate. (Amir, 31 years old, fourteen years served)

Despite the strain attributed to managing the duality of his lived experiences, Amir's increased willingness to consider life beyond the walls for fear of losing his mother, and his impending release date, compelled him to reconnect and reengage with those who he once rejected. He reflected on the moment he decided to restore his presence within the family:

> Man, once the cancer came on, something happened. I gave her the green light ... I can't let much time go by without seeing her.

After Amir's shift in thinking, he had weekly phone calls scheduled with his mother, welcomed visits from his mother and brother, and worked to share the emotional toll/ stress associated with her diagnosis. In order to do this he risked losing further freedom by relying on prohibited resources (i.e. mobile phone) to maintain contact. Amir's situation illustrated the complexities and fluidity in men's approaches to visitation during various stages of their sentences and as family circumstances changed.

Conclusion

Through incarcerated men's accounts of their visitation experiences, we find that engaging in visits with people from the outside served a number of key purposes. To

---

[7] Inmates are placed in these minimum-security housing units when approaching release.

start, the men expressed feeling a sense of belonging to their families, and to some extent the broader society, rather than the prison system. The visits reminded these men that they exist in the broader society and are more than property of the state. We do, however, see limitations as both the men and their families still encountered the duality of marginalization, invisibility, and exclusion from the broader society, and hyper surveillance and control of their lives, particularly within the confines of the prison. Moreover, some men coped with incarceration by limiting visits from family members.

Legally, prison officials have 'absolute discretion' in the manner in which they implement visitation programmes and are only required to consider their legal obligation to prisoners as opposed to moral duties (Rosen, 2001, 71). In the case of visitation, managerial needs of the prisons upstage the commitment to their moral duties. The restrictiveness, arbitrariness, and degradation associated with the implementation of policies governing prison visiting make maintaining contact through visitation challenging for prisoners, families, and friends. As extant research has documented, the families of the prisoners are burdened in myriad ways, from paying the collect phone call bills originated from the correctional facility, to undergoing the secondary prisonization Comfort (2008) so vividly described.

One recent development in the United States and other countries, is the use of video visitation, often times requiring family members to pay a fee for the services, with little empirical evidence about the experience for the incarcerated or family members. Video visitation lacks the humanizing aspects we found were central to men's descriptions of the visitation experience. In particular, family practices such as touching, hugging, and praying together are not possible through video visits. In addition, the men valued the dynamic and reciprocal aspects of visits, in which family gauged and reacted to their wellbeing, and the men returned in kind. The empathic, connective aspects of in person visits may be lost through a video monitor.

Prior research has highlighted the important and meaningful functions of visitation, particularly for the family members on the outside. Comfort (2002) found that during visits the carceral environment became a *domestic satellite* for 'kinship gatherings, family celebrations, and romance' (470). Visits function as a direct portal for family members and incarcerated men to continue their relationship with one another and represent an opportunity for family members to 'bridge' the primary loss associated with incarceration (Arditti, 2003). Families are permitted to share physical and intimate moments and communicate, face-to-face, about family matters, providing or receiving counsel, advice, and encouragement and/or assisting with decision making.

In this study, we illuminate how visitation affords men 'a place' in a familial unit despite being rendered socially invisible in the larger society. Building on previous research, we demonstrate how visitation changes (even if temporarily) men's experiences of the prison environment. Interactions with family members during visitation provide a sense of belonging, inclusion, and equality, in stark contrast to their other interactions within the prison. These findings highlight the need for theoretically enriched research, and carceral policies, that situate prison visitation as a means to advance social justice and inclusion for the incarcerated and their family members.

References

Arditti, J. A. 2003. 'Locked Doors and Glass Walls: Family Visiting at a Local Jail'. *Journal of Loss and Trauma*, 8(2), 115–38.

Arditti, J. A. 2005. 'Families and Incarceration: An Ecological Approach'. *Families in Society*, 86(2), 251–60.

Boxer, P., Middlemass, K., and Delorenzo, T. 2009. 'Exposure to Violent Crime During Incarceration: Effects on Psychological Adjustment Following Release'. *Criminal Justice and Behavior*, 36(8), 793–807.

Breyer, T. 2015. 'Social Visibility and Perceptual Normativity', in Doyon, M. and Breyer, T. (eds.) *Normativity in Perception.* 140–60. Basingstoke: Palgrave Macmillan.

Brunton-Smith, I. and McCarthy, D. J. 2016. 'The Effects of Prisoner Attachment to Family on Re-entry Outcomes: A Longitudinal Assessment'. *British Journal of Criminology*, 57(2), 463–82.

Casey-Acevedo, K., Bakken, T. and Karle, A. 2004. 'Children Visiting Mothers in Prison: The Effects on Mothers' Behavior and Disciplinary Adjustment'. *Australian New Zealand Journal of Criminology*, 37(3), 418–30.

Christian, J. 2005. 'Riding the Bus Barriers to Prison Visitation and Family Management Strategies'. *Journal of Contemporary Criminal Justice*, 21(1), 31–48.

Clear, T. R. 2009. *Imprisoning Communities: How Mass Incarceration Makes Disadvantaged Neighborhoods Worse*. Oxford University Press.

Cochran, J. C. 2012. 'The Ties that Bind or the Ties that Break: Examining the Relationship between Visitation and Prisoner Misconduct'. *Journal of Criminal Justice*, 40(5), 433–40.

Cochran, J. C. 2014. 'Breaches in the Wall: Imprisonment, Social Support, and Recidivism'. *Journal of Research in Crime and Delinquency*, 51(2), 200–29.

Cochran, J. C. and Mears, D. P. 2013. 'Social Isolation and Inmate Behavior: A Conceptual Framework for Theorizing Prison Visitation and Guiding and Assessing Research'. *Journal of Criminal Justice*, 41(4), 252–61.

Comfort, M. 2002. '"Papa's House": The Prison as Domestic and Social Satellite'. *Ethnography*, 3(4), 467–99.

Comfort, M. 2008. *Doing Time Together: Love and Family in the Shadow of the Prison*. Chicago: University of Chicago Press.

Crewe, B. 2011. 'Depth, Weight, Tightness: Revisiting the Pains of Imprisonment'. *Punishment & Society*, 13(5), 509–29.

Crewe, B., Warr, J., Bennett, P., and Smith, A. 2014. 'The Emotional Geography of Prison Life'. *Theoretical Criminology*, 18(1), 56–74.

Eason, J. M. 2017. *Big House on the Prairie: Rise of the Rural Ghetto and Prison Proliferation*. Chicago: University of Chicago Press.

Glaze, L. E. and Maruschak, L. M. 2008. 'Parents in Prison and their Minor Children'. *Bureau of Justice Statistics Special Report*. Washington, DC: Department of Justice, Office of Justice Programs.

Green, K. M., Ensminger, M. E., Robertson, J. A., and Juon, H. S. 2006. 'Impact of Adult Sons' Incarceration on African American Mothers' Psychological Distress'. *Journal of Marriage and Family*, 68(2), 430–41.

Holligan, C. 2016. 'An Absent Presence: Visitor Narratives of Journeys and Support for Prisoners during Imprisonment'. *Howard Journal of Crime and Justice*, 55(1–2), 94–110.

Irwin, J. 1987. *The Felon*. Berkeley: University of California Press.

Kaeble, D. and Glaze, L., 2016. *Correctional Populations in the United States, 2015*. Washington, DC: Bureau of Justice Statistics.

Lee, H., McCormick, T., Hicken, M. T., and Wildeman, C. 2015. 'Racial Inequalities in Connectedness to Imprisoned Individuals in the United States'. *Du Bois Review: Social Science Research on Race*, 12(2), 269–82.

Liebling, A. 2004. *Prisons and their Moral Performance: A Study of Values, Quality, and Prison Life*. Oxford: Oxford University Press.

Nurse, A. M. 2002. *Fatherhood Arrested: Parenting from Within the Juvenile Justice System*. Nashville: Vanderbilt University Press.

Pettit, B. and Western, B. 2004. 'Mass Imprisonment and the Life Course: Race and Class Inequality in U.S. Incarceration'. *American Sociological Review*, 69(2), 151–69.

Pierce, M. B. 2015. 'Male Inmate Perceptions of the Visitation Experience: Suggestions on how Prisons can Promote Inmate–family Relationships'. *Prison Journal*, 95(3), 370–96.

Porter, L. C. and Novisky, M. A. 2016. 'Pathways to Depressive Symptoms among former inmates'. *Justice Quarterly*, 34(5), 847–72.

Ricciardelli, R., Maier, K., and Hannah-Moffat, K. 2015. 'Strategic Masculinities: Vulnerabilities, Risk and the Production of Prison Masculinities'. *Theoretical Criminology*, 19(4), 491–513.

Rosen, D. M. 2001. 'Mass Imprisonment and the Family: A Legal Perspective'. *Marriage and Family Review*, 32(3–4), 63–82.

Smith, P. S. 2014. *When the Innocent are Punished: The Children of Imprisoned Parents*. Basingstoke: Palgrave.

Sykes, G. M. 1958. *The Society of Captives: A Study of a Maximum Security Prison*. Princeton, NJ: Princeton University Press.

Tasca, M., Mulvey, P., and Rodriguez, N. 2016. 'Families Coming Together in Prison: An Examination of Visitation Encounters'. *Punishment & Society*, 18(4), 459–78.

Thomas, S. S. 2011. *Negotiating Family and Prison behind the Wall: Incarcerated Men's Role Management Strategies*. Ph.D. dissertation, Rutgers University–Graduate School-Newark.

Toch, H. and Gibbs, J. C. 1992. *Living in Prison: The Ecology of Survival*. Lawrenceville, NJ: American Psychological Association.

Travis, J., Western, B., and Redburn, F. S. 2014. *The Growth of Incarceration in the United States: Exploring Causes and Consequences*. Washington, DC: National Academic Press.

Wacquant, L. 2001. 'Deadly Symbiosis: When Ghetto and Prison Meet and Mesh'. *Punishment & Society*, 3(1), 95–133.

Wakefield, S. and Wildeman, C. 2014. *Children of the Prison Boom: Mass Incarceration and the Future of American Inequality*. Oxford: Oxford University Press.

Western, B., Braga, A. A., Davis, J., and Sirois, C. 2015. 'Stress and Hardship after Prison'. *American Journal of Sociology*, 120(5), 1512–47.

Wildeman, C., Schnittker, J., and Turney, K. 2012. 'Despair by Association? The Mental Health of Mothers with Children by Recently Incarcerated Fathers'. *American Sociological Review*, 77(2), 216–43.

19
The Systemic Invisibility of Children of Prisoners

Else Marie Knudsen

Introduction

In beginning a study of children of prisoners in Canada 2011, I immediately faced a significant hurdle: no one seemed to know anything about my topic. As I widened my net to approach policy makers, advocacy organizations, social service agencies, child welfare agencies, probation services, and anyone else I could think of, I kept receiving a variation of the same response: 'Oh that's interesting. We don't have any data/programs/experience, but there must be someone who does?' Few had any information, resources, or leads, which is curious given there are likely around 40,000 children in Canada who *currently* have a parent in prison (Knudsen, 2016). Even as I began to meet families of prisoners, I found that few wanted to participate, and a common reason given was that their child didn't know where the incarcerated parent was.

While I eventually met with several very knowledgeable key informants[1] and generous participant families, the pervasive ignorance about the experiences of Canadian children of prisoners was striking. Indeed, writing about families of prisoners often begins with a mention of their virtual absence from academic research until the 2000s. Until the recent escalation of research, this topic was under-examined, equivocal, and poorly understood, and continues to be so in some country-specific contexts including Canada. McCormick et al. (2014) write, 'children of criminally incarcerated parents are an invisible population in Canada'. This invisibility extends beyond the lack of academic research; parental incarceration is often enrobed in secrecy, confusion, and misunderstanding—within families, in communities, and in public policy.

In this chapter, I will argue that children of prisoners are rendered invisible from the micro to the macro level, through a series of interconnected processes I will call *systemic invisibility*. While these children make up a sizeable population, and the experience and outcomes of parental incarceration appear to be significant, they are often hidden from view, subject to layers of invisibility. Starting from children's own families, to their relationship with their schools and communities, to the policies and practices of the prison systems in which they are so tightly intertwined, and finally to the broader social policy context, I will discuss the ways in which parental incarceration is kept secret, enigmatic, and poorly understood. Finally, I will discuss the meanings and reasons behind these connected layers of invisibility.

---

[1] I am deeply indebted to the organizations that generously supported my research and allowed me to meet potential participants: Jessica and Derek Reid of FEAT for Children, as well as the John Howard Society of Hamilton, Cpt. Laura Burrell of the Salvation Army Kingston, Judith Laus of Prison Fellowship International's Angel Tree program, and Louise Leonardi and Lloyd Withers of Canadian Families and Corrections Network.

Prisons, Punishment, and the Family: Towards a New Sociology of Punishment? First Edition. Rachel Condry and Peter Scharff Smith. © The several contributors 2018. Published 2018 by Oxford University Press.

This discussion will be illustrated with data from my doctoral research into the experiences of Canadian children of prisoners, and thus make particular reference to the Canadian context, a jurisdiction in which there is a particular lack of policy attention. The study involved qualitative interviews with twenty-two children and youths, aged between 6 and 17, as well as their caregivers and a variety of key informants; study methodology is extensively described in Knudsen (2016).

Secrecy within families of prisoners

A challenge that immediately arose in my attempts to recruit families for the present study was a seemingly pervasive secrecy within families about parental incarceration. While this could not be a target of this study of self-reported experiences of parental incarceration, I found much anecdotal evidence of caregivers misleading children about their incarcerated parents' whereabouts. Many caregivers I met reported that they had not, or 'not yet', told their child the truth, including some I met while on trips with their children to prisons. One parent reported she'd told her son that they were going to an 'electricity factory' to explain why their parent would be behind glass in the remand centre. Several of my child participants had been lied to in the past. For example, 10-year-old Sophia described a trip to prison, at which the family was in fact refused the visit after travelling over 350km from their home to the prison due to not being properly registered for the visit:

> Mom kinda had to lie to us, she was like 'oh we're gonna see [family friend] in his new place' and I was, 'cool.' And then after that, I found out, they said 'Oh guys you can't go visit your dad.' And we're like, 'wait, we're supposed to visit our dad?'

Okay, so you didn't know?

> Yeah, I didn't know. None of us did besides [15-year-old-brother]

So you didn't know it was a prison, either?

> I didn't know, I thought it was a food tasting place. (Sophia, 10)

Question about lying to children about parental incarceration is a common topic of discussion for caregivers. For example, discussing parental incarceration with children is a common topic of factsheets and flyers provided to families of prisoners by charitable organizations (such as Adalist-Estrin, 2014 and CFCN, n.d.). An American online support network for prisoners' families, 'Prison Talk Online' has a sub-forum for people raising children who have a parent in prison, and the issue of whether to tell children about their parent's incarceration is a common topic of conversation (Prison Talk Online, 2017); the advice varies between those who tell children that dad is away at work or college, and those who tell them that dad is in prison or use 'developmental explanations' (Poehlmann, 2005) such as that the parent is 'away on a time-out'.

Scholars have long relied on anecdotal evidence to suggest that children are pervasively lied to (Ayre et al., 2011; Hairston, 2002; Caddle and Crisp, 1997) and empirical data on the issue of children being lied to beginning to emerge (Smith, 2014; Lockwood and Raikes, 2015). Poehlmann (2005) studied children with a mother in prison, their caregiver and their incarcerated mother, and found the following: 57 per cent of caregivers gave honest information or developmental explanations of their mother's incarceration; 35 per cent gave distorted explanations (such as that she was away at college) or did not tell the child where their mother was; and 8 per cent told the child about their mother's incarceration but included developmentally inappropriate details. Poehlmann (2005, 692) found that children are slightly more likely to have a positive view of their incarcerated mother when they are told about her imprisonment in a way that was 'simple, honest, and developmentally appropriate'.

The focus on maternal incarceration in Poehlmann's study renders it less generalizable and suggests that the rate of distorted explanations could be much higher. Men make up over 90 per cent of the prison population, thus paternal incarceration is much more prevalent. The vast majority (90 per cent) of children with incarcerated fathers in the United States live with their mothers and have not faced any change in caregiver with the incarceration of their father, where children of incarcerated mothers are more likely to live with someone other than their father (which 28 per cent do) (Mumola, 2000). It would seem logical that caregivers of children who have changed caregivers due to parental incarceration are much less likely to provide a distorted explanation or no explanation at all.

The low rate of physical contact between prisoners and their children may also support the hypothesis of widespread secrecy. Only 20–25 per cent of US prisoner parents have monthly or more frequent visits with their children, and the majority of parents in prison have never had a visit from their children since their admission (Mumola, 2000). The reasons for this low contact likely include a range of explanations that are both consistent with pervasive family secrecy, as well as a variety of other explanations such as prohibitive travel costs, lack of meaningful relationship, or the unwillingness of the custody holder to support contact (Smith, 2014). Hutton's chapter in this volume provides further insight into the challenges faced by visitors to prison.

If one begins with the assumption that caregivers seek to optimize their child's best interest, and that decisions that appear inconsistent with this aim are due to ignorance or external barriers, this decision can be seen as not at all surprising. Parents might be concerned that a child may not be developmentally ready to receive this information (Crenshaw and Lee, 2011), that it will cause distress, that it may damage their relationship with the incarcerated parent, or that a child will tell others and be ill-treated or otherwise stigmatized (e.g. by teachers). In my conversations with caregivers of children of prisoners, reasons for lying that were less active decisions emerged, such as wanting to wait until the outcome of a trial in case the parent was acquitted; these lies was therefore a type of denial, 'vital lie' (Cohen, 2001). Given the oppression and marginalization more likely to be faced by families of prisoners, who are more likely to be Black or Indigenous, living in poverty, and have lower educational attainment, this fear of mistreatment by figures in authority is unsurprising (Juristat, 2009, 2015; Statistics Canada, 2007; Glaze and Maraschuk, 2008; Murray and Farrington, 2005; Social Exclusion Unit, 2002). Caregivers may be also be prioritizing short-term goals or delaying full explanations when making the decision not to tell children about parental incarceration. Given the uncertain and chaotic nature of initial periods of incarceration, such as prior to bail decisions being made, caregivers may feel that children need not be told about parental incarceration that is not (or hoped not to be) long term.

This seemingly pervasive lying to children about their incarceration caregivers is not innocuous. First, a widespread practice of lying to children about their parent's incarceration suggests that caregivers understand parental incarceration as needing to be kept secret because this knowledge would present risks or vulnerabilities for their children. Both the reasons for these fears and whether they are borne out present significant concerns and need for attention. Second, the decision to keep the incarcerated parent's whereabouts a secret from a child is not a neutral choice; it may have negative emotional implications for children. Arditti (2012, 104) notes that secrecy towards children about their parent's incarceration, due to families colluding to keep secrets and not socially validating the child's experience of loss, contributed to the disenfranchised nature of the grief they experience. Loss that is disenfranchised is thought to inhibit the progress and resolution of that grief (Doka, 1989). Scholars warn that children may also experience anger, frustration, distrust, and fear associated with being lied to about a parent being in prison and (Robertson, 2007; Glover, 2009; Ayre et al., 2006; Loureiro, 2010; Katz, 2002). A key informant in the present study, a mental health professional around the prison system, links parents' decisions to lie to their own confusion with the system, but notes the harm this may pose to children:

> If they think their parent has just chosen a job somewhere to go to construction or is working in a prison and you only get to see [them there]. So is the child thinking, 'did you choose a job far away rather than be with me?' (Key informant 2)

Finally studies on children experiencing other types of loss further support the possibility that lying to children about parental incarceration may be harmful to children. For example, research into children's experience of divorce and other family transitions have highlighted the gulf between parents' and children's perceptions about how well an event or transition has been explained (Dunn et al., 2001; Smart, 2002), as well as children's desire to be heard and resentment at poor communication by their caregivers (Pryor and Rodgers, 2001; Dunn et al., 2001; Smart, 2002).

In this vein, one participant in the present study, 17-year-old Josh, reported that when he found out that his mother was in prison, one of his main concerns was that his caregiver (his maternal aunt) had lied to him about his mother's whereabouts:

> Then my mom told me, she was, was like, 'yeah I was in the hospital for the time your aunt's letting you know I was in the hospital. Just recently I actually got put into the prison.' So I was like, 'oh okay, makes sense, lovely. She didn't lie to me or anything?' I was like 'okay cool, that's all I want to know, makes sense'. (Josh, 17)

Secrecy by children in their communities

While secrecy from children about parental incarceration was an anecdotal element of my study, secrets kept *by* children about their parent in prison was a significant finding; every child participant reported that keeping their parent's incarceration secret from everyone outside the home was their default response; most told no one but closest friends, and all of those who disclosed did so with caution. Children all seemed to understand their parent's incarceration to be a risky or vulnerable piece of information to them, even if some could not articulate the risk it posed. Some had been explicitly instructed by caregivers to keep this a secret. Ten-year-old Darcy reported:

> *Do you tell anyone, any of your friends that dad is in prison?*
>
> No.
>
> *Is it a secret?*
>
> Hmm ... I'm not sure 'cause my mom just said 'don't tell people'.
>
> *Gotcha. What do you think about that?*
>
> I think that it's right 'cause like ... I'm not sure. I just think it's right. (Darcy, 10)

The children who were able to describe the reasons for their secrecy did so in three broad categories: First, several feared negative responses such as ridicule or shaming. For example, 10-year-old Sophia reported that she did not tell others 'Cause I thought that like they'd make fun of me about it'. Second, some older children reported a concern over potentially awkward or uncomfortable reactions. Fourteen-year-old Amy reported, for example, that she disliked being pitied for having a parent in prison, saying:

> And I don't like that, when people [say] 'oh I'm sorry'. I don't care if you're sorry for me, it's fine […] I'm not a big fan of [pity]. No, like it's, it's been like a whole life thing. (Amy, 14)

Finally, several children noted a concern about people finding out about their parent's incarceration due to the breach of privacy itself, regardless of any emotional or concrete impact. The harm here appears to be solely the thought process of the potential 'listener', regardless of what that person might do or say as a result. For example, 15-year-old Oliver explained:

> Like everybody that I know knows pretty much. But like only my, I only tell like certain things to my best friend. […] … Because I can trust him, not to tell anybody
>
> *Okay, okay. What would happen if somebody did tell somebody, like what's the concern? For you?*
>
> It wasn't their business to know. (Oliver, 15)

These findings are consistent with the research in this area; studies consistently find that children tend to keep parental incarceration a closely guarded secret from both peers and adults in their community (Lockwood and Raikes, 2015). Nesmith and Ruhland (2008) found that every participant in their study of thirty-four children and youths of prisoners reported concerns and confusion about whether to disclose to friends and teachers that they have a parent in prison. They presented as keenly aware of the risks and negative associations that this information holds and reported a desire for privacy. Another study found children expressing a desire to keep parental incarceration a secret from others and fear that others knowing would lead to bad consequences (Boswell, 2002).

This seemingly pervasive secrecy can have direct and indirect negative effects for children. First, secrecy prohibits community caregivers from the opportunity to provide potentially useful support. Ideally, having teachers, doctors, and other key caregiving figures in children's lives aware of their parental incarceration will provide them with insights into, and opportunities for responsive care to meet the child's emotional and behavioural needs. Effective social support networks have been shown to have an array of benefits to children's outcomes and wellbeing (Hagen and Myers, 2003).

> Connecting children's microsystems via increased communication between caring teachers and concerned caregivers could help improve children's outcomes, as children may have access to more caring individuals who are committed to helping them deal with their parent's incarceration. (Dallaire et al., 2010, 289).

Indeed, a few youths in one study reported positive experiences such as a new friendship and feelings of solidarity which resulted from finding another youth with a parent in prison after disclosing (Nesmith and Ruhland, 2008). The present study also found several children reported that when they did make the decision to tell others of their parent's incarceration, the experience was positive. Ten-year-old Phoebe reported the experience of telling a peer 'was awesome, to have friends on my side' and others found that adults could be surprising sources of support and reassurance.

Further, keeping secrets can in itself be an isolating, disconnecting experience and limit the ways in which these children can connect to, participate in, and be known to their communities. Studies of partners of prisoners have consistently found this group experiencing social isolation (Arditti et al., 2003; Condry, 2007; Smith et al., 2008).

Harter et al. (2005, 322) write about their similarly secretive subjects, homeless youths: 'when the hidden homeless remain invisible, their life experience too often are sequestered, opportunities for emancipation too often diminished, and potentialities too often suppressed rather than actualized'. Thus while efforts to pass as normal may be a tactic to meet short-term goals of relieving risk and discomfort, the invisibility of children of prisoners from their communities may exclude them, and have profoundly negative effects on their social capital.

However there is a counter perspective, that secrecy around parental incarceration is protective for children. Hagen and Myers (2003) studied a large sample of children of female prisoners and found that for children with low levels of social support, those who did not keep maternal incarceration a secret had higher internalizing and externalizing problem scores. That is, those children with few people to talk to but who spoke freely about their mother being in prison had the worst outcomes. They note that keeping secrets is a normal, pervasive, and positive developmental step for children, and further that parents requiring that their children keep this potentially stigmatizing information secret may be wise and protective (Hagen and Myers, 2003).

One explanation for this last finding is that secrecy about parental incarceration is an effective stigma management tool and that stigma is damaging to children's outcomes. Stigma, the convergence of labelling, stereotyping, and separation (Link and Phelan, 2001), is a concept that has been widely applied by researchers to aid in understanding familial incarceration—including in the chapter by Hutton in this volume—some arguing that stigma may be one of the mediators of negative outcomes in children of prisoners (Hannem, 2010; Phillips and Gates, 2011; Hagan and Foster, 2012; Arditti, 2012). Studies of the partners of prisoners have similarly found that they experience shame and stigma through association with, or 'contamination' by, the offender (Condry, 2007; Nesmith and Ruhland, 2008; Cunningham, 2001; Lowenstein, 1986). Harter et al. (2005) describe the serious lengths that their similar respondents, homeless youths, went to in their efforts at secrecy, to 'remain invisible and thereby pass as normal rather than deviant ... when participants shed their protective anonymity, they risk stigmatisation'.

This fear may be well-founded. In an intriguing study, Dallaire et al. (2010) found that teachers who assessed a fictional student describe a student whose mother is away in prison as less competent than a student whose mother is away for other reasons. Further, the teachers, all of whom expressed support and care about students with a parent in prison, reported concerns that *other* teachers would have lower expectations of and stigmatize these students (Dallaire et al., 2010).

However secrecy may, in a circular fashion, reinforce the very stigmatizing attributes that children seek to hide. Harter et al. (2005) note that: 'Stigmatization not only creates definitions of acceptable and non-acceptable individuals and groups, it creates powerful cognitive maps of acceptable and non-acceptable places (and the types of people to be encountered in particular social settings).' Children of prisoners learn that incarceration is socially negative and any connection to prisons a negative attribute, but through their secrecy, they reinforce for themselves and others that prisons and prisoners require secrecy. Their efforts at self-protection through secrecy render children of prisoners invisible to the communities with which they interact, and may contribute to the notable lack of policy attention to the topic of parental incarceration;

in turn, the lack of policy attention to parental incarceration and lack of government funded or provided programming in Canada (described further below) may contribute to children feeling invisible and isolated. In this way, the invisibility of children of prisoners becomes contagious, systemically crossing through the layers of children's lives.

Lack of community between prisoners' families

Another element of the invisibility of children of prisoners is the lack of political organizing or advocacy by and for this group in the public sphere. Unlike other groups of parents with concerns about the ways their children are being treated by state systems, caregivers of children who have a parent in prison appear, in Canada, to rarely engage in resisting, organizing, or even meeting each other (Knudsen, 2016).

There are a variety of practical issues that may prevent the formation of connections and sense of 'community' between family members of prisoners. The nature of being a prisoner's family member means that one only meets peers in person if paths cross in the strange space of prison waiting rooms. If prisoners' families find each other online, the initial period of remand may be marked by much confusion, or hopes that the situation is temporary (and thus not be worth investing in forging new peer relationships). Moreover, the common denominator between them is highly negative and unwanted, and stigma or fear may also prevent efforts to meet others. These families may also simply be too exhausted to take on advocacy activities; given the demands on their finances, time, and emotions that are involved in having a loved one in prison, there may be no resources left with which to enact resistance.

Further, while families of prisoners share a greater likelihood of facing social risks such as poverty, they are far from homogenous in other aspects of their lives, experiences, and interests. Wacquant (2016, 1078) warns:

> The sociology of marginality must fasten not on vulnerable 'groups' (which often exist merely on paper, if that) but on the institutional mechanisms that produce, reproduce and transform the network of positions to which its supposed members are dispatched and attached. And it urges us to remain agnostic as to the particular social and spatial configuration assumed by the resulting district of dispossession. In particular, we cannot presume that the emerging social entity is a 'community' (implying at minimum a shared surround and identity, horizontal social bonds and common interests), even a community of fate, given the diversity of social trajectories that lead into and out of such areas.

While peer support groups, which exist in many jurisdictions, might seem to be effective in supporting prisoners' partners to advocate for themselves and their families' rights, this does not necessarily constitute collective resistance faced by families of prisoners, both because it may not challenge systemic stigma or other repressive structures, and because, as Cornish (2006) notes, the advocacy is not widely known.

Cornish (2006) argues that self-stigma is challenged by problematising it, through using the language of rights, showing equivalencies with other repressed groups and movements which have successfully organised for change, and showing the group's own positive achievements. It is interesting, then, that existing organisations working with families of prisoners tend not problematise the treatment of prisoners' families by prison systems, at least in their public materials (Knudsen, 2016). For example, the security processes faced by visitors is widely presented as challenging but necessary, infallible and politically neutral.

As these groups would be the natural source for organizing collective resistance, their lack of criticism and problematization is not benign. Organized resistance has the potential to improve the conditions faced by aggrieved groups, but even if ineffective at promoting change in conditions, these actions can 'give voice' to invisible groups. In this way, the processes that pose barriers to organizing, both pragmatic and structural, contribute to the invisibility of families of prisoners at the political and policy level.

Invisibility in prison and children's policy

The invisibility of children of prisoners in Canada runs deeper than can be explained by their and their caregivers' individual secrecy. As researchers began to explore the outcomes of parental incarceration in the 1990s and 2000s, the data suggested that children of prisoners faced gravely poor outcomes, and the sheer number of these children with the late modern penal explosion meant that even small differences were massively consequential. Murray (2006, 771) writes that these findings:

> ... should have prompted large-scale epidemiological and intervention studies to assess the risks associated with parental imprisonment and to evaluate programs aimed at supporting prisoners' children. Penal and social policies should have been implemented to prevent harmful effects on children. Neither the research nor the social policy has been forthcoming.

While this appears to be starting to change in Europe, Canadian children of prisoners have not been recognized in social policy, they are markedly absent from a variety of discussions, policies, and systems in which they would be expected to be recognized, and their absence causes contradictions in stated policy intentions. Formal policies and legislation around Canadian prisons, at both the federal and provincial level, make virtually no mention of children of prisoners (Knudsen, 2016), as Oldrup and Frederikson note was the case in European states until the 2000s (Oldrup and Frederikson, this volume).

Even policies that are seemingly explicitly about children, such as the Canadian Mother–Child programme, which allows women prisoners to reside with their young children inside federal institutions under certain conditions, is marked by an absence of children. The programme is extremely difficult to access and thus consistently 'hardly used' since its 2001 inception; the part-time programme in particular has been 'rarely used' at any point (Brennan, 2014). There are around 900 women incarcerated in federal institutions (Juristat, 2015), around half of them mothers, and the programme (both its full and part-time iterations) has been used by an average of 2.9 mothers per year since its inception (Brennan, 2014.).

Children of prisoners are also absent from the broader children and family policy context. While this group of children can easily be described as high needs and high risk, and number in the hundreds of thousands, they simply do not exist in Canadian social policy (Knudsen, 2016). There is no special mention of this group in government documentation at the Ontario provincial or federal level, despite both levels of government having a stated focus on supporting children and families, and making special mention of a variety of other sub-groups of children who have special needs or interests (Canada, 2015; Government of Ontario, 2015). Systems and institutions in Canada who would seem to have an interest in understanding and attending to this particularly vulnerable group of children similarly, such as primary education Boards and child welfare agencies, appear to have no policy, research, or programming related specifically to children of prisoners.

Similarly, there is a marked paucity of research about Canadian families of prisoners. While there has been an explosion of research in this area internationally in recent years, rigorous research into parental incarceration of Canadian children continues to be virtually non-existent (Bayes, 2002; McCormick et al., 2014. Exceptions include these aforementioned sources, and Withers and Folsom, 2007). This is undoubtedly related to the lack of available data to work from; like the Irish system described by Parkes and Donson in this volume, neither the Canadian federal system nor the Ontario provincial system keep any recorded statistics on children, parenting status, or visits of their prisoners. Lack of research evidence can, in turn, only support the lack of prison policy or broader social policy attention to children of prisoners.

Understanding children of prisoners' systemic invisibility

Having described the ways in which children of prisoners are rendered invisible in all of the layers of their lives, from the micro to the macro level, and several ways in which these layers of invisibility are interconnected, I seek now to consolidate these arguments, suggesting that this invisibility is systemic.

I suggest that the secrecy around parental incarceration is both pervasive and contagious. As argued above, the widespread secrecy from and by children about their parent's incarceration may contribute to a broader ignorance by the communities that serve them about parental incarceration. This in turn may contribute to the large-scale paucity of attention to children of prisoners by the many people, organizations and systems who would otherwise be considered knowledgeable about the experiences of marginalized children or criminalized people, such as child welfare agencies, or prisoner rights organizations. Perhaps the relationship may also travel in the other direction; the profound lack of Canadian programming, policy, or research may affect children's decisions to disclose parental incarceration to peers and teachers by communicating implicitly that this is an unknown, misunderstood, and even shameful topic. I posit three overarching reasons that contribute to children of prisoners being rendered invisible at every level.

1. Intersecting Invisibility

The lack of research data, public policy, and programming focused on children of prisoners stands in sharp contrast to the amount of data, policy, and programming focused on prisoners themselves. Indeed, stigma cannot be the main reason for the lack of policy and programme attention to children of prisoners.

Purdie-Vaughns and Eibach's (2008) concept of intersectional invisibility provides a useful explanation. Specifically, they argue that less prototypical members of oppressed groups that also belong to another subordinate group are not recognized as members of either group. Like any group, people connected by subordination are heterogeneous, subject to internal power hierarchies that see the most powerful members as controlling elites, even if they occupy a limited social space as a group (Hannem, 2012). In this way, the marginal members of marginalized groups become 'acutely socially invisible' (Purdie-Vaughns and Eibach, 2008). Cornish (2006) notes that 'the most profound stigmatisation often occurs at the intersection of multiple forms of exclusion'. This corresponds to Crenshaw's work on intersectionality, which argues that there is a unique marginalization at the intersection of forms of oppression such as racism and sexism (Crenshaw, 2002).

I suggest that intersectional invisibility contributes to the absence of any significant advocacy work, research, service provision, or other attention to children of prisoners in Canada. Children are clearly marginal and less powerful members (in both abstract and practical terms) of groups that include adults. Their interests are particularly rendered invisible when they are assumed to have identical interests to the more powerful members of a series of more specific groups: the criminalized, secondarily criminalized people, or even the family of an individual prisoner.

Children's interests may fail to be privileged even in services that explicitly seek to support them. For example, many jurisdictions offer transportation or visiting services aimed explicitly at supporting or even encouraging children to visit incarcerated parents. However this approach to prison visits is grounded in several uncritical and unfounded beliefs. One is that visits are always and necessarily beneficial to children and that prisoners' and children's interests and wishes coincide. While it is certainly the case that family visits are beneficial for prisoners, having been shown to reduce violence and recidivism (Schafer, 1994; Bales and Mears, 2008; Derkzen et al., 2009), the outcomes of children of prisoners is much less clearly positive. Poehlmann's (2005) study found negative emotional outcomes associated with children visiting prisons in some situations, and Poehlmann et al.'s (2010) review of the literature on visiting a parent in prison found that the research suggested that visits with incarcerated parents in non-'child-friendly' visitation environments are associated with attachment concerns, and attention and behavioural problems. Thus, any blanket recommendation that children visit incarcerated parents, or programme that seeks to encourage visits to take place without support or assessment is privileging the prisoner's and the prison service's interests over the child's.

Another problematic belief is that prisoners' needs for reintegration success is a goal for which a child's visit can and ought to be a means, an issue of instrumentalizing discussed in the chapters by Hutton and Loucks and Loureiro in this volume. Codd (2007, 258) notes the concerns about using children as tools to increase the wellbeing and interests of their parent: 'it is more appropriate to support families for their own sake, rather than as instruments of penal policy'. To become 'visible', children must be both attended to in policy and practice, but also have their needs and wishes privileged as worthy in themselves.

i. Less accountability

Another reason for the invisibility of children of prisoners in the criminal justice system is, I argue, that it serves the needs of this system for these children to be unknown, empirically. As noted, no quantifiable data is collected about Canadian children of prisoners or parenting in prison and without basic knowledge about families of prisoners, it is possible to not take (or be given) any responsibility for their wellbeing or outcomes. A senior official responded as follows to my questions about the lack of available data about children of prisoners:

> We don't know. If you were to ask me the question how many have children and age ranges and what happens to them, and are they involved in child welfare or Children's Aid Societies, I could not tell you.
>
> *Why?*
>
> Let me be careful but, it serves no purpose to know ... (Key informant 1)

The data, if known, could lead to the government being given challenging responsibilities for children of prisoners' wellbeing and for addressing the impact of parental incarceration. For example, public awareness of the numbers and plight of children of prisoners could create political pressure to provide a variety of services and supports. Further, basic data about children of prisoners, combined with recognition of their needs and outcomes, could lead to administrative, judicial, or quasi-judicial demands that children of prisoners be treated as clients of the prison service. This would not be unfounded; children enter prisons, are subject to prison rules, enter into communication with prison residents which is mediated by the prison, and are profoundly emotionally and materially affected by prison policies. That the prison service has responsibilities to its child visitors can certainly be argued, as Donson and Parkes set out in the European context in this volume.

If children of prisoners were seen as secondary clients of the prison service, responsibilities would be a high financial cost in the short term; providing, for example, transportation services, financial resources to support family visiting, further visiting options including video visits, structured and supported family visits, bespoke programming for child of prisoners, would all be associated with high financial cost, particularly in development. These costs may actually also be a wise long-term financial investment, potentially recuperated through lower recidivism rates, and meet other correctional and social justice goals, however short political cycles may make such investments unattractive.

In addition to financial costs, responsibility for children of prisoners might be seen as adding to the risk and liability faced by the prison service. If 40,000 Canadian children became clients of the prison service, and their wellbeing and outcomes thereby fell under the purview and mandate of the service, a secondary concern after cost might likely be the security risks and other changes the prison would see this as presenting. Watson (2015, 342) argues that the Correctional Service of Canada (CSC) resists research by external sources in an effort to avoid criticism, transparency, and change: 'Asking for [in her case] staff perceptions could potentially open a door to problems or criticisms that would demand organisational attention and modification of the status quo.' Remaining in the 'knowing-not knowing' state allows the institution to deny a potentially uncomfortable state (Cohen, 2001).

The prison system has also long been argued to take an actuarial approach, reducing prisoners to their risk assessment (Hannah-Moffatt, 2016). Lives reduced to actuarial rates and devoid of social context are surely less messy to manage. A striking piece of evidence of this faith in actuarial assessments, and reluctance to discuss experiences is found in Watson's (2015) case study of her failed attempt to gain research access to federal prisons. She received the following response from CSC to her proposal to ask staff about their perceptions (of substance abuse programming):

CSC currently uses a variety of actuarial tools to assess change and the impact of a program, which have been demonstrated to be more effective than clinical assessment. Accordingly, the basis for asking for opinions is not supported by research. (Quoted in Watson 2015, 342)

Munn (2012) invokes Foucault to argue that prisoners' lives are lived under regulation, discipline, and surveillance, all through the language of risk assessment but which, she suggests, sends the message of undesirability and unfitness. Reduced to their level of cost, liability, and risk to the institution is, like being reduced to their utility, surely a process of dehumanization, rendering children of prisoners invisible.

ii. Political utility

The final reason for the invisibility of children in penal policy is, I suggest, that the construction of prisoners as parents is incompatible and disruptive to the political narrative of criminals in late modernity. The invisibility of children of prisoners therefore serves the ideological needs of the system. Canadian criminal justice policy has changed dramatically since the Conservative Party formed the first of three consecutive governments in 2006. An explicit push by that government to change the penal landscape of the country saw a myriad of legislative changes in line with the punitive trend across English-speaking and Western European countries.

The government introduced broad-ranging mandatory minimum prison sentences, actively resisted research- and court-supported safe injection sites, and introduced a 'dangerous offender' designation which allows prisoners to be kept incarcerated indefinitely (CBC, 2011). The 2015 Election platform by the incumbent Conservative Party continued to use criminal justice policy as a major election issue and to use a punitivism narrative with a promise to introduce 'Life means life' legislation (removal of parole for certain life sentences) and attack the other two major political parties for their criminal justice stances. While the centrist Liberal Party gained power in 2015 and campaigned on promises to reverse some of these Law and Order policies, they have, to date, failed to take any meaningful action (Brown and Lacy, 2018).

Under this ideology, criminals are constructed as unredeemable, deviant 'others,' and people in prison exemplify the extreme binary on which the punitive Law and Order approach to criminal justice relies. In this normative and strict binary, the category of 'criminal' is constructed as mutually exclusive from other law-abiding and hardworking citizens. This is seen in the frequent use of a 'zero-sum game' to suggest that criminals having rights harms or preclude the rights of victims (Reiner, 2007). For example, one press release stated that another party leader's 'dangerous, ideology driven criminal justice policy would make our communities less safe by putting the so-called "rights" of criminals ahead of the rights of victims' (Conservative Party of Canada, 2015). This narrative crosses through layers of Canadians' lives, impacting or reflecting everything from policy to service, to everyday conversation.

To this strict binary, the presence of children and parenting roles is, I would argue, disruptive. Outside of the prison context, young children are constructed as universally innocent, and parenting as valuable and worthy of policy support. Further, parenting is profoundly human and complex, an irreconcilable contrast to the construction of prisoners as narrowly deviant, less-human 'others.'

Giddens (1984, 192) describes ideology as functioning to legitimate and favour dominant interests by constructing narrow interests as universal, denying contradictions, and bolstering existing social structures. As such, children of prisoners and prisoners' parenting roles certainly present a contradiction to the current criminal justice ideology and thus rendering these invisible, from the micro to the macro level, is a method of maintain the ideology's legitimation and sense.

Conclusion

This chapter has outlined an argument that children of prisoners are 'invisible' at a variety of levels of their lives. Secrecy by and towards these children renders them hidden in their families and communities, and lack of policy and data hides them from public debate or attention. These types of invisibility may be interconnected and be exacerbated by factors, such as intersectional invisibility, as well as the liability and ideological interests that these children's absence may serve for prison systems. The breadth and reach of this absence across and between the micro to the macro level suggests it is a systemic invisibility. This invisibility is likely to be far from innocuous; children of prisoners deserve the practical and abstract benefits of being recognized, heard, and valued.

References

Adalist-Estrin, A., 2014. *Fact and issues: Questions Children Ask. Children of Incarcerated Parents Library Factsheet*. National Resource Centre on Children and Families of the Incarcerated. Available at: http://nrccfi.camden.rutgers.edu/files/cipl103-conversations-questionschildrenask.pdf.

Arditti, J. A. 2012. *Parental Incarceration and the Family*. New York: New York University Press.

Arditti, J. A., Lambert-Shute, J., and Joest, K. 2003. 'Saturday Mornings at the Jail: Implications of Incarceration for Families and Children'. *Family Relations*, 52(3), 195–204.

Ayre, E., Gampell, L., and Smith, P. S. 2011. 'Introduction', in Smith, P. S. and Gampell, L. (eds.) *Children of Imprisoned Parents*. Denmark. 3–11. The Danish Institute for Human Rights, European Network for Children of Imprisoned Parents, University of Elster and Bambinisenzasbarre.

Bales, W. D. and Mears, D. P. 2008. 'Inmate Social Ties and the Transition to Society: Does Visitation Reduce Recidivism?'. *Journal of Research in Crime and Delinquency*, 45(3), 287–321.

Bayes, S. 2002. *A Snowball's Chance: Children of Offenders and Canadian Social Policy*. Vancouver: Elizabeth Fry Society of Greater Vancouver.

Boswell, G. 2002. 'Imprisoned Fathers: The Children's View'. *The Howard Journal*, 41(1), 14–26.

Brennan, S. 2014. 'Canada's Mother-Child Program: Examining Its Emergence, Usage and Current State'. *Canadian Graduate Journal of Sociology and Criminology*, 3(1), 11–33.

Brown, D. and Lacy, M. 2018. 'Trudeau Government is Falling Short on Justice reform'. *The Toronto Star*. 30 January. Available at: https://www.thestar.com/opinion/contributors/2018/01/30/trudeau-government-is-falling-short-on-justice-reform.html.

Caddle, D. and Crisp, D. 1997. *Imprisoned Women and Mothers*. Home Office Research Study 162. London: Home Office.

Canada, Government of. 2015b. *Helping Families Prosper*. Available at: https://www.budget.gc.ca/efp-peb/2014/overview-apercu-eng.html.

Canadian Families and Corrections Network (CFCN), n.d. 'Telling the Children: How to talk to Children about a loved One's Incarceration'. Available at: https://www.cfcn-rcafd.org/resources-children.

CBC. 2011. 'Tory Crime Bill Cracks Down on Drug, Sex Offences'. 20 September. Available at: http://www.cbc.ca/news/politics/tory-crime-bill-cracks-down-on-drug-sex-offences-1.1003225.

Christensen, E. 1999. *Forældre i fængsel—en undersøgelse af børn og forældres erfaringer*. Copenhagen: Socialforskningsinstituttet.

Codd, H. 2007. 'Prisoners' Families and Resettlement: A Critical Analysis'. *The Howard Journal of Criminal Justice*, 46(3), 255–63.

Cohen, S. 2001. *States of Denial: Knowing about Atrocities and Suffering*. Cambridge: Polity.

Condry, R. 2007. *Families Shamed: The Consequences of Crime for Relatives of Serious Offenders*. Cullompton: Willan.

Conservative Party of Canada. 2015. 'Harper Announces "Life Means Life" as his Government's Top Justice Priority'. Press Release. 18 August. Available at: http://www.conservative.ca/harper-announces-life-means-life-as-his-governments-top-justice-priority/.

Cornish, F. 2006. 'Challenging the Stigma of Sex Work in India: Material Context and Symbolic Change'. *Journal of Community & Applied Social Psychology*, 16(6), 462–71.

Crenshaw, D. A. and Lee, J. 2011. 'The Disenfranchised Grief of Children', in Webb, N. B. (ed.) *Helping Bereaved Children: A Handbook for Practitioners*. 91–108. (3rd ed.). New York: Guilford Press.

Crenshaw, K. W. 2002. 'First Decade: Critical Reflections, or a Foot in the Closing Door'. *The UCLA Law Review*, 49, 1343–72.

Cunningham, A. 2001. 'Forgotten Families—The Impacts of Imprisonment'. *Family Matters*, 59, 35–8.

Dallaire, D. H., Ciccone, A., and Wilson, L. C. 2010. 'Teachers' Experiences with and Expectations of Children with Incarcerated Parents'. *Journal of Applied Developmental Psychology*, 31(4), 281–90.

Derkzen, D. M., Gobeil, R., and Gileno, J. 2009. *Visitation and Post-Release Outcome among Federally-Sentenced Offenders*. Correctional Service of Canada.

Doka, K. J. 1989. *Disenfranchised Grief: Recognizing Hidden Sorrow*. Lexington, MA: Lexington Press.

Dunn, J., Davies, L. C., O'Connor, T. G., and Sturgess, W. 2001. 'Family Lives and Friendships: The Perspectives of Children in Step-, Single-Parent, and Nonstep Families'. *Journal of Family Psychology*, 15(2), 272–87.

Garland, D. 2001. *The Culture of Control: Crime and Social Order in Contemporary Society*. Oxford: Clarendon Press.

Giddens, A. 1984. *The Constitution of Society: Outline of the Theory of Structuration*. Berkley: University of California Press.

Glaze, L. and Maruschak, L. 2008. *Parents in Prison and Their Minor Children*. US Department of Justice, Bureau of Justice Statistics.

Glover, J. 2009. *Every Night you Cry: The Realities of Having a Parent in Prison*. Barnado's Believe in Children Report. Available at: http://www.barnardos.org.uk/everynightyoucry_briefing_final_double.pdf.

Government of Ontario. 2015. 'Ontario Launches Enhanced Youth Action Plan'. News Release. 26 June. Available at: https://news.ontario.ca/mcys/en/2015/06/ontario-launches-enhanced-youth-action-plan.html.

Hagan, J. and Foster, H. 2012. 'Children of the American Prison Generation: Student and School Spillover Effects of Incarcerating Mothers'. *Law & Society Review*, 46(1), 37–69.

Hagen, K. A. and Myers, B. J. 2003. 'The Effect of Secrecy and Social Support on Behavioral Problems in Children of Incarcerated Women'. *Journal of Child and Family Studies*, 12(2), 229–42.

Hairston, C. 2002. 'Prisoners and Families: Parenting Issues During Incarceration'. Paper presented at the US Department of Health and Human Services conference: 'From Prison to Home: The Effect of Incarceration and Reentry on Children, Families and Communities', January.

Hannah-Moffat, K. 2016. 'A Conceptual Kaleidoscope: Contemplating "Dynamic Structural Risk" and an Uncoupling of Risk from Need'. *Psychology, Crime & Law*, 22(1), 33–46.

Hannem, S. 2010. 'Stigma, Marginality, Gender and the Families of Male Prisoners in Canada', in Doyle, A. and Moore, D. (eds.) *Critical Criminology in Canada: New Voices, New Directions*. 183–218. Vancouver: University of British Columbia Press.

Hannem, S. 2012. 'The Mark of Association: Transferred Stigma and the Families of Male Prisoners', in Hannem, S. and Bruckert, C. (eds.) *Stigma Revisited: Implications of the Mark*. 95–117. Ottawa: University of Ottawa Press.

Harter, L. M., Berquist, C., Scott Titsworth, B., Novak, D., and Brokaw, T. 2005. 'The Structuring of Invisibility among the Hidden Homeless: The Politics of Space, Stigma, and Identity Construction'. *Journal of Applied Communication Research*, 33(4), 305–27.

Juristat. 2015. *Adult Correctional Services Survey 2013/2014*. Canadian Centre for Justice Statistics, Statistics Canada.

Katz, A. 2002 'Parents in Prison'. *Criminal Justice Matters*, 50(1), 18–19.

Knudsen, E. M. 2016. *The Experiences of Canadian Children of Prisoners*. PhD thesis, The London School of Economics and Political Science.

Link, B. G. and Phelan, J. C. 2001. 'Conceptualizing Stigma'. *Annual Review of Sociology*, 27(1), 363–85.

Lockwood, K. and Raikes, B. 2015. 'A Difficult Disclosure: The Dilemmas Faced by Families Affected by Parental Imprisonment Regarding What Information to Share', in Reeves, C. (ed.) *Experiencing Imprisonment: Research on the Experience of Living and Working in Carceral Institutions*. 230–47. London: Routledge.

Loureiro, T. 2010. *Perspectives of Children and Young People with a Parent in Prison*. Scotland's Commission for Children and Young People.

Lowenstein, A. 1986. 'Temporary Single Parenthood—The Case of Prisoners' Families'. *Family Relations*, 35(1), 79–85.

McCormick, A. V., Millar, H. A., and Paddock, G. B. 2014. 'In the Best Interests of the Child: Strategies for Recognizing and Supporting Canada's At-risk Population of Children with Incarcerated Parents'. University of the Fraser Valley. Centre for Safe Schools and Communities.

Mumola, C. 2000. *Incarcerated Parents and Their Children* (NCJ-182335). Washington, DC: Department of Justice.

Munn, M. 2012. 'The Mark of Criminality Rejections and Reversals, Disclosure and Distance: Stigma and the Ex-Prisoner', in Hannem, S. and Bruckert, C. (eds.) *Stigma Revisited: Implications of the Mark*. University of Ottawa Press. 147–69.

Murray, J. 2006. 'Review: All Alone in the World: Children of the Incarcerated'. *British Journal of Criminology*, 46(4), 771–74.

Murray, J. and Farrington, D. P. 2005. 'Parental Imprisonment: Effects on Boys' Antisocial Behaviour and Delinquency Through the Life-Course'. *Journal of Child Psychology and psychiatry*, 46(12), 1269–78.

Nesmith, A. and Ruhland, E. 2008. 'Children of Incarcerated Parents: Challenges and Resiliency, in Their Own Words'. *Children and Youth Services Review*, 30(10), 1119–30.

Phillips, S. D. and Gates, T. 2011. 'A Conceptual Framework for Understanding the Stigmatization of Children of Incarcerated Parents'. *Journal of Child and Family Studies*, 20(3), 286–94.

Poehlmann, J. 2005. 'Representations of Attachment Relationships in Children of Incarcerated Mothers'. *Child Development*, 76(3), 679–96.

Poehlmann, J., Dallaire, D., Loper, A. B., and Shear, L. D. 2010. 'Children's Contact with Their Incarcerated Parents: Research Findings and Recommendations'. *American Psychologist*, 65(6), 575–98.

Prison Talk Online. 2017. 'When to tell children'. Bulletin Board Post. Available at: http://www.prisontalk.com/forums/showthread.php?t=683883.

Pryor, J., and Rodgers, B. 2001. *Children in Changing Families: Life After Parental Separation*. Oxford: Wiley-Blackwell.

Purdie-Vaughns, V. and Eibach, R. P. 2008. 'Intersectional Invisibility: The Distinctive Advantages and Disadvantages of Multiple Subordinate-Group Identities'. *Sex Roles*, 59(5–6), 377–91.

Reiner, R. 2007. *Law and Order: An Honest Citizen's Guide to Crime and Control*. London: Polity.

Robertson, O. 2007. *The Impact of Parental Imprisonment on Children*. Geneva: Quaker United Nations Office.

Schafer, N. E. 1994. 'Exploring the Link between Visits and Parole Success: A Survey of Prison Visitors'. *International Journal of Offender Therapy & Comparative Criminology*, 38(1), 17–32.

Smith, P. 2014. *When the Innocent are Punished: The Children of Imprisoned Parents*. Basingstoke: Palgrave Macmillan.

Smart, C. 2002. 'From Children's Shoes to Children's Voices'. *Family Court Review*, 40(3), 307–19.

Smith, R., Grimshaw, R., Romeo, R., and Knapp, M. 2008. 'Prisoners' Families: Civic Virtue and Policies of Impoverishment'. *Benefits*, 16(1), 3–17.

Social Exclusion Unit. 2002. *Reducing Re-Offending by Ex-Prisoners*. Report. Available at: https://www.bristol.ac.uk/poverty/downloads/keyofficialdocuments/Reducing%20Reoffending.pdf.

Statistics Canada. 2007. *Population and Dwelling Counts, 2006 Census*. Statistics Canada Catalogue no. 97-550-XWE2006002. Ottawa, Ontario.

Wacquant, L. 2016. 'Revisiting Territories of Relegation: Class, Ethnicity and State in the Making of Advanced Marginality'. *Urban Studies*, 53(6), 1077–88.

Watson, T. M. 2015. 'Research Access Barriers as Reputational Risk Management: A Case Study of Censorship in Corrections'. *Canadian Journal of Criminology and Criminal Justice*, 57(3), 330–62.

Withers, L. and Folsom, J. 2007. Incarcerated Fathers: A Descriptive Analysis'. Research Report. Available at: http://publications.gc.ca/collections/collection_2010/scc-csc/PS83-3-186-eng.pdf.

Index

Note: Locator following *fig.* refers to figure

abuse
  child 10–11, 96, 136, 225
  from other children 91
  from the state 17, 133
  substance 42, 48, 59, 96, 107, 267, 269, 298
  verbal 189, 260
  of women 47, 267–8
  see also domestic violence
accountability 297–8
activities in contemporary family life 89
adaptation 249–52
addiction issues 8, 73, 146, 170, 173, 191, 267–8
  see also alcohol; drugs
adjustment 217
adoption (child) 13, 141
adulthood 90, 107, 198–9
  conceptions of 82
adversarial interactions 18, 122, 175
adverse outcomes 8, 183
affiliation 34, 37
African American population 28, 35, 42, 47–8, 58, 65
age
  adolescents and parental incarceration 67, 81, 93, 106, 174
  adult male prisoners 215–16, 225, 235, 273, 278–83
  child development 153
  dependent children 143, 162, 276
  infant mortality and 35
  sociological variable 10, 13, 19, 41, 159, 186, 214, 235, 248, 278
  substance abuse and 138
alcohol abuse 8, 107, 138, 188, 191
ambiguous loss 8, 249–51
  concept of 246
ambivalent emotions 10
  see also emotion
American Society of Criminology 2
Angiolini Commission on Women Offenders 155–6, 158
antisocial behaviour 8–9, 42, 107, 137, 153
arrest
  criminal justice contact 20, 66, 181, 197
  emotional effects of parental 18, 103, 122, 131, 153, 160
  house 159
  impact assessments 157
  pain and trauma of 190, 247–50
  police procedures 9–10
arts-based workshops 16, 226
Assault Definitive Guideline 138–9
attachment theory 11
Australia
  children of prisoners 16
  generations through prison 224
  housing 96
  imprisonment rates 67
  indigenous communities 16, 214
  PEMA survey 89
  social exclusion 91–2
  use of imprisonment 2, 181
  see also Vulnerable Families Project

Bangkok Rules 139, 156, 159, 201
behavioural problems 5, 7, 9, 15, 43, 50, 59–61, 96, 102, 111, 138, 140, 297
belonging
  visibility and 281–4
benefits agencies 18
'benefits of the least advantaged' 31–2
'best interests' principle 198, 206
  Better Outcomes, Brighter Futures: The National Policy Framework for Children and Young People 196
Black–White dichotomy 15, 58–67
  child wellbeing and inequality 60*fig.*
  comparisons 63–5
blended families 13
bodily health 33, 35
bodily integrity 34, 37
breach of duty of care 18
breadth 18, 181–5, 188–9, 191–3
British Society of Criminology 2

Canada
  imprisonment rates 67
  systemic invisibility 19, 288–300
Capabilities Approach 28, 33, 35
  substantive freedoms and 33–5

Care Assessment (Scotland) 155
care-giving arrangements 7, 19, 29
'causes vs effects' 8–9
change 252–5
   see also pains of imprisonment
Child and Family Impact Assessments
      (C&FIA) 152, 157, 159, 161
   attempts to introduce 156–8
   in Scotland 153–4
   tools 155–6
   see also Scotland
child development theories 105
child inequality
   material hardship and 45
   notions of 42–3
   parenting/caregiving quality 50
   system effects 95
Child Rights and Wellbeing Impact
      Assessments (CRWIA) 158
child rights approach
   to prison visits in Ireland 196–208
childcare 7, 44, 51, 82, 104, 171, 187, 198,
      262, 264
child-centred perspectives 102–15
   child-centred research
      approach 104–5
   context 102–4
   discussion 114–15
   methods 107–8
   results 109
   see also social exclusion
child-derived concepts 88–9
children's rights 17–18
   background to 136
   Irish prison visiting system 201–2
   primary carer sentencing 140–3
   principles 204, 207
   see also dependent children
citizenship 9, 18, 27–8, 30, 35–8, 83, 144,
      172–3, 176
   concept of 3
civic participation 2, 7, 41
civil liberties 28, 30–1, 196
   citizenship and 35–8
civil society 10
class advantage 19
   see also social class
co-desistance 224
coercion 3
cohabitation 13
collateral
   effects 2, 6, 12

consequences 1, 32, 126–7, 137–8, 140,
      150–4, 158, 167, 171, 181, 183, 188,
      191, 214, 231, 238, 273
   damage 18, 37, 123, 125, 226, 246, 290
communitarianism 145
community
   education principles 169, 177
   lack of between prisoners' families 294–5
   relations 167–78
confinement experience 20, 63, 66
'confounding grief' 19, 138
control over one's environment 34–5, 37
coping 244–56
   see also pains of imprisonment theory
corporal punishment 4
corrosive disadvantage 33
costs of incarceration 7
courtesy stigma 19–20, 188–9, 231,
      233–4, 240–2
   see also stigmatization
criminal history 19, 278
criminology 3–4, 7, 12, 14, 58, 125
cross-national comparisons 66–8
custodial citizenry 36

darkness 185–6
decent life 88
democracy 9, 32
   democratic society 2, 38
demographic characteristics 8, 28
Denmark
   Danish Institute for Human Rights 200
   data on families of prisoners 28
   imprisonment rates 67
   prison visits and supervision 277
   risk of maternal and paternal
      incarceration 67
   Scandinavian prison reform 200
   social and administrative
      exclusion 16, 102–14
   US–Danish comparisons 4, 15–16, 67, 127
Department of Corrections guidelines 277n
dependent children
   impact on 136–8
   international sentencing process 143–5
   sentencing process in England and
      Wales 138–40
depth 7, 18, 181–7, 191–2, 274
   definition of 182, 184
desert 28, 266
   concept of 31–2
   equality and 30–1

deterrence
    general 1–2, 197
    individual 1–2, 197
developmental science
    principles of 51
difference principle
    concept of 31–2
direct importation model 127
disadvantage
    cumulative 8, 29, 33, 173
    multiple 15–19, 95
    pre-existing 8, 28–9, 33, 44, 49, 90
discrimination 17, 29, 33–4, 38, 47, 131, 142, 201, 231, 233, 235–42, 260
    associative 241
    discriminatory practices 19–20
    race 35
    structural 236
    see also non-discrimination principle
disenfranchisement 8, 30, 33
    felon 35, 37
    see also voting restrictions
distance 185–6
divorce 13, 94–5, 106, 112, 141, 151, 284, 291
domestic violence 10–11, 29, 34, 267–8
    see also abuse
domination (institutional) 3, 28, 32–3
drugs
    controlled 203
    involvement with 138, 221–2, 230, 268, 282–3
    passing 174
    selling 81
    smuggling 204, 237–8
    see also abuse: substance; addiction issues
duration of imprisonment 9–10

ecological theory 42, 105, 111
economic deprivation 8, 225
economic impact of imprisonment 262–5
economic security 19
economic strain 7–8, 46
education
    attainment 8–9, 105, 214, 225, 290
    courses 16, 226
    parental 59
    see also community; training
'effects vs causes' 8–9
emotion 18, 34, 77, 127
    see also ambivalent emotions
employment 74, 77, 81–3, 107, 175, 225

    caregivers' 44–6
    effects of imprisonment on 8, 9
    exclusion of ex-offenders from 41
    history of 214
    restricted access to 2, 105, 193
    right to seek 34
    rules and regulations of 191
    under-employment 45
    unemployment 45, 51, 81, 96
    women's 45
equality
    concept of 31
    desert and 30–2
    see also family inequality
ethical duties of society 17
ethnicity 3, 10, 13, 19, 34, 63–4, 248, 259, 278–9
    imprisonment rates of male prisoners 64*fig*.
    incarceration by 64*fig*.
European Prison Rules 4, 199, 203, 276
exclusionary model 127–8
(ex)intimates 218–20
expenses 7, 45, 92, 106, 153, 263

fairness 3, 37, 168–9, 176–7, 246–7, 275
    justice as 31
family
    child-centred perspectives 106
    complexity of 19–20
    concept of 12, 96, 169, 219
    definitions of 12–14, 42–3, 216–17
    heterogeneity of 19–20
    membership 14–15
    punishment and society 2–3
    social organization and 5
    social relations and 109–10, 113
    state and society 17–19
    status of members 2
    'upside down' world of 123–4
family inequality 15
    background and significance 41–2
    definition of 46
    family instability 46–7
    recommendation to promote equality 50–2
    sources of 43–4
    in the United States 41–52
Family Inequality Framework (FIF) 41–6
    schema 44*fig*.
family life
    right to 17, 139–40, 156, 160, 200

family perspective 15, 17, 41, 132
family relationships 7–8, 275–6
family resources/processes 9n
family strengths
  definition of 52
Family Stress Proximal Process Model 43, 50
family stress theory 42–3, 46
family structure 7, 9, 46, 107–8, 112
family studies 3, 14
family type 109
  comparisons 113
  differences between prisoners' children 111–14
'fertile functioning' 33
finance
  hardship 8–9, 90
  help 18, 82
  problems 5, 187
foster care 7, 48–9, 65–6, 189, 214

gay marriage and parenting 13
gender
  background and context 73–4, 83
  constructions of masculinity 75–8
  dynamics among couples during and after prison 73–83
  financial pressures 80–3
  identity 77, 201
  lack of employment 80–3
  methods 75
  norms and roles 7, 16, 29, 248, 253–4, 259, 264
  of the offender 8
  of officers 239
  oppression 29
  prevalence of prison 216
  sociological variable 3, 10, 19, 41, 214, 235, 241
  see also women
'goodness' 34
guilt 10, 145, 171, 231, 263
  concept of 124

harm 17, 28–30, 32–3, 37–8
health 7
  bodily 33, 35
  healthcare 2, 34, 87, 90
  problems 8–9, 35, 48, 59, 61, 96, 108, 138, 146, 153
  see also mental health; physical health
heterogeneity of prisoners' families 19–20, 33, 49–50, 63, 65–6

Hispanics 15, 63–6
history of penal practice 3–4
'home' 222–4
homelessness 2, 6, 9, 15, 43, 59–61, 87, 90, 173, 225
housing 2, 51, 79, 81, 83, 96, 105–6, 140, 151, 160, 167, 214, 221, 225, 263, 284
  assistance 18
human rights 2, 17, 34
  approach 130–2, 269
  concept of 3
  context 121
  European Convention on 140, 156, 200, 232
  European Court of 140, 160, 200
  family and 121–33, 156n
  justice and 126–7
  law 232
  legitimacy and 126–7
  treaties 158, 198
  Universal Periodic Review of 140, 157
  see also Universal Declaration of Human Rights

identity
  children's 87–8
  gender 77, 201, 274
  of prisoners 246, 252, 255, 281–2
  of prisoners' families 187, 190, 235, 241
  social 138, 145, 232
  social visitors 235
  threats to 19
imagination 17, 34
impact on children 8, 155–8, 162
importation theory 274
Imposition of Community and Custodial Sentences: Definitive Guideline 2017 139
'imprisonment', definition of 12
incarceration history 279
  see also participant characteristics
'incarceration', definition of 12
income loss 7, 49
  see also finance
inequality see family inequality; intersectional inequality
infant mortality 7, 9, 15, 35, 43, 59–62, 66
Information and Communications Technologies (ICTs) 4
informed justice 130
  see also justice
insecure attachment 8

institutionalization 183, 188, 255
  concept of 28, 246
  institutional frameworks 145
  institutional practices 8
integrity 37, 80, 235, 241
  bodily 34
intensive parenting 13
intergenerational disadvantage 6–7
intergenerational incarceration 15–16
international imprisonment rates 67*fig.*
intersecting invisibility 296–9
  less accountability 297–8
  political utility 299
  see also invisibility
intersectional inequality 15–19
intersectional invisibility
  concept of 19, 296
intersectionality 296
invisibility
  in prison and children's policy 295–6
  see also intersecting invisibility; systemic invisibility
Irish prisons 18, 196–208
  children's rights 204–6
  children's rights within the Irish prison visiting system 201–2
  child visits and Irish prison policy 202–4
  context 196–7
  family visits 205–6
  opportunities 207–8
  prison perspectives 204–5
  state obligations 197–201
  tensions 207–8
isolation
  of imprisonment 4, 15, 129, 217, 282–3
  social 42, 95, 167, 182, 185, 273, 293

justice
  communitarian conception of 18
  concept of 121, 124
  enabling conception of 32
  as fairness theory 31
  idea of 192
  legitimacy and 126–7
  liberal theories of 145
  meaning of 2, 27
  naya (Indian concept) 192
  public sense of 126–7
  punishment vs 145–7
  'uninformed' and 'informed' senses of 130
  see also social justice

kin relationship 8, 19, 27, 36

labelling 233–5, 293
  definition of 233
  theories 11
legal cynicism 167
legitimacy 2–3, 18
  concept of 121, 126, 168, 177
  context 167–9, 177–8
  dialogical model of 176, 178
  effect of imprisonment and criminal justice on families 175–7
  erosion of 167–78
  framework of 168
  justice and human rights 126–7
  methods 169
  social marginality and 170–2
leisure
  activities 16, 87, 91–2, 102, 107, 114
  risk behaviour and 107, 110–13
lesbian marriage and parenting 13
less eligibility principle 223
level of contact 185
liberal theory 145
liberty
  deprivation of 1, 9, 12, 274
lies 10, 290
life 33
life-chances 2
linguistic expressions 178
living conditions 16, 88, 91, 97
  customary 89
longitudinal models 49, 74–5, 184

male incarceration 273–85
manhood
  conceptions of 80–2, 277
marginalization 15–17, 29–38, 61, 122, 190, 290, 296
  duality of 285
  social 3, 19–20, 89, 170–1, 173, 175, 177, 224
marriage 13, 42, 61
masculinity 16, 74, 83, 275–6
  constructions of 75–8
  see also gender
mass imprisonment/incarceration 1, 6, 42, 146
  arguments 58–62
  context 58, 68
  effect on childhood inequality 58–68
material hardship 42–52, 92, 96, 187

material welfare 9, 16, 105–10, 114
mediational models 49
mediators 8–10, 49, 293
mental health 6
   of adults 90, 183
   of caregivers 48
   of children 43, 138, 146, 153, 183
   disadvantage 29
   maternal 45, 108
   parental prisoners 42, 76, 81, 96
   of partners of incarcerated men 273
   paternal 59, 103–4
   problems 8, 9, 29, 35, 153
   professionals 291
minimum living standards
   definition of 89
'missing out' for prisoners' children 15, 91–7
   see also social exclusion
modelling theories 11
moderators 8–11
morality 17, 213, 220
mothering frameworks 48
multidisciplinary 14
multiple disadvantage 15–19, 95

national welfare policies 8
Native Americans 15, 63–5
naya (Indian concept of justice) 192
'need,' concept of 31
negative stereotyping 231–6, 241–2
Nelson Mandela Rules 160, 201
neo-liberal risk management 1, 193
Netherlands, the 4, 67, 155, 159
networks
   family 10, 16, 106, 193, 216, 259, 263–4
   non-carceral 280
   professional 207
   social 51, 73, 103, 173–4, 177, 260, 292
non-discrimination principle 34, 131, 136, 141–3, 198
non-governmental organizations (NGOs) 10, 20, 102, 160
Nordic exceptionalism 104
normalization
   principle of 34
Norway 4, 17, 67, 200
nuclear family 13, 109, 112–13

obesity 7
offence type 8, 10
official visitors 19, 231, 235–42

open prisons 9, 182, 185–6
oppression
   definition of 32–3
   elimination of institutional 32–3
organizational power 3
'other mediating factors' 11
'other species' 34
Overarching Principles, Seriousness guideline 138
Oxford Dictionary of Sociology 14

pains of imprisonment theory 7–8
   acute and chronic pain 190–1
   context 244–7, 255–6
   'coping' and 244–56
   methods and sample 247–8
   penal power and 182–3
   social justice and 191–3
   theoretical framework 245–7
   see also adaptation; separation (parental): settling, time of
paramountcy principle 144
parental socialization 8
parenting quality 11, 43–4, 48–50, 52
participant characteristics 278–9
   incarceration history 279
pedagogical principles *see* community: education principles
penal populism 1, 124, 126, 128–9
penal power 18, 181–93
   context 181–2
   lives of research families 184–91
   pains of imprisonment and 182–3
   prisoners' families and 183–4
   research studies 184
penal practice 124
   history of 3–4
   societal consequences of 3–5
perceptions of punishment 11
philosophy of punishment 3, 7
physical health 6, 9, 12, 45
play-based activities 15–16, 32, 34, 89, 91–2, 97, 189, 266
police
   arrest procedures 9, 37, 185
   practices 10
political utility 299
Portugal 10, 159
   sharing imprisonment 258–69
post-release period 19, 74–7, 214–15, 246, 254

poverty 16, 29, 32, 41–2, 45, 51, 61, 88–9, 95, 103, 260, 263, 290, 294
   definition of 88
power *see* penal power
practical reason 34, 37
presence of absence 269
pre-trial detention 10, 12
prevalence of prison 216
primary and secondary effects 8
primary carers 18, 19
   children's rights and 136–47
   responsibilities 139
   sentencing in the criminal courts 140–3
principled sentencing 127–8, 130
prison
   boom 6, 34, 58–68
   conditions 7–11, 126
   definition of 12–14
   environment 74, 182, 232, 265, 273–9, 285
   as an institution of punishment 4, 192
   perspectives 204–5
   regimes 8, 10, 34, 126, 132
   sentences 14–15, 193, 269, 299
   sociology, concepts of 18, 256
   type 19
   visits *see* visitation
Prisoners and their families Study 5
prisoners' family *see* family
Prison Reform Trust 29, 68, 234
Prison Service Instructions 232, 240
prisonization theory 7, 11, 183
privacy
   right to 17, 200, 205
processing (security) 230, 236–9
professional status 241
proportionality principle 158, 238
proximity model of sentencing policy 192
psychological discourse 182
psychology 14, 146
public issues 17
public sense of justice 127–30
   legitimacy and 126–7
   see also justice
public shaming 4
punishment creep 65, 181
punishment theories 12, 30, 125, 145
   punishment as a social institution 124
punishment vs justice 145–7

qualified public input model 128, 130
quality of parental relationships
   see parenting quality
quasi-inmates
   status of 29–30, 183

race
   jail incarceration by 63–4
   participant characteristics 279
   racial disadvantage 7
   risk of parental incarceration 59
   sociological variable 3, 15, 28–9, 34–5, 41, 47–8, 142, 201, 241, 259, 278
recreational activities 16, 34
   see also leisure; play-based activities; sport
rehabilitation 1–2, 83
   strategies towards offenders 1, 130, 188, 197, 205–7, 268
reintegration 207, 213, 224–6, 273, 276, 297
relational approach 3
religion 4, 127, 196
resilience 7–10, 19, 47–8, 191, 215
respect
   by authorities 3
   for the views of the child, principle of 198
rights of the child 141–4, 151, 156–8, 198–201, 203, 205
   see also United Nations Convention on the Rights of the Child (UNCRC)
risk behaviour 9, 105
   leisure and 107–13
role modelling 8, 80

same-sex partnerships 13
schooling 9, 106–7, 110–13, 223–5
   see also education
Scotland 18
   background 151–2, 162
   good international practice 158–60
   impact of imprisonment on children and families 151–62
   knowledge about children affected by imprisonment 152–3
   potential pitfalls 160–1
   recent developments in 161–2
   see also Child and Family Impact Assessments (C&FIA)
Scotland's Commissioner for Children and Young People (SCCYP) 153, 155, 158, 162
Scottish Prisons Commission 168

searches 36, 187, 236–9
second and third generation
    prisoners 213–26
  background and literature 214
  context 213
  data 214–15
  ripple effects 221–2
  themes 215–24
secondary prisonization 30, 37, 181, 231, 276, 285
  concept of 11, 183, 186–7
  definition of 183
secrecy 10, 103, 138, 153n, 185, 288
  by children in their communities 291–4
  within families of prisoners 289–300
secure attachment 8, 19, 137
self/problem distinction 245
senses 34
sentence length 19, 278–9
sentencing guidelines
  England and Wales 18, 138–9, 151–2, 160–1
  principles 152
separateness 233–5, 293
  damage caused by 5–6
  definition of 233
separation (parental) 131, 140–2, 152–3, 185–6, 199, 248, 274–5, 280, 293
  enforced 222
  settling 249–52
  time of 248–9
  traumatic 8, 11, 192, 217
sexuality 19, 29
  see also gender
shame 4, 7, 8, 10, 30, 35, 88–9, 91, 95, 219, 222, 260, 293, 296
  web of 188–9
SHANARRI framework 155
sharing imprisonment
  complex effects 267–8
  context 258–9, 268–9
  creative negotiation of family involvement 265–7
  economic and familial implications 262–5
  methodology 261–2
  in Portugal 258–69
  visibility 260–1
shock 18, 81, 145, 185–6, 190, 252
single-headed households 13
Skype 4

social and administrative exclusion 8, 12, 15, 18, 123, 128, 130, 174
  see also social exclusion
social capital 19, 167, 293
social class 3
  see also class advantage
social cohesion 17, 126, 133, 145
social exclusion 2, 7, 87–97, 102–15
  background and context 87–8, 97
  children in general vs 109–11
  concept of 3, 15, 87–91, 97, 104
  consequences of 95–6
  current research 89–91
  definition of 16, 87, 89–90
  nature of children's social exclusion 88–9
  see also child-centred perspectives
social justice 27–38
  civil and political liberties 35
  concept of 3, 27, 32, 177
  context 27–8
  definition of 28, 30, 32
  harm to prisoners' families 30–8
  pains of imprisonment and 191–3
  principles of 27–8, 31, 269
  theories of 27–8, 31, 38
  threats to 15
  see also harm
social labelling 8, 152
social learning theories 8, 11
social life 7, 32, 245, 258
social marginalization 3, 19, 89, 170–7, 224
  concept of 3, 224
  criminal justice contact 172–5
  legitimacy and 170–2
  social marginality 168, 170–2
social organization 4–5
social policy 3, 14, 214, 288, 295–6
social relations 4, 9, 16, 102–3, 105, 247
  family and 108–13
social services 10, 160–1
social visibility 273–85
  belonging and visibility 281–4
  context 273–4, 284–5
  family relationships and prison visitation 275 6
  findings 278–84
  literature review 274–6
  methods 276–8
  participant characteristics 278–9
  prison environment 274–5
  setting 276–8
  visits as a reprieve 279–81

social workers 18, 154–5, 175, 189, 193
sociology of punishment 3, 124–6
  analytical frameworks 14
  context 1–2
  effects of imprisonment on 8–10
  literature on the effects on family and children 7–8
  positive effects 10–11
  punishment and society 2–3
  research trends 5–7
  themes 14–20
  theoretical explanations 11–12
solitary confinement 9
sport 16, 93, 110–13
State, the
  'enemy' status 121–3
  obligations of 197–201
status
  economic/social 10, 13, 29, 90, 185, 187
  loss of 231, 235–6
stepfamilies 5, 13
stereotyping
  negative 231–6, 293
stigmatization 8, 19, 293
  conceptualizing 'stigma' 7, 11, 232–3, 293
  context 230–1, 240–2
  of prisoners 230–42
  research context and approach 231–2
  see also courtesy stigma
strain theories 11
stress 7, 48–50, 81, 92, 95, 106, 140, 250, 284
  see also family stress theory
structural injustice 33
structures of prisoners' children
  vs children in general 112
substantive freedoms 28–30
  capabilities and 33–5
supervision (parental) 8, 48, 182, 249–50, 273, 277
support *see* networks
surveillance
  concentrated 30
  exposure to 61
  female 78–80, 175
  penal 261, 269
  police 36
  of prisoners 36, 285, 298
  prison staff 240–1
  punitive 260
symbiotic harms 12
systemic invisibility 19
  of children of prisoners 288–300
  context 288–9, 299–300
  perspectives 296–9
  see also invisibility

third generation prisoners *see* second and third generation prisoners
thought 34
tightness 7, 18, 181–5, 188, 191–3, 245, 254, 274
  concept of 184
training
  industry options and facilities 16, 225–6
  staff 201, 203–7
transactional theory 275
transportation 4, 171, 263, 297–8
trauma theories 11
traumatic separation *see* separation (parental)
travel distance 10
trust 3, 122, 146, 161, 167–9, 177, 234–5, 241–2, 246–7, 255, 267, 275, 292
tuchthuis model 4

UN Prison Rules 205
unemployment 2
uninformed justice 130
  see also justice
United Kingdom
  black and minority ethnic (BME) groups 28
  children of prisoners 214
  data on prisoners' families 28
  disenfranchisement 35
  long sentences 245
  National Prison Survey in England and Wales 214
  prison statistics 68
  serious offenders 260
  social inequality 29
  social welfare policy 175
  UNCRC 140, 152
  UPR process 157–8
  use of imprisonment 1, 181
  voluntary sector 18
  see also pains of imprisonment; Scotland
United Nations Convention on the Rights of the Child (UNCRC)
  principles 18, 139–41, 152–62, 198
United States
  children of prisoners 214
  correctional supervision 273
  data infrastructure 20

United States (*cont.*)
  disenfranchisement 35
  family inequality 41–52
  impact statements 155, 161
  imprisonment rates 67, 73, 181
  mass imprisonment 58–68, 146, 168
  maternal incarceration 137
  penal policy 183, 188
  prisoner focus groups 274
  prison regulations 1, 6, 29, 261
  prison visitation sessions 274
  probation services 151
  processing procedures 244
  racialized nature of imprisonment 15, 28, 58–68, 127, 167
  risk of maternal and paternal incarceration 67
  social inequality 6, 29
  stratification system 15
  video visitation 285
  visitation and travel 249
  see also African American population; family inequality; mass imprisonment
Universal Declaration of Human Rights 5, 131
utilitarianism 126–7

valued activities 88
video conferencing 4, 226, 285, 298
visibility 260–1
  belonging and 281–4
  see also social visibility
visitation 4, 11, 18
  children's rights in prison visit development 204–6
  family visits as interventions 205–6
  location and conditions of 239–40
  'playing the visits game' 217–18
  prison 275–6
  visiting process, definition of 277
  visits as a reprieve 279–81
Visitors' Centre at HMP Edinburgh 169–78
voluntary sector 18
voting restrictions 2, 35, 37
  see also disenfranchisement
Vulnerable Families Project 91–7

weight 7, 18, 181–7, 191–3, 274
  concept of 182, 184
welfare
  agencies 191–3, 288, 295–6
  benefit system 2, 42, 66, 95, 249
  carceral 188
  child system of 18, 48, 65, 104, 139, 141–2, 159, 200, 288, 295–7
  courts 145
  penal services 183
  policies 8, 10
  of prisoners 29
  social 51, 114–15, 131, 175, 186, 189–92
  'society' 259
  see also material welfare
wellbeing 9, 33, 43, 224–6
  black-white inequalities 60*fig.*
  of children 43, 45–6, 50, 58–62, 65–6, 68, 88, 95–6, 102–8, 111–15, 162n, 187, 199, 292, 298
  family 47–8, 51–2, 170, 174, 191, 218, 224–6, 268
  poor and ethnic minority populations 37
  of prisoners 126, 185–6, 192, 221, 263, 275, 285, 297–8
  SHANARRI indicators of 155
  see also Child Rights and Wellbeing Impact Assessments (CRWIA)
women
  African American 273
  care-taking role 45, 82–3, 264
  incarceration of 61, 65, 137, 139, 142, 151, 155–6, 160, 169, 171, 173, 175, 192, 201, 261, 264, 276, 295
  mothers in prison with young children 18, 295
  non-incarcerated partners and mothers 16, 41, 43, 45, 48, 50, 74, 90, 106, 111
  relationships with incarcerated men 74–7, 183, 245, 261
  role in discipline and surveillance 78–80
  in Scottish prisons 151
  status of 183
  views of criminal justice system 246–56
  see also gender
wrong-doing 12